# WILLMINGTON'S
# GUIDE TO THE BIBLE

# Willmington's
# GUIDE
## to the
# BIBLE

# Dr. H. L. Willmington

## VOLUME 1  OLD TESTAMENT

TYNDALE HOUSE
PUBLISHERS, INC.
WHEATON, ILLINOIS

*Willmington's Guide to the Bible*, Volume 1

Third printing, November 1988

H. L. Willmington's Charts and Illustrations
designed by Hugh Claycombe

Library of Congress Catalog Card Number 86-51140
ISBN 0-8423-8810-9

Printed in the United States of America

# Contents

## HEBREW BIBLE
### OLD TESTAMENT ARRANGEMENT

| *LAW*<br>*5 books* | GENESIS<br>EXODUS<br>LEVITICUS<br>NUMBERS<br>DEUTERONOMY | | |
|---|---|---|---|
| *PROPHETS*<br>*8 books* | *4 FORMER*<br>JOSHUA<br>JUDGES<br>SAMUEL<br>KINGS | *4 LATTER*<br>ISAIAH<br>JEREMIAH<br>EZEKIEL<br>THE TWELVE | |
| *WRITINGS*<br>*II books* | *3 POETICAL*<br>PSALMS<br><br>PROVERBS<br><br>JOB | *5 ROLLS*<br>SONG OF<br>SOLOMON<br><br>RUTH<br><br>LAMENTATIONS<br><br>ESTHER<br><br>ECCLESIASTES | *3 HISTORICAL*<br><br>DANIEL<br><br>EZRA<br>NEHEMIAH<br><br>CHRONICLES |

## ENGLISH BIBLE
### OLD TESTAMENT ARRANGEMENT

| *LAW*<br>*5 books* | • GENESIS<br>• EXODUS<br>• LEVITICUS<br>• NUMBERS<br>• DEUTERONOMY | | |
|---|---|---|---|
| *HISTORY*<br>*12 books* | • JOSHUA<br>• JUDGES<br>• RUTH<br>• 1 SAMUEL<br>• 2 SAMUEL<br>• 1 KINGS | • 2 KINGS<br>• 1 CHRONICLES<br>• 2 CHRONICLES<br>• EZRA<br>• NEHEMIAH<br>• ESTHER | |
| *POETRY*<br>*5 books* | • JOB<br>• PSALMS<br>• PROVERBS<br>• ECCLESIASTES<br>• SONG OF SOLOMON | | |
| *PROPHECY*<br>*17 books* | *5 MAJOR*<br>• ISAIAH<br>• JEREMIAH<br>• LAMENTATIONS<br>• DANIEL<br>• EZEKIEL | *12 MINOR*<br>• HOSEA<br>• JOEL<br>• AMOS<br>• OBADIAH<br>• JONAH<br>• MICAH | • NAHUM<br>• HABAKKUK<br>• ZEPHANIAH<br>• HAGGAI<br>• ZECHARIAH<br>• MALACHI |

# Why the Child of God Should Study the Word of God

At first glance it would seem totally unnecessary to discuss reasons for studying God's Word. One might assume that, upon conversion, the most natural thing for a new believer to do would be to begin a lifelong study of that Book which originally brought him to Christ. But personal observation, as well as church history, proves the facts to be quite the opposite. The truth is, most Christians know very little about the Bible! Here then are some sound reasons for studying the Scriptures.

    I. Because of its Author.

Often God is thought of as a Creator, a Redeemer, a Shepherd, a Judge, etc. This is correct thinking, of course, for he does indeed function in all these roles. But there is one great accomplishment of God which is almost always left off the divine attribute lists compiled by men. This wonderful but forgotten role is that of Author! God has written a book, and that profound and priceless book is the Bible. As testified to by any human author, the nicest thing one can say to an author is, "Oh, yes, I've read your book."

It is a tragic but true fact that many of the Christians who will someday (along with all believers) stand before the judgment seat of Christ will be sadly forced to admit that, while they were saved by heeding the salvation message in God's Book, they nevertheless failed to take the time to read it. Thus, if for no other reason, the Bible should be carefully read to allow the believer to proclaim to Christ on that day: "Dear Jesus, there were many things I did not do on earth that I should have done, as well as other things I did do that I should not have, but one thing I did—I read your book!"

    II. Because of the often-repeated command to read it.

"This book of the law shall not depart out of thy mouth; but thou shalt meditate therein day and night, that thou mayest observe to do according to all that is written therein: for then thou shalt make thy way prosperous, and then thou shalt have good success" (Josh. 1:8).

"Study to shew thyself approved unto God, a workman that needeth not to be ashamed, rightly dividing the word of truth" (2 Tim. 2:15).

"But he answered and said, It is written, Man shall not live by bread alone, but by every word that proceedeth out of the mouth of God" (Mt. 4:4).

Especially to be noted is this last verse. Jesus said *every word*.

    III. Because the Bible is God's chosen way to accomplish his divine will.

      A. Sinners are saved through the message of the Bible.

"For whosoever shall call upon the name of the Lord shall be saved.

How then shall they call on him in whom they have not believed? and how shall they believe in him of whom they have not heard? and how shall they hear without a preacher? And how shall they preach, except they be sent? as it is written, How beautiful are the feet of them that preach the gospel of peace, and bring glad tidings of good things! But they have not all obeyed the gospel. For Esaias saith, Lord, who hath believed our report? So then faith cometh by hearing, and hearing by the word of God" (Rom. 10:13-17).

"But Peter, standing up with the eleven, lifted up his voice, and said unto them, Ye men of Judaea, and all ye that dwell at Jerusalem, be this known unto you, and hearken to my words" (Acts 2:14).

"Now when they heard this, they were pricked in their heart, and said unto Peter and to the rest of the apostles, Men and brethren, what shall we do?" (Acts 2:37).

"Therefore they that were scattered abroad went every where preaching the word. Then Philip went down to the city of Samaria, and preached Christ unto them. And the people with one accord gave heed unto those things which Philip spake, hearing and seeing the miracles which he did. For unclean spirits, crying with loud voice, came out of many that were possessed with them: and many taken with palsies, and that were lame, were healed. And there was great joy in that city" (Acts 8:4-8).

"Being born again, not of corruptible seed, but of incorruptible, by the word of God, which liveth and abideth for ever" (1 Pet. 1:23).

"Of his own will begat he us with the word of truth—that we should be a kind of firstfruits of his creatures" (Jas. 1:18).

B. Saints are sanctified through the message of the Bible.

"Sanctify them through thy truth: thy word is truth" (Jn. 17:17).

"As newborn babies, desire the sincere milk of the word, that ye may grow thereby" (1 Pet. 2:2).

"For this is the will of God, even your sanctification, that ye should abstain from fornication" (1 Thess. 4:3).

"Wherewithal shall a young man cleanse his way? by taking heed thereto according to thy word. With my whole heart have I sought thee: O let me not wander from thy commandments. Thy word have I hid in mine heart, that I might not sin against thee" (Ps. 119:9-11).

"Every word of God is pure: he is a shield unto them that put their trust in him. Add thou not unto his words, lest he reprove thee, and thou be found a liar" (Prov. 30:5, 6).

"If ye abide in me, and my words abide in you, ye shall ask what ye will, and it shall be done unto you" (Jn. 15:7).

"And now, brethren, I commend you to God, and to the word of his grace, which is able to build you up, and to give you an inheritance among all them which are sanctified" (Acts 20:32).

IV. Because our enemy the devil has read it.

During the account in Matthew 4, Christ is tempted three times by the devil. On each occasion the Savior answered Satan with the phrase, "It is written," and then proceeded to quote from the Word of God as found in the book of Deuteronomy. But what is almost always overlooked is the fact that the phrase "it is written" is repeated four times in Matthew 4, and that the fourth time it is the devil using it to quote Scripture to Christ! Note the background at this point.

"Then the devil taketh him up into the holy city, and setteth him on a pinnacle of the temple, and saith unto him, If thou be the Son of God, cast thyself down: for it is written, He shall give his angels charge concerning thee: and in their hands they shall bear thee up, lest at any time thou dash thy foot against a stone" (Mt. 4:5, 6).

Here Satan quotes from Psalm 91:11, 12. It is taken completely out of context, to be sure, but how did Satan know about it in the first place? The answer is painfully obvious. One day when the devil had nothing better to do, he must have sat down and studied Psalm 91. Many Christians today have probably never even read this Psalm, but the devil apparently has it memorized! Thus, we need to read God's Word lest Satan get an advantage upon us.

V. Because of the example of Paul.

Paul was probably the greatest Christian that ever lived. His spiritual accomplishments are nothing short of staggering. Here was a man who made the first three missionary journeys, who founded and pastored the first fifty or more Bible-believing churches, who wrote over half of the New Testament, and who on five occasions saw the resurrected Christ, and at least once was actually caught up into the third heaven itself! But then he was arrested, condemned to death, and placed in prison. Note carefully his final words to Timothy just prior to his execution.

"For I am now ready to be offered, and the time of my departure is at hand. I have fought a good fight, I have finished my course, I have kept the faith: Henceforth there is laid up for me a crown of righteousness, which the Lord, the righteous judge, shall give me at that day: and not to me only, but unto all them also that love his appearing. The cloak that I left at Troas with Carpus, when thou comest, bring with thee, and the books, but especially the parchments" (2 Tim. 4:6-8, 13).

What were these parchments? They were his copies of the Old Testament scrolls. The point to be made here is that in spite of all his marvelous achievements, the old apostle still felt he could profit from studying the Word of God on the eve of his death.

VI. Because the Bible alone provides answers to life's three sixty-four-trillion-dollar questions. These questions, pondered by every generation, are:

A. Where did I come from?

"And God said, Let us make man in our image, after our likeness: and let them have dominion over the fish of the sea, and over the fowl of the air, and over the cattle, and over all the earth, and over every creeping thing that creepeth upon the earth. So God created man in his own image, in the image of God created he him; male and female created he them" (Gen. 1:26, 27).

"Know ye that the Lord he is God: it is he that hath made us, and not we ourselves; we are his people, and the sheep of his pasture" (Ps. 100:3).

B. Why am I here?

"Let us hear the conclusion of the whole matter: Fear God, and keep his command-ments: for this is the whole duty of man" (Eccl. 12:13).

"Thou are worthy, O Lord, to receive glory and honour and power: for thou hast created all things, and for thy pleasure they are and were created" (Rev. 4:11).

C. Where am I going?

"For God so loved the world, that he gave his only begotten Son, that whosoever believeth in him should not perish, but have everlasting life. For God sent not his Son into the world to condemn the world; but that the world through him might be saved. He that believeth on him is not condemned: but he that believeth not is condemned already, because he hath not believed in the name of the only begotten Son of God" (Jn. 3:16-18).

"The Lord is my shepherd; I shall not want. Surely goodness and mercy shall follow me all the days of my life: and I will dwell in the house of the Lord for ever" (Ps. 23:1, 6).

"And whosoever was not found written in the book of life was cast into the lake of fire" (Rev. 20:15).

VII. Because we'll never have the opportunity to apply many of its verses after we leave this earth.

A. There will be no opportunity to apply 1 Corinthians 10:13 in heaven.

"There hath no temptation taken you but such as is common to man: but God is faithful, who will not suffer you to be tempted above that ye are able; but will with the temptation also make a way to escape, that ye may be able to bear it" (1 Cor. 10:13).

*Reason:* In heaven there will be no temptation.

B. There will be no opportunity to apply 1 John 1:9 in heaven.

"If we confess our sins, he is faithful and just to forgive us our sins, and to cleanse us from all unrighteousness" (1 Jn. 1:9).

*Reason:* In heaven there will be no sin.

C. There will be no opportunity to apply Philippians 4:19 in heaven.

"But my God shall supply all your need according to his riches in glory by Christ Jesus" (Phil. 4:19).

*Reason:* In heaven there will be no need.

D. There will be no opportunity to apply John 14:1-3 in heaven.

"Let not your heart be troubled: ye believe in God, believe also in me. In my Father's house are many mansions: if it were not so, I would have told you. I go to prepare a place for you. And if I go and prepare a place for you, I will come again, and receive you unto myself; that where I am, there ye may be also" (Jn. 14:1-3).

*Reason:* In heaven there will be no sorrow.

E. There will be no opportunity to apply Psalm 23:4 in heaven.

"Yea, though I walk through the valley of the shadow of death, I will fear no evil: for thou art with me; thy rod and thy staff they comfort me" (Ps. 23:4).

*Reason:* In heaven there will be no death.

VIII. Because the only ultimate proof for our faith is the Bible.

To introduce the eighth and final reason for studying God's Word, the following imaginary situation is proposed. Often the unbeliever hurls the following accusation at the believer: "Oh, you Christians—you're all alike! You're so dogmatic. You think you alone are right and everybody else is dead wrong. How can you possibly be so sure what you believe is true?" This question, though often asked in a scoffing manner, is nevertheless a fair one. How *does* the child of God know his faith is the only correct one?

Let us suppose that you are invited to an important social function in your hometown. Attending this gathering are people from all over the world. As the introductions are being made, it slowly dawns upon you that the only professing Christian there is yourself. You are subsequently introduced to a Buddhist, a Confucianist, a Shintoist, a Moslem, and other individuals, all belonging to various non-Christian religions. After a pleasant dinner, the conversation gradually turns to matters of religion. Your hostess, realizing this subject to be of general interest, suddenly announces:

"I have a wonderful idea! Since everyone here seems to have a great interest in religion, may I suggest that we share with one another by doing the following: Each person will be allowed to speak uninterrupted for ten minutes on the subject, 'Why I feel my faith is the right one.'"

The group quickly agrees with this unique and provocative idea. Then with no warning she suddenly turns to you and exclaims, "You go first!" All talk immediately ceases. Every eye is fixed on you. Every ear is turned to pick up your first words. What would you say? How would you start? Let us quickly list a few arguments which you could *not* use.

1. You *couldn't* say, "I know I'm right because I *feel* I'm right! Christ lives in my heart!"

This, of course, is a wonderful truth experienced by all believers, but it would not convince the Buddhist, who would doubtless *feel* that he was right too.

2. You *couldn't* say, "I know I'm right because Christianity has more followers in this world than any other religion."

   This is simply not true today. Actually, the sad truth is that evangelical Bible-believing Christianity is a distinct minority in the world today. The Moslem would doubtless quickly point this out to you.

3. You *couldn't* say. "I know I'm right because Christianity is the oldest of all religions.

   Ultimately, of course, this is true. But the Confucianist might contend that Confucius presented his teachings centuries before the Bethlehem scene. Of course, he would not understand the eternal existence of our Lord Jesus Christ. These then are arguments you could *not* use. What *could* you say? In reality you would have at your disposal only one single argument. But that argument, that weapon, used in the right way, would be more than enough to overwhelmingly convince any honest and sincere listener at that social gathering. That wonderful weapon, that unanswerable argument, is one's own personal copy of the Bible! What could you say? Well, you could hold up your Bible and confidently proclaim the following:

   "Look at this! I know I'm right because the Author of my faith has given me a Book which is completely unlike any of the books of your faiths."

   You could then continue (until your time ran out) by pointing out the unity, the indestructibility, and the universal influence of the Bible. You could discuss its historical, scientific, and prophetical accuracy. Finally, you might relate exciting examples of perhaps the greatest single proof of the supernatural nature of the Bible, that is, its marvelous life-transforming power!

   Of course, it must be pointed out that neither the Word of God nor the God of the Word can be scientifically analyzed in a laboratory test tube. The divine Creator still desires and demands faith on the part of his Creation. (See Heb. 11:1-6.) But he has presented us with a heavenly textbook to aid us in this needed faith. In fact, the Gospel of John was specifically written ". . . that ye might believe that Jesus is the Christ, the Son of God; and that believing ye might have life through his name" (Jn. 20:31).

## THE FORTY-EIGHT MOST IMPORTANT CHAPTERS IN THE OLD TESTAMENT

The Old Testament has 929 chapters. The following forty-eight chapters have been selected because of their historical, prophetical, theological, or practical significance.

**GENESIS**
- 1—**Creation** of all things
- 3—**Fall** of man
- 6—The universal **flood**
- 11—The Tower of **Babel**
- 12—The call of **Abraham**
- 15—The confirmation of the **Abrahamic Covenant**

**EXODUS**
- 3—The call of **Moses**
- 12—The **Passover**
- 14—The **Red Sea** crossing
- 16—The giving of the **Sabbath**
- 20—The giving of the **Law**
- 40—The completion of the **tabernacle**

**LEVITICUS**
- 8—The anointing of **Aaron** as Israel's first high priest
- 23—The **feasts** of Israel

**NUMBERS**
- 14—The **rebellion** at Kadesh-barnea
- 21—The serpent of **brass**

**DEUTERONOMY**
- 28—**Israel's future** predicted by Moses

**JOSHUA**
- 4—Israel enters the **Promised Land**

**RUTH**
- 4—The marriage of Boaz and **Ruth**

**I SAMUEL**
- 9—The anointing of **Saul** as Israel's first king
- 16—The anointing of **David**

**2 SAMUEL**
- 6—**Jerusalem** becomes the capital of Israel
- 7—The giving of the **Davidic Covenant**

**I KINGS**
- 8—The dedication of the **Temple** by **Solomon**
- 12—The **divided kingdom** of Israel

**2 KINGS**
- 17—The **capture** of the northern kingdom by Assyria
- 19—The **saving** of Jerusalem by the death angel
- 24—The **capture** of the southern kingdom by Babylon

**EZRA**
- 1—The decree of Cyrus and the **return** to Jerusalem

**JOB**
- 1—The confrontations between **God and Satan** (see also Job 2)

**PSALMS**
- 22—The Psalm of **Calvary**
- 23—The Psalm of the **Good Shepherd**
- 51—The great confession of **sin** chapter
- 119—The Psalm of the **Word of God**

**ISAIAH**
- 7—The **prophecy** of the virgin birth
- 14—The fall of **Satan**
- 35—The **Millennium**
- 53—The sufferings of **Christ**

**JEREMIAH**
- 31—The **promise** of the new covenant to Israel

**EZEKIEL**
- 10—The **departure** of the glory cloud from Israel
- 28—The prehistorical life of **Satan**
- 37—The dry bone **vision** of Israel's restoration
- 38—The **future** Russian invasion into Palestine (see also Ezekiel 39)
- 40—The **future millennial temple**

**DANIEL**
- 2—The **dream** of the future Gentile world powers (see also Daniel 7)
- 9—The **vision** of the seventy weeks

**JONAH**
- 2—The **great fish** and Jonah

**ZECHARIAH**
- 14—The **Second Coming** of Christ

## THE MOST IMPORTANT OLD TESTAMENT EVENTS

1. Creation of **Adam** and **Eve** (Gen. 1:26, 27; 2:7, 21, 22)
2. Institution of **marriage** (Gen. 2:23–25)
3. **Fall** of man (Genesis 3:6)
4. Promise of the **Redeemer** (Gen. 3:15)
5. Universal **flood** (Gen. 6–8)
6. Institution of human **government** (Gen. 9:1–19)
7. Tower of **Babel** (Gen. 11:1–9)
8. Conversion and call of **Abraham** (Gen. 12:1–3)
9. Giving of Abrahamic **Covenant** (Gen. 12:7; 13:14–17; 15:1–21)
10. Abraham's marriage to **Hagar** (Gen. 16:1–16)
11. The birth of **Isaac** (Gen. 21:1–8)
12. The flight of **Jacob** (Gen. 28)
13. The selling of **Joseph** into Egyptian slavery (Gen. 37)
14. The enslavement of **Israel** in **Egypt** (Ex. 1)
15. The call of **Moses** (Ex. 3:1–10)
16. The ten **plagues** (Ex. 7–12)
17. The institution of the **Passover** (Ex. 12)
18. The appearance of the **glory cloud** (Ex. 13:21, 22)
19. The **Red Sea** crossing (Ex. 14)
20. The giving of the **manna** (Ex. 16:4)
21. The institution of the **Sabbath** (Ex. 16:29)
22. The giving of the **Law** (Ex. 20:1–17)
23. The completion of the **tabernacle** (Ex. 40:33, 34)
24. The anointing of **Aaron** (Lev. 8:1–12)
25. The **unbelief** at Kadesh-barnea (Num. 14)
26. The death of **Moses** (Deut. 34:5–8)
27. The **Jordan River** crossing into Palestine (Josh. 3)
28. The victory over **Jericho** (Josh. 6)
29. The death of **Joshua** (Josh. 24:29)
30. The marriage of **Ruth** to Boaz (Ruth 4)
31. The capture of the **ark** by the Philistines (1 Sam. 4)
32. The rejection of **Samuel** by Israel (1 Sam. 8:1–9)
33. The anointing of **Saul** (1 Sam. 9, 10)
34. The rejection of **Saul** (1 Sam. 15:23)
35. The anointing of **David** (1 Sam. 16:13)
36. The capture of **Jerusalem** by David (2 Sam. 5:9)
37. The recovery of the **ark** by David (2 Sam. 6:15, 16)
38. The giving of the Davidic **Covenant** (2 Sam. 7:8–17)
39. The anointing of **Solomon** (1 Ki. 1:39)
40. The completion of **Solomon's Temple** (1 Ki. 6:38)
41. The Israeli **civil war** (1 Ki. 12)
42. The deliverance of **Joash** from murderous Queen Athaliah (2 Chron. 22:10–12)
43. The **Assyrian captivity** of the northern kingdom (2 Ki. 17:6)
44. The **deliverance** of **Jerusalem** from the Assyrians (2 Ki. 19:32–35)
45. The death of **Josiah** (2 Ki. 23:29, 30)
46. The departure of the **glory cloud** (Ezek. 10:18)
47. The **destruction** of the **Temple** of Solomon (2 Ki. 25:8, 9)
48. The **Babylonian captivity** of the southern kingdom (2 Ki. 25:11)
49. The return under **Cyrus'** decree (Ezra 1)
50. The completion of the new Temple under **Zerubbabel** (Ezra 3)
51. The salvation of the Jews by **Esther** (Est. 4–7)

# The Chronological Method

Nearly every Bible institute and Christian college offers courses in Old Testament and New Testament survey. The usual approach is to briefly examine the sixty-six books, suggesting a key thought, verse, truth, character, etc., for each book. The main problem with this method is the difficulty in connecting the many "keys" with the proper biblical "locks."

A simpler method would be to place every book into twelve logical and historical divisions. This we have done in this *Guide to the Bible*. Nine divisions are contained in this Old Testament Volume 1. A separate companion volume, *Willmington's Guide to the Bible*, Volume 2—New Testament, contains an additional three divisions.

Each stage describes a particular and unique period of time in God's progressive revelation to man. These twelve divisions are historical, *not* dispensational in nature.

A quick survey of the nine divisions in this Old Testament Volume 1 reveals the following:

| | |
|---|---|
| *Creation Stage* | 1. Creation |
| | 2. Fall |
| | 3. Flood |
| | 4. Tower of Babel |
| *Patriarchal Stage* | 1. Lives of Abraham, Isaac, Jacob, Joseph, and Job |
| | 2. Beginning of Hebrew nation |
| | 3. Arrival of Jews in Egypt |
| *Exodus Stage* | 1. Deliverance from Egypt |
| | 2. Giving of Law |
| | 3. Building of tabernacle |
| | 4. Failure at Kadesh |
| *Conquest Stage* | 1. Invasion of the land |
| | 2. Subjection of the land |
| | 3. Division of the land |
| *Judges Stage* | 1. Ministry of twelve military reformers |
| | 2. Marriage of a Moabite girl |
| | 3. Call and ministry of Samuel |
| *United Kingdom Stage* | 1. Reigns of Saul, David, and Solomon |
| | 2. Recovery of the ark and capture of Jerusalem |
| | 3. Construction of first Temple |
| *Chaotic Kingdom Stage* | 1. Civil War |
| | 2. Capture of ten tribes by Assyria |
| | 3. Capture of two tribes by Babylon |
| *Captivity Stage* | 1. Ministry of Daniel and Ezekiel |
| | 2. Fall of Babylon |
| | 3. Rise of Persia |
| *Return Stage* | 1. Decree of Cyrus |
| | 2. Construction of second Temple |
| | 3. Deliverance of Jews in Persia |

# THE CREATION STAGE

## INTRODUCING THE CREATION STAGE (Genesis 1-11)

These eleven chapters are absolutely vital in rightly understanding the remaining 1178 in the Bible. If one accepts them at face value, he will have no difficulty concerning the rest of the Old and New Testament.

### THE CREATION STAGE

GENESIS, CHAPTERS ONE THROUGH ELEVEN

The three important men of this stage are Adam, Enoch, and Noah.

The four important events are, the Creation, the Fall, the Flood, and the Tower of Babel.

The Creation account includes everything, from electrons to galaxies, from dinosaurs to dandelions, and from Adam to angels!

This stage is the only one which describes God as resting (Gen. 2:2, 3).

It gives us the first human to be created (Adam) and the first human to be born (Cain) (Gen. 1:26; 4:1).

It records the first man to die (Abel) and the first not to die (Enoch) (Gen. 4:8; 5:24).

We are introduced to a serpent, a raven, and a dove (Gen. 3:1; 7:1, 8).

The glory of God in creation (Gen. 1:1) and the grace of God in salvation (Gen. 6:8) are both clearly seen.

We see the world's earliest civilization (Cainite) and the world's oldest citizen (Methuselah) (Gen. 4:17; 5:27).

This stage describes the first marriage, the first murder, and the first promise of the Messiah (Gen. 2:23-25; 4:8; 3:15).

It gives us the first illustration of human religion (the fig leaves), and the first example of divine redemption (the coats of skin) (Gen. 3:7, 21).

In its pages sinners are drowned, and a saint is drunken (Gen. 7:21; 9:20, 21).

A ship settles on a mountain and a tower rises on a plain (Gen. 8:4; 11:1-4).

## AN OVERALL VIEW OF GENESIS 1-11

I. The *Creation* of All Things (Gen. 1-2)
   A. First day
   B. Second day
   C. Third day
   D. Fourth day
   E. Fifth day
   F. Sixth day
   G. Seventh day
II. The *Corruption* of All Things (Gen. 3-5)
   A. The subtlety of Satan (3)
   B. The sin of Adam (3)
   C. The redemption of God (3)
   D. The story of Cain and Abel (4)
   E. The ministry of Enoch (5)
III. The *Condemnation* of All Things (Gen. 6-9)
   A. The conditions prior to the flood (6)
   B. The salvation through the flood (7-8)
   C. The tragedy following the flood (9)
IV. The *Confusion* of All Things (Gen. 10-11)
   A. The arrogance of man
   B. The judgment of God
   C. The origin of nations

## THE GEOGRAPHY OF GENESIS 1-11

## THE CREATION STAGE

I. The Creation of All Things (Gen. 1-2).
   "In the beginning God created the heaven and the earth" (Gen. 1:1). The word *heaven* is plural in the Hebrew. There are three heavens mentioned in the Bible. God created all three.

## GENESIS 1–11: "IN THE BEGINNING...

# GOD

# CREATION

### ORIGIN OF ALL THINGS—GEN. 1–2

- SIX DAYS OF CREATION
- ONE DAY OF REST

# CORRUPTION

### SIN OF ADAM—GEN. 3–5

- SUBTLETY OF SATAN
- SIN OF ADAM
- REDEMPTION OF GOD
- MARTYRDOM OF ABEL
- MINISTRY OF ENOCH

# CONDEMNATION

### FLOOD OF NOAH—GEN. 6–9

- CONDITIONS BEFORE THE FLOOD
- SALVATION THROUGH THE FLOOD
- THE TRAGEDY AFTER THE FLOOD

# CONFUSION

### TOWER OF BABEL—GEN. 10–11

- THE ARROGANCE OF MAN
- THE JUDGMENT OF GOD
- THE ORIGIN OF NATIONS

*First Heaven*—home of the birds and clouds.

"The leaves thereof were fair, and the fruit thereof much, and in it was meat for all: the beasts of the field had shadow under it, and the fowls of the heaven dwelt in the boughs thereof, and all flesh was fed of it" (Dan. 4:12).

"Behold the fowls of the air: for they sow not, neither do they reap, nor gather into barns; yet your heavenly Father feedeth them. Are ye not much better than they?" (Mt. 6:26).

*Second Heaven*—home of the sun, moon, and stars.

"The heavens declare the glory of God; and the firmament sheweth his handiwork" (Ps. 19:1).

*Third Heaven*—home of the angels and departed saints.

"I knew a man in Christ above fourteen years ago, (whether in the body, I cannot tell; or whether out of the body, I cannot tell: God knoweth;) such an one caught up to the third heaven" (2 Cor. 12:2).

Note now the work of the first six days.

A. First day: the creation of light (1:2-5).

The Holy Spirit moved (vibrated) upon the earth. From this omnipotent, vibrating energy source began to flow our energy waves—waves of heat and sound magnetism. Thus, the created uni-

verse was energized. The earth rotating on its axis also began at this time. Both energy and matter were now present in the space, mass, time framework. The three basic types of force fields were now in effect.

1. gravitational—the force between two objects
2. electro-magnetic—the force between the electron and the nucleus of an atom
3. nuclear—the force between the proton and neutron within the atom.

Some mistakenly believe that the Holy Spirit first came to earth at Pentecost in Acts 2, and that he will leave at the rapture. But here he is pictured in the second verse in the Bible.

## "In the Beginning GOD Created the Heaven and the Earth"

| THIS IS A SUMMARIZATION STATEMENT | THIS IS A REFUTATION STATEMENT | |
|---|---|---|
| 1:1 TELLS US WHAT GOD DID. | PHILOSOPHY REFUTED | HOW REFUTED |
| | ATHEISM | THERE IS A GOD |
| 1:2–2:25 TELLS US HOW HE DID IT. | POLYTHEISM | THERE IS BUT ONE GOD |
| | EVOLUTION | HE CREATED ALL THINGS |
| | PANTHEISM | HE IS APART FROM HIS CREATION |
| | MATERIALISM | THERE WAS A BEGINNING TO CREATION |
| | FATALISM | THERE WAS A PURPOSE TO CREATION |

B. Second day: the separating of the waters (1:6-8). This water was in two forms:
   1. regular land-based water in shallow ocean, river, and lake beds
   2. atmospheric water—in the form of invisible translucent vapor

C. Third day: the creation of plant life (1:9-13). Lush green vegetation and exotic flowers now grace the newly emerged dry ground.

These verses alone totally refute the harmful doctrine of theistic evolution which says life began aeons ago from a glob of scum floating on some remote ocean surface. But to the contrary, Moses tells us life was supernaturally created on the third day of Creation and began on dry ground.

D. Fourth day: the creation of the sun, moon, and stars (1:14-19). On the first day God created physical light. He now creates special light sources. These heavenly bodies were to function in a threefold manner:
   1. As signs—they teach and remind men of God's creative work.

"When I consider thy heavens, the work of thy fingers, the moon and the stars, which thou hast ordained" (Ps. 8:3).

"Because that which may be known of God is manifest in them; for God hath shewed it unto them. For the invisible things of him from the creation of the world are clearly seen, being understood by the things that are made, even his eternal power and Godhead; so that they are without excuse" (Rom. 1:19, 20).

## THE THREE HEAVENS OF CREATION

(See Gen. 1:1; 2:1)

**THIRD HEAVEN**
(2 COR. 12:2)

**SECOND HEAVEN**
(PS. 19:1)

**FIRST HEAVEN**
(DAN. 4:12; MT. 6:26)

**EARTH**

FATHER SON GOD HOLY SPIRIT

2. As seasons—they function as a calendar, dividing seasons, days, and years, enabling men to accurately plan their work.
3. As lights—they replace the temporary light source of the early days.

It may be asked why God created the earth on the first day, but waited until the fourth day before establishing the sun, stars, and moon. Two possible reasons are suggested for this, one dealing with *priority*, the other with *prevention*.

a. That of priority. God created the earth first because it was the most important in his mind. It was upon *planet earth* that he planned to create on the sixth day a creature made in his own image. This creature, man, would live on earth, and not the moon. Then, plans had already been made in the fullness of time for the second person in the Trinity to wrap human flesh and bone about him and come to planet earth. Finally, it will be upon the earth, not Pluto or Venus, that the King of kings shall someday touch down upon the Mount of Olives to establish his millennial Kingdom.

b. That of prevention. Almost without exception every ancient civilization has worshiped the sun. But God wanted his people to worship its Creator, namely, himself. Thus, he informs us that life and light existed before the sun, and that "every good gift and every perfect gift is from above and cometh down from the Father of lights . . ." (Jas. 1:17).

E. Fifth day: the creation of fish and fowl (1:20-23).

What a contrast is seen here, from the tiny hummingbird to the massive blue sperm whale. It is not generally known, but the blue sperm whale is longer and heavier than a modern 737 Boeing jet passenger plane. It can reach a length of 110 feet, and weigh 150 tons.

## THE DAYS OF CREATION

### THE LENGTH OF THESE DAYS

QUESTION: **ARE THESE LITERAL TWENTY-FOUR-HOUR DAYS?**

ANSWER: **YES, BECAUSE:**
1. THE NUMERICAL ADJECTIVE USED WITH THE WORD "DAY" (HEBREW *YOM*) INDICATES THIS.
2. MOSES BELIEVED IT (EX. 20:11; 31:17)
3. DAVID BELIEVED IT (PS. 33:6–9)
4. MOST HEBREW LANGUAGE SCHOLARS BELIEVE IT.
5. HEBREW STRUCTURE ITSELF SEEMS TO TEACH IT.

### THE CORRELATION OF THESE DAYS

FIRST THREE DAYS **PROVIDE THE BACKDROP FOR THE CREATION DRAMA**

LAST THREE DAYS **PROVIDE THE ACTUAL ACTORS IN THE CREATION DRAMA**

**THE BACKDROP**

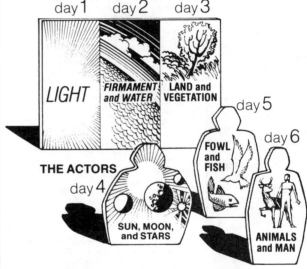

day 1 — LIGHT
day 2 — FIRMAMENT and WATER
day 3 — LAND and VEGETATION
day 4 — SUN, MOON, and STARS
day 5 — FOWL and FISH
day 6 — ANIMALS and MAN

**THE ACTORS**

### THE TWOFOLD ACCOUNT OF THESE DAYS

THE FLOODLIGHT ACCOUNT (GEN. 1)
A GENERAL DESCRIPTION OF THE CREATION OF THE UNIVERSE.
A CHRONOLOGICAL ACCOUNT

THE SPOTLIGHT ACCOUNT (GEN. 2)
A SPECIFIC DESCRIPTION OF THE CREATION OF MAN
A TOPICAL ACCOUNT

F. Sixth day: the creation of land creatures and man (1:24-31). Man immediately becomes the highlight of this day and of the entire creation week.

Note the divine account of this act. "And God said, Let us make man in our image, after our likeness . . ." (Gen. 1:26). This is the first strong evidence of the Trinity in the Old Testament. (See also Gen. 11:7; Ps. 2:7; 45:7; 110:1; Isa. 48:16.)

"Come ye near unto me, hear ye this; I have not spoken in secret from the beginning; from the time that it was, there am I: and now the Lord God, and his spirit, hath sent me" (Isa. 48:16).

1. He was made in the image of God and possessed the highest kind of life.
   a. Plant life possessed *unconscious* life.
   b. Animal life possessed *conscious* life.
   c. Man alone possessed *self-conscious* life.
   Thus, here was a creature who could not only eat of Eden's delicious food, but would glance heavenward first and thank that One who created both eater and food. No dandelion or dinosaur could do this.
2. He was to subdue the earth and fill it (1:28).
3. He was encouraged to enjoy the Tree of Life and all other trees of creation except one (2:9, 16).
4. He was forbidden to partake of the Tree of the Knowledge of Good and Evil (2:17).
5. He was to name all the animals (2:19).
6. He was given a wife (2:18-25). Here is the first of three great institutions given by God

## THE CREATION WEEK

| DAY | ACTION | COMMENT |
|---|---|---|
|  | **CREATION of earth, light and probably angels** | • Created universe now energized.<br>• Earth's rotation on its axis begins.<br>• Gravitational electromagnetic and nuclear force fields now in effect. |
|  | **SEPARATION of the upper and lower waters by space** | • Upper atmosphere may have had more water vapor than today.<br>• Would help explain longevity before the flood.<br>• Would help explain the flood itself. |
|  | **CREATION of plant life** | • Totally refutes theistic evolution.<br>• Darwin said life began in ancient ocean.<br>• MOSES said it began on dry ground. |
|  | **CREATION of the sun, moon, and stars** | Why was the EARTH created before the SUN?<br>• TO SHOW GOD'S PRIORITY.<br>• To prevent sun worship. |
|  | **CREATION of fish and fowl** | • Included the tiny humming bird.<br>• Included the mighty blue whale. |
|  | **CREATION of land animals and man** | Included all land animals from the dog to the dinosaur. |
|  | **CREATION COMPLETED. GOD RESTS** | • The seventh day now becomes a symbol of a finished creation.<br>• The only time God is pictured as resting. |

to man, that of *marriage, human government* (Gen. 9), and the *church* (Mt. 16).
This records the second of four methods used by God to bring human beings into this world.
   a. a man without mother or father (Adam)
   b. a woman without a mother (Eve)
   c. a man without a father (Christ)
   d. individuals having both mothers and fathers (all other human beings)
G. Seventh day: God rests (2:1-3).
This is the only place where God is described as resting. Sin would soon enter the picture and the entire Trinity will become involved in redemption.

The first law of thermodynamics is now in effect. This law says that energy can be changed from one form to another, but it cannot be created or destroyed.

Here we have in fifty-six simple but sublime verses (Gen. 1 and 2) the concise but complete account of creation. The first of these verses (1:1) should be looked upon as a summary statement. God here tells us just *what* he did. The remaining fifty-five verses then become detailed statements informing us just *how* he went about doing all he said he did.

The creation of angels is not mentioned in the original week. However, in the book of Job (38:7) the Bible seems to place their creation at the same time as that of the stars. If this is correct, the angels came into being on the fourth day. Others feel this same chapter (38:4) indicated angels were present at the creation of the earth. If this is true, then angels must have been created sometime during the very first day of the Creation week.

II. The Corruption of All Things (Gen. 3-5).
At a later place in this study we will consider a popular (but in our opinion erroneous) position known as the Gap Theory. In a nutshell this theory locates the fall of Satan between Genesis 1:1 and 1:2. To the contrary, however, Moses seems to place it between the second and third chapters of Genesis. Helpful background material concerning the events transpiring between these two chapters can be found in Isaiah 14 and Ezekiel 28.
   A. The subtlety of Satan (3:1).
      1. He speaks through the serpent. Eve is tempted to disobey God by the devil who talks with her through the serpent's body. Adam and Eve could apparently communicate with the animal kingdom prior to the Fall in ways totally unknown to us today.

      Prior to the Fall, the serpent was not only the most intelligent creature of all, but perhaps the most beautiful also. It is clear from the later account (see 3:14) that the serpent did not crawl as it does today. It may even have had wings and stood upright. The serpent is the first of three creatures besides man which speaks in the Bible. (For the other two, see Num. 22:28, where an ass speaks; and Rev. 8:13, where an eagle talks.) From this point on, the serpent becomes a symbol for treachery and sin.

      "Their poison is like the poison of a ser-

## THE GAP THEORY

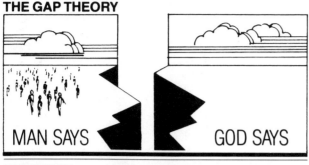

MAN SAYS                    GOD SAYS

| | |
|---|---|
| **MEANING OF** | • In Gen. 1:1 God created a perfect and complete universe. • Between 1:1 and 1:2 Satan's rebellion marred this perfect universe. • From 1:2 on, God remolds this sin-marred creation. |
| **POPULARITY OF** | Made popular and well known by two men: • George H. Pember in 1876 • C.I. Scofield in 1917 |

### CONSIDERATION OF

| | *Arguments FOR Gap Theory* | | *Arguments AGAINST Gap Theory* |
|---|---|---|---|
| WORDS | "Without form and void" always indicate judgment. (See Isa. 34:11; 45:18; Jer. 4:23.) | FALSE. | Words can often simply refer to lifelessness and empty space. (See Job 26:7; Deut. 32:10.) |
| VERB | "Was" in 1:2 should be translated "became." | FALSE. | Hebrew word *hayetha* (was) is almost always translated "was." It is used 264 times in the Pentateuch. Of these, it is translated "was" 258 times. See Jonah 3:3 for an example. |
| THERE IS A DIFFERENCE BETWEEN CREATED *(BARA)* AND MADE *(ASAH)* | | FALSE. | Words are used interchangeably. EXAMPLE: 1. GOD created *(bara)* the great sea monsters (1:21). 2. GOD made *(asah)* the beast of the earth (1:15). 3. "Let us make [*asah*] man" (1:26). 4. "So God created [*bara*] man" (1:27). |
| WORD "DARKNESS" INDICATES JUDGMENT. (SEE 1:2.) | | FALSE. | Darkness here is simply the absence of light and is sometimes spoken of as being good. (See Ps. 104:20, 24.) |
| WORD "REPLENISH" IN 1:28 INDICATES THE WORLD WAS ONCE FILLED. | | FALSE. | Hebrew word *male* almost always means simply "to fill." (See Ex. 40:34; 1 Ki. 18:33; Ps. 107:9.) |

pent: they are like the deaf adder that stoppeth her ear" (Ps. 58:4).

"Ye serpents, ye generation of vipers, how can ye escape the damnation of hell" (Mt. 23:33).

"And the great dragon was cast out, that old serpent, called the Devil, and Satan, which deceiveth the whole world: he was cast out into the earth, and his angels were cast out with him" (Rev. 12:9).

"And he laid hold on the dragon, that old serpent, which is the Devil, and Satan, and bound him a thousand years" (Rev. 20:2).

2. He begins by doubting God's Word.

"Yea, hath God said . . .?" (3:1). Eve now foolishly attempts to match her wits with the devil. No child of God should even try this. We are to resist him (1 Pet. 5:8, 9; Jas. 4:7), but never to debate him!

"Be sober, be vigilant; because your adversary the devil, as a roaring lion, walketh about, seeking whom he may devour: Whom resist stedfast in the faith, knowing that the same afflictions are accomplished in your brethren that are in the world" (1 Pet. 5:8, 9).

"Submit yourselves therefore to God. Resist the devil, and he will flee from you" (Jas. 4:7).

To make matters worse, Eve adds to God's Word during the debate (3:3). God did not tell her not to touch the fruit. The devil laughs with hellish glee when he can trick someone into either adding to or subtracting from God's Word.

"Every word of God is pure: he is a shield unto them that put their trust in him. Add thou not unto his words, lest he reprove thee, and thou be found a liar" (Prov. 30:5, 6).

"For I testify unto every man that heareth the words of the prophecy of this book, If any man shall add unto these things, God shall add unto him the plagues that are written in this book: And if any man shall take away from the words of the book of this prophecy, God shall take away his part out of the book of life, and out of the holy city, and from the things which are written in this book" (Rev. 22:18, 19).

3. He ends by denying God's Word.

"And the serpent said . . . ye shall not surely die" (3:4). Are there any lies in the Bible? There are indeed and here is the first one. God told Adam and Eve they would die if they disobeyed, but Satan says they will not. It should, of course, be quickly noted here that while the Bible certainly *teaches* no lies whatsoever, it does, on occasion, faithfully *record* the lies of both sinners (Saul, for example—see 1 Sam. 15:20) and saints (David, see 1 Sam. 21:2).

Many centuries later the apostle John would warn all believers to beware of three deadly temptations. These are (1) the lust of the flesh, (2) the lust of the eyes, and (3) the pride of life. See 1 John 2:15-17. In the Garden, Satan now subjects Eve to all three.

a. "The woman saw the tree was good for food" *(lust of the flesh).*
b. "And that it was pleasant to the eyes" *(lust of the eyes).*
c. "And a tree to . . . make one wise" *(pride of life).*

Our Lord would later be tempted in a similar manner by the devil in the wilderness. (See Mt. 4:3-10.)

a. "Command that these stones be made bread" *(lust of the flesh).*
b. "He showeth him all the kingdoms of the world" *(lust of the eyes).*
c. "Cast thyself down [from the pinnacle of the temple] . . . for he shall give his angels charge concerning thee . . ." *(pride of life).*

Note Satan's work in Genesis 3:5—"for God doth know that in the day ye eat thereof, then your eyes shall be opened, and ye shall be as God, knowing good and evil."

In one sense, Satan's promises were true. Their eyes *were* opened, and they *did* know good and evil, *but not as God did!* Thus, a half-truth presented as the whole truth is an untruth. God wanted Adam to know what the good *is* and what the evil *would* be, but instead he now would discover what the evil *was* and what the good *would have been!*

Instead of recognizing the evil from the summit of the good, they now must recognize the good from the abyss of evil. Often, experience is *not* the best teacher, for sometimes the tuition is too expensive!

- **THE HIGHLIGHT OF GOD'S CREATION**
- **ABSOLUTELY UNIQUE**
- **MADE IN GOD'S IMAGE**
- **DECLARED KING OF CREATION**
- **COMMANDED NOT TO EAT OF THE TREE OF THE KNOWLEDGE OF GOOD AND EVIL**
- **ENCOURAGED TO EAT OF ALL OTHER TREES**
- **GIVEN A WIFE**

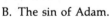

## SEVEN FACTS ABOUT ADAM

B. The sin of Adam.
1. He becomes the first human sinner.
   Chronologically, Eve ate first, but theologically, Adam is declared by the New Testament to be the original sinner. The reason for this is that Adam was the head of the human race, and, therefore, responsible for its actions.

   "Wherefore, as by one man sin entered into the world, and death by sin; and so death passed upon all men, for that all have sinned" (Rom. 5:12).

   "But I fear, lest by any means, as the serpent beguiled Eve though his subtilty,

so your minds should be corrupted from the simplicity that is in Christ" (2 Cor. 11:3).

   "And Adam was not deceived, but the woman being deceived was in the transgression" (1 Tim. 2:14).

2. He attempts (at first) to hide his nakedness before God (3:7). Apparently some drastic change occurred concerning Adam's physical as well as his spiritual condition. It may be that the bodies of Adam and Eve were, at creation, covered with a soft light of innocence. Our Lord was clothed with a light brighter than the sun during his transfiguration. (See Mt. 17:2.)

   But now this protection is gone. In a desperate effort to correct the situation, they "sewed fig leaves together and made themselves aprons" (3:7).

   We now have the first example of manmade religion in history. Religion is any attempt to clothe ourselves apart from the righteousness of Christ. Adam and Eve tried it with fig leaves. Men today try it with education, church membership, baptism, tithing, confirmation, good works, etc. But all to no avail.

   "But we are all as an unclean thing, and all our righteousnesses are as filthy rags; and we all do fade as a leaf; and our iniquities, like the wind, have taken us away" (Isa. 64:6).

3. He attempts (at last) to hide himself from God.

   "Adam and his wife hid themselves from the presence of the Lord . . ." (3:8).

   This is the ultimate tragic result of sin. It not only separates man from God, but makes him actually desire to hide from God. But this cannot be done!

   "O God, thou knowest my foolishness; and my sins are not hid from thee" (Ps. 69:5).

   "Whither shall I go from thy spirit? or whither shall I flee from thy presence?" (Ps. 139:7).

   "Fear them not therefore: for there is nothing covered, that shall not be revealed; and hid, that shall not be known" (Mt. 10:26).

   "And the kings of the earth, and the great men, and the rich men, and the chief captains, and the mighty men, and every bondman, and every free man, hid themselves in the dens and in the rocks of the mountains; And said to the mountains and rocks, Fall on us, and hide us from the face of him that sitteth on the throne, and from the wrath of the Lamb: For the great day of his wrath is come; and who shall be able to stand?" (Rev. 6:15-17).

C. The redemption of God.
Up to this point we have seen only those attributes of God directly involved in his *creative* acts. These would include his power and wisdom. In this chapter, however, after man's sin, we are in-

Genesis 3

## THE FIVEFOLD JUDGMENT UPON SIN

**UPON MAN**
Wearisome toil

**UPON WOMAN**
Suffering in childbirth
Subordination to man

**UPON NATURE**
Thorns and thistles
Aimlessness

**UPON THE SERPENT**
To crawl upon its belly

**UPON SATAN**
To suffer a fatal head wound

HE PROMISED ADAM A SAVIOR

HE SOUGHT ADAM OUT

HE CLOTHED ADAM

HE REMOVED ADAM FROM THE GARDEN

## THE FOURFOLD GRACE OF GOD

troduced to his *redemptive* attributes, those of his holiness and his grace.

1. His holiness, as God deals with *sin*. God now pronounces a fivefold judgment sentence.
   a. Upon the man (3:17).
   "Cursed is the ground for thy sake." God is careful never to put a curse on Adam. He curses the serpent, Satan, and the soil, but not mankind. The reason, of course, is that he desired to redeem man and, therefore, would not curse that which he planned to later save. Even so, the un-saved man can expect nothing good in this life apart from Christ.
   "Yet man is born unto trouble, as the sparks fly upward" (Job 5:7).
   "Man that is born of a woman is of few days, and full of trouble" (Job 14:1).
   b. Upon the woman (3:16).
   "In sorrow thou shalt bring forth chil-dren." It should be noted that the suffer-

ing of childbirth is not so much a direct judgment from God, but rather an in-direct result of sin. Sin always causes suf-fering, sickness, separation, and sorrow.
   c. Upon all nature (3:18).
   "Thorns . . . and thistles shall it bring forth." From this point on, man's para-dise becomes a wilderness. The roses now contain thorns and the docile tiger suddenly becomes a hungry meat eater! This will continue to be the case until the curse is lifted during the millennium. In the New Testament Paul writes about all this in Romans 8:19-22:
   "For the earnest expectation of the creature waiteth for the manifestation of the sons of God. For the creature was made subject to vanity, not will-ingly, but by reason of him who hath subjected the same in hope, because the creature itself also shall be deliv-ered from the bondage of corruption into the glorious liberty of the chil-dren of God. For we know that the whole creation groaneth and travail-eth in pain together until now."
At this point, that immutable scientific principle called the Second Law of Ther-modynamics came into being. This law states that when energy is being trans-formed from one state to another, some of it is turned into heat energy which cannot be converted back into useful form. In other words, this universe may be looked upon as a wound-up clock that is slowly running down. This law is ex-panded in Psalm 102:26 and Hebrews 1:10-12.
   "And, Thou, Lord, in the beginning hast laid the foundation of the earth; and the heavens are the works of thine hands: They shall perish; but thou remainest; and they all shall wax old as doth a garment; And as a ves-ture shalt thou fold them up, and they shall be changed: but thou art the same, and thy years shall not fail" (Heb. 1:10-12).

## THE VICIOUS VOCABULARY OF SIN

| AS INTRODUCED BY THE FIRST ADAM | | | AS DEALT WITH BY THE SECOND ADAM | | |
|---|---|---|---|---|---|
| *BY* **GEN. 2:17** | *HE INTRODUCED...* | **DEATH** | *BY* **HEB. 2:9** | *HE DEALT WITH...* | **DEATH** |
| *BY* **GEN. 3:17** | *HE INTRODUCED...* | **NAKEDNESS** | *BY* **JN. 19:23** | *HE DEALT WITH...* | **NAKEDNESS** |
| *BY* **GEN. 3:14** | *HE INTRODUCED...* | **CURSE** | *BY* **GAL. 3:13** | *HE DEALT WITH...* | **CURSE** |
| *BY* **GEN. 3:17** | *HE INTRODUCED...* | **SORROW** | *BY* **ISA. 53:3** | *HE DEALT WITH...* | **SORROW** |
| *BY* **GEN. 3:18** | *HE INTRODUCED...* | **THORNS** | *BY* **JN. 19:5** | *HE DEALT WITH...* | **THORNS** |
| *BY* **GEN. 3:19** | *HE INTRODUCED...* | **SWEAT** | *BY* **LK. 22:44** | *HE DEALT WITH...* | **SWEAT** |
| *BY* **GEN. 3:24** | *HE INTRODUCED...* | **SWORD** | *BY* **JN. 19:34** | *HE DEALT WITH...* | **SWORD** |

d. Upon the serpent (3:14).

"And . . . God said unto the serpent . . . upon thy belly shalt thou go."

The serpent is not offered a chance to explain its actions as God allowed Adam and Eve to do. Judgment is passed out immediately. For lending its body to Satan, the serpent was cursed to crawl in the dust from that point on. Isaiah indicates that this judgment will continue to be binding upon the serpent even during the millennium!

"The wolf and the lamb shall feed together, and the lion shall eat straw like the bullock: and dust shall be the serpent's meat. They shall not hurt nor destroy in all my holy mountain, saith the Lord" (Isa. 65:25).

e. Upon the devil (3:15).

"And I will put enmity between thee and the woman, and between thy seed and her seed; it shall bruise thy head, and thou shalt bruise his heel" (Gen. 3:15).

At first glance this verse would merely seem to predict the natural hatred of man for snakes. But for centuries devout Bible students have seen a far more precious and profound truth underlying these words. For in this verse they claim to see no less than a thrilling prediction of the Cross and the resurrection, of the Savior's great victory over Satan. Theologically, then, verse 15 may be translated as follows:

"And there will be intense hatred between Satan and Christ. Eventually Christ will crush the head of Satan, while suffering a heel wound in the process."

This all-important verse is known as the "Proto-Evangel," the first Gospel.

See also:

"And the God of peace shall bruise Satan under your feet shortly. The grace of our Lord Jesus Christ be with you. Amen" (Rom. 16:20).

"But he was wounded for our transgressions, he was bruised for our iniquities: the chastisement of our peace was upon him; and with his stripes we are healed" (Isa. 53:5).

2. His grace, as God deals with sinners.

a. In seeking out Adam (3:9).

"And the Lord God called unto Adam." Sometimes foolish and wicked college professors tell their students that the Bible is simply a record of man's search after God; but it is instead the opposite. The Bible is a record of God's search after man! Here God takes the first step in reconciling man back to himself.

"Come now, and let us reason together, saith the Lord: though your sins be as scarlet, they shall be as white as snow; though they be red like crimson, they shall be as wool" (Isa. 1:18).

"Ho, every one that thirsteth, come ye to the waters, and he that hath no money; come ye, buy, and eat; yea, come, buy wine and milk without money and without price. Wherefore do ye spend money for that which is not bread? and your labour for that which satisfieth not? hearken diligently unto me, and eat ye that which is good, and let your soul delight itself in fatness. Incline your ear, and come unto me: hear, and your soul shall live; and I will make an everlasting covenant with you, even the sure mercies of David" (Isa. 55:1-3).

"In the last day, that great day of the feast, Jesus stood and cried, saying, If any man thirst, let him come unto me, and drink. He that believeth on me, as the scripture hath said, out of his belly shall flow rivers of living water" (Jn. 7:37, 38).

"And the Spirit and the bride say, Come. And let him that heareth say, Come. And let him that is athirst come. And whosoever will, let him take the water of life freely" (Rev. 22:17).

"For the Son of man is come to seek and to save that which was lost" (Lk. 19:10).

b. In promising them a Savior (3:15).

c. In clothing them (3:21).

"God made coats of skins and clothed them."

Although we are not specifically told so, it would seem probable that some innocent animal had to die so that Adam and his wife might be clothed. Thus, here we have the first example of that great biblical doctrine, the innocent dying for the guilty.

"But he was wounded for our transgressions, he was bruised for our iniquities: the chastisement of our peace was upon him; and with his stripes we are healed. All we like sheep have gone astray; we have turned every one to his own way; and the Lord hath laid on him the iniquity of us all" (Isa. 53:5, 6).

"For Christ also hath once suffered for sins, the just for the unjust, that he might bring us to God, being put to death in the flesh but quickened by the Spirit" (1 Pet. 3:18).

Note: We have already seen the first symbol in the Bible when the serpent became a type for sin. We now observe the second symbol—righteousness and salvation are likened to right clothes. (Compare Isa. 64:6 with Rev. 19:7, 8.)

"But we are all as an unclean thing, and all our righteousnesses are as filthy rags; and we all do fade as a leaf; and our iniquities, like the wind, have taken us away" (Isa. 64:6).

"Let us be glad and rejoice, and give honour to him: for the marriage of the Lamb is come, and his wife hath made herself ready. And to her was granted that she should be arrayed in fine linen, clean and white: for the fine linen is the righteousness of saints" (Rev. 19:7, 8).

d. In removing them from the Garden of Eden (3:24).

"So he drove out the man."

Man's expulsion from Eden by God was really an act of mercy rather than judgment. As we are told in 3:22, God did this to prevent mankind from partaking of the tree of life and living forever in immorality. Adolf Hitler killed himself a few days after reaching his fifty-sixth birthday. Yet during his brief life span, he was directly responsible for the slaughter of literally millions of human beings by shooting, bombing, hanging, burning, gassing, and other forms of torture and death too horrible to mention. But what if this Nazi monster had lived to be 500 or even 5000? Or worse still, what if he could have lived forever? This is why God drove Adam from Eden.

"He placed . . . cherubims and a flaming sword" (3:24).

The cherubims are apparently a special kind of angelic being who concern themselves with matters relating to the holiness of God. (See Ex. 25:18–22; Ezek. 10:1–20; Rev. 4:6–8.) This is the first of two kinds of angels mentioned in the Bible. The other kind are known as the seraphims. (See Isa. 6.)

"In the year that king Uzziah died I saw also the Lord sitting upon a throne, high and lifted up, and his train filled the temple. Above it stood the seraphims: each one had six wings; with twain he covered his face, and with twain he covered his feet, and with twain he did fly. And one cried unto another, and said, Holy, holy, holy, is the Lord of hosts: the whole earth is full of his glory. And the posts of the door moved at the voice of him that cried, and the house was filled with smoke" (Isa. 6:1–4).

"To keep the way of the tree of life" (3:24).

At this point, the tree of life disappears from the pages of the Bible. It reappears once again during the millennial and eternal age.

"And he shewed me a pure river of water of life, clear as crystal, proceeding out of the throne of God and of the Lamb. In the midst of the street of it, and on either side of the river, was there the tree of life, which bare twelve manner of fruits, and yielded her fruit every month: and the leaves of the tree were for the healing of the nations" (Rev. 22:1, 2).

D. The Martyrdom of Abel (Gen. 4).
1. Eve gives birth to Cain and exclaims, "I have gotten a man from the Lord" (4:1). Here she apparently felt this baby was the fulfillment of Genesis 3:15. She would soon know differently. Abel is then born (4:2).

The birth of these two babies illustrates the fourth of four methods God has chosen to bring human beings into this world.
   a. Adam—born without father or mother.
   b. Eve—born without a mother.
   c. Christ—born without a father.
   d. All others—both with father and mother.

2. Cain brings a bloodless offering to God and is rejected (4:5). Not only was the sacrifice bloodless, but it had already been cursed by God; therefore, Cain added insult to injury. (See 3:17). Cain may have thought it to be far more refined and cultured to bring fresh fruit and vegetables rather than a bloody animal offering, but not so!

"There is a way which seemeth right unto a man, but the end thereof are the ways of death" (Prov. 14:12).

We have in this verse the first plank of that great scriptural platform of truth that without the shedding of blood there is no remission of sin. (See Lev. 17:11; Heb. 9:22.)

"And almost all things are by the law purged with blood; and without shedding of blood is no remission" (Heb. 9:22).

Abel offers a lamb sacrifice and is accepted (4:4).

Dr. Barnhouse has written the following:

"The highway to the cross was now firmly established. Here the first lamb is seen, one lamb for one man. Later, at the Passover, there will be one lamb for one household (Ex. 12). Then, on the Day of Atonement, there will be one sacrifice for the nation (Lev. 16). Finally, it is Christ who takes away the sin of the world" (Jn. 1:29).

This was God's way then of illustrating the awesome power of the bleeding Lamb. One Lamb saves a man, then a household, then a nation, and finally is available through the Lamb of God for the whole world.

3. Cain slays his brother. Cain now becomes the first murderer (4:8). He also becomes the first human liar (see 4:9).

4. Cain is driven from the blessings of God. He marries one of his sisters (4:17; 5:4) and dwells in the land of Nod. Let us observe some recorded facts concerning earth's first civilization.
   a. *Cain* builds the first city and names it Enoch (after his own son), which means "dedication." This urban project was no doubt an attempt to counteract God's curse in 4:12.
   b. *Lamech*, Cain's great-great-great-grandson becomes:

(1) the first recorded polygamist (4:19)
(2) the first recorded songwriter (the word "speech" in 4:23 may refer to a poem or ballad)
(3) the second recorded murderer (4:23)

c. *Jabal* becomes the inventor of the tent and developer of the Nomadic life style. He also devised formal systems for domesticating and commercially producing animals apart from sheep. His name means "wanderer" (4:20).

d. *Jubal* becomes the inventor of both stringed and wind musical instruments. His name means "sound" (4:21).

e. *Tubal-Cain* becomes the inventor of metallurgy both in bronze and iron (4:22).

E. The ministry of Enoch.

1. He is one of two men who was said to have walked with God before the flood. (The other was Noah—see 6:9.) Note: It does not say he walked with God, however, until his first son, Methuselah, was born. In the Hebrew language, the name Methuselah literally means, "When he is dead it shall be sent." Why did Enoch walk with God? Because God had apparently told him that when Methuselah died the world was going to be destroyed by the terrible flood. This is probably why Methuselah lived longer than any man in the history of the world (969 years), for God was not willing that any should perish and was giving sinful mankind as much time for repentance as possible.

"The Lord is not slack concerning his promise, as some men count slackness; but is longsuffering to us-ward, not willing that any should perish, but that all should come to repentance" (2 Pet. 3:9).

"Who will have all men to be saved, and to come unto the knowledge of the truth" (1 Tim. 2:4).

2. Enoch was the first recorded preacher and he preached on the coming judgment. In Jude 1:14, 15 we actually have his recorded message:

"And Enoch also, the seventh from Adam, prophesied of these, saying, Behold, the Lord cometh with ten thousands of his saints, To execute judgment upon all, and to convince all that are ungodly among them of all their ungodly deeds which they have ungodly committed, and of all their hard speeches which ungodly sinners have spoken against him."

3. Enoch was a man of great faith (Heb. 11:5). "By faith Enoch was translated that he should not see death; and was not found, because God had translated him: for before his translation he had this testimony, that he pleased God."

But just how did Enoch demonstrate this great faith ascribed to him? Well, here was a preacher who fervently spoke of Christ's *second* coming centuries before his *first* coming had taken place.

4. Enoch was one of two human beings who got to heaven without dying physically. (For the other, see 2 Ki. 2:11.) Someday, however, millions of Christians will experience the same thing.

"Behold, I shew you a mystery; We shall not all sleep, but we shall all be changed, in a moment, in the twinkling of an eye, at the last trump: for the trumpet shall sound, and the dead shall be raised incorruptible, and we shall be changed" (1 Cor. 15:51, 52).

"For the Lord himself shall descend from heaven with a shout, with the voice of the archangel, and with the trump of God: and the dead in Christ shall rise first: Then we which are alive and remain shall be caught up together with them in the clouds, to meet the Lord in the air: and so shall we ever be with the Lord" (1 Thess. 4:16, 17).

III. The Condemnation of All Things (Gen. 6–9).

A. The conditions prior to the Flood.

1. A great population explosion took place (6:1). Man has consistently broken every single command given by God with the exception of the very first one. This one he has consistently obeyed! "Be fruitful, and multiply, and fill the earth . . ." (Gen. 1:28).

2. There was an outpouring of satanic activity (6:2).

3. All humanity had become depraved. Wickedness, both in word and deed, was both universal and unparalleled (6:5, 11).

4. As a result of all this, "it repented the Lord that he had made man on earth, and it grieved him at his heart" (6:6). The Hebrew (*nacham*) and Greek (*metanoia*) words for repentance have both a literal and a theological meaning.

a. the literal meaning—to be eased, to be comforted (*nacham*)

b. the theological meaning—to change one's mind (*metanoia*)

Combining both meanings, it may be said that God's original creation had ceased to reflect his glory (see Rev. 4:11) to the extent that he was no longer comforted by it. He, therefore, changed his previous course of action toward humanity and determined to destroy it by a mighty universal flood.

5. The Flood would occur 120 years from this point (6:3).

B. The salvation through the Flood.

1. God informs Noah (who had found grace in his sight) to construct a 450 × 75 × 45-foot floating barge.

Some have limited the word *law* to the Old Testament, and the word *grace* to the New Testament. But this is a serious error. Here in Genesis 6, early in Old Testament history, and long before the Mosaic Law, Noah experiences the marvelous *grace* of God. A more correct summary of the Old and New Testament would thus be:

a. The Old Testament is the account of how God *in grace* dealt with the nation of Israel and sinners.

b. The New Testament is the account of

how God in grace deals with the church and sinners.

2. Noah was to cover both the outside and inside of the ark with pitch. The Hebrew word here translated pitch is *kaphar*. In almost every other instance in the Old Testament *kaphar* is translated by the word *atonement*. (See Ex. 30:10.) To atone is to cover with blood. As the oily pitch protected the ark from the Flood judgment, so the blood of Christ protects the believer from the sin judgment. Thus far, we may note the following Old Testament types:

   a. Enoch is a type of the church, being saved *from* the Flood judgment. (The church will not go through the great tribulation.)

   b. Noah is a type of Israel, being saved *through* the Flood judgment. (Israel will go through the great tribulation.)

3. Noah gathered a male and female of all earth's animals (including seven pairs of clean animals, such as the ox and lamb) and, along with his wife, three sons, and their wives, at the command of God, boarded the ark.

   This passage (Gen. 7:1) is the first to record the word *come* in the Bible.

   "And the Lord said unto Noah, Come thou and all thy house into the ark. . . ."
   The final reference to this word is:

   "And the Spirit and the bride say, Come. And let him that heareth say, Come. And let him that is athirst come. And whosoever will, let him take the water of life freely" (Rev. 22:17).

4. God "remembered" Noah during the flood as he later would remember:

   a. Lot in Sodom.
   "And it came to pass, when God destroyed the cities of the plain, that God remembered Abraham, and sent Lot out of the midst of the overthrow, when he overthrew the cities in the which Lot dwelt" (Gen. 19:29).

   b. Israel in Egypt.
   "And God heard their groaning, and God remembered his covenant with Abraham, with Isaac, and with Jacob" (Ex. 2:24).
   "And I have also heard the groaning of the children of Israel, whom the Egyptians keep in bondage; and I have remembered my covenant" (Ex. 6:5).

   c. The thief on the cross.
   "And he said unto Jesus, Lord, remember me when thou comest into thy kingdom" (Lk. 23:42).

5. The flood passes and the ark rests upon the mountains of Ararat. Noah is told by God to "be fruitful and multiply upon the earth" (8:17; 9:1). Adam had once heard similar words (1:28), but here after the flood the word *subdue* is left out. Scofield writes the following concerning Genesis 1:28.

   "This is the divine magna charta for all true scientific and material process. Man

began with a mind that was perfect in its finite capacity for learning, but he did not begin knowing all the secrets of the universe. He is commanded to 'subdue,' i.e., acquire a knowledge and mastery over his material environment, to bring its elements into the service of the race." (*New Scofield Bible*, p. 4)

But now Eden's sin and the Flood judgment had so radically changed man's environment that he would find it quite impossible to fully subdue anything.

These verses in Genesis, if rightly understood, help explain a rather strange miracle performed by Christ in the New Testament. It all began when Simon Peter came to Jesus concerning the needed payment of a certain tribute tax. The Savior responded by ordering his apostle to "go thou to the sea, and cast a hook, and take up the fish that first cometh up; and when thou hast opened his mouth thou shalt find a piece of money: that take, and give unto them for me and thee" (Mt. 17:27). This miracle, if properly considered, demonstrates more clearly the Savior's perfect *humanity* than his *deity*, for Adam could have (and possibly did) exercised this same power over both fish and fowl. Again, consider the divine command given to Adam:

"Be fruitful, and multiply, and fill the earth, and subdue it; and have dominion over the fish of the sea, and over the fowl of the air, and over every living thing that moveth upon the earth" (Gen. 1:28).

6. God now establishes a rainbow covenant with Noah. The covenant elements are as follows:

   a. God would never again destroy the earth of men through a flood (8:21, 22; 9:9-17). But the earth will be destroyed again, this time through a fire. (See 2 Pet. 3:1-13.)
   "But the day of the Lord will come as a thief in the night; in the which the heavens shall pass away with a great noise, and the elements shall melt with fervent heat, the earth also and the works that are therein shall be burned up" (2 Pet. 3:10).

   b. God would require the life of a man who murdered another man (9:6).

   c. The order and seasons of nature are confirmed (8:22).

   d. The fear of animals for man is prophesied (9:2).

   e. The flesh of animals for man's diet is permitted (9:3).

C. The tragedy following the Flood (9:20-29).

   1. Noah becomes drunken from his own vineyard and exposes himself within his tent.

   2. His son Ham and grandson Canaan view this nakedness. Canaan especially, incurs the wrath of his grandfather for the part he played in this.

   3. Noah predicts the future physical and spiritual life style of his three sons and their descendants.

4. Noah dies at the age of 950. The ultimate tragedy in his life may be seen by the fact that no spiritual accomplishments whatsoever are recorded during his final 350 years. He apparently experienced that thing so dreaded by Paul—being set on a shelf by God. (See 1 Cor. 9:19-27.)

"But I keep under my body, and bring it into subjection: lest that by any means, when I have preached to others, I myself should be a castaway" (1 Cor. 9:27).

IV. The Confusion of All Things (Gen. 10–11).
   A. The arrogance of man.
      A rebel named Nimrod (grandson of Ham) instigates a religious building program (consisting of both an astrological tower and a city) on the plains of Shinar near Babylon (11:1-4).
   B. The judgment of God.
      God punishes this evil attempt and separates mankind into small ethnic groups by confusing their once universal language into many dialects (11:5-9).
   C. The origin of nations.
      The ancient world is now settled by the descendants of Noah's three sons.
      1. The descendants of Japheth (10:2-5).
         Some of his descendants and the peoples they founded would be:
         a. Gomer (Germany)
         b. Magog, Tubal, and Mechech (Russia)
         c. Madai (Persia)
         d. Javan (Greece)
         e. Tiras (Italy)
         f. Togarmah (Armenia)
         g. Tarshish (Spain)
         h. Kittim (Cyprus)
      2. The descendants of Ham (10:6-20).
         Some of his descendants and the peoples they founded would be:
         a. Cush (Ethiopia)
         b. Mizraim (Egypt)
         c. Phut (Africa)
         d. Canaan (the Canaanites of Palestine)
         e. Nimrod (Babylon and Assyria)
         f. Sidon (Phoenicia)
         g. Heth (Hittites)
         h. Jebus (the Jebusites, the occupants of Jerusalem prior to David's reign)
         i. Pilistim (the Philistines)
         j. Sin (possible founder of the oriental peoples, China, Japan, India, etc.)
      3. The descendants of Shem (10:21-32; 11:10-32).
         a. Through Abraham, Isaac, and Jacob: the nation Israel.
         b. Through Abraham, Ishmael, and Esau: the Middle East Arab countries.
         Anthropologist Arthur Custance writes:
         "And thus we conclude that from the family of Noah have sprung all the peoples of the world, prehistoric and historic. The events described in connection with Genesis 6 to 10 and particularly the prophetic statements of Noah himself in Genesis 9:25-28 with respect to the future of his three sons, Shem, Ham, and Japheth, together combine to provide us

## NOAH—GENESIS 9:20–27

THE FAILURE OF NOAH: DRUNKENNESS
THE SIN OF CANAAN: UNKNOWN, PERHAPS THAT OF HOMOSEXUALITY

### THE THREEFOLD PROPHECY OF NOAH

| CONCERNING HAM AND CANAAN: | CONCERNING JAPHETH: | CONCERNING SHEM: |
|---|---|---|
| General servitude to seed of Shem and Japheth. | "God shall enlarge Japheth, and he shall dwell in the tents of Shem." | |
| **"A SERVANT OF SERVANTS"** | **"GOD SHALL ENLARGE JAPHETH"** | **"BLESSED BE THE LORD GOD OF SHEM"** |
| • Joshua, David, and Solomon subdued them. <br> • Alexander the Great subdued them. <br> • The Romans subdued them. | • Since 539 B.C., with the defeat of the Babylonians by Cyrus the Great, no Semitic or Hamitic race has succeeded in breaking the world supremacy of the Japhethic race. | • Here is obviously a reference to the special favor bestowed upon Shem's descendants, beginning with Abraham, and ending in a Bethlehem manger. |
| **TECHNICAL PROFICIENCY** | **"AND HE SHALL DWELL IN THE TENTS OF SHEM."** | |
| The famous Christian anthropologist Arthur C. Custance states that all the earliest civilizations of note were founded and carried to the highest technical proficiency by Hamitic peoples. | This glorious prophecy is fully explained by Paul in Rom. 11:13-25. | |

### THE THREEFOLD CONTRIBUTION OF NOAH'S SONS

| HAM | JAPHETH | SHEM |
|---|---|---|
| • Technical proficiency. <br> • Responsible for man's physical well-being. | • Application of philosophy. <br> • Development of the scientific method. <br> • Responsible for man's mental well-being. | • Religious insights. <br> • Responsible for man's spiritual well-being. |

with the most reasonable account of the early history of mankind, a history which, rightly understood, does not at all require us to believe that modern man began with the stature of an ape and only reached a civilized state after a long, long evolutionary history, but made a fresh start as a single family who carried with them into an unpeopled earth the accumulated heritage of the pre-flood world.

In summary, then, what we have endeavored to show in this paper may be set forth briefly as follows:

(1) The geographical distribution of fossil remains is such that they are most logically explained by treating them as marginal representatives of a widespread and, in part, forced dispersion of people from a single multiplying population, established at a point more or less central to them all, which sent forth successive

waves of migrants, each wave driving the previous one further towards the periphery.

(2) The most degraded specimens are representatives of this general movement who were driven into the least hospitable areas where they suffered physical degeneration as a consequence of the circumstances in which they were forced to live.

(3) The extraordinary physical variability of their remains stems from the fact that they were members of small, isolated, strongly inbred bands; whereas the cultural similarities which link together even the most widely dispersed of them indicate a common origin for them all.

(4) What is true of fossil man is equally true of vanished and of living primitive societies.

(5) All these initially dispersed populations are of one basic stock—the Hamitic family of Genesis 10.

(6) They were subsequently displaced or overwhelmed by the Indo-Europeans (i.e., Japhethites) who nevertheless inherited, or adopted and extensively built upon, their technology and so gained the upper hand in each geographical area where they spread.

(7) Throughout this movement, both in prehistoric and historic times, there were never any human beings who did not belong within the family of Noah and his descendants.

(8) Finally, this thesis is strengthened by the evidence of history, which shows that migration has always tended to follow this pattern, has frequently been accompanied by instances of degeneration both of individuals or whole tribes, and usually results in the establishment of a general pattern of cultural relationships, which are paralleled to those that archaeology has since revealed from antiquity." (*Genesis and Early Man*, pp. 56, 57)

# QUESTIONS AND ANSWERS ABOUT GENESIS 1-11

1. How vast is our universe?

It is so vast that it takes a beam of light (which travels some 700 million miles per hour) over 100,000 years just to cover the distance length of our galaxy called the Milky Way. But our galaxy is only one among many billions in the known universe. To illustrate the size of our universe, consider the following four examples:

a. paper stack model

(1) Let us say the thickness of a sheet of paper represents the distance from the earth to the sun (some ninety-three million miles).

(2) To represent the distance to the nearest star we would need a seventy-one-foot high stack of paper.

(3) To cover the diameter of our Milky Way galaxy would require a 310-mile high stack.

(4) To reach the edge of the *known* universe would demand a pile of paper sheets thirty-one *million* miles high.

b. orange and grain of sand model

(1) Here an orange would represent the sun.

(2) A grain of sand is the earth, circling the orange at a distance of thirty feet.

(3) Pluto (most remote planet in our solar system) is another grain of sand, circling the orange at ten city blocks away.

(4) Alpha Centauri (the nearest star) is 1300 miles away from the orange.

c. hollow sun illustration

(1) If the sun were hollow, one million, three hundred thousand earths could fit inside.

(2) A star named Antares (if hollow) could hold sixty-four million of our suns.

(3) In the constellation of Hercules there is a star which could contain 100 million of Antares.

(4) The largest known star, Epsilon, could easily swallow up several million stars the size of the one in Hercules!

d. the relative speed illustration

(1) Our earth is traveling around its own axis at 1000 m.p.h.

(2) It moves around the sun at 67,000 m.p.h.

(3) It is carried by the sun across our galaxy at a speed of 64,000 m.p.h.

(4) It moves in orbit around our galaxy at 481,000 m.p.h.

(5) It travels through space at one million, three hundred and fifty thousand m.p.h.

(6) Every twenty-four hours we cover 57,360,000 miles.

(7) Each year we travel 20,936,400,000 miles across empty space.

All the above is, of course, but a feeble attempt to illustrate the magnitude of space and of a universe which contains as many stars as there are grains of sand on all the seashores of the world. Furthermore, in Psalm 147:4 (also Isa. 40:26), we are told that God has both numbered and named each star.

"He telleth the number of the stars; he calleth them all by their names" (Ps. 147:4).

"Lift up your eyes on high, and behold who hath created these things, that bringeth out their host by number: he calleth them all by names by the greatness of his might, for that he is strong in power; not one faileth" (Isa. 40:26).

But more glorious than all this is the statement that this same omnipotent and omniscient God "healeth the broken in heart and bindeth up their wounds" (Ps. 147:3).

"Great is our Lord, and of great power: his understanding is infinite" (Ps. 147:5).

2. How minute is our universe?

Simply stated, it is as unbelievably small as it is big. Consider the following:

a. All material in the universe consists of *atoms*. Atoms in turn are made up of three "building blocks," which are *protons* and *neutrons* (which two go to make up the center of an atom called the nucleus), and *electrons* (which circle the nucleus as our earth does the sun).

b. On the tip of a ball point pen are so many atoms that if they were carried by an army, marching four abreast, an atom to a man, it would take over 20,000 years for a march-past.

c. It would take 25 trillion protons laid side by side to span a linear inch.

d. There are as many protons in a cubic inch of copper as there are drops of water in the oceans of the world, or grains of sand on the seashores of our earth.

e. The size of an electron is to a dust speck as the dust speck is to the entire earth.

f. The *space* between an electron and the nucleus is 10,000 times as great as the size of that nucleus. For example, if the outer shell of electrons in an atom were the size of the Houston Astrodome, the nucleus would be the size of a Ping-Pong ball in the center of that stadium.

*Question:* If most of the atom is empty space, why does a table top offer so much resistance when you push at it with your finger?

*Answer:* The surface of the table (like the tip of one's finger) consists of a wall of electrons, belonging to the outermost layer of atoms in both objects. Both the speed and force attraction of these electrons thus prohibit your finger from going through the table as a fast-moving bicycle wheel would prevent you from placing your finger through the spokes.

3. How much energy exists within our universe?

a. The protons and neutrons within the nucleus of an atom are held together with a density of one billion tons per cubic inch. This is around forty pounds of energy between each proton.

b. This energy force is one followed by thirty eight zeros times stronger than regular gravitational forces. How big is this number? It is over 100 trillion times larger than the number of all the grains of sand on earth's seashores.

c. German physicist Otto Gail has calculated that a single drop of gasoline, if totally utilized in an automobile, would be sufficient for 400 journeys around the world (a trip involving ten million miles).

d. Albert Einstein estimated the total amount of energy released from one ounce of water could easily lift 200 million tons of steel one mile above the earth.

e. The various stars and galaxies were created by the conversion of energy into mass. It has been determined that the amount of energy used in the creation of only one gram of matter (1/450th of a pound) is equal to 2.5 times the amount of energy generated by Niagara Falls in one entire day. This would be ten million kilowatts.

4. What mysterious secrets lie within our universe?

A prominent scientist once said that man's universe is both unknown and unknowable. Consider:

a. Quasars: These are light sources discovered by Dr. M. Schmidt of the California Institute of Technology in 1963. They are relatively small, yet produce more energy than a cluster of ten trillion stars!

b. Super novaes: These are stars that suddenly increase their luminosity by more than ten million times.

c. Neutron stars: This is a star that implodes (falls in on itself) rather than exploding. The gravitational forces would crush the atoms into nuclear particles called neutrons. A neutron star would have an unbelievable density, as a teaspoon of its material would weigh a billion tons on earth. In fact, its weight would be sufficient to drive itself all the way through our earth. If we collapsed the whole earth to neutron star density, it would be approximately 300 feet in diameter. If you took all the human beings in the world today and put them in one raindrop, you would have such density as exists in a neutron star.

d. Black holes: A black hole occurs when an imploding star continues beyond the neutron stage. Its gravitational forces thus become so strong that even light itself cannot escape. Dr. Kip Thorne, of the California Institute of Technology, writes:

"A black hole is the end product of the catastrophic collapse of a really large star, the ultimate concentration of matter. We believe a black hole is an extremely smooth structure; it can never have ripples or mountains. Anything it traps can never escape. The black hole can neither split nor decrease in size; it can only grow, and nothing can prevent it from growing. Ultimately if the universe itself does not collapse and die first, the black holes will eat up all the matter in our galaxy. Already, as much as one ten thousandth of the universe might be down black holes. We would like to sweep this fact under the rug, but occasionally we drag it out and look it in the face and shudder." (*National Geographic*, May, 1974)

e. Time-light mysteries: As an object reaches the speed of light, time (we are told) slows down. Thus, a rocket ship manned by several men sets out to explore the universe traveling at near the speed of light.

| Destination | Years lapsed aboard ship | Years lapsed on earth |
|---|---|---|
| (1) Alpha Centauri (our closest star) | 3 years, 6 months | ten years |
| (2) Center of our Milky Way | 21 years | 50,000 years |
| (3) Andromeda Galaxy (our nearest galaxy) | 28 years | 2 million years |

f. Length and weight-time mysteries: Not only does time on a space craft (moving at near the speed of light) slow down, but its length and weight are also affected. Imagine a space ship which is 1000 feet long and weighs 1000 tons. At 162,000 miles-per-second, it would measure only 500 feet, but weigh 2000 tons.

It has furthermore been speculated that if a thirty-year old man could somehow remove himself to a planet exactly thirty light years away from our earth and from there point a telescope back to earth, he could actually watch himself being born.

5. How complex is our universe?

Here we refer to life itself. The wonders of the atom

and the glory of the galaxies are but drab tinker toys when compared to the miracle of living organisms.

a. The smallest insect on this earth is made up of millions of living cells. There are some seventy-five trillion such cells in the body of an average man. But each individual cell is unbelievably complex. It has been demonstrated that the simplest living cell is vastly more complicated than the most sophisticated giant computer on earth.

b. Each cell is a world brimming with as many as 200 trillion tiny groups of atoms called protein molecules. It is a micro-universe in itself.

c. The largest molecule is called the DNA (deoxyribonucleic acid). The DNA strand carries the hereditary information from the parent to the offspring in all living things. It contains the genetic code and determines whether you will turn out to be a man, mushroom, dandelion, or dinosaur.

## INDICATIONS OF A RECENT CREATION DATE

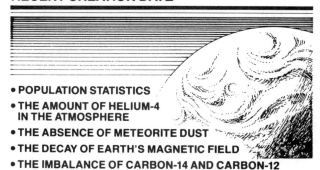

- **POPULATION STATISTICS**
- **THE AMOUNT OF HELIUM-4 IN THE ATMOSPHERE**
- **THE ABSENCE OF METEORITE DUST**
- **THE DECAY OF EARTH'S MAGNETIC FIELD**
- **THE IMBALANCE OF CARBON-14 AND CARBON-12**

d. The total length of the DNA strand in one cell is six feet. If all the DNA strands in the body were bunched up they could fit into a box the size of an ice cube. But if unwound and joined together, the string could stretch from the earth to the sun and back more than 400 times.

e. Each of the seventy-five trillion cells in a man's body contains the information found in all other cells. Thus, a cell in a man's little toe has all the data in its DNA for making another man physically identical to himself.

f. If the coded DNA instructions of a single human cell were put into English, they would fill a 1000-volume encyclopedia.

g. During cell division, two strands of DNA (called the double helix), which have been interwoven around each other in ladder-like fashion, separate to form a new cell. It is believed that the rotation during this unwinding occurs at the rate of more than seventy-five turns a second. This would be somewhat like attempting in a split second to uncoil and separate a huge cathedral packed from top to bottom with twisted and intertwined microphone cord. After the double helix is separated it then duplicates itself into a new cell. This duplication is so accurate that it would correspond to a rate of error of less than one letter in an entire set of the *Encyclopedia Britannica*.

h. A human cell in a laboratory, free from bodily influence, may divide some fifty times before dying. If all of our cells divided that often, we would eventually reach a weight of more than eighty trillion tons.

6. When was the universe created?

Some scientists would confidently tell us its origin occurred via a big bang from five to fifty billion years ago. How are these dates arrived at? One time calendar is called radiometric dating—the dating of rocks. In certain rocks the element uranium 238 decays into lead 206 with a half-life of 4.5 billion years (that is, the decay involves 50% of the original uranium each 4.5 billion years). It is claimed, therefore, that the age of a rock may be determined through this method.

However, there are serious problems at times with radiometric dating. For example, radiometric dating has shown certain rocks from volcanoes in Russia to be five billion years old, whereas it is known they were formed within the last 200 years.

In opposition to the above radical ancient dates, a number of creation scientists now feel there is mounting evidence that our earth may be much younger than supposed, perhaps less than 12,000 years old. These indications are as follows:

a. Population statistics. If man appeared over one million years ago, the present world population would be thousands of times greater than it actually is. In fact, our entire galaxy could not provide the needed space for so many.

The present world population is around 4.3 billion. Assuming the average life span to be seventy years and the average generation length to be thirty-five years, then starting with one family, the present world population would result in about thirty doublings. These doublings would carry us back in history from today to around 3500 B.C. This date is suggested by several creationist scientists to mark the time of the Flood.

Thus, the creation model dovetails beautifully with known world population statistics. But what of the evolutionary model? Morris writes:

"Now, if the first man appeared one million years ago, and these very conservative growth rates applied during that period, the world population would be at present 10 (27000 zeros following) people. However, no more than 10 (with 100 zeros) people could be crammed into the known universe!" (*Science and Creation*, p. 154)

b. The amount of helium-4 in the atmosphere. This suggests that our atmosphere is less than 15,000 years old.

c. The absence of meteorite dust. Some fifteen million tons of nickel meteorite dust settle to earth each year. If the earth has indeed existed for five billion years, then there should now be a layer of this dust at least 200 feet thick all over the planet. Of course, no such layer is found.

d. The decay of earth's magnetic field. This field, it has been shown, has a half-life of 1400 years. This means it is weakened by 50 percent each fourteen centuries. It also means the magnetic field was twice as strong 1400 years ago as it is now, four times as strong 2800 years ago, and so on. Only 7000 years ago it must have been thirty-two times as strong. It is very doubtful that it could have been much stronger than this.

e. The imbalance of carbon-14 and carbon-12. It can be shown that it would take a period of 30,000

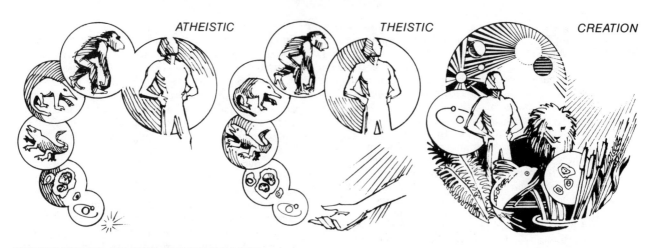

ATHEISTIC    THEISTIC    CREATION

## THREE VIEWS ON THE ORIGIN OF LIFE

| BELIEF | ATHEISTIC MATERIALISM | THEISTIC EVOLUTION | SPECIAL CREATION |
|---|---|---|---|
| Source | Accidental arrangement of molecules | God through evolution | God in six literal days |
| Time | One billion years ago | One billion years ago | Less than 10,000 years |
| Method | Mutations | Mutations | Supernatural act from the hand of God |
| Purpose | No purpose | To glorify God | To glorify God |
| First Man | Some remote, sub-human male ape | Some remote, sub-human male ape | Adam |
| First Woman | Some remote sub-human female ape | Some remote sub-human female ape | Eve |
| View of Gen. 1–3; Rom. 5:12–21 | Pure myth | Spiritual allegory | Historical fact |
| Proponent | Darwin and his followers | Those who would attempt to reconcile Moses and Darwin | Moses |
| Reason for View | Contempt for supernatural possibility | Mistaken view that evolution has been proven and must be accepted | Literal interpretation of Genesis 1; 2 |
| Problem | First law of thermodynamics, second law of thermodynamics, law of biogenesis | Cannot take at face value (Gen. 1–2; Rom. 4:12–21) | No real problem |
| Scriptural Proof | None | None | Gen. 1:31; 2:1–3; Ex. 20:11; 31:17; Ps. 33:6–9; I Cor. 11:8–9; 15:39; I Tim. 2:13 |
| Scientific Support | None | None | First law of thermodynamics, second law of thermodynamics, law of biogenesis |

years to attain an equilibrium between these two. However, at present C-14 still exceeds C-12 by some 50 percent.

The above are but five of over eighty facts which would indicate a recent creation date.

f. Another time calendar is known as the radiocarbon method. This method, unlike the first three, is used only in determining the age of organic fossils. Radioactive carbon is formed in the earth's upper atmosphere resulting from the incoming cosmic radiation and atmospheric nitrogen-14. It then unites with oxygen to form carbon dioxide and is absorbed by all plants and animals. At the moment of death, plants and animals cease to absorb C-14. It then begins to decay back into nitrogen 14. This has a half-life of 5730 years. Five "half-lives" of C-14 would equal 29,000 years, and would leave only $^1/_{32}$ of the original C-14 content. Therefore, the C-14 method becomes increasingly weak past a few thousand years. As with the other dating methods, C-14 has its problems. Many living systems are not

in equilibrium for the C-14 exchange. It has been found that the shells of living mollusks may show radiocarbon ages up to 2300 years.

The amount of natural carbon may have varied in the past. It is known that the earth once had far more vegetation than today. This is indicated by the vast amounts of coal deposits now known all over the world. Consequently, organisms living at that time would be subjected to only a very small C-14/C-12 ratio, and their remains now would contain no radio carbon at all, even if they had lived 6000 years ago. On the other hand, during the ice age there would have been much less C-12 than during the vegetation age.

However, one must exercise care in attempting to pinpoint exactly a recent creation date. For example, the Irish seventeenth century theologian Archbishop James Ussher and his contemporary Dr. John Lightfoot stated that creation week occurred on October 18–24 in the year 4004 B.C., and that the creation of Adam took place on Friday of that week, October 23, 4004 B.C., at 9:00 A.M., forty-fifth meridian time!

7. How did life come into being?

The real question today is not the survival of the species, but rather the *arrival* of it. Three theories have been advocated to explain the problem of origin.

a. Atheistic materialism.

This interesting theory boldly assures us that everything once came from nothing. In other words, if one gives enough mud enough time, it will, all by itself, produce the music of a Beethoven, the paintings of a Raphael, the writings of a Shakespeare, and the teachings of a Christ.

*Question:* How long would it take one million monkeys typing away day and night on one million typewriters for just one monkey to accidentally type out the first ten words in the Bible? ("In the beginning God created the heaven and the earth.")

*Answer:* Consider a rock which reached from the earth to the nearest star (some twenty-six trillion miles away). Once every million years a tiny bird flies to this massive rock and removes the smallest grain of sand from it. When four rocks this size have been completely carried away, then one of those monkeys will have accidentally typed out Genesis 1:1.

But this accomplishment would be absolutely nothing as compared to the probabilities that a living cell would by random processes be formed. Consider the following: Dr. Harold Morowitz of Yale estimated the theoretical limits for the smallest free-living thing which could duplicate itself. It would require 239 individual protein molecules. What are the chances that the first protein molecule would form all their amino acids into left-handed chains? (For some unknown reason all life consists only of these left-handed protein molecule chains). Well, the minimal number of amino acids in a protein is 410. This then would be like flipping a coin 410 times and coming up with heads *every* time! The answer is one chance in $10^{123}$ (the figure 1 followed by 123 zeros). But then even *if* this occurred in one protein, it would have to be repeated in at least 238 other proteins also. The chances are now one in $10^{29345}$ (one followed by 29,345 zeros). This would be about twenty $8\frac{1}{2} \times 11$ pages of typed zeros! How big is this number? Consider the following:

There are $10^{18}$ seconds in 15 billion years.
The known universe weighs $7 \times 10^{41}$ pounds.
The universe contains $5 \times 10^{78}$ atoms.
The universe contains $10^{130}$ electrons.

*Conclusions:* Suppose each atom could expand until it was the size of the present universe. There would then be $3 \times 10^{157}$ atoms in the universe.

By comparison, the odds against a single protein forming by chance in earth's entire history is 4000 times larger than the number of atoms in this super-universe. Imagine an amoeba traveling a line stretched across our known universe, some fifteen billion light years in length. Its speed is one inch per year. It has one task, to carry one atom across and come back for another. Each trip takes $2 \times 1^{28}$ years. The time it would take to carry all the atoms across the entire diameter of the known universe is the expected time it would take for one protein to

form by chance. Suppose the amoeba has only traveled one inch since the universe has existed (fifteen billion years to cover one inch). He could still carry $6 \times 10^{53}$ universes while one protein is forming.

From time to time sensational claims are made concerning attempts to create life in a laboratory. But has this actually been done?

*Stanley Miller* (University of California) showed that certain amino acids (which are basic components of proteins) could be generated by discharging electricity through a mixture of methane, water vapor, and ammonia.

*Sidney Fox* (Florida State University) heated a dry mixture of amino acids at 175°C for six hours and showed that under certain artificial conditions a number of amino acids could be randomly linked together. He called them "coacervates" and thought them to be similar to protein molecules.

*Arthur Kornberg* (Stanford) was able to make DNA replicate itself after extracting it from a living cell and placing it in a bath of the four nucleotides which constitute DNA, provided the proper enzymes and other constituents were also present. He also showed that virus DNA could be made to reproduce outside a host cell, contrary to usual virus behavior, provided the proper enzymes were present. A virus, however, is *not* a living cell.

*H. G. Khorana* (University of Wisconsin) was successful in the synthesis of a gene. He started with a certain simple DNA structure, considered to be a particular gene, and with the presence of enzymes again, was able to copy this gene. In 1970 J. P. Danielli (Buffalo University) claimed to have accomplished the first artificial synthesis of a living and reproducing cell. However, he had started with living amoebas in the first place, then partially dismantling and finally reassembling them, using components from different amoebas.

However, if life is to be defined as a self-contained, self-sufficient, and self-reproducing unit, such as in a cell, then we see the experiments above have yet to take the first tiny step in the journey of a billion light years in the creation of life. Thus, the theory of atheistic materialism is not only interesting, but idiotic and impossible also.

b. Theistic evolution.

This theory may be thought of as the Mosaic-Darwinian theory, for it earnestly attempts to unify two seemingly irreconcilable philosophies. It is known as the molecule-to-man theory. Theistic evolution says we must look to Darwin for the *when* and *how* of creation, and then learn from Moses concerning the *who* and *why* of all things. There are, however, two serious flaws in this theory. One is a *scientific* problem. Evolution runs contrary to the Second Law of Thermodynamics which describes this universe as a wound-up clock which is slowly running down. Instead, evolution has all life being built up from the simple to the complex.

The second problem confronting evolution is a scriptural one. For example, Moses informs us that life began on dry land during the third day of creation (Gen. 1:9-13), while evolution says it originated in some slimy sea. Furthermore, evolution is in direct contradiction to the creation of Eve. Finally, evolution would reduce Adam to a spiritually transformed ape, but the Scripture says he was originally and suddenly made in the very image of God.

In an attempt to get around this, it is claimed by some that our world in this area is not governed by the Second Law, for it receives the necessary energy from the sun to account for evolution. But the complexity of life calls for more than a source of energy. It also demands a purposeful direction of that energy. As an example, a builder might expose bricks, sand, nail, paint, wires, wood, and other building materials to the heat and energy of the sun and to the refreshing gentle rains, but these objects would never by themselves unite and form a house! In the light of all this many have concluded with Dr. Henry Morris that evolution is clearly, strongly, and completely refuted by the Bible. Morris observes:

"*Genesis* teaches that life began on dry land (Gen. 1:11, 12) while evolution says it began in some remote sea bottom.

*Genesis* declares birds existed before insects while evolution reverses this order (Gen. 1:20, 24).

*Genesis* states that birds and fishes were created at the same time (Gen. 1:21) but evolution says fishes evolved hundreds of millions of years before birds developed.

*Genesis* stresses ten times that the entities created were to reproduce "after their kinds," while evolution postulates the slow ascent of all organisms from a common ancestor.

*Genesis* says that Adam was made from the dust of the ground into the image of God, while evolution claims Adam descended from a sub-ape creature.

*Genesis* records woman coming from man's side, while evolution teaches both man and woman developed simultaneously.

*Genesis* tells us that man was originally a vegetarian (Gen. 1:29) while evolution teaches he was probably a head-hunting cannibal!"

c. Special creation.

This simply affirms that God said just what he meant and meant just what he said in the first two chapters of the Bible, as he did in the remaining 1187 chapters.

8. How many false philosophies does the first verse in the Bible refute?
   a. It refutes *atheism,* for creation is the work of God's hand.
   b. It refutes *evolution,* for the universe was created and did not evolve.
   c. It refutes *materialism,* for the universe did not always exist.
   d. It refutes *polytheism,* for there is only one God.
   e. It refutes *pantheism,* for God is apart from and independent of his creation.

9. Why was the earth made on the first day but the sun, moon, and stars not until the fourth day of creation? We have already briefly touched upon this.
   a. To emphasize the importance of this earth. God would soon (during the sixth day) place a creature created in his own image upon the earth. Years later his only Son would be born upon this planet and die upon it. Furthermore, upon this earth the King of kings will someday once again return.

b. To discourage the worship of the sun. All ancient civilizations worshiped the sun. It gave them light and warmth. But God wanted his people to know that light and life come from him—that the earth existed *before* the sun, and that *he* created both.
Dr. John Witcomb writes:
   "But if the sun, moon, and stars are not ultimately essential to the earth's existence, then why did God create them? Three basic reasons are listed in Genesis 1:14. They are for lights, for seasons (a calendar), and for signs.
   As lights, they replaced the special and temporary light of the early days.
   As a calendar, dividing seasons, days, and years, they enable men to plan their work accurately into the distant future, thus reflecting the purposive mind of God.
   As signs, they teach and ever remind men of vastly important spiritual truths concerning the Creator.
   David learned from the heavens the transcendence of God and his own comparative nothingness. 'When I consider the heavens, the work of thy fingers, the moon and the stars which thou hast ordained, what is man that thou art mindful of him?' (Ps. 8:3). The Apostle Paul insisted that men are utterly without excuse for their idolatry." (*The Early Earth,* pp. 58, 59)

10. Are the days of Genesis 1 really literal twenty-four-hour days?
There is strong scholarly and scriptural evidence that the days are indeed literal.
   a. The use of a numerical adjective with the word "day" in Genesis 1 would limit it to a normal day.
   b. The natural reading of the Genesis account would suggest it.
   c. Moses believed it. See Exodus 20:11; 31:17.
   d. Edward Young (outstanding Hebrew scholar) believed it.
   e. Benjamin Warfield (one of the great Orthodox theologians of all time) believed it.
   f. Departmental professors of Oriental language in nine leading universities were once asked the following question by a research scholar:
      "Do you consider that the Hebrew word Yom (day) as used in Genesis 1 accompanied by a numeral should properly be translated as (a) a day, as commonly understood, (b) an age, or (c) either a day or an age without preference?"
      The nine universities polled were: Oxford, Cambridge, London, Harvard, Yale, Columbia, Toronto, McGill, and Manitoba. Of these, seven universities responded that it should be translated as a day as commonly understood.
   g. As indicated by the genealogies found in Genesis 5 and 11. If evolution is correct and man is really a million years old, then we would be forced to allow a fifty-thousand-year gap between each name in these two chapters. Furthermore, if life itself is nearly five billion years old, then each day in Genesis 1 would have to stand for approximately seven hundred million years!

11. Did something horrible take place between the first and second verse in the Bible? Many believe something terrible indeed occurred, and that something was the fall of Satan. The following arguments are offered to support this.

a. The phrase in Genesis 1:2, "without form and void" (Hebrew: *tohu wa-bohu*), appears elsewhere in Isaiah 34:11; 45:18; and Jeremiah 4:23 and speaks of judgment. However, in other passages it simply means space. (See Job 26:7; Deut. 32:10; Job 6:18; 12:24; Ps. 107:40.)

b. The verb translated "was" in Genesis 1:2 (Hebrew: *hayetha*) should be translated "became." Scriptural evidence, however, would deny this. The Hebrew verb *hayetha* is found 264 times in the Pentateuch, and of these, in 258 instances the word is correctly translated *was*. See, for example, Jonah 3:3.

c. There is a difference between the verbs *bara* (created, Genesis 1:1) and *asah* ("made," Genesis 1:7). But, to the contrary, these verbs are used synonymously. Note:

"And God *created [bara]* the great sea monsters . . ." (1:21).

"And God *made [asah]* the beast of the earth . . ." (1:25).

"Let us *make [asah]* man in our image . . ." (1:26).

"So God *created [bara]* man in his own image . . ." (1:27).

d. Genesis 1:2 says "darkness was upon the face of the deep," and darkness is a symbol of evil.

This is not always the case, as seen in Psalm 104:20, 24: "Thou makest darkness, and it is night, wherein all the beasts of the forest do creep forth. . . ."

Although traces of this theory can be traced back in Christian writings as early as the fourth century A.D., it was not until the ministries of Dr. Thomas Chalmers, Scottish scholar, and George H. Pember (1876) that the theory really caught on. In 1917 C.I. Scofield included it in his notes and its popularity was assured. These last two dates are significant, for by 1880 Darwin's theory of evolution, as propounded in his book, *The Origin of the Species,* was universally accepted by the scientific world. This theory taught that the world was many millions of years old, as indicated by the vast fossil

## THE THREEFOLD PROBLEM OF THE GAP THEORY

### IT IS UNSCIENTIFIC
- THE GAP THEORY WAS (IN PART) A CHRISTIAN ATTEMPT TO RECONCILE THE CREATION ACCOUNT WITH THE LONG PERIODS OF TIME IN THE THEORY OF EVOLUTION.
- BUT EVOLUTION ITSELF AS A THEORY IS TOTALLY UNSCIENTIFIC, DEFYING THE SECOND LAW OF THERMODYNAMICS.

### IT IS UNSCRIPTURAL
- THE GAP THEORY WOULD DESCRIBE ADAM WALKING ATOP A GIGANTIC FOSSILIZED ANIMAL GRAVEYARD.
- PAUL, HOWEVER, IN ROM. 5:12 AND 8:20–22 STATES THAT MAN'S SIN BROUGHT ABOUT DEATH, EVEN OF ANIMALS.

### IT IS UNNECESSARY
- THE MOST NATURAL INTERPRETATION OF GEN. 1 AND 2 IS TAKING IT AT FACE VALUE, WITHOUT ADDITION OR SUBTRACTION.
- GEN. 1:1 THUS BECOMES A SUMMARY STATEMENT OF CREATION.
  1. IN THE FIRST VERSE GOD TELLS US *WHAT* HE DID.
  2. IN THE REMAINING VERSES HE TELLS US *HOW* HE DID IT.

record and the claims of uniformitarian geology. The Christian theologian was then confronted with a serious problem. How could all this be reconciled with Genesis 1? An answer was found—uncounted millions of years could be conveniently tucked into that bottomless hole which was thought to exist between Genesis 1:1 and 1:2. Thus the gap theory may be viewed in part as an attempt by the Christian theologian to appease the non-Christian evolutionist.

In summary, the gap theory faces a real problem in the New Testament, for Paul states in Romans 5:12 and 8:20-22 that man's sin brought about death, even of animals. But the gap theory would have Adam walking on top of a gigantic fossilized animal graveyard! One may thus conclude that Genesis 1:1 is a summary statement for the first two chapters. In this verse God tells us *what* he originally did. In the remaining verses he then informs us *how* he did it!

In conclusion at this point it may be asked: "If Satan did not fall between Genesis 1:1 and 1:2, then where do we place his fall?" A probable answer is somewhere between Genesis 2:25 and 3:1. We do know that Lucifer had become the devil at the time of Genesis 3:1. Bible students have pondered for centuries over why Lucifer sinned in the first place. Two suggestions have been offered: One, Satan may have doubted God's word that he had been created. Maybe God was lying. Second, he was no doubt jealous over man's nature (especially his ability to reproduce himself—something angels cannot do), and the responsibilities given to Adam. (See Gen. 1:26-28; Ps. 8:3-6; Heb. 2:5-9.) This last suggestion would of course indicate that Lucifer did not sin until *after* the creation of Adam.

12. What was God doing before he created man?

a. He was having fellowship with his Son. (See Prov. 8:22-30; Jn. 17:5, 24.)

"The Lord possessed me in the beginning of his way, before his works of old. I was set up from everlasting, from the beginning, or ever the earth was. When there were no depths, I was brought forth—when there were no fountains abounding with water. Before the mountains were settled, before the hills, was I brought forth; while as yet he had not made the earth, nor the fields, nor the highest part of the dust of the world. When he prepared the heavens, I was there; when he set a compass upon the face of the depth; when he established the clouds above; when he strengthened the fountains of the deep; when he gave to the sea its decree, that the waters should not pass his commandment; when he appointed the foundations of the earth, then I was by him, as one brought up with him; and I was daily his delight, rejoicing always before him" (Prov. 8:22-30).

"And now, O Father, glorify thou me with thine own self with the glory which I had with thee before the world was" (Jn. 17:5).

"Father, I will that they also, whom thou hast given me, be with me where I am, that they may behold my glory, which thou hast given me; for thou lovedst me before the foundation of the world" (Jn. 17:24).

Why did God make man in the first place? Well, whatever else may be involved, he did not create Adam because he was lonely. God had, he has, and always will have a beloved Son called Jesus Christ.

b. He was creating angels and stars.

"Where wast thou when I laid the foundations of the earth? declare, if thou hast understanding" (Job 38:4).

"When the morning stars sang together, and all the sons of God shouted for joy" (Job 38:7). Both were there at the creation of Adam. The starlight fell upon that beautiful garden and the angels hovered over it.

c. He was choosing the elect.

"According as he hath chosen us in him before the foundation of the world, that we should be holy and without blame before him, in love" (Eph. 1:4).

"Who hath saved us, and called us with an holy calling, not according to our works, but according to his own purpose and grace, which was given us in Christ Jesus before the world began" (2 Tim. 1:9).

Theologians may argue over the reason *for* this election, but not the fact *of* the matter!

d. He was planning for a church.

"Unto me, who am less than the least of all saints, is this grace given, that I should preach among the Gentiles the unsearchable riches of Christ, and to make all men see what is the fellowship of the mystery, which from the beginning of the ages hath been hidden in God, who created all things by Jesus Christ" (Eph. 3:8, 9).

Before God created the upper atmosphere he had in mind the Upper Room.

e. He was preparing for a kingdom.

"Then shall the King say unto them on his right hand, Come, ye blessed of my Father, inherit the kingdom prepared for you from the foundation of the world" (Mt. 25:34).

Thus, in God's mind the thousand-year period of the millennium preceded the one-week period of Creation.

f. God was planning for a Savior.

"Forasmuch as ye know that ye were not redeemed with corruptible things, like silver and gold, from your vain conversation received by tradition from your fathers; but with the precious blood of Christ, as of a lamb without blemish and without spot: Who verily was foreordained before the foundation of the world, but was manifest in these last times for you" (1 Pet. 1:18-20).

"And all that dwell upon the earth shall worship him, whose names are not written in the book of life of the Lamb slain from the foundation of the world" (Rev. 13:8).

Long before he placed the first Adam in the Garden, God prepared the second Adam for the cross.

13. Why did God create man in the first place?

We have already stated that he did not create Adam because he was lonely! Some have suggested that prior to man's creation God had ample opportunity to express many of his attributes. In creating the stars, his omnipotence was shown. In fashioning angels, his omniscience was seen. In judging Lucifer (Ezek. 28; Isa.

14) his holiness was demonstrated. But one attribute very close to his heart had not been exercised. This was his grace. It is therefore not unreasonable to suggest that God created Adam knowing full well he would sin (but in no way encouraging him to do so) and then, in the fullness of time, he planned to send his only Son to die in man's place and thus display his marvelous grace! All this is indicated in the following verses:

"Thou art worthy, O Lord, to receive glory and honour and power: for thou hast created all things, and for thy pleasure they are and were created" (Rev. 4:11).

"Moreover the law entered, that the offence might abound. But where sin abounded, grace did much more abound" (Rom. 5:20).

"That in the ages to come he might shew the exceeding riches of his grace in his kindness toward us through Christ Jesus" (Eph. 2:7).

"For we are his workmanship, created in Christ Jesus unto good works, which God hath before ordained that we should walk in them" (Eph. 2:10).

14. How was man made in the image of God?

a. Perhaps because of man's trinity—man consists of spirit, soul, and body.

"And the very God of peace sanctify you wholly; and I pray God your whole spirit and soul and body be preserved blameless unto the coming of our Lord Jesus Christ" (1 Thess. 5:23).

"For the word of God is quick, and powerful, and sharper than any two-edged sword, piercing even to the dividing asunder of soul and spirit, and of the joints and marrow, and is a discerner of the thoughts and intents of the heart" (Heb. 4:12).

b. Perhaps because man (like God) knows the differences between good and evil. Only man, among all creatures, has self-consciousness.

c. Perhaps God had in mind the future work of Jesus when he took upon himself the body of a man.

"And the Word was made flesh, and dwelt among us, (and we beheld his glory, the glory as of the only begotten Father,) full of grace and truth" (Jn. 1:14).

"And without controversy great is the mystery of godliness: God was manifest in the flesh, justified in the Spirit, seen of angels, preached unto the Gentiles, believed on in the world, received up into glory" (1 Tim. 3:16).

"Let this mind be in you, which was also in Christ Jesus: Who, being in the form of God, thought it not robbery to be equal with God: But made himself of no reputation, and took upon him the form of a servant, and was made in the likeness of men: And being found in fashion as a man, he humbled himself, and became obedient unto death, even the death of the cross" (Phil. 2:5-8).

d. Perhaps God had in mind the future life of the believer when all Christians shall be like Jesus.

"Who shall change our vile body, that it may be fashioned like unto his glorious body, according to the working whereby he is able even to subdue all things unto himself" (Phil. 3:21).

"For whom he did foreknow, he also did predestinate to be conformed to the image of his

Son, that he might be the firstborn among many brethren" (Rom. 8:29).

"Beloved, now are we the sons of God, and it doth not yet appear what we shall be: but we know that, when he shall appear, we shall be like him, for we shall see him as he is" (1 Jn. 3:2).

15. What was Adam really like?

a. Adam was the highlight of God's creation. It has been estimated that the most brilliant genius uses but one tenth of 1 percent of his total potential brain ability. This means Adam was at least one thousand times superior to today's intellectuals. We are probably 95 percent blind to the total color scheme displayed by nature and 98 percent deaf to her many sound patterns. But Adam's five senses were tuned to absolute perfection. He may even have possessed E.S.P. He perfectly understood both himself and his environment. He apparently was able to communicate with animals (Gen. 3:1, 2) and perhaps all nature also!

The following article appeared in the April 1977 issue of *Reader's Digest*:

"*Six-Million-Dollar Original*

Tired of hearing that the human body is worth only about three dollars? And of the humbling and humiliating realization that a chicken or a salmon sells for more than you are worth? There's news to heal our bruised egos.

Yale University biophysicist Harold J. Morowitz says that the human body is actually worth $6 million. And that price covers only the raw materials—hormones, proteins, enzymes, etc. The intricate work of fashioning the material into human cells might cost six thousand trillion dollars. And assembling these cells into a functioning human being would drain all the world's treasures. 'Each human being is priceless' is the professor's understatement" (p. 144).

b. Adam was absolutely unique. Over the years a pile of shattered skulls and moldy bones have been dug up and presented by the evolutionist to "prove" the existence of ancient subhuman creatures who finally evolved into man. Again, one must either choose between Moses or Darwin on this subject. Some of the more "important" of these lost links in man's chronological chain are:

*Neanderthal man*—Found in Neander Valley, near Dusseldorf, Germany, in 1856 by Johann C. Fuhlrott. The find consisted of a skull and several bones. He was first portrayed as a semi-erect brutish subhuman. It is now believed these "creatures" were real people who suffered severely from rickets, caused by a deficiency of vitamin D. This condition results in the softening of bones and consequent malformation.

"It is now known that Neanderthal man was fully erect and in most details was indistinguishable from modern man, his cranial capacity even exceeding that of modern man. It is said that if he were dressed in a business suit, and were to walk down one of our city streets, he would be given no more attention than any other individual. Today he is classified *Homo Sapiens*—full human" (*Evolution? The Fossils Say No*, Duane T. Gish, p. 103).

*Java man* (*Pithecanthropus erectus*, "erect ape man")—Found in Trinil, Java, in 1891, by Eugene Dubois, a Dutch physician. The "find" consisted of a single skull cap. One year later a thigh bone, along with two molar teeth, was discovered fifty feet from where the skull cap had been. Dubois estimated they all belonged together, and dated back one-half million years! He did not reveal, however, until thirty-one years later, that he had also found two obviously human skulls at the same time and in the same level. Most evolutionists of the day were convinced of the validity of this 500-thousand-year-old creature. But prior to his death, Dubois sadly concluded his Java man was actually the remains of a large gibbon.

*Piltdown man* (*Eanthropus dawsoni*, "Dawn Man")—Found in Piltdown, England, in 1912, by Charles Dawson. The find was a skull part and a few teeth. Soon the consensus of the world's greatest authorities was that here indeed was a genuine link in the evolution of man. It was dated to be from 500 to 750 thousand years old! The praises of the Piltdown man were sung by Dr. Arthur Smith Woodward, eminent paleontologist at the British museum, and Dr. Henry Fairfield Osborn, paleontologist of the American Museum of Natural History. However, in 1950 the Piltdown bones were carefully examined by fluoride tests and discovered to be a colossal hoax. The "skull" had been stained with iron salts and the teeth filed down to give it the appearance of age. Thus, the world-famed Piltdown man was simply the doctored remains of a recent age.

*Peking man*—Found near Peking, China, in 1912 (and 1937) by Davidson Bolack. Find consisted of the fragments of thirty skulls and 147 teeth. This find disappeared in 1941 when it was moved from Peking by a U.S. Marine detachment to escape the oncoming Japanese invasion. It is now believed by some that this find was simply the remains of some large monkeys or baboons killed and eaten by workers in an ancient lime-burning quarry!

*Nebraska man* ("Western ape man")—Found in western Nebraska in 1922 by Harold Cook. The find was exactly one tooth! It was immediately declared by Dr. H. F. Osborn of the American Museum to be the vaunted missing link. He placed it at the very bottom of the tree of man's ancestry. Dr. William K. Gregory, curator of the American Museum of Natural History and professor of Paleontology at Columbia University, called it "the million dollar tooth." Sir Grafton Elliott Smith of the *London Illustrated News* assigned an imaginative artist to draw the ape man that once carried the tooth around in his mouth some six thousand centuries ago. During the famous Scopes evolutionary trial in Dayton, Tennessee, William Jennings Bryan (Bible defender) was confronted and ridiculed for his ignorance concerning this tooth and other "facts" of evolution by a delegation of authorities, led by Professor H. H. Newman of the University of Chicago. In 1927, to the supreme embarrassment of many, the tooth was discovered to be that of an extinct pig.

*East Africa ape* (*zinjanthropus*)—Found in 1959 in Olduvia, Tanzania, by Louis S. B. Leakey. Find consisted of a skull cap and a few bone fragments.

This "discovery" was sensationalized through the *National Geographic Magazine*, which society had sponsored Leakey. His find was dated from two to four million years in age, thus making East Africa man by far the oldest "link" known at the time. However, prior to his death, Leakey indicated he felt his vaunted discovery was but a variety of *australopithecus* (Southern ape) found in 1924.

One of the most respected scholars of the twentieth century is Dr. Mortimer J. Adler, co-editor of the monumental fifty-four-volume set, *Great Books of the Western World*. In one of his many books, *Great Ideas from the Great Books*, Adler answers a question asked him concerning the difference between men and animals.

"Dear Dr. Adler,

Is there any basic difference between man and animals, or is man an animal like all the others? Some people say that man is the only creature that can think and learn. But I don't regard this as a real distinction, since biologists and psychologists have demonstrated that animals can construct things and solve problems. I have known some very intelligent dogs and some very thoughtless human beings. What is the essential difference between man and the animals?                                    A.M.P.

Dear A.M.P.

Until comparatively recent times, few philosophers doubted that man was essentially different from all other animals. In the great tradition of Western thought, from Plato right down to the nineteenth century, it was almost universally held that man and man alone is a rational animal. This philosophical view of man's distinctive nature accords with the Biblical view that man and man alone is created in the image of God—a person, not a thing.

Since the time of Darwin, the opposite view has come to prevail, not only among scientists but among the educated classes generally. The Darwinian theory of man's origin, as you know, is that man and that anthropoid apes have descended from a common ancestral form; and along with this view of man's evolutionary origin goes the view that man and the higher mammals differ only in degree. Thus, for example, instead of regarding man alone as rational, the evolutionists find the same kind of intelligence in man and other animals. Man simply has more of it.

You say in your letter that you think the traditional arguments for man's distinctive nature are weak, because animals as well as men can reason, because animals as well as men can make things, etc. Let me answer your question by defending the traditional point of view about man as a very special creature.

The strongest evidence that men have certain powers which no other animals possess in any degree whatsoever consists in the thing which men can do but which other animals cannot do at all. One such indication is man's power of making things.

I know that bees make hives, birds make nests, and beavers make dams. But such productions are entirely instinctive on their part. A given species of bird makes its nests in the same way generation after generation. This shows that the nest is a product of instinct not of art, which involves reason and free will. In making houses, bridges, or any other of their artifacts, men invent and select. They are truly artist, as animals are not.

In addition, only men build machines which are themselves productive. Other animals may use rough tools, but no other animal makes a die press which stamps out an indefinite number of a product when the raw materials are fed into it. This is another indication of man's special power as a maker of things.

You say that other animals can reason. In my opinion it is more correct to say that other animals can solve problems when they are confronted by the biological urgency of finding a way of getting what they need. All so-called 'thinking' by animals is on this level. But no animal ever sits down to think, the way a philosopher or a mathematician does when he has no biologically urgent need to do so.

The fact that human thinking is discursive and involves language is another indication that it is quite different from animal problem-solving. Animals, of course, do make sounds and communicate their emotions or impulses to one another. But no animal communicates thought; no animal ever utters a sentence which asserts something to be true or false. Only a rational animal can do that.

I could go on and give you many other items of evidence that man has certain powers which no other animal possesses in the least degree. But I shall content myself with one more fact.

Man is the only animal with an historical development. Other animals may change in their biological constitution over the course of hundreds of thousands of generations; but such changes result entirely from changes in the germ plasm, which is the only thing that is transmitted from one generation to another. Men transmit ideas and institutions, a whole tradition of culture, from one generation to another, and it is this which accounts for the history of the human race.

In my opinion the empirical evidence is overwhelmingly in favor of the view that men are essentially different in kind from the brutes. Like the brutes, they, too, are animals. But unlike them, men are rational. This, of course, if true, would require us to reject Darwin's theory of man's evolutionary origin. But theories after all must be made to fit the facts, not facts theories."

(*Great Ideas from the Great Books*, pp. 173–275)

c. Adam was declared the king of creation, commanded to subdue the earth, to name the animals, and to care for his beautiful home in Eden's garden (Gen. 1:28–31; 2:8–15, 19, 20).

d. He was commanded to abstain from the tree of the Knowledge of Good and Evil, lest he die (Gen. 2:17). The Hebrew language indicates here that if Adam sinned he would die twice. This phrase can also be translated, "and in dying thou shalt surely die." In the Bible there are two kinds of death and both can be defined by a single word. The word is separation. The two kinds of death are physical and spiritual. When a person dies physically, his soul is separated from his body. The body is put in the ground, but the soul lives on. It can never die. The more serious kind of death, however, is spiritual death. This will occur when the unsaved sinner will someday be forever separated from God. This is sometimes called the second death.

"And then I will profess unto them, I never knew you: depart from me, ye that work iniquity" (Mt. 7:23).

"Then shall he say also unto them on the left hand, Depart from me, ye cursed, into everlasting fire, prepared for the devil and his angels" (Mt. 25:41).

"And I saw a great white throne, and him that sat on it, from whose face the earth and the heaven fled away; and there was found no place for them. And I saw the dead, small and great, stand before God; and the books were opened: and another book was opened, which is the book of life: and the dead were judged out of those things which were written in the books, according to their works. And the sea gave up the dead which were in it; and death and hell delivered up the dead which were in them: and they were judged every man according to their works. And death and hell were cast into the lake of fire. This is the second death. And whosoever was not found written in the book of life was cast into the lake of fire" (Rev. 20:11-15).

"But the fearful, and unbelieving, and the abominable, and murderers, and whoremongers, and sorcerers, and idolaters, and all liars, shall have their part in the lake which burneth with fire and brimstone: which is the second death" (Rev. 21:8).

With this background in mind, let us ponder this tremendous truth: to be born once means to die twice, but to be born twice means to die once (and maybe not even once, if one is alive at the rapture). (See 1 Cor. 15:51-53; 1 Thess. 4:16, 17.)

e. Adam was encouraged to participate in the Tree of Life and all other trees (the trees of music, literature, art, etc.?). (See Gen. 1:29; 2:9, 16.)

Even though Adam had a perfect body at creation, it was apparently necessary for him to partake of this fruit tree in order to assure that his body continued in top running order. Many centuries later the early Spanish explorers in America looked in vain for the fountain of youth. But they searched for the wrong thing!

f. Adam was given a wife (2:22-24). The first wedding in history was conducted in Eden and performed by God himself. Note the account:

(1) "And the rib . . . from man made he a woman" (2:22). It has often been noted that God did not take Eve from Adam's feet, that she might be his slave, nor did he take her from Adam's head, that she might be his master, but rather from under his heart, that she might love and be loved by Adam.

"For the man is not of the woman; but the woman of the man. Neither was the man created for the woman; but the woman for the man" (1 Cor. 11:8, 9).

The word rib should be translated side. The Hebrew here is *tsela* and is almost always translated side.

"And thou shalt cast four rings of gold for it, and put them in the four corners thereof; and two rings shall be in the one side of it, and two rings in the other side of it" (Ex. 25:12).

"His strength shall be hunger-bitten, and destruction shall be ready at his side" (Job 18:12).

16. What seven words were missing from Adam's vocabulary? We are told in Genesis 2:19 that "Adam called every living creature . . . the name thereof." Adam must have had a tremendous vocabulary. Today there are over 3500 different mammals, 8600 birds, 5500 reptiles and amphibians. Doubtless there existed many more in Adam's day. And he named them all! In spite of this, however, there were seven simple words unknown and unexperienced by Adam prior to his fall. These words were:

**Death:**

"But of the tree of the knowledge of good and evil, thou shalt not eat of it: for in the day that thou eatest thereof thou shalt surely die" (Gen. 2:17).

**Nakedness:**

"And the eyes of them both were opened, and they knew that they were naked; and they sewed fig leaves together, and made themselves aprons" (Gen. 3:7).

**Cursed:**

"And unto Adam he said, Because thou hast hearkened unto the voice of thy wife, and hast eaten of the tree, of which I commanded thee, saying, Thou shalt not eat of it: cursed is the ground for thy sake; in sorrow shalt thou eat of it all the days of thy life" (Gen. 3:17).

**Sorrow:**

(Gen. 3:17)

**Thorns:**

"Thorns also and thistles shall it bring forth to thee; and thou shalt eat the herb of the field" (Gen. 3:18).

**Sweat:**

"In the sweat of thy face shalt thou eat bread, till thou return unto the ground; for out of it wast thou taken, for dust thou art, and unto dust shalt thou return" (Gen. 3:19).

**Sword:**

"So he drove out the man; and he placed at the east of the garden of Eden Cherubims, and a flaming sword which turned every way, to keep the way of the tree of life" (Gen. 3:24).

After the Fall, Adam soon added these bitter and bloody words to his vocabulary. The echo of these wicked words would haunt Adam and mankind for over forty long centuries. Then came the Second Adam. He successfully met and dealt with each word.

**Death:**

"Jesus said unto her, I am the resurrection, and the life: he that believeth in me, though he were dead, yet shall he live" (Jn. 11:25).

**Nakedness:**

"Then the soldiers, when they had crucified Jesus, took his garments, and made four parts, to every soldier a part; and also his coat: now the coat was without seam, woven from the top throughout" (Jn. 19:23).

**Cursed:**
"Christ hath redeemed us from the curse of the law, being made a curse for us: for it is written, Cursed is every one that hangeth on a tree" (Gal. 3:13).

**Sorrow:**
"He is despised and rejected of men; a man of sorrows, and acquainted with grief: and we hid as it were our faces from him; he was despised, and we esteemed him not" (Isa. 53:3).

**Thorns:**
"Then came Jesus forth, wearing the crown of thorns, and the purple robe. And Pilate saith unto them, Behold the man!" (Jn. 19:5)

**Sweat:**
"And being in an agony he prayed more earnestly: and his sweat was as it were great drops of blood falling down to the ground" (Lk. 22:44).

**Sword:**
"But one of the soldiers with a spear pierced his side, and forthwith came there out blood and water" (Jn. 19:34).

Paul shouts out the glorious results of Christ's mission. "Blotting out the handwriting of ordinances that was against us, which was contrary to us, and took it out of the way, nailing it to his cross" (Col. 2:14).

17. How long were Adam and Eve in the Garden?
In Genesis 4:1 we are told that Adam "knew his wife." This is a reference to sexual union. Inasmuch as this is the first time it is mentioned, it would appear they spent a very short time in Eden, perhaps only a few hours or days.

18. Will we see Adam in heaven?
We know he was created perfect and we know he sinned. But was he saved later? There are two verses that indicate he was saved.
   a. Genesis 3:21—God clothed Adam and Eve in coats of animal skins. Doubtless some innocent animal died to provide this clothing. This act is a type of salvation.
   b. Genesis 4:4—Abel knew the right way to God was by the blood of a lamb. It seems reasonable to assume this knowledge came from Adam.

19. Where did Cain get his wife?
Perhaps no other question concerning the Bible has been asked more than this one. To say the least, it is absolutely insignificant as compared to the one asked by a Philippian jailor, "What must I do to be saved?" (Acts 16:30). According to Genesis 5:4, Adam and Eve had sons and daughters. Thus, Cain doubtless married one of his sisters. This verse also explains what Cain was afraid of after he had murdered his brother in Genesis 4:14. He no doubt assumed his parents would bear other sons and daughters and that one of them might someday come looking for him.

20. Do the genealogies in Genesis 5 and 10 contain any gaps?
   a. The names in Genesis 5 are repeated in exact order in 1 Chronicles 1:1-4 and Luke 3:36-38, so it might seem there are none. However, if this is true, then one must conclude the following:
      (1) That Creation took place around 4000 B.C.
      (2) That the Flood occurred around 2400 B.C. (1656 years after Creation).

(3) That Adam was a contemporary with Enoch for 308 years and died fifty-seven years before his translation.
(4) That Seth (Adam's son) lived to see Enoch's translation and died just fourteen years before the birth of Noah.
(5) That Noah was a contemporary with Abraham for fifty-eight years.
(6) That Shem (Noah's son) actually outlived Abraham by thirty-five years. However, few conservative Bible scholars would concur with all these conclusions.
   b. In Genesis 10 there is at least one gap. Note:
      (1) Genesis 10:24 tells us that Arpachs begat Shelah who begat Eber.
      (2) Luke 3:34, 36 informs us that Arpachs begat Cainan who begat Shelah, who begat Eber.
   c. In Matthew chapter one three names are left out.
      (1) Matthew 1:8, 9 tells us that Asa begat Jehoshaphat, who begat Jehokam, who begat Uzziah.
      (2) In 2 Chronicles chapters 17-26 we are told that Asa begat Jehoshaphat, who begat Jehoram, who begat Ahaziah, who begat Joash, who begat Amaziah, who begat Uzziah.

21. Who were those mysterious sons of God in Genesis 6? Much controversy has surrounded these verses. Who were the sons of God who married the daughters of men? There are two basic approaches to this. The simple interpretation is that the sons of God were those individuals belonging to the line of Seth while the daughters of men were the unsaved girls who belonged to the line of Cain. The second and more involved interpretation holds that the sons of God were wicked and fallen angelic beings of some kind who committed immoral and unnatural physical acts with women in general.
   a. Basic arguments for the first view.
      (1) This is the most natural way to interpret the passage.
      (2) It is supported by Jesus' statement in Matthew 22:30:
         "For in the resurrection they [saved human beings in heaven] neither marry, nor are given in marriage, but are as the angels of God in heaven."
      (3) Because of the law of biogenesis, life begets similar life. (Note the statement "after its kind" in Gen. 1:11, 12, 21, 24, 25.)
      (4) Paul's statement in 1 Corinthians 15:38-40, "There are also celestial bodies, and bodies terrestrial," would indicate these two can never co-join.
      (5) Moses did not use the regular Hebrew word for angel (*malak*) which he later employs at least twenty-eight times in the Pentateuch.
      (6) "Mighty men" (supposed offspring of angels and women) is the Hebrew word *gibbor* (Gen. 6:4) which is used dozens of times in the Old Testament and always refers to human men (see Jdg. 6:12).
   b. Basic arguments for the second view:
      (1) The Hebrew language seems to favor it.
         (a) The Hebrew phrase "bne-elohim" (Sons of God) always refers to angels in the Old

Testament. (See Job 1:6; 2:1; 38:7; Dan. 3:25.)

(b) The Hebrew word *"nephilim"* (translated "giants" in 6:4) actually should be rendered "fallen ones." The normal word for a huge man is *rapha*. Thus, men like Og and Goliath were described by the word *rapha*. (See Deut. 3:11; 1 Chron. 20:6.)

(2) There is almost always a basis for commonly held ancient legends, however weird and distorted they might have become. In 6:4 we read concerning the "men of renown," which some believe is the historical basis for the legends of Hercules and other children of the gods of mythology. This later corresponds to such Babylonian figures as Gilgamesh, the supposed son of a goddess and a mortal. He was called "two-thirds god and one-third man."

(3) The common opinion of Jewish scholars: Josephus, the great Jewish historian, brings this out in his writings. The Septuagint (the Greek translation of the Hebrew Old Testament and the Bible used by Jews) translates Genesis 6:2 as the "angels of God."

(4) The interpretation of the early church: it was not until the fourth century that another view opposed to the angels of God theory was offered. Dr. James M. Gray (past President of Moody Bible Institute) writes, "There is reason to believe this view would not have changed . . . had it not been for certain erroneous opinions and practices of Christendom" (from his book, *Spiritism and the Fallen Angels*). Gray then suggests two such reasons:

(a) One of these was angel worship. The church sometime after the fourth century began worshiping angels, so the natural thing would be to deny any angel could do such vile things with humanity.

(b) The other reason was celibacy. If indeed these sons of God were human men, then the monks would have scriptural justification for indulging in sexual activities in spite of their official vows of celibacy.

(5) Various New Testament passages support this view. For example: 1 Peter 3:18-20—"For Christ also hath once suffered for sins, the just for the unjust, that he might bring us to God, being put to death in the flesh but quickened by the Spirit: By which also he went and preached unto the spirits in prison; which sometime were disobedient, when once the long-suffering of God waited in the days of Noah, while the ark was a preparing wherein few, that is, eight souls were saved by water."

It is thought by some that these spirits here were those sons of God in Genesis 6. The reason for their iniquity was a satanic attempt to corrupt human flesh and thus prevent the promised Incarnation (Gen. 3:15) from taking place. But here Peter describes Christ as telling them their foul plan didn't work! For another suggested passage along this line, see Jude 1:5-7.

(6) Two kinds of fallen angels exist: the unchained and those already chained. The *unchained* now have access to high places and to the bodies of unsaved men. (See Eph. 6:12; Lk. 8:27; Mk. 1:23.) The *chained* are at present already incarcerated. (See 2 Pet. 2:4; Jude 1:5-7.) The thought is that these are chained because of their involvement in Genesis 6.

In conclusion it should be noted that in recent times a third view has been advocated which says the sons of God were indeed fallen angels who totally controlled and possessed all the evil men living before the flood. These demons may have even attempted to change (by genetic engineering, as we see today) the DNA code of future babies, as would some deadly virus.

22. What was the pre-flood world like? Life prior to the flood was doubtless very different than today.
a. It was probably universally warm, with a pleasant and mild climate.
b. It may have had no deserts or ice caps.
c. The land surface was more extensive and the oceans much smaller.
d. The topography was gentle, without the rugged mountains or deeper canyons which affect our weather so much today.
e. Lush vegetation may have thrived worldwide.
f. There was apparently no rainfall, the earth being watered by early ground dews and from artesian springs. In addition to scriptural inferences, the presence of great oil deposits and plant fossils found near both North and South Poles give conclusive evidence that the world's climate was once temperate or even sub-tropical.

23. How advanced was the pre-flood civilization? One of the most popular books of the early seventies was *Chariots of the Gods?* by Erich Von Daniken. He attempts to prove by the following data that our earth was once visited by "little green men":
a. a landing strip, built many centuries ago, in Peru
b. long, ancient concrete constructions in Bolivia
c. drawings of space ships in Mexico

## THE PHYSICAL FEATURES OF THE ANCIENT WORLD

- **UNIVERSALLY WARM WITH PLEASANT AND MILD CLIMATE**
- **NO DESERTS OR ICE CAPS**
- **MORE LAND SURFACE THAN TODAY**
- **SMALLER AND SHALLOWER OCEAN BASINS**
- **NO RUGGED MOUNTAINS OR DEEP CANYONS**
- **CONSTANT, GENTLE WEATHER CONDITIONS**
- **WORLDWIDE LUSH VEGETATION**
- **NO RAINFALL, EARTH PROBABLY WATERED BY GROUND DEWS AND FROM ARTESIAN SPRINGS**

d. glass-like bits of rocks called "tektites" in which radioactive aluminum isotopes have been discovered in Lebanon

e. finds of cut crystal lenses, indicating electro-chemical activity

f. electric dry batteries found in Baghdad

g. ornaments of smelted platinum in Peru

h. parts of a belt made of aluminum in an ancient grave in China

While one would immediately reject Von Daniken's unscriptural conclusions, there is nevertheless a remote possibility that the above objects are but faint evidences of a highly sophisticated (and, alas, highly sinful) pre-flood society.

24. How much spiritual light did the pre-flood world have?

a. They had the witness of nature.

"Because that which may be known of God is manifest in them; for God hath shewed it unto them. For the invisible things of him from the creation of the world are clearly seen, being understood by the things that are made, even his eternal power and Godhead; so that they are without excuse" (Rom. 1:19, 20).

b. They had the witness of conscience.

"For when the Gentiles, which have not the law, do by nature the things contained in the law, these, having not the law, are a law unto themselves: Which shew the work of the law written in their hearts, their conscience also bearing witness, and their thoughts the mean while accusing or else excusing one another" (Rom. 2:14, 15).

c. They had the promise of a Redeemer.

"And I will put enmity between thee and the woman, and between thy seed and her seed; it shall bruise thy head, and thou shalt bruise his heel" (Gen. 3:15).

d. They had the knowledge of the sacrifice.

"And Abel, he also brought of the firstlings of his flock and of the fat thereof. And the Lord had respect unto Abel and to his offering" (Gen. 4:4).

e. They had the preaching of Enoch.

"And Enoch also, the seventh from Adam, prophesied of these, saying, Behold, the Lord cometh with ten thousands of his saints, to execute judgment upon all, and to convince all that are ungodly among them of all their ungodly deeds which they have ungodly committed, and of all their hard speeches which ungodly sinners have spoken against him" (Jude 1:14, 15).

f. They had the preaching of Noah.

"And spared not the old world, but saved Noah the eighth person, a preacher of righteousness, bringing in the flood upon the world of the ungodly" (2 Pet. 2:5).

g. They had the ministry of the Holy Spirit.

"And the Lord said, My spirit shall not always strive with man, for that he also is flesh: yet his days shall be an hundred and twenty years" (Gen. 6:3).

But all this *light* produced *life* for only eight human beings.

# THE MORAL FAILURES OF THE ANCIENT WORLD

- **PREOCCUPATION WITH PHYSICAL APPETITES (LK. 17:27)**
- **RAPID ADVANCES IN TECHNOLOGY (GEN. 4:22)**
- **GROSSLY MATERIALISTIC ATTITUDES AND INTERESTS (LK. 17:28)**
- **UNIFORMITARIAN PHILOSOPHIES (HEB. 11:7; 2 PET. 3:4)**
- **INORDINATE DEVOTION TO PLEASURE AND COMFORT (GEN. 4:21)**
- **NO CONCERN FOR GOD IN EITHER BELIEF OR CONDUCT (2 PET. 2:4; JUDE 15)**
- **DISREGARD FOR THE SACREDNESS OF MARRIAGE RELATIONSHIP (MT. 24:38)**
- **REJECTION OF THE INSPIRED WORD OF GOD (1 PET. 3:19)**
- **POPULATION EXPLOSION (GEN. 6:1, 11)**
- **WIDESPREAD VIOLENCE (GEN. 6:11, 13)**
- **CORRUPTION THROUGHOUT SOCIETY (Gen. 6:12)**
- **PREOCCUPATION WITH ILLICIT SEX ACTIVITY (GEN. 4:19; 6:2)**
- **WIDESPREAD WORDS AND THOUGHTS OF BLASPHEMY (JUDE 1:15)**
- **ORGANIZED SATANIC ACTIVITY (GEN. 6:1–4)**
- **PROMULGATION OF SYSTEMS AND MOVEMENTS OF ABNORMAL DEPRAVITY (GEN. 6:5, 12)**

25. How did their age compare with ours? Our Lord once said:

"And as it was in the days of Noah, so shall it be also in the days of the Son of man. They did eat, they drank, they married wives, they were given in marriage, until the day that Noah entered into the ark, and the flood came, and destroyed them all" (Lk. 17:26, 27).

Dr. Henry Morris suggests some fifteen similarities between their age and ours:

a. preoccupation with physical appetites (Lk. 17:27)

b. rapid advances in technology (Gen. 4:22)

c. grossly materialistic attitudes and interests (Lk. 17:28)

d. uniformitarian philosophies (Heb. 11:7; 2 Pet. 3:3–6)

"Knowing this first, that there shall come in the last days scoffers, walking after their own lusts, and saying, Where is the promise of his coming? for since the fathers fell asleep, all things continue as they were from the beginning of the creation. For this they willingly are ignorant of, that by the word of God the heavens were of old, and the earth standing out of the water and in the water: Whereby the world that then was, being overflowed with water, perished" (2 Pet. 3:3–6).

e. inordinate devotion to pleasure and comfort (Gen. 4:21)

f. no concern for God in either belief or conduct (2 Pet. 2:4; Jude 1:15)

g. disregard for the sacredness of the marriage relationship

"For as in the days that were before the flood they were eating and drinking, marrying and giving in marriage, until the day that Noe entered into the ark" (Mt. 24:38).

## FLOOD FACTS

| | |
|---|---|
| **WHEN** DID THE FLOOD BEGIN? | It began in November. This month is lamented by many people around the world as the day of the dead. |
| **HOW LONG** DID THE FLOOD LAST? | **371 DAYS** |
| **WHAT** MAY HAVE TRIGGERED THE FLOOD? | **A.** An earthquake may have released vast and pressured water reservoirs in the earth's mantle (Gen. 7:11) <br><br>**B.** This may have blown immense amounts of dust skyward which would then initiate the condensation and precipitation of the watery canopy. |
| **WAS** THE FLOOD WORLDWIDE? YES! | **A.** Because of the need for the ark <br><br>**B.** Because of the wide distribution of man before the flood. (See Gen. 4:16.) <br><br>**C.** Because of the comparison made in 2 Peter 3:3–7 <br><br>**D.** Because of the universal flood traditions <br><br>**E.** Because of the marine fossils found on mountains <br><br>**F.** Because of the many fossil fish beds <br><br>**G.** Because of the worldwide animal fossil graveyards <br><br>**H.** Because of the evidence of recent water bodies in present desert areas <br><br>**I.** Because of the evidence of a recent drastic rise in the sea level <br><br>**J.** Because of the evidence from the geologic column |

**HOW BIG** WAS THE ARK?

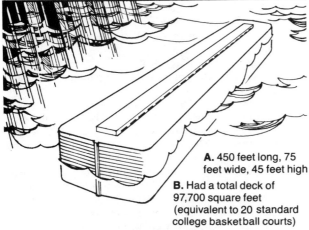

**A.** 450 feet long, 75 feet wide, 45 feet high

**B.** Had a total deck of 97,700 square feet (equivalent to 20 standard college basketball courts)

**C.** Largest ship ever built until 1884 A.D.

**D.** Nearly one half the length of the Queen Mary

| | |
|---|---|
| **HOW** DID NOAH FIND ROOM FOR ALL THE ANIMALS? | **A.** Total animal population would not have exceeded 35,000 vertebrates <br><br>**B.** Average size would be that of a sheep <br><br>**C.** Modern train of 150 boxcars could carry this <br><br>**D.** Ark had carrying capacity of over 520 boxcars! |

h. rejection of the inspired Word of God

"But there were false prophets also among the people, even as there shall be false teachers among you, who privily shall bring in damnable heresies, even denying the Lord that bought them, and bring upon themselves swift destruction" (2 Pet. 2:1).

i. population explosion (Gen. 6:1, 11)
j. widespread violence

"The earth also was corrupt before God, and the earth was filled with violence" (Gen. 6:11).

"And God said unto Noah, The end of all flesh is come before me; for the earth is filled with violence through them; and, behold, I will destroy them with the earth" (Gen. 6:13).

k. corruption throughout society (Gen. 6:12)
l. preoccupation with illicit sex activity

"And Lamech took unto him two wives: the name of the one was Adah, and the name of the other Zillah" (Gen. 4:19).

"That the sons of God saw the daughters of men that they were fair; and they took them wives of all which they chose" (Gen. 6:2).

m. widespread words and thoughts of blasphemy (Jude 1:15)
n. organized satanic activity (Gen. 6:1-4)
o. promulgation of systems and movements of abnormal depravity (Gen. 6:5, 12)

26. How could men live so long at that time? The average age of the patriarchs mentioned in Genesis 5 was 912 years. Several factors doubtless contributed to this amazing phenomenon.

a. As a slow developing cancer will often take several years to destroy a healthy body, so the physical results of sin settled down upon the bodies of men.

b. Prior to the flood there apparently existed many times the amount of water vapor in the upper atmosphere that there is today. (Compare Gen. 1:7 with 7:11.) This vapor, although invisible to the eye, would nevertheless function as a filtering protection and shield against the amount of intense radiation falling upon the earth from the sun. Scientific research is now demonstrating that radiation can appreciably reduce the life span of living tissue and actually cause the cells to speed up the process. Of course, after the flood that protective watery canopy disappeared as it fell upon the earth in the form of rain.

27. When did the flood begin? Creation scientist F. Filby suggests that it began in November (the seventeenth day of the second month on Noah's calendar; Gen. 7:11). He points out that this fact and date is indelibly enshrined in the memory of the human race, pointing out that to many people around the world, November brings the Day of the Dead (in the western world, November 2 is All Soul's Day).

28. How long did the flood last? It is believed that 371 days elapsed from the time Noah entered the ark (Gen. 7:11) until the day he stepped out (8:18).

29. What may have triggered the flood? Dr. Henry Morris suggests the following:

a. A secondary source of water is postulated, existing in vast subterranean heated and pressurized reservoirs in the earth's mantle.

b. The actual trigger to unleash these stored waters may have been an earthquake.

c. This earthquake would not only allow the underground waters to surface through the fractured earth, but would also result in immense amounts of dust blown skyward which would then initiate the condensation and precipitation of the water canopy.

30. Was the flood really worldwide? Both scriptural and secular evidence would strongly support that it was indeed universal.
This is verified by:
   a. The need for the ark. God commanded Noah to build an ark to save both a remnant of humanity and the animal creation. But if the flood were local, then all the effort to build it would be totally unnecessary and the whole story becomes ridiculous. Noah could have just trotted down the road a few miles and escaped.
   b. The wide distribution of man before the flood. In Genesis 4:16, Cain "went out from the presence of the Lord and dwelt in the land of Nod, on the east of Eden." Some believe this to be a reference to China.
   c. The comparison between the historical flood judgment and the coming fire judgment. The Apostle Peter (2 Pet. 3:3-7) states definitely that as God once destroyed the world by a flood, he will someday do likewise through a fire. As the Bible clearly teaches, the entire earth will be burned (2 Pet. 3:10; Rev. 21:2), we logically conclude that the entire earth was once flooded. Few local flood advocates would propose a "local-fire" theory.
      "And as it was in the days of Noe, so shall it be also in the days of the Son of man. They did eat, they drank, they married wives, they were given in marriage, until the day that Noe entered into the ark, and the flood came, and destroyed them all. Likewise also as it was in the days of Lot; they did eat, they drank, they bought, they sold, they planted, they builded; but the same day that Lot went out of Sodom it rained fire and brimstone from heaven, and destroyed them all. Even thus shall it be in the day when the Son of man is revealed" (Lk. 17:26-30).
   d. If the flood was local, then God lied to Noah when he promised never to send a destructive flood again (Gen. 9:11). But there have been, of course, many local destructive floods since.
   e. Flood traditions can be found in the history of every ancient civilization culture. The early aborigines of nearly every country of the world have preserved records of the universal flood. Dr. Richard Andree collected forty-six flood legends from North and South America, twenty from Asia, five from Europe, seven from Africa, and ten from South Sea islands and Australia.
   f. Marine fossils have been found atop mountains. Scientists of the nineteenth century were dismayed to find that, as high as they climbed, the rocks yielded skeletons of marine animals, ocean fish, and shells of mollusks. Thus, in ancient days, flood waters streamed over Mount Everest and all other mountains. A whale's skeleton was once found on the top of Mount Sanhorn on the Arctic Coast, and other similar skeletons a mile high on California's coastal range.
   g. Many fossil "fish beds" exist all over the world. The *Science Magazine,* January 9, 1959, states:
      "More than a billion fish averaging 6 to 8 inches in length died on 4 square miles of bay bottom off the California Coast line."
      Ivan Velikovsky writes:
      "When a fish dies its body floats on the surface or sinks to the bottom and is devoured rather quickly, actually in a matter of hours, by other fish. However, the fossil fish found in sedimentary rocks is very often preserved with all its bones intact. Entire shoals of fish over large areas, numbering billions of specimens, are found in a state of agony, but with no marks of a scavenger's attack." (*Earth in Upheaval,* p. 222)
   h. Because of the worldwide animal fossil graveyards. Robert Broom, South African paleontologist, estimated 800 *billion* skeletons of vertebrate animals exist in the Karroo formation alone. To this can be added the tens of thousands of fossils of all kinds found in the LaBrea tar pits in Los Angeles, California.
   i. Evidence of water bodies in present desert areas.
   j. Evidence of a recent drastic rise in the sea level.
   k. The universal occurrence of rivers in valleys too large for the present system.
   l. Evidence from the geologic column suggests two things:
      (1) That there was a continuous deposition of the stratum layers from beginning to end. There is no erosion in between the layers. In fact, in some layers there are actual ripple marks. In other stratums there exists one or more vertical tree trunks, with the same tree making its way up from top to bottom!
      (2) That fossils from supposed different "ages" in the evolutionary theory actually lived at the same time!

31. How destructive would a worldwide flood be? In his book entitled, *Disasters,* author John Godwin related the following terrifying information concerning just one kind of power which can spring from the ocean. This is called Tsunami or "killer waves." He lists three examples.
   a. Hilo, Hawaii, May, 1960. At this time a hundred-foot wave traveling at 550 m.p.h. hit the coast, drowning 665 people and causing property damage of 50 million dollars.
   b. Lisbon, Portugal, Nov. 1, 1755. This city was hit by a seventy-foot wave which drowned 65,000 people.
   c. Indonesia, May 20, 1883. On this date the volcano Krakatoa exploded and caused a 150-foot wave to rush ashore. It sunk thirty-three European vessels, buried many islands beneath a nine-foot layer of mud, destroyed over 1000 coastal cities, and left over 50,000 dead in its terrible wake. One of the most descriptive summaries of the destruction wrought by a worldwide flood is from the pen of Dr. Henry Morris, Ph.D., and expert in hydrology (the nature of moving water). Morris writes:
      "Visualize, then, a great hydraulic cataclysm bursting upon the present world, with currents of water pouring perpetually from the skies and erupting continuously from the earth's crust, all over the world, for weeks on end, until the entire globe was submerged, accompanied by out-

pourings of magma from the mantle, gigantic earth movements, landslides, tsunamis, and explosions.

Sooner or later all land animals would perish. Many, but not all, marine animals would perish. Human beings would swim, run, climb, and attempt to escape the floods but, unless a few managed to ride out the cataclysm in unusually strong watertight sea-going vessels, they would eventually all drown or otherwise perish.

Soils would soon erode away and trees and plants be uprooted and carried down toward the sea in great mats on flooding streams. Eventually, the hills and mountains themselves would disintegrate and flow downstream in great landslides and turbidity currents. Slabs of rock would crack and bounce and gradually be rounded into boulders and gravel and sand. Vast seas of mud and rock would flow downriver, trapping many animals and rafting great masses of plants with them.

On the ocean bottom, upwelling sediments and subterranean waters and magmas would entomb hordes of invertebrates. The waters would undergo rapid changes in heat and salinity, great slurries would form, and immense amounts of chemicals would be dissolved and dispersed throughout the seaways.

Eventually, the land sediments and waters would commingle with those in the ocean. Finally, the sediments would settle out as the waters slowed down, dissolved chemicals would precipitate out at times and places where the salinity and temperature permitted, and great beds of sediment, soon to be cemented into rock, would be formed all over the world.

The above, of course, is only the barest outline of the great variety of phenomena that would accompany such a cataclysm." (*Scientific Creationism*, pp. 117, 118)

32. How big was Noah's Ark? The size of the ark was approximately 450 feet long, seventy-five feet wide, and forty-five feet high. It had a deck total of 97,700 square feet, or the equivalent to more than an area of twenty standard college basketball courts. Its total volume was around 1,500,000 cubic feet and the gross tonnage exceeded some 14,000 tons. (See Gen. 6:14-16.) It was not until 1884 A.D. that this huge boat was exceeded by modern man (when the Italian vessel, *Eturia*, was built). The *Queen Mary* ocean liner had a total length of 1018 feet, so the ark was nearly half this size. Author Frederick Filby writes:

"The Ark was, according to the specifications laid down, to be 300 cubits long by 500 cubits wide by 30 cubits high. The ratios of these numbers are very interesting. They obviously reflect an advanced knowledge of ship building. The Babylonian account which speaks of the Ark as a cube betrays complete ignorance. Such a vessel would spin slowly around. But the Bible ratios leave nothing to be desired." (*The Flood Reconsidered*, p. 90)

33. How did Noah possibly gather all the needed animals from the various remote areas and nations of the world? In the first place, we are told that God himself gathered these animals (Gen. 7:8, 9). In addition, the indication is strong that prior to the flood the conti-

nents of the earth were not separated by vast bodies of water as they are today.

34. How did Noah possibly pack all those animals on board? First it must be asked how many animals were involved here? Millions? Hundreds of thousands? Hardly. One of America's leading systematic taxonomists lists the following numbers for animal species according to the best estimates of modern taxonomy:

| | |
|---|---|
| Mammals | 3,500 |
| Birds | 8,600 |
| Reptiles and amphibians | 5,500 |
| Worms | 25,500 |

Taking this into consideration, one may reasonably conclude that no more than 35,000 individual vertebrate animals the size of a sheep (overall average) boarded the Ark. It has been estimated that a modern train hauling 150 boxcars could easily handle these animals. But the Ark had a carrying capacity of more than 520 stock cars! In other words, there was more than enough room in the Ark. Noah and his family could have played shuffleboard on deck had they chosen to do so.

35. How did Noah feed and keep these animals for an entire year? Of course, we may only speculate. A possible solution might have involved that mysterious and remarkable factor of animal physiology known as hibernation. Hibernation is generally defined as a specific physiological state in an animal in which normal functions are suspended or greatly retarded, enabling the animal to endure long periods of complete inactivity. This suggestion would not seem to be unreasonable, for the animals went aboard two by two (the clean animals by sevens) and came off the same way—including the rabbits.

36. Were there dinosaurs on board the Ark? Perhaps no other single question concerning the flood will more quickly bring out the agnostic's sneers and the believer's fears than will this one. But there is now mounting evidence that man and dinosaurs did indeed live on earth at the same time.

a. In Rhodesia paintings on cave walls by bushmen known to have left the caves in 1500 B.C. include paintings of brontosaurs. According to the nature of their art, cavemen only painted from what they could actually see. Thus, they would have had to see a brontosaur in order to paint one.

b. Evidence of these large reptiles has been found since the flood. Dinosaur footprints have been located in the same strata with human footprints in Glen Rose, Texas.

c. To conclude this argument, we quote again from Henry Morris:

"The Book of Job is one of the oldest in the Bible and reflects living conditions in the early centuries after the flood. The climax of the book is when God speaks directly to Job and his friends in Job 38, 39, 40, and 41. God is calling attention to His great power in creating and sustaining all things (exactly the message urgently needed by the world today.)

Finally, He calls attention to His two greatest creations in the animal kingdom, behemoth (Job 40:15-24) and leviathan (Job 41:1-34). Most commentators today suggest behemoth is either the elephant or hippopotamus and that leviathan is the crocodile. However, the actual descriptions (and these, coming as they do from the mount of God Himself, certainly refer to real animals) obviously do not apply to any animals known today. The most reasonable interpretation, therefore, is that they refer to extinct animals. Perhaps, then behemoth is a land dinosaur and leviathan a marine dinosaur. Suddenly these chapters become very much alive and meaningful! These great animals were still living in Job's day, even though they may have become extinct since.

In reading God's description of behemoth, one can clearly visualize a giant brontosaur, with his long neck projecting out to eat the swamp vegetation and to wash it down with great quantities of water, with his powerful legs and tail easily capable of demolishing his enemies with their overwhelming blows. 'Behold now behemoth,' God remarks . . . 'he eateth grass as an ox . . . his strength is in his loins, and his force is in the navel of his belly. He moveth his tail like a cedar.' (Ever see an elephant's tail?) His bones are as strong pieces of brass, his bones are like bars of iron (no wonder so many fossil dinosaur bones have been preserved so long). Finally, God states, 'He is the chief of the ways of God' (thus the greatest animal God ever made); 'He that made him can make his sword to approach unto him' (thus God Himself can destroy the dinosaurs, even though man could not). 'Behold he drinketh up a river . . . his nose pierceth through snares.' " (*The Remarkable Birth of the Planet Earth*, pp. 32, 33)

Thus, to answer the question concerning whether dinosaurs were on the ark, it may be said that inasmuch as they definitely existed with man prior to the flood, the chances are good that a young pair of these huge reptiles may well indeed have been aboard!

37. Why do we not find animal fossils in Asia Minor, the place where the Ark landed? Both agnostics and local flood advocates have often pointed out this fact to those who hold the universal flood view. Dr. Russell L. Mixter, professor of Zoology at Wheaton College, writes:

"If kangaroos were in the ark and first touched land in Asia, one would expect fossils of them in Asia. According to Romer, the only place where there are either fossil or living kangaroos is in Australia. What shall we conclude? If the fossil evidence means that there never have been kangaroos in Asia, then kangaroos were not in the ark or if they were, they hurried from Australia to meet Noah, and as rapidly returned to their native land. Is it not easier to believe that they were never in the ark, and hence were in an area untouched by the flood, and that the flood occurred only in the area inhabited by man?" (*Creation and Evolution*, p. 15)

This objection, however, may be quickly refuted by pointing out the fact that fossils are only formed under unusual conditions and that, apart from these conditions, all dead animals rapidly decompose and disappear. Note the following examples to undergird this:

a. Concerning lions in Palestine: There is no fossil evidence of lions in Palestine, but the Old Testament informs us that the land was once infested with these animals. (See Jdg. 14:5; 1 Sam. 17:34; 2 Sam. 23:20; 1 Ki. 13:24; 20:36; 2 Ki. 17:25.)

b. Concerning buffalo (or bison) in the American West:

"The Buffalo carcasses strewn over the plains in uncounted millions two generations ago have left hardly a present trace. The flesh was devoured by wolves and vultures within hours or days after death, and even the skeletons have now largely disappeared, the bones dissolving and crumbling into dust under the attack of the weather." (Carl Dunbar, *Historical Geology*, p. 39)

38. How did the animals get from Asia Minor to their present location? Professor Paul A. Moody of the University of Vermont writes:

"In times of flood, large masses of earth and entwining vegetation, including trees, may be torn loose from banks of rivers, and swept out to sea. Sometimes such masses are encountered floating in the ocean out of sight of land, still lush and green, with palms twenty to thirty feet tall. It is entirely probable that land animals may be transported long distances in this manner. Mayr records that many tropical ocean currents have a speed of at least two knots; this would amount to fifty miles in a day, 1000 miles in three weeks." (*Introduction to Evolution*, p. 262)

"It seems certain that land animals do at times cross considerable bodies of water where land connections are utterly lacking . . . floating masses of vegetation, such as are sometimes found off the mouths of the Amazon, may be one means of effecting this type of migration." (Alfred S. Romer, Harvard University, *Vertebrate Paleontology*)

"One glance at a world map will show that, with the exception of the narrow break at the Bering Strait, a dryland path leads from Armenia to all lands of the globe except Australia. In the case of the latter (Australia) the East Indies even today form a fairly continuous bridge of stepping-stones to that southern continent. As regards the Bering Strait, there is no doubt that a land connection once existed between Asia and North America." (Frank L. Marsh, *Evolution, Creation, and Science*)

39. Where did all the flood waters go? Hebrew scholar John Whitcomb writes:

"Even as the beginning of the flood year was characterized by supernatural intervention, so also the end of the flood was brought about by a stupendous miracle of God. Apart from this, the waters would have covered the earth forever, and all terrestrial-like would soon have come to an end.

Two passages of Scripture, in widely separated Old Testament books, deal with this particular activity of God. The first, in Genesis 8:2-3, tells us that 'the fountains . . . of the deep . . . were stopped . . . and the waters returned from off the earth continually.' Since the breaking up of the fountains of the great deep involved the uplift of ocean floors, the stopping of these 'fountains' must refer to a reversal of this action, whereby new and much deeper ocean basins were formed to serve as vast reservoirs for the two oceans which were separated from each other by the atmospheric expanse before the flood (Gen. 1:7). A natural result of this subsidence was that 'the waters returned from off the earth continually' permitting continents to emerge from the oceans again, as they had done on the third day of creation.

A second passage that sheds important light upon the termination of the flood is Psalm 104:6-9.

'Thou coveredst it with the deep as with a garment: the waters stood above the mountains. At thy rebuke they fled; at the voice of thy thunder they hasted away. They go up by the mountains; they go down by the valleys unto the place which thou hast founded for them. Thou hast set a bound that they may not pass over; that they turn not again to cover the earth' (Ps. 104:6-9).

Though it contains several figures of speech, the passage is clearly historical in its reference to the flood. Note, for example, the statement of verse 6—'the waters stood above the mountains' and that of verse 9—'thou hast set a bound that they may not pass over; that they turn not again to cover the earth.' The latter is obviously a reference to the rainbow covenant of Genesis 9, in which God assured mankind that there would never again be a universal flood (cf. Isa. 54:9).

Now the key statement in this passage (Ps. 104:8) for our purposes is in the beginning of verse 8: 'The mountains rose, the valleys sank down' (ASV; cf. RSV, Berkeley, Amplified, NASB). We have already seen in Genesis 8:2 that the ocean basins were lowered at the termination of the flood, and with this concept the phrase 'the valleys sank down' is in agreement. God supernaturally depressed various parts of the earth's crust, and into those places which God 'founded for them' the waters 'fled' and 'hasted away,' there to abide while this earth exists (cf. Rev. 21:1), never again to cover the continents."

(*The World That Perished*)

40. Has the Ark been sighted since it landed on Mt. Ararat? Introduction: On the evening of June 2, 1840, a terrific earthquake shook the highest mountain of the Armenian plains, located north of Lake Van in Turkey. The name of this shattered mountain was Aghri Dagh, better known as Mt. Ararat. The power released was beyond that of hundreds of atomic bombs. It totally wiped out the little village of Ahora and the monastery of St. Jacob.

Since 1840, a number of reports have come to the world's attention concerning the sighting of an ark-like structure of hand-tooled timber on treeless Mt. Ararat. Even prior to this there have been many ancient reports about this very thing, which includes the testimonies of Herodotus (the Greek historian), Josephus (the Jewish historian), the Koran (sacred book of the Islamic faith), and Marco Polo (famous European explorer).

A summary of the eyewitness reports since 1840 proves fascinating reading indeed. Their testimonies bear striking similarities.

a. The ship is half buried in a partly melted lake.
b. Its altitude is around 13 thousand feet.
c. The inside of the ark is filled with wooden separators (like bars in a cage).
d. The outside and inside are covered with a heavy varnish or lacquer.
e. The wood is extremely hard, almost petrified.
f. The main door is missing.

*The witnesses themselves are an interesting lot:*

g. Haji Yearman (date of Ark sighting, 1865). He was an Armenian who lived at the base of Mt. Ararat. He died in Oakland, California, in 1916.
h. John Joseph. The Archbishop of Babylon and head of the Christian Nestorian Church. Joseph reported his experience at the World's Fair in Chicago in 1893.
i. W. Roskovitsky. A Russian airman. The sighting was in 1915 during World War I. Later, in 1917, a Russian expedition numbering 150 men saw it.
j. Carveth Wells. A popular radio commentator over KFI in Los Angeles reported seeing wood from the Ark while at the site in 1933.
k. Various airmen (both Russian and American) during World War II. Mount Ararat was on a direct flight between the allied base in Tunisia and the Russian base at Brivan. One of the Russians claiming to have seen it was Major Jasper Maskelyn, wartime chief of Camouflage (1941-1945).
l. Resit. A Kurdish farmer. His experience was published in an Istanbul newspaper on November 13, 1948.
m. Dr. Donald M. Liedman. Dr. Liedman is a Jewish scientist and medical doctor. He has given sworn testimony that he was shown actual snapshots of the Ark on two occasions while in Hamburg, Germany, by a Russian air force major who had personally taken the pictures during World War II.
n. George Jefferson Greene. Greene was on a helicopter research mission for his company in 1953. While flying over Mt. Ararat he spotted a strange object and took a number of pictures from ninety feet. When developed, they showed a large wooden object. These pictures were seen by many. Greene was later found murdered. The pictures were never located.
o. Bernard Navarra. This French explorer visited Mount Ararat and later wrote a book on the subject entitled, *Noah's Ark, I Touched It.* Navarra cut some wood from an object on Mt. Ararat and subjected it to C-14 testings at two universities.

"This fossilized wood was derived from an epoch of great antiquity." (official statement from the University of Bordeaux)

"Our analysis estimated the age of the fragment at 5000 years." (from the Forest Institute in Madrid)

*Concluding statements:*

p. In the thirties, Dr. Alexander A. Koor, Russian Colonel, scholar, researcher, author, historian, and etymologist of ancient languages discovered and translated an ancient Sumerian inscription found at Karada Pass near Mt. Ararat. It read:

"God sowed the seeds of the world into the waters . . . the waters filled the earth, descending from above . . . His children came to rest on the mountain peak."

q. The following quotes are taken from Viola Cumming's book, *Noah's Ark, Fable or Fact?*

"Silhouetted against the sky at the crest of a rocky eminence some distance away, the sharply-carved outlines of a nobly-proportioned patriarchal head rose perhaps eight to ten feet above the top of the hill. For some reason, the ancient sculptor had faced the bearded, turbaned profile so that its sightless gaze would forever rest on the towering heights of Mt. Ararat. Did the same hand that recorded the story of the Deluge on the Karada Cliff not far away also carve the majestic patriarchal head atop a hill facing the heights of Mt. Ararat?

One of the still greater wonders of Ararat is the rainbow which can frequently be seen in the afternoon from the north and north-eastern slopes."

41. Was there an Ice Age?

Author Reginald Daly writes the following:

"The Ice Age automatically follows the Universal Flood. There could not have been a universal flood without a glacial age following. The deserts were sopping wet for centuries following the flood. There were lakes everywhere. Evaporation kept humidity at 100%. There was rain every day in the north country. Winds carried moisture-laden clouds, super-saturated, to northern Canada, Scotland, Norway, Sweden, where snow poured down every day and every hour from November until April, probably five hundred or a thousand feet thick the first winter. Multiply 500 feet of snow by 100 years of wet weather. This makes 50,000 feet of snow which would settle down into approximately 5000 feet of ice—the glacial age. The tops of these mountains, a mile high, would be so cold that snow would continue to pile up all spring and early fall as well as all winter, leaving such a brief, chilly July-August summer that only a small amount of snow would melt. The small amount melting in July would be many times over-balanced by the prodigious winter snowfall. The effect would be cumulative: the higher the mountain, the colder the temperature, the shorter the summers, and the greater the snowfall. The weight of a mile or two of ice would cause it to flow outwards, across the Baltic Sea, depositing boulders all over the north German plain, as we find them today. Also downward over North America, across Lake Erie, leaving moraines, eskers, drumlins and boulders across Ohio and Missouri as far south as the Missouri River." (*Earth's Most Challenging Mysteries*, p. 142)

Few other men have written as extensively on the Ice Age from a Christian viewpoint as has Donald Patten. He writes:

"Mammoths were, along with mastodons, the largest members of the elephant family. They have become mummified in two manners, both of which suggest cataclysm and suddenness. In Alaska and Siberia mammoths have been mummified, apparently by the millions, both in ice and in sedimentary strata. It is as if they had been deposited in watery graves in some areas, but encased in ice in other areas, ice which has remained unmelted. Their entombment and refrigeration have been so effective that mammoth carcasses have been thawed to feed sled dogs, both in Alaska and Siberia; in fact, mammoth steaks have even been featured on restaurant menus in Fairbanks.

Every indication is that the mammoths died suddenly, in intense cold, and in great numbers. Death came so quickly that the swallowed vegetation is yet undigested in their stomachs and their mouths." (*The Ice Age*, p. 105)

42. What was involved in Noah's prophecy concerning his three sons after the flood?

Noah became drunk and exposed his nakedness to Ham. Upon awaking he pronounced a judgment upon Ham's son, Canaan. He then issued a prophecy concerning all three sons, Ham, Shem, and Japheth.

"And Noah began to be an husbandman, and he planted a vineyard: And he drank of the wine, and was drunken; and he was uncovered within his tent.

And Ham, the father of Canaan, saw the nakedness of his father, and told his two brethren without.

And Shem and Japheth took a garment, and laid it upon both their shoulders, and went backward, and covered the nakedness of their father; and their faces were backward, and they saw not their father's nakedness. And Noah awoke from his wine, and knew what his younger son had done unto him. And he said, Cursed be Canaan; a servant of servants shall he be unto his brethren. And he said, Blessed be the Lord God of Shem; and Canaan shall be his servant.

God shall enlarge Japheth, and he shall dwell in the tents of Shem; and Canaan shall be his servant.

And Noah lived after the flood three hundred and fifty years. And all the days of Noah were nine hundred and fifty years: and he died" (Gen. 9:20-29).

a. What was this horrible sin which prompted a curse?

Some believe the crime involved here was homosexuality. Reasons for holding this view are:

(1) The Hebrew language seems to suggest it.

(2) The phrase "nakedness of his father" in 9:22 is definitely connected with sexual immorality in Leviticus 18 and 20.

(3) Ham's son, Canaan, was the progenitor of the Canaanite people who later populated Palestine and who were noted for their horrible habits of sexual perversion.

"And the border of the Canaanites was from Sidon, as thou comest to Gerar, unto Gaza; as thou goest, unto Sodom, and Gomorrah, and Admah, and Zeboim, even unto Lasha" (Gen. 10:19).

"And there came two angels to Sodom at even; and Lot sat in the gate of Sodom: and Lot seeing them rose up to meet them; and he bowed himself with his face toward the ground; and he said, Behold now, my lords, turn in, I pray you, into your servant's house, and tarry all night, and wash your feet, and ye shall rise up early, and go on your ways. And they said, Nay; but we will abide in the street all night. And he pressed upon them greatly; and they turned in unto him, and entered into his house; and he made them a feast, and did bake unleavened bread, and they did eat.

But before they lay down, the men of the city, even the men of Sodom, compassed the house round, both old and young, all the people from every quarter:

And they called unto Lot, and said unto him, Where are the men which came into thee this night? bring them out unto us, that we may know them.

And Lot went out at the door unto them, and shut the door after him, and said, I pray you, brethren, do not so wickedly. Behold now, I have two daughters which have not known man; let me, I pray you, bring them out unto you, and do ye to them as is good in your eyes: only unto these men do nothing; for therefore came they under the shadow of my roof.

And they said, Stand back. And they said again, This one fellow came in to sojourn, and he will needs be a judge: now will we deal worse with thee, than with them. And they pressed sore upon the man, even Lot, and came near to break the door.

But the men put forth their hand, and pulled Lot into the house to them, and shut to the door.

And they smote the men that were at the door of the house with blindness, both small and great: so that they wearied themselves to find the door" (Gen. 19:1-11).

"And there were also sodomites in the land: and they did according to all the abominations of the nations which the Lord cast out before the children of Israel" (1 Ki. 14:24).

"Wherefore God also gave them up to uncleanness through the lusts of their own hearts, to dishonour their own bodies between themselves: Who changed the truth of God into a lie, and worshipped and served the creature more than the Creator, who is blessed for ever. Amen.

For this cause God gave them up unto vile affections: for even their women did change the natural use into that which is against nature: And likewise also the men, leaving the natural use of the woman, burned in their lust one toward another; men with men working that which is unseemly, and receiving in themselves that recompence of their error which was meet" (Rom. 1:24-27).

b. Why was Canaan cursed (9:25) when it would appear that Ham, "his younger son," had instigated the crime?
    *Lange's Commentary* suggests that the phrase "his younger son" should be translated "his youngest one," and was actually a reference to Noah's youngest grandson, which was Canaan. To lend weight to this, if the account in Genesis 5:32 can be taken at face value, Japheth was Noah's youngest son, and not Ham.

c. What was involved in Noah's threefold prophecy?
    (1) To Ham and Canaan—"a servant of servants shall he be unto his brethren."
        (a) Negative—it did not result in a special curse upon black people. Ham had four sons. These were:
            *Cush*—the progenitor of the Ethiopians
            *Mizriam*—of the Egyptians
            *Phut*—of the Libyans and peoples of Africa
            *Canaan*—of the Canaanites

Thus, as the curse was specifically leveled at Canaan and not Phut (who may have founded the African nations), there exist absolutely no racial implications whatsoever within the curse. In fact, the skin texture of Israelites and Canaanites at the time of Joshua's invasion was probably very similar. The problem concerning the Canaanites was not in the color of their *skin* but rather in the condition of their *hearts*.

        (b) Positive—but the wider scope of Noah's words accurately foretells that the descendants of Ham would be in some measure subjected to the descendants of both Shem and Japheth. History attests to this. *Joshua, David,* and *Solomon* had subdued them by 1000 B.C.
        *Alexander the Great* (a descendant of Japheth) defeated the Phoenicians in 331 B.C.
        *The Romans* (of Japheth) defeated Hannibal of Carthage (founded by the Hamitic Phoenicians in 850 B.C.) during the Second Punic War in 202 B.C. at Zama. German theologian Eric Sauer writes:
            "With Nimrod began, with Hannibal ended the drama of Hamitic World Empire, and Rome's brilliant victory sealed conclusively the . . . establishment of the world-rule of the Japhetic race. 'Let Canaan be his servant'—this it is which stands as written, as with letters of fire, over the battlefield of Zama." (*Dawn of World Redemption*, p. 80)
    (2) To Shem—"Blessed be the Lord God of Shem." Here is obviously a reference to the special favor bestowed upon Shem's descendants, beginning with Abraham, Isaac, and Jacob, and ending in a Bethlehem manger.
    (3) To Japheth—"God shall enlarge Japheth." Some nineteen centuries later this prophecy came to pass. During those centuries the Hamites ruled in the Nile Valley and the Semites reigned in Mesopotamia. But in October of 538, the decisive hour struck, as Cyrus the Persian (a descendant of Japheth) defeated Belshazzar (Dan. 5) and the proud Semitic capital fell. Since then no Semitic or Hamitic race has succeeded in breaking the world supremacy of the Japhethic race. Shortly after this, Cambyses, successor of Cyrus, conquered Egypt and ended the Hamitic rule. As recent as A.D. 732 Japhethic descendant Charles Martel defeated the combined hordes of both Semitics and Hamitics at the historic battle of Tours.

    It should also be noted that the second part of the prophecy concerning Japheth reads, "and he shall dwell in the tents of Shem." Paul himself would later explain this glorious fulfillment in Romans 11:13-25.

        "For I speak to you Gentiles, inasmuch as I am the apostle of the Gentiles, I magnify mine office: If by any means I may provoke to emulation them which are my flesh, and might save some of them. For if the casting away of them be the reconciling of the world, what shall the receiving of them be, but life from the dead?

For if the firstfruit be holy, the lump is also holy: and if the root be holy, so are the branches.

And if some of the branches be broken off, and thou, being a wild olive tree, wert grafted in among them, and with them, and with them partakest of the root and fatness of the olive tree; boast not against the branches. But if thou boast, thou bearest not the root, but the root thee.

Thou wilt say then, The branches were broken off, that I might be grafted in.

Well; because of unbelief they were broken off, and thou standest by faith. Be not highminded, but fear: For if God spared not the natural branches, take heed lest he also spare not thee. Behold therefore the goodness and severity of God: on them which fell, severity, but toward thee, goodness, if thou continue in his goodness: otherwise thou also shalt be cut off. And they also, if they abide not still in unbelief, shall be grafted in: for God is able to graft them in again. For if thou wert cut out of the olive tree which is wild by nature, and wert grafted contrary to nature into a good olive tree; how much more shall these, which be the natural branches, be grafted into their own olive tree? For I would not, brethren, that ye should be ignorant of this mystery, lest ye should be wise in your own conceits; that blindness in part is happened to Israel, until the fulness of the Gentiles be come in" (Rom. 11:13-25).

43. How have the descendants of each of Noah's three sons contributed to mankind?

Dr. Arthur C. Custance, renowned scholar and anthropologist writes the following:

"In the case of Ham and his descendants, history shows that they have rendered an extraordinary service to mankind from the point of view of the physical developments of civilization. All the earliest civilizations of note were founded and carried to their highest technical proficiency by Hamitic people. There is scarcely a basic technological invention which must not be attributed to them. As we shall show later, neither Shem nor Japheth made any significant contribution to the fundamental technology of civilization, in spite of all appearance to the contrary. This is a bold statement but it is not made in ignorance of the facts.

The contribution of Japheth has been in the application of philosophy to technology and the consequent development of the scientific method. As the application of Japheth's philosophy to the technology of Ham produced science, so the application of his philosophy to the religious insights of Shem produced theology. The Hamitic people never developed science and the Semitic people did not develop theology, until the influence of Japhetic philosophy was brought to bear . . . most of us have been brought up to believe that we, Indo-Europeans, are the most inventive people in the world. It is exceedingly difficult to escape from this culturally conditional prejudice to take a fresh objective look at the origins of our technological achievements. One may take almost any essential element of our highly complex civilization—aircraft, paper, weaving, metallurgy, propulsion of various kinds, painting, explosives, medical techniques, mechanical principles, food, the use of electricity, virtually anything technological in nature—and an examination of the history of its development leads us surely and certainly back to a Hamitic people and exceedingly rarely to Japheth or Shem. The basic inventions which have been contributed by Shem or Japheth can, it seems, be numbered on the fingers of one hand. This seems so contrary to popular opinion, yet it is a thesis which can be supported—and has been documented—from close to 1000 authoritative sources.

What we have been trying to show is that the historical process reflects the interaction between three families of people descended respectively from the three sons of Noah whom God appears to have apportioned specific responsibilities and equally specific capabilities for the fulfillment of them; to Shem, responsibility for man's religious and spiritual well-being; to Japheth, his mental well-being; and to Ham, his physical well-being . . . all the great religions of the world—true and false—had their roots in the family of Shem, all true philosophical systems have originated within the family of Japheth, and the world's basic technology is a Hamitic contribution . . . when these three work together in balanced harmony, civilization as a whole has advanced.

It is important to observe that all three are necessary for this. If any one element is given overemphasis the ultimate effect is detrimental! No society prospers which is over materialistic, or overly intellectual, or overly spiritual." (*Noah's Three Sons*, pp. 26, 37, 38, 263, 264)

In another book, Custance has written:

"I believe that in Adam and his descendants, until the Flood brought an end to the old world, these three capacities were by and large combined within each person individually though, of course, not always in exactly the same measure, just as not everyone now has the same level of intelligence. But each man carried within himself a threefold potential which after the Flood was very greatly reduced and more often than not was limited to a capacity chiefly in one direction. In another work, the thesis has been examined rather carefully that *science* results only where philosophy (the contribution of Japheth) is wedded to technology (the contribution of Ham), just as *theology* only arises where philosophy is wedded to spiritual insight based upon revelation (which was the specific contribution of Shem). On the whole, those who are highly inventive and mechanically minded are rarely of a philosophical turn of mind, and philosophers tend to be rather impractical. Whenever these two capacities do happen to appear in one man, we have the scientific individual. Unfortunately, scientifically minded people tend to be somewhat indifferent about spiritual things that are matters of faith. And since man is primarily a spiritual creature, science has often tended to be one-sided and inadequate, sometimes rather futile, and frequently dangerous because it encourages a sceptical attitude. But consider what would happen if every man had within himself a large capacity for invention and could extend the application of his own inventiveness as greatly as scientists have recently extended the basic technology of the previous 6,000 years of civilization. The progress of the past 100 years might have been crowded into the first few centuries of human history, and Adam's grandson might have seen the development of city life, the erection of very large buildings, the appearance of the arts including all kinds of music, the extended use of metals, and the establishment of cattlemen and farmers on a large scale—as evidently Cain's children did (Gen. 4:17-22).

But, as always seems to have been the case, man's spiritual capacity tended to suffer from disuse, or even abuse, and the evil in man was fortified very rapidly to an extraordinary degree by the exercise of the other capabilities, until the Lord looked down from Heaven and saw that it was too dangerous for the individual to be endowed so fully. After the Flood, what had been combined in Adam was thenceforth divided between Shem, Ham, and Japheth. During pre-flood times, however, it seems that the capacity of the individual was so much greater that the processes of civilization were all enormously accelerated." (*Genesis and Early Man*, pp. 138, 139)

44. What really took place at the Tower of Babel?
"And the whole earth was of one language, and of one speech. And it came to pass, as they journeyed from the east, that they found a plain in the land of Shinar; and they dwelt there. And they said one to another, Go to, let us make brick, and burn them throughly. And they had brick for stone, and slime had they for morter. And they said, Go to, let us build us a city and a tower, whose top may reach unto heaven; and let us make us a name, lest we be scattered abroad upon the face of the whole earth" (Gen. 11:1-4).

The passage in Genesis 11 does not teach that early mankind stupidly attempted to build a tower which would reach into outer space! Especially to be noted are the words in verse four "may reach." They are in italics to show they are supplied by the translators and therefore not in the original Hebrew text. In reality the phrase should read: "whose top is heaven."

Archaeological evidence suggests that the Tower of Babel was in reality a building given over to astrology, or the heathen worship of the heavens. Among the ruins of ancient Babylon is a building 153 feet high with a 400 foot base. It was constructed of dried bricks in seven stages, to correspond with the known planets to which they were dedicated. The lowermost was black, the color of Saturn, the next orange, for Jupiter, the third red, for Mars, and so on. These stages were surmounted by a lofty tower, on the summit of which were the signs of the Zodiac. Dr. Barnhouse writes:

"It was an open, definite turning to Satan and the beginning of devil worship. This is why the Bible everywhere pronounces a curse on those who consult the sun, the moon, and the stars of heaven."
"Lest we be scattered abroad" (11:4).
Years prior to this, the world's first murderer, Cain, heard God say, "A fugitive and a vagabond shalt thou be in the earth" (Gen. 4:12). Now Cain's spiritual children were rebelling against the same God, but were anxious to stay together, lest they share Cain's fate.

German theologian Erich Sauer has written:
"The original language in which Adam in Paradise had named all the animals was, as it were, a great mirror in which the whole of nature was accurately reflected. But now God shattered this mirror, and each people retained only a fragment of it, the one a larger, the other a smaller piece, and now each people sees only a piece of the whole, but never the whole completely." (*Dawn of World Redemption*, p. 82)

Thus, the many earphones and translation booths at the United Nations in New York today give eloquent testimony to the tragic episode at Babel. "Therefore is the name of it called Babel" (11:9). This tower project may have been named by Nimrod himself. Babel literally means "gate of God." Thus, while mankind had rejected the true God, they nevertheless attempted to assuage their uneasy consciences by acknowledging some vague and impersonal "grand architect of the universe." But it didn't work! God changed the meaning of the word Babel to mean "confusion."

45. When, where, and how did the distinct racial characteristics of modern mankind begin?
Dr. Henry Morris writes:
"As each family and tribal unit migrated away from Babel, not only did they each develop a distinctive culture, but also they each developed distinctive physical and biological characteristics. Since they would communicate only with members of their own family unit, there was no further possibility of marrying outside the family. Hence, it was necessary to establish new families composed of very close relatives, for several generations at least. It is well established genetically that variations take place very quickly in a small inbreeding population, but only very slowly in a large interbreeding population. In the latter, only the dominant genes will find common expression in the outward physical characteristics . . . even though the genetic factors for specifically distinctive characteristics are latent in the gene pool of the population. In a small population, however, the . . . genes will have opportunity to become openly expressed and even dominant under these circumstances. Thus, in a very few generations of such inbreeding, distinctive characteristics of skin color, height, hair texture, facial features, temperament, environmental adjustment, and others, could come to be associated with particular tribes and nations." (The *Genesis Record*, p. 176)

# THE PATRIARCHAL STAGE

## INTRODUCING THE PATRIARCHAL STAGE (Genesis 12–50; Job)

1. The important men who appear during this stage are Abraham, Isaac, Jacob, Joseph, and Job. Abraham is considered to be the second of the seven greatest men who ever lived. These are: Adam, Abraham, Moses, David, John the Baptist, Peter, and Paul.

2. In the Creation Stage God dealt with the entire earth in general. For example, Genesis 1–11 deals with the world of men as a whole. Now, however, in the Patriarchal Stage, he will employ the rifle instead of the shotgun. The floodlight will give way to the spotlight. Our attention is now drawn from the world to a nation (Israel), then to a tribe in that nation (Judah), then to a family within that tribe (Jesse), and finally to an individual within the family (Jesus Christ).

3. This stage spans a period of some 350 years.

4. Here a city is destroyed on the plains (Sodom) and a boy is spared on a mountain (Isaac) (Gen. 19, 22).

5. Here a son (Jacob) deceives his father (Isaac) and is later himself deceived by his sons (brothers of Joseph) (Gen. 27, 37).

6. Here we read of the first barren wife (Sarah) and the first dying mother (Rachel) (Gen. 16, 35).

7. This stage records how God's friend (Abraham) speaks to him concerning a city (Sodom), and how his enemy (Satan) speaks to him concerning a saint (Job) (Gen. 18; Job 1–2).

8. Jerusalem (a type of the heavenly) and Egypt (a type of the worldly) are first mentioned in this stage (Gen. 13–14).

9. Here we first learn of a king called Melchizedek and a cave named Machpelah (Gen. 14, 25).

10. Here the first of three great biblical covenants is introduced.
    a. The Abrahamic Covenant, promising a goodly land (Gen. 15).
    b. The Davidic Covenant, promising a glorious king (2 Sam. 7).
    c. The new covenant, promising a godly people (Jer. 31).

## THE PATRIARCHAL STAGE

The remaining thirty-nine chapters of Genesis (12–50) summarize the lives of Abraham, Isaac, Jacob, and Joseph. Although there is some overlapping, the following chapter division may be noted:

Genesis 12–24—The story of Abraham
Genesis 24–27—The story of Isaac
Genesis 28–36—The story of Jacob
Genesis 37–50—The story of Joseph

THE PATRIARCHAL STAGE

ABRAHAM  ISAAC  JACOB  JOSEPH

GENESIS 12-50      JOB

The Old Testament World

I. Abraham (Gen. 12–24).
   A. His conversion (Acts 7:2).
      The God of glory appeared unto our father, Abraham, when he was in Mesopotamia . . .
      1. Abraham was born around 2166 B.C. We know nothing of his early life or how he was led to God. It has been speculated that either Job, Shem, or even Melchizedek showed him the way of salvation. The importance of his life cannot be underestimated. He is mentioned some 308 times in the Bible; 234 times in the Old Testament; and seventy-four in the New Testament. These quotes came from twenty-seven books: sixteen in the Old Testament and eleven in the New Testament. Abraham was the reason the southern kingdom was spared as long as it was. (See 2 Ki. 13:23.)

The book of Genesis spans a period of around 2350 years. The first eleven chapters, which describe the Creation of the universe, the Fall, Flood, and Tower of Babel, cover a period of 2000 years. The last thirty-nine chapters concern themselves with Abraham and his seed, covering some 350 years. In other words, God gave us more detail about Abraham than about the origin of the universe!

2. Abraham was born and raised in the city of Ur of the Chaldees. Ur was a seaport on the Persian Gulf, at the mouth of the Euphrates River, some twelve miles from the traditional site of the Garden of Eden. But preceding the time of Abraham, it was the most magnificent city in all the world; a center of manufacturing, farming, and shipping, in a land of fabulous fertility and wealth, with caravans going in every direction to distant lands, and ships sailing from the docks of Ur down the Persian Gulf with cargoes of copper and hard stone. For years the skeptic ridiculed the actual existence of Ur. But during the years of 1922-1934 C. T. Wooley of the British museum thoroughly explored the secrets of these ruins.

The most conspicuous building of the city in Abraham's day was the ziggurat, or the temple tower, which was probably patterned after the Tower of Babel. This tower was square, terraced, and built of solid brick. Each successive terrace was planted with trees and shrubbery. The city had two main temples, one dedicated to Nannar, the Moon-god, and the other to his wife, Ningal.

(The information concerning Ur was gleaned in part from *Halley's Handbook*, pp. 88, 89.)

B. His calling (Gen. 11:31; 12:1; Josh. 24:3; Acts 7:2). He was to leave Ur and his father's house for a land that God would show him.

C. His commission (Gen. 12:2, 3; Acts 7:3) was sevenfold:
   1. I will make of thee a great nation.
   2. I will bless thee.
   3. I will make thy name great.
   4. Thou shalt be a blessing.
   5. I will bless them that bless thee.
   6. I will curse him that curseth thee. (See the book of Esther.)
   7. In thee shall all families of the earth be blessed. (A reference to Christ; see Mt. 1:1.)

D. His caution (11:31, 32).
   God had told Abraham to leave his father's house and proceed to Canaan. But he was disobedient concerning both matters in that he took his father with him, and allowed himself to get bogged down in Haran. Haran was the last green outpost of civilization before one entered the vast desert of Arabia. The city was 700 miles northwest of Ur and about sixty miles from the Euphrates River. It was located on a main caravan road connecting the cities of the east with Damascus and Egypt. This was considered a strategic location. The city also worshiped the moon god and goddess as did Ur.

Abram might have been content to settle in Haran permanently, but once more God stepped in and Terah his father died. After that, Abram quickly moves on! The name "Terah" means "delay." Only God knows the multitudes of Christians that have left Ur, bound for Canaan, only to get bogged down in Haran.

E. His Canaan (12:4-9).
   1. He entered the Promised Land and pitched camp near Shechem, some thirty miles north of Jerusalem.
   2. God again appeared to him. It should be noted that the Lord had simply promised to show him a land when he was in Ur, but now adds the words, "Unto thy seed will I give this land." (Compare 12:1 with 12:7.)
   3. Abram built his first recorded altar here.
   4. He then moved on to Bethel, a place meaning "house of God" which would later become a very sacred place in Canaan. (See Gen. 28:1-22; 35:7.) At Bethel he built his second altar to the Lord.

F. His carnality (12:10-20).
   1. After a short while, the land was hit with famine. Thus far, he had obeyed God and was dwelling victoriously in the Promised Land. But now comes the temptation from Satan. There was a famine in the land.
   2. He then left Palestine and went to Egypt. This is the first mention of Egypt in the Bible. Egypt in the Scriptures is pictured as a symbol or type of the world, an instance of dependence upon some human source or help apart from God. As God himself once warned: "Woe to them that go down to Egypt for help . . . and trust in chariots . . . and in horsemen . . . but . . . look not unto the Holy One of Israel, neither seek the Lord" (Isa. 31:1). The Christian therefore "goes to Egypt," spiritually speaking, when he depends upon something or someone else for guidance instead of God. (Carefully read Prov. 3:5, 6; 2:6, 8; Mt. 6:31-33.)
   3. Pharaoh planned to marry Sarai, but was plagued by God and eventually found out the deception of Abraham. The angry king rightfully took Abram to task for this. After a frustrating, dangerous, and embarrassing time, Abram returned to Palestine, where he should have stayed in the first place. Notice the tragic results of his disobedience:
      a. He grieved God—Abram's sin (and our sin) always grieves God. (See Ps. 78:40; Eph. 4:30; Ps. 95:10; Mk. 3:5.)
      b. He weakened his own faith—later Abram failed God in this same matter of lying about his wife. (See Gen. 20.) After we once commit a sin, the second time becomes much easier.
      c. He became a poor testimony to his nephew Lot—some of Abram's worldliness rubbed off on Lot, with tragic results. (See Gen. 13, 19.)
      d. He caused the Pharaoh to be afflicted. (See 12:17.) Sometimes the children of the world suffer for the sins of Christians.

We note Pharaoh's rebuke to Abram here. There is no sadder situation in the world than when an unbeliever rebukes a Christian for some wrong action.

    e. He picks up Hagar the Egyptian handmaid (Gen. 16:3). Hagar would later become Abram's mistress and would give birth to Ishmael, the father of the modern Arabs. Thus the agony of the world's most troubled hot spot, the Middle East, has been caused in part by Abram's sin some thirty-nine centuries ago.

    f. He provided a bad example for his son, Isaac. Even though unborn at the time of the sin, Isaac doubtless was told of it as a young man; he failed God likewise by lying about his wife Rebekah. (See Gen. 26.)

Lest we forget—our sins always affect others.

G. His condescension (13:1-18).

1. Upon returning to Palestine he once again worshiped the Lord at Bethel—right where he had left God's blessing by going to Egypt. (See Isa. 30:15; Rev. 2:4, 5.)

2. The servants of Abraham and his nephew Lot began arguing over grazing rights. Abraham was concerned about this and graciously allowed the younger man to pick his choice of land. Lot foolishly selected that area near Sodom. Lot now left the Promised Land, never to return.

3. God appeared to Abraham for the third time and reassured him of a mighty posterity and of their eventual rights to Palestine.

H. His courage (14:1-16).

1. This chapter records the first war in the Bible. The last great battle can be found in Revelation 19:11-21. Until that time human wars will continue. On the headquarters of the United Nations there is inscribed the words of Micah 4:3: " . . . and they shall beat their swords into plowshares, and their spears into pruning hooks; nation shall not lift up a sword against nation, neither shall they learn war any more." This, of course, will be literally realized some glorious day. But not until the Prince of Peace comes to reign on this earth. Until that day, both Daniel (Dan. 9:26) and Jesus (Mt. 24:6) warned of continued war. It has been pointed out by the Society of International Law at London that there have been only 268 years of peace during the past 4000 years of human history, despite the signing of more than 8000 separate peace treaties. So then, until the coming of Christ, the United Nations should have more correctly inscribed the fearful words of Joel 3:9, 10: "Proclaim ye this among the Gentiles; Prepare war, wake up the mighty men; let all the men of war draw near; let them come up; beat your plowshares into swords, and your pruning hooks into spears."

2. Nine nations were involved in this war. It began when five kings, located in the Dead Sea area, revolted against Ched-or-Laomer, King of Elam, and his three allies. The Dead Sea Confederation, which included Sodom, was wiped out during a pitched battle. Lot, who had moved into the wicked city, was taken captive along with thousands of others. God would scarcely have bothered to record this pagan dog fight between nine heathen cities were it not for these four little words, "and they took Lot!" Lot still belonged to God. He didn't act like it, he didn't look, talk, dress, or walk like it, but God knows his own. (See 2 Tim. 2:19; 2 Pet. 2:7.)

3. Abraham learned of this and immediately armed his 318 trained servants for battle. We learn a number of things about Abraham's character from this single action.

    a. He was a man of sympathy.
He could have said, "It serves him right," or, "He had it coming to him," but he didn't. Abram was fulfilling the truth that would later be written in Matthew 7:1 and Galatians 6:1.

    b. He was prepared.
Abram kept in shape, spiritually, socially, mentally, and physically. God often cannot use a Christian, not because he is unclean, but because he is unprepared. The Bible has much to say about preparation. (See 2 Chron. 12:14; 19:3; 27:6; Mt. 3:3; Lk. 12:47; 2 Tim. 2:21.)

4. After a forced night march, Abraham caught up with them just north of Damascus and defeated them after a sudden surprise attack.

I. His communion (14:17-24).

1. As Abram returned from defeating Ched-or-Laomer, he was met by Melchizedek, the King of Salem (Jerusalem), who was also a priest of God. Who was this mysterious king-priest? There are three main theories as to his identity:

    a. That he was Shem. This is the Hebrew tradition. If so, he would have been the world's oldest living person at the time. Shem died at the age of 600.

    b. That he was Christ himself. This is referred to by theologians as a Christophany (a pre-Bethlehem Old Testament appearance of the Savior). Those who advocate this theory offer Hebrews 7:1-4 to support their claim.

    c. That he was simply the first mentioned king of Jerusalem. Melchizedek literally means "King of Righteousness," and Salem is thought to be an early name for Jerusalem. Melchizedek is mentioned again in Psalm 110. (In the New Testament, he is found in Heb. 5:6-10; 7:1-22.)

2. Melchizedek brought him bread and wine and blessed him. This is the first mention of bread and wine in the Bible, and depicts the future work of Christ on the cross.

3. The word priest first appears in the Bible at this time. (See 14:18.) At this point it is appropriate to point out briefly the three great offices in the Old Testament. These are: The offices of prophet, priest, and king.

    a. The prophet was one who represented God to man (1 Ki. 19:16).

b. The priest was one who represented man to God (Lev. 8:12; Ps. 133:2).
c. The king was one who under God ruled over man (1 Sam. 10:1; 16:13)
In the New Testament, however, all three of these offices belong to our Lord Jesus Christ.
a. He was a prophet (his past ministry) (Jn. 1:18; Mt. 21:11; Lk. 7:16; Jn. 4:19; Heb. 1:1, 2).
b. He is a priest (his present ministry) (Rom. 8:34; Heb. 4:14-16; 7:24, 25; 1 Jn. 1:1).
c. He will be a king (his future ministry) (Rev. 19:11-16).
4. After Melchizedek had blessed him, Abram gave him tithes of all he had. Some believe the practice of tithing (giving one's money to God) was only to be done by the nation Israel under the Law and therefore is not for us now. But this is not the case. Abram tithed long before Israel became a nation, and some 400 years before the Law was given. When we come to the New Testament, we are told that not just a tenth, but everything the Christian has belongs to God. (See 1 Cor. 6:19, 20.) This includes his *time* (Eph. 5:16; Ps. 90:12); his *talents* (Rom. 12:6; 1 Cor. 7:7; 2 Tim. 1:6); and his *treasures* (1 Cor. 16:1, 2; 2 Cor. 9:7).
5. Abram refused the materialistic offer of the ungodly Bera, who was King of Sodom. Bera wanted him to split the loot from the war.

J. His covenant (15:1-21).
1. God spoke to Abram in a vision, saying, "Fear not, Abram: I am thy shield, and thy exceedingly great reward" (15:1). Here we read for the first time those two wonderful little words, "fear not." Abram needed this reassurance at this time, for he had made some powerful enemies as a result of his actions in Genesis 14.
2. Abram "reminded" God that he and Sarai were still childless and suggested that a young servant boy named Eliezer of Damascus become his adopted heir. But this request was refused. Eliezer would later be used to aid Abram in another way. (See Gen. 24:1-4.)
3. God once again promised his old servant a child, this time adding the words, "Look now toward heaven, and count the stars, if thou be able to number them: and he said unto him, So shall thy seed be" (15:5). Here is another little proof of the Bible as God's Word. Today we know there are probably as many stars in the heavens as there are grains of sand on the seashores of the world. But in Abram's time men believed the total number of stars to be less than twelve hundred.
4. When God had finished, we are told that Abram "believed in the Lord; and he counted it unto him for righteousness" (15:6). This is the first biblical mention of three great words and each deserves our consideration.
a. Believed.
(1) This does not mean that Abram was the first man to believe in God, but rather that his faith is to be a pattern for all future believers. (See Rom. 4; Gal. 3:6-9; Heb. 11:8-10, 17, 19.)
(2) It does not say Abram pleased God or appeased him, but that he *believed* in God.
b. Counted. In the New Testament, this word is translated "imputed." To impute means to add to one's account. There are three main imputations in the Bible.
(1) The imputation of Adam's sin upon the human race (Rom. 3:23; 5:12).
(2) The imputation of the race's sin upon Christ (Isa. 53:5, 6; Heb. 2:9; 2 Cor. 5:14-21; 1 Pet. 2:24).
(3) The imputation of God's righteousness upon the believing sinner (Phil. 3:9; Jas. 2:23; Rom. 4:6, 8, 11, 22, 23, 24).
c. Righteousness—This word, simply defined, means "right clothing." The Bible teaches that all sinners are naked before God (Gen. 3:10; Heb. 4:13; Rev. 3:17). Some realize this and attempt to make their own set of spiritual clothes, but God looks upon such clothes as filthy rags (Isa. 64:6). Therefore, whenever a sinner realizes his nakedness and calls on the mercy of God, he gets a new suit of clothes. (See 2 Cor. 6:7; Eph. 6:14; Rev. 19:7, 8.)
5. When Abram asked how he could be sure all these things were true, especially the promise concerning the land, God ordered him to gather some animals and birds. Dr. Donald Barnhouse writes concerning this answer in 15:9:
"This is one of the strangest answers ever given to a question. Yet, it was the only possible answer. The question was, 'How am I to know that I shall possess the promised land?' The answer is, 'Bring me a heifer!' One might think that the dial of the radio had slipped from one program to another. The question is asked on a program of legal advice. The answer comes from a broadcast of a department of agriculture. But as we shall soon see, both the heifer and the inheritance are bound together in the mind of God." (*Genesis*, Vol. 1)
6. Abram gathered the creatures as ordered. In our culture today, whenever two parties determine to enter an agreement, a contract is drawn up and signed by both parties. But in Abram's time it was different. Back then the two parties would slaughter some animals, carve them up, and arrange the pieces in two lines. Then both parties would join hands and solemnly walk together down the middle path. By so doing they would pledge in the presence of blood and suffering and death, their intention to keep the terms of the contract. This is the first of three kinds of legal convenants in the Bible. These are:
a. The covenant of blood (Gen. 15:10; Jer. 34:18, 19).

b. The covenant of a shoe (Ruth 4:7, 8).
c. The covenant of salt (Num. 18:19; 2 Chron. 13:5).

7. Just prior to God's physical presence upon this scene (in the form of a smoking fire-pot and a flaming torch), Abram was put into a deep sleep. As he slept, God's presence passed through these bloody pieces alone, thus indicating that the promises of Jehovah concerning Abram's salvation and his possession of Palestine were both unconditional, with no heavenly strings attached whatsoever. Thus, the Abrahamic Covenant which was *announced* in Genesis 12:1-4, and *confirmed* in 13:14-17; 15:1-7, is now officially and legally *ratified* here in 15:8-18.

8. In Genesis 15:13-16 God utters a sevenfold prophecy to Abram. *All seven have eventually come to pass.*
   a. That Abram's descendants would be strangers in a foreign land. (See Gen. 46:2-4.)
   b. That they would be servants in that land. (See Ex. 1:7-14.)
   c. That this servitude would last some 400 years. (See Ex. 12:40.)
   d. That God himself would later judge that nation which enslaved Israel. (See Ex. 7-12.)
   e. That Abram would be spared all of this. (See Gen. 25:7, 8.)
   f. That after spending four long generations in Egypt, Israel would return to Canaan. (See Ex. 6:16-20. Here we learn that Levi, Abram's great-grandson, was the first generation. Levi's son Kohath, was the second; Kohath's son, Amram, was the third; and Amram's son, Moses, was the fourth.)
   g. That Israel would come out of Egypt with great substance. (See Ex. 12:35, 36; Ps. 105:37.)

9. God would take a long time to accomplish this, however, "for the iniquity of the Amorites is not yet full" (15:16). Here we have another expression of that important principle first discussed in Genesis 6:3. Sin accumulates until the time when God's anger and judgment explode down upon it. In this case the Amorites were those wicked descendants of Canaan (Gen. 10:16) who had been dwelling in Palestine for some 400 years at the time of Abraham. But God would allow them yet another four or five hundred years before destroying them. (See Josh. 10.) (This truth is brought out by Paul in Rom. 2:4, 5. See also 2 Pet. 3:1-9; 2 Chron. 36:15, 16.) Thus, while God's patience and forgiveness have no *depth* limit (Rom. 5:20), they *do* have a *length* limit (Prov. 27:1).

K. His compromise (16:1-15).
   1. Sarai persuaded Abram to father a child through her Egyptian maiden girl Hagar. They would then adopt this child as their own.
   2. Hagar became pregnant and her arrogant attitude soon caused trouble, resulting in her dismissal from Abram's household by Sarai. This one verse alone refutes the doctrine of polygamy. God permitted it, but never approved it. (See Gen. 2:23; 1 Tim. 3:2.)
   3. Hagar was found by the angel of the Lord beside a desert spring and commanded to return to Abram and Sarai. The sex (male) and name (Ishmael) of her unborn child were prophesied by this angel. This is the first mention of the angel of the Lord. Some theologians believe that when this title is found in the Old Testament, it is actually another name for the Lord Jesus Christ. At any rate, this special angel played an important part in the history of Israel.
      a. The angel of the Lord wrestles with Jacob (Gen. 32:24-30).
      b. The angel of the Lord redeems Jacob (Gen. 48:16).
      c. The angel of the Lord speaks to Moses from a burning bush (Ex. 3:2).
      d. The angel of the Lord protects Israel at the Red Sea (Ex. 14:19).
      e. The angel of the Lord prepares Israel for the Promised Land (Ex. 23:20-23; Ps. 34:7; Isa. 63:9; 1 Cor. 10:1-4).
      f. The angel of the Lord commissions Gideon (Jdg. 6:11).
      g. The angel of the Lord ministers to Elijah (1 Ki. 19:7).
      h. The angel of the Lord reassures Joshua (Josh. 5:13-15).
      i. The angel of the Lord saves Jerusalem (Isa. 37:36).
      j. The angel of the Lord preserves three Hebrew young men (Dan. 3:25). In this verse the angel of the Lord locates and comforts a pagan Egyptian woman named Hagar. Hagar does not fare well in the Bible, for she possesses little or no spirituality, is brazen, hateful, proud, disrespectful, and is a poor mother. Yet God loves her, and sends his blessed messenger to help her.
   4. Ishmael is born. Abram was eighty-six years old at this time.
L. His circumcision (17:1-27).
   1. As chapter 16 ends, Abram is at his lowest spiritual point. He has sinned and is out of fellowship with both his God and his family. But the Lord seems to do nothing to his erring child. Is Abram going to get away with all this?
      To answer we need only note that he was eighty-six years old when Ishmael was born (16:16), but is 99 when God again speaks with him. Abram thus apparently suffered a thirteen-year period of God's grieved silence. Here the words of the Psalmist concerning Israel's history comes to mind: "And he gave them their request; but sent leanness into their soul" (Ps. 106:15).
   2. In spite of this, a gracious God now forgives and restores him (Ps. 51) back into fellowship. The title "Almighty God" in the Hebrew is *El Shaddai*. The word *Shadd* refers to

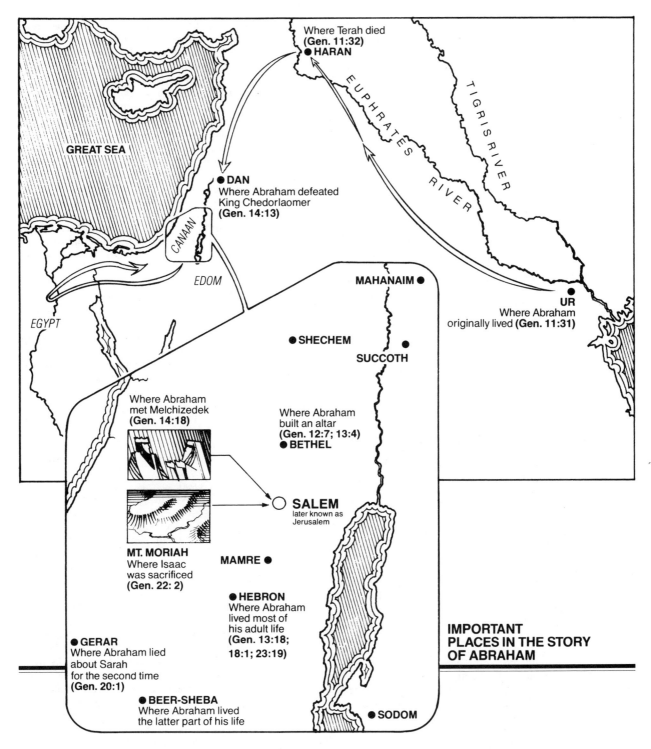

Where Terah died
**(Gen. 11:32)**
● **HARAN**

**GREAT SEA**

EUPHRATES RIVER

TIGRIS RIVER

● **DAN**
Where Abraham defeated
King Chedorlaomer
**(Gen. 14:13)**

CANAAN

EDOM

EGYPT

**MAHANAIM** ●

**UR**
Where Abraham
originally lived **(Gen. 11:31)**

● **SHECHEM**

**SUCCOTH**

Where Abraham
met Melchizedek
**(Gen. 14:18)**

Where Abraham
built an altar
**(Gen. 12:7; 13:4)**
● **BETHEL**

○ **SALEM**
later known as
Jerusalem

**MT. MORIAH**
Where Isaac
was sacrificed
**(Gen. 22: 2)**

**MAMRE** ●

● **HEBRON**
Where Abraham
lived most of
his adult life
**(Gen. 13:18;
18:1; 23:19)**

**IMPORTANT
PLACES IN THE STORY
OF ABRAHAM**

● **GERAR**
Where Abraham lied
about Sarah
for the second time
**(Gen. 20:1)**

● **BEER-SHEBA**
Where Abraham lived
the latter part of his life

● **SODOM**

the bosom of the nursing mother. The word
*El* means "the strong one."
  a. God comforts Jacob with his name (Gen. 35:10, 11).
  b. He reassures Moses with this name (Ex. 6:3).
  c. Jacob blesses Joseph with this name (Gen. 49:25).
  This title is found more often in the book of Job (thirty-one times) than in any other Old Testament book. And that suffering patriarch needed it. Perhaps the most sublime

passage in which it is used is Psalm 91:1: "He that dwelleth in the secret place of the most High shall abide under the shadow of the Almighty."
3. His name was now changed from Abram, which means "exalted father," to Abraham, which means, "Father of a great multitude." Dr. Donald Barnhouse has summarized Abram's life at this time in a wonderful and witty way:
  "And the point of the story lies in the fact that Abram had no seed. This may not be

a disaster in our western lands, but in the Orient it must have been particularly galling.

There are some things in the Bible that cause me to chuckle, and there is a thought in connection with this verse that always has had that effect on me. I cannot help think of what must have happened when Abraham broke the news to his family and servants that he was now changing his name. They all knew that his former name was Abram, father of many, and they knew it had been somewhat of a thorn to him. So we can imagine the stir of interest and curiosity when he announced, 'I am going to change my name.' 'The old man couldn't take it. It finally got under his skin.' After all, to be father of nobody for eighty-six years, and then to be father of only one, with a name like he has—father of many—must have its rough moments. So he is going to change his name. I wonder what it will be."

And then the old man spoke, 'I am to be known as Abraham—father of a multitude.' We can almost hear the silence of the stunned moment as the truth breaks upon them. Father of a multitude? Then the laughter broke forth behind the scenes. 'The old man has gone crazy. He had one child when he was eighty-six and now at ninety-nine he is beginning to get ideas. Father of a multitude! Was there anything more ridiculous for a man of his age?'" (*God's Remedy*, Vol. III, p. 316)

4. For the fourth time now God reaffirms the land and seed covenant to his old servant. (See Gen. 12:2, 3, 7; 13:14-17; 15:5.) On this occasion (17:9-14), God commanded Abraham to circumcise himself, all the males of his household, and each future male baby on the eighth day of birth. Following is a brief summary of circumcision as found in the Bible.

a. Abraham was the first man to be circumcised.
   This in itself was a real act of faith, for it rendered completely helpless all the males in the camp.

b. Circumcision was to be the seal (or sign) of God's promise, but not the source.

c. Faith in God's Word was the source.

d. Circumcision of the flesh without circumcision of the heart was absolutely worthless.
   Years later, Moses would remind Israel: "And now, Israel, what doth the Lord thy God require of thee, but to fear the Lord thy God, to walk in all his ways, and to love him, and to serve the Lord thy God with all thy heart and with all thy soul. Circumcise therefore the foreskin of your heart, and be no more stiffnecked" (Deut. 10:12, 16).

e. Circumcision was set aside in Acts 15:29.

5. Abraham's wife's name is now changed from Sarai (contentious) to Sarah (a princess).

6. Abraham laughs for joy (Rom. 4:19-21) at the thought of his own physical heir and asks God to bless Ishmael.

7. God promises to bless Ishmael and then commands Abraham and Sarah to name the future heir of the covenant, Isaac.

8. Abraham obeys God's command to circumcise all males.

M. His compassion.
   1. Abraham is personally visited by the Lord and two angels. As he ministers to them, God again promises him an heir, and this time sets a date (18:10, 14).
   2. Sarah overhears this conversation and laughs in disbelief. God rebukes Abraham for his wife's unbelief. Sarah then denies that she laughed (18:10-15).
   3. Both Sarah and Abraham then hear God's thrilling words (18:14): "Is anything too hard for the Lord?" (See also Lk. 1:26-37; Mt. 19:23-26.)
   4. The two angels depart to complete a secret mission to Sodom. God then reveals to Abraham his intention to destroy that wicked cesspool of sin on the desert sand (18:16-22).
   5. Abraham then begins his remarkable plea for Sodom. This is one of the most compassionate and persistent prayers in all the Bible.
      a. It was definite. He did not pray for "that soul nearest hell," or for "the missionaries around the world," or for "Aunt Tilly's sore toe."
      b. It was reverent. "I . . . am but dust and ashes" (v. 27).
      c. It was mixed with faith. "Shall not the Judge of all the earth do right?" (v. 25).
   6. At first he asks God to spare the city if but fifty righteous persons can be found there. God agrees. Then the request is for forty-five; then forty; then thirty; then twenty; and finally ten. Here Abraham stops. Why did he not press for five? The answer is that he probably felt there were at least ten saved people. There were, after all, Lot, Lot's wife, their two unmarried daughters, and the married daughters and their husbands. This group he thought would surely total more than ten! But Abraham was to be heartbroken, for it would appear that only Lot and his two unmarried daughters were saved.

N. His corrupted kin (19:1-38).
   1. In this chapter we have the dramatic account of the destruction of Sodom, which is the second of two Old Testament events referred to by our Lord as illustrations of the coming day of judgment. The first event was the flood in Noah's day. Note Christ's words in Luke 17:26-30.
   2. The angels find Lot at the gate of Sodom. He was probably an alderman of some sort, with delegated authority. He has now come the full circle of compromise. Note the sad order of his tragic fall:

a. He first looked longingly at Sodom (Gen. 13:10).
b. He then chose the area of ground near Sodom (Gen. 13:11).
c. He next pitched his tent toward Sodom (Gen. 13:12).
d. He thereupon moved into the city of Sodom (Gen. 14:12).
e. He finally gives both his daughters and his energies to Sodom (Gen. 19). Surely the New Testament words apply here: "Behold, how great a matter a little fire kindleth!" (Jas. 3:5). Sin is like cancer and leprosy. It starts off ever so small, but winds up eating at the vital organs of the body.

In the New Testament Simon Peter's great sin of cursing the Lord Jesus also began very small. He warmed his hands at the camp of the enemy (Lk. 22:54–56).
f. He began by boasting of his loyalty (Mk. 14:29)
g. He then slept when he should have prayed (Mk. 14:37)
h. He thereupon followed Christ from afar off (Mt. 26:58)
i. He next is found associating with Christ's enemies (Mt. 26:69)
j. He finally curses the Savior (Mt. 26:70–74)

Lot makes a feast for these two angels and prepares unleavened bread. This action suggests two facts: The fact that he served them unleavened bread indicates he recognized the identity of his heavenly guests. The fact that he and not his wife did the baking suggests her unconcern for her husband's position or the things of God.

3. The angels tell Lot of the impending destruction of Sodom. Conditions were so corrupt that they were forced to blind some sexual perverts who had surrounded Lot's home where they were staying. These men had absolutely no respect for the backslidden Lot.
4. Lot had become so carnal that he attempted to appease those Sodomite sinners by offering them his two virgin daughters. He also refers to them as "brethren." (See 2 Jn. 10, 11.)
5. He spends the rest of the night in a frantic but fruitless attempt to convince his married daughters to flee to the city with him.
6. At daybreak the angels literally drag Lot, his wife, and their two daughters out of Sodom, telling them to flee to the mountains.
7. Lot begins arguing, begging that they allow him to settle in a nearby little city called Zoar instead of the mountains.
8. Lot's family receives one final warning: "Haste thee, escape there; for I cannot do anything till thou be come there" (19:22). Sodom's destruction is a foreshadow of the coming tribulation, and Lot's departure may be pictured as a type of the Rapture of all believers. (See 2 Thess. 2:6, 7.)

9. The Lord then "rained upon Sodom and upon Gomorrah brimstone and fire from . . . out of heaven" (19:24). Brimstone is often used in the Bible to denote punishment and destruction (Deut. 29:23; Job 18:15; Ps. 11:6; Isa. 30:33; Ezek. 38:22; Lk. 17:29; Rev. 9:17). Some feel it to be a reference to sulphur. We are told in Genesis 14:10, that the surrounding area of Sodom was "full of slime pits" (or asphalt pits).
10. Lot's wife looked back and she became a pillar of salt. In Luke 17:32, the Lord Jesus admonishes all men to "remember Lot's wife." And so we should. Her life is proof of the saying: "You can take the boy out of the farm, but not the farm out of the boy." In her case the proverb would read: "You can take a worldly person out of the world, but you can't take the world out of a worldly person."

The unbeliever has often ridiculed the account of Lot's wife turning into a hundred-pound bag of salt! Of course God could have literally done this, but a more reasonable explanation would be that a flaming glob of sulphur fell upon her and encrusted her with its salty substance.

God remembered Abraham, and sent Lot out. A gracious God has promised to forget the confessed sins of all believers (Heb. 8:12), but in his faithfulness he does remember at least two things:
a. The prayers of a believer (see Gen. 18:23; Rev. 5:8).
b. The works of a believer (Heb. 6:10).

Thus carnal and worldly Lot was saved through the faithful prayers of Abraham. Perhaps Jude had Lot in mind when he later wrote:
"And of some have compassion, making a difference: And others save with fear, pulling them out of the fire; hating even the garment spotted by the flesh" (Jude 1:22, 23).

11. In his terrible fear, Lot bypasses Zoar and takes refuge in a cave with his two unmarried daughters. Here the ultimate is shown of the high cost of low living. Lot's daughters, fearing they will never marry, get their own father drunk, and have sexual relations with him. Both bear him children. The oldest daughter names her son Moab (father of the Moabites) and the younger daughter calls her boy Ben-ammi (father of the Ammonites). Both nations would later cause Israel much heartache. (See Gen. 19:30-38.)

O. His carnality (20:1-17).
1. Abraham falls into the same sin pattern here as he had once done in Egypt. On this occasion he moves into the land of the Philistines and lies to Abimelech concerning Sarah as he previously lied to Pharaoh.
2. God warns Abimelech in a dream not to touch Sarah.
3. Abimelech rebukes Abraham for lying to him.

# Abraham

| EVENT | DETAILS | SCRIPTURE REFERENCE |
|---|---|---|
| **1.** **CONVERSION AT UR** | **SEVENFOLD PROMISE**<br>1. I will make of thee a great nation.<br>2. I will bless thee.<br>3. I will make thy name great.<br>4. Thou shalt be a blessing.<br>5. I will bless them that bless thee.<br>6. I will curse him that curseth thee.<br>7. In thee shall all the families of the earth be blessed. | **Acts 7:2**<br>**Gen. 11:31**<br>**Gen. 12:1-4**<br>**Josh. 24:3** |
| **2.** **AT HARAN** | **PARTIAL OBEDIENCE:** He takes his father and settles in Haran | **Gen. 11:31, 32** |
| **3.** **ARRIVAL IN CANAAN** | He builds an altar and is promised the land | **Gen. 12:4-9** |
| **4.** **TRIP TO EGYPT** | **REASON:** A famine in Canaan<br>**SIN:** Doubt (concerning God) and deceit (concerning Sarai)<br>**TYPE:** Egypt is a type of the world<br>**RESULTS:** 7 tragic consequences:<br>1. He grieved God<br>2. He weakened his own faith<br>3. He weakened the faith of Sarai<br>4. He became a poor testimony to his nephew Lot<br>5. He caused the Pharaoh to be afflicted<br>6. He picked up Hagar, the Egyptian handmaid<br>7. He provided a bad example for his son, Isaac | **Gen. 12:10-20** |
| **5.** **MEETS MELCHIZEDEK** | **BACKGROUND:** Abram had won a war and rescued his nephew<br>**IDENTITY OF MELCHIZEDEK:** Christ? Shem? Unknown priest?<br>**IMPORTANCE OF MEETING:** Four firsts recorded:<br>1. FIRST COMMUNION (bread and wine)<br>2. First mention of HOLY CITY (Salem)<br>3. First mention of PRIEST<br>4. First example of TITHING | **Gen. 13, 14** |
| **6.** **RATIFICATION OF HIS COVENANT** | **BACKGROUND:** This covenant was:<br>1. Announced in Genesis 12:1-4<br>2. Confirmed in Genesis 13:14-17; 15:1-7<br>3. Ratified in Genesis 15:8-18<br>**METHOD EMPLOYED:** A blood agreement<br>**FEATURES:** A land (Palestine) and a people (Israel)<br>**TERMS:** Unconditional, no strings attached<br>**LANGUAGE:** Three key words: **BELIEVED, COUNTED, RIGHTEOUSNESS**<br>**PROPHECY INVOLVED:** The 400-year Egyptian captivity and deliverance of Israel | **Gen. 15** |
| **7.** **MARRIAGE TO HAGAR** | The **PLAN** of Sarai<br>The **PLIGHT** of Hagar<br>The **AID** of an angel<br>The **BIRTH** of Ishmael | **Gen. 16** |

4. Abraham prays for God's blessing to fall upon Abimelech.

P. His celebration (21:1–34).

1. Isaac is born as God had promised. His name meant "laughter."
2. A great celebration is held to mark the weaning of Isaac.
3. Hagar and her fourteen-year-old son Ishmael are sent away from Abraham's household for mocking Isaac during this happy occasion. (Paul discusses the significance of this event in Gal. 4:22–31.)
4. God graciously ministers to Hagar and Ishmael after they are lost in the wilderness of Beer-sheba, by pointing her to a fresh well. Ishmael later marries an Egyptian girl and becomes an expert archer.

Q. His "calvary" (22:1–24).

1. God "tempts" Abraham by ordering him to "take now thy son, thine only son Isaac, whom thou lovest, and get thee into the land of Moriah: and offer him there for a burnt offering . . . " (22:2) This was in reality a *test* to help Abraham grow spiritually. (Contrast Gen. 22:2 with Jas. 1:13.)
2. The land of Moriah was that district around Jerusalem where the Temple was much later built (see 2 Chron. 3:1). Just what did God

# Abraham

| | | | |
|---|---|---|---|
| **8.** | **ABRAM AT 99** | **SOME NEW NAMES**<br>1. Abram changed to Abraham (father of nations)<br>2. Sarai changed to Sarah (a princess)<br>3. God introduced as *El Shaddai* (the fruitful one)<br>**A NEW SEAL:** circumcision now becomes the sign of God's covenant | **Gen. 17** |
| **9.** | **GOOD NEWS AND BAD NEWS** | **ABRAHAM** is visited by the Lord and two angels<br>The **GOOD** news: His long-promised heir would be born the next spring<br>The **BAD** news: God planned to destroy Sodom, Lot's home city<br>**SODOM** is destroyed. Only Lot and his two daughters survive | **Gen. 18, 19** |
| **10.** | **ABRAHAM IN PHILISTIA** | During a famine he again leaves Canaan and lies about Sarah | **Gen. 20** |
| **11.** | **THE HEIR OF THE COVENANT** | Isaac is born<br>Hagar and Ishmael are sent away | **Gen. 21** |
| **12.** | **FORESHADOWS OF CALVARY** | The **TYPE:** 1. Sacrifice of Isaac<br>2. Substitute for Isaac<br>The **LOCATION:** Mt. Moriah, thought to be Golgotha<br>The **REVELATION:** A new name for God, Jehovah-Jireh ("the Lord will provide") | **Gen. 22** |
| **13.** | **DEATH OF SARAH** | Sarah dies at 127 and is buried in the cave of Machpelah | **Gen. 23** |
| **14.** | **COMMANDING HIS SERVANT** | **ABRAHAM'S COMMAND:** To fetch a bride for Isaac<br>**THE SERVANT'S PRAYER:** Show me the right girl<br>**THE LORD'S ANSWER:** Rebekah is the one<br>**THE SCRIPTURAL TYPES:** This is the most type-filled chapter in the Bible<br>1. Abraham is a type of the Father<br>2. Isaac is a type of the Son<br>3. The servant is a type of the Holy Spirit<br>4. Rebekah is a type of the Church | **Gen. 24** |
| **15.** | **HIS MARRIAGE TO KETURAH** | She bore him six sons<br>**The fourth was Midian, father of the Midianites** | **Gen. 25:1-6** |
| **16.** | **HIS DEATH** | **AGE:** 175<br>Place of **BURIAL:** The cave of Machpelah<br>**EPITAPH:**<br>**HEB. 11:8-10**<br>"By faith Abraham, when he was called to go out into a place which he should after receive for an inheritance, obeyed; and he went out, not knowing whither he went. By faith he sojourned in the land of promise, as in a strange country, dwelling in tabernacles with Isaac and Jacob, the heirs with him of the same promise: For he looked for a city which hath foundations, whose builder and maker is God." | **Gen. 25:7-10;**<br>**Heb. 11:8-10** |

BY FAITH ABRAHAM... BY FAITH ABRAHAM... BY FAITH

order Abraham to do to Isaac? (Later, in Lev. 1:1-9, Moses is given instructions about the burnt offering.)

a. The offering had to be a male animal without blemish.
b. It had to be offered voluntarily by the owner.
c. It was killed and the blood sprinkled.
d. It was then cut into pieces.
e. Finally, it was washed and burned.

How much of this was known to Abraham, we are not told. But this the old man did know: God was ordering him to slaughter his beloved son.

3. They arrived on the third day. Abraham left a day after God commanded him, and it took three days to get to Moriah, thus making a total of four days. This corresponds perfectly to Exodus 12:3, where the Passover Lamb was to be kept for four days before killing it. (See Gen. 22:3, 4.)

4. Abraham then instructs his servants, saying: "Abide ye here with the ass; and I and the lad will go yonder and worship, and come again to you" (22:5). Here we see a glimpse of Abraham's faith. Notice he tells the men that both he and his son would come back again. Thus even though Abraham fully

meant to sacrifice Isaac, he believed God would raise him from the dead! So then the two highest points in this grand old man's life would be:

    a. Believing God concerning the supernatural birth of his son (Rom. 4:18-21).

    b. Believing God concerning the supernatural resurrection of his son (Heb. 11:17-19).

5. Isaac then asked, "Behold the fire and the wood: but where is the lamb for a burnt offering?" (22:7). This question is still being asked by a frightened and confused world today. Where is that lamb? Where do we look for our salvation? The world asks the right question, but looks for the wrong thing. Some look for this lamb in various directions:

    a. The lamb of education.

    b. The lamb of good works.

    c. The lamb of the U.N.

    d. The lamb of baptism.

    e. The lamb of church membership.

But the salvation lamb cannot be found in any of these.

6. The heartbroken old patriarch softly answers his son: "My son, God will provide himself a lamb for a burnt offering . . ." (22:8). This one sentence is a complete summary of the Bible. Theologically we could read it in either of the following ways:

    a. God will provide *for* himself a lamb—that is, the lamb will come from God.

    b. God will provide himself *for* a lamb—that is, the lamb offered will be God.

    Either way is correct, for in the New Testament, both meanings come true.

7. Abraham builds an altar and binds his only son to it. This little statement speaks highly of Isaac, for he was not the small boy some have pictured him to be, but probably a full grown man. Yet he willingly allows his old father to tie and bind him to a death altar (22:9).

8. The Spirit of God records for us in dramatic phrases the breathtaking action which now takes place on that windswept hill: "And Abraham stretched forth his hand, and took the knife to slay his son" (Gen. 22:10).

    However, before he can do this, God shows him a nearby ram and orders this animal to be sacrificed in place of Isaac. A grateful Abraham obeys and names this place Jehovah-jireh.

9. The title Jehovah-jireh is one of God's great names in the Old Testament, and it literally means, "the Lord will provide." Does it really pay to serve God? Just for the record, God had already provided Abraham with the following "fringe benefits."

    a. eternal salvation (Gen. 15:6).

    b. guidance (Gen. 12:1).

    c. courage (Gen. 14:15).

    d. spiritual blessings (Gen. 14:19).

    e. earthly needs (Gen. 13:2).

    f. social security (Gen. 15:15).

    g. forgiveness (Gen. 20:17).

    h. a son in his old age (Gen. 21:3).

    i. continued protection (Gen. 15:1).

    j. the promise of a heavenly city (Heb. 11:10).

10. Before leaving this chapter, let us notice some striking similarities between Abraham the father and God the Father:

    a. Both had a beloved son (Mt. 3:17; 17:5). Both were born miraculously (Lk. 1:35).

    b. Both had willing sons—that is, sons that were willing to be offered up (Jn. 10:18).

    c. Both offered up their sons (Jn. 3:16; both on the same spot).

    d. Both received their sons back with great joy (Ps. 24:7-10).

    (Note: Some believe this Psalm refers to the Lord Jesus' coming back to the glory of heaven after his death and resurrection.)

    e. Both made careful preparations for their sons' weddings. In Genesis 24, Abraham sends his trusted servant out to find a bride for Isaac. In the New Testament, we read, of course, of the Heavenly Father's preparation for his Son's wedding (Mt. 22:1, 2).

11. The angel of the Lord again announces the features of the Abrahamic Covenant.

12. Upon returning home Abraham learns a message has arrived bringing him up to date concerning his brother Nahor, whom he apparently had not seen since leaving Ur. Nahor had moved into Haran and God had blessed him and his wife Milcah with eight sons. The fifth son, Bethuel, would become important in the biblical record, for he had a daughter named Rebekah and a son named Laban. Rebekah would, of course, later marry Isaac; and Laban's daughters, Rachel and Leah, were to be Jacob's wives (22:19-24).

R. His cave (23:1-20).

1. Sarah dies at the age of 127. There are those today who would advocate the adoration of Mary, but in the New Testament it is the life of Sarah that is called to our attention. (See 1 Pet. 3:1-6.)

2. Abraham buys a cave at Machpelah for 400 pieces of silver and buries his beloved wife there. Later he himself will be laid there.

S. His command (24:1-67).

1. Abraham commands his trusted servant (Eliezer) to go to Haran and choose a wife for Isaac.

2. Upon reaching his destination, the servant kneels down outside the city and prays for wisdom. This is one of the most remarkable prayers in all the Bible, not only because of its great faith, but because it was answered even before the prayer was finished. The servant asks God to show which girl he desired for Isaac by causing her to offer both him and the thirsty camels some water. Note the result:

    "And it came to pass, before he had done speaking, that, behold, Rebekah came out, who was born to Bethuel, son of Milcah, the wife of Nahor, Abraham's brother, with her pitcher upon her shoulder" (24:15).

3. Rebekah unknowingly fulfills his prayer by offering water both to the servant and his camels.

4. The servant is introduced to Rebekah's mother and her brother Laban. He informs them of his mission, and also of the amazing answer to his prayer.

5. Rebekah agrees to go with the servant and become Isaac's wife.

6. Isaac anxiously awaits his bride in a field near Hebron. They become husband and wife.

This is one of the great typical chapters in all the Bible. Note:

a. Abraham is a perfect type of the Heavenly Father. It is the Father who is planning a marriage for his beloved Son (see Mt. 22:2).

b. Isaac is a perfect type of the Lord Jesus Christ. Isaac, like Jesus, had been offered up as a sacrifice (compare Gen. 22 with Mt. 27) and seeks his bride. Isaac, like Christ, had been given all things of his father. (Compare 24:36 with Phil. 2:9, 10.) Finally Isaac, like Christ, loves his bride dearly. (Compare 24:67 with Eph. 5:25.)

c. Eliezer is a perfect type of the Holy Spirit. Abraham's servant came to Mesopotamia for one sole reason—to take a bride for Isaac. Years later (Acts 2) the Holy Spirit would come at Pentecost for one purpose—to gather a bride for the Son. While at Mesopotamia, Eliezer gave honor constantly to the father and son. Today the Holy Spirit does likewise. (See Jn. 15:26.)

d. Rebekah is a perfect type of the church. Before anyone can enter God's true church, he or she must first favorably answer the question of the Father's servant: "And they called Rebekah, and said unto her, Wilt thou go with this man? And she said, I will go" (24:58).

T. His Keturah (25:1-6).

1. Abraham marries a woman named Keturah, who bears him six sons.

2. The most important son was Midian, the fourth boy, who became the father of the Midianites. This nation would later cause Israel much grief.

U. His city (25:7-10; Heb. 11:8-10).

"And these are the days of the years of Abraham's life which he lived, an hundred threescore and fifteen years.

Then Abraham gave up the ghost, and died in a good old age, an old man, and full of years; and was gathered to his people.

And his sons Isaac and Ishmael buried him in the cave of Machpelah, in the field of Ephron, the son of Zohar the Hittite, which is before Mamre;

The field which Abraham purchased of the sons of Heth: There was Abraham buried, and Sarah his wife" (25:7-10).

"By faith Abraham, when he was called to go out into a place which he should after receive for an inheritance, obeyed; and he went out, not knowing whither he went. By faith he sojourned in the land of promise, as in a strange country, dwelling in tabernacles with Isaac and Jacob, the heirs with him of the same promise: For he looked for a city which hath foundations, whose builder and maker is God" (Heb. 11:8-10).

II. Isaac (Gen. 25-27).

Isaac has been described as the mediocre son of a great father (Abraham) and the mediocre father of a great son (Jacob). The main action of his life occurs at the following five places: on a mountain, by a field, alongside some desert wells, in a Philistine apartment, and at a supper table.

A. On a Jerusalem mountain (22:1-14).
*The submissive son.* Isaac meekly submits to being used as a burnt offering.

B. By a Hebron field (24:61-67; 25:9-11, 19-26); *the gentle groom.*

1. He meets Rebekah for the first time (24:61-67).

2. He and Ishmael his brother bury their father Abraham (25:9).
Abraham had lived thirty-eight years after the death of Sarah.

3. Ishmael dies at the age of 137 (25:17).

4. Isaac prayed that God would give him and his wife children (25:21).
This is the second of five recorded biblical prayers for a child. Note:

a. Abraham's prayer (Gen. 15:2).

b. Isaac's prayer (Gen. 25:21).

c. Rachel's prayer (Gen. 30:1, 22).

d. Hannah's prayer (1 Sam. 1:10, 11; 2:1-10).

e. Zachariah's prayer (Lk. 1:5-7, 13-17).

5. Rebekah gives birth to twin boys. They are named Esau and Jacob (25:24-26).

C. In a Philistine home (26:1-14); the copy cat.

1. Isaac repeats the sin of his father many years back. (See 1 Cor. 10:13.)

a. In time of famine, he forsakes Palestine and moves into the Philistine area (as Abraham had once gone to Egypt).

b. He lies to King Abimelech concerning Rebekah, saying she is his sister.

2. Abimelech discovers the truth of the matter and reproves a totally embarrassed Isaac about his lying.

3. In spite of his carnality, God reaffirms the Abrahamic Covenant to Isaac and blesses him greatly in material things.

D. Alongside some desert wells (26:15-34); the willing worker.

1. The Philistines soon became jealous of his great success and retaliated by filling up with earth some old wells once dug by his father, Abraham. Isaac spends a great deal of time clearing the debris from these clogged water holes.

The young minister of God can derive some profitable lessons from these verses. Throughout history our spiritual forefathers had, with patience and pleasure, dug down deep into the Word of God and beautifully exposed those clear, fresh cold water wells of the virgin birth, the sinless life of Christ, his death, resurrection, ascension, and future second coming. But of late these wells have been clogged in the minds of many because of the hateful actions of false critics. Therefore, the main job of the young man of God today is to clean out these wells, that the life-giving fluids may once again satisfy the parched hearts of humanity.

2. Isaac (as did once his father Abraham) enters into a nonaggressive pact with King Abimelech (Prov. 16:7).

3. God appears to Isaac again.

4. Isaac and Rebekah are grieved over the marriage of Esau, who at forty years of age, picks a pagan girl for his wife.

E. At a supper table in his own home (27:1-46); the frustrated father.

1. Isaac, at age 137, felt he was at the point of death. Actually, he would live another forty-three years and reach 180 (Gen. 35:28). His brother Ishmael had died at 137 (25:17) and this may have influenced his thinking. In addition, he was half-blind at this time.

2. He instructs Esau to kill a deer and prepare him a venison meal that he might eat and bless him before he dies. At the very point of death (or so he thought) Isaac's last thoughts were on his stomach! His spiritual condition had apparently seriously deteriorated (see Phil. 3:18, 19).

3. Rebekah overhears this conversation and immediately enters a plot with Jacob to deceive Isaac, that he (Jacob) might obtain the blessing. Rebekah was right in concluding that God desired the blessing to go to Jacob (Gen. 25:23), but she was totally wrong by taking matters into her own hands. The end never justifies the means. It is never right to do wrong that right might be done (see Rom. 3:8).

4. Jacob feels the plot will never work. In spite of being half-blind, the lad knew his father would want to lay hands on him, and he complains: "Behold, Esau, my brother, is a hairy man, and I am a smooth man" (27:11). He surely was, and in more ways than one. You surely would not have wanted to buy a used car from Jacob!

5. His mother reassures him, "Upon me be thy curse, my son" (see Mt. 27:24, 25), and prepares Jacob for his deceitful action by cooking a dish similar to that of venison. She then dressed him in Esau's rough clothing and put "the skins of the kids of the goats upon his hands, and upon the smooth of his neck" (27:16).

6. Jacob then presents himself to Isaac as Esau. When asked how he found the venison so quickly, Jacob lies, "Because the Lord thy God brought it to me" (27:20).

7. After some initial doubts concerning his identity, Isaac gives the blessing.

8. Jacob kisses his father. This is the first of three kisses of treachery in the Bible.
   a. Jacob kisses Isaac in order to deceive him (Gen. 27:27).

# Isaac

## The Submissive Son
**GEN. 22:1-4**
● He is offered up by his father Abraham

## The Gentle Groom
**GEN. 24:62-67**
● He meets Rebekah for the first time

## The Praying Parent
**GEN. 25:19-26**
● He prays that God would bless them with children
● Rebekah gives birth to twins—Esau and Jacob

## The Copy-Cat
**GEN. 26:1-11**
● Like his father, he leaves Palestine during a famine
● Like his father, he lies about his wife

## The Willing Worker
**GEN. 26:17-33**
● Some jealous Philistines had filled up Abraham's wells with debris
● Isaac redigs and cleans out those wells

## The Frustrated Father
**GEN. 27:1-45**
● At ninety-seven Isaac feels his death is near
● Esau is instructed to prepare him a meal and receive the patriarchal blessing
● Rebekah arranges to deceive the dim-eyed Isaac by substituting Jacob
● Jacob receives the blessing intended for Esau
● Isaac sends Jacob away that his son might escape Esau's revenge

b. Joab kisses Amasa in order to murder him (2 Sam. 20:9).
c. Judas kisses Christ in order to betray him (Mt. 26:49).

9. Jacob had no sooner walked out than Esau came in and the plot was discovered. Esau wails aloud over this deception (Heb. 12:16, 17) and determines to kill him after his father's funeral (27:41).

10. Rebekah learns of this plot and asks Isaac that Jacob might be sent to Haran to seek a wife. Her main reason, however, was to save his life.

11. Isaac calls in Jacob, blesses him, and sends him to Haran, saying: "Thou shalt not take a wife of the daughters of Canaan" (28:1). At this point Isaac drops out of the biblical account, even though he lived another forty-three years. Isaac was not a man who dreamed dreams and conquered continents. A summary of his rather uneventful life, listing both strong and weak points, would include:
   a. He was a submissive son.
      (1) As shown by his willingness to be sacrificed (Gen. 22:7-10).
      (2) As shown by his willingness to allow a bride to be picked for him (Gen. 24).
   b. He was a sensual man.
      (1) As shown by the "window" passage (Gen. 26:8).
      (2) As shown by his craving for food (Gen. 27:1-4).
   c. He was an indulgent father and husband.

(1) He had little control over Esau, who married two heathen girls (Gen. 26:34).

(2) He had little control over Rebekah, who felt free to deceive him at will (Gen. 27:5-13).

(3) He had little control over Jacob, who looked to his mother instead of him for authority (Gen. 27:13).

d. He was, nevertheless, at times a man of faith (Gen. 28:1-4; 22:7-10; Heb. 11:20).

III. Jacob (Gen. 25; 27-36; 38).

A. The devising brother (25:27-34).

1. Jacob was the second born of twins. The birth of these boys is vividly paraphrased for us by *The Living Bible* (25:25, 26).

"The first was born so covered with reddish hair that one would think he was wearing a fur coat! So they called him 'Esau.' Then the other twin was born with his hand on Esau's heel! So they called him Jacob (meaning 'grabber')."

2. Both these boys had the same background. But one grew to love God, while the other looked down upon spiritual things.

3. Esau became a skilled hunter and the favorite of Isaac's while Jacob was the quiet type and appealed more to his mother.

4. Jacob connives to get his famished brother to trade his birthright. This applied to certain advantages, privileges, and responsibilities of firstborn baby boys during Old Testament Israelite history. Note:

a. The *advantages* and privileges were that this baby became the object of special affection and would legally receive a double portion of his father's estate.

b. The *responsibilities* were that he was expected to assume the spiritual leadership of the family. He also was required to provide food, clothing, and other necessities for his mother until her death and all unmarried sisters until their marriage. But, we are told, "Esau despised his birthright" (25:34). In the New Testament we read the following concerning Esau and this birthright: "Lest there be any fornicator, or profane person, as Esau, who, for one morsel of meat, sold his birthright" (Heb. 12:16).

5. With all this background in mind, much light can be thrown upon the character of Esau, who counted as nothing his birthright.

a. He was apparently not interested in any double-portion slice of his father's estate. While Isaac his father would gather much wealth later (Gen. 26:12-14), he may have possessed very little of this wealth during these early days. At any rate, Esau was not interested in the material advantages of his birthright.

b. He certainly was not interested in maintaining any spiritual responsibilities. Nor was he concerned with providing for his mother. He may have sensed her special affection for Jacob (Gen. 25:28).

c. His actions reflected his carnal attitude for as we have already seen, he was both a fornicator and a profane person. The term fornicator refers to his immorality, while the word profane calls attention to his utter disregard for spiritual things. It literally means, "one outside the temple."

B. The deceitful son (27:1-46).

1. Rebekah overhears Isaac's plan to bestow the patriarchal blessing upon Esau.

2. She immediately plots with Jacob to obtain this for him.

3. Isaac is deceived by Jacob and he receives that blessing meant for Esau.

4. Esau discovers this trickery and vows revenge. The question may be raised as to why Esau who once had despised his birthright now is so concerned with the blessing. The answer seems to be in the nature of the two. As we have previously noted, Esau was not interested at all in assuming the spiritual responsibilities of the birthright. But the blessing was something different, for it carried with it a good and wholesome prophecy concerning the future.

C. The dreaming pilgrim (28:1-22).

1. Jacob leaves Beer-sheba and starts toward Haran. After a long hard journey he arrives at Bethel, some forty miles from Beer-sheba.

2. Using a stone for a pillow, Jacob soon falls into an exhausted sleep.

3. As he sleeps, he dreams, "and behold a ladder set up on the earth, and the top of it reached to heaven: and behold the angels of God ascending and descending on it" (28:12). According to Hebrews 1:14, <u>angels are the ministering spirits to the heirs of salvation.</u> Jacob's grandfather Abraham had received their blessed ministry (Gen. 18:1-16) as had Lot (Gen. 19:1). Now Jacob would also share in this experience.

4. At the top of this ladder Jacob sees the presence of God himself, and (for the first time) hears the Lord's voice confirming to him the Abrahamic Covenant. (See 28:1-15.) Especially thrilling are the words, "I will not leave thee" (28:15).

"Most precious of all promises is that of the presence of the Lord. It was made here to Jacob in pure grace; to Moses for all the people before they crossed the Jordan with Joshua (Deut. 31:6); to Joshua as he assumed leadership and faced battle (Josh. 1:5, 8); and to Solomon for the building of the Temple (1 Chron. 28:20). It was made to the disciples just before the Lord ascended into heaven (Mt. 28:20), and confirmed to us here today" (Heb. 13:5, 6). (*Genesis*, Vol. 2, p. 86, D. G. Barnhouse)

5. Jacob awakens and makes a vow (Gen. 28:20-22).

In spite of the rather pitiful conditions of this carnal prayer, a sovereign God graciously chose to answer it.

D. The love-struck suitor (29:1-20).
1. Jacob arrives in Haran and meets his cousin (and future wife) Rachel. After rolling away a heavy well stone, which allowed her to water her sheep, Jacob introduces himself, accompanied by kissing and crying (29:1-12). This is the first of several important meetings in the Bible which took place beside wells. (See Ex. 2:15; Jn. 4:6, 7.)
2. Jacob then meets Laban (his uncle) and future father-in-law. Jacob agrees to work seven years for the hand of Rachel in marriage (29:13-15). Here begins one of the great love stories of all time.
E. The frustrated family man (29:21—30:24).
1. Jacob is deceived on his wedding night by a crafty Laban who had secretly substituted his oldest girl named Leah in place of Rachel, his youngest (29:16-24). Jacob, the deceiver, is now himself deceived.
2. Jacob is furious, but agrees to work another seven years for Rachel without pay. He is, however, permitted to marry her within a week (29:25-30).
3. Jacob now has two wives and would gather two more, as Leah and Rachel each present him their personal handmaidens for childbearing purposes. These four women will bear Jacob twelve sons and one daughter.
   a. From Leah:
      (1) Reuben ("see, a son"), his first son (29:32).
      (2) Simeon ("hearing"), his second son (29:33).
      (3) Levi ("joined"), his third son (29:34).
      (4) Judah ("praise"), his fourth son (29:35).
      (5) Issachar ("he brings wages"), his ninth son (30:18).
      (6) Zebulun ("dwelling"), his tenth son (30:20).
   b. From Bilhah (Rachel's handmaiden):
      (1) Dan ("judge"), his fifth son (30:6).
      (2) Naphtali ("wrestling"), his sixth son (30:8).
   c. From Zilpah (Leah's handmaiden):
      (1) Gad ("troop"), his seventh son (30:11).
      (2) Asher ("gladness"), his eighth son (30:13).
   d. From Rachel:
      (1) Joseph ("adding"), his eleventh son (30:24).
      (2) Benjamin ("son of my right hand"), his twelfth son (35:18).
4. The following interesting conclusions may be drawn at this point:
   a. Half of Jacob's sons were born to a wife (Leah) he had no intention or knowledge of marrying. This included:
      (1) Levi—from which tribe all priests would eventually come.
      (2) Judah—from which tribe the Lord Jesus would eventually come.
   b. Leah gave Jacob his only recorded daughter, whose name was Dinah (30:21).

c. Rachel bore him his two final and favorite sons. Joseph would later, of course, become the most famous of all.
d. After her first four children, Leah becomes temporarily barren and attempts to stimulate her womb by eating some mandrakes, a leafy plant (sometimes referred to as love apples), eaten by peasant women in the Near East in the belief that this would aid them in becoming pregnant. Leah was now attempting to bear children with the aid of artificial methods. The mandrake fruit, as used here, serves as an example of the various artificial and Christ-dishonoring methods used by some to fill the house of God, such as church bazaars, bingo parties, rock-and-roll sessions, etc. Earthly children are only born when the bride comes into contact with her bridegroom. So it is with souls. When the Bride prays Rachel's prayer, "Give me children, or else I die" (30:1), the Bridegroom will bless.
F. The enterprising employee (30:25—31:55).
1. After the birth of his children, Jacob wants to return home but is persuaded by Laban to remain for awhile (30:25-28).
2. He agrees under the condition that he be allowed to keep as his own all speckled or spotted goats, and all black sheep (30:29-36).
3. Jacob then attempts to increase the size of his herd by removing some of the bark from certain kinds of tree branches and placing them in that area used by the animals for mating purposes (30:37-39).
4. After a period of six years Jacob becomes a very wealthy man. Jacob is commanded by God to return to Palestine again (30:43; 31:3).
5. Jacob quickly breaks camp and leaves for home without bothering to inform Laban (31:17-21).
6. Laban, upon hearing of the flight three days later, sets out in hot pursuit and catches up with them, after a week's journey, at Mt. Gilead. God had already warned the angry father-in-law not to harm Jacob (31:22-25).
7. Laban rebukes Jacob for sneaking off without saying goodbye, and accuses him of stealing his household gods (31:26-30). *The New Scofield Bible* offers the following comment concerning these gods:
   "This incident has long been a puzzle. Why was Laban so greatly concerned about recovering these images which Rachel had stolen? Attempting to recapture them he conducted a long (275 miles) and expensive expedition.
   Excavations at Nuzi in northern Mesopotamia, in the region in which Laban lived, show that the possession of the household gods of a father-in-law by a son-in-law was legally acceptable as proof of the designation of that son-in-law as principal heir. . . . It is no wonder that Jacob was angry that he should be accused of such a deed, and that the two

men set up a boundary and promised not to cross it to injure one another. Jacob never made evil use of these images which Rachel had stolen, but ordered that they should be buried at Shechem" (Gen. 35:2–4). (*New Scofield Bible*, p. 46)

8. Jacob angrily denies stealing these images (unaware of Rachel's actions) and directs a tirade against Laban, accusing him of grossly inconsistent and inhuman treatment during their twenty-year employment relationship (31:36–42).

9. These idols, hidden in Rachel's camel saddle, were never discovered. She remained seated during the search, saying, "I cannot rise up before thee, for the custom of women is upon me" (31:35).

10. At Laban's suggestion, the two men entered a covenant by building a pile of stones and calling it Mizpah, or "the watchtower." Laban then added these words upon completion: "The Lord watch between me and thee, when we are absent one from another" (31:49).

   Dr. Donald Barnhouse writes:

   "Careless reading of the Word of God has made this statement familiar to millions in a totally false application. That it should be engraved on rings, made the motto of a youth organization, and used for a benediction to close a meeting is preposterous. It did not stand for blessing, communion and fellowship; rather, it indicates armistice, separation, menace, and warning. In effect the pillar of Mizpah meant, 'If you come over on my side of this line, . . . I'll kill you!' The covenant-breaker would need God to take care of him, because the other would shoot to kill!" (*Genesis, Vol. 2*, p. 110).

G. The determined wrestler (32:1—33:20).

1. Jacob is again ministered to by angels on his route homeward as he had been when leaving home some twenty years before. (See Gen. 28:12 and compare with 32:1, 2.) Jacob here mentions for the first time in the Bible the armies of heaven. That is what he meant by the phrase "God's host." This host is composed of angels. There are many instances in the Scripture showing this divine army in action.

   a. *Joshua* was visited by the captain of this host (Josh. 5:14).

   b. *Elisha* and his young servant were reassured by this mighty army (2 Ki. 6:13–17).

   c. *The Savior* announced to Peter that he could call upon this divine army to save him from the Cross, had he wanted to. But thank God he did not choose to do so. (See Mt. 26:52, 53 where he states he could easily call down twelve legions, or seventy-two thousand, angels!)

   As David would write in Psalm 34:7: "The angel of the Lord encampeth round about them that fear him and delivereth them."

2. At this time he learns the terrifying news that Esau his brother was en route to meet him with 400 men. Jacob is petrified with fear. He immediately does three things:

   a. He divides his household into two groups, saying, "If Esau comes to the one company, and smite it, the other company which is left shall escape" (32:8).

   b. He cries out to God in prayer (32:9–11). At this time Jacob acknowledges, perhaps for the very first time that: "I am not worthy of the least of all the mercies, and of all the truth, which thou hast shown unto thy servant" (32:10).
   Paul would testify to this truth also. (See 1 Tim. 1:12–15.)

   c. He sends out a bribe gift to Esau consisting of 550 animals (32:13–21).

3. There occurred that night by the river Jabbok one of the most mysterious and wondrous events in all the Bible. (See 32:24–29.)

4. Whatever theology one may glean from these strange verses of God and man engaged in an all-night wrestling match, two facts clearly emerge:

   a. His name is changed from Jacob (the crooked heel-catcher) to Israel, which signifies "one who has power with God" (32:28).

   b. He never walked the same after this soul-struggling session with God (32:31, 32).

5. Afterward Jacob called the name of this place Peniel (the Face of God). God had touched his heart at Bethel, but here at Peniel God claimed his life. The former place saw his conversion and salvation, but this place witnessed his consecration and sanctification. The first had *introduced him* to the peace of God; the second freely *gave him* that peace of God. He now possessed not only life, but abundant life. (See Rom. 5:1; Phil. 4:7; Jn. 10:10.)

6. Jacob, bowing and trembling, meets Esau. To his surprise and immense relief, Esau embraces him (33:1–4).

7. Esau wanted Jacob to accompany him to the land of Seir. This was the farthest thing from Jacob's mind, but instead of simply telling Esau this, he hides behind his children: "My lord knoweth that the children are tender, and the flocks and herds with young are with me: and if men should overdrive them one day, all the flock will die" (33:13).

8. Jacob promises, however, to meet him in Seir. This was, of course, a brazen lie. Jacob was headed for Succoth, which was northwest, while Seir was southeast. One wonders what Esau thought about Jacob's glowing testimony concerning God's grace when he learned his brother had once again deceived him. (See 33:14–16.)

H. The enraged father (34:1; 38:1–30).

1. Over the sin of murder, committed by Levi and Simeon (34:1–31).

   a. Jacob allows his daughter Dinah to run loose, resulting in her being seduced by

Shechem, the son of King Hamor of the Hivites. Jacob, like his father Isaac, had little idea what his children did or whom they saw. It was an accepted assumption among the Egyptians and Canaanites that unmarried and unattended women were legitimate prey. (See Gen. 12:14; 20:2; 26:7.) Dinah was approximately fourteen years of age at this time.

b. Shechem then determines to marry Dinah and asks Jacob for the necessary permission. In fact, the Hivites suggested to Jacob, "Make ye marriages with us and take our daughters unto you. And ye shall dwell with us . . ." (34:9, 10).

c. This line of reasoning is, of course, one of Satan's favorite tactics. The Christian is urged to raise his tolerance level and lower his standards, to appease his flesh and to abandon his faith. (For the answer to this satanic suggestion, see 1 Cor. 6:15-20; 2 Cor. 6:14-18.)

d. Dinah's brothers, inwardly boiling with anger, cruelly deceived Shechem by agreeing to his request with the stipulation that all male Hivites circumcise themselves (34:13-24).

e. On the third day, when their wounds were sore and sensitive to every movement, Levi and Simeon walked boldly into the camp and slaughtered every man there, including Shechem and his father. They then plundered the city, taking all its spoil, including the widows and orphans (34:25-30).

f. Jacob was furious and soundly rebuked his two murderous sons: "Ye have troubled me to make me stink among the inhabitants of the land, among the Canaanites and the Perizzites: and I being few in number, they shall gather themselves together against me, and slay me; and I shall be destroyed, I, and my house" (34:30).

Even at this late stage in Jacob's life we sadly note:

(1) He expresses no sorrow over the defilement of his only daughter Dinah.

(2) He voices no regrets over an entire town being exterminated.

(3) He apparently is unconcerned about God's feelings in all this.

(4) His main (perhaps only) concern is that he be hurt because of his sons. He assumes no personal responsibility whatsoever.

2. Over the sin of adultery, committed by Judah (38:1-30).

Although Jacob's name does not occur in this chapter, we may assume he was well aware of the tragic facts and disapproved of them.

a. Judah, Jacob's fourth son, marries a Canaanite girl, who bears him three sons, Er, Onan, and Shelah (38:1-5).

b. His oldest son, Er, marries a girl named Tamar, but God soon kills him for an un-

recorded act of wickedness. Judah then commands his second son, Onan, to marry her. He also is soon slain for wickedness.

c. Judah promises Tamar to give her his youngest son Shelah in due time, although he secretly had no intention of doing this (38:11, 12).

d. After awhile Tamar realizes this and, disguising herself as a common harlot, entices Judah into her tent for sexual purposes. For payment she demands and receives his signet, bracelets, and staff (38:13-19). Tamar soon becomes pregnant from this relationship.

e. Some three months later an indignant Judah orders her to be burned to death. Tamar then shows him his signet, bracelets, and staff. A remorseful and doubtless red-faced Judah immediately sets her free (38:24-26).

f. Tamar has twins and calls them Perez and Zerah. Both this Canaanite prostitute woman and her illegitimate firstborn son would later be included through the amazing grace of God in the sacred genealogy of the Lord Jesus Christ! (See Mt. 1:3.)

I. The obedient patriarch (35:1-7).

1. God again reminds Jacob of his previous command to return to Bethel (35:1). (See also 31:11-13.) Jacob had been living in Shechem for ten years, and Bethel was only thirty miles away. How tragically easy it is to move toward surrender and yet fall short of it. (See Heb. 4:1, 9, 11.)

2. Jacob instructs his entire household to destroy their idols, to wash themselves, and to put on fresh clothing in preparation for the Bethel trip. These idols and earrings are then collected and buried under an oak tree near Shechem. This is the first recorded revival in God's Word.

3. Jacob arrives at Bethel and builds an altar there, naming it El-Bethel. As we have already seen, the name Bethel means "House of God," but El-Bethel means, "The God of the House of God." The difference between these two concepts is the difference between knowing the Word of God and of knowing the God of the Word! We are to read the pages of the first to acquaint us with the Person of the second (35:7).

J. The sorrowing saint (35:8-29).

1. Jacob loses, in rapid succession, three loved ones.

a. His old nurse, _Deborah_ (35:8). This woman, first mentioned here, apparently came to live with Jacob after the death of her mistress (and Jacob's mother) Rebekah.

b. His beloved wife _Rachel_ dies giving birth to her second (and Jacob's twelfth) son, who is named Benjamin, "Son of my Right Hand" (35:16-20).

c. His father _Isaac_ (35:27-29) dies at age of 180 and is buried by Jacob and Esau

# Jacob

## THE DEVISING BROTHER
**GEN. 25:27-34**
- He pressures Esau into trading his birthright.

## THE DECEITFUL SON
**GEN. 27:6-29**
- He tricks his father to receive the blessing.

## THE DREAMING PILGRIM
**GEN. 28:10-22**
- He sees a ladder set up from earth to heaven at Bethel.
- Angels are ascending and descending upon it.
- God confirms to him the Abrahamic Covenant.
- Upon awakening he anoints a rockpile and vows to serve God.

## THE LOVE-STRUCK SUITOR
**GEN. 29:1-20**
- He meets Rachel, his cousin and future wife, beside a well.
- Here begins one of history's great love stories.
- He promises Rachel's father Laban (Jacob's uncle and future father-in-law) he will work seven years for her hand in marriage.

## THE FRUSTRATED FAMILY MAN
**GEN. 29:21—30:24**
- He is deceived on his wedding night by Laban who secretly substitutes Leah (Rachel's older sister) for Rachel.
- Jacob is furious, but agrees to work yet another seven years for Rachel.
- He now has two wives and would gather yet another two, for both Rachel and Leah present to him their personal handmaids for childbearing purposes.

These four women would bear Jacob twelve sons and one daughter.

| wife | **Leah** | **Bilhah** (Rachel's handmaid) | **Zilpah** (Leah's handmaid) | **Rachel** |
|------|----------|----------|----------|----------|
| son | 1. Reuben | | | |
| | 2. Simeon | | | |
| | 3. Levi | | | |
| | 4. Judah | | | |
| | | 5. Dan | | |
| | | 6. Naphtali | | |
| | | | 7. Gad | |
| | | | 8. Asher | |
| | 9. Issachar | | | |
| | 10. Zebulun | | | |
| | | | | 11. Joseph |
| | | | | 12. Benjamin |
| daughter | Dinah | | | |

## THE ENTERPRISING EMPLOYEE
**GEN. 30:25—31:55**
- Jacob goes into business with Laban and becomes a wealthy man.
- Upon being ordered by God to return home, he breaks camp without telling Laban.
- Laban chases him down and accuses Jacob (among other things) of stealing his household gods.
- Laban and Jacob come to a truce and build a memorial pile of stones.

## THE DETERMINED WRESTLER
**GEN. 32:1—33:20**
- Jacob learns that Esau is on his way to meet him, riding with 400 men.
- Filled with fear, Jacob wrestles with God in prayer all night long by the Brook Jabbok.
- He is reassured by God for this and his name is changed from Jacob to Israel.
- The ensuing meeting between Israel and Esau is very friendly.

## THE ENRAGED FATHER
**GEN. 34:1-31; 35:22; 38:1-30**
- Over the sin of murder, committed by Levi and Simeon
  1. These boys trick a group of desert men (whose leader had seduced Dinah, their sister) into circumcising themselves.
  2. On the third day when they are helpless to defend themselves because of their self-inflicted wounds, Jacob's two sons slaughter them like animals.
- Over the sin of adultery, committed by Reuben "And it came to pass, when Israel dwelt in that land, that Reuben went and lay with Bilhah, his father's concubine: and Israel heard it . . ." (Gen. 35:22).
- Over the sin of adultery, committed by Judah
  1. To seek revenge upon Judah (for refusing a request of hers) Tamar, his daughter-in-law, disguises herself as a common harlot and entices him into her tent for sexual purposes.
  2. Tamar becomes pregnant and Judah orders her death for immorality until he learns who the father of the child really is!

## THE OBEDIENT PATRIARCH
**GEN. 35:1-15**
- Jacob is ordered by God back to Bethel.
- In preparation for this trip, Jacob instructs his household to destroy their idols and prepare their hearts.
- He builds an altar at Bethel and calls it "El-Bethel"—the God of the house of God.

## THE SORROWING SAINT
**GEN. 35:16-20; 37:31-35**
- He loses his beloved wife, Rachel, in childbirth.
- He buries his father Isaac.
- He is led to believe that Joseph has been killed and eaten by a wild beast

alongside Abraham in the Cave of Machpelah at Hebron.

2. There are two important "first mentions" in these verses.
   a. The first mention of the drink offering (35:14).
   b. The first reference to Bethlehem (35:19). Here Rachel dies giving birth to the son of Jacob's right hand. Many centuries later a young virgin would give birth to another baby in Bethlehem. This Babe would be known as the Son of God's Right Hand.

IV. Joseph (Gen. 37, 39–50).
   A. The favored son (37).
      1. The dreams of Joseph.
         a. The remaining chapters in Genesis now describe the life of Joseph, Jacob's second youngest son, born to him of his beloved Rachel. (See Gen. 30:24.)
         b. Joseph had brought down upon him the wrath of his ten half-brothers. Three factors had led to this sad situation.
            (1) Because he had reported to his father some of the bad things the ten were doing (37:2).

(2) Because he had become Jacob's favorite son. To show this special affection, the old man gave Joseph a long-sleeved brightly colored tunic (37:3).

(3) Because of Joseph's strange dreams.

    (a) In one of his dreams they were all in the field binding sheaves, when suddenly his sheaf stood up and their sheaves all gathered around it and bowed low before it.

    (b) During his second dream he saw the sun, moon, and eleven stars bow low before him (37:9).

c. Joseph is sent from his home in Hebron to Shechem to check on his half-brothers and their grazing flocks. He finally finds them at Dothan, some fifteen miles from Shechem, and sixty-five miles from Hebron.

2. The deceit of his brothers.

a. His ten brothers see him in the distance and determine to kill him (37:18).

b. Reuben, Jacob's firstborn (Gen. 29:32), apparently had second thoughts, however, for he suggested that they simply throw him in a pit and let him die. Reuben was then planning to secretly return him to his father (37:21, 22).

c. Joseph is stripped of his coat and cast into a pit (37:24).

d. Ignoring his pitiful cries (Gen. 42:21), the cruel brothers sat down to eat. Suddenly a slave caravan of Ishmaelites and Midianites came into view en route to Egypt. The nine brothers made a hasty and heartless decision to sell Joseph as a slave (37:25-27). Reuben was apparently not present at the time. Judah is the ringleader in this disgraceful deal.

e. Joseph is sold for twenty pieces of silver (the going price of a slave) and carried into Egypt (37:28). Reuben returns and weeps over the action his brothers have taken (37:29).

3. The despair of his father.

a. To conceal their horrible crime, they take Joseph's coat, smear it with goat's blood, and deceive Jacob into believing his beloved son has been slain and eaten by a wild animal (37:31-35).

b. Joseph is sold as a slave to Potiphar, a captain in Pharaoh's Egyptian palace guard (37:36). That immutable law of retribution which runs so strongly throughout the Bible (see Gal. 6:7) is clearly seen here in this chapter. Jacob, who once deceived his father by using the skin of a kid (Gen. 27:16), is himself now deceived in a similar manner. Other examples would include:

(1) Pharaoh, who ordered the destruction of Israel by the waters of the Red Sea, was himself drowned there. (Compare Ex. 14:5 with 14:28.)

(2) Korah, who caused a division in the congregation of Israel, was swallowed by a division in the ground. (Compare Num. 16:1-3 with 16:31, 32.)

(3) Haman, who built the gallows to execute a godly Hebrew, later himself was hanged from the same gallows. (Compare Est. 5:14 with 7:10.)

B. The faithful steward (39).

1. His service.

a. Joseph is sold as a slave to Potiphar, an officer in Pharaoh's Egyptian palace guard (38:30; 39:1).

b. Under the blessings of God, he was quickly entrusted with the entire administration of Potiphar's household (39:2-6).

2. His self-control.

a. Joseph is enticed to commit immorality by the wife of Potiphar, but refuses her continued advances (39:7-10).

b. In an act of revenge, she accuses Joseph of rape (39:11-18).

3. His sufferings.

Joseph is thrown into prison (39:9-20).

C. The forgotten servant (40).

1. The jailor, like Potiphar, soon recognized Joseph's beautiful and talented character and put him in charge of the entire prison administration (39:21-23).

2. For some reason, the anger of Pharaoh is aroused against both his chief baker and butler and he sends them to Joseph's prison (40:1-4).

3. While in prison these two men have mysterious dreams. God gives Joseph the ability to correctly interpret each dream.

a. The *details* of the butler's dream. He had seen a vine with three branches that began to bud and blossom and soon produced clusters of ripe grapes. In his dream, the butler then squeezed the juice from the grapes and served it to Pharaoh in the royal wine cup (40:9-11).

b. The *meaning* of the butler's dream. The three branches meant that within three days Pharaoh would free him and restore him to his old employment. Joseph then asked the butler to mention him to Pharaoh, and ask him to remember the injustices he suffered (40:12-15).

c. The *details* of the baker's dream. He saw himself carrying upon his head three baskets of pastries. The top basket contained special goods for the Pharaoh. But suddenly some birds flew down and ate this food (40:16, 17).

d. The *meaning* of the baker's dream. It meant that within three days the Pharaoh would take off the baker's head and impale his body on a pole, and that the birds would come and pick off his flesh (40:18, 19).

4. Three days later, on his birthday, the Pharaoh dealt with the butler and baker exactly as Joseph had predicted he would do. But the

butler forgot to mention anything about Joseph (40:20-23).

D. The famed statesman (41-44).
  1. The revelation of Joseph.
    a. One night two years later Pharaoh experienced two mysterious dreams.
      (1) The contents of the first dream. He was standing on the bank of the Nile River when suddenly seven sleek, fat cows came up out of the river and began grazing in the grass. Then seven other cows came up, but they were very skinny and all their ribs stood out. Suddenly the skinny cows ate the fat cows (41:1-4).
      (2) The contents of the second dream. He saw seven heads of grain on one stalk, with every kernel well formed and plump. Then suddenly seven more heads appeared on the stalk, but these were shriveled and withered by the east wind. The dream ended as the thin heads devoured the plump ones (41:5-7).
    b. Pharaoh consults his magicians about these dreams the next morning but they are unable to interpret them (41:8).
    c. The butler suddenly remembers the amazing talent of Joseph and relates to the Pharaoh those events which occurred in prison two years back (41:9-13).
    d. Joseph is cleaned up, shaven, and brought before Pharaoh. After hearing the contents of the dreams, he immediately interprets them, giving God the glory. According to Joseph, both dreams meant the same thing (41:14-25).
      (1) The seven fat cows and the seven plump heads of grain meant that there were seven years of prosperity ahead (41:26).
      (2) The seven skinny cows and the lean heads of grain meant that a seven-year famine period would follow the years of plenty (41:27).
    e. Joseph then advises Pharaoh to appoint a capable administrator over a nationwide farm program, and divide Egypt into five districts. The officials of these districts should then gather into the royal storehouses all the excess crops of the next seven years (41:33-36).
  2. The elevation of Joseph (41:37-57).
    a. The Pharaoh appoints Joseph to this high office on the spot.
    He then:
      (1) Places his own signet ring on Joseph's finger.
      (2) Dresses him in beautiful clothing.
      (3) Hangs the royal golden chain about his neck.
      (4) Gives him the chariot of his second-in-command.
      (5) Decrees that all shall bow down to him.
      (6) Changes his name to Zaph-enath-paneah, which means, "the one who

furnishes the sustenance of the land."
      (7) Presents him with a wife, Asenath, the daughter of Potiphera, priest of Heliopolis. Joseph thus marries into a family of high nobility, his father-in-law being a major priest-politician of the time.
    b. Joseph is now thirty years of age (41:46). In one day he has been elevated from the prison to the palace. But it has taken God thirteen years to bring him to this place of service, for he was seventeen when he first arrived in Egypt. (See Ps. 105:17-21.)
    c. Joseph's wife presents him with two boys. The first is named Manasseh (meaning "made to forget"), and the younger Ephraim (meaning "fruitful"). (See 41:50, 52.)
    d. As Joseph had predicted, the seven fat years were followed by seven lean ones, causing people from many lands to buy their food in Egypt (41:53-57).
  3. The consternation of Joseph's brothers (Gen. 42-44).
    a. Jacob sends his ten older sons into Egypt from Hebron to buy food (42:1-5).
    b. They arrive in Egypt and bow low before Joseph, but do not recognize him, thus fulfilling his dream some twenty years back (42:6).
    c. Joseph does not reveal himself at first but accuses them of being foreign spies. The frightened brothers attempt to convince him otherwise (42:7-13).
    d. He throws them into jail for three days and then releases them, but keeps Simeon as a hostage until they can return with Benjamin, as he demands they bring him to him (42:14-20).
    e. The terrified brothers acknowledge to each other that their present misfortunes have doubtless been caused by the terrible sin committed twenty years back, not realizing that Joseph can understand every word (42:21-23).
    f. After leaving the room to weep, he orders his servants to fill the men's sacks with grain and also to put each brother's payment at the top of his sack. The nine then start for home (42:24-26).
    g. En route home, one of the men discovers his payment, and when they reach Hebron the rest find theirs and are filled with fear concerning the safety of Simeon. In spite of their earnest pleas, Jacob at first refuses to allow Benjamin to accompany them on a future trip into Egypt (42:27-38).
    h. The famine intensifies in Hebron and Jacob is forced to allow Benjamin to go back with them into Egypt for food. Judah attempts to guarantee the safety of Benjamin (43:1-14).
    i. They again present themselves to Joseph, who takes them to his palace for a feast.

The brothers attempt to convince Joseph's household manager that they have not stolen the payment of their former trip. Simeon is released and joins the group. For the first time in twenty years all twelve brothers are together, but only one is aware of it (43:15-25).

j. The brothers are fed at a separate table from that of Joseph. But to their amazement he seats them in order of their ages, giving Benjamin five times as much food as the others (43:26-34).

k. Before they return the next morning Joseph once again secretly places the payment money in each man's sack, along with Joseph's own silver cup at the top of Benjamin's sack (44:1, 2).

l. The brothers have but left the city when they are arrested (at Joseph's command) and accused of stealing his silver cup (44:4-6).

m. They quickly deny this charge and agree to serve as slaves if any stolen loot can be found on them. A search quickly reveals the cup in Benjamin's sack (44:7-12).

n. Standing before Joseph for the third time, Judah steps forward and begs him to accept his life in place of Benjamin. He tearfully reminds Joseph that their old father Jacob would simply die if anything happened to Benjamin (44:13-34).

E. The forgiving saint (45-48).
1. Joseph and his brothers.
   a. Joseph cannot contain himself any longer and reveals his identity to his brothers (45:1-3).
   b. After a time of tearful reuniting, Joseph informs them that the two-year drought they have already experienced will continue another five years and urges that they bring Jacob back with them and all make plans to live in Egypt (45:4-15).
   c. Joseph reassures his brothers (still in semi-shock) he has no hard feelings, but feels God has overruled their evil plot so as to guarantee Israel will indeed be a great nation (45:5-8).
   d. Pharaoh rejoices along with Joseph over his restored brethren and also invites the entire clan to live in Egypt (45:16-20).
2. Joseph and his father.
   a. The old patriarch, Jacob, at first cannot comprehend the thrilling news concerning Joseph, but then believes the report and plans his trip to Egypt (45:26-28).
   b. En route at Beer-sheba, God reassures Jacob he will still bless him, even in Egypt. Jacob is told he is to die there, but God will bring his descendants back to Palestine someday (46:1-4).

   Note: There has been some controversy as to whether Jacob's trip to Egypt was God's perfect will or his permissive will. One benefit, however, was the fact that Egypt was a country in which Jacob's descendants would be forced to remain a separate and distinct people, for they were shepherds, and shepherds were an abomination to the Egyptians (Gen. 43:32; 46:34). There would thus be no intermarriage. In Canaan, this had apparently occurred. Simeon had married a girl from Canaan (46:10).

   c. Jacob enters Egypt with his entire household. Here three separate numbers are given.
      (1) Sixty-six (Gen. 46:26). This was the number of those going to Egypt, his own descendants, not counting his son's wives.
      (2) Seventy (Gen. 46:27). This was the number after adding Jacob himself, Joseph, and Joseph's two sons, Ephraim and Manasseh.
      (3) Seventy-five (Acts 7:14). Here Stephen refers to the "kindred," a probable reference to the five surviving wives of Jacob's sons.
   d. Joseph and Jacob meet in Goshen for the first time in twenty-two years. The son is now thirty-nine and the father 130 (46:28-30).
   e. Joseph introduces his father to the Pharaoh and Jacob is given choice land to live upon (47:1-12).
   f. As the famine continues, Pharaoh becomes richer and Joseph's wise food administration plan saves untold thousands from outright starvation (47:13-26).
   g. The population of Israel in Goshen rapidly expands in spite of the famine everywhere else (47:27).
   h. At the age of 147 Jacob realizes his time is near and thus calls for his beloved son Joseph and his favorite grandsons, Ephraim and Manasseh (48:1).
   i. Joseph promises his father he will not be buried in Egypt (47:29-31).
3. Joseph and his sons.
   a. Joseph's two sons stand before their grandfather waiting to be blessed. The old man adopts them as his own sons and assures them of an equal inheritance (48:3-9).
   b. Jacob lays his right hand on Ephraim's head and his left hand on Manasseh's head. A displeased Joseph attempts to reverse this, pointing out that Manasseh is the older and therefore should have the right hand on his head (48:10-18).
   c. Jacob refuses to change hands, however, for he predicted the tribe of Ephraim would be even greater than the tribe of Manasseh (48:19-22).
F. The fruitful shade tree (49-50).
   1. Joseph receives his father's blessing (49). (See also Heb. 11:21.) Jacob gathers his twelve sons around his bedside just before his death, "that I may tell you that which shall befall you in the last days" (49:1). The *New Scofield Bible* has the following note on this verse:

"This is the first occurrence of the term 'the last days,' a most important concept in Biblical prophecy. In general, the expression refers to that terminal period in the history of a particular group of people or nations when God's announced purpose for them is about to be consummated" (p. 68).

Jacob then pronounces the following prophecies:

a. Upon Reuben (49:3, 4)

    (1) He was as unruly as the wild waves of the sea. As the first-born he was entitled to a double share of honor and inheritance (Deut. 21:17), but Jacob passes him over because of his immorality with Bilhah, Jacob's own concubine (Gen. 35:22).

    (2) The Reubenites later settled east of Jordan (along with the tribe of Gad and half-tribe of Manasseh). (See Josh. 1:12-16.)

    (3) They unintentionally almost caused a civil war by putting up a large monument on the west bank of Jordan (Josh. 22:10).

    (4) They later refused to help the armies of Israel, led by Barak and Deborah, in their war against a pagan named Sisera and his 900 iron chariots. (See Jdg. 4:1-3; 5:15, 16.)

b. Upon Simeon and Levi (49:5-7).

    (1) These were men of violence and injustice. They slaughtered the inhabitants of Shechem by deceit (Gen. 34:25). Jacob also bypasses them both.

    (2) Their descendants would thus be scattered throughout Israel. This meant that they would not be given regular land holdings as were their brother tribes. Levi's children dwelled in various cities throughout Palestine, and the Simeonites had to share that portion of land given to Judah. (See Num. 18:24; Josh. 19:1-9.)

c. Upon Judah (49:8-12).

    (1) The other brothers were to praise Judah and bow before him.

    (2) Judah would destroy his enemies, and would be left undisturbed, like a young lion.

    (3) The scepter would not depart from Judah until Shiloh (Christ) came. (See Num. 24:17; Rev. 5:5.) With the anointing of David (1 Chron. 28:4; 5:2; 2 Sam. 7:13), this was assured.

d. Upon Zebulun (49:13).

    (1) He would dwell near the seashore.

    (2) His borders would extend to Sidon.

e. Upon Issachar (49:14, 15).

    (1) He would be a strong beast of burden.

    (2) He would give up liberty for security.

f. Upon Dan (49:16-18).

    (1) Dan would become a serpent in the pathway that bit horses' heels, causing the riders to fall off. An old tradition has it that the antichrist will come from this tribe.

    (2) Samson was from Dan (Jdg. 13:2, 24).

g. Upon Gad (49:19).

Gad would be the opposite of Issachar, and would often bravely fight for liberty. (See 1 Chron. 5:18; 12:8-15.)

h. Upon Asher (49:20).

"Asher would produce rich food, fit for kings." Anna was from the tribe of Asher (Lk. 2:36).

i. Upon Naphtali (49:21).

He would become known for his mobility and swiftness (as a released deer) and for his eloquence with words.

j. Upon Joseph (49:22-26).

    (1) He would be a fruitful tree beside a fountain whose branches shaded the wall.

# Joseph

## The Favored Son
**(GEN. 37)**

- The dreams of Joseph
- The deceit of his brothers
- The despair of his father

## The Faithful Steward
**(GEN. 39)**

- His service
- His self-control
- His sufferings

## The Forgotten Servant
**(GEN. 40)**

- Joseph finds himself in the same cell with the Pharaoh's butler and baker who were also imprisoned.
- These two men experience strange dreams. Joseph interprets both, predicting that within three days the king will free the butler but execute the baker.
- All this comes true. However, upon his release, the butler forgets all about Joseph.

## The Famed Statesman
**(GEN. 41-44)**

- The revelation by Joseph
- The elevation of Joseph
- The frustration of Joseph's brothers

## The Forgiving Saint
**(GEN. 45-48)**

- Joseph and his brothers
- Joseph and his father
- Joseph and his sons

## The Fruitful Shade Tree
**(GEN. 49-50)**

- He receives his father's blessing
  *"Joseph is a fruitful bough . . . by a well, whose branches run over the wall. . . . His hands were made strong by . . . the mighty God . . .*
  *. . . the Almighty . . . shall bless thee with the blessings of heaven above . . ."* (Gen. 49:22-25).
- He returns his father's body

(2) He would be severely injured by vicious archers, but their weapons were shattered by the mighty one of Jacob, the Shepherd, the Rock of Israel.

(3) Jacob predicts and pronounces the richest divine blessing of all the twelve (with the exception of Judah) upon Joseph.

k. Upon Benjamin (49:27).

(1) He was to be as a wolf on the prowl.

(2) He would devour his enemies in the morning and divide the spoils in the evening. For examples of this trait, see Judges 20.

(3) Both the Saul of the Old Testament (1 Sam. 9:1, 2) and the Saul of the New Testament (Phil. 3:5) were from this tribe.

2. Joseph returns his father's body (50).

a. Jacob dies at age of 147 (47:28; 49:33).

b. His body is embalmed in Egypt during a forty-day preparation period (50:2, 3).

c. All Egypt mourns over him for seventy days (50:3).

d. He is carried by his sons in Palestine and buried alongside Abraham and Isaac in the Cave of Machpelah (50:13).

e. Joseph reassures his troubled brothers that favorable conditions would remain as before the funeral (50:15-21). He gently reminds them, "Ye thought evil against me; but God meant it unto good, to bring to pass, as it is this day, to save much people alive" (50:20).

f. Joseph dies at age of 110 (50:26).

G. The foreshadow of the Savior.

Joseph is the most complete type of Christ in all the Bible. Note the amazing similarities between these two:

1. Both were beloved by their fathers (37:3; Mt. 3:17).

2. Both regarded themselves as shepherds (37:2; Jn. 10:11-14).

3. Both were sent to their brethren by their fathers (37:13, 14; Lk. 20:13; Jn. 3:17; Heb. 10:7).

4. Both were hated by their brethren without cause (37:4, 5, 8; Jn. 1:11; 7:5; 15:25).

5. Both were plotted against by their brethren (37:20; Jn. 11:53).

6. Both were severely tempted (39:7; Mt. 4:1).

7. Both were taken to Egypt (37:36; Mt. 2:14, 15).

8. Both were stripped of their robes (37:23; Jn. 19:23, 24).

9. Both were sold for the price of a slave (37:28; Mt. 26:15).

10. Both were bound (39:20; Mt. 27:2).

11. Both remained silent and offered no defense (39:20; Isa. 53:7).

12. Both were falsely accused (39:16-18; Mt. 26:59, 60).

13. Both experienced God's presence through everything (39:2, 21, 23; Jn. 16:32).

14. Both were respected by their jailors (39:21; Lk. 23:47).

## JOSEPH .. THE FORESHADOW OF THE SAVIOR

| JOSEPH GENESIS | Note the amazing similarities between these two | JESUS |
|---|---|---|
| 37:3 | Beloved by their fathers | MT. 3:17 |
| 37:2 | Regarded themselves as shepherds | JN. 10:11-14 |
| 37:13, 14 | Sent by their fathers to their brethren | LK. 20:13; HEB. 2:12 |
| 37:4, 5, 8 | Hated by their brethren without a cause | JN. 1:11; 7:5; 15:25 |
| 37:20 | Plotted against by their brethren | JN. 11:53 |
| 39:7 | Severely tempted | MT. 4:1 |
| 37:26 | Taken to Egypt | MT. 2:14, 15 |
| 37:23 | Stripped of their robes | JN. 19:23, 24 |
| 37:28 | Sold for the price of a slave | MT. 26:15 |
| 39:20 | Bound | Mt. 27:2 |
| 39:20 | Remained silent and offered no defense | ISA. 53:7 |
| 39:16-18 | Falsely accused | MT. 26:59, 60 |
| 39:2, 21, 23 | Experienced God's presence through everything | JN. 16:32 |
| 39:21 | Respected by their jailors | LK. 23:47 |
| 40:2, 3 | Placed with two prisoners, one of which was later lost, the other saved | LK. 23:32 |
| 41:46 | Both around thirty at the beginning of their ministry | LK. 3:23 |
| 41:41 | Both highly exalted after their sufferings | PHIL. 2:9-11 |
| 41:45 | Both took non-Jewish brides | EPH. 3:1-12 |
| 42:7, 8 | Both lost to their brethren for awhile | ROM. 10:1-3; 11:7, 8 |
| 45:1-15 | Both forgave and restored their repentant brothers | ZECH. 12:10-12 |
| 41:57 | Both visited and honored by all earthly nations | ISA. 2:2, 3; 49:6 |

15. Both were placed with two prisoners, one of which was later lost, and the other saved (40:2, 3, 21, 22; Lk. 23:32, 39-43).

16. Both were around thirty when their ministry began (41:46; Lk. 3:23).

17. Both were highly exalted after their sufferings (41:41; Phil. 2:9-11).

18. Both took Gentile brides (41:45; Eph. 3:1-12).

19. Both were lost to their brothers for awhile (42:7, 8; Rom. 10:1-3; 11:7, 8).

20. Both forgave and restored their repentant brothers (45:1-15; Micah 7:18, 19; Zech. 12:10-12; Rev. 1:7).

21. Both were visited and honored by all earthly nations (41:57; Isa. 2:2, 3; 49:6).

V. Job (Job 1-42). Introduction:
1. This is one of the most ancient books of the entire Bible.
   Note:
   a. The ancient historical allusions, e.g., the pyramids (3:14), the cities of the plains (15:28), and the Flood (22:16).
   b. The mission of Israel's history. No reference is made to the Law, the Exodus, the Red Sea crossing, Canaan, or any of the kings of Israel.
2. Job was a historical character, mentioned later by both Ezekiel (Ezek. 14:14, 20) and James (5:11).
3. The Greek Septuagint identifies Job with Jobab, the second king of Edom (Gen. 36:33).
4. The land of Uz may have been located northeast of the Sea of Galilee, running toward the Euphrates River. (See Gen. 36:28; Lam. 4:21.)
5. Job's disease may have been leprosy, complicated with elephantiasis, one of the most loathsome and painful diseases known in the world of his time.
6. Job's sufferings are intensified by three false friends, a bitter wife, and an impetuous youth.
   a. Eliphaz, who bases his advice on personal experience. (See 4:8, 12-16; 5:3, 27; 15:17.) Eliphaz was a descendant of Esau. (See Gen. 36:11.)
   b. Bildad, who bases his advice on tradition. (See 8:8-10; 18:5-20.) Bildad was a descendant of Abraham and Keturah. (See Gen. 25:2.)
   c. Zophar, who bases his advice on pure dogmatism. (See 11:6; 20:4.) Zophar was from the land of Naamah.
   d. Elihu, who seems to base his advice on youth alone. (See 32:6-10.) Elihu was a descendant of Nahor, Abraham's brother. (See Gen. 22:21.)
   e. Job's wife, who bases her advice on sheer unbelief. (See 2:9.)
7. The statements from Job's various "friends" cannot be used for doctrinal purposes, for they are often wrong.
   a. God rebukes them for not speaking the truth about him; see 42:7.
   b. They were also wrong in calling Job a hypocrite. (See 8:12; 15:34; 20:5; 34:30.) God, however, had found *no fault* in him. (See 1:8; 2:3.)

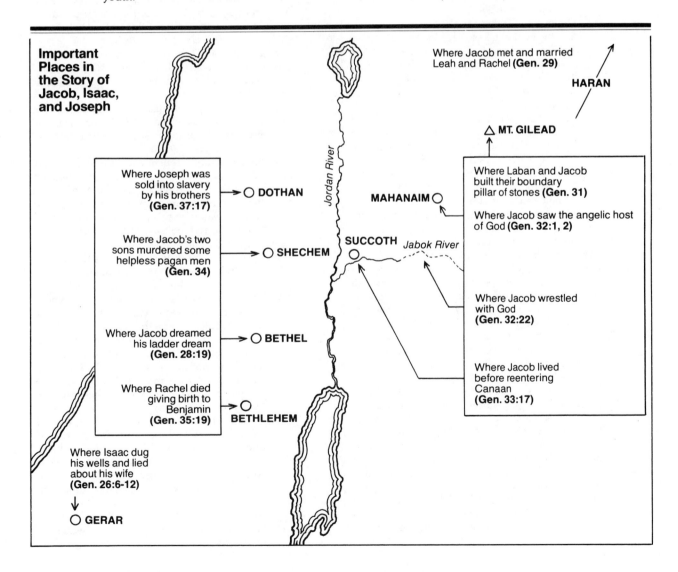

**Important Places in the Story of Jacob, Isaac, and Joseph**

Where Jacob met and married Leah and Rachel **(Gen. 29)**

HARAN

△ MT. GILEAD

Where Joseph was sold into slavery by his brothers **(Gen. 37:17)** → ○ DOTHAN

Where Laban and Jacob built their boundary pillar of stones **(Gen. 31)**

Where Jacob saw the angelic host of God **(Gen. 32:1, 2)**

MAHANAIM ○

Where Jacob's two sons murdered some helpless pagan men **(Gen. 34)** → ○ SHECHEM

SUCCOTH ○ *Jabok River*

Jordan River

Where Jacob wrestled with God **(Gen. 32:22)**

Where Jacob dreamed his ladder dream **(Gen. 28:19)** → ○ BETHEL

Where Jacob lived before reentering Canaan **(Gen. 33:17)**

Where Rachel died giving birth to Benjamin **(Gen. 35:19)** → ○ BETHLEHEM

Where Isaac dug his wells and lied about his wife **(Gen. 26:6-12)**
↓
○ GERAR

8. The book of Job is an extended commentary on Luke 22:31, 32 and Hebrews 12:7-11.
9. The following opinions have been given concerning the book of Job.
   a. Victor Hugo: "The book of Job is perhaps the greatest masterpiece of the human mind."
   b. Thomas Carlyle: "Call this book . . . one of the grandest things ever written. There is nothing written, I think, of equal literary merit."
   c. Alfred, Lord Tennyson: "The greatest poem, whether of ancient or modern literature."

A. Job's terrible trials (Job 1-2).
   1. The nature of these trials.
      a. First trial: His oxen and donkeys are stolen and his farm hands are killed by a Sabean raid.
      b. Second trial: His sheep and herdsmen are burned up by fire.
      c. Third trial: His camels are stolen and his servants killed by a Chaldean raid.
      d. Fourth trial: His sons and daughters perish in a mighty wind.
      e. Fifth trial: Job himself is struck with a terrible case of boils.
   2. The reason for these trials.
      A conversation takes place in the heavenlies between God and Satan concerning Job. The devil sneeringly charges that Job only worships God because of two selfish benefits:
      a. Because God has given his servant much wealth.
      b. Because God has given his servant good health. Satan argues that if he could but remove these two elements, that Job would curse God to his face. Thus, to shut the devil's mouth, God gives him permission to remove both Job's wealth and health. It should be noted here that Satan cannot tempt a believer apart from God's specific permission.
B. His whimpering wife (2:9, 10).
   "Then said his wife unto him, Dost thou still retain thine integrity? Curse God, and die. But he said unto her, Thou speakest as one of the foolish women speaketh. What? Shall we receive good at the hand of God, and shall we not receive evil? In all this did not Job sin with his lips."
C. His fickle friends (4-37).
   It has been pointed out that his friends came to sympathize, but stayed on to sermonize. At any rate, Job's three "friends" delivered eight full-blown messages, all with three points and a poem, to the long-suffering patriarch. Eliphaz preached three of these (Job 4-5; 15; 22); Bildad, three (ch. 8; 18; 25); and Zophar, being less-winded, came up with two (11; 20). No sooner, however, had this tiresome trio finished than the filibuster began again by a young "preacher boy" named Elihu who drones on for six chapters (32-37). Perhaps at no other Bible conference in history have so many preachers preached to so few in attendance where the congregation enjoyed it less!

Following is a brief summary of their speeches and of Job's defense.

*The speeches of Eliphaz* (ch. 4, 5, 15, 22).
See Genesis 36:10.
   1. He claimed Job was suffering for his sins. "Remember, I pray thee, who ever perished, being innocent? Or where were the righteous cut off? Even as I have seen, they that plow iniquity, and sow wickedness, reap the same" (4:7, 8).
   "Thine own mouth condemneth thee, and not I: yea, thine own life testify against thee" (15:6).
   He then accuses Job of the following:
      a. That he had cheated the poor (22:6).
      b. That he had withheld bread from the hungry (22:7).
      c. That he had mistreated widows and orphans (22:9).
      d. That he was a windbag (15:2).
   2. He bases his conclusions on personal experience. (See 4:8, 12-16; 5:3, 27; 15:17.)
   3. He relates his night vision "ghost story" (4:12-17).
   4. He urges Job to repent and turn back to God (22:21-28). "If thou return to the Almighty, thou shalt be built up, thou shalt put away iniquity very far from thy tents" (22:23).

*The speeches of Bildad* (ch. 8; 18; 25).
   5. He claimed Job was suffering for his sins. "Behold, God will not cast away a perfect man, neither will he help the evildoers" (8:20).
   6. He bases his conclusions on tradition. "For inquire, I pray thee, of the former age, and prepare thyself to the search of their fathers" (8:8). (See also 8:9, 10.)
   7. He urges Job to repent and turn back to God. "If thou wouldest seek unto God betimes, and make thy supplication to the Almighty; If thou wert pure and upright; surely now he would awake for thee, and make the habitation of thy righteousness prosperous" (8:5, 6).

*The speeches of Zophar* (11:4, 5).
   8. He claimed Job was suffering for his sins. "For thou hast said, My doctrine is pure, and I am clean. . . . But oh, that God would speak, and open his lips against thee. . . . Know, therefore, that God exacteth of thee less than thine iniquity deserveth" (11:4-6).
   "Knowest thou not this of old, since man was placed upon the earth, that the triumphing of the wicked is short, and the joy of the hypocrite but for a moment" (20:4, 5).
   9. He bases his conclusions on sheer dogmatism. (See 11:6; 20:4.)
   10. He urges Job to repent and turn back to God. "If thou prepare thine heart, and stretch out thine hands toward him. If iniquity be in thine hand, put it far away, and let not wickedness dwell in thy tents. For then shalt thou lift up thy face without spot; yea, thou shalt be steadfast, and shalt not fear" (11:13-15).

*The speech of Elihu* (ch. 32-37).
   11. He waits awhile before speaking because of his youth (32:4-7).

12. However, once begun, he feels as confident and qualified to straighten out Job as the former three did. In fact, he actually suggests that he is the one whom Job seeks! "Behold, I am according to thy wish in God's stead; I also am formed out of the clay" (33:6).

13. Elihu is angry at all four, at Job because of his self-righteousness, and at the three friends because they had "found no answers, and yet had condemned Job" (32:3).

14. He accuses Job of both foolish speaking (34:35–37; 36:16) and false righteousness (35:2).

15. He exhorts Job to consider God's glory and his greatness (37:14–24).

D. The defenses and dialogues of Job.
The suffering patriarch responds to his accusers in nine separate speeches.

First: chapter 3; Second: 6–7; Third: 9–10;
Fourth: 12, 13, 14; Fifth: 16–17; Sixth: 19;
Seventh: 21; Eighth: 23–24; Ninth: 26–31

During these nine speeches Job discusses fourteen topics. These are:

1. I am righteous, and therefore not suffering for my sin (27:6; 31:1–30). "My righteousness I hold fast, and will not let it go; my heart shall not reproach me as long as I live" (27:6).

2. In the past I have performed many good works (29:12–17; 30:25).

3. Oh, for those good old days when I enjoyed health, wealth, and respect (29:1–11, 20–25).

4. But now I am being unfairly punished by God (9:16, 17, 30, 31, 32, 33; 13:26, 27; 10:2, 7, 8; 19:6–11; 30:20, 21).

5. My three so-called friends are miserable comforters (12:2; 13:4; 16:2; 19:3).

6. If they were in my place I would help them and not unjustly accuse them (16:4, 5).

7. Even my neighbors, associates, and servants have turned against me (19:13–22; 30:1, 9, 10).

8. I wish I could find the answers for all this (28:12–28).

9. I wish I could find God (23:8, 9).

10. My flesh is clothed with worms (7:5; 30:17, 18, 30).

11. I wish I had never been born (3:3–11, 16; 10:18).

12. I wish I were dead (6:8, 9; 7:15, 16).

13. I have no hope (10:20–22).

14. In spite of all, I'll trust God (13:15; 16:19; 23:10).

E. His glorious God (38–41).
Suddenly from out of a whirlwind comes the mighty voice of God. The sullen Job is then subjected to a sixty-question quiz. Note God's first series of questions (Job 38–39).

1. Job 38:4: "Where wast thou when I laid the foundations of the earth? Declare, if thou hast understanding."

2. Job 38:18: "Hast thou perceived the breadth of the earth? Declare if thou knowest it all."

3. Job 38:19: "Where is the way where light dwelleth? and as for darkness, where is the place thereof?"

4. Job 38:24: "By what way is the light parted, which scattereth the east wind upon the earth?"

5. Job 38:28: "Hath the rain a father? or who hath begotten the drops of dew?"

6. Job 40:2: "Shall he that contendeth with the Almighty instruct him? He that reproveth God, let him answer it."

Job's reply (40:4, 5): "Behold, I am vile; what shall I answer thee? I will lay mine hand upon my mouth. Once have I spoken; but I will not answer: yea, twice; but I will proceed no further."

God's second series of questions (40:6—41:34).

7. Job 40:15: "Behold now behemoth, which I made with thee; he eateth grass as an ox."

8. Job 41:1: "Canst thou draw out leviathan with an hook? Or his tongue with a cord which thou lettest down?"

Note: These two creatures may very well refer to a land dinosaur and a sea dinosaur.

Job's reply (42:1–5):
"I know that thou canst do every thing, and that no thought can be withholden from thee. Who is he that hideth counsel without knowledge? Therefore have I uttered that I understood not; things too wonderful for me, which I knew not. Hear, I beseech thee, and I will speak: I will demand of thee, and declare thou unto me. I have heard of thee by the hearing of the ear; but now mine eye seeth thee: Wherefore I abhor myself, and repent in dust and ashes."

F. His bountiful blessings (42:7–17).
Job has been subjected to five fiery trials and has participated in five painful debates, but now he receives at the hand of God a tenfold blessing.

1. He is allowed to see the glory of God.

2. He sees himself as God sees him. (This is always a blessing.)

3. He is vindicated by God before the eyes of his three critical friends.

4. He discovers the joy of praying for these three friends.

5. His former health is fully restored.

6. He is comforted by his brothers and sister.

7. He is given double his former wealth.

8. He is given seven more sons and three more daughters.

9. He lives to enjoy his grandchildren and great-grandchildren.

10. He is given an additional 140 years—twice the number normally accorded a man. (See Ps. 90:10.)

## CLASSIC STATEMENTS IN JOB

1. "He taketh the wise in their own craftiness . . . " (5:13). Quoted by Paul in 1 Corinthians 3:19.

2. "Behold, happy is the man whom God correcteth; therefore, despise not thou the chastening of the Almighty" (5:17). Quoted in Hebrews 12:5, 6.

3. "Neither is there any daysman between us that might lay his hand upon us both" (9:33). The word daysman refers to a mediator. In the New Testament of course, all this would change. See 1 Timothy 2:5.

4. "Man that is born of a woman is of few days, and full of trouble. He cometh forth like a flower, and is cut

# Job

## HIS TERRIBLE TRIALS

**Nature of trials (1-2)**
1. Oxen and donkeys stolen and farmhands killed
2. Sheep and herdsmen burned by fire
3. Camels are stolen and servants killed
4. Sons and daughters die in a mighty wind
5. Job himself is struck with boils

**Background of trials**
Job's motives for worshiping God had been challenged by Satan during a confrontation in the heavenlies.

A sovereign God thereupon allows the five trials.

## HIS WHIMPERING WIFE

"Then said his wife unto him, Dost thou still retain thine integrity? Curse God. and die" **(2:9).**

## HIS FICKLE FRIENDS

### ELIPHAZ
**SERMON LOCATION 4, 5, 15, 22**
**SERMON AUTHORITY** PERSONAL EXPERIENCE 4:8, 12-16
**SERMON CONCLUSION**
"You are suffering because of your sin!" **(4:7, 8; 15:6)**
1. You have cheated the poor **(22:6)**
2. You have not fed the hungry **(22:7)**
3. You have mistreated widows and orphans **(22:9)**
4. You are a windbag **(15:2)**
"My advice: Repent and turn back to God!" **(22:21-28)**

### BILDAD
**SERMON LOCATION 8, 18, 25**
**SERMON AUTHORITY** TRADITION 8:8-10
**SERMON CONCLUSION**
"You are suffering because of your sin!" **(8:20)**
"My advice: Repent and turn back to God!" **(8:5, 6)**

### ZOPHAR
**SERMON LOCATION 11, 20**
**SERMON AUTHORITY** DOGMATISM 11:6; 20:4
**SERMON CONCLUSION**
"You are suffering because of your sin!" **(11:4-6; 20:4, 5)**
"My advice: Repent and turn back to God!" **(11:13-15)**

### ELIHU
**SERMON LOCATION 32-37**
**SERMON AUTHORITY** Elihu thought he was God's answer to Job's problem 33:6
**SERMON CONCLUSION**
1. You are guilty of foolish speaking **(34:35-37; 36:16)**
2. You are guilty of false righteousness **(35:2)**
3. Consider God's glory and greatness **(37:14-24)**

## HIS DEFENSES and DIALOGUES

The suffering patriarch responds to his accusers in nine separate speeches.

| ONE **CHAPTER 3** | FOUR **12, 13, 14** | SEVEN **21** |
|---|---|---|
| TWO **6-7** | FIVE **16, 17** | EIGHT **23, 24** |
| THREE **9-10** | SIX **19** | NINE **26-31** |

**During these nine speeches Job discusses fourteen topics. These are:**
1. Righteousness and suffering (27:6; 31:1-40)
2. Good works (29:12-17; 30:25)
3. Health, wealth, and respect (29:1-11, 20-25)
4. Unfair punishment (9:16, 17, 30-33; 13:26, 27; 10:2, 7, 8; 19:6-11; 30:20, 21)
5. So-called friends (12:2; 13:4; 16:2; 19:3)
6. "If they were in my place" (16:4, 5)
7. False neighbors, associates, and servants (19:13-22; 30:1, 9, 10)
8. Answers (28:12-28)
9. God (23:8, 9)
10. The flesh (7:5, 13, 14; 30:17, 18, 30)
11. "I wish I had never been born" (3:3-11, 16; 10:18)
12. "I wish I were dead" (6:8, 9; 7:15, 16)
13. "I have no hope" (10:20-22)
14. "In spite of all, I'll trust God" (13:15; 16:19; 23:10)

## HIS GLORIOUS GOD

**Suddenly from out of a whirlwind comes the mighty voice of God. The sullen Job is then subjected to a quiz:**

**GOD'S FIRST SERIES OF QUESTIONS: JOB 38-39**

1. **JOB 38:4** "Where wast thou when I laid the foundations of the earth? Declare, if thou hast understanding."
2. **JOB 38:18** "Hast thou perceived the breadth of the earth? Declare if thou knowest it all."
3. **JOB 38:19** "Where is the way where light dwelleth? And as for darkness, where is the place thereof?"
4. **JOB 38:24** "By what way is the light parted, which scattereth the east wind upon the earth?"
5. **JOB 38:28** "Hath the rain a father? Or who hath begotten the drops of dew?"
6. **JOB 40:2** "Shall he that contendeth with the Almighty instruct him? He that reproveth God, let him answer it."

**JOB'S REPLY: 40:4, 5**

**GOD'S SECOND SERIES OF QUESTIONS: JOB 40:6—41:33**

1. **JOB 40:15** "Behold now the behemoth, which I made with thee; he eateth grass as an ox."
2. **JOB 41:1** "Canst thou draw out leviathan with an hook? or his tongue with a cord which thou lettest down?"
   NOTE: These two creatures may very well refer to a land dinosaur and a sea dinosaur.

**JOB'S REPLY: 42:1-5**

## HIS BOUNTIFUL BLESSINGS

**JOB 42:7-17**

**Job has been subjected to five fiery trials and has participated in five painful debates, but now he receives at the hand of God a tenfold blessing**
1. He is allowed to see the glory of God.
2. He sees himself as God sees him. (This is always a blessing.)
3. He is vindicated by God before the eyes of his three critical friends.
4. He discovers the joy of praying for these three friends.
5. His former health is fully restored.
6. He is comforted by his brothers and sister.
7. He is given double his former wealth.
8. He is given seven more sons and three more daughters.
9. He lives to enjoy his grandchildren and great-grandchildren.
10. He is given an additional 140 years—twice the number normally accorded a man. **(See Ps. 90:10.)**

## Some reasons for Job's sufferings
1. That Satan might be silenced **(1:9-11; 2:4, 5).**
2. That Job might see God **(42:5).**
3. That Job might see himself **(40:4; 42:6).**
4. That Job's friends might learn not to judge **(42:7).**
5. That Job might learn to pray for, rather than to lash out against, his critics **(42:10).**
6. To demonstrate that all God's plans for his own eventually have happy endings **(42:10).**

down; he fleeth also as a shadow, and continueth not" (14:1, 2).

5. "They have gaped upon me with their mouth; they have smitten me upon the cheek reproachfully; they have gathered themselves together against me. God hath delivered me to the ungodly, and turned me over into the hands of the wicked" (16:10, 11).

These words are repeated (in paraphrase fashion) in Psalms 22:13; 35:21, in reference to the sufferings of Christ on the cross.

6. "Also now, behold, my witness is in heaven, and my record is on high" (16:19).

7. "But he knoweth the way that I take; when he hath tested me, I shall come forth as gold" (23:10).

8. "He stretcheth out the north over the empty place, and hangeth the earth upon nothing" (26:7).

9. "Oh, that I knew where I might find him, that I might come even to his seat!" (23:3). This problem was solved through the *incarnation* of Christ. See John 1:18, 45.

10. "How then can man be justified with God? Or how can he be clean that is born of a woman?" (25:4). Problem solved through the *death* of Christ. See Romans 4:24, 25; 5:1.

11. "If a man die, shall he live again?" (14:14). Problem solved through the *resurrection* of Christ.

12. "For I know that my redeemer liveth, and that he shall stand at the latter day upon the earth: And though after my skin worms destroy this body, yet in my flesh shall I see God" (19:25, 26).

## SOME REASONS FOR JOB'S SUFFERINGS

1. That Satan might be silenced (1:9–11; 2:4, 5).
2. That Job might see God (42:5).
3. That Job might see himself (40:4; 42:6).
4. That Job's friends might learn not to judge (42:7).
5. That Job might learn to pray for, rather than to lash out against his critics (42:10).
6. To demonstrate that all God's plans for his own eventually have happy endings (42:10).

## INTRODUCING THE EXODUS STAGE
### (Exodus, Leviticus, Numbers, Deuteronomy)

1. The four most important men during this stage are: Moses, Aaron, Caleb, and Joshua.
2. The Exodus Stage covers a period of some 325 years.
3. It includes the following key events:
   a. The captivity and deliverance of Israel from Egypt by Moses (Ex. 1-14).
   b. The failure of Israel to enter the Promised Land because of unbelief (Num. 13-14).
   c. The appearance of the manna (Ex. 16:14), the institution of the Sabbath (Ex. 16:23-30), and the giving of the Ten Commandments (Ex. 20:3-17).
   d. The building of the tabernacle (Ex. 40).
   e. The aimless wandering in the wilderness (Num. 14:33, 34).
   f. The sin and death of Moses (Num. 20:7-13; Deut. 34:5-8).
   g. The choice of Joshua as Israel's new leader (Num. 27:15-23; Deut. 34:9).
4. Here we read of a bloody river, a backed up sea, and a bitter brook (Ex. 7, 14, 15).
5. We are told of a golden calf, a talking ass, and a bronze snake (Ex. 23; Num. 22; 21).
6. We see a burning bush in the desert and a bright cloud in the sky (Ex. 3, 13).
7. Here Moses ascends to the pleasures of heaven (Ex. 33) while Korah descends to the pits of hell (Num. 16).

## THE EXODUS STAGE

I. Israel, Enslaved in Egypt (Ex. 1:1—12:36).
   A. God's people.
      1. After the death of Joseph there arose a new king over Egypt, "which knew not Joseph" (1:8).
      2. This king cruelly persecuted Israel, enslaved them, and ordered the death of all male Hebrew babies (1:10-16).
   B. God's grace.
      "And God heard their groaning, and God remembered his covenant with Abraham, with Isaac, and with Jacob. And God looked upon the children of Israel, and God had respect unto them" (2:24, 25).
   C. God's man.
      1. The prince of Egypt.
         a. Moses is born of godly parents, hidden for three months, and then set afloat in a basket on the Nile River (2:3).
         b. Moses is discovered by Pharaoh's daughter and, upon the advice of Miriam (Moses' sister, who had watched all this), secures the nursing services of his own mother (2:8, 9).
         c. Moses grows up in Pharaoh's court, but at the age of forty flees the land of Egypt. This he does:
            (1) Because of his involvement in murder. Moses slays an Egyptian who is beating a Hebrew slave (2:12).
            (2) Because of his involvement with the Messiah—Hebrews 11:24-26: "By faith Moses, when he was come to years, refused to be called the son of Pharaoh's daughter; choosing rather to suffer affliction with the people of God, than to enjoy the pleasures of sin for a season."
      2. The shepherd of Midian.
         a. Moses finds refuge in Midian and marries Zipporah, the daughter of Jethro, and lives the next forty years as a shepherd (2:21).
         b. Moses receives his divine call from the burning bush to deliver Israel (3:1-10). The command was: "Draw not nigh hither: put off thy shoes from off thy feet, for the place whereon thou standest is holy ground" (3:5).
            Note: Moses was told to take his shoes off at this time, for he was on holy ground. This he did. But it should be observed that he later put them back on again. All too often Christians hear God speak to them concerning special service for him. They take their spiritual shoes off at some church altar, perhaps, but then do nothing about that call. God needs individuals who will both take off and put back on their shoes today. A worship experience should be followed by a working experience.
         c. He resisted this call, listing five lame excuses why he could not perform God's command:
            (1) I have no ability (3:11).
            (2) I have no message (3:13).
            (3) I have no authority 4:1).
            (4) I have no eloquence (4:10).
            (5) I have no inclination (4:13).
         d. God answered all these arguments for Moses, just as he does today for those whom he calls for service. Thus:
            (1) The objection, "I have no ability" is answered by Philippians 4:13.

(2) The objection, "I have no message" is answered by 1 Corinthians 15:3, 4.

(3) The objection, "I have no authority" is answered by Matthew 28:18-20.

(4) The objection, "I have no eloquence" is answered by Philippians 2:13.

(5) The objection, "I have no inclination" is answered by Philippians 2:13.

e. God answers all these arguments and gives Moses a twofold demonstration of his powers (4:2-7).

  (1) His shepherd's rod temporarily becomes a snake.

  (2) His right hand temporarily becomes leprous.

f. God graciously allows Moses to take his older brother Aaron with him (4:14, 15).

g. Moses had carelessly neglected to circumcise his own son, Gershom, which was a serious blunder on his part. Zipporah finally steps in at the last minute and saves Moses from divine judgment (4:24-26).

D. God's enemy.

1. Pharaoh not only refuses to free Israel, but puts more work upon the slaves, making them gather their own straws to make the bricks (5:1-9).

2. Pharaoh's treatment embitters the leaders of Israel against Moses, who complains to God and is reassured (5:20—6:8).

E. God's plagues.

1. Moses (now eighty) and Aaron (eighty-three) work their first miracle against Pharaoh, causing a rod to become a snake (7:10).

2. The Pharaoh's magicians (Jannes and Jambres—see 2 Tim. 3:8) perform the same trick, but see their snakes swallowed up by Moses' snake (7:12).

3. Moses calls down the ten plagues.

  a. First plague—water into blood (7:20).

  b. Second plague—a frog invasion (8:6).

  c. Third plague—lice (8:17).

  d. Fourth plague—flies (8:24).

  e. Fifth plague—cattle disease (9:6).

  f. Sixth plague—boils (9:10).

  g. Seventh plague—hail mingled with fire (9:24).

  h. Eighth plague—locusts (10:13).

  i. Ninth plague—a three-day darkness (10:22).

  j. Tenth plague—slaying of the firstborn (12:29).

4. Pharaoh offers Moses four compromises during these plagues, but all are refused.

  a. First compromise—don't leave, but do your thing here in Egypt (8:25).

  b. Second compromise—leave, but don't go too far (8:28).

  c. Third compromise—leave, but allow your children to remain here (10:10).

  d. Fourth compromise—leave, but without your flocks and herds (10:24).

5. Pharaoh's heart is hardened some eleven times during this period. We note that on at least seven occasions in the book of Exodus we are told that God hardened the heart of Pharaoh (see 4:21; 7:3; 9:12; 10:1, 20, 27; 11:10). How are we to understand this? A partial (and only partial) answer may be found in the following observation: The manner in which a given object will react when confronted by an outside influence is wholly dependent upon the nature of that object. For example, imagine a winter scene. Yonder is a frozen river. On either side is a bank of yellow clay. Suddenly the sun comes from behind the clouds and shines brightly down upon the river and the banks. What happens next? The reaction is this—the ice will melt but the clay will harden. Thus we see in nature the same outside and heavenly influence softening one object but hardening the other. Furthermore it should be pointed out that on four occasions we are informed that Pharaoh hardened his own heart. (See Ex. 7:22; 8:15, 19; 9:35.)

F. God's salvation (Ex. 11-12).

At this point let us summarize briefly both the nature and purpose of these plagues.

1. The nature of the plagues:

  a. The turning of the Egyptian waters into blood (7:20). Some have attempted to view this plague as the result of a natural event, such as the polluting of the Nile by excessive red soil or the sudden increase of certain bacteria microcosms, but it is doubtful if such natural occurrences would make the slightest impression upon the watching Pharaoh.

  b. The vast horde of frogs (8:2).

Dr. John David quotes Harry Rimmer, who writes: "Like the blanket of filth the slimy, wet monstrosities covered the land, until men sickened at the continued squashing crunch of the ghastly pavement they were forced to walk upon. If a man's feet slipped on the greasy mass of putrid uncleanness, and when he sought water to cleanse himself, the water was so solid with frogs, he got no cleansing there." (*Moses and the Gods of Egypt*, p. 101)

  c. The lice (8:16).

Some Hebrew scholars believe a more accurate translation here is "gnats," or "mosquitoes." Small insects have always been a problem in Egypt. Many devices were constructed by the ancient Egyptians in an attempt to get relief from them (such as ostrich plumes on the end of a stick which would be waved by servants to keep such insects away from the faces of the king and lords; floors and walls were often washed with a solution of soda).

  d. The swarm of flies (8:24).

This may have been the large bloodsucking dog fly.

e. The grievous murrain cattle disease (9:3). This plague doubtless had grave economic and religious consequences for the Egyptians. Oxen were depended upon for heavy labor in agriculture, while camels, asses, and horses were used for transportation. Cattle not only provided milk, but the bull was one of the most sacred objects in the worship services of the land.

f. The blains and boils (9:10). The Hebrew language indicates these were leprous, pus-filled, open, and running sores.

g. The hail mingled with fire (9:24). This crushing hailstorm was possibly accompanied by severe lightning which set fires to the Egyptian fields already ruined by the massive icy pellets from heaven. Because of the first of six plagues, some of the Egyptians apparently believed the word of God and brought their cattle and slaves in from the field (9:20).

h. The invasion of locusts (10:13). A locust is capable of eating its own weight daily and one square mile of a swarm will normally contain up to 200 million of the creatures. Swarms covering more than 400 square miles have been recorded. A plague this size would carry some eighty billion locusts.

i. The three-day darkness (10:22). This plague was surely the most frightening of all that had previously fallen. The darkness was so complete it could actually be felt. For seventy-two agonizing hours this horrifying blackness deprived its victims of food, water, and the slightest freedom of movement. More than one mind must have snapped under its terrible torture.

j. The death angel visitation (12:29). God instructs Israel on preparing for that first Passover. An unblemished year-old male lamb was to be selected by each family on the tenth of April. This animal was to be killed on the fourteenth day. Its blood was to be drained into a basin. A cluster of hyssop branches was to be dipped into the basin and blood smeared against the lintel and two side panels of the door. The flesh of the lamb was to be roasted and eaten on the night of the fourteenth along with bitter herbs and unleavened bread.

Note: This is the first mention of leaven in the Bible, and from this point on it becomes a symbol of evil. In the New Testament, leaven stands for:
(1) Hypocrisy (Lk. 12:1)
(2) Rationalism (Mt. 16:6, 12)
(3) Worldliness (Mk. 8:15)
(4) Evil conduct (1 Cor. 5:6)
(5) False doctrine (Gal. 5:9)

The Passover lamb was of course a beautiful type and foreshadow of the Lord Jesus Christ. (See Jn. 1:29; 1 Cor. 5:6, 7; 1 Pet. 1:18, 19.) The hyssop here may represent faith. It was a common plant of the field. As the hyssop plant was used to apply the lamb's blood in the Old Testament, so faith applies the blood to the human heart in the New Testament. (See Eph. 2:8, 9.) It should be observed, however, that the mere death of the lamb did not automatically save anyone *until* the shed blood was applied.

Israel ate unleavened bread that night, and were to do this each April to remind them of their great deliverance (12:39–51).

2. The purpose of the plagues. The purpose of the plagues was apparently twofold:
a. To demonstrate to Israel the strength of their God.
b. To show the Egyptians the total inability of their gods. It may be observed that each plague was directed against a particular Egyptian god. Thus:

# 1
## ISRAEL, ENSLAVED IN EGYPT

**GOD'S PEOPLE:** Persecuted by a Pharaoh who did not know Joseph **(Ex. 1)**
**GOD'S GRACE:** He remembered his covenant with Abraham and heard their cries **(2:23-25)**

**GOD'S MAN:**

# MOSES

**HIS FIRST FORTY YEARS AS A PRINCE IN EGYPT** (2:1-14)
● He is rescued by an Egyptian princess as a baby
● Later he rescues an Israeli slave
**HIS SECOND FORTY YEARS AS A SHEPHERD IN MIDIAN** (2:15—4:31)
● He marries a girl named Zipporah
● He receives his "burning bush" call
**GOD'S ENEMY:** Pharaoh refuses to free the Jews and increases their work burden **(Ex. 5:2, 4-9)**
**GOD'S PLAGUES: EXODUS 7-10**
PURPOSE
1. To show Israel their true God.
2. To show Egypt their false gods.

| NATURE | EGYPTIAN GOD DEFEATED | |
|---|---|---|
| 1. Water into blood | OSIRIS | Exodus 7:20 |
| 2. A frog invasion | HEKT | 8:6 |
| 3. Lice | SEB | 8:17 |
| 4. Flies | HATKOK | 8:24 |
| 5. Cattle disease | APIS | 9:6 |
| 6. Boils | TYPHON | 9:10 |
| 7. Hail with fire | SHU | 9:24 |
| 8. Locust | SERAPIA | 10:13 |
| 9. Three-day darkness | RA | 10:22 |
| 10. Death of firstborn | ALL gods | 12:29 |

**GOD'S CHOICE**

| FACT | REASON |
|---|---|
| ● That the firstborn be sanctified | ● He wanted a nation of priests. |
| ● That the southern route be taken | ● Israel needed to spend time with him. |

(1) The first plague of bloody waters was directed against Osiris, the god of the Nile.

(2) The second plague of frogs was against the frog goddess Hekt.

(3) The third plague of lice was against Seb, the earth god.

(4) The fourth plague of beetles (or flies) was against Hatkok, the wife of Osiris.

(5) The fifth plague of cattle disease was against Apis, the sacred bull god.

(6) The sixth plague, boils, was against Typhon.

(7) The seventh plague, hail and fire, was against Shu, the god of the atmosphere.

(8) The eighth plague, locusts, was against Serapia, the god who protected Egypt against locusts.

(9) The ninth plague, darkness, was against Ra, the sun god.

(10) The tenth plague, the death of the firstborn, was an attack on *all* gods.

3. The result of the final plague.

    a. At midnight, April 14, the death angel passes over Egypt, taking the firstborn sons from all unprotected homes, including the household of Pharaoh himself.

    b. During the early morning hours of the fifteenth, all Israel (600,000 men plus their families) cross the border of Egypt.

    c. They are accompanied by a mixed multitude.

G. God's selection.

    1. The sanctification of the firstborn—God originally planned for a nation of priests, but finally, due to Israel's constant sin, limited his selection to the tribe of Levi (Ex. 13:2; 19:6; Num. 8:16).

    2. The selection of the safer route (13:17).

II. Israel, En Route to Mt. Sinai (Ex. 12:37—18:27).

Ten key events took place between Rameses, their departure city in Egypt, and the arrival at the base of Mt. Sinai. The distance was approximately 150 miles. These events are:

A. The appearance of God's shekinah glory cloud (13:21, 22).

From Succoth to Etham. At Etham the pillar of cloud and fire is manifested to lead Israel by day or night. This marks the first appearance of the shekinah, that visible and luminous indication of God's presence (13:21, 22). Other Old Testament and New Testament appearances would include:

    1. At the Red Sea (Ex. 10:19, 20).

    2. In the tabernacle Holy of Holies (Lev. 16:2).

    3. In the Temple Holy of Holies (2 Chron. 5:11-13).

    4. Disappearance in Ezekiel's time (Ezek. 10).

    5. At the birth of Christ (Lk. 2:9-11).

    6. On the Mount of Transfiguration (Mt. 17:5).

    7. At the Ascension (Acts 1:9).

    8. At the rapture (1 Thess. 4:17).

    9. At the Second Coming (Mt. 24:30; Mk. 8:38).

    10. During the millennium (Isa. 4:5, 6; 60:19).

B. The chase by Pharaoh, who had regretted his action of letting Israel go (14:5-10).

From Etham to Pi-hahiroth (14:1-4).

    1. The decision of Pharaoh—to follow up. Pharaoh regrets his decision to free Israel and determines to fall upon them and recapture them in the desert near the Red Sea through his crack chariot corps.

    2. The despair of the people (Ex. 14:11, 12) to give up.

    3. The declaration of the prophet (Ex. 14:13, 14) to look up.

C. The parting of the Red Sea (14:13-31).

D. The subsequent celebration of Israel over their deliverance and the destruction of Pharaoh's armies (15:1-21).

From Pi-hahiroth through the Red Sea (14:15—15:21).

    1. The cloudy pillar—protecting. This is the second greatest miracle in all the Bible. The greatest of course is the resurrection of Christ from the dead—see Ephesians 1:20. The Red Sea crossing is mentioned many times in the Word of God. See Psalm 78:53; 106:11, 12, 22; Hebrews 11:29. This miracle was actually threefold in nature:

      a. The first part was the shift in position of the glory cloud which placed itself between the camp of the Israelites and that of the Egyptians. It then settled down upon Pharaoh's armies like a fog, but gave light to God's people.

      b. The second part was the actual dividing of the waters, clearing a path of perhaps a mile wide. Concerning this, Dr. Leon Wood writes:

        "A marching line of 2,000,000 people, walking ten abreast with an average five feet separating each rank, would be 190 miles long. Had this path been only as wide as a modern highway, the first Israelites through would have been in Canaan before the last started, and several days would have elapsed." (*A Survey of Israel's History*, p. 133)

      c. The third part was the actual closing of the water.

    2. The Red Sea parting.

    "And Moses stretched out his hand over the sea; and the Lord caused the sea to go back by a strong east wind all that night, and made the sea dry land, and the waters were divided" (14:21).

    3. The Egyptian army perishing.

    "And the waters returned, and covered the chariots, and the horsemen, and all the host of Pharaoh that came into the sea after them; there remained not so much as one of them" (14:28).

    4. The Lord's people praising.

    "Then sang Moses and the children of Israel this song unto the Lord, and spake, saying, I will sing unto the Lord, for he hath triumphed gloriously: the horse and his rider hath he thrown into the sea" (Ex. 15:1).

E. Marah's bitter waters made sweet by the casting in of a tree (15:22-26). God at this time promised them freedom from sickness if they would but obey him.

From the Red Sea to Marah (15:22-26).
1. The galling water.
"And when they came to Marah, they could not drink of the waters of Marah, for they were bitter: therefore the name of it was called Marah" (15:23).
2. The goodly tree.
"And he cried unto the Lord; and the Lord shewed him a tree, which when he had cast into the waters, the waters were made sweet: there he made for them a statute and an ordinance, and there he proved them" (Ex. 15:25).
3. The Great Physician.
"And said, If thou wilt diligently hearken to the voice of the Lord thy God, and wilt do that which is right in his sight, and wilt give ear to his commandments, and keep all his statutes, I will put none of these diseases upon thee, which I have brought upon the Egyptians: for I am the Lord that healeth thee" (Ex. 15:26).
From Marah to Elim (Ex. 15:27).
"And they came to Elim where were twelve wells of water and threescore and ten palm trees: and they encamped there by the waters."

F. The giving of the manna (16:4, 14, 35).
This heavenly bread would become their staple diet for the next forty years.
From Elim to the Wilderness of Zin (16:1-36).
1. The complaining crowd.
"And the whole congregation of the children of Israel murmured against Moses and Aaron in the wilderness: And the children of Israel said unto them, would to God we had died by the hand of the Lord in the land of Egypt, when we sat by the flesh pots, and when we did eat bread to the full; for ye have brought us forth into this wilderness, to kill this whole assembly with hunger" (Ex. 16:2, 3).
2. The miraculous manna (16:14, 15).
Beginning now and continuing for the next forty years God would feed them six days a week with manna, a white, flat, coriander-like seed which tasted like honey bread. It would only cease when Israel entered the Promised Land. (See Josh. 5:12.)
It was to be picked up each morning and eaten that same day for six days, and on the sixth, a double portion was to be taken for the seventh, when no manna would fall. The word manna in the Hebrew literally means, "What is it?" This is what the people said when they first saw it, and the name stuck. Jesus would later apply this event to his own ministry. (See Jn. 6:30-63.) Dr. John Davis writes the following helpful words on the subject of manna:
"It should not be assumed from these passages that manna constituted the only part of the diet of the Hebrews during the forty-year period. We know that the Is-

raelites had sheep and cattle (12:38; 17:3) and they continued to possess these not only in Sinai (34:3) but had them when they reached Edom and the country east of the Jordan (Num. 20:19; 32:1). It appears that on some occasions the Hebrews bought food and even water from the Edomites (Deut. 2:6, 7). That wheat and meats were available is clearly implied in such references as Exodus 17:3; 24:5; Leviticus 8:2, 26, 31; 9:4; 10:12; 24:5; and Numbers 7:13, 19." (*Moses and the Gods of Egypt*, p. 181)

G. The institution of the Sabbath (16:23, 26-30; 31:13).
The solemn Sabbath (16:23-30).
"See, for that the Lord hath given you the sabbath, therefore he giveth you on the sixth day the bread of two days; abide ye every man in his place, let no man go out of his place on the seventh day. So the people rested on the seventh day" (Ex. 16:29, 30).
Following is a brief summary on the biblical teaching concerning the Sabbath:
1. Sabbath first mentioned in Exodus 16:23. For the first 2500 years of human history no one observed it but God himself. (See Gen. 2:2.)
2. Sabbath was then given to Israel (Ex. 31:13, 17) who previously knew *nothing* about it whatsoever. (See Ex. 16:29.) This day was never given to the church (see Col. 2:16; Gal. 4:9-11).
3. Sabbath is not a Hebrew word for seven but means "Rest or cessation." Hebrew words for seven are *sheba* and *shibah*. Thus, a literal translation of the fourth commandment would read, "Remember the rest day, to keep it holy."
4. There were many "Sabbaths" given to Israel:
   a. The weekly seventh day Sabbath (Ex. 20:8-11).
      (1) It began at sundown on Friday and ended at sundown Saturday.
      (2) It was a day of absolute rest, with no services or gatherings.
   b. The first day of the seventh month Sabbath (Lev. 23:24, 25), feast of trumpets.
   c. The tenth day of the seventh month Sabbath (Lev. 16:29, 30), day of atonement.
   d. The fifteenth day of the seventh month Sabbath (Lev. 23:34), feast of tabernacles.
   e. The seventh year Sabbath (Lev. 25:1-4), land was to be idle for entire year.
   f. The fiftieth year Sabbath (Lev. 25:8).
      The seventy-year Babylonian captivity was primarily due to Israel's disobedience to observe these rest years. In approximately 500 years they had accumulated until Israel owed the Promised Land seventy rest years. (See Lev. 26:27-35; 2 Chron. 36:21; Jer. 25:11.)
5. Sabbath had never been changed but has been set aside because the nation Israel has been set aside. (See Mt. 21:43.)
6. The Sabbath will be observed again during the kingdom age. (See Isa. 66:23.)

Question: Where then does the church receive authority to worship on Sunday?

Answer: This authority was laid out in pattern form through the resurrection, which occurred on the first day—Sunday. This fact is reported by all four Gospels (Mt. 28:1; Mk. 16:2, 9; Lk. 24:1, 13; Jn. 20:1, 19). Thus, as the seventh day commemorates a finished creation (Ex. 20:8-11), so the first day commemorates a finished redemption. (See Acts 20:7; 1 Cor. 16:1, 2; Heb. 7:12.) It is true that Paul often preached to the Jews on the Sabbath (Acts 13:14; 16:13; 17:2; 18:4), but he only did so because this was the day the Jews regularly gathered together. (See 1 Cor. 9:19, 20.)

H. Striking the rock at Rephidim (17:1-7). This was done to provide water, which God supernaturally gave from the side of that rock. Nearly forty years later Moses will strike another rock in a distant place, but at that time he will be out of God's will. (See Num. 20:7-13.)

From the Wilderness to Rephidim (Ex. 17:1-18:27).

Moses strikes the rock (17:6). The fickle Israelites were almost ready to stone Moses because of their thirst when God stepped in. "Behold, I will stand before thee there upon the rock in Horeb; and thou shalt smite the rock, and there shall come water out of it that the people may drink. . . ."

## 2 ISRAEL, EN ROUTE TO MT. SINAI   EXODUS 12-18

**A. APPEARANCE OF GLORY CLOUD (EX. 13:21, 22)**
The first of ten biblical appearances

**B. CHASE BY PHARAOH (14:5-10)**
The decision of the Pharaoh—to follow up
The despair of the people—to give up
The declaration of the prophet—to look up

**C. THE MIRACLE AT THE RED SEA (14:13—15:21)**
The cloudy pillar—*PROTECTING*
The Red Sea—*PARTING*
The Egyptian army—*PERISHING*
The Lord's people—*PRAISING*

**D. THE EPISODE AT MARAH (15:22-26)**
The galling waters
The good tree
The Great Physician

**E. THE GIVING OF MANNA (16:4, 14, 35)**
The sarcastic crowd
The supernatural food

**F. THE INSTITUTION OF THE SABBATH (16:23, 26-30)**
Given to Israel as a spiritual wedding ring
Commemorated a finished creation

**G. THE WATER-FILLED ROCK (17:1-7)**
In obedience Moses strikes this rock
In disobedience he will later strike another rock
(See **Num. 20:7-13**)

**H. VICTORY OVER THE AMALEKITES (FOUR "FIRSTS" NOW OCCUR) (17:8-16)**
First mention of Joshua
First intercession of Moses for Israel
First part of Bible to be written (?)
First reference to God as *Jehovah-Nissi*

**I. MOSES REUNITED WITH HIS FAMILY (18:5)**
He greets his father-in-law, wife, and two sons

I. Israel's Victory over the Amalekites (Ex. 17:8-16). Here four important "firsts" should be noted:

1. The first mention of Joshua, who was selected by Moses to lead the armies of Israel (17:9).
2. The first prayer of Moses for Israel (17:11, 12).
3. The first part of the Bible to be written (17:14).
4. The first reference to one of God's great names—*Jehovah-nissi* (the Lord is my banner). (See 17:15.)

Moses smites an enemy (17:11). The enemy—the Amalekites. These descendants of Esau (Gen. 36:12), a roving and raiding desert band, had probably been tracking Israel for some time now, and chose this moment to strike (17:8).

The general—Joshua. This is the first mention of one of the most remarkable military men who ever lived. In spite of his youth (probably in his early twenties), Moses chose him to head up Israel's fighting forces. His ability and bravery were matched by his love for God (17:9).

The intercessor—Moses. This grand old man ascends a nearby hill, extends his arms upward, and begins praying for Joshua and Israel fighting below (17:11).

The helpers—Aaron and Hur. These two aided Moses in keeping his weary arms heavenward so that God could give victory below. Israel is victorious, one of the first sections of the Bible is written, and Moses builds an altar to God, calling it *Jehovah-nissi,* meaning "Jehovah is my Flag."

J. The meeting of Moses with his family (18:5). Moses salutes his family (18:7).

1. He is greeted by Jethro, Zipporah, and his two sons Gershom and Eliezer.
2. At Jethro's advice, Moses appoints capable men to help him judge the problems of Israel (18:17-27).

III. Israel, Settled down at Sinai (Ex. 19:1—Num. 10:10). On June 15, 1445 B.C., Israel arrived at Mt. Sinai. They would be there for eleven months and five days (Num. 10:11). Three major events took place during this time. These are:

The commandment of the law (requirement for fellowship).

The corruption of the golden calf (ruination of that fellowship).

The construction of the tabernacle (restoration of that fellowship).

We shall now look at an introduction *to* and a consideration *of* these three events.

A. An introduction to the action at Mt. Sinai.

1. Israel arrives at Mt. Sinai and is given notice that God will meet with them in three days. They are therefore to wash their clothes and prepare their hearts (Ex. 19:9, 10).
2. On the third day, God manifests himself on Mt. Sinai, accompanied by thunderings, lightnings, a thick cloud, the voice of a trumpet, an earthquake, smoke, and fire (Ex. 19:16-18).

3. Moses is ordered to climb Mt. Sinai to meet God. At this time, God gives him orally both the Ten Commandments and the seventy laws which compose the Book of the Covenant. Moses then descends the mountain and repeats God's words to Israel (Ex. 19:20—23:33).

4. The people agree to all that God has told Moses (24:3).

5. Moses then writes down for Israel's record all that he has told them, builds an altar of twelve pillars, and sacrifices blood upon it to satisfy this covenant agreement (24:4-8).

6. Moses once again ascends the mountain and this time is accompanied part way by Joshua (24:13).

7. Here he will spend the next forty days, at which time he will receive the pattern for the tabernacle and two tables of stone written by God himself and containing the Ten Commandments. During this entire period, Moses fasts (Ex. 24:18; 31:18; 34:28; Deut. 9:9).

8. He then is warned to get down immediately to deal with the golden calf episode below (Ex. 32:7).

9. He prays for Israel that God would not destroy her (Ex. 32:11-13).

10. He picks up Joshua halfway down (Ex. 32:17).

11. Upon viewing Israel's terrible immorality, he breaks into pieces the stones containing the Ten Commandments (Ex. 32:19).

12. He rebukes Aaron and judges Israel the second time (32:20-29).

13. He prays for Israel the second time (32:30-32).

14. He then fasts for the next forty days (Deut. 9:18).

15. He again ascends the mountain and is ordered by God to carve out two new rocks, upon which the Lord rewrites the Ten Commandments (Deut. 10:2).

16. He is commanded to make an ark-box of shittim wood and to place the two tablets of stone in this box. Moses then returns to the valley below with the ark (Deut. 10:5).

17. Moses asks to see the glory of God. The Lord replies:

"And he said, I will make all my goodness pass before thee, and I will proclaim the name of the Lord before thee; and I will be gracious to whom I will be gracious, and will shew mercy on whom I will shew mercy. And he said, Thou canst not see my face: for there shall no man see me, and live. And the Lord said, Behold there is a place by me, and thou shalt stand upon a rock. And it shall come to pass, while my glory passeth by, that I will put thee in a clift of the rock, and will cover thee with my hand while I pass by. And I will take away mine hand, and thou shalt see my back parts: but my face shall not be seen" (Ex. 33:19-23).

B. A consideration of the action at Mt. Sinai.
*The Commandment of the Law.* There were three basic sections of the Mosaic Law.

1. The moral code. This section is commonly known as the Ten Commandments (Ex. 20:3-17; Deut. 5:7-21).
   a. Thou shalt have no other gods before me.
   b. Thou shalt not make unto thee any graven image.
   c. Thou shalt not take the name of the Lord thy God in vain.
   d. Remember the Sabbath day to keep it holy.
   e. Honor thy father and thy mother.
   f. Thou shalt not kill.
   g. Thou shalt not commit adultery.
   h. Thou shalt not steal.
   i. Thou shalt not bear false witness.
   j. Thou shalt not covet.

2. The spiritual code. This section deals with the ordinances, all of which foreshadow Christ and salvation. (See Heb. 10:1.) It includes the Levitical feasts, offerings, etc. (Ex. 35-40; Lev.).

3. The social code. This section deals with the judgments and divine laws of God's new establishment for Israel. It includes rules for diet, sanitation, quarantine, soil conservation, taxation, military service, marriage, divorce, etc.

   There are some seventy basic regulations in the social code. Of these, twenty of the more important are as follows:
   a. "And if a man smite his servant, or his maid, with a rod, and he die under his hand; he shall be surely punished (Ex. 21:20).
   b. "And he that smiteth his father, or his mother, shall surely be put to death" (21:15).
   c. "And he that stealeth a man, and selleth him, or if he be bound in his hand, he shall surely be put to death" (21:16).
   d. "Eye for eye, tooth for tooth, hand for hand, foot for foot" (21:24).
   e. "And he that curseth his father, or his mother, shall surely be put to death" (21:17).
   f. "And if a man smite the eye of his servant, or the eye of his maid, that it perish; he shall let him go free for his eye's sake" (21:26).

# 3
## ISRAEL, SETTLED DOWN AT SINAI

## Three main events occurring at Sinai
1. **EXODUS 20:3-17**
   **THE COMMANDMENTS OF THE LAW**
   Requirement for divine fellowship
2. **EXODUS 32**
   **THE CORRUPTION OF THE CALF**
   Ruination of divine fellowship
3. **EXODUS 25-31, 35-40**
   **CONSTRUCTION OF THE TABERNACLE**
   Restoration to divine fellowship

g. "If a man shall steal an ox, or a sheep, and kill it, or sell it; he shall restore five oxen for an ox, and four sheep for a sheep" (22:1).

h. "And if a man entice a maid that is not betrothed, and lie with her, he shall surely endow her to be his wife" (22:16).

i. "Thou shalt not suffer a witch to live" (22:18).

j. "Whosoever lieth with a beast shall surely be put to death" (22:19).

k. "He that sacrificeth unto any god, save unto the Lord only, he shall be utterly destroyed" (22:20).

l. "Thou shalt neither vex a stranger, nor oppress him: for ye were strangers in the land of Egypt" (22:21).

## THE THREEFOLD DIVISION OF THE LAW

# Moral Code

1. Thou shalt have no other gods before me.
2. Thou shalt not make unto thee any graven image.
3. Thou shalt not take the name of the Lord thy God in vain.
4. Remember the Sabbath day to keep it holy.
5. Honor thy father and thy mother.
6. Thou shalt not kill.
7. Thou shalt not commit adultery.
8. Thou shalt not steal.
9. Thou shalt not bear false witness.
10. Thou shalt not covet.

## The Revelation from Christ
**(1 CORINTHIANS 10:4)**

# Spiritual Code

This section dealt with those special ordinances which foreshadowed Christ and his full redemption. It included:

1. The seven **Levitical feasts.**
2. The five **Levitical offerings.**

EXODUS 35-40; LEVITICUS

## The Realization in Christ
**(MATTHEW 5:17, 18; ROMANS 10:4; 1 CORINTHIANS 5:7)**

# Social Code

This section included rules governing Israel's diet, sanitation, quarantine, soil conservation, taxation, military service, marriage, childbirth, divorce, etc.

BOOK OF LEVITICUS

## The Regulation Until Christ
**(GALATIANS 3:24)**

m. "Ye shall not afflict any widow, or fatherless child" (22:22).

n. "If thou lend money to any of my people that is poor by thee, thou shalt not be to him as an usurer, neither shalt thou lay upon him usury" (22:25).

"If thou at all take thy neighbour's raiment to pledge, thou shalt deliver it unto him by that the sun goeth down" (22:26).

"For that is his covering only, it is his raiment for his skin: wherein shall he sleep? and it shall come to pass, when he crieth unto me, that I will hear; for I am gracious" (22:27).

o. "Thou shalt not revile the gods, nor curse the ruler of thy people" (22:28).

p. "Thou shalt not delay to offer the first of thy ripe fruits, and of thy liquors: the firstborn of thy sons shalt thou give unto me" (22:29).

q. "If thou meet thine enemy's ox or his ass going astray, thou shalt surely bring it back to him again" (23:4).

"If thou see the ass of him that hateth thee lying under his burden, and wouldest forbear to help him, thou shalt surely help with him" (23:5).

r. "Thou shalt not wrest the judgment of thy poor in his cause" (23:6).

s. "And six years thou shalt sow thy land, and shalt gather in the fruits thereof: But the seventh year thou shalt let it rest and lie still; that the poor of thy people may eat: and what they leave the beast of the field shall eat. In like manner thou shalt deal with thy vineyard, and with thy oliveyard" (23:10, 11).

t. "Behold, I send an Angel before thee, to keep thee in the way, and to bring thee into the place which I have prepared" (23:20).

Simply stated, the moral code acted as the *revelation* of God's law, the social code as the *regulation* of that law, and the spiritual code as the *realization* of that law—in Christ. (See Mt. 5:17, 18; Rom. 10:4.)

C. The corruption of the golden calf (Ex. 32).

1. During the final days of Moses' first forty-day meeting with God atop Mr. Sinai, the fickle Israelites in the valley below demand that Aaron make them a god.

2. Aaron agrees, and, using their own golden earrings, forms a golden calf god.

3. After the "worship service" the people throw a wild party and indulge in sexual immorality. The verb translated "to play" in 32:6 means to sexually caress. (See Gen. 26:8 for a similar situation.)

4. God informs Moses of all this on the mountain and declares his intention to destroy the entire bunch. A trembling Moses then begins his respectful "debate with deity." He pleads for God to turn his wrath away for two reasons:

a. Because of his enemies (32:12).

b. Because of his friends (32:13).

5. Moses and Joshua return to the camp and in righteous anger Moses breaks the Ten Commandment tablets of stone. He then burns the golden calf, grinds it into powder, mixes it with water, and makes the people drink it.
6. He reprimands Aaron and demands to know who is on the Lord's side. The tribe of Levi, to a man, declare themselves to be, and from that day are chosen to become the priests of God.
7. God then sends a plague to punish Israel and orders the execution of 3,000 troublemaking ring leaders.

D. The construction of the tabernacle (Ex. 25–31: 35–41; Lev.).
   1. A general description of the tabernacle:
      a. The three sections—the outer court, the inner court, and the Holy of Holies. The outer court, a glorified picket fence construction, measured 150 feet in length, seventy-five feet wide, and seven-and-a-half feet high. In the center of the "picket fence" was a tent, forty-five feet long, fifteen feet wide, and fifteen feet high.

There were two rooms in this tent, separated by a thick veil. The eastern room section of this tent (the entire tabernacle faced east) was the holy place, and the western section was the Holy of Holies. The tent was made of forty-eight upright boards and was covered by four kinds of cloth. Three of these were animal skins, and the fourth was a fine linen. The colors involved were white, blue, purple, and scarlet.
      b. The various materials used—gold (3,140 pounds), and silver (9,575 pounds), bronze (7,540 pounds), animal cloth, acacia wood, olive oil, spices, onyx stones.
      c. Overall supervisor, Bezaleel, grandson of Hur, from tribe of Judah.
      d. Time of construction, approximately six months.
      e. Method of construction—the tabernacle was the production of willing hands and hearts. God's house was financed by God's people, and not through suppers,

## THE CONSTRUCTION OF THE TABERNACLE

### DESCRIPTION AND SIZE

Consisted of three sections: (1) outer court (2) inner court (3) holy of holies
Outer court: similar to a picket fence—150 ft. long, 75 ft. wide, 7½ ft. high
Tent within the outer court—45 ft. long, 15 ft. wide, 15 ft. high
Tent had two rooms which were separated by a thick veil
Eastern tent room known as the inner court or Holy Place
Western tent room known as the Holy of Holies

### BUILDING MATERIALS

Gold, silver, bronze, animal cloth, acacia wood, onyx stones

### FURNITURE
**EX. 25, 27, 30, 37, 38**

In outer court: a bronze altar and a bronze laver
In inner court: shewbread table, lampstand, and incense altar
In Holy of Holies: the Ark of the Covenant

### TIME OF CONSTRUCTION

Six months

### METHOD OF CONSTRUCTION

Made by willing hands and hearts (See **Ex. 35; Num. 7**)

### THE PRIESTS
**EX. 28-29**
Had to come from the tribe of Levi
Were anointed with water, oil, and blood

### THE HIGH PRIEST

Had to come from the line of Aaron of the tribe of Levi
Clothing: two ephods (outer and inner robes) breastplate, mitre, Urim and Thummim
Duties: to care for the physical needs of the tabernacle and the spiritual needs of the people

### OFFERINGS

| | |
|---|---|
| BURNT OFFERING **Lev. 1** | Offered primarily to **maintain** fellowship with God. |
| MEAL OFFERING **Lev. 2** | |
| PEACE OFFERING **Lev. 3** | |
| SIN OFFERING **Lev. 4** | Offered primarily to **restore** fellowship to God. |
| TRESPASS OFFERING **Lev. 5** | |

### HOLY FEASTS
**(LEV. 23, 25)**

| | |
|---|---|
| WEEKLY SABBATH | These three speak of God's first great work, that of **creation**. (See **Rev. 4:11**) |
| SEVEN-YEAR SABBATH | |
| FIFTY-YEAR SABBATH | |
| PASSOVER Speaks of Calvary | These six speak of God's second great work, that of **redemption**. (See **Rev. 5:9.**) |
| FIRST FRUITS The resurrection | |
| PENTECOST Coming of Holy Spirit | |
| TRUMPETS Rapture and Second Coming | |
| ATONEMENT The tribulation | |
| TABERNACLE The millennium | |

### THE PURPOSE OF THE TABERNACLE

To provide for Israel a visible center of worship.
To preview the work of Christ. Note similarities between the language of Moses and John.

| MOSES | JOHN |
|---|---|
| Describes the brazen altar | Describes the Lamb of God **(Jn. 1:29)** |
| Speaks of the brazen laver | Speaks of the water of life **(Jn. 4:14)** |
| Writes of the table of shewbread | Writes of the bread of life **(Jn. 6:35)** |
| Talks of the lampstand | Talks of the light of the world **(Jn. 9:5)** |
| Presents the altar of incense | Presents the great prayer of Christ **(Jn. 17)** |
| Witnesses of the mercy seat | Witness of Christ our mercy seat **(1 Jn. 2:2)** |

### DEDICATION OF TABERNACLE

THE TRIUMPH: God's glory cloud fills the place **(Ex. 40:33-38)**
THE TRAGEDY: God's judgment falls upon Aaron's two wicked sons **(Lev. 10:1-11)**

### CENSUS OF TABERNACLE

The first Exodus census (of two) now takes place **(Num. 1)** (For second census see **Num. 26.**)

### NAZARITE VOW

THREE RULES: (1) not to drink wine (2) not to cut hair (3) avoid contact with dead objects **(Num. 6).**

junk sales, and bingo parties. Some of the most inspiring verses in the Old Testament speak of this sweet and sacrificial spirit (35:5, 21, 22, 29).

Another precious truth involved in the tabernacle project was the fact that God personally observed each gift which was given, no matter how small. This is dramatically brought out in Numbers 7, where twelve tiny gold boxes of incense are given by twelve different individuals. In spite of the fact that the gifts were identical and inexpensive (approximately $6.50 per box) God nevertheless acknowledged each person and each gift. (See also Rev. 2:2, 9, 13; 3:1, 8, 15.)

2. The furniture of the tabernacle.
There were six main objects:
a. The brazen (or bronze) altar—Exodus 27:1-8; 38:1-7.
This was the first piece of furniture as one enters the tabernacle from the east. It was a box-like structure made of acacia wood overlaid with bronze. It was approximately seven-and-a-half feet wide and three feet high. There was a grate midway between the top and the bottom. A horn was located on each corner of the altar to help hold the animal sacrifices which were offered at this altar.
b. The brazen (or bronze) laver—Exodus 30:18; 38:8.
A brass basin which was filled with water, resting on a pedestal, covered by mir-

rors. It was used by the priests for actual and ceremonial cleansing of both hands and feet.
c. The table of shewbread—Exodus 25:23-30; 37:10-16.
A table was made of acacia wood and covered with gold. On this table were placed twelve cakes of bread, renewed each week, one for each tribe in Israel. This table was approximately one-and-a-half feet wide by two-and-a-half feet high. This table, unlike the first two pieces of furniture, was on the inside of the tent, resting on the northern side of the first room.
d. The lampstand—Exodus 25:31-40; 37:17-24.
One of the most ornate objects in the tabernacle. It was made of pure gold and consisted of an upright shaft from each side of which three branches extended upward in pairs. The lamps were trimmed every morning and evening and were never to be extinguished all at one time. The lamp had to be regularly supplied with pure olive oil. The entire lamp required 107 pounds of gold and cost approximately $175,000. Jewish tradition says the lampstand was five feet high and three-and-a-half feet wide. It rested on the south side of the first room (also called the holy place).

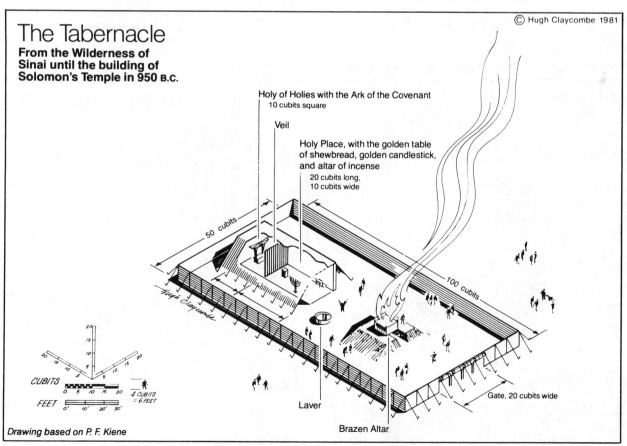

© Hugh Claycombe 1981

# The Tabernacle
**From the Wilderness of Sinai until the building of Solomon's Temple in 950 B.C.**

Holy of Holies with the Ark of the Covenant
10 cubits square

Veil

Holy Place, with the golden table of shewbread, golden candlestick, and altar of incense
20 cubits long,
10 cubits wide

50 cubits

100 cubits

CUBITS

FEET

4 CUBITS = 6 FEET

Gate, 20 cubits wide

Laver

Brazen Altar

*Drawing based on P. F. Kiene*

e. The altar of incense—Exodus 30:1-10; 37:25-28.

This foot-and-a-half square by three feet high acacia wood table overlaid with gold was symbolic of prayer. Sweet spices were burned on this table each morning and evening. (See Rev. 8:3, 4.) Once each year the horns on this altar were smeared with blood. The incense table occupied the western position of the holy place.

f. The Ark of the Covenant—Exodus 25:10-22; 37:1-9.

The most important piece in all the tabernacle, also made of acacia wood covered with gold. It resembled a cedar chest, and was approximately four feet long and two feet high. It contained several objects, the most important being the two stones upon which was written the Ten Commandments. The lid of this box was made of solid gold and called the mercy seat. On top of the box stood two golden angelic cherubims. Once each year during the great day of atonement in October, the high priest would enter the Holy of Holies (which was separated from the holy place by a thick veil) and sprinkle blood upon the mercy seat for the sins of Israel. Above the entire ark dwelled the Shekinah Glory cloud of God. Perhaps the most thrilling truth of the tabernacle is seen here: the one thing that stood between the broken law that man could not keep and the holy and righteous wrath of God was the blood of the lamb.

3. The priesthood of the tabernacle.

a. Their ordination—one of the most impressive ceremonies in the Old Testament world was undoubtedly the consecration of a young Levite boy to the Israelite priesthood. The sacred procedure was as follows:

(1) He was first washed with water (Ex. 29:4).

(2) He was then clothed (29:5).

(3) He was then anointed with oil (29:7).

(4) He was finally to identify himself with a sacrifice (29:15-20). This was done by the placing of his hand upon a dying lamb. The blood of this lamb was then placed upon his right ear, his right thumb, and his right big toe.

b. Their clothing. Following is a description of the garments worn by the high priest (Ex. 28:2-43).

(1) The ephod—a sleeveless outer garment reaching from the shoulders to below the knees. It consisted of two pieces, one covering the back and the other the front side of the body, fastened on each shoulder by a golden clasp on the top of which were two onyx stones with the names of six tribes on each stone. The ephod was woven of blue, purple, scarlet, and fine linen yarn, embroidered with figures of gold and held to the body by a girdle.

(2) The breastplate of judgment (28:15-20)—a square piece of cloth

## THE FURNISHINGS OF THE TABERNACLE AND THE BRAZEN ALTAR

Altar of Incense

Location of shewbread

Golden Candlestick

Laver

Brazen Altar

## THE ARK OF THE COVENANT

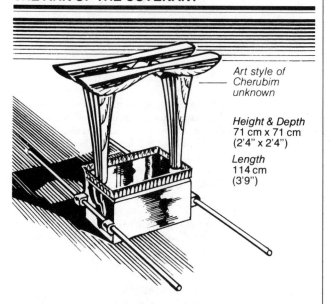

Art style of Cherubim unknown

*Height & Depth*
71 cm x 71 cm
(2'4" x 2'4")

*Length*
114 cm
(3'9")

attached to the ephod over the priest's heart upon which were twelve precious stones set in gold and arranged in four rows. On top of the stones were engraved the names of the twelve tribes of Israel.

(3) The Urim and Thummim (28:30).
The nature of this apparel is not certain. The Hebrew words literally mean "lights" and "perfection." They could have been two especially costly stones. It is thought by some that they were used by the high priest in times of crisis to determine the will of God. (See Num. 27:21; 1 Sam. 28:6.)

(4) The robe of the ephod (28:31–35).
This was a blue seamless garment worn under the ephod and was a lit-

## THE HIGH PRIEST AND HIS GARMENTS

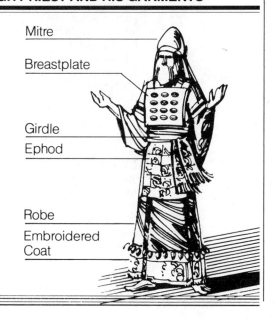

Mitre

Breastplate

Girdle

Ephod

Robe

Embroidered Coat

tle longer than the ephod. Along its hem were blue, purple, and scarlet pomegranates and golden bells which tinkled as the priest served in the tabernacle.

(5) The mitre (28:36–38).
The fine white linen turban head-dress of the high priest. On its front was a golden nameplate with the words "Holiness to the Lord" engraved on it.

c. Their duties. The various responsibilities of the priesthood would fall into two basic categories:

(1) That of Temple service—this would include the burning of incense, the care of the lamps, the placing of the bread, and the sacrificial offerings (Num. 3:5–9).

(2) That of personal service—to inspect unclean persons, especially lepers, to instruct the people of Israel in the law of God, and to take a general interest in the spiritual welfare of the people (Num. 6:23–27; Deut. 17:8, 9).

d. Their personal obligations.

(1) They must not consume strong drink (Lev. 10:9).

(2) They must not clip bald spots on their heads, beards, or flesh (Lev. 21:5).

(3) They must not marry a harlot, divorced woman, widow, or someone from another tribe. Their wife must be a virgin from Levi (Lev. 21:7, 14).

(4) They could not have any bodily defects such as blindness or lameness (Lev. 21:16–21).

4. The offerings of the tabernacle.

a. There were five main offerings and each kind is described by a separate chapter in Leviticus 1–5.

(1) The burnt offering (Lev. 1).
(2) The meal offering (2).
(3) The peace offering (3).
(4) The sin offering (4).
(5) The trespass offering (5).

b. These five offerings can be placed into two general categories:

(1) Those offerings to be used for the purpose of restoring broken fellowship. This would include the sin and trespass offerings.

(2) Those offerings to be used for the purpose of maintaining fellowship. These would include the burnt, the meal, and the peace offerings. The special red heifer offering of Numbers 19 would also be included in this category.

5. The holy feasts of the tabernacle. There were nine special feasts and rest times in Israel's calendar. The first three were to remind the believers of God's creative work and the last six of his redemptive work.

a. His creative work.
  (1) The weekly Sabbath (Ex. 20:8-11; Lev. 23:1-3).
  (2) The seven-year Sabbath feast (Ex. 23:10, 11; Lev. 25:2-7).
  (3) The fiftieth year Sabbath feast (Lev. 25:8-16).
  Note: These three speak of God's creation, as they come in endless cycles of seven, just as God rested on the seventh day.
b. His redemptive work.
  (1) The Passover feast (Lev. 23:4-8). This speaks of *Calvary* (1 Cor. 5:7).
  (2) The feast of the first fruits (Lev. 23:9-14) speaks of the resurrection (1 Cor. 15:23).
  (3) The feast of Pentecost (Lev. 23:15-25). This speaks of the coming of the Holy Spirit (Acts 2).
  (4) The feast of trumpets (Lev. 23:23-25). This speaks of the rapture and Second Coming (1 Thess. 4:13-18).
  (5) The day of atonement feast (Lev. 23:26-32). This speaks of the tribulation (Rev. 6-19). In the Hebrew this is *Yom Kippurim* and it occurred on October 10 of each year. The order of service on this all-important day is detailed for us in Leviticus 16.
   (a) The high priest would offer a bull sacrifice for himself. Preachers need to be saved and cleansed too!
   (b) Lots would then be cast over two goats to determine which one would become a scapegoat, and which would be killed.
   (c) The high priest would then sprinkle the blood of the slaughtered bull and goat seven times upon the mercy seat.
   (d) He would finally place his hands upon the scapegoat, confess over it all the sins of Israel, and then appoint a man to lead the goat into the desert.
  (6) The feast of tabernacles (Lev. 23:33-44). This speaks of the *millennium* (Rev. 20:1-6).
c. To picture the entire program of salvation.
6. The handbook of the tabernacle. The remaining chapters in Leviticus are given over to various dos and don'ts which cover the religious, social, and physical life of each Israelite.
  a. Certain foods may be eaten, while other kinds must be avoided. The general invitation to eat all animals given to Noah (Gen. 9:3) is now being restricted.
  b. Two chapters (12; 15) are given over to the ceremonial cleansing involved in sex and childbirth. Here it should be pointed out that nowhere does the Bible in any remote way equate sin with sex and childbirth. What God was undoubtedly attempting to do through these laws was to teach the tragic truth that all men are born with sin natures (see Rom. 5:12).
  c. The subject of leprosy occupies two chapters (13-14). This is the first mention of the word, and from this point on, leprosy becomes a symbol of sin. Among the many thousands of lepers in the Old Testament only two were healed by God. In Numbers 12, Miriam is healed, and in 2 Kings, Naaman is cured.
  d. Blood is discussed in chapter 17 to explain that great biblical principle: "It is the blood that maketh an atonement for the soul" (17:11; see also Heb. 9:22).
  e. Chapters 18-21 involve themselves with personal separation. Note the following commands as taken from *The Living Bible*: "None of you shall marry a near relative . . ." (18:6).
  "Homosexuality is absolutely forbidden, for it is an enormous sin" (18:22).
  "A medium or a wizard . . . shall surely be stoned to death . . ." (20:27).
  A specific listing of the regulations in this handbook would include the following:
  (1) concerning diet
   (a) animal life (Lev. 11:2, 3)
   (b) marine life (11:9)
   (c) bird life (11:20)
   (d) insect life (11:21, 22)
  (2) concerning motherhood (Lev. 12)
  (3) concerning leprosy (13-14)
   (a) recognizing the leper (13:2, 3)
   (b) rules for the leper (13:45-56)
   (c) restoring the leper (14:2, 3)
  (4) concerning issues from the body (Lev. 15)
  (5) concerning morality among one's kin (18)
   (a) the father (18:7)
   (b) the mother (18:8)
   (c) the sister (18:9)
   (d) the daughter-in-law (18:10)
   (e) the aunt (18:12)
   (f) the uncle (18:14)
   (g) the sister-in-law (18:16)
  (6) concerning benevolence (Lev. 19)
  (7) concerning apostasy (20:1-9)
   (a) worshiping Molech (20:3)
   (b) consulting wizards (20:6)
   (c) cursing one's parents (20:9)
  (8) concerning perversion (20:10-21)
   (a) adultery (20:10)
   (b) incest (20:12)
   (c) sodomy (20:13)
   (d) polygamy (20:14)
   (e) indecent exposure (20:17)
  (9) concerning kinsman redemption (25:47-49)
  (10) concerning disobedience (Lev. 26)
   (a) the principle stated (26:1-13)
   (b) the punishment cited (26:14, 15)
    [1] first punishment (26:14, 15)

[2] second punishment (26:14, 15)

[3] third punishment (26:21, 22)

[4] fourth punishment (26: 23-26)

[5] fifth punishment (26:27-31)

(c) the punishment certain (26: 32-39)

(11) concerning dedication (Lev. 27)

7. The dedication of the tabernacle. (Ex. 30:22-33; 40:33-35).

Thus was dedicated the most important building ever constructed on this earth. There was however one tragic event which marred the otherwise happy celebration, and that was the death of Nadab and Abihu, Aaron's two priest sons. These two foolish and wicked young men had offered unholy fire before the Lord. Furthermore, the account indicates (see Lev. 10) that both were drunk at the time.

8. The census of the tabernacle (Num. 1:1-54). There are two occasions when Israel was numbered during their march from Egypt to Palestine. The first occurred here at Sinai on April 15 (see Num. 1-2), and the second took place some thirty-eight years later in the desert of Moab (Num. 26). The census here counted all the men twenty years of age and up. The total was 603,550 men.

It is sad to know that of these men, 603,550 in number, 603,548 would later perish in the wilderness (cf. Num. 14:29). The only two men who would later enter Canaan were Joshua and Caleb.

Much speculation has centered around this census figure. If taken literally it would strongly suggest a total Israelite population of over two million. The problem therefore arises concerning the care and feeding of this multitude for nearly forty years; much of it spent in a desolate and arid desert. For example, it has been estimated that it would require nearly fifty railway box cars of manna per day just to feed the people. This would not take into account the physical needs of the thousands of animals which accompanied them. The water needs would likewise be immense: some twelve million gallons per day. In fact the ground area needed to accommodate this multitude when they camped at night would exceed one hundred square miles.

Some have attempted to solve these problems by a watering down of the text. For example, it is suggested that the Hebrew word 'elep translated by the King James Version as "thousand" could as easily be rendered by the word "family" or "clan."

Thus, we would have six hundred and three families with each family contributing perhaps an average of five fighting men each for a total of 3,015 soldiers. Assuming each man was married with two children we then would arrive at the figure of some fifteen thousand or the grand total of Israel's camp.

But this approach raises far more problems than it solves. Gleason Archer writes:

"It is true that there is an 'elep which means family or clan (1 Sam. 10:19, etc.); but it is very clear from the numeration chapters (Num. 1-4; 26) that 'elep is intended in the sense of 'thousand,' for the smaller unit below this 'elep is me' ot, 'hundreds' (cf. Num. 1:21, 23, 25, etc.). The most that a 'family' could contribute to the national army would be four or five men on the average, and it would be absurd to suppose that 'hundreds' would be mentioned or the next lower numerical unit after an average contingent of five men each.

Further corroboration is given by the total amount of ransom money—at the rate of half shekel apiece—recorded in Exodus 38:25 as 100 talents, 1775 shekels. Since there were 3000 shekels to the talent, this comes out to exactly 603,550 contributors. It is therefore safe to say that no objective handling of the textual evidence can possibly sustain the thesis that 'elep in Numbers signifies anything less than a literal thousand." (Gleason Archer, *A Survey of Old Testament Introduction*, pp. 246, 247)

This number did not include the men of Levi, which was the tribe to be excluded from the census. The total number of the Levitical priesthood is given as 8,580 in 4:48. If the estimated Israelite population of that time, some two million, is divided by the number of the priesthood—8,580—it comes out that each priest was responsible for around two-hundred-thirty-three people. The largest tribe was Judah (74,600) and the smallest was Manasseh with 32,200. The descendants of Gershon, Kohath, and Merari, Levi's three sons, were placed in charge of the entire tabernacle. God's original plan, of course, was to have the eldest sons of all the tribes act as priests (see Ex. 13:1), but because of Israel's constant sin, he had limited his choice to the Levites (Num. 3:11-13). The priest had to be thirty years of age before he could fully enter into the service of God. (See Num. 4:3; Lk. 3:23.)

9. The arrangement of the tribes around the tabernacle (Num. 2:1-34). Especially to be noted are the actual location arrangements of the various tribes. On the east were Issachar, Judah, and Zebulun. On the west were the tribes of Benjamin, Ephraim, and Manasseh. On the north were Asher, Dan, and Naphtali, while the south was occupied by Gad, Reuben, and Simeon. Rabbinical tradition suggests that Judah (leader of the eastern section) carried with it a standard of green because it was on an emerald that the name of Judah was engraved upon the breastplate of the high priest, and that its emblem was that of a lion because of the prophecy in Genesis 49:9.

Reuben, leader of the southern flank, flew a red standard to commemorate their name

## TRIBAL ENCAMPMENT POSITION

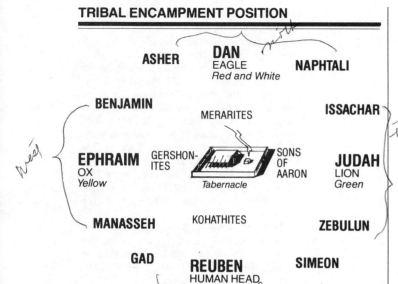

written on a sardius stone. Their emblem was that of a human head. The chief tribe of the western side was Ephraim. It displayed a golden flag, for it was upon a golden stone that their name was engraved. Ephraim's emblem was a calf, it is said, because Joseph (their founder) was elevated to power in Egypt through a calf vision. (See Gen. 41:1–32.) Finally the color of Dan (northern leader) was red and white, for their stone was the jasper. An eagle was the emblem of this tribe. We are not sure, of course, just how much of all this is based on fact. If it is true, however, it blends in beautifully with the visions of both Ezekiel and John (see Ezek. 1 and Rev. 4).

10. The Nazarite vow of the tabernacle (Num. 6:1–21).

This especially concerned itself with that individual (man or woman) who desired to consecrate himself to the Lord in a special way, either for life or for a certain period of time. The rules were:
a. He could not taste the fruit of the vineyard in any manner.
b. He could not cut his hair.
c. He could not come in contact with any dead person.

The most well-known Old Testament Nazarite of course was Samson. (See Jdg. 13:7).

11. The great benediction of the tabernacle (Num. 6:22–27).

"And the Lord spake unto Moses, saying, Speak unto Aaron and unto his sons, saying, On this wise ye shall bless the children of Israel, saying unto them, The Lord bless thee, and keep thee: The Lord make his face shine upon thee, and be gracious unto thee: The Lord lift up his countenance upon thee, and give thee peace. And they shall put my name upon the children of Israel; and I will bless them" (Num. 6:22–27).

12. The two silver trumpets of the tabernacle

(Num. 10:1–9). These trumpets were to be sounded on four specific occasions.
a. To summons (v. 2). If both trumpets were blown, then the entire congregation was to gather at the tabernacle (v. 3). If, however, but one trumpet blew, only the heads of the divisions were to appear (v. 4).
b. To give warning in case of attack (v. 5).
c. When Israel itself would go to war (v. 9).
d. At Israel's appointed feasts (v. 10).

IV. Israel, from Sinai to Kadesh-barnea (Num. 10:11—12:16).

This was also a distance of 150 miles.

A. En route to Kadesh (10:11—12:16).

1. A balking brother-in-law. Moses attempts to secure the scouting services of Hobab, his brother-in-law, but the offer is refused (10:29–32).

2. A continuing cloud (10:34–36).

"And the cloud of the Lord was upon them by day, when they went out of the camp. And it came to pass, when the ark set forward that Moses said, Rise up, Lord, and let thine enemies be scattered; and let them that hate thee flee before thee. And when it rested, he said, Return, O Lord, unto the many thousands of Israel" (Num. 10:34–36).

The distance between Mt. Sinai and Kadesh is less than two hundred miles. In Numbers 33:16–36 Moses lists some twenty stops from these two places. The Sinai area is dotted with mountains, rugged valleys, and sandy ground. But their journey was never too long or difficult for "the cloud of the Lord was upon them."

3. A murmuring multitude (11:4–6).
a. Once again this unsaved Egyptian-controlled group stirred up the people to complain, this time about their food. Note their words:
"We remember the fish, which we did eat in Egypt freely; the cucumbers, and the melons, and the leeks, and the onions, and the garlick: But now our soul is dried away; there is nothing at all, beside this manna, before our eyes" (11:5, 6).
b. God sends a fire to punish this rebellion. The people cry to Moses who again intercedes for them and the plague is stopped.

4. A provoked prophet (11:10–15).
a. Moses concludes that God has simply given him too heavy a burden in leading Israel and demands additional help. The despair becomes so severe that Moses demands from God either deliverance or death. (See v. 15.) Elijah the prophet would later require a similar thing from God in a moment of despondency (cf. 1 Ki. 19:4).

It is tragic that in his great hour of need Moses did not respond as the Apostle Paul would do when facing an unbearable burden.

"And lest I should be exalted above measure through the abundance of

**THE EXODUS STAGE**

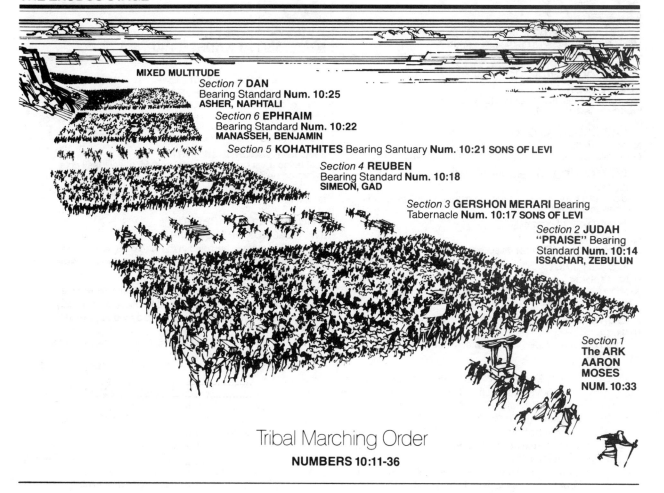

MIXED MULTITUDE
*Section 7* **DAN**
Bearing Standard **Num. 10:25**
**ASHER, NAPHTALI**

*Section 6* **EPHRAIM**
Bearing Standard **Num. 10:22**
**MANASSEH, BENJAMIN**

*Section 5* **KOHATHITES** Bearing Santuary **Num. 10:21** SONS OF LEVI

*Section 4* **REUBEN**
Bearing Standard **Num. 10:18**
**SIMEON, GAD**

*Section 3* **GERSHON MERARI** Bearing
Tabernacle **Num. 10:17** SONS OF LEVI

*Section 2* **JUDAH**
**"PRAISE"** Bearing
Standard **Num. 10:14**
**ISSACHAR, ZEBULUN**

*Section 1*
**The ARK
AARON
MOSES
NUM. 10:33**

Tribal Marching Order
**NUMBERS 10:11-36**

the revelations, there was given to me a thorn in the flesh, the messenger of Satan to buffet me, lest I should be exalted above measure. For this thing I besought the Lord thrice, that it might depart from me. And he said unto me, My grace is sufficient for thee; for my strength is made perfect in weakness. Most gladly, therefore, will I rather glory in my infirmities, that the power of Christ may rest upon me" (2 Cor. 12:7-9).

b. God grants this regrettable request by taking some of the power of the Holy Spirit from Moses and distributing it equally to seventy chosen Hebrew elders (11:25).

c. Two of these men, Eldad and Medad, begin prophesying (11:26-29).

5. A deadly diet (11:31-34).
To silence the people's constant bickering, God sent an immense flock of quail over the camp, flying approximately three feet in the air. Millions of these birds were knocked down and eaten, but with the meat God sent a plague also. (See Ps. 106:15.)

6. A suffering sister (Num. 12:1-15).

a. Aaron and Miriam criticize their younger brother Moses on two counts:

(1) Because of his wife. They could have been referring to Zipporah, but it is possible that she had died and this Cushite wife was his second one. It is indeterminate from the text as to whether the criticism was because she was a Gentile or because of her color (if indeed she was of different color). At any rate, the marriage was not contrary to the law which forbade marriage only to Canaanites. (See Gen. 24:37.)

(2) Because of his strong leadership. How often has this sin been committed by deacons and officials in a local church since this time. Aaron and Miriam would soon learn the truth of Psalm 105:15: "Touch not mine anointed, and do my prophets no harm."

b. God rebukes them for their criticism, telling them that Moses was his special friend.

c. Miriam, the ring leader, is suddenly struck with leprosy. Aaron begs forgiveness and asks Moses to plead with God concerning her restoration.

# 4
## ISRAEL, EN ROUTE TO KADESH-BARNEA

### A Balking Brother-In-Law
**NUM. 10:29-31**
Moses unsuccessfully attempts to secure the services of his brother-in-law as a guide.

### A Continuing Cloud
**NUM. 10:34-36**
God's faithful guide continues to show them the way.

### A Murmuring Mixed Multitude
**NUM. 11:1-3**
God sends a fiery plague to stop the bitter and blasphemous complaints of Israel.

### A Provoked Prophet
**NUM. 11:14-25**
At Moses' request, God sends seventy men to help him.

### A Deadly Diet
**NUM. 11:31-34**
To show their hatred for the manna, the people turn to a diet of quail meat. A deadly plague follows.

### A Suffering Sister
**NUM. 12**
For criticizing both Moses and his wife, Miriam is punished with leprosy.

    d. Moses does this, and after a period of seven days she is restored to fellowship and health.

V. Israel at Kadesh-barnea (Num. 13-14).
  A. The penetration.

Moses is instructed to send a leader from each of the twelve tribes to spy out the land of Canaan. Among these leaders were Joshua, from the tribe of Ephraim, and Caleb, from Judah.

In Numbers 13 it would seem that this command of God was indicative of his perfect will that Canaan be spied out first, but Moses adds more information as recorded in Deuteronomy 1:19-24, which gives the entire background. "And ye came near unto me, every one of you, and said, we will send men before us, and they shall search out the land, and bring us word again . . ." (Deut. 1:22).

Thus it would seem that the original expedition idea came from man and not from God.

  B. The lamentation.

After forty days of searching out the land, the twelve return with these reports:

    1. The majority report—composed of the leaders of ten tribes: "We can't take the land!" (13:32, 33).

    2. The minority report—by Joshua and Caleb: "Let us go up at once and possess it, for we are well able to conquer it" (Num. 13:30).

    3. The vote of the people: "We won't go!" (14:1-3). This sad episode marked the tenth occasion when Israel rebelled against God. He had graciously brought them out of captivity through ten mighty plagues only to have them turn against his grace ten times (14:22).

These ten occasions of rebellion are as follows:

# 5
## ISRAEL, AT KADESH-BARNEA

### The Two-Fold Report
**TEN-MAN MAJORITY REPORT**
"We are not able to go up against the people; for they are stronger than we." **(Num. 13:31)**

"And there we saw giants . . . and we were . . . as grasshoppers . . . in their sight." **(Num. 13:33)**

**TWO-MAN MINORITY REPORT**
"Let us go up at once, and possess it; for we are well able to overcome it." **(Num. 13:30)**

" . . . Neither fear ye the people of the land . . . for . . . the Lord is with us . . ." **(Num. 14:9)**

### The Two-Fold Reaction
**THE REACTION OF THE PEOPLE**
"Would God that we had died in the land of Egypt!" **(Num. 14:2)**

"Let us make a captain, and let us return into Egypt." **(Num. 14:4)**

**THE REACTION OF GOD**
This marked their tenth rebellion against him. **(Num. 14:22)**

Their carcasses would fall in the wilderness. **(Num. 14:29)**

No one over twenty (Joshua and Caleb excepted) would enter Palestine. **(Num. 14:29)**

They would wander forty years, a year for each day the spies spent in the land. **(Num. 14:34)**

The majority-report members would die of a plague. **(Num. 14:37)**

    a. At the Red Sea (Ex. 14:11, 12).
    b. At Marah (Ex. 15:24).
    c. In the wilderness of Sin (Ex. 16:2, 3).
    d. At Rephidim (Ex. 17:1-3).
    e. At Sinai (Ex. 32:1-6).
    f. En route to Kadesh (three occasions) (Num. 11:1-3; 4-9; 31-34).
    g. At Kadesh (two occasions) (Num. 14:1-4; 14:10).

  C. The condemnation.

God determined that not one person twenty years or over would be allowed to enter Canaan. "Since the spies were in the land for forty days, you must wander in the wilderness for forty years—a year for each day, bearing the burden of your sins" (Num. 14:34).

During the next four decades, then, Israel was to linger in the desert until the last person twenty years and older died and was buried. Dr. Leon Wood makes the following observation:

"Figuring 1,200,000 (600,000 of both men and women) as having to die in 14,508 days (38½ years), gives 85 per day. Figuring 12 hours per day maximum for funerals, gives an average of seven funerals per hour for all 38½ years, a continuous foreboding reminder of God's punishment upon them." (*A Survey of Israel's History*, p. 159)

Thus, the sad period of Kadesh ends with these words:

"Then the ten spies who had incited the rebellion against Jehovah by striking fear into the hearts of the people were struck dead before the Lord. Of all the spies, only Joshua and Caleb remained alive" (Num. 14:36-38, *TLB*).

VI. Israel, from Kadesh-barnea to the Eastern Bank of Jordan (Num. 15-36).

During this period of aimless wanderings, the following events transpire:

A. A futile attack stopped (Num. 14:40–45).

The fickle and foolish Israelites suddenly change their minds and attempt to push their way into the land, but are quickly defeated by the Canaanites.

B. A Sabbath-breaker stoned (15:32–36).

C. A troublemaker swallowed (16:1–32).

1. A very influential descendant of Levi named Korah led a 250-strong conspiracy against the authority of Moses.

2. The entire matter led to a showdown on the following day at which time God stepped in and caused the ground to open up and swallow the troublemakers. In spite of this terrible object lesson, Israel continued to murmur, actually accusing Moses of killing God's people. Before the tragic incident was over, 14,700 more people would be killed by a special judgment plague from God. The New Testament writer Jude (1:11) mentions this event in his epistle as a stern warning against apostasy.

D. A stick that sprouted—the budding of Aaron's rod (17:1–13).

To emphasize the authority he had invested in Moses and Aaron, the Lord ordered the leaders from each tribe to place a rod in the tabernacle with his personal name inscribed on it. Aaron was commanded to do the same. The next morning it was discovered that Aaron's rod had budded, was blossoming, and had ripe almonds hanging from it!

E. A red heifer slain (Num. 19:1–22).

1. The rite of the red heifer (19:1–10). Laws had already been given whereby a living person coming in contact with a corpse would be considered unclean (disqualified from religious life and service) for a period of seven days. But a crisis had probably now arisen. Due to the recent plague (Num. 16:49) no less than 14,700 corpses had come upon the scene. This event alone had, doubtless, contributed to the defilement of tens of thousands of people. What could be done about this? The rite of the red heifer was God's answer to this problem.

2. The rules for cleansing (19:11–32). "He who toucheth the dead body of any man shall be unclean (v. 11)." The cleansing of a defiled Israelite was fourfold.

a. Eleazar was to slaughter an unblemished red heifer outside the camp (vs. 2, 3).

b. Its blood was to be sprinkled toward the tabernacle seven times (v. 4).

c. The red heifer was to be burned along with cedar, wood, hyssop, and some scarlet cloth material (vs. 5, 6).

d. Finally water was to be added to the ashes of the heifer and sprinkled upon the defiled Israelite (vs. 17–19).

F. An angry man snared (20:1–13).

1. Miriam died and was buried near Kadesh (20:1).

2. After years of hard work, the devil finally snared Moses, the meekest man on earth (Num. 12:3), into the trap of anger and pride. The wicked and fickle Israelites were, as usual, complaining about the lack of water (it would seem they held a protest meeting against God at least once a day). God thereupon instructed Moses to speak to a certain rock and order it to pour out its water.

3. But the longsuffering Moses suddenly "blew his cool," and in an act, due partly to unbelief and anger, screamed at the people and disobeyed the Lord by striking the rock twice instead of speaking to it once as God had commanded (20:8).

4. God sent water in spite of Moses' disobedience, but told him this sin would keep him from the Promised Land (20:12).

5. Evidently Moses petitioned God later about going to Palestine until the Lord finally ordered him not to even mention it again (Deut. 3:26, 27).

G. A simple request scorned (20:14–22).

The Edomites, descendants of Esau, refused to allow Israel to march through their land, thus forcing God's people to trek an additional 180 miles in a hot and hostile desert.

H. A high priest stripped (20:23–29).

1. God ordered Moses to strip Aaron of his priestly garments and place them upon his son, Eleazar.

2. Aaron died at the age of 123 and was buried on Mt. Hor.

3. C. I. Scofield observes that the death of Aaron marks the end of Israel's wanderings. From this point the nation either marched or halted, but did not wander (*New Scofield Bible*, p. 195). It should be noted here that the wilderness experience, but not the wanderings, was originally in the perfect will of God for Israel (Ex. 13:17, 18).

I. A serpent problem solved (21:5–9).

1. God sent poisonous serpents to punish rebellious Israel.

2. The people repented and a cure was provided.

3. A serpent of brass was placed atop a pole where all could view it.

4. Anyone bitten needed only to look upon the brass serpent to be healed. Jesus used this event as an illustration to win Nicodemus. (See Jn. 3:14, 15.) Years later, in 700 B.C., King Hezekiah destroyed this serpent, for the people were worshiping it. (See 2 Ki. 18:4.)

J. The Amorites slaughtered (21:21–24).

As did the Edomites, the Amorites refused Israel passage, but on this occasion the armies of Moses fought and won a great victory.

K. A perverted prophet (Num. 22–24).

1. Balak, the frightened King of Moab, offers Balaam, a pagan diviner from Mesopotamia, tempting riches if he will put a hex on the advancing Israelites and thus save Moab (22:1–8).

2. God warns Balaam not to accept this bribe (22:9–12).

3. The offer is increased and Balaam agrees to go with Balak's men (22:15–21).

4. En route to Moab, Balaam is soundly re-

buked by the very animal he rode and narrowly escapes death at the hand of God's angel (Num. 22:22-35).

5. Balaam arrives in Moab and, looking down upon Israel's armies in a nearby valley, attempts to curse them on four occasions. But, in every case, words of blessing proceed from his mouth, to his amazement and Balak's anger. These four blessings are as follows: Numbers 23:8-10; 23:22-24; 24:5-9; 24:7.

Especially to be noted is the language found in some of Balaam's prophecies.

"How shall I curse, whom God hath not cursed? or how shall I defy, whom the Lord hath not defied? For from the top of the rocks I see him, and from the hills I behold him: lo, the people shall dwell alone, and shall not be reckoned among the nations. Who can count the dust of Jacob, and the number of the fourth part of Israel? Let me die the death of the righteous, and let my last end be like his!" (Num. 23:8-10).

"I shall see him, but not now: I shall behold him, but not nigh: there shall come a Star out of Jacob, and a Sceptre shall rise out of Israel, and shall smite the corners of Moab, and destroy all the children of Sheth. And Edom shall be a possession for his enemies; and Israel shall do valiantly" (Num. 24:17-19).

Of the thousands of characters in the Old Testament, surely Balaam is the most mysterious, and in some ways, the most tragic. He is mentioned by no less than three New Testament writers, each of whom writes concerning a particular aspect of his character.

His way—". . . the *way* of Balaam . . . who loved the wages of unrighteousness . . ." (2 Pet. 2:15).

His error—". . . the *error* of Balaam . . ." (Jude 1:11). His error was his conclusion that God would simply have to curse Israel because of their many sins. M. F. Unger writes:

"He was ignorant of God's election of Israel as a nation, and the immutability of God's choice (Rom. 11:29) and the nation's preservation. He failed to see how God can be 'Just and the Justifier' of the believing sinner through the cross, to which all Israel's tabernacle ritual pointed." (*Unger's Bible Dictionary*, pp. 133, 134)

His doctrine—". . . the *doctrine* of Balaam who . . . cast a stumbling block before the children of Israel, to eat things sacrificed unto idols, and to commit fornications" (Rev. 2:14). Even though this wicked prophet failed in his attempts to curse Israel, his corrupt and clever suggestions that God's people mix with the Moabites was highly successful. Before it was all over, this perverted preacher would cause the death of 24,000 Israelites (Num. 25:9), resulting in a punishment from God. Balaam was later killed by the invading armies of Israel (Num. 31:8). Thus, even though Balaam could not turn God away

from Israel, he did, for a while, turn Israel away from God. The hero of this tragedy was Phinehas, the grandson of Aaron. A controversy had been imagined between the number Moses gives here (24,000), and the number Paul later gives in the New Testament (23,000) (see 1 Cor. 10:8), but the solution would seem to be a simple one—Moses gives the entire number while Paul gives the number who died on the first day.

L. A patriotic priest (Num. 25).
1. In spite of his failure to curse Israel, Balaam nearly succeeded in destroying that nation by craftily arranging for the Moabite women to sexually seduce the Israelite men (Num. 25:1; 31:16).
2. Phinehas, godly grandson priest of Aaron, averted the full wrath of Almighty God by his drastic action in executing an especially brazen sexual couple, a prince from the tribe of Simeon and his harlot lover from Midian. In spite of this, 24,000 died (25:7-18).

Because of his faithfulness and fearlessness, God promised Phinehas his covenant of peace (v. 12), and from his family was to come Israel's high priest, and two priestly sons (two had already died through a divine punishment because of their sin). These were Eleazar and Ithamar. Phinehas was the son of Eleazar. But for some unknown reason the high priesthood was later switched from Eleazar to Ithamar in the person of Eli (1 Sam. 1), a descendant of Ithamar. However, in the days of David it returned to the promised line here through Zadok, a descendant of Eleazar. (See 1 Ki. 1:8.)

M. The second census (Num. 26).
1. The total of the second census is given as 601,730. (See v. 51.) This census, about thirty years after the first (1:46) was 1820 fewer.
2. Not one individual was alive who had been over twenty at the Kadesh rebellion, except for Moses, Caleb, and Joshua (26:64, 65).
3. The greatest decrease from the first census was in Simeon's tribe (37,100) and the greatest increase was in Manasseh (20,500).

N. Five determined daughters (27:1-11).
Zelophehad, a man from the tribe of Manasseh, had died, leaving five daughters but no sons. Those daughters then appealed to Moses and received the right to inherit their father's land when Palestine was later divided.

O. A change in commanders (27:12-23).
1. Eleazar the high priest is instructed to lay hands upon Joshua in a public ceremony, thus transferring Moses' authority over to him.
2. Joshua then becomes the new leader. Moses himself delivers the ordination address.

P. The mortification of Midian (31).
1. Moses' final order from God as Commander was to defeat and judge the Midianites for their former sin in refusing Israel passage through their land (25:6-18; 31:1, 2).
2. This Moses does by picking a thousand choice warriors from each of Israel's twelve tribes (31:3-7).

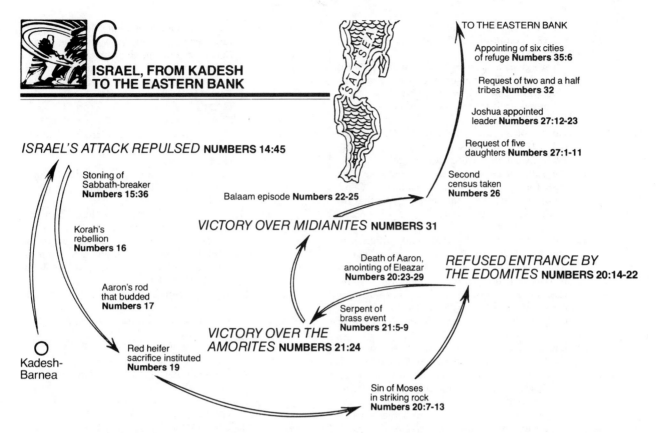

**6 ISRAEL, FROM KADESH TO THE EASTERN BANK**

*ISRAEL'S ATTACK REPULSED* **NUMBERS 14:45**

Stoning of Sabbath-breaker **Numbers 15:36**

Korah's rebellion **Numbers 16**

Aaron's rod that budded **Numbers 17**

Red heifer sacrifice instituted **Numbers 19**

Kadesh-Barnea

Balaam episode **Numbers 22-25**

*VICTORY OVER MIDIANITES* **NUMBERS 31**

*VICTORY OVER THE AMORITES* **NUMBERS 21:24**

Serpent of brass event **Numbers 21:5-9**

Death of Aaron, anointing of Eleazar **Numbers 20:23-29**

*REFUSED ENTRANCE BY THE EDOMITES* **NUMBERS 20:14-22**

Sin of Moses in striking rock **Numbers 20:7-13**

TO THE EASTERN BANK

Appointing of six cities of refuge **Numbers 35:6**

Request of two and a half tribes **Numbers 32**

Joshua appointed leader **Numbers 27:12-23**

Request of five daughters **Numbers 27:1-11**

Second census taken **Numbers 26**

The Midianites were descendants of Abraham through his wife Keturah (Gen. 25:2). Some forty years back Moses (a descendant of Abraham through Sarah) had married a Midianite, Zipporah. But in the ensuing years, this tribe had degenerated until they were no different from a dozen other pagan desert people.

A great contrast can be seen at this point, as one compares the account here with that described in the tribulation. In the first (Num. 31) God sends out 12,000 Israelite soldiers to consume their enemies, but in the second (Rev. 7) he will send out 144,000 Israelite preachers to convert their enemies.

Q. Some worldly warriors (Num. 32).
   1. The Reubenites, Gadites, and half-tribe of Manasseh come to Moses and ask permission to settle in Gilead, an area east of Palestine, just across the Jordan River.
   2. Moses sadly issues the requested permission, providing these two-and-a-half tribes would cross over with the remaining tribes and help defeat the Canaanites. To this they agree.
R. A summary of the sojournings (33).
   In this chapter Moses lists each camp site of Israel from Rameses, Egypt, to Shittim, Moah. They made no less than forty-two stops, thus moving to a new location every eleven months for forty years.
S. Six cities of salvation (35).
   1. These cities were: on the eastern side of Jordan—Bezer, Golan, and Ramoth. On the western side (in Palestine itself)—Kadesh, Shechem, and Hebron (Num. 35:10-14; Deut. 4:43; Josh. 20:7-9).

   2. These six were part of the forty-eight cities given to the Levites who did not receive a regular section of land as did the other tribes when the land was later divided by Joshua.
   3. The six were designated as refuge for all accidental manslayers to avoid the dead man's avenging relatives.
   4. The manslayer was safe as long as he remained in one of these six cities until the death of the high priest, at which time he could safely return home (35:25-28).
VII. Israel, on the Eastern Side of the River Jordan (Deuteronomy).
   On the banks of the Jordan Moses delivers three sermons to Israel, issues a challenge to Joshua, pronounces a blessing upon the individual tribes, composes a song, and departs for heaven.
   A. His three sermons.
      *First sermon* (Deut. 1-4).
      1. He relates the splendor of God they had experienced while at Mt. Sinai (4:10-19, 32, 33).
      2. He reviews their tragic sin at Kadesh-barnea (1:27). Thus a trip that should have taken but eleven days (from Mt. Sinai to Canaan) actually took some thirty-eight years (1:2).
      3. He reminds them of his own sin which would keep him from the Promised Land (3:23-27; 4:21, 22). (See also 31:1.)
      4. He urges Israel to encourage their new leader Joshua (1:38; 3:28). (See also 31:7, 8, 23.)
      5. He sets apart the three eastern cities of refuge (4:41-43).
      *Second sermon* (5-26).
      6. The Ten Commandments are repeated (5:7-21).

7. A warning is issued against immorality (23:17), compromise (7:1-5), and witchcraft (18:9-14).

8. Moses gives a description of Canaan (8:7, 8).

9. He reviews his personal experiences with God while upon Mt. Sinai (9:9-21).

10. He reminds them of their financial obligations to God (26).

11. Laws concerning clothing (22:5), divorce (24:1-4), woman's rights (21:10-17; 22:13-20), and warfare (20) are given.

12. He summarizes God's overall purpose and plan for that generation of Israelites. "And he brought us out from there [Egypt] that he might bring us in [Canaan] . . . ." (See 6:23.)

*Third sermon (27-30).*

13. He orders the blessings and judgments (curses) of the law to be read by the Levites upon two mountains when Israel entered the Promised Land. The blessings were to be read on Mt. Gerizim, and the curses upon Mt. Ebal. (See 11:26-29; 27:1-14.) The specific blessings are referred to in 28:1-14, and the curses in 27:15-26; 28:15-68.

14. Deuteronomy 28-30 records in seven parts the features of the Palestinian Covenant.

   a. Israel to be dispersed for disobedience (28:36, 49-53, 63-68; 30:1). This takes in the Assyrian, Babylonian, and Roman captivities, in addition to Israel's trials during the past twenty centuries. It would almost seem that Moses had Hitler's armies in mind when he wrote 28:64-67. During this time Israel would become a byword (28:37), and be the tail instead of the head (cf. 28:13 with 28:44).

   b. Israel will repent while in dispersion (30:2).

   c. The return of Christ will occur (30:3).

   d. Israel will be restored to the land (30:5).

   e. The nation will receive a new heart (30:6).

   f. Israel's oppressors will be judged (30:7).

   g. The nation will experience prosperity (30:9).

15. Moses offers his generation a choice between God's judgment or blessing (30:15-20). During these three sermons Moses expounds upon the following great theological themes:

   a. The faithfulness of God (2:7; 4:33-38; 7:6-8; 8:3, 4; 9:4-6; 29:5, 6; 32:9-14).

   b. The Word of God (4:1, 2, 7, 9; 11:18-21; 30:11-14).

   c. The Person of God (6:4, 5; 7:9; 32:39).

   d. The love of God (7:13).

   e. The glory of God (4:39; 10:17, 18).

   f. The grace of God (7:6-9; 9:4-6).

   g. The coming great prophet of God (18:15-20).

   h. The will of God (10:12-16).

   i. The kings of God (17:14-20).

   j. The Israel of God (4:25-31; 11:16, 17).

## Moses THE THEOLOGIAN

During these three sermons Moses expounds upon ten great theological themes.

1. THE **FAITHFULNESS** OF GOD
   **DEUTERONOMY 2:7; 4:33-38; 7:6-8; 8:3, 4; 9:4-6; 29:5, 6; 32:9-14**

2. THE **WORD** OF GOD
   **4:1, 2, 7, 9; 11:18-21; 30:11-14**

3. THE **PERSON** OF GOD
   **6:4, 5; 7:9; 32:39**

4. THE **LOVE** OF GOD
   **7:13**

5. THE **GLORY** OF GOD
   **4:39; 10:17, 18**

6. THE **GRACE** OF GOD
   **7:6-9; 9:4-6**

7. THE COMING **GREAT PROPHET** OF GOD
   **18:15-19**

8. THE **WILL** OF GOD
   **10:12-16**

9. THE **KINGS** OF GOD
   **17:14-20**

10. THE **ISRAEL** OF GOD
    **4:25-31; 11:16, 17**

   B. His challenges to Joshua (31). See especially 31:7, 8, 14, 23.

   C. His song. See 31:19-22, 30; 32:1-47.
      At this time Moses also completes the Pentateuch (first five books of the Bible). (See 31:9, 24.)

   D. His blessings upon the individual tribes (33).

   E. His departure for heaven (31:2, 14-18; 32:48-52; 34:1-12).

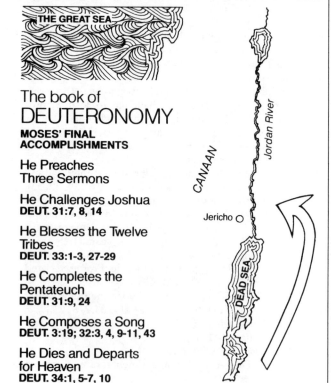

# 7
## ISRAEL, AT THE EASTERN BANK

THE GREAT SEA

## The book of DEUTERONOMY

**MOSES' FINAL ACCOMPLISHMENTS**

He Preaches Three Sermons

He Challenges Joshua
**DEUT. 31:7, 8, 14**

He Blesses the Twelve Tribes
**DEUT. 33:1-3, 27-29**

He Completes the Pentateuch
**DEUT. 31:9, 24**

He Composes a Song
**DEUT. 3:19; 32:3, 4, 9-11, 43**

He Dies and Departs for Heaven
**DEUT. 34:1, 5-7, 10**

CANAAN

Jordan River

Jericho O

DEAD SEA

**THE EXODUS STAGE**

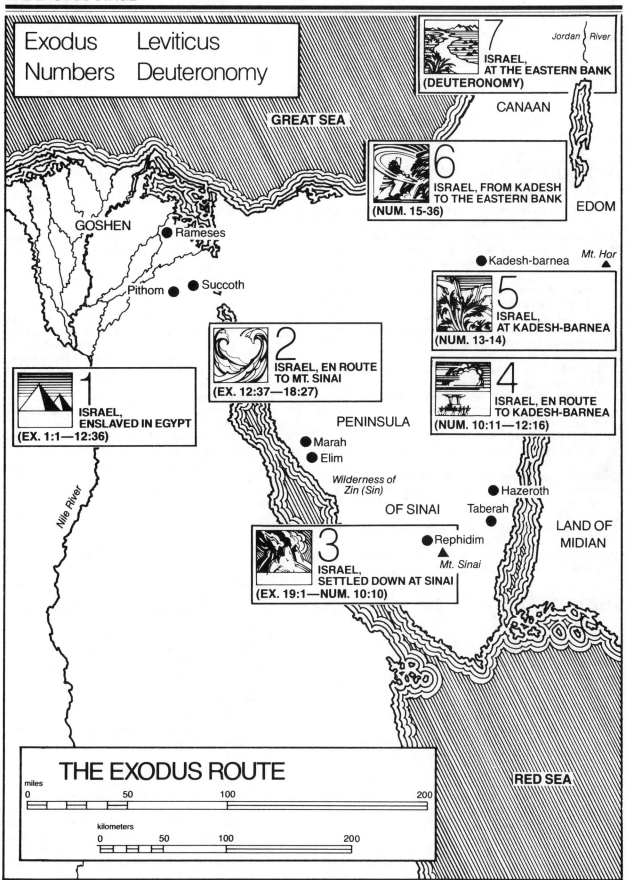

Exodus    Leviticus
Numbers   Deuteronomy

**7**
ISRAEL,
AT THE EASTERN BANK
(DEUTERONOMY)

*Jordan River*

CANAAN

GREAT SEA

**6**
ISRAEL, FROM KADESH
TO THE EASTERN BANK
(NUM. 15-36)

EDOM

GOSHEN

● Rameses

● Kadesh-barnea      *Mt. Hor* ▲

Pithom ●   ● Succoth

**5**
ISRAEL,
AT KADESH-BARNEA
(NUM. 13-14)

**2**
ISRAEL, EN ROUTE
TO MT. SINAI
(EX. 12:37—18:27)

**4**
ISRAEL, EN ROUTE
TO KADESH-BARNEA
(NUM. 10:11—12:16)

PENINSULA

**1**
ISRAEL,
ENSLAVED IN EGYPT
(EX. 1:1—12:36)

● Marah
● Elim

*Wilderness of
Zin (Sin)*

● Hazeroth

*Nile River*

OF SINAI

Taberah ●

LAND OF
MIDIAN

**3**
ISRAEL,
SETTLED DOWN AT SINAI
(EX. 19:1—NUM. 10:10)

● Rephidim
▲ *Mt. Sinai*

**THE EXODUS ROUTE**

miles
0          50          100                    200

kilometers
0      50      100              200

**RED SEA**

# THE CONQUEST STAGE

## INTRODUCING THE CONQUEST STAGE (Joshua)

1. The three most important individuals in this stage are Joshua, Caleb, and Rahab.
2. It covers a period of about twenty-five years.
3. The book describes the invasion, conquest, and settlement of Palestine by the nation Israel.
4. The book of Joshua is the counterpart of Exodus. *Exodus* records how God led his people *out of* the land of *bondage,* while Joshua tells us how he led his people *into* the land of *blessing.* Moses summarizes both books in Deuteronomy 6:23: "And he brought us out from there, that he might bring us in, to give us the land which he swore to give unto our fathers."
5. In Exodus God had parted the waters of the Red Sea to bring his people out of Egypt. Now in Joshua he will part the waters of the Jordan River to bring his people into Canaan. God performs whatever is necessary to assure both the exit and entrance of his people (Ex. 14:21, 22; Josh. 3:13-17).
6. Joshua has been called the Ephesians of the Old Testament.
7. In this stage we see the salvation of a harlot from the town of Jericho (Rahab) and the condemnation of a Hebrew from the tribe of Judah (Achan) (Josh. 6:25; 7:24-26).
8. We view a prince from glory and some beggars from Gibeon (Josh. 5:13-15; 9:3-15).
9. Joshua records the twin miracles of the falling walls and a standing sun (Josh. 6:20; 10:12-14).

## THE CONQUEST STAGE

I. The Invasion of the Land—Israel claims its possessions (1-5).
  A. The preparation (1:1-9).
    1. God speaks to Joshua.
       a. He was to lead Israel across the Jordan into Palestine.
       b. He was to be strong and courageous.
       c. He was to observe and meditate upon the Law of God.
       d. He could then be absolutely confident that, "The Lord thy God is with thee wherever thou goest" (1:9).
    2. Joshua speaks to Israel.
       "Prepare you victuals; for within three days ye shall pass over this Jordan . . ." (1:11).
  B. The penetration (2:1).
    1. Two men are sent to spy out Jericho.
    2. The King of Jericho learns of their mission and sends out a search party.

3. The spies are hidden by a newly converted ex-harlot named Rahab. Rahab had not only heard of the mighty power of God (2:9-11), but apparently come to trust him also. She must have possessed some kind of testimony, for it was to her house the spies first went, and later the King of Jericho guesses they might be hiding there also. This converted harlot is mentioned in three New Testament passages (Mt. 1:5; Heb. 11:31; Jas. 2:25). She later married a Hebrew man named Salmon, who may have been one of the spies. At any rate, this former pagan would later become the great-great-grandmother of King David. This is perhaps one of the most beautiful illustrations of the grace of God in the Bible.
  C. The passage (3:13).
    1. The priests were to lead the way to the Jordan River, carrying the Ark of God.
    2. The congregation was to follow them about a half-mile behind.
    3. When the priests put their feet into Jordan, the river immediately stopped flowing, thus allowing Israel to cross on dry ground.
  D. The pile of stones (4:1, 8, 9, 21).
    1. Upon crossing, Israel was to construct two memorial piles of twelve stones each. One pyramid was to be placed in the middle of the river and the other on the west side of Jordan.
    2. The pyramid on the western bank was there as a silent witness to future generations of God's faithfulness in rolling back Jordan's waters.
  E. The purification of the people (5:3).
     Upon reaching the western side of Palestine, God ordered the males of Israel to be circumcised. This was done, and the name of the place was called Gilgal, which means, "to roll away."
  F. The Passover (5:10).
     "And the Children of Israel encamped in Gilgal, and kept the passover on the fourteenth day of the month at even in the plains of Jericho."
  G. The passing diet (5:11, 12).
     "And they did eat of the old corn of the land on the morrow after the passover, unleavened cakes, and parched corn in the selfsame day. And the manna ceased on the morrow after they had eaten of the old corn of the land; neither had the children of Israel manna anymore; but they did eat of the fruit of the land of Canaan that year."

## THE CONQUEST STAGE

# The book of JOSHUA

## INVASION OF THE LAND

## Israel CLAIMS Its Possessions
### JOSHUA 1-5

**The PREPARATION 1:1-9**
God speaks to Joshua: I will be with you.

Joshua speaks to Israel: Get prepared, for we move out in three days.

**The PENETRATION 2:1-24**
Two Israeli spies search out Jericho. Upon being discovered, they are hidden by a newly converted harlot named Rahab.

**The PASSAGE 3:1-17**
The message from God: Step out as if the Jordan was solid rock.

The miracle from God: The waters of the Jordan are rolled back.

**The PILE OF STONES 4:1-24**
Israel was to place twelve huge stones on the western bank as a memorial reminder of the supernatural crossing.

**The PURIFICATION 5:2-9**
Upon reaching the western bank, the Israeli males are circumcised.

**The PASSOVER 5:10**
The Passover is observed upon the plains of Jericho.

**The PASSING DIET 5:11-12**
The manna ceases and they eat the food of the Promised Land.

**The PRINCE FROM HEAVEN 5:13-15**
Joshua is visited and reassured by Jesus himself.

H. The prince from heaven (5:13-15).
   1. Joshua receives a heavenly visitor, apparently Jesus himself on the eve of the battle against Jericho.
   2. Joshua is reassured of victory and is told (as once was Moses—Ex. 3:5) to remove his shoes.
II. The Subjection of the Land—Israel conquers its possessions (6-12).
   A. The central campaign (Josh. 6-8).
      1. Jericho—a city shouted down (6:20).
         a. This was the first recorded example of psychological warfare in history. Dr. John Davis writes the following about the actual march:

         "A single march around the nine-acre mound area probably took twenty-five to thirty-five minutes. It should not be concluded that every Israelite took part in this march. Such a feat would not only be impractical, but would be impossible. It is more probable to assume that the march was carried out by tribal representation." (*Conquest and Crisis,* p. 45)
         b. The command to destroy all the humanity in Jericho except Rahab and her household has been a problem to both saved and unsaved. Why would the God

of love and grace order this wholesale destruction? While God owes no living man an explanation for anything he does, there are nevertheless, certain factors undoubtedly involved.
   (1) When a culture or a city (like that of Sodom, Gen. 19) reaches a certain point of perversion, the holiness and justice of God demand that he step in and destroy it. The entire Canaanite society had long since reached that point. According to 1 Kings 14:24, the entire land was populated with loathsome sexual perverts.
   (2) God desired to keep Israel as pure as possible for as long as possible to assure the future purity of the line of Christ. Had Mary been an immoral woman, God would not and could not have used her.
   c. In verse 26 of this chapter, Joshua makes an amazing threefold prophecy about this fallen city. He predicted:
      (1) That Jericho would be rebuilt again by one man.
      (2) That the builder's oldest son would die when the work on the city had begun.
      (3) That the builder's youngest son would die when the work was completed.
   d. Joshua uttered these words around 1406 B.C. Did all this happen? Some five centuries later, in 930 B.C., we are told the following:
      (1) That a man named Hiel from Bethel rebuilt Jericho. That as he laid the foundations, his oldest son, Abiram, died.
      (2) That when he had completed the gates, his youngest son, Segub, died. (See 1 Ki. 16:34.)
   2. Ai—arrogance knocked down (7:3).
      a. After Jericho, Israel became overconfident and determined to send out only a token fighting force to subdue the next enemy, a little city called Ai.
      b. Israel's armies are totally routed by Ai and suffer a great loss of troops.
   3. Achan—a sinner sought (7:19).
      a. Joshua is told that this defeat was due to sin in the camp. Someone had disobeyed God and stolen some forbidden loot from Jericho.
      b. A divinely conducted manhunt begins and eventually points to Achan, from the tribe of Judah, as the criminal.
      c. He confesses to stealing a Babylonian robe, some silver, and a bar of gold.
      d. Achan is executed for this in the Valley of Achor.
   4. Gerizim and Ebal—the law handed down (8:30-35). As Moses had previously commanded, the blessings and curses of the law are read from Mt. Gerizim and Ebal.

B. The southern campaign (Josh. 9-10).
  1. Gibeon—the wool pulled over (9:3-6).
     a. When news of Jericho and Ai reached Gibeon, the people resorted to trickery to save themselves. They sent to Joshua ambassadors wearing worn-out clothing, as though they had come on a long journey. They had patched shoes, weather-worn saddle bags on their donkeys, old and patched wine skins, and dry moldy bread.
     b. Upon arriving, they persuaded Joshua to make a nonaggression treaty. They probably were aware of the Law of Moses (Deut. 7:1, 2; 20:10-15) which permitted Israel to make peace with far-off cities when Joshua entered Palestine, but not with the Canaanite nations living in close proximity to them.
  2. Ajalon—the sun shone down (10:12, 13).
     a. When the King of Jerusalem heard of the Gibeonite alliance with Israel, he formed a pact with four other kings for the purpose of destroying both Israel and Gibeon.
     b. Upon hearing this, Joshua is instructed to attack this alliance before they can attack him. During the battle, he is aided by a divinely sent hailstorm.
     c. Joshua then prayed God would allow the sun to give prolonged additional light for the mopping-up exercises. This happened, for the sun stopped in the heavens and stayed there for almost twenty-four hours.

Apart from the whale and Jonah, perhaps no other biblical miracle has caused such ridicule from unbelievers and so much uncertainty among believers. What really happened here? Three basic views can be found in the writings of sound Bible scholars.
     d. The total eclipse view. Dr. John Davis writes: "The essence of this view is that God brought darkness rather than light on this occasion" (*Conquest and Crisis*, p. 66).
     This prayer was then a petition from Joshua to shade his weary troops from the fierce Mideast sun. God, it would seem, answered this prayer by sending a massive hailstorm which not only cooled off Joshua's weary troops, but killed their enemies. No less a scholar than Dr. Robert Dick Wilson of Princeton advocates this theory, pointing out that the Hebrew word *dom*, translated "stand thou still" in the KJV, can also be correctly rendered "be silent," "cease," and "leave off." However, two serious objections would seem to discredit this view.
       (1) The account in Joshua 10:11 would indicate that the hailstorm occurred *before* Joshua's petition, and not after.
       (2) In verse 14, we are told that this day was absolutely unique in history, which simply would not be true if the miracle here involved only a massive hailstorm.
     e. The slowing down of the earth's rotation. The late scientist and Bible student Dr. Harry Rimmer held this view and cited Professor Pickering of Harvard Observatory along with Dr. Totten of Yale among those who favored this position. Another believer in this view is Immanuel Velikovsky, who suggests in his famous book, *Worlds in Collision*, that the miracle was caused by a comet which came near the earth, exerted its gravitational pull, and disrupted normal movement. The comet's icy tail, according to Velikovsky, could have provided the hailstones. Finally, in listing the various points which favor the second view, it may be said that research has brought to light reports from Egyptian, Chinese, and Hindu sources of such a long day. But the second view is not without its problems.
       (1) One consideration is the sheer staggering power it would take to slow down or stop the earth on its own axis. Our planet weighs some six trillion tons and at the equator is moving about a thousand miles an hour. It has been estimated that it would take roughly twenty million billion of our largest hydrogen bombs to stop the earth. Of course, God is capable of anything, but compared to this the impressiveness of the universal flood (the greatest Old Testament miracle) would shrink significantly. In fact, this would require more raw power than anything God had ever done since creation, either before or after. If this really occurred, however, it would seem strange that the only other reference to it is found in Habakkuk 3:11.
       (2) If the second view is correct, then God would be required to do this same stupendous thing again for Hezekiah. Dr. John Davis writes:
         "It is extremely doubtful that such a miracle was performed on that occasion. In fact, the parallel passage found in 2 Chronicles 32:24-31 seems to imply that it was a local miracle. Verse 24 of this passage indicates that God gave a special sign to Hezekiah. That sign was evidently witnessed only in Palestine, for verse 31 records the fact that ambassadors from Babylon were sent down to Hezekiah to 'inquire of the wonder that was done in the land'! If the miracle performed in the days of Hez-

ekiah was universal, there would be little need for ambassadors to come all the way from Babylon to inquire of the miracle." (*Conquest and Crisis*, p. 69)

  f. The extension of refraction of the sun's rays on a local level. Taking everything into consideration, this would seem to be the most scriptural approach. At least two other instances come to mind when God did a similar thing concerning light and darkness on a local level. These are:

   (1) The three-day darkness upon the land of Egypt (Ex. 10:21–23).
   (2) The three-hour darkness surrounding the area of the cross (Mk. 15:33).

 3. Makkedah—five kings cut down (10:10, 28).

  a. During the battle, the king of Jerusalem, the one who organized and led the southern campaign against Israel, and four other kings took refuge in a cave at Makkedah.
  b. Joshua had these kings taken from the cave and, in a victory celebration, ordered the captains of his army to put their feet on the kings' necks. They were then executed.

C. The northern campaign (Josh. 11–12).

 1. Hazor—a capital burned down (11:13).
  Jaban, King of Hazor, organized and led the northern attack against Israel. He was soundly defeated and had his capital burned to the ground.
 2. Merom—the horses slowed down (11:6, 9). Here, Joshua hamstrung the horses, thus rendering them useful for farm work but useless for warfare.

III. The Distribution of the Land—Israel colonizes its possessions (13–24).

 A. The land divided.
  The land was now partitioned under the supervision of Joshua, Eleazar, and the key tribal leaders by the casting of lots (14:1, 2; 19:51).

  1. The land east of Jordan: Reuben, Gad, and one half tribe of Manasseh.
  2. The land west of Jordan: Judah, Ephraim, one half tribe of Manasseh, Benjamin, Simeon, Zebulun, Issachar, Asher, Naphtali, Dan.
  3. The land for Levi: Levi was given no land, as God himself would be its portion (13:33). However, the tribe was given forty-eight special cities from the remaining eleven tribes (21:41).

 B. A warrior excited.
  Caleb visits with Joshua and gives one of the most thrilling testimonies in all the Bible. Note his challenging words in 14:7–12.

 C. An altar indicted (22).
  1. After the land was divided, Israel set up the tabernacle at Shiloh (18:1).
  2. Joshua called together the armies of the two

## SUBJECTION OF THE LAND

### Israel CONQUERS Its Possessions
**JOSHUA 6-12**

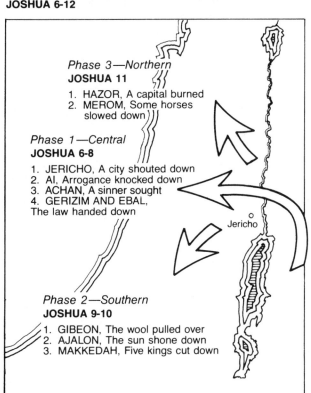

*Phase 3—Northern*
**JOSHUA 11**
1. HAZOR, A capital burned
2. MEROM, Some horses slowed down

*Phase 1—Central*
**JOSHUA 6-8**
1. JERICHO, A city shouted down
2. AI, Arrogance knocked down
3. ACHAN, A sinner sought
4. GERIZIM AND EBAL, The law handed down

Jericho

*Phase 2—Southern*
**JOSHUA 9-10**
1. GIBEON, The wool pulled over
2. AJALON, The sun shone down
3. MAKKEDAH, Five kings cut down

## DISTRIBUTION OF THE LAND

### Israel COLONIZES Its Possessions
**JOSHUA 13-24**

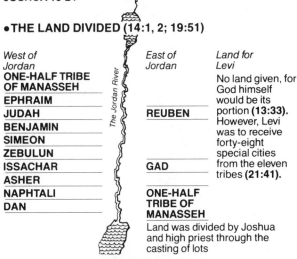

● **THE LAND DIVIDED (14:1, 2; 19:51)**

| West of Jordan | East of Jordan | Land for Levi |
|---|---|---|
| **ONE-HALF TRIBE OF MANASSEH** | | No land given, for God himself would be its portion **(13:33)**. However, Levi was to receive forty-eight special cities from the eleven tribes **(21:41)**. |
| **EPHRAIM** | | |
| **JUDAH** | **REUBEN** | |
| **BENJAMIN** | | |
| **SIMEON** | | |
| **ZEBULUN** | | |
| **ISSACHAR** | **GAD** | |
| **ASHER** | | |
| **NAPHTALI** | **ONE-HALF TRIBE OF MANASSEH** | |
| **DAN** | | |

Land was divided by Joshua and high priest through the casting of lots

● **A WARRIOR EXCITED (14:7-12)**
Caleb visits Joshua and relates one of Scripture's most thrilling testimonies.

● **AN ALTAR INDICTED (chapter 22)**
1. The tabernacle was set up in Palestine at Shiloh (18:1).
2. The two-and-one-half eastern tribes set up an altar on the Jordan bank as a reminder of their common heritage with the western tribes.
3. This was at first misinterpreted as an act of rebellion and a civil war was narrowly averted.

● **A FINAL SERMON RECITED (23-24)**
Joshua's last words to Israel

and a half tribes at Shiloh, blessed them, and sent them to their chosen home on the east side of Jordan.

3. Before crossing the river, these two and a half tribes erected a large monument in the shape of an altar to remind them and their unborn children of their common heritage with the tribes on the west side of Jordan.

4. This was misinterpreted by the nine and a half tribes as an act of rebellion and an ugly civil war was threatened.

5. The misunderstanding was cleared up just in time by an eleven man delegation from the nine and a half tribes led by Aaron's grandson, Phinehas.

D. A final sermon recited (23–24).
   Joshua's last words to Israel.
   1. He reminds them of God's goodness (23:3).
   2. He warns them concerning disobedience (23:11–13).
   3. He reviews this history (24:1–13).
   4. He challenges them to serve God (24:14–18).

## INTRODUCING THE JUDGES STAGE
### (Judges; Ruth; 1 Samuel 1–7)

1. This stage records the saddest and most sordid period in the entire history of Israel. It is the dark ages of that nation.
2. Important names in this period would include Gideon, Samson, Naomi, Ruth, Boaz, Eli, and Samuel.
3. The book spans a period of some 300 years.
4. In brief, it records seven apostasies on Israel's part, seven servitudes to seven heathen nations, and seven deliverances.
5. The following two outlines have been suggested which summarize the Judges Stage.
   a. Rebellion, retribution, repentance, and restoration (or)
   b. Sin, servitude, supplication, and salvation.
6. Counting Eli and Samuel, there were fifteen judges in all. One was a woman, Deborah. These judges were not so much legal experts, as military reformers.
7. The root of Israel's problem was that when Joshua died, God could find no man to take his place as he did when Moses died. The statement, "In those days there was no king in Israel; every man did that which was right in his own eyes," is repeated on four separate occasions in the book of Judges. (See 17:6; 18:1; 19:1; 21:25.) This period is thus the antithesis of the millennium when King Jesus will rule with a rod of iron (see Ps. 2).
8. The fruit of Israel's problems could be seen in her:
   a. Compromise—not doing what God told her to do, that is, to drive out the enemy. (See 1:21, 27–33; 2:1–5.)

      "And an angel of the Lord came up from Gilgal to Bochim, and said, I made you to go up out of Egypt, and have brought you unto the land which I sware unto your fathers; and I said, I will never break my covenant with you. And ye shall make no league with the inhabitants of this land; ye shall throw down their altars: but ye have not obeyed my voice; why have ye done this? Wherefore I also said, I will not drive them out from before you; but they shall be as thorns in your sides, and their gods shall be a snare unto you."

   b. Apostasy—doing what God told her not to do, that is, to worship the gods of her enemies. (See 2:11–15; 6:8–10.)

      "And the children of Israel did evil in the sight of the Lord, and served Baalim: And they forsook the Lord God of their fathers, which brought them out of the land of Egypt, and followed other gods, of the gods of the people that were round about them, and bowed themselves

      unto them, and provoked the Lord to anger. And they forsook the Lord, and served Baal and Ashtaroth" (Jdg. 2:11–13).

9. In spite of all this God still loved Israel. In the Old Testament the angel of the Lord is mentioned eighty times. It is thought by most theologians that the angel of the Lord in the Old Testament was none other than Christ himself. No less than twenty of these instances are in the book of Judges. Thus, during no other stage does God so minister to his people.
10. The final part of Galatians 5 provides an excellent summary of the books of Joshua and Judges. (See 5:22–26 concerning Joshua and 5:17–21 concerning Judges.)

    "Now the works of the flesh are manifest, which are these; Adultery, fornication, uncleanness, lasciviousness, idolatry, witchcraft, hatred, variance, emulations, wrath, strife, seditions, heresies, envyings, murders, drunkenness, revellings, and such like: of the which I tell you before, as I have also told you in time past, that they which do such things shall not inherit the kingdom of God. But the fruit of the Spirit is love, joy, peace, longsuffering, gentleness, goodness, faith, meekness, temperance: against such there is no law" (Gal. 5:19–23).

    Note the overall contrast between these two stages:

    | Joshua | Judges |
    |---|---|
    | a. victory | defeat |
    | b. freedom | slavery |
    | c. faith | unbelief |
    | d. progress | declension |
    | e. obedience | disobedience |
    | f. heavenly vision | earthly emphasis |
    | g. joy | sorrow |
    | h. strength | weakness |
    | i. unity among tribes | disunity among tribes |
    | j. strong leader | no leader |

11. Judges is the classic example of Hosea 8:7 and Galatians 6:7.

    "For they have sown the wind, and they shall reap the whirlwind" (Hosea 8:7a).

    "Be not deceived; God is not mocked: for whatsoever a man soweth, that shall he also reap. For he that soweth to his flesh shall of the flesh reap corruption; but he that soweth to the Spirit shall of the Spirit reap life everlasting" (Gal. 6:7, 8).

    Note especially Judges 6:3.

    "And so it was, when Israel had sown, that the Midianites came up, and the Amalekites, and the children of the east, even they came up against them" (Jdg. 6:3).

    This almost seems to be a play on words. Read it again carefully.

12. Judges also offers seven illustrations of 1 Corinthians 1:27.

"But God hath chosen the foolish things of the world to confound the wise; and God hath chosen the weak things of the world to confound the things which are mighty."

In Judges, God used:
a. an oxgoad (3:31)
b. a nail (4:21)
c. some trumpets (7:20)
d. some pitchers (7:20)
e. some lamps (7:20)
f. a millstone (9:53)
g. the jawbone of an ass (15:15)

13. In Judges we thus see:
a. The first Nazarite recorded in history (Jdg. 13:2–5).
b. The strongest man recorded in history (15:15).
c. A bloodthirsty son (Abimelech) and a heartbroken father (Jephthah) (9, 11).
d. An evil spirit and the Spirit of God (9:23; 13:24, 25).
e. An army put to death for mispronouncing a word (12).
f. Three hundred victorious men and 600 desperate men (7:7; 20:46, 47).
g. One of the two fables in the Bible (9:7–15).
h. A new name for God (6:24).
i. Fox catching, riddle telling, fleece throwing, and hair cutting (15:4; 14:14; 6:36–40; 16:19).

14. The book of Ruth in brief.
a. It is the first of two biblical books to bear the name of a woman.
b. Ruth becomes the third of four women to be included by Matthew in his genealogy of Christ (See Mt. 1.)
c. The history of this book, which took place during the Judges Stage, is like a pure lily floating on the vast cesspool of sin.
d. It records the first of three all-important trips to the little city of Bethlehem in the Bible (Ruth 1:19). (For the other two, see 1 Sam. 16:4; Lk. 2:4.)
e. It offers the greatest example of Christ as our Kinsman Redeemer in the entire Bible.
f. Ruth becomes the second of two women in the Old Testament who foreshadow the church in the New Testament. (The other is Rebekah; see Gen. 24.)

15. The first seven chapters of 1 Samuel in brief.
a. We find one of the greatest dedicatory prayers for one's child ever uttered.

"And she said, Oh my lord, as thy soul liveth, my lord, I am the woman that stood by thee here, praying unto the Lord. For this child I prayed; and the Lord hath given me my petition which I asked of him: Therefore also I have lent him to the Lord; as long as he liveth he shall be lent to the Lord. And he worshipped the Lord there" (1 Sam. 1:26–28).

b. The description of one of Israel's saddest moments—the capture of their beloved Ark of the Covenant (1 Sam. 4:10, 11).
c. A divine midnight call to a young boy (1 Sam. 3:1–10).
d. The agony of a dying mother and the ecstasy of a grateful prophet.
(1) The agony is seen in the word *Ichabod.*

"And his daughter in law, Phinehas' wife, was with child, near to be delivered: and when she heard the tidings that the ark of God was taken, and that her father in law and her husband were dead, she bowed herself and travailed; for her pains came upon her.

And about the time of her death the women that stood by her said unto her, Fear not; for thou hast born a son. But she answered not, neither did she regard it.

And she named the child Ichabod, saying, The glory is departed from Israel: because the ark of God was taken, and because of her father in law and her husband.

And she said, The glory is departed from Israel: for the ark of God is taken" (1 Sam. 4:19–22).

(2) The ecstasy is seen in the word *Eben-ezer.*

"And as Samuel was offering up the burnt-offering, the Philistines drew near to battle against Israel: but the Lord thundered with a great thunder on that day upon the Philistines, and discomfited them; and they were smitten before Israel.

And the men of Israel went out of Mizpeh, and pursued the Philistines, and smote them, until they came under Beth-car.

Then Samuel took a stone, and set it between Mizpeh and Shen, and called the name of it Eben-ezer, saying, Hitherto hath the Lord helped us" (1 Sam. 7:10–12).

## THE JUDGES STAGE

"In those days there was no king in Israel, but every man did that which was right in his own eyes" (17:26). See also 19:1; 21:25.

"And the children of Israel did evil in the sight of the Lord, and served Baalam" (2:11).

"And the anger of the Lord was hot against Israel, and he delivered them into the hands of the spoilers . . ." (2:14).

"Nevertheless the Lord raised up judges, who delivered them out of the hand of those who spoiled them" (2:16).

The main action of the Judges stage. The key events during this period center around the following individuals or groups of individuals.

I. Twelve Military Reformers.
II. A Bloody Butcher.
III. An Idol-Worshiping Son.
IV. A Cowardly Levite.
V. A Moabite Girl.
VI. A Dedicated Mother.
VII. An Undisciplined Priest.
VIII. Some Frustraed Philistines.
IX. A Circuit-riding Preacher.

We shall now examine in some detail each of these nine.

I. Twelve Military Reformers—The Judges.
A. First judge: Othniel (1:12, 13; 3:8–11).
1. Oppressing nation: Mesopotamia
2. Length of oppression: eight years
3. Years of peace he gave: forty
4. Accomplishments:
Othniel was both the nephew and the son-in-law of Caleb (1:13). He won his wife by

successfully defeating a strong enemy city which his tribe Judah was attempting to capture (1:12). Othniel had already proven his bravery. (See Josh. 15:15-20.) He was one of the many judges said to be filled with the Holy Spirit (3:10). He defeated the King of Mesopotamia (3:10) which had plagued Israel for eight long years (3:8). The land now had rest for forty years (3:11).

B. Second judge: Ehud (3:12-30).
1. Oppressing nation: Moab
2. Length of oppression: eighteen years
3. Years of peace: eighty years
4. Accomplishments:
Ehud was a left-handed Benjaminite (Jdg. 3:15). In Old Testament times God often especially blessed left-handed warriors. (See Jdg. 20:16; 1 Chron. 12:2.)

Ehud was chosen to carry Israel's annual (and hated) tax money to the Moabite capital. Israel had been doing this for eighteen years (3:14, 15).

After paying the tax, Ehud secured a private meeting with Eglon, the fat Moabite king, claiming he had a "message from God" for the king. He thereupon stabbed Eglon with a double-edged eighteen-inch dagger (Jdg. 3:16-23). We note however that the Bible does not say he did this by the Spirit of God.

He then fled to the hill country of Ephraim where he sounded the war trumpet, raised an army, attacked the Moabites (killing 10,000), and gave rest to the land for the next eighty years (Jdg. 3:26-30).

C. Third judge: Shamgar (3:31).
1. Oppressing nation: Philistia
2. Length of oppression: unrecorded
3. Years of peace: unrecorded
4. Accomplishments: With an ox goad this soldier killed 600 Philistines.

D. Fourth judge: Barak (as helped by Deborah, Jdg. 4-5).
1. Oppressing nation: northern Canaanites
2. Length of oppression: twenty years
3. Years of peace: forty years
4. Accomplishments:
Israel (at this time) had been in bondage to King Jaban of Hazor (a Canaanite ruler) for twenty years (4:3). Jaban had a five-star general named Sisera, who commanded 900 iron chariots plus a huge marching army (4:2, 3).

At this time Israel was judged by a woman whose name was Deborah (4:4, 5). She informed Israel's army commander, a man named Barak, that God had chosen him to mobilize 10,000 men from the tribes of Naphtali and Zebulun. He was then to lead them to Mt. Tabor and do battle with Sisera (4:6, 7).

At his insistence, Deborah agrees to go with him, but warns him that the honor of conquering Sisera will not be credited to him, but to another woman (4:8, 9).

Barak leads his 10,000 men down the slopes of Mt. Tabor and, through God's in-tervention, totally routs and defeats Sisera (4:14, 15).

Sisera escapes and takes refuge in the tent of a Kenite housewife named Jael. Pretending to befriend him, she lulls him to sleep and kills him by driving a peg through his brain (4:17-21). Deborah and Barak thereupon sing their "duet of deliverance" hymn of praise to God.

The land then was to enjoy rest for forty years (5:31). Barak is later included in the New Testament hall of fame (Heb. 11:32). This fifth chapter of Judges is the third great song of praise in the Bible thus far. The other two are Exodus 15 and Deuteronomy 32.

E. Fifth judge: Gideon (6-8).
1. Oppressing nation: Midian
2. Length of oppression: seven years
3. Years of peace: forty years
4. Accomplishments:
After Barak's death, Israel returned to idolatry and God delivered them into the hands of the cruel Midianites for seven years. (Note their sad plight: Jdg. 6:2-6.)

A nameless (and fearless) prophet reminded Israel that their terrible circumstances were due to sin (6:8-10). An angel of the Lord (Jesus?) appeared at this point to Gideon, who was threshing wheat by hand in the bottom of a grape press to hide it from the Midianites (6:11).

Gideon is divinely commissioned to defeat the Midianites, and thereupon builds an altar to God, calling it *Jehovah-shalom* ("the Lord send peace," Jdg. 6:12-24).

Note: In spite of his many doubts, Gideon shows real faith at this time of famine by offering a young goat and baked bread sacrifice. Gideon thus, like Abraham, prepared a meal for God himself. (See Gen. 18.)

That very night, at God's command, Gideon pulls down the family altar of Baal and replaces it with an altar to Jehovah (6:25-27). Gideon's father, Joash, calms down an angry crowd the next morning who would have killed Gideon for his brave act. God's Spirit then comes upon Gideon. Gideon blows a trumpet and sounds a call to arms (6:34, 35).

He then throws out the fleece (twice) and is thus reassured concerning his call by God (6:36-40). Was Gideon justified in doing this? Is it ever God's will for a believer to throw out a fleece? Is the old cliche "testing is not trusting" correct? Let us consider the following:
5. Biblical examples of fleece throwing:
a. The servant of Abraham (Gen. 24:14). He was sent to find a bride for Isaac in a foreign land. Upon arriving, he prayed and threw out a fleece. God obviously accepted this fleece prayer. Especially thrilling are the words, "and it came to pass, before he had done speaking, that, behold, Rebekah came out" (v. 15).
b. King Ahaz (Isa. 7:11).
"Moreover the Lord spake again unto Ahaz saying, Ask thee a sign of the

Lord thy God; Ask it either in the depth, or in the height above. But Ahaz said, I will not ask, neither will I tempt the Lord" (Isa. 7:10-12).

In this instance, God himself invited this wicked Judean king who was threatened by outside enemies to ask for any sign he wanted and God would perform it to prove that Jerusalem would be saved from her enemies. But the evil ruler refused.

c. King Hezekiah (2 Ki. 20:10, 11).

God caused the sundial shadow to go back ten degrees, showing he would be healed. Again, it may be observed that God honored this requested sign.

d. Satan (Mt. 4:6).

"Then the devil taketh him up into the holy city, and setteth him on a pinnacle of the temple, And saith unto him, If thou be the Son of God, cast thyself down: for it is written, He shall give his angels charge concerning thee: and in their hands they shall bear thee up, lest at any time thou dash thy foot against a stone. Jesus said unto him, It is written again, Thou shalt not tempt the Lord thy God" (Mt. 4:5-7).

Here the Savior rightly refused to perform the perverted fleece-throwing as suggested by the devil.

e. Gideon (Jdg. 6:37).

Several facts may be immediately seen:

(1) The Lord had already on two previous occasions clearly assured Gideon of what he was to do. (See 6:14, 16.)

(2) The Lord had on one occasion actually given a sign that Gideon had requested. (See 6:17-21.)

6. Basic conclusions on fleece-throwing:

a. On certain occasions the believer may rightfully seek God's will through a fleece of some sort. This may be done:

(1) *If* the Scriptures have not already answered his request. In other words, it would be totally in error to throw out a fleece concerning whether God desired a believer to quit body-harming habits, for to do so is clearly implied in many passages. (See 1 Cor. 6:19, 20.)

(2) *If* the immediate circumstances are indefinite and unclear. Let us suppose a missionary feels strongly about entering a country whose doors have just been closed to all Christian work. He then would be perfectly justified in asking God to open those doors if it is his perfect will.

(3) *If* his fleece does not limit the action God must take. To illustrate this, it would be unwise for a pastoral candidate, when preaching a trial sermon, to pray that God would show

him this was the church he should accept by having exactly seven come forward during the invitation for salvation. What if there were eight present that morning whom God desired to save? Or what if there were indeed seven there under conviction, all being dealt with by the Holy Spirit, but it was not God's perfect will for the pastoral candidate to accept that church?

b. In Gideon's case, while God did honor his fleece-prayer, it was nevertheless unnecessary (for he already knew what he should do), and unprofitable, for he later needed reassurance again. (See Jdg. 7:10.)

God thereupon cut down his army from 32,000 to 22,000, and finally down to 300 (7:2-7). With these 300 he would face 135,000 enemy troops (see 8:10). Gideon and his servant made their way behind enemy lines on the eve of the battle and were once again reassured of victory by overhearing an enemy conversation (7:10-15). Gideon divided his army into three companies, and upon the signal, each man blew a trumpet, broke a clay jar, raised up a blazing torch, and shouted, "The sword of the Lord, and of Gideon" (7:16-20). The army of Midian was thrown into panic and completely routed (7:21-24). Gideon pursued them across the Jordan River where he finished defeating them. He thereupon returned to Palestine and severely punished two towns which had refused to feed his 300 hungry troops (8:4-17).

Gideon then executed the two pagan Midianite kings for killing his brothers at Tabor (8:18-21). He refused an offer by Israel to become king over them, but requested the gold earrings captured in battle, plus other war booty (8:22-26).

From this gold he made an ephod. Soon Israel began worshiping this, and it became a snare for the nation (8:27).

Note: An ephod was part of the apparel worn by the high priest. Gideon had previously declined to offer to become king, but he may have had aspirations for the priestly office.

Gideon eventually settled down, married many wives, and raised seventy-one sons (and doubtless many daughters also). One of these sons was named Abimelech, who would later cause much bloodshed after Gideon's death (8:29-31). Because of Gideon's work the land would enjoy rest for forty years (8:28).

F. Sixth judge: Tola (10:1).

1. Oppressing nation: unrecorded
2. Length of oppression: unrecorded
3. Years of peace: twenty-three
4. Accomplishments: unrecorded

G. Seventh judge: Jair (10:3-5).

1. Oppressing nation: unrecorded
2. Length of oppression: unrecorded
3. Years of peace: twenty-two

4. Accomplishments: He and his thirty sons delivered thirty Israeli cities from oppression.

H. Eighth judge: Jephthah (10:6—12:17).
   1. Oppressing nation: Ammon
   2. Length of oppression: eighteen years
   3. Years of peace: six
   4. Accomplishments:

After Abimelech's death, Israel was judged by Tola for twenty-three years. The clan of Tola was later known in David's time for its men of valor (1 Chron. 7:1, 2). After Tola's death, God raised up a man called Jair, who judged for twenty-two years. When Jair died, Israel once again "did evil in the sight of the Lord," and was turned over to the Philistines and Ammonites for a period of eighteen years (10:6-8). Fickle and foolish Israel once again turned to God in their hour of great need. As usual, he was filled with compassion and promised deliverance, but not before delivering a soul-searching message. Note its content: Judges 10:10-16. This passage in Judges should be compared with Isaiah 63:7-9. God now raised up Jephthah, the son of a harlot. He had been rejected by his own brethren due to his illegitimate birth (11:1-11).

Jephthah attempts to negotiate with the Ammonites concerning some disputed land east of Jordan. He argues that:

a. The land was originally the Amorites' and not the Ammonites' (Num. 21:21-30).

b. God gave the land to Israel and she had been there for the last 300 years.

At this statement a state of war existed between the two countries. God's Spirit came upon him, and Jephthah prepared for battle (11:28, 29). On the eve of the battle, however, Jephthah did something which would later cause him much pain and anguish. We read in Judges 11:30, 31:

"And Jephthah vowed a vow unto the Lord, and said, If thou shalt without fail deliver the children of Ammon into mine hands, then it shall be, that whatsoever cometh forth of the doors of my house to meet me, when I return in peace from the children of Ammon, shall surely be the Lord's, and I will offer it up for a burnt offering."

God delivered the Ammonites into Jephthah's hands (11:32, 33). But his real problem was just beginning. We read in Judges 11:34, 35:

"And Jephthah came to Mizpeh unto his house, and, behold, his daughter came out to meet him with timbrels and with dances: and she was his only child; beside her he had neither son nor daughter.

And it came to pass, when he saw her, that he rent his clothes, and said, Alas, my daughter! Thou hast brought me very low, and thou art one of them that trouble me: for I have opened my mouth unto the Lord, and I cannot go back."

Much ink has been used throughout the years by theologians concerning this passage. What was involved in Jephthah's vow here? Dr. John J. Davis writes:

"There are, therefore, today, two prevailing interpretations of this portion of chapter 11. The *first* is that he did not kill his daughter. This view is suggested by a number of conservative writers. The arguments for this view are as follows: (1) Jephthah was too well acquainted with the law to be ignorant of God's condemnation of human sacrifices (11:15-27). (2) He must have known that a human being would come out of the home. Furthermore, an animal would have been too small a sacrifice for such a victory. (3) Jephthah must have been a godly man, or his name would not have appeared in Hebrews 11. (4) If his daughter were to be slain, there would be no point in emphasizing her virginity (37-39). (5) Jephthah could not have done this, especially after the Spirit of God came upon him (29). (6) There were women at this time who gave their lives to serving the Lord in the tabernacle at Shiloh (1 Sam. 2:22). Thus, Jephthah could have vowed that in case of victory, he would dedicate to God for tabernacle service one member of his household. The fact that it turned out to be his daughter was tragic for him. Because she was his only child, he would never expect to see grandchildren; and he would seldom, if ever, see her again. (7) It is argued that the conjunction which appears in the vow in verse 31 should be translated 'or' rather than 'and.' In other words, Jephthah is thought to have said, 'Whatever comes from the doors of my home to meet me as I return shall be devoted to the Lord's service if it is human, or if it is a clean animal, I will offer it up as a whole burnt offering. (8) It is argued by those holding this view that the expression 'to lament' in verse 40 should be translated 'to talk to,' indicating that the daughter remained alive.

The *second* view with regard to Jephthah's vow and its fulfillment is that he did offer his daughter as a human sacrifice. Again this view is supported by many well-known writers. The arguments for this view are as follows: (1) The Hebrew word for burnt offering is *olah* which always has the idea of a burnt sacrifice in the Old Testament. (2) Jephthah was the son of a common heathen prostitute *Zonah* and spent a great deal of time with various peoples on the east side of the Jordan (11:1-3). Furthermore, it should be observed that later individuals engaged in such human sacrifice. Second Kings 3:26, 27 records the action of the king of Moab in offering his eldest son for a burnt offering on the wall of his city. Second Chronicles 28:3 tells of Ahaz's burning of his children, and 2 Kings 21:6 tells of Manasseh's sacrifice of his son. If such practices were followed by leaders in Israel at the later period, it is not impossible that they could have been introduced at this earlier period. (3) The fact that Jephthah was a judge of Israel does not remove the possibility of his making a rash vow. The dominant philosophy of this day was a moral and spiritual relativism in which 'every man did that which was right in his own eyes' (Jdg. 21:25). Many of Israel's leaders were affected by this attitude. Recall that Gideon made a golden ephod which led Israel to idolatry, and Samson engaged in activities that were obviously in opposition to the law of Moses. (4) If Jephthah could lead in the slaughter of 42,000 Israelites (Jdg. 12), he would therefore be capable of this vow and its fulfillment. (5) The fact that her virginity is bewailed in verses 36-40 seems to imply that there was no hope for children in the future because of her impending death. This discussion 'is probably mentioned to give greater force to the sacrifice, as it would leave him without issue, which in the east was considered a special misfortune.' Finally, the argument based upon the Hebrew word for 'lament' in verse 40 by those holding the dedication view is rather tenuous. The verb *tanah* occurs only once elsewhere in the Hebrew Bible (Jdg. 5:11). The best translation of this form appears to be 'to recount.' " (*Conquest and Crisis*, pp. 125-128)

After all this, Jephthah's troubles were not yet over, for he was provoked into battle by the jealous tribe of Ephraim (Jdg. 12:4-7). This tragic battle, won by Jephthah, resulted in the loss of 42,000 Ephraimite troops. It was one of the strangest ever fought, because many of those troops lost their lives due to their inability to pronounce the word *Shibboleth* (Hebrew for "stream") correctly.

I. Ninth judge: Ibzan (12:8-10).
   1. Oppressing nation: unrecorded
   2. Length of oppression: unrecorded
   3. Years of peace: seven
   4. Accomplishments: unrecorded
J. Tenth judge: Elon (12:11, 12).
   1. Oppressing nation: unrecorded
   2. Length of oppression: unrecorded
   3. Years of peace: ten
   4. Accomplishments: unrecorded
K. Eleventh judge: Abdon (12:13-15).
   1. Opposing nation: unrecorded
   2. Length of oppression: unrecorded
   3. Years of peace: eight
   4. Accomplishments: unrecorded
L. Twelfth judge: Samson (13-16).
   1. Opposing nation: Philistia
   2. Length of oppression: forty
   3. Years of peace: twenty (16:31)

4. Accomplishments:
   Prior to Samson's birth, Israel had been in bondage to the Philistines for forty years (13:1).
   Samson's mother is visited by the angel of the Lord, who tells her of his future birth (13:2, 3). She thus becomes one of the four biblical women who received such a pre-birth angelic promise. The three others were:
   a. Sarah (Gen. 18:10-14)
   b. Elisabeth (Lk. 1:13)
   c. Mary (Lk. 1:30, 31)
   This heavenly messenger instructed the parents that their child was to be raised a Nazarite (13:4, 5). According to Numbers 6:1-6, the Nazarite had three restrictions placed upon him.
   d. He was not to touch wine.
   e. His hair was to remain untouched by a razor.
   f. He must not touch a dead body.
      (Note: Samson's mother was also commanded not to drink wine, 13:4, 14.)
   On this occasion Samson's parents prayed a prayer all expectant Christian parents should pray (Jdg. 13:8, 12). Who was this angel of the Lord: The parents attempted to discover his name, but were told, "it is secret" (v. 17). The Hebrew word here translated "secret," can also be rendered "wonderful," and is very similar to the word used in Isaiah 9:6, where we are told concerning Christ's birth that, "his name shall be called Wonderful, Counsellor, The Mighty God, The Everlasting Father, The Prince of Peace." This would strongly indicate a pre-Bethlehem appearance of the Lord Jesus Christ.
   Samson was born and empowered by the Holy Spirit even as he grew up (13:24, 25).
   He determined to marry an unbelieving Philistine girl, to the dismay of his parents. Already Samson's carnal nature is seen coming to the surface. In spite of his sensuality, God used him for his glory (14:1-4).
   En route to Philistia Samson kills a lion. Later he discovers that a swarm of bees had chosen the carcass of the lion to make honey in. At his wedding feast Samson uses this experience as a basis for a riddle (Jdg. 14:12-14).

## THE JUDGES STAGE

The books of
# JUDGES; RUTH; 1 SAMUEL (1-7)
### THE JUDGES

| Othniel | Gideon | Ibzan |
| --- | --- | --- |
| Ehud | Tola | Elon |
| Shamgar | Jair | Abdon |
| Deborah | Jephthah | Samson |
| Barak | | |

The guests eventually would dishonestly solve this riddle, getting the answer from Samson's bride. He becomes furious at this and pays his debt to the wedding guests, but only at the expense of thirty Philistine victims (14:15-19).

He returns only to find that the girl's father had given his bride to Samson's best man! In an act of revenge, the Hebrew strong man does the following:

"And Samson went and caught three hundred foxes, and took firebrands, and turned tail to tail, and put a firebrand in the midst between two tails. And when he had set the brands on fire, he let them go into the standing corn of the Philistines, and burnt up both the shocks, and also the standing corn, with the vineyards and olives" (Jdg. 15:4, 5).

He then killed many Philistines (15:8). After this, the Philistines threaten to destroy the tribe of Judah unless Samson is bound and delivered to them. Samson meekly allows himself to be tied up, but as the enemy comes in view he breaks the ropes, grabs the jawbone of an ass, and slaughters 1,000 Philistines (15:9-17).

He then prays one of his only two recorded prayers. Both are totally carnal and self-centered. (Compare 15:18 with 16:28.)

At Gaza (a Philistine city) Samson once again avoids capture, this time by ripping apart the iron gate of the city (16:1-3). Samson is finally done in by a Philistine woman named Delilah, who discovers the source of his great strength (16:4-20).

Note: At this point, Samson has violated

## TWELVE MILITARY REFORMERS

### Othniel JUDGES 1:12, 13; 3:8-11
Oppressing nation—**Mesopotamia**
Length of oppression—**8 years**
Years of peace **40 years**
He was both nephew and son-in-law of Caleb.
He captured a strong Canaanite city.

### Ehud (3:12-30)
Oppressing nation—**Moab** Length of oppression—**18 years**
Years of peace **80 years**
He assassinated a fat Moabite enemy king named Eglon.
He organized an Israeli army which killed 10,000 enemy troops.

### Shamgar (3:31)
Oppressing nation—**Philistia** Length of oppression—**unrecorded**
Years of peace **unrecorded**
He killed 600 Philistines with an oxgoad.

### Barak (4-5)
Oppressing nation—**Canaanites**
Length of oppression—**20 years**
Years of peace **40 years**
He raised an army of 10,000 at Deborah's encouragement.
He defeated enemy general named Sisera at base of Mt. Tabor.
Sisera is killed later by Jael while in her tent sleeping.
Barak and Deborah sang a duet of praise over their victory.

### Gideon (6-8)
Oppressing nation—**Midian** Length of oppression—**7 years**
Years of peace **40 years**
He was commissioned by God to defeat the Midianites.
He prepared for this by destroying the family idols.
He threw out the fleece twice.
He raised an army of 10,000.
He saw this army reduced to 300 by God.
He defeated 135,000 enemy troops with his 300.
He caused Israel to sin by making a golden ephod.

### Tola (10:1)
Oppressing nation—**unrecorded** Length of oppression—**unrecorded**
Years of peace **23 years**
Unrecorded

### Jair (10:3-5)
Oppressing nation—**unrecorded** Length of oppression—**unrecorded**
Years of peace **22 years**
He and his 30 sons delivered 30 Israeli cities from oppression.

### Jephthah (10:6—12:17)
Oppressing nation—**Ammon** Length of oppression—**18 years**
Years of peace **6 years**
He was a harlot's son who became a mighty warrior.
On the eve of battle he made a rash vow to God: if victorious he would offer the first thing that greeted him. His daughter met him and he sadly performed his vow.
He is later provoked into battle with the jealous tribe of Ephraim.

### Ibzan (12:8-10)
Oppressing nation—**unrecorded** Length of oppression—**unrecorded**
Years of peace **7 years**
Unrecorded

### Elon (12:11, 12)
Oppressing nation—**unrecorded** Length of oppression—**unrecorded**
Years of peace **10 years**
Unrecorded

### Abdon (12:13-15)
Oppressing nation—**unrecorded** Length of oppression—**unrecorded**
Years of peace **8 years**
Unrecorded

### Samson (13-16)
Oppressing nation—**Philistia** Length of oppression—**40 years**
Years of peace **20 years**
He was to be raised as a Nazarite.
He killed a lion en route to his wedding.
He killed 30 Philistines to pay off a clothing debt.
Upon losing his wife, he burned the wheat fields of the Philistines.
He killed 1000 Philistines with the jawbone of an ass.
He ripped off an iron gate at Gaza.
He was betrayed into the hands of the Philistines by Delilah.
He was shaven, blinded, and enslaved.
He was supernaturally empowered to destroy many Philistines in their own temple by pulling it down.
He himself was killed at this time.

# THE JUDGES STAGE

The action during this period centers around nine individuals or groups of individuals.

**TWELVE MILITARY REFORMERS**

**A BLOODY BUTCHER**

**AN IDOL-WORSHIPING SON**

**A COWARDLY LEVITE**

**A MOABITE GIRL**

**A DEDICATED MOTHER**

**AN UNDISCIPLINED PRIEST**

**SOME FRUSTRATED PHILISTINES**

**A CIRCUIT-RIDING PREACHER**

all three Nazarite vows. He had touched the carcass of a lion (14:8, 9). He had drunk wine (14:10). He had allowed his hair to be cut (16:19).

Samson now learns the high cost of low living (Jdg. 16:21).

"But the Philistines took him, and put out his eyes, and brought him down to Gaza, and bound him with fetters of brass; and he did grind in the prison house."

In prison he regains his strength as his hair grows out again. He is then allowed by God to destroy thousands of Philistines who had gathered in their heathen temple for a drunken orgy. In the following destruction Samson himself perished (Jdg. 16:22–31).

II. A Bloody Butcher—Abimelech (9).
  A. Abimelech was the son of Gideon by a concubine in Shechem (8:31). He arranged for the brutal murder of sixty-nine of his seventy half-brothers and was crowned "king" of his mother's hometown, Shechem (9:1–5).

  Jotham, the half-brother who escaped, relates one of the two fables in the Bible (for the other, see 2 Ki. 14:9), and directs it at Abimelech, whom he ridicules as a "thornbush bramble king." Note his dripping sarcasm in Judges 9:8–14.

  Three years later God stirred up trouble between King Abimelech and the citizens of Shechem. In the ensuing struggle, Abimelech was killed (Jdg. 9:22–57). Some Christians have been bothered concerning the statement recorded in Judges 9:23:

  "Then God sent an evil spirit between Abimelech and the men of Shechem; and the men of Shechem dealt treacherously with Abimelech."

This is the first of at least three Old Testament instances when such action took place. Let us briefly examine each occasion.
  1. Saul (1 Sam. 16:14, 23)
  2. Ahab (2 Chron. 18:18–22)
How are we to understand these verses? Two basic interpretations have been offered:
  a. That these were angelic messengers sent from God to do his works of judgment as the seven elect angels will one day do during the coming tribulation. (See Rev. 8:2.)
  b. That these were demonic fallen angels. The context, it would seem, favors this view. They are described as evil, and the word used is the same Hebrew word found in Genesis 6:5, where we are told God destroyed mankind for their evil hearts. But why would evil spirits request to be used of God, and why would the Lord comply? Here one should carefully read Job 1 and 2. Satan himself had requested permission to torment Job. God allowed it, but only to fulfill his divine purpose.

In Abimelech's case, God had pronounced doom upon this mad dog through a woman of Shechem, thus making way for a godly ruler named Tola, who would defend the sheep of Israel, and not butcher them as Abimelech had done. (See Jdg. 10:1.) The evil spirit obviously had a different motive in mind for the removal of Abimelech. He had proven to be an inept bungler who for three years had failed to extend his wicked reign beyond the city boundaries of Shechem. Perhaps the evil spirit had hoped to work through another wicked man. But it didn't succeed! In Saul's case, the evil spirit apparently hoped to totally control him in an attempt to remove from the scene the hated David. But again, it would fail, for God had already set in motion those plans which would lead to his death on a Philistine battlefield.

In Ahab's case, the evil spirit may have wanted the wicked king to go into battle, willing to sacrifice this faithful devil worshiper in order to get to Jehoshaphat. As things turned out, had not God stepped in, the foolish Jehoshaphat would indeed have fallen in battle (see 2 Chron. 18:28–32). Thus, God often uses the wrath of wicked men and even demons for his glory (Ps. 76:10). For two New Testament instances in which God will use both wicked men and demons for his glory, consider the following passages:
  (1) Revelation 16:13, where he will use demons to entice men to Armageddon.
  (2) Revelation 17:16, 17, where he will cause the antichrist to destroy the false church.

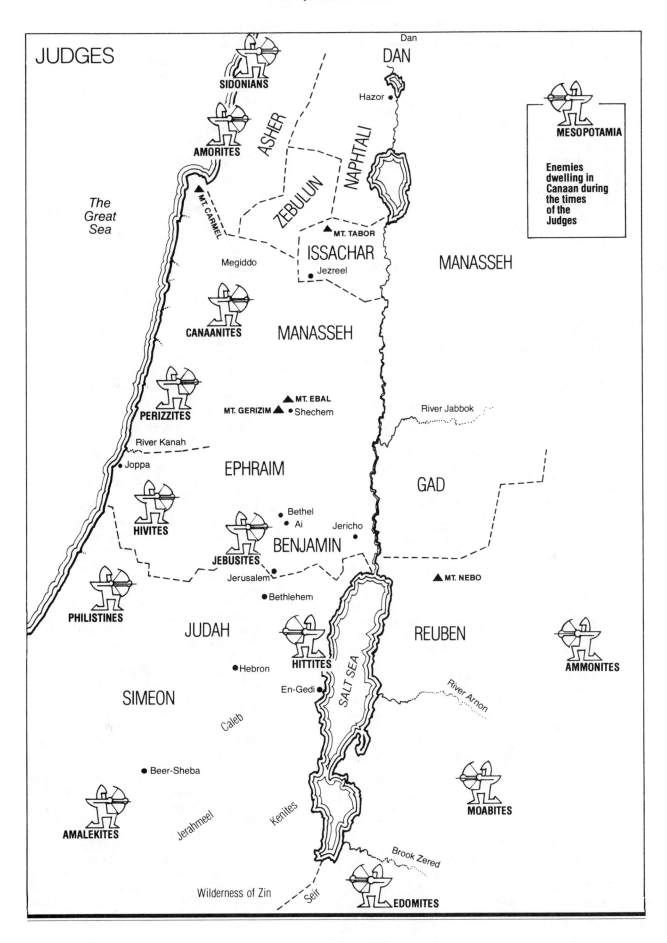

JUDGES

SIDONIANS

DAN

Dan

Hazor

ASHER

AMORITES

ZEBULUN

NAPHTALI

MESOPOTAMIA

Enemies dwelling in Canaan during the times of the Judges

The Great Sea

MT. CARMEL

MT. TABOR

ISSACHAR

MANASSEH

Megiddo

Jezreel

CANAANITES

MANASSEH

PERIZZITES

MT. EBAL

MT. GERIZIM · Shechem

River Jabbok

River Kanah

· Joppa

EPHRAIM

GAD

HIVITES

Bethel

Ai

Jericho

JEBUSITES

BENJAMIN

Jerusalem

MT. NEBO

· Bethlehem

PHILISTINES

JUDAH

REUBEN

AMMONITES

· Hebron

HITTITES

SALT SEA

SIMEON

En-Gedi

River Arnon

Caleb

· Beer-Sheba

Jerahmeel

Kenites

MOABITES

AMALEKITES

Brook Zered

Wilderness of Zin

Seir

EDOMITES

## A TERRIBLE TRIO

### Abimelech, the bloody butcher— Judges 9

1. He was the mad-dog son of Gideon.
2. He arranged for the murder of sixty-nine of his half-brothers. Only a man named Jotham escaped.
3. He set up his "kingdom" at Shechem.
4. He was later killed by God, who used an evil spirit and an old woman to perform his will.

### Micah, a mother-spoiled thief and idol worshiper— Judges 17-18

1. He is encouraged by his indulgent mother to "start his own religion."
2. He does this by hiring his own personal priest, a money-hungry Levite from Bethlehem.
3. This perverted "private pastor" is later enticed by the tribe of Dan to become their official priest.

### A cowardly and emotionally sick Levite— Judges 19-21

1. A Levite and his concubine are threatened by a mob of sex perverts while visiting in the land of Benjamin.
2. He saves his miserable hide by allowing this corrupt crowd to sexually murder the woman.
3. He then cuts up her dead body into twelve pieces and sends a bloody chunk to each tribe in Israel.
4. An army of 450,000 is raised, but the Benjamin tribe officials refuse to hand over the guilty men.
5. A civil war breaks out, which leaves but 600 Benjaminite soldiers alive.
6. A plan is effected by the eleven tribes to provide wives for these 600, lest the tribe of Benjamin disappear.

III. An Idol-Worshiping Son—Micah (17-18).

Micah, a thief and idol worshiper, is encouraged by his indulgent mother to "start his own religion." This he does by (among other things) hiring his own personal priest, a money-grabbing Levite from Bethlehem (17:1-13). This perverted "private pastor" is later enticed by the tribe of Danites to become their official priest (18:1-31).

IV. A Cowardly Levite (19-21).

A. These three chapters are among the most depressing in all the Bible. The story began when a Levite and his unfaithful concubine wife stopped overnight in Gibeah, a city located in the tribal territory of Benjamin (19:1-15).

B. The couple stayed with an old man. That night his house was surrounded by a group of sex perverts who demanded the Levite come out and partake of their disgusting and degrading actions. The cowardly Levite saved himself by giving his wife over to this miserable mob. By morning time the perverts had sexually murdered her (19:16-27).

C. The Levite (who apparently was emotionally sick himself) thereupon cut her dead body into twelve pieces, and sent a bloody chunk to each tribe in Israel along with the story of what happened (19:28, 29).

D. Israel was enraged at this sexual crime and gathered an army of some 400,000 troops to punish the guilty perverts of Gibeah (19:30—20:11).

E. The citizens of Benjamin, however, refused to surrender the criminals and a civil war broke out. After an especially bloody three-battle war in

which Israel lost 40,000 men, Benjamin was defeated. When the body "dead count" was in, only 600 out of some 26,000 soldiers of Benjamin were left alive. A sobered and saddened Israel then provided wives for these 600, lest the very name of Benjamin disappear from the face of the earth (20:12—21:25).

V. A Moabite Girl—Ruth (Ruth 1-4).

A. Chapter one: Ruth renouncing.

1. During a famine, a Bethlehem citizen named Elimelech (which means, "God is King"), his wife Naomi ("the sweet one") and their two sons, Mahlon and Chilion ("sick" and "pining") leave Palestine and go into Moab (Ruth 1:1, 2).

2. The two boys marry, but soon tragedy strikes, for at first the father dies, and then both sons, leaving three saddened widows (1:3-5).

3. Naomi decides to return to Palestine and is accompanied by her older daughter-in-law, Ruth. Naomi attempts to persuade Ruth to go back to her own home. Ruth's answer must be counted as one of the most beautiful statements ever to come from the human throat. She says (in Ruth 1:16, 17):

"And Ruth said, Intreat me not to leave thee, or to return from following after thee: for whither thou goest, I will go; and where thou lodgest, I will lodge: thy people shall be my people, and thy God my God: where thou diest, will I die, and there will I be buried: the Lord do so to me, and more also, if ought but death part thee and me."

4. Ruth and Naomi begin their difficult trip, walking nearly 100 miles and crossing mountains a mile high. Upon their return, a disillusioned Naomi instructs her old neighbors to call her "Mara," which means, "bitter," and not Naomi (1:20-22).

B. Chapter two: Ruth requesting.

1. Ruth goes out to glean wheat and, in the providence of God, picks a field belonging to Boaz, a near relative of Elimelech (2:1-3). Boaz was the son of the ex-harlot, Rahab (Mt. 1:5).

2. Boaz sees her, and apparently falls in love with her. He treats her kindly and orders his hired hands to do the same (2:15, 16).

3. Ruth brings home some thirty pounds of barley and reports the kindness of Boaz to Naomi, who immediately begins planning a wedding (2:19-23).

C. Chapter three: Ruth resting.

1. Naomi sends Ruth to Boaz with instructions for her to assume a position at his feet. This has been looked upon by some as an immoral act, but no one who knew the custom of Israel and the ancient oriental world would make such a claim. According to Hebrew law, Ruth was entitled to call upon her nearest of kin to fulfill the various duties of a kinsman redeemer. By this course of action, Ruth was doing just this. Boaz understood fully her request to: "spread therefore thy

skirt over thine handmaid; for thou art a near kinsman" (3:9).

From this point on, Boaz took the necessary steps to marry Ruth. This custom is still practiced to some extent among the Arabs today.

2. Boaz then explains to Ruth why he had not proposed marriage to her before this time: "There is a kinsman nearer than I" (3:12).
3. Ruth returns home to Naomi with a full report. Naomi reassures her concerning Boaz by the following words:

"Then said she, Sit still, my daughter, until thou know how the matter will fall: for the man will not be in rest, until he have finished the thing this day" (3:18).

D. Chapter four: Ruth reaping.
1. Boaz called a council meeting to determine whether the nearest kinsman (who may have been a brother to Elimelech) wanted to assume his obligations (4:1-4).

Note: Boaz's heart must have dropped to his knees when the man said, "I will redeem

# RUTH
## A Moabite Girl

## Chapter One
### Ruth Renouncing
- A citizen from Bethlehem named Elimelech, his wife Naomi, and their two sons move to Moab during a famine.
- The boys marry Moabite girls, but soon both father and sons die, leaving three widows.
- Naomi returns to Bethlehem, accompanied by one of her daughters-in-law, named Ruth, who had renounced her Moabite gods for the true God of Israel.

## Chapter Two:
### Ruth Requesting
- In the providence of God Ruth gleans wheat in a field owned by Boaz, a near relative of Elimelech.
- At their first meeting, Boaz falls in love with Ruth.
- Upon learning of this, Naomi begins planning for the wedding.

## Chapter Three:
### Ruth Reaping
- Naomi sends Ruth to Boaz, that she might request of him to fulfill his responsibility as a kinsman redeemer.
- Boaz is thrilled with Ruth's request, but tells her there is a kinsman redeemer closer than he.
- Ruth returns home and leaves the matter with God.

## Chapter Four:
### Ruth Rejoicing
- Boaz arranges a meeting with the closer kinsman redeemer.
- Upon hearing the facts, he steps aside and allows Boaz to fulfill the kinsman redeemer responsibilities, including marriage to Ruth.
- Ruth presents Boaz with a male baby which is named Obed.

it" (4:4). But Boaz continues the meeting, saying:

"What day thou buyest the field of the hand of Naomi, thou must buy it also of Ruth the Moabitess, the wife of the dead, to raise up the name of the dead upon his inheritance" (4:5).

With a great sigh of relief, and no doubt a silent prayer of thanksgiving to God, Boaz hears the nearest kinsman conclude:

"I cannot redeem it for myself, lest I mar mine own inheritance: redeem thou my right to thyself; for I cannot redeem it" (4:6).

2. The issue was no longer in doubt. Boaz would now marry Ruth. To confirm this decision, the man plucked off his shoe. It was the custom at that time in Israel for a man transferring a right of purchase to pull off his sandal and hand it to the other party. This publicly validated the transaction (4:7-10).
3. In time, God gave Boaz and Ruth a son named Obed. Obed would grow up and father a boy named Jesse, who would in turn have a son called David. Thus a Moabite girl who was once heathen would become the great-grandmother of King David, and be included in the New Testament genealogy of the Lord Jesus Christ. (See Mt. 1:5). This is perhaps one of the most thrilling examples of God's marvelous grace in all the Bible.

IV. A Dedicated Mother—Hannah (1 Sam. 1:1—2:11, 18-21).

A. The account begins when a barren woman stands weeping and praying at the altar in Shiloh. Her name was Hannah. We note her prayer in 1 Samuel 1:11.

We observe several factors in this request:
1. Part of Hannah's sorrow was due to constant ridicule from her husband's other wife, Peninnah (1:6). God never sanctioned polygamy, for it always brought grief and frustration. (See Gen. 21:9-11; 30:1.)
2. Dr. John Davis writes concerning this prayer of Hannah:

"In great bitterness of soul she prayed to the Lord and the essence of this prayer is wrapped up in two words found in verse 11, 'remember me.' These words have a familiar ring to them. One is reminded of the simplicity of Samson's prayer recorded in Judges 16:28. In blindness and helplessness he cried out to his God and asked to be 'remembered.'

This prayer was also found on the lips of a man being crucified at Calvary. One of the malefactors who was hanged with Jesus looked to Him with faith and said, 'Lord remember me when thou comest into thy kingdom.' " (See Lk. 23:42.) (*Conquest and Crisis*)

3. Hannah vows that if a son is given to her, she will raise him as a Nazarite. Thus her boy, Samuel, would become one of the three Nazarites mentioned in the Bible. The other two were Samson (Jdg. 13) and John the Baptist (Lk. 1).

## THE SORROWING, SINGING SAINT

# Hannah

### Her Sorrow 1 SAMUEL 1:1-19
- Hannah was a barren and ridiculed woman.
- Even her anguished prayer was misinterpreted in the Temple by Eli the priest.
- She promised God that any son given her would be raised as a Nazarite.
- She is reassured about this from God through Eli.

### Her Song 1 SAMUEL 1-2
- Hannah gives birth to Samuel.
- Upon weaning him she brings him to Eli for Temple service unto God.
- She sings a hymn of praise to God for:
  1. Blessing the poor and humble over the rich and proud
  2. Keeping the feet of his saints
  3. Rightfully judging the earth
- In her hymn she utters a Messianic prophecy:
  "He shall give strength unto his king, and exalt the horn of his anointed" **(2:10).**
- Hannah later has three additional sons and two daughters. **(1 SAM. 1:20—2:11, 18-21).**

4. In her soul's agony, Hannah moves her lips, but makes no audible sound, which causes the old high priest Eli (who has been secretly watching her) to conclude that she is drunk (1:12, 13).
B. Upon being rebuked for this supposed drunkenness, Hannah immediately denies the charge and then shares with Eli the true nature of her heartache. The old priest thereupon reassures her that God will indeed answer her prayer (1:14-18).
C. In the course of time God did "remember" Hannah (compare with Gen. 8:1) with a son whom she called Samuel. When he was weaned (probably at two or three years of age) Hannah brought him to Eli to dedicate him to God (1 Sam. 1:26-28).
D. After the dedication, Hannah utters a beautiful ode of praise which appears to be the basis of Mary's song found in Luke 1:46-55. (See 1 Sam. 2:1-11.)
VII. An Undisciplined Priest—Eli (1 Sam. 2:12-17, 22-36; 4:1-22).
A. A sad note is now introduced concerning the priestly sons of Eli. According to the sacred account:
  1. They were unsaved (2:12).
  2. They regarded Belial as the true God (2:12).
  3. They stole the offerings from God (2:14).
  4. They bullied the people of God (2:14).
  5. They committed adultery right in the tabernacle (2:22).
  6. They caused God's people to transgress (2:17, 24).

B. Eli attempts to correct this by a mild and weak "slap on the wrist," but his wicked sons remain unmoved and unrepentant (2:22-25).
C. Eli was warned by an unnamed prophet of God concerning the following:
  1. That his two wicked sons would both die on the same day (2:34).
  2. That God would raise up a faithful priest (2:35).
  Note: There has been some speculation concerning the identity of this "faithful priest." Let us briefly examine this:
  3. God originally instituted the priesthood through Aaron, who was a descendant of Levi (Ex. 28:43; 29:9).
  4. Aaron had four sons. Two were slain by God due to their wickedness (Lev. 10). The other two were Eleazar and Ithamar. The line of the high priest was apparently to continue through Eleazar. At his death, Phinehas took office (Num. 25:11-13).
  5. However, after this, for some unexplained reason, the line was shifted from Eleazar's line to that of Ithamar in the person of Eli.
  6. Some Bible students feel that the verse in 1 Samuel 2:35 is a reference to Zadok, from the line of Eleazar, who would later be the faithful spiritual advisor to King David (1 Ki. 1:7, 8). This prophecy also indicates that there would never lack a descendant of Zadok to walk before God's anointed kings. Zadok's seed will walk before Christ in the millennial temple (Ezek. 44:15; 48:11; 43:19).
D. God revealed himself to Samuel one night as the boy lay in his bed in the Temple. The bulk of this divine message was the future judgment of Eli's household. The next morning a reluctant Samuel relates all this to Eli (3:1-18).
E. Samuel is now elevated by God to the office of a prophet (3:19-21).

## Eli
### THE UNDISCIPLINED PRIEST FATHER

### SINS OF HIS SONS
They were unsaved **(1 Sam. 2:12)**
They regarded Belial as the true god **(2:12)**
They stole the offerings from God **(2:14)**
They bullied the people of God **(2:14)**
They committed adultery right in the tabernacle **(2:22)**
They caused God's people to transgress **(2:17, 24)**

### WARNINGS TO HIS SONS
By God through an unnamed prophet **(2:34)**
By God through the boy Samuel **(3:1-18)**

### DEATH OF HIS SONS
Israel is defeated by the Philistines **(1 Sam. 4:1-10)**
The ark is captured **(4:11)**
Eli's sons are killed **(4:11)**
Eli learns of this, falls from his seat, and dies **(4:12-18)**
His daughter-in-law dies in childbirth, but not before naming her baby boy Ichabod **(4:19-22)**

F. After this, Israel is soundly defeated by the Philistines. During the battle, the Ark of the Covenant is captured, and Eli's two sons, Hophni and Phinehas, are killed (4:1–11).

G. The tragic news is brought back to Shiloh, which results in the death of Eli and the total despair of his daughter-in-law (1 Sam. 4:14, 18–22).

VIII. Some Frustrated Philistines (1 Sam. 5–6).

A. The captured Ark of the Covenant proved a curse among the Philistines wherever it was taken.

　1. At Ashdod, it destroyed the statue of the idol god Dagon and smote the people with boils (5:1–7).

　2. At Gath it wrought great destruction and similar boils (5:8, 9).

　3. At Ekron it brought great fear and more boils (5:10).

　　Note: Dr. John Davis writes the following concerning the various plagues suffered by the Philistines:

　　"Many feel that this is one of the first references to the 'black death,' or bubonic plague. This is inferred from the mention of tumors and mice (possibly rats) that 'marred the land.'" (See 6:4, 5.) (*Conquest and Crisis*)

B. The ark is then placed by the Philistines on a wooden cart hitched to two cows. On this cart are also placed five golden mice (6:1–11).

C. The ark is carried to an Israelite town called Beth-shemesh, where it is first received with great rejoicing, but later brings great sorrow, for some foolish men look into the ark and cause a divine punishment from God (6:12–19).

D. From Beth-shemesh, the ark is taken to another Israelite town named Kirjath-jearim. Here it was to remain for twenty years (7:1, 2).

IX. A Circuit-riding Preacher—Samuel (1 Sam. 7).

"And Samuel grew, and the Lord was with him, and did let none of his words fall to the ground. And all Israel from Dan even to Beer-sheba knew that Samuel was established to be a prophet of the Lord. And the Lord appeared again in Shiloh . . . [and] revealed himself to Samuel" (1 Sam. 3:19–21).

A. At this time the great prophet and priest Samuel gathers all of Israel at Mizpeh (another town in Palestine) for a great revival (7:3–6).

B. When the Philistines hear of this gathering, they mobilize their armies and prepare to attack. But at Samuel's cry, God steps in and utterly routs the Philistines (7:7–14).

"So the Philistines were subdued, and they came no more into the coast of Israel: and the hand of the Lord was against the Philistines all the days of Samuel" (7:13).

"And Samuel judged Israel all the days of his life. And he went from year to year in circuit to Bethel, and Gilgal, and Mizpeh, and judged Israel in all those places. And his return was to Ramah; for there was his house; and there he judged Israel; and there he built an altar unto the Lord" (7:15–17).

## SAMUEL, THE CIRCUIT-RIDING PREACHER

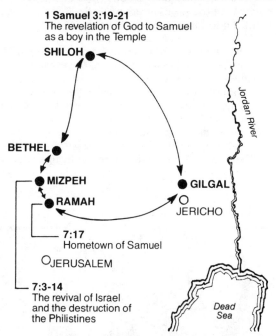

**1 Samuel 3:19-21**
The revelation of God to Samuel as a boy in the Temple

SHILOH

BETHEL

MIZPEH

RAMAH

GILGAL

JERICHO

**7:17**
Hometown of Samuel

JERUSALEM

**7:3-14**
The revival of Israel and the destruction of the Philistines

Jordan River

Dead Sea

*"And Samuel judged Israel all the days of his life. And he went from year to year in circuit to Bethel, and Gilgal, and Mizpeh, and judged Israel in all those places. And his return was to Ramah; for there was his house, and there he judged Israel, and there he built an altar unto the Lord"*
**1 SAMUEL 7:15-17**

## THE TRAVELING ARK

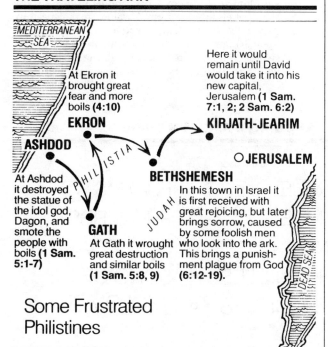

MEDITERRANEAN SEA

At Ekron it brought great fear and more boils (4:10)

Here it would remain until David would take it into his new capital, Jerusalem (**1 Sam. 7:1, 2; 2 Sam. 6:2**)

**EKRON**

**KIRJATH-JEARIM**

**ASHDOD**

PHILISTIA

○ **JERUSALEM**

At Ashdod it destroyed the statue of the idol god, Dagon, and smote the people with boils (**1 Sam. 5:1-7**)

**BETHSHEMESH**

JUDAH

**GATH**
At Gath it wrought great destruction and similar boils (**1 Sam. 5:8, 9**)

In this town in Israel it is first received with great rejoicing, but later brings sorrow, caused by some foolish men who look into the ark. This brings a punishment plague from God (**6:12-19**).

DEAD SEA

## Some Frustrated Philistines

# THE UNITED KINGDOM STAGE

## INTRODUCING THE UNITED KINGDOM STAGE (1 Samuel 8-31; 2 Samuel; 1 Kings 1-11; 1 Chronicles; 2 Chronicles 1-9; Psalms; Proverbs; Ecclesiastes; Song of Solomon)

1. This stage, covering a period of approximately 120 years, records the history of Israel's first three kings. Each ruled for forty years. The kings are Saul, David, and Solomon.
2. Most of Israel's beautiful songs and words of wisdom were composed during this period. These would include: Psalms, Proverbs, Song of Solomon, and Ecclesiastes.
3. The period begins with the selection of a ruler (Saul, 1 Sam. 9) and ends with the rejection of another ruler (Rehoboam, 1 Ki. 12).
4. It includes a visit to the witch of En-dor (1 Sam. 28) and a visit by the Queen of Sheba (1 Ki. 10).
5. The death of two babies is noted. The first (2 Sam. 12) pointed out the wages of sin, while the second (1 Ki. 3) pointed out the wisdom of Solomon.

   "And David said unto Nathan, I have sinned against the Lord. And Nathan said unto David, The Lord also hath put away thy sin; thou shalt not die. Howbeit, because by this deed thou hast given great occasion to the enemies of the Lord to blaspheme, the child also that is born unto thee shall surely die" (2 Sam. 12:13, 14).

   "And the king said, Divide the living child in two, and give half to the one, and half to the other. Then spake the woman whose the living child was unto the king, for her bowels yearned upon her son, and she said, O my lord, give her the living child, and in no wise slay it. But the other said, Let it be neither mine nor thine, but divide it. Then the king answered and said, Give her the living child, and in no wise slay it: she is the mother thereof. And all Israel heard of the judgement which the king had judged; and they feared the king: for they saw that the wisdom of God was in him, to do judgement" (1 Ki. 3:25-28).

6. During this period a city is saved (1 Sam. 11), some animals are spared (1 Sam. 15), and a giant is slain (1 Sam. 17).
7. It describes a fearless prophet (Nathan, 2 Sam. 12), and a faithful priest (Zadok, 2 Sam. 15).
8. The Ark of God on two occasions is carried to Jerusalem, once during a celebration (2 Sam. 6), and again during a revolution (2 Sam. 15).

   "So David and all the house of Israel brought up the ark of the Lord with shouting, and with the sound of the trumpet. And they brought in the ark of the Lord, and set it in his place, in the midst of the tabernacle that David had pitched for it: and David offered burnt-offerings and peace-offerings, he blessed the people in the name of the Lord of hosts" (6:15, 17).

   "And David said unto all his servants that were with him at Jerusalem, Arise, and let us flee; for we shall not else escape from Absalom: make speed to depart, lest he overtake us suddenly, and bring evil upon us, and smite the city with the edge of the sword. And lo Zadok also, and all the Levites were with him, bearing the ark of the covenant of God:

**THE UNITED KINGDOM STAGE**

| | |
|---|---|
| 1 SAMUEL 8-31 | PSALMS |
| 2 SAMUEL | PROVERBS |
| 1 KINGS 1-11 | ECCLESIASTES |
| 1 CHRONICLES | SONG OF |
| 2 CHRONICLES 1-9 | SOLOMON |

and they set down the ark of God; and Abiathar went up, until all the people had done passing out of the city. And the king said unto Zadok, Carry back the ark of God into the city: if I shall find favour in the eyes of the Lord, he will bring me again, and shew me both it, and his habitation" (15:14, 24, 25).

9. A sister is raped (2 Sam. 13) and a son is hanged (2 Sam. 18).
10. A father's son (Jonathan) protects young David from the son's father (Saul, Sam. 20).
11. A heathen city becomes the Holy City (2 Sam. 5).

"And the king and his men went to Jerusalem unto the Jebusites, the inhabitants of the land: which spake unto David, saying, Except thou take away the blind and the lame, thou shalt not come in hither: thinking, David cannot come in hither. Nevertheless David took the strong hold of Zion: the same is the city of David. And David said on that day, Whosoever getteth up to the gutter, and smiteth the Jebusites, and the lame and the blind, that are hated of David's soul, he shall be chief and captain. Wherefore they said, The blind and the lame shall not come into the house" (2 Sam. 5:6–8).

12. Solomon is instructed (1 Ki. 2) and the Temple is constructed (1 Ki. 6).

# THE UNITED KINGDOM STAGE

"And the Lord said to Samuel, hearken unto their voice, and make them a king" (1 Sam. 8:22).

## The Rulers of This Stage

I. Saul, Israel's First King.
   A. The selection of Saul.
      1. The circumstances leading to his selection.
         a. Israel's elders gather at Ramah and demand that Samuel give them a king (8:3–20).
         b. Samuel is displeased and lists the many disadvantages of having a king (8:11–18).
         c. God nevertheless informs Samuel of his decision to give Israel a king and that he can expect the new leader at his doorstep in twenty-four hours (1 Sam. 9:16).
         d. The next day Saul unknowingly fulfills this prophecy by seeking Samuel's help in locating some lost animals (1 Sam. 9:18–20).
      2. The chronology of his selection.
         a. He is privately anointed by Samuel at Ramah (10:1).
         b. He is publicly acclaimed by Samuel at Mizpeh (10:24).
            Note: At this stage Saul was a very humble man. He felt he was unworthy of being king (9:21) and actually had to be brought out of hiding when Samuel officially proclaimed him king (10:21).
      3. The confirmation of his selection.
         a. Following his inaugural service, Saul returns to his farm in Gibeah (10:26).
         b. He later raises an army of 330 thousand to rescue a surrounded Israelite city called Jabesh-Gilead from a cruel enemy and thus establishes his ability to lead the kingdom (11:8–15).
         c. Samuel then gathers Israel to Gilgal, and

there delivers his final recorded sermon to the people.
      (1) He warns both people and their king of the follies of disobeying God (12:25).
      (2) God emphasizes this warning by the miracle of thunder and rain (12:18).
   B. The rejection of Saul (1 Sam. 13:1—15:9). This Saul caused:
      1. By offering the sacrifice of a priest (13:9).
      2. By ordering the death of his own son. Saul had foolishly ordered no food to be eaten by his troops until the Philistines were defeated. Jonathan, his son, unaware of the command, ate some honey. The people, however, refused to let Saul carry out his foolish law and thus saved Jonathan (14:45). God saved Israel that day; this was done in spite of Saul's stupidity, through three things:
         a. Jonathan's battle plan and personal courage (14:6)
         b. a divine earthquake (14:15)
         c. panic among the Philistine troops (14:19)
      3. By opposing the command of God to destroy a pagan named Agag and his city (15:9). This event was significant because:
         a. It marked the total rejection of Saul by God (15:11).
         b. It illustrated a great biblical principle. When Saul lamely excused his actions in not killing the animals as instructed, but in saving them for sacrificial reason, he heard the stern rebuke of Samuel:

         "And Samuel said, Hath the Lord as great delight in burnt offerings and sacrifices, as in obeying the voice of the Lord? Behold, to obey is better than sacrifice, and to hearken than the fat of rams. For rebellion is as the sin of witchcraft, and stubbornness is as iniquity and idolatry. Because thou hast rejected the word of the Lord, he hath also rejected thee from being king" (1 Sam. 15:22, 23).

         In other words, it is better to obey than to sacrifice (for sins) because when one obeys God in the first place, he need not offer a sacrifice. (It is therefore better to apply the principle laid down in Eph. 6:13 than the one found in 1 John 1:9.)
         c. It was the last meeting between Saul and Samuel until Samuel died (15:35).
II. David, Israel's Finest King (1 Sam. 16—2 Sam. 31; 1 Chron. 11–29).
   A. David the shepherd (16:1–13).
      1. Samuel is instructed to visit the house of Jesse in Bethlehem and anoint one of his eight sons as King of Israel.
      2. Samuel is furthermore admonished to, "Look not on his countenance, or on the height of his stature . . . for the Lord seeth not as man seeth; for man looketh on the outward appearance, but the Lord looketh on the heart" (16:7).
      3. After God rejects the first seven sons, David is fetched from the sheep pasture and anointed by Samuel (16:11–13).

B. David the singer (16:14-23).
   1. King Saul is from this point on troubled by an evil spirit.
   2. The fame of David's skill as an accomplished harpist causes Saul to issue a "command performance," and David readily agrees.
   3. David's beautiful music helps the troubled Saul.

C. David the soldier (17).
   1. Jesse sends David with some food for his brothers who are soldiers in Saul's army.
   2. Israel at this time was engaged in battle with the Philistines.
   3. Upon arriving, David views a giant Philistine warrior who had for forty days (17:16) brazenly insulted the armies of Israel and their God, taunting them to send forth a soldier to do battle with him and thus determine the war. The giant's name was Goliath; he was approximately ten feet high. He wore a bronze helmet, a 200-pound coat of mail, bronze leggings, and carried a bronze javelin several inches thick, tipped with a twenty-five-pound iron spearhead.
   4. David accepts this challenge and, armed with only the sling of a shepherd, kills the giant with a stone which he hurls into his forehead.

D. David the sought (1 Sam. 18-31).
   1. He now begins his lifelong friendship with Jonathan, Saul's son (1 Sam. 18:1-4).
   2. He is made commander-in-chief of Saul's armies (1 Sam. 18:5).
   3. He receives the praise of the Israelite women for slaying Goliath (1 Sam. 18:6, 7). These women sang concerning how Saul had slain his thousands, but David his ten thousands. Apparently the Philistines would also later hear of this song. (See 1 Sam. 21:11; 29:5.)
   4. He incurs the wrath of Saul (1 Sam. 18:8).
   5. Saul makes his first attempt to kill David (1 Sam. 18:11).
   6. He is demoted from general to a captain in Saul's armies (1 Sam. 18:13).
   7. Saul attempts to have the Philistines kill David, by falsely promising his daughter to wife for defeating the enemy (1 Sam. 18:19).
   8. Saul then promises his second daughter, Michal, to David if he can kill 100 Philistines. David thereupon goes out and kills 200 (1 Sam. 18:20-27).
   9. David marries his first of many wives, Michal (1 Sam. 18:27, 28).
   10. Saul attempts to kill him again with a javelin (1 Sam. 19:10).
   11. David escapes Saul's next murderous attempt by being lowered down through his own bedroom window with the help of Michal (1 Sam. 19:12).
   12. David goes to Ramah and reports all this to Samuel (1 Sam. 19:18).
   13. Jonathan warns David of Saul's renewed efforts to kill him (1 Sam. 20:18-22, 35-42).
   14. David goes to Nob and (after lying about the nature of his visit) receives bread and a sword from Ahimelech, the high priest (1 Sam. 21:1-9).

15. He then goes to the Philistine city of Gath and fakes insanity before King Achish (1 Sam. 21:10-15).
16. David makes the Cave of Adullam his headquarters and begins gathering his "outlaw army." This army at first totaled 400 men (1 Sam. 22:1, 2).
17. During this period three of his mighty men slipped through enemy lines to bring David the drink of water from the well in Bethlehem he had so longed for. David was so impressed that he refused to drink it, but poured it out as an offering to God (1 Chron. 11:16-19).
18. David goes to Moab, but is ordered back to Judah through the mouth of Gad, the prophet of the Lord (1 Sam. 22:3-5). God had already gone to the trouble of bringing David's great grandmother from Moab into Judah. (See Ruth 1.)
19. A vicious Edomite named Doeg betrays Ahimelech to Saul, whereupon the insane king orders the slaughter of eighty-five priests at Nob simply because Ahimelech had offered some bread to David (22:12-19).
20. David receives Abiathar, one of Ahimelech's sons, who alone had escaped Saul's bloody slaughter of the priests at Nob (1 Sam. 22:20-23).
21. David saves the Israelite city of Keilah from the Philistines (1 Sam. 23:5).
22. He then is warned by God to flee the city, for the fickle citizens were preparing to hand him over to Saul (1 Sam. 23:10-12).
23. He now has an army of 600 men (1 Sam. 23:13).
24. Jonathan and David meet in the woods of Ziph and renew their friendship (1 Sam. 23:16-18).
25. Saul surrounds David in the wilderness of Maon, but upon hearing the report of a Philistine invasion, is forced to leave before capturing him (1 Sam. 23:26-28).
26. David spares Saul's life in a cave in the wilderness of En-gedi, by cutting off a piece of Saul's coat when he could have sliced off his head (1 Sam. 24:1-15).
   a. After his sin with Bath-sheba (2 Sam. 12:13).
   b. After numbering the people of Israel (2 Sam. 24:10). (Psalm 7 may have been written at this time.)
27. David's heart immediately smote him for this act of disrespect (1 Sam. 24:5). (This "smiting" was to be recorded on two future occasions, as well.)
28. Saul acknowledges both his stupidity and the fact that he knew God had chosen David to rule Israel (1 Sam. 24:16-22).
29. David marries his second wife, Abigail. She was the widow of an arrogant and rich Judean sheepherder who had refused to help David in his time of need and for this reason was slain by the Lord ten days later (25:1-42). (Just prior to this, Samuel had died and was buried at Ramah.)
30. David marries his third wife, Ahinoam

(1 Sam. 25:43). Note: His first wife, Michal, had been given by Saul to another man (25:44). Ahinoam would later give birth to Amnon (see 2 Sam. 3:2).

31. David spares Saul's life the second time on a hillside in the wilderness of Ziph. To prove this to Saul, he orders one of his men to take the spear and water canteen while the king lies sleeping (1 Sam. 26:1-16).

32. Saul once again acknowledges his wickedness and promises no more to seek his life (1 Sam. 26:17-24). Note: The wicked and frustrated king, apparently, this time, kept his word.

33. David backslides and moves to the Philistine city of Ziklag (1 Sam. 27:1).

34. David now completes his army of mighty men. These men were known for:
   a. their strength (1 Chron. 12:2, 8)
   b. their spiritual perception (1 Chron. 12:18)

35. During this time, a period of sixteen months, David carries out numerous plundering raids upon various non-Israelite cities, but convinces the Philistine king, Achish, that the cities are indeed Israelite ones. (See 1 Sam. 27:8-12.)

36. Saul visits the witch of En-dor in a desperate attempt to call up Samuel from the dead in order to receive advice concerning a fearful Philistine military threat (28:1-11).

37. Samuel appears, apart, however, from any actions of the evil witch, and predicts Saul's defeat and death on the battlefield the following day (28:12-25).

Note: The appearance of Samuel on this occasion has created a great deal of discussion among Bible scholars and has produced a number of viewpoints with regard to the precise nature of this event. They are as follows:
   a. "The appearance of Samuel was not a literal one, but merely the product of psychological impressions. According to this view, the woman had permitted herself to become emotionally involved and psychologically identified with the prophet, so that she was convinced that he had actually appeared when called. Two objections can be raised against this view. The first is derived from verse 12, which indicates that when Samuel did appear, the medium cried out with a loud voice, apparently surprised or startled by his appearance. Such would not be the case if she were merely seeking a vision produced by 'psychological excitement.' Second, the general reading of the text leads one to the conclusion that not only did the woman speak with Samuel, but Saul spoke with him as well (cf. v. 15).
   b. A demon or Satan impersonated Samuel. Those holding this view argue for the idea that a visible form of Samuel himself appeared, which was in reality merely an impersonation of him. Many who defend this view argue that God would not permit a woman of this type to actually disturb the rest of a godly man. The whole affair is therefore considered a satanic or demonic deception of Saul. The advocates of this view remind us that Satan can appear as 'an angel of light' (2 Cor. 11:14) and, therefore, has the ability to carry out such deceptions. In evaluating this view, it should be pointed out that the basic reading of the biblical text leads one to the conclusion that this was actually Samuel and not an impersonation. While it is true that Satan can perform such deception, it is highly doubtful that he has the prophetic knowledge necessary to reveal that which was given to Saul in this chapter. Furthermore, if this were a demon or an evil spirit, it is improbable that he would have given the prediction found in this passage. More likely, in the light of the godly character of David and the wickedness of Saul, the demonic power would have flattered Saul with a positive prophecy.
   c. The whole thing was a deliberate imposture practiced upon Saul. The witch really did not see Samuel, but fooled Saul into believing that her voice or that of someone else was that of Samuel. Those maintaining this view point out that only the woman saw Samuel and reported his words. Saul heard and saw nothing. A number of objections may be raised against this view. In the first place, the Bible does not specifically say that the woman reported Samuel's words; on the contrary, it makes it clear that Samuel spoke directly to Saul. Orr's statement that the king 'saw and heard nothing' is in direct conflict with the obvious reading of the text (cf. v. 15ff). It is also highly doubtful that she was in a position to predict the outcome of the battle and specifically forecast the death of Saul's sons. It is also unlikely, from a practical point of view, that she would give such a forecast to a man obviously aligned with the Israelite camp.
   d. The most popular view and that which is maintained by most orthodox commentators is that this was a genuine appearance of Samuel brought about by God himself. In favor of this proposal is the Septuagint reading of 1 Chronicles 10:13 which is as follows: 'Saul asked counsel of her that had a familiar spirit to inquire of her, and Samuel made answer to him.' Furthermore, the fact that she cried out when she saw Samuel indicated that she did not bring up Samuel and did not expect him to appear in this manner. The fact that Saul bowed himself to the ground and did obeisance is a further indication that this was a real appearance of Samuel. It is doubtful that he would have reacted merely on the grounds of a verbal description or a false impression.

Samuel's statement to Saul in verse 15 should not be regarded as a proof of the fact that the witch of En-dor or Saul brought him back from the dead. What, then, was the purpose of God in bringing Samuel back for this appearance? This unusual act on the part of God was certainly designed to emphasize the doom of Saul and God's displeasure for his coming to a necromancer. Robert Jamieson suggests three additional reasons: (1) To make Saul's crime an instrument of his punishment, (2) To show the heathen world God's superiority in prophecy, and (3) to confirm a belief in a future state after death. Two other men who made an appearance on the earth after death were Moses and Elijah at the transfiguration of Christ (Mt. 17:3; Lk. 9:30, 31). They, however, appeared 'in glory,' but Samuel appeared in the mantle which he had worn while on earth. Therefore, in a real sense the appearance of Samuel after death was a completely unique event." (*The Birth of a Kingdom,* John J. Davis, pp. 96–99)

38. David foolishly volunteers to join the Philistines as they march to fight with Israel at Jezreel. But he is not fully trusted by the Philistine leaders, and his offer is refused (1 Sam. 29:1-11).

39. David avenges the sudden destruction of his adopted Philistine city Ziklag by totally slaughtering the guilty Amalekites (1 Sam. 30:1-18).

40. After this successful battle, David institutes an important statute and ordinance in Israel, which reads:

"But as his part is that goeth down to the battle, so shall his part be that tarrieth by the stuff: they shall part alike" (1 Sam. 30:21-25).

41. Saul is defeated by the Philistines and is sorely wounded. He thereupon falls upon his sword to avoid torture at the hands of the enemy. His sons, including Jonathan, are also killed in battle (31:1-7).

E. David the sovereign (2 Sam. 1-10; 1 Chron. 11-19).

1. David hears the news of the death of Saul and Jonathan and grieves for them in Ziklag (2 Sam. 1:1-27). He orders the execution of an Amalekite soldier who attempted to take the credit for Saul's death.

2. At God's command, he returns to Palestine and is anointed at Hebron by the men of Judah as their king. This was his second anointing (2 Sam. 2:1-4). David is now around thirty and he will rule over Judah for the next seven and a half years (2 Sam. 5:5).

3. Abner, Saul's general, makes Ish-bosheth, Saul's son, king over the eleven tribes (2:8-10).

4. Joab arranges a meeting with Abner and murders many of his men. Abner is forced to kill Joab's brother Asahel in self-defense (2:18-23).

5. After a long war between Saul's house and David's house, Abner breaks with Ish-bosheth and attempts to negotiate with David (3:1, 21). David agrees to cooperate.

6. Joab hears of this and murders Abner (3:30).

7. At this time David gets Michal, his first wife, back. He then marries four more women, for a grand total of seven wives, while in Hebron (2 Sam. 3:2-5; 1 Chron. 3:1-4). It was in Hebron that four (of his many) children were born who would later bring sorrow to his life. They were:

a. Amnon, who would rape his half-sister Tamar (2 Sam. 13:1-14)

b. Tamar (2 Sam. 13:1)

c. Absalom, who would kill Amnon for this and later lead a revolt against the king himself (2 Sam. 13:28; 15:13, 14)

# King Saul, HIS RISE AND FALL

RISE

**1 SAMUEL 8**
**Israel demands a king. Reasons for this:**
Samuel was getting old.
His sons were wicked.
Israel wanted to be like all other nations.
**1 SAM. 9**
**Saul is chosen by Samuel at God's command.**
Saul seeks Samuel's advice concerning some lost animals.
Samuel tells him of God's plans.
**1 SAM. 10**
**Saul is anointed at Ramah and acclaimed at Mizpah.**
He begins as a humble and somewhat reluctant ruler.
See 9:21; 10:22, 27; 11:12-15.
**1 SAM. 11-12**
**His leadership is confirmed at the rescue of Jabesh-Gilead.**
This Israelite city is surrounded by the Ammonites.
Saul raises an army and delivers the city.
He is urged by Samuel to always serve God.

_____*FALL*

| | |
|---|---|
| **STEP ONE:** | He intrudes into the office of the priesthood **(1 Sam. 13)**. |
| **STEP TWO:** | He orders the death of his own son **(1 Sam. 14)**. |
| **STEP THREE:** | He spares Amalek, God's enemy **(1 Sam. 15)**. |
| **STEP FOUR:** | He is possessed by an evil spirit **(16:14; 18:10; 19:9)**. |
| **STEP FIVE:** | He attempts to kill David **(18:11, 21, 25; 19:1, 10, 15)**. |
| **STEP SIX:** | He curses and attempts to kill his own son **(20:30-33)**. |
| **STEP SEVEN:** | He slaughters eighty-five priests of God at the city of Nob **(22:17-19)**. |
| **STEP EIGHT:** | He goes to the witch of Endor and is slain on a battlefield **(1 Sam. 28, 31)**. |

d. Adonijah, who also would later attempt to steal David's throne while the old king lay dying (1 Ki. 1)

8. David learns of and bitterly laments the brutal murder of Abner (Saul's ex-captain) by Joab (David's captain) (2 Sam. 3:31-39). David would never forget this vicious act of revenge done by Joab to Abner. Nor did Joab stop here, for the king's beloved (and prodigal) son, Absalom, would later be murdered by Joab (see 2 Sam. 18:14). The viciousness of this crime was intensified in that it was done in Hebron, a city of refuge (see Josh. 21:13). In such a city not even the avenger of blood might slay the murderer without a trial (Num. 35:22-25). Joab probably murdered Abner for two reasons:
   a. To avenge the slaying of his brother Asahel (2:23) by Abner. However, Abner had done this only in self-defense.
   b. To protect his own position as commander-in-chief of David's armies.

   Joab was the son of David's half-sister, Zeruiah (1 Chron. 2:16; 2 Sam. 17:25) and was therefore his nephew.

9. David avenges the murder of Ish-bosheth, Saul's fourth son, by executing his two murderers (2 Sam. 4:9-12). This was the turning point, for after the death of Ish-bosheth, nothing could stop David from having the kingdom of Israel. Much blood had now been shed to purchase David's throne. Death had claimed eighty-five priests, Saul, Jonathan, an Amalekite, Asahel, many Israelite soldiers, Abner, Ish-bosheth, and two captains. David was indeed (even though at that time unintentionally so) a bloody man. (See 1 Chron. 22:8.) How different would be David's perfect Son who shed only his own blood to obtain his eternal throne! (See 1 Pet. 1:18, 19.)

10. David is anointed king over all Israel at Hebron. This marked his third anointing. It was a fantastic three-day celebration with nearly 400 thousand honor troops from the twelve tribes of Israel taking part (2 Sam. 5:1-5; 1 Chron. 12:23-40). Especially helpful must have been those soldiers from the tribe of Issachar, for we are told they were: "Men that had understanding of the times, to know what Israel ought to do" (1 Chron. 12:32).

11. David then captured Jerusalem and made it his permanent capital. He enlarges his kingdom, hires Hiram, the King of Tyre, to build him a palace, and marries more wives and concubines (5:6-16).

12. He is victorious over the Philistines twice during this time. Both victories were at the hand of God (2 Sam. 5:17-25).

13. David brings the Ark of the Covenant (2 Sam. 6:1-19; 1 Chron. 13:1-14; 15:1—16:43).
   a. His method of carrying the ark (in a new cart) displeases God, resulting in the death of a man called Uzzah, and brings a three-month delay (2 Sam. 6:3, 7, 11).

b. Finally, with much shouting, singing, and making of music, the ark enters the city. A history of the ark up to this time is as follows:
   (1) It was first made by Moses at God's command (Ex. 25:10-22).
   (2) It was then transported along with the other tabernacle furniture through the forty-year wilderness journey.
   (3) It was eventually set up in Shiloh, the first Israelite capital (Josh. 18:1).
   (4) It was carried into battle and captured by the Philistines (1 Sam. 4:11).
   (5) It was passed on among the Philistine cities like a hot potato (1 Sam. 5).
   (6) It was brought to the city of Bethshemesh, where it caused a fearful plague (1 Sam. 6:19).
   (7) It was brought to Kirjath-jearim where it resided twenty years (1 Sam. 7:1, 2).
   c. David then appointed some of the Levites to "minister before the ark of the Lord, and to record, and to thank and praise the Lord God of Israel" (1 Chron. 16:4; 25:7). This choir, numbering 288, was to do nothing but praise and thank the Lord.
   d. David now delivers his first recorded Psalm (1 Chron. 16:7-36).

14. Upon returning home, he is severely rebuked for all this "religious emotional nonsense" by his wife Michal (2 Sam. 6:20-23).

15. He desires to build a temple, but this request is not allowed by God (2 Sam. 7:17; 1 Chron. 17:4).

16. He is now given the Davidic Covenant from God (2 Sam. 7:8-17). This all-important covenant stated:
   a. David is to have a child, yet to be born, who will succeed him and establish his kingdom.
   b. This son (Solomon) shall build the Temple instead of David.
   c. The throne of his kingdom shall be established forever.
   d. The throne will not be taken away from him (Solomon) even though his sins justify chastisement. (See Ps. 89:33-37.)
   e. David's house, throne, and kingdom shall be established forever. (See also Lk. 1:28-33, 68-75; Acts 15:13-18.)

17. He responds to this by offering a beautiful prayer of thanksgiving (2 Sam. 7:18-29).

18. He now consolidates his kingdom by defeating in rapid succession the Philistines, the Moabites, the Syrians, and the Edomites (2 Sam. 8:1-14).

19. He seeks out and shows kindness to Mephibosheth, Jonathan's lame son (2 Sam. 9:1-13).

20. The Ammonites spurn his act of kindness by humiliating his ambassadors and are soundly punished for this (2 Sam. 10:1-19).

# The life of
# DAVID

## 1. The Shepherd  1 SAMUEL 16:1-13

1. David, the eighth son of Jesse, is brought from a sheep field near Bethlehem and anointed by Samuel **(1 Sam. 16:1-12).**
2. The Spirit of God comes upon David **(16:13).**

## 2. The Singer  1 SAM. 16:14-23

1. King Saul is troubled by an evil spirit.
2. David's beautiful music on the harp helps soothe the troubled king **(1 Sam. 16:14-25).**

## 3. The Soldier  1 SAM. 17:1-58

1. A giant Philistine warrior named Goliath had defied the armies of Israel for forty days **(17:16).**
2. With but a sling and a stone, David kills this mighty soldier **(17:49).**

---

''The Lord hath sought him a man after his own heart. . . .'' **1 SAM. 13:14**

---

## 4. The Sought  1 SAM. 18-31

1. He begins his lifelong fellowship with Jonathan **(1 Sam. 18:1-4; 20:41, 42; 23:16-18).**
2. His growing popularity incurs Saul's insane jealousy. Saul attempts to do him in by:
   A. Jonathan **(compare 18:5 with 18:13)**
   B. Private attempts on his life **(18:11, 21, 25; 19:1, 10, 15)**
   C. Trickery **(18:25-27)**
   D. Openly hunting him as a wild animal **(23:15, 26; 24:2; 26:2, 17-20)**
3. He marries Michal, the first of many wives **(18:27).**
4. He flees to the city of Nob, and in desperation lies to the high priest there **(21:1-9).**
5. He then travels to the Philistine city of Gath and fakes insanity **(21:10-15).**
6. He begins gathering his army of "spiritual outlaws" **(22:1, 2; 23:13).**
7. He goes to Moab but is ordered to Judah by God **(22:3-5).**
8. He spares the life of Saul on two occasions:
   A. In a cave in En-gedi **(24:1-15)**
   B. In a wilderness in Ziph **(26:1-16)**
9. He marries his second wife, a widow named Abigail **(25:1-42).**
10. Again he backslides and settles in the Philistine city of Ziklag **(27:1-6).**

## 5. The Sovereign  2 SAM. 1-10 / 1 CHRON. 11-19

1. Upon the death of Saul, by God's command he comes to Hebron and is anointed by the men of Judah as their king **(2 Sam. 2:1-4).**
2. After a seven-year war, David is successful over the house of Saul and is anointed at Hebron by all twelve tribes **(2 Sam. 3-5).**
3. He captures the city of Jerusalem and makes it his new capital **(2 Sam. 5:6-10).**
4. He then brings the Ark of the Covenant into Jerusalem **(2 Sam. 6:1-19; 1 Chron. 15-16).**
5. He desires to build a Temple for God, but is not allowed to do so **(2 Sam. 7:17; 1 Chron. 17:4).**
6. He now receives the all-important Davidic Covenant from God **(2 Sam. 7:8-17; 1 Chron. 17:7-15).** This covenant in essence predicted the millennial reign of Christ, the seed of David, upon the earth someday.
7. He seeks out and shows kindness to Mephibosheth, Jonathan's lame son **(2 Sam. 9:1-13).**

## 6. The Sinner  2 SAM. 11

1. David commits adultery with Bath-sheba.
2. He then arranges to have her husband, Uriah, killed on a battlefield **(2 Sam. 11).**

## 7. The Sorrowful  **2 SAM. 12-31**
**1 CHRON. 20, 21**

1. Nathan the prophet confronts David about this, and the king confesses **(2 Sam. 12:1-12; Ps. 32, 51).**
2. God forgives him, but determines David will pay back fourfold. **(Compare 12:5, 6 with 12:9-12.)** This will involve:
   A. The death of his infant son **(12:18)**
   B. The rape of Tamar, his daughter, by Amnon, his son **(13:14)**
   C. The murder of Amnon by his half-brother (and David's son) Absalom **(13:29)**
   D. The rebellion of Absalom against his father's own throne **(15-18)**

## 8. The Statesman  **2 SAM. 21:1-14**

1. God had sent a three-year plague upon Israel to punish them for Saul's past sins against the nation Gibeon.
2. He stays the plague by negotiating with the Gibeonites, who agree justice can only be served by permitting them to execute seven of Saul's guilty sons **(2 Sam. 21:1-14).**

## 9. The Statistician  **2 SAM. 24**

1. He succumbs to the temptation of Satan and numbers Israel **(1 Chron. 21:1-6).**
2. A divine plague occurs, which is finally stopped by David as he pleads with the death angel **(2 Sam. 24:15-25; 1 Chron. 21:18-30).**

## 10. The Sponsor  **1 CHRON. 22-29**

1. He presides over a great dedicatory service for the future Temple **(1 Chron. 22:5, 9, 10).**
2. He himself contributes millions of dollars and helps raise additional millions **(1 Chron. 29:4, 6, 7).**
3. He gives the Temple blueprints he received from God to Solomon **(28:19).**
4. He then offers one of Scripture's most beautiful prayers **(29:10-19).**

## 11. The Scribe  **2 SAM. 22:1; 23:1-3**

David writes over half of the Psalms in the Word of God. "The spirit of the Lord spoke by me, and his Word was in my tongue" **(2 Sam. 23:2). See also 23:1-3; 22:1.**

## 12. The Sage  **1 KINGS 2**

On his deathbed David exhorts Solomon to do the following:
1. Act like a man of God **(1 Ki. 2:2)**
2. Be true to the Word of God **(2:3)**
3. Rely on the promises of God **(2:4)**
4. Execute the judgment of God **(2:5)**

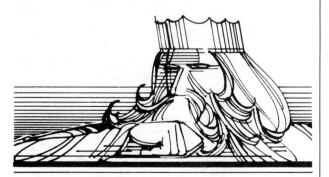

F. David the sinner (2 Sam. 11).
   1. The indulgent king lusts after and lies with Bath-sheba, the wife of Uriah, one of his soldiers.
   2. Bath-sheba becomes pregnant and reports this to David.
   3. Uriah is hurriedly called home from the battlefield under a pretext that he might visit his wife and thus later believe that the unborn child would be his.
   4. Uriah apparently realizes the truth of the situation and refuses to cooperate.
   5. In an act of desperation, David sends him back with a sealed letter to Joab to arrange for his death in battle.
   6. Uriah is killed and David marries Bath-sheba.
G. David the sorrowful (2 Sam. 12–31; 1 Chron. 20, 21).
   1. After Bath-sheba's child is born, Nathan the prophet relates to David a story of how a rich farmer who owned thousands of sheep stole a little pet lamb from a poor farmer, his only one, butchered and ate it (12:1-4).
   2. David's anger knows no limit and he vows that the cruel rich man will pay back fourfold for his sin (12:5, 6).
   3. Nathan then boldly points out to David that he, the king, is that man.
   4. David confesses his sin and repents (12:13).
   5. God forgave David, but would require his servant to pay back fourfold, the same price the king would have made the rich man pay.
   6. Seven days after David's confession, the first installment comes due, for the child dies (12:18).
   7. The king accepts this by faith, believing he will someday see him again (12:23).
   8. Solomon is born (12:24).
   9. David fights his last recorded battle against an outside enemy and defeats Rabbah, the capital city of Ammon (12:29).
   10. David's son, Amnon, lusts after and eventually rapes his own half-sister, Tamar. The second installment on David's debt had come due (13:14).
   11. Absalom, the full brother of Tamar, begins plotting the murder of Amnon and kills him two years later. This would be installment number three (13:29).
   12. Absalom flees into the desert and stays with his pagan grandfather for three years (13:38).
   13. Joab employs a crafty woman from Tekoah to trick David into permitting Absalom to return to Jerusalem.
   14. Absalom returns, but is refused an audience with his father for two years. Finally, after Absalom burned a barley field to get attention, David agrees to see him (14:33).
   15. Absalom begins planning a revolt against his father. After four years, he is ready, and instigates the plot in Hebron (15:12).
   16. The rebellion gathers strength and David is forced to leave Jerusalem. God had now exacted the fourth installment (15:14).

17. David is accompanied into the wilderness by Ittai (a foreign guest who, along with his 600 soldiers, sides in with him) (2 Sam. 15:18–22).
18. Abiathar and Zadok also accompany him. However, David orders these joint high-priests back to Jerusalem. They return, carrying God's ark with them (2 Sam. 15:24–29).
19. David walks up the road to the Mount of Olives and weeps (2 Sam. 15:30).
20. Upon learning that his advisor Ahithophel has joined Absalom's rebellion, the king prays, "O Lord, I pray thee, turn the counsel of Ahithophel into foolishness" (2 Sam. 15:31).
21. David then orders another advisor, Hushai, also to pretend to sell out to Absalom, that he might frustrate and counter Ahithophel's advice (2 Sam. 15:34). Absalom listens to both counselors. Ahithophel advises an immediate "hit-'em-where-they-aren't" frontal attack, before David can muster his forces. Hushai, however, appeals to the vain pride of Absalom by suggesting that they wait until a larger army can be raised and that Absalom himself lead the attack. This inferior advice was heeded, whereupon Ahithophel went home and hanged himself (17:1–23).
22. He now meets Ziba, the manager of Mephibosheth's household, who brings him food, but who lies about his master to feather his own nest (2 Sam. 16:1–4).
23. David is cursed out and has stones thrown at him by Shime-i, a member of Saul's family (2 Sam. 16:5–8). In spite of this, David refuses to order his execution (16:10–12).
24. Absalom enters Jerusalem and possesses David's concubines (16:22).
25. David is warmly greeted by Shobi (an Ammonite), and others, who offer him mats to sleep upon and food to eat (2 Sam. 17:27–30).
26. Out of loving concern, David's armies refuse to allow him into the battle with Absalom (2 Sam. 18:3).
27. He sends his troops into battle in the woods of Ephraim, but orders the life of Absalom to be spared (2 Sam. 18:5, 6).
28. Absalom's green soldiers are no match for David's seasoned troops and they quickly lose some twenty thousand men and the entire battle (18:7).
29. Absalom attempts to escape, but is caught in some underbrush and killed by Joab (18:14).
30. David learns of Absalom's death at Joab's hand and grieves over his dead son (18:33; 19:1–4).
31. Joab severely rebukes him for this (19:5–7).
32. He begins his trip back to Jerusalem and promises to appoint his nephew Amasa as head of his armies if Amasa can get the people of Judah (who had been miffed at David) to back his return to power (19:13, 14).
33. He spares the life of Shime-i, who falls at his feet at the river Jordan and begs forgiveness (19:23).
34. He meets Mephibosheth and hears why his lame friend did not join him in the wilderness (19:24–30).
35. He meets Barzillai, who had befriended him in the wilderness, and invites the old man to accompany him to Jerusalem and live there (19:34–37).
36. Upon crossing Jordan, David is confronted with yet another rebellion, this one led by Sheba, a Benjaminite. Ten tribes now desert David. Only Judah and Benjamin remain loyal (20:1–3).
37. David instructs Joab to crush this revolt. This Joab does at a city called Abel, but prior to this, Joab brutally murders Amasa, thus eliminating a dangerous rival (20:6–22).
38. David thereupon once again returns to Jerusalem, a sadder and wiser man. He would have more troubles later, but they would not include wars and rebellions. He could now burn the mortgage on his sin-debt with Bathsheba.

H. David the statesman (2 Sam. 21:1–14).
1. A three-year plague from God had settled down upon Israel. David is told it was because of the bloody house of Saul in the past when he slew the Gibeonites.
2. In Joshua 9, Israel had made a covenant with these Gibeonites that they would not be harmed. This sin was now being punished.
3. David negotiates with the Gibeonite leaders, and they determine that justice can be done only by allowing them to execute seven of Saul's sons, all of whom doubtless had participated in the former Gibeon massacre. This is done and the plague is stayed.

I. David the statistician (2 Sam. 24).
1. David succumbs to the temptation of Satan and numbers Israel (1 Chron. 21:1–6).
2. He later repents of this and is offered by God one of three kinds of punishment:
   a. seven years of famine
   b. to flee ninety days before his enemies
   c. a three-day pestilence
3. He chooses the third (2 Sam. 24:15).
4. As a result, 70,000 men die. The plague is stopped by David at a threshing floor as he pleads with God's death angel. David later buys this floor (2 Sam. 24:15–25; 1 Chron. 21:18–30).

J. David the sponsor (1 Chron. 22–29).
1. David is now nearly seventy. When he was but thirty-seven, he determined to build the Temple for God, but was forbidden by the Lord to do so (22:7, 8).
2. The old king is, however, allowed to lead in the preparations for the Temple which Solomon will construct (22:5, 9, 10).
3. David therefore makes the following preparations:
   a. the blocks of squared stone which will be used in the Temple (22:2)
   b. great quantities of iron for the Temple nails (22:3)
   c. a huge supply of cedar logs (22:4)
   d. three million dollars in gold bullion (22:14)
   e. two million dollars' worth of silver (22:14)

f. 24,000 Levites to supervise the Temple work (23:4)

g. 6,000 Levites to be Temple bailiffs and judges (23:4)

h. 4,000 Levites to act as Temple guards (23:5)

i. 4,000 Levite musicians to head up the praise service (23:5)

j. a special Temple choir of 288 skilled singers (25:1, 7)

4. David then calls a special dedicatory service and does the following:

a. He hands over the Temple blueprints to Solomon, which plans he received directly fom God's hand (28:19).

b. He personally contributes to the work of an offering totaling 85 million dollars of gold and 20 million dollars of silver (29:4).

c. His action immediately prompts Israel's leaders to pledge $145 million in gold, $50 thousand in foreign currency, $30 million in silver, 800 tons of bronze, and 4600 tons of silver, in addition to great amounts of jewelry (29:6, 7). Thus the total of David's preparation must have exceeded $200 million.

d. He then offers one of the most beautiful prayers in all the Bible (1 Chron. 29: 10-19).

e. This dedicatory service was ended by a massive sacrificial service, which included a thousand young bulls, a thousand rams, and a thousand lambs, all offered up as burnt offerings (29:21).

K. David the scribe: Of the 150 Psalms, David wrote seventy-seven. The Psalms are discussed at the end of this stage.

L. David the sage (1 Ki. 2:2-5).

III. Solomon, Israel's fabulous king (1 Ki. 1-11; 2 Chron. 1-9).

A. His triumph over his enemies (1 Ki. 1:1—2:46).

1. Over Adonijah.

a. While David is on his deathbed, his oldest living son, Adonijah, attempts to steal the throne from his half-brother, Solomon. He is supported by Joab and Abiathar (1:7).

b. Solomon, however, is supported by Nathan, the Prophet; Bath-sheba, his mother; Zadok, the high priest; and Benaiah, one of David's mighty men of old (1:8-11).

c. Bath-sheba visits her dying husband, and arranges for Solomon to be anointed by Zadok (1:39).

d. Adonijah is placed on probation, but later executed when he makes a power play for the throne by attempting to marry Abishag, who had been David's last concubine (1:3; 2:17, 25).

2. Over Abiathar (2:26, 27). Because of his faithfulness to David, Abiathar is allowed to live but is banished from the priesthood.

3. Over Joab (2:28-34). This bloody general is finally executed, not only for his part in Adonijah's rebellion, but for many past crimes which included the murders of Abner and Amasa.

4. Over Shimei (2:36-46). Shimei, like Adonijah, is for a while placed on parole, but he breaks this trust and suffers the death penalty for it. At the execution of Shimei, David's dying request has been fulfilled by Solomon, for he had asked that justice be done to both Joab and Shimei (2:5, 8).

B. His talent from God (3:4-28).

1. Solomon is visited by the Lord in a dream while in Gideon to make sacrifice. God tells him he may have anything he desires and the new king asks for wisdom (3:6-9).

2. When he returns to Jerusalem, he is immediately confronted with a situation which tests his newly acquired wisdom. Two harlot mothers approach him concerning two babies, one dead and the other living. Both mothers claim the living one as theirs. Solomon suggests he divide the living child with a sword and give half to each woman. The real mother, of course, is horrified at this, and thus her true identity is revealed (3:16-28).

C. His total and tranquil reign over all Israel (1 Ki. 4:1-34). Solomon's reign at this time is a beautiful foreshadowing of Christ's perfect millennial reign. Thus we see:

1. Solomon had twelve cabinet members to aid in his reign (1 Ki. 4:7). Jesus will confer this upon his twelve disciples (Mt. 19:28).

2. Solomon ruled "over all kingdoms" in the Holy Land area (1 Ki. 4:21), while Christ will rule over all kingdoms everywhere (see Rev. 11:15).

3. Solomon's subjects served him as we will serve Christ (1 Ki. 4:21; Rev. 22:3).

4. Solomon brought in local peace (1 Ki. 4:24), as Christ will usher in universal peace (Isa. 2:2-4).

5. Judah and Israel dwelt safely, "every man under his vine" (1 Ki. 4:25). So will it be during Christ's reign (Jer. 23:6; Micah 4:4; Zech. 3:10).

D. His Temple of worship (1 Ki. 5-8; 2 Chron. 2-7).

1. The preparation.

a. It was begun in May during Solomon's fourth year and completed in November of his eleventh year, thus making a total of seven years (1 Ki. 6:38).

b. It was exactly twice the size of Moses' tabernacle, ninety feet long, thirty feet wide, and forty-five feet high. (Compare with Ex. 26:16, 18.)

c. It was built by the partial slave labor project instituted by Solomon, which consisted of 100,000 Israelites, 80,000 stone cutters, and 330 foremen.

d. The floors and walls were made of stone covered with cedar and overlaid with gold (1 Ki. 6:16, 21, 22).

e. It was built without the sound of hammer, axe, or any other tool (1 Ki. 6:7).

f. It had ten lampstands and ten tables of shewbread (1 Ki. 7:49), as opposed to one each in Moses' tabernacle.

g. Solomon paid King Hiram of Tyre nearly a million bushels of wheat and some 840 gallons of pure olive oil for the timber alone from the forest of Lebanon to construct the Temple shell (5:8-11).

h. There were two golden cherubim in the Holy of Holies (1 Ki. 8:7).

2. The dedication. Solomon briefly reviews the historical circumstances which led up to this glad day (1 Ki. 8:12-21; 2 Chron. 6:1-11).

3. The supplication (1 Ki. 8:22-53; 2 Chron. 6:12-42). Solomon prays that the influence of this beautiful Temple will extend itself in a threefold manner:

a. Over the individual (1 Ki. 8:31, 32).
(1) That sinners will be judged.
(2) That the righteous will be justified.
b. Over the nation.
(1) That its sins might be forgiven (vs. 33-35).
(2) That its land might be healed (vs. 36, 37).
(3) That Israel might be preserved in captivity (vs. 44-50).
c. Over the heathen (vs. 41-43).

4. The benediction (1 Ki. 8:54-61).

5. The manifestation (2 Chron. 7:1-3).
"Now when Solomon had made an end of praying, the fire came down from heaven and consumed the burnt offering and the sacrifices; and the glory of the Lord filled the house."

6. The presentation (1 Ki. 8:62-66; 2 Chron. 7:4-10). This offering, consisting of 120 thousand sheep and twenty-two thousand oxen, was the largest in the Bible, and perhaps of all time.

E. His treasury of riches.
1. He had 700 wives and 300 concubines (1 Ki. 11:3).
2. He had fantastic quantities of gold.
a. from Hiram he acquired three and a half million (9:14)
b. from his navy, 420 talents of gold (9:27, 28)
c. from the Queen of Sheba, three and a half million (10:10)
d. from yearly taxes and revenue, upwards of 20 million (10:14)
3. He owned 40,000 horses (4:26).
4. He owned 1400 chariots, each costing $400 apiece (10:26).
5. He commanded 12,000 cavalrymen (10:26).
6. He owned an extensive fleet of ships (1 Ki. 9:26-28; 10:22; 2 Chron. 8:17, 18).
7. He built a huge ivory throne and overlaid it with pure gold. It had six steps and a rounded back with arm rests. It was surrounded by twelve lions, two resting on each step (10:18-20).
8. He constructed an iron-smelting industry at Ezion-Geber (1 Ki. 9:17).

F. His testimony throughout the land (1 Ki. 4:29-34; 10:1-13).
1. The ruler of Arabia came to see for herself the riches of Solomon and also to test his

# Solomon

## Triumph over his enemies

**1 KINGS 1-2**
- Adonijah
- Abiathar
- Joab
- Shimei

## Talent from God

**1 KINGS 3:4-28**
- The talent—wisdom
- The test—a baby and a sword

## Total and tranquil reign

**1 KINGS 4**
A beautiful type of Christ's millennial rule

## Temple of worship

**1 KINGS 5-8; 2 CHRONICLES 2-7**
- Twice the size of the tabernacle
- Seven years in construction

## Treasury of riches

**4:26; 9:17, 26-28; 10:22, 26; 11:3**
- Much gold
- Many horses and chariots
- A fleet of ships

## Testimony throughout land

**4:29-34; 10:1-13**
As testified by the Queen of Sheba

## Transgressions against God

**1 KINGS 11**
He disobeyed (**Deut. 17:14-17**) and accumulated:
- Much gold
- Many wives
- Many horses

universally famed wisdom. She entered Jerusalem a skeptic, but left with this testimony:

"I believed not the words, until I came and mine eyes had seen it: and behold, the half was not told me: thy wisdom and prosperity exceedeth the fame which I heard" (1 Ki. 10:7).

Some nine centuries later the Savior would refer to this historic visit. (See Mt. 12:42.)

2. Solomon's wisdom was testified to universally in matters of:
   a. jurisprudence (1 Ki. 3:28)
   b. administration (1 Ki. 4:29; 5:12)
   c. poetry (1 Ki. 4:32) (Solomon's writings are discussed at the end of this stage.)
   d. natural science (1 Ki. 4:33)
   e. architecture and engineering (1 Ki. 5:1-7; 9:15-22)
   f. commercial enterprise (1 Ki. 9:26—10:29)
   g. philosophy (Eccles. 2:3)
   h. horticulture (Eccles. 2:5)

G. His transgressions against God:
   1. The warnings to Solomon against transgressing.
      a. from David
         (1) first warning (1 Chron. 22:13)
         (2) last warning (1 Ki. 2:3)
      b. from God
         (1) first warning (1 Ki. 3:14)
         (2) second warning (9:6, 7)
         (3) last warning (11:11)
   2. The nature of Solomon's transgressions. Some four and one-half centuries before Solomon, God had written the following qualifications concerning all future kings of Israel:

      "When thou art come unto the land which the Lord thy God giveth thee, and shalt possess it, and shalt dwell therein, and shalt say, I will set a king over me, like as all the nations that are about me; thou shalt in any wise set him king over thee, thou mayest not set a stranger over thee, which is not thy brother. But he shall not multiply horses to himself, nor cause the people to return to Egypt, to the end that he should multiply horses: forasmuch as the Lord hath said unto you, Ye shall henceforth return no more that way. Neither shall he multiply wives to himself, that his heart turn not away: neither shall he greatly multiply to himself silver and gold" (Deut. 17:14-17).

      But Solomon disobeyed in all three areas.
      a. He had much gold and silver (1 Ki. 10:14-27).
      b. He owned thousands of horses (4:26).
      c. He gathered hundreds of wives and concubines (11:3).
   3. The results of Solomon's transgressions:
      a. That he would, for the first time in his reign, be plagued with troublemakers and minor revolts (11:14-25).
      b. That after his death, God would take the kingdom from Solomon's son and give a large portion of it to another (11:9-13, 26-40).

## The Writings of This Stage

I. The Psalms. There are three basic ways to study the Psalms: (1) by book division, (2) by authorship, and (3) by subject matter.
   A. By book division (each ends with a doxology).
      1-41 (corresponds to Genesis) Key word is *man*.

      "Blessed is the man that walketh not in the counsel of the ungodly, nor standeth in the way of sinners, nor sitteth in the seat of the scornful" (1:1).

      "What is man, that thou art mindful of him? and the son of man, that thou visitest him?" (8:4).

      "What man is he that feareth the Lord: him shall he teach in the way that he shall choose" (25:12).

      "O taste and see that the Lord is good: blessed is the man that trusteth in him" (34:8).

      "What man is he that desireth life, and loveth many days, that he may see good?" (34:12).

      "The steps of a good man are ordered by the Lord: and he delighteth in his way" (37:23).

      "Mark the perfect man, and behold the upright: for the end of that man is peace" (37:37).

      "Blessed is that man that maketh the Lord his trust, and respecteth not the proud, nor such as turn aside to lies" (40:4).

      42-72 (corresponds to Exodus) Key word is *deliverance*.

      "And call upon me in the day of trouble: I will deliver thee, and thou shalt glorify me" (50:15).

      "For he hath delivered me out of all trouble: and mine eye hath seen his desire upon mine enemies" (54:7).

      "For thou hast delivered my soul from death: wilt not thou deliver my feet from falling, that I may walk before God in the light of the living?" (56:13).

      "Deliver me from mine enemies, O my God: defend me from them that rise up against me" (59:1).

      "Deliver me out of the mire, and let me not sink: let me be delivered from them that hate me, and out of the deep water" (69:14).

      "Deliver me in thy righteousness, and cause me to escape: incline thine ear unto me, and save me" (71:2).

      "For he shall deliver the needy when he crieth; the poor also, and him that hath no helper" (72:12).

      73-89 (corresponds to Leviticus) Key word is *sanctuary*.

      "Until I went into the sanctuary of God; then understood I their end" (73:17).

      "They have cast fire into thy sanctuary, they have defiled by casting down the dwelling place of thy name to the ground" (74:7).

      "Thy way, O God, is in the sanctuary: who is so great a God as our God?" (77:13).

      "And he built his sanctuary like high palaces, like the earth which he hath established for ever" (78:69).

      90-106 (corresponds to Numbers) Key words are *unrest, wanderings*. (See chapters 90 and 106.)

      107-150 (corresponds to Deuteronomy) Key phrase is *Word of God*. (See chapter 119.)

B. By authorship.
 1. David
  a. The Shepherd Psalms: 8, 19, 23, 29, 144
  b. The Sinner Psalms: 32, 51, 38
  c. The Suffering Psalms: 3, 4, 5, 6, 7, 11, 12, 13, 14, 17, 22, 25, 26, 27, 28, 31, 34, 35, 39, 40, 41, 53, 54, 55, 56, 57, 58, 59, 61, 62, 63, 64, 69, 70, 86, 109, 140, 141, 142, 143
  d. The Satisfied Psalms: 2, 9, 15, 16, 18, 20, 21, 24, 30, 36, 37, 52, 60, 65, 68, 72, 95, 101, 103, 105, 108, 110, 122, 124, 131, 133, 138, 139, 145
 2. Korah: 42, 44, 45, 46, 47, 48, 49, 84, 85, 87
 3. Asaph: 50, 73, 74, 75, 76, 77, 78, 79, 80, 81, 82, 83
 4. Heman: 88
 5. Ethan: 89
 6. Solomon: 127
 7. Moses: 90
 8. Hezekiah: 120, 121, 123, 125, 126, 128, 129, 130, 132, 134
 9. Anonymous: 1, 10, 33, 43, 66, 67, 71, 91, 92, 93, 94, 96, 97, 98, 99, 100, 102, 104, 106, 107, 111, 112, 113, 114, 115, 116, 117, 118, 119, 135, 136, 137, 146, 147, 148, 149, 150
C. By subject matter.
 1. The Devotional Psalms: 4, 9, 12, 13, 14, 16, 17, 18, 19, 22, 23, 24, 27, 30, 31, 33, 34, 35, 37, 40, 42, 43, 46, 50, 55, 56, 61, 62, 63, 66, 68, 69, 71, 73, 75, 76, 77, 80, 81, 84, 85, 88, 90, 91, 94, 95, 100, 103, 106, 107, 111, 115, 116, 118, 119, 122, 123, 126, 133, 136, 138, 139, 141, 142, 144, 147, 148, 149, 150
 2. The Penitential Psalms: 6, 32, 38, 51, 102, 130, 143
 3. The Imprecatory Psalms: 35, 55, 58, 59, 69, 83, 109, 137, 140
 4. The Degree or Ascent Psalms: 120 through 134
 5. The Hallel (Hallelujah) Psalms: 113 through 118
 6. The Historical Psalms: 78, 105, 106
 7. The Acrostic Psalms: 9, 10, 25, 34, 37, 111, 112, 119, 145
 8. The Messianic Psalms: 2, 8, 16, 22, 23, 24, 31, 34, 40, 41, 45, 55, 68, 69, 72, 89, 102, 109, 110, 118, 129
We shall now study the Psalms by the subject matter method.

## The Devotional Psalms

These seventy Psalms have been titled "devotional" because they contain (among other things) precious and personal promises which all believers can feed upon. In dealing with these, sometimes only the promise itself will be quoted with no comment. On other occasions, a word or so may be added. These Psalms include both sobbing and singing. The authors will at times pout, doubt, and shout. They review the past and preview the future. Here the naked soul of man is manifested as perhaps in no other writings.
 1. Psalm 4
  Selection:
  "But know that the Lord hath set apart him that is godly for himself; the Lord will hear when I call unto him" (4:3).

"I will both lay me down in peace, and sleep: for thou, Lord, only makest me dwell in safety" (4:8).
Reflection:
Here David's praying brought him peace and sleep. One of the sweetest fringe benefits of the Christian life is peace. Note: "The Lord . . . will bless his people with peace" (Ps. 29:11).
"Great peace have they which love thy law: and nothing shall offend them" (Ps. 119:165).
 2. Psalm 9
 Selection:
 "The wicked shall be turned into hell, and all the nations that forget God" (9:17).
 Reflection:
 This will someday become a horrible reality. (See Ps. 11:6; Mt. 25:31-46; Rev. 14:10; 19:20; 20:11-15; 21:8.)
 3. Psalm 13
 Selection:
 "How long wilt thou forget me, O Lord? for ever? how long wilt thou hide thy face from me?" (v. 1).
 "How long shall I take counsel in my soul, having sorrow in my heart daily? How long shall mine enemy be exalted over me?" (v. 2).
 Reflection:
 One popularly held misconception about the Bible is that its heroes were men who differed entirely from other men; they never suffered defeat, they never became discouraged, they were at all times successful, saintly, and supremely happy. Absolutely nothing could be further removed from the truth. The fact is that all of them were "subject to like passions as we are" (Jas. 5:17). These men had all borne the bitter burden of defeat on many occasions. They were at times overwhelmed with despair as the sons and daughters of Adam are today. This despondency was often evident in their praying. Psalm 13 is such an example of soul-suffering supplication. Other notable examples are as follows:
  David's prayer in Psalms 6:1-7; 31:1-14
  Asaph's prayer in Psalm 77:1-20
  Heman's prayer in Psalm 88:1-18
  Unknown author's prayer in Psalm 102:1-11
  Jewish prisoner's prayer en route to Babylon in Psalm 137:1-6
  Moses' prayer in Numbers 11:1, 12, 14, 15
  Joshua's prayer in Joshua 7:6-9
  Elijah's prayer in 1 Kings 19:4, 10, 14
  Job's prayers in Job 3:3-12; 10:18-22
  Jeremiah's prayers in Jeremiah 4:10; 20:7-9, 14-18
  Jonah's prayer in Jonah 4:1-3
  Habakkuk's prayer in Habakkuk 1:2-4
  Korah's prayer in Psalms 42:3-11; 44:8-26
 4. Psalm 14
 Selection:
 "The fool hath said in his heart, there is no God. They are corrupt, they have done abominable works, there is none that doeth good" (14:1).
 Reflection:
 David here describes the atheistic fool. In biblical terms, a fool is a person with heart trouble, not head trouble. Note other kinds of fools in the Bible.
  a. The sin-mocking fool (Prov. 14:9).
  b. The wisdom-hating fool (Prov. 15:5).
  c. The strife-causing fool (Prov. 20:3).
  d. The glory-seeking fool (1 Sam. 26:21).
  e. The money-loving fool (Lk. 12:20).

f. The Christ-honoring fool (1 Cor. 4:10; the only "wise" fool in the bunch).

5. Psalm 17
Selection:
"Keep me as the apple of the eye, hide me under the shadow of thy wings" (17:8).
Reflection:
Here David uses two tender terms depicting God's affection for the believer.
a. Apple of the eye. (See also Deut. 32:10; Zech. 2:8.)
b. Shadow of thy wings. (See also Deut. 32:11, 12; Ps. 36:7; 57:1; 91:1, 4; Mt. 23:37.)

6. Psalm 18
Selection:
"He sent from above, he took me, he drew me out of many waters" (18:16).
"He brought me forth also into a large place: he delivered me, because he delighted in me" (18:19).
"For thou wilt light my candle: the Lord my God will enlighten my darkness" (18:28).
"Thou hast also given me the shield of thy salvation: and thy right hand hath holden me up, and thy gentleness hath made me great" (18:35).
Reflection:
In verse 16 he speaks of being drawn out of many waters. Water is often employed in the Psalms as a symbol for trouble and anguish. (See Ps. 69:1, 2; 144:7; Isa. 43:2.) In a very real sense, the daughter of Pharaoh, upon fetching a baby from the Nile, unconsciously nicknamed every child of God when she "called his name Moses . . . because I drew him out of the water" (Ex. 2:10). David here claims the Lord drew him out of many waters. Years later the Apostle John would write: "The Lamb . . . shall lead them unto living fountains of waters . . ." (Rev. 7:17).

7. Psalm 23
Selection:
(The entire Psalm) "The Lord is my shepherd; I shall not want."
Reflection:
This is undoubtedly the most famous prayer of all times, with the possible exception of the so-called Lord's prayer in Matthew 6:9-13.
David says the Lord is his Shepherd. Because of this, he continues, "I shall not want." Thus:
a. When his soul needed spiritual refreshment, the Shepherd provided green pastures.
b. When his soul was weary, the Shepherd provided still waters.
c. When his soul needed revival, the Shepherd restored him.
d. When his soul needed guidance, the Shepherd led him in right paths.
e. When his soul was confronted with death, the Shepherd went with him.
f. When his soul was confronted with enemies, the Shepherd provided his victory table.
g. When his soul was wounded, the Shepherd anointed his head with oil.
h. When his soul needed companionship, the Shepherd appointed goodness and mercy to accompany him.
i. When David would leave this temporary earthly dwelling place, the Shepherd would provide a permanent heavenly dwelling place. Thus David's testimony was, "I shall not want." What a contrast to

compare this statement with the one that would later be written on a Babylonian banquet wall addressed to Belshazzar.
The message was:
". . . God hath numbered thy kingdom, and finished it" (Dan. 5:26).
"Thou art weighed in the balances, and art found wanting" (Dan. 5:27).

j. At this point, it is appropriate to consider what is known as the trilogy of the Psalms, that is, a comparison of Psalms 22, 23, 24. Note:
Psalm 22 (Jn. 10:11)
   (1) the Good Shepherd
   (2) the Savior
   (3) the Foundation
   (4) Christ dying
   (5) the Cross
   (6) he gives his *life*
   (7) Grace
Psalm 23 (Heb. 13:20)
   (8) the Great Shepherd
   (9) the Satisfier
   (10) the manifestation
   (11) Christ living
   (12) the Comforter
   (13) he gives his *love*
   (14) guidance
Psalm 24 (1 Pet. 5:4)
   (15) the Chief Shepherd
   (16) the Sovereign
   (17) the expectation
   (18) Christ coming
   (19) the crown
   (20) he gives his *light*
   (21) glory

8. Psalm 34
Selection:
"This poor man cried, and the Lord heard him, and saved him out of all his troubles. The angel of the Lord encampeth round about them that fear him, and delivereth them. O taste and see that the Lord is good: blessed is the man that trusteth in him. O fear the Lord, ye his saints: for there is no want to them that fear him (34:6-9).
Reflection:
Our gracious heavenly Father often uses his angelic messengers to aid, protect, and encourage his earthly children. (See 2 Ki. 6:17; Heb. 1:14; Acts 12:7.)

9. Psalm 35
Selection:
"False witnesses did rise up; they laid to my charge things that I knew not. They rewarded me evil for good to the spoiling of my soul. But as for me, when they were sick, my clothing was sackcloth: I humbled my soul with fasting; and my prayer returned into mine own bosom" (35:11-13).
Reflection:
This type of praying is indeed difficult—to intercede for those in their need who perhaps do not even want to be prayed for and who would rejoice if the same calamity overtook you. But the believer is nevertheless commanded to pray such a prayer.

10. Psalm 37
Selection:
"Fret not thyself because of evildoers, neither be thou envious against the workers of iniquity. For they shall

soon be cut down like the grass, and wither as the green herb. Trust in the Lord, and do good; so shalt thou dwell in the land, and verily thou shalt be fed" (37:1-3).

"Delight thyself also in the Lord; and he shall give thee the desires of thine heart" (v. 4).

"Commit thy way unto the Lord; trust also in him; and he shall bring it to pass" (v. 5).

"Rest in the Lord, and wait patiently for him: fret not thyself because of him who prospereth in his way, because of the man who bringeth wicked devices to pass" (v. 7).

"The wicked plotteth against the just, and gnasheth upon him with his teeth" (v. 12).

"The Lord shall laugh at him: for he seeth that his day is coming" (v. 13).

"The Lord knoweth the days of the upright: and their inheritance shall be for ever" (v. 18).

"The steps of a good man are ordered by the Lord: and he delighteth in his way" (v. 23).

"Though he fall, he shall not be utterly cast down: for the Lord upholdeth him with his hand" (v. 24).

"I have been young, and now am old; yet have I not seen the righteous forsaken, nor his seed begging bread" (v. 25).

"For the Lord loveth judgment, and forsaketh not his saints; they are preserved for ever; but the seed of the wicked shall be cut off" (v. 28).
Reflections:
This prayer Psalm could be called "the climb to the sublime," or, "from frustration (v. 1) to exaltation" (v. 34). There are five rungs in this ladder of ascent as given in the first several verses. Fret not—I have a problem.
Trust—I believe God can answer my problem.
Delight—I believe he will answer my problem.
Commit—I bring my problem to him.
Rest—I leave my problem with him.

In the Psalms God is pictured as laughing at two things:
a. the attempts of the wicked to dethrone his son (Ps. 2:2-4)
b. the attempts of the wicked to destroy his saints (Ps. 37:13; 59:8)
Often in the Psalms the one praying will ask the Lord to impress upon him the brevity of this life, so that he might commit each precious day to his Creator. This is referred to here (37:18) and in other prayers:
"My times are in thy hand . . ." (Ps. 31:15).
"Lord, make me to know mine end, and the measure of my days, what it is: that I may know how frail I am" (Ps. 39:4).
"So teach us to number our days, that we may apply our hearts unto wisdom" (Ps. 90:12).
"How many are the days of thy servant?" (Ps. 119:84) In this Psalm verses 23, 24, 25 and 28 describe God's Social Security plan for his workers along with all its fringe benefits.

11. Psalm 40
Selection:
"I waited patiently for the Lord; and he inclined unto me, and heard my cry. He brought me up also out of an horrible pit, out of the miry clay, and set my feet upon a rock, and established by goings. And he hath put a new song in my mouth, even praise unto our

God: many shall see it, and fear, and shall trust in the Lord" (40:1-3).

"Many, O Lord my God, are thy wonderful works which thou hast done, and thy thoughts which are to us-ward: they cannot be reckoned up in order unto thee: if I would declare and speak of them, they are more than can be numbered" (v. 5).
Reflections:
Verses 1-3 illustrate the differences between Christianity and all other religions. Consider this story: Here is a man who has fallen into a dark and foul pit, breaking his legs and arms as he lands. Soon his helpless and pain-wracked cries for air proceed from the pit. In this illustration, Confucius comes by, looks down, and says: "Friend, let me give you this sage advice: If you ever get out of there, take heed where you walk, that you fall not again into such a place." With this, the Chinese philosopher walks on.

Awhile later, Buddha passes by and views the helpless man. He says: "Friend, you need help. If you can meet me halfway, I'll aid in your escape. Just climb a bit and stretch your hands toward me." But the broken and bleeding victim cannot move. Buddha then sadly walks away. The desperate man huddles in his prison of pain, his hope almost gone. But he utters one final cry for salvation. Then the Savior of all men gazes down upon him with loving compassion. Without a word of advice or admonishment, he slips down into the pit, tenderly places the fallen traveler over his strong shoulders, and climbs out of the pit with him. He then sets the broken bones, points the man's feet toward heaven, and puts a song in his heart! This is *salvation*. In verse 5 of this prayer, David mentions God's wonderful works performed for him, and God's countless thoughts about him. Other passages bring this precious truth into focus (see Ps. 92:5; 139:17, 18; Jer. 29:11).

12. Psalm 42
Selection:
"Why art thou cast down, O my soul? and why art thou disquieted in me? Hope thou in God: for I shall yet praise him . . . (42:5). (See also 42:11; 43:5.)
Reflection:
These three verses are mentioned here because of their remarkable repetition. It is often rather jokingly observed by the world that it is all right for a man to talk to himself, but if he answers himself—this is bad. But not according to Korah! He both asks *and* answers his own questions. This self-assurance of one's own soul is a good practice. Sometimes it is helpful for a person to lecture and console himself as he would another.

13. Psalm 46
Selection:
"God is our refuge and strength, a very present help in trouble. Therefore will not we fear, though the earth be removed, and though the mountains be carried into the midst of the sea: Though the waters thereof roar and be troubled, though the mountains shake with the swelling thereof" (46:1-3).

"The heathen raged, the kingdoms were moved: he uttered his voice, the earth melted. The Lord of hosts is with us; the God of Jacob is our refuge. Selah. Come, behold the works of the Lord, what desolations he hath made in the earth. He maketh wars to cease unto the end of the earth; he breaketh the bow, and cutteth the spear in sunder; he burneth the chariot in the fire" (vs. 6–9).

Reflection:

This may become a favorite Psalm of that frightened Israelite remnant which may hide from the antichrist in Petra during the last terrible period of the great tribulation. (Isa. 26:19, 20; Rev. 6:12–14; especially Mt. 24:15, 16; Rev. 12:14).

14. Psalm 50

Selection:

"Gather my saints together unto me; those that have made a covenant with me by sacrifice" (50:5).

"For every beast of the forest is mine, and the cattle upon a thousand hills. I know all the fowls of the mountains: and the wild beasts of the field are mine. If I were hungry, I would not tell thee: for the world is mine, and the fulness thereof. Will I eat the flesh of bulls, or drink the blood of goats? Offer unto God thanksgiving; and pay thy vows unto the most High" (50:10–14).

Reflections:

There are those critics that have charged the Old Testament with presenting a bloodthirsty Hebrew tribal god who was more interested in gory sacrifices than in helping men. In this Psalm, Asaph lays the axe to that lie. He says God was more interested in the man's soul than in his sacrifices. Burning devotion was far more precious to him than bloody beasts. It was not the outward brazen altar that pleased the Lord, but the inward, heart altar. Moses had reminded Israel some four centuries previous to this of the same great principle. (See Deut. 10:12–16.)

15. Psalm 56

Selection:

"Thou tellest my wanderings: put thou my tears into thy bottle: are they not in thy book?" (56:8).

"For thou hast delivered my soul from death: wilt not thou deliver my feet from falling, that I may walk before God in the light of the living?" (56:13).

Reflections:

The sweet words in verse 8 here should comfort and cheer the most despondent heart. David asks God to preserve his tears. The author once traced the trail of human tears across the pages of the Bible during a personal study of his own. What a study it was. This sea of soul sorrow begins in Genesis and flows through every book, finally to crest itself in the Revelation of John.

One of the first instances of a believer weeping occurred when Abraham buried his beloved Sarah in a lonely and desolate cave somewhere in Hebron (Gen. 23:2).

This trickle continues and becomes a current as it is fed by the tears of Jacob for Joseph (Gen. 37:35), of Moses for Miriam (Num. 12:13), of Hannah for a son (1 Sam. 1:10), of Samuel for Saul (1 Sam. 15:11, 35), and of David for Absalom (2 Sam. 18:33). By this time the current has become a torrent, but is still growing. Hezekiah weeps for himself (2 Ki. 20:2, 3), Nehemiah for Jerusalem (Neh. 1:4), a father for his little girl (Mk. 5:39), and two sisters over their dead brother (Jn. 11).

This torrent, now an uncontrollable river, finds itself carrying the most precious tears of all, those belonging to our Savior. He weeps over Lazarus (Jn. 11:35) and over Jerusalem (Lk. 19:41). But at last, in the Book of Revelation, this swollen sea is dramatically and deci-

sively stopped! The last recorded instance of a believer weeping is found in Revelation 5:5. Finally, God himself mops up all remaining traces (in Rev. 21:4).

16. Psalm 63

Selection:

"When I remember thee upon my bed, and meditate on thee in the night watches" (63:6).

Reflection:

In the Psalms we read of David praying at various times of the day. But especially did he enjoy seeking his Shepherd in the still of the night, as he relates here in verse 6. Consider his midnight messages to God: "Commune with your own heart upon your bed, and be still" (Ps. 4:4).

"Thou hast visited me in the night . . ." (Ps. 17:3).

"I cry . . . in the night season . . ." (Ps. 22:2).

"In the night his song shall be with me, and my prayer . . ." (Ps. 42:8).

"I call to remembrance my song in the night . . ." (Ps. 77:6).

"To shew forth . . . thy faithfulness every night" (Ps. 92:2).

"I have remembered thy name, O Lord, in the night . . ." (Ps. 119:55).

"Let the saints be joyful in glory: let them sing aloud upon their beds" (Ps. 149:5).

17. Psalm 66

Selection:

"If I regard iniquity in my heart, the Lord will not hear me" (66:18).

Reflection:

This absolute prayer principle is stated throughout the entire Bible and refers to both sinners and saints alike. The blood of Christ will forgive us of all our confessed sins, but will not cover even one of our miserable excuses. (See Prov. 15:29; 28:9; Isa. 1:15; 59:1, 2; Jn. 9:31; Jas. 4:3.)

18. Psalm 68

Selection:

"The chariots of God are twenty thousand, even thousands of angels" (68:17).

Reflection:

In verse 17 David numbers the angels in heaven among the thousands. This estimate is undergirded by other biblical references such as in Daniel 7:10, Mt. 26:53, and Revelation 5:11. Some five centuries later, a lonely and broken prophet would sit amid the debris of a dying and desolate Jerusalem, only recently leveled by the invading Babylonians. As he sat there he may have recalled David's testimony here in Psalm 68:19. At any rate, the prophet with the pierced heart wrote his testimony, based upon David's earlier one: "This I recall to mind, therefore have I hope. It is of the Lord's mercies that we are not consumed, because his compassions fail not. They are new every morning: great is thy faithfulness" (Lam. 3:21–23).

19. Psalm 69

Selection:

"But as for me, my prayer is unto thee, O Lord, in an acceptable time: O God, in the multitude of thy mercy hear me, in the truth of thy salvation" (69:13).

Reflection:

When is this "acceptable time"? A teacher once said to his Sunday school class: "Boys, the best time for a fella to prepare to meet God is the day before he dies." This at first seemed to be acceptable to the class, but then one small boy raised his hand and exclaimed: "But teacher, sometimes a guy doesn't know about it twenty-four hours before he dies! What should he do then?" The teacher wisely replied: "Then boys, the *next* best time for a fella to prepare to meet God is today!" One of the most important theological concepts in the Scriptures is the doctrine of the present tense—of to-day.

God desires:

a. That the sinner give his heart to Christ today (2 Cor. 6:2).

b. That the saint give his body to Christ today (Rom. 6:19; 12:1-3; Heb. 3:7, 13, 15).

The obvious reason for all this haste is found in the following verses: Proverbs 27:1; James 4:13-15.

20. Psalm 71

Selection:

"For thou art my hope, O Lord God: thou art my trust from my youth" (71:5).

"Cast me not off in the time of old age; forsake me not when my strength faileth" (71:9).

"O God, thou hast taught me from my youth: and hitherto have I declared thy wondrous works" (71:17).

"Now also when I am old and grayheaded, O God, forsake me not; until I have shewed thy strength unto this generation, and thy power to every one that is to come" (71:18).

Reflection:

This could rightly be called, "The Psalm of the Old Man." One of the greatest "fringe benefits" afforded to the believer is that old age simply brings him all the closer to that glorious goal of being like Christ. This is totally different from all other earthly goals, such as in the field of sports and other professional careers, where youth, brains, strength, and looks are cruel taskmasters, and the unfortunate individual is crudely and rudely cast aside in his old age (see Ps. 25:7; 37:25; Eccles. 11:9, 10; 12:1).

21. Psalm 73

Selection:

"But as for me, my feet were almost gone; my steps had well nigh slipped" (73:2).

"For I was envious at the foolish, when I saw the prosperity of the wicked" (v. 3).

"They are not in trouble as other men; neither are they plagued like other men" (v. 5).

"Their eyes stand out with fatness: they have more than heart could wish" (v. 7).

"Behold, these are the ungodly, who prosper in the world; they increase in riches" (v. 12).

"Verily I have cleansed my heart in vain, and washed my hands in innocency" (v. 13).

"For all the day long have I been plagued, and chastened every morning" (v. 14).

"When I thought to know this, it was too painful for me; until I went into the sanctuary of God; then understood I their end. Surely thou didst set them in slippery places: thou castedst them down into destruction. How are they brought into desolation, as in a moment! They are utterly consumed with terrors" (73:16-19).

Reflections:

Asaph here asks a question that has bothered countless Christians throughout history: Why do the wicked prosper while the righteous suffer? Lazarus must have pondered it as he sat ill-clothed, ill-fed, and covered with running sores beside the gates of a heartless and thoughtless millionaire (Lk. 16:19-31). Samuel was doubtless pained by the thought as he watched the anointed David fleeing from the arrogant Saul.

It is reported that some years ago an editor wrote in a farm magazine that while he was not a particularly religious man, yet he did see the wisdom of the biblical command to work six days and rest on the seventh. Soon after the publication of the article, an irate farmer wrote the editor, informing him that his article was pure hogwash! To prove this, he pointed out that that very year he had planted his crops on Sunday, cared for them on Sunday, and harvested them on Sunday. He closed gleefully with the words: "Now here it is October already and I have made more money this year than any of my so-called Christian farmer friends who did not work on Sunday!" The editor, upon receiving his letter, published it in the following issue along with his own terse observation which read:

"Dear Sir, God does not settle all his accounts in October!"

22. Psalm 75

Selection:

"For promotion cometh neither from the east, nor from the west, nor from the south. But God is the judge: he putteth down one, and setteth up another" (75:6, 7).

Reflection:

Perhaps no other king in all history attested more to the fearful accuracy of these words than did the mighty Babylonian monarch Nebuchadnezzar. He had dreamed of a mighty tree which had been cut down at God's command. Daniel rightly prophesied that God was warning the proud ruler to humble himself, lest he be cut down to size. Not only would this happen, but he would also suffer a seven-year period of insanity. But the haughty king refused to bend or bow. Then, the storm broke. (See Dan. 4:29-37.)

23. Psalm 76

Selection:

"Surely the wrath of man shall praise thee" (76:10).

Reflection:

Scriptural illustrations abound which prove the prayer statement found here. Consider:

a. The wrath of Esau caused Jacob to flee afar off, where he met Rachel—to the praise of God (Gen. 27:41-45; 29:10).

b. The wrath of eleven brothers sent Joseph to Egypt as a slave, where he later became prime minister—to the praise of God (Gen. 37:23-28; 41:38-44).

Later Joseph would remind his brothers of all this:

"But as for you, ye thought evil against me; but God meant it unto good, to bring to pass, as it is this day, to save much people alive" (Gen. 50:20).

c. A Moabite king in wrath attempted to curse Israel through a hireling prophet, but this resulted in a beautiful prophecy about Christ—to the praise of God (Num. 22:1-6; 24:17).

d. The wrath of Haman built a gallows to destroy a Jew but was himself hanged upon that same gallows—to the praise of God (Est. 5:12-14; 7:10).

e. The wrath of an Israelite king burned a book from God, but the book was thereupon rewritten with an addition which prophesied his own doom—to the praise of God (Jer. 36:22, 23, 27, 28, 29, 30, 31, 32).

f. The wrath of the Pharisees placed Christ on the cross between two thieves, which resulted in the salvation of the dying thief—to the praise of God (Lk. 23:39–43).

g. The wrath of a Roman emperor banished the Apostle John to a lonely isle to prevent him from preaching the gospel, resulting in the book of Revelation—to the praise of God (Rev. 1:9).

24. Psalm 80
Selection:
"Give ear, O Shepherd of Israel, thou that leadest Joseph like a flock; thou that dwellest between the cherubims, shine forth" (80:1).

"Thou hast brought a vine out of Egypt: thou hast cast out the heathen, and planted it" (80:8).

Reflection:
Here a reference is made to the cherubim. The two golden cherubim statues, some fifteen feet high, which stood over the mercy seat of the Ark of the Covenant in the Holy of Holies, were apparently meant to be representative of actual beings. They are mentioned some sixty-four times in the Bible. Note:

a. Both Moses and Solomon placed them in the Holy of Holies (Ex. 25:19; 1 Ki. 6:27).

b. God spoke to Moses from between the cherubim (Num. 7:89).

c. Hezekiah spoke to God through the cherubim (2 Ki. 19:15).

d. Ezekiel sees the glory of the Lord amid four flying cherubim (Ezek. 10).

e. The millennial Temple is described as featuring the cherubim (Ezek. 41:17–20).

Aside from what has already been said about the cherubim, this psalm prayer of Asaph could rightly be titled "The Dying Vine Psalm." The vine is often used in the Bible as a symbol for Israel. Note what Asaph says about this vine. He declares:

f. God brought it out of Egypt (v. 8).

g. He planted this vine in his chosen land (v. 8).

h. He cleared the ground and tilled the soil for his vine (v. 9).

i. The vine took root and grew for awhile (v. 9).

j. The vine covered the mountains and grew as high as cedar trees (v. 10).

k. It traveled from the Great Sea to the Euphrates River (v. 11).

l. But then God broke down the hedge protecting his vine (v. 12).

m. Strangers then took their plunder of its grapes (v. 12).

n. The wild boar rooted it and the wild beast ate it (v. 13).

o. Its enemies chopped it and burned it (v. 16).

Why did God treat his vine like this? The answer is given very clearly. (See Isa. 5:1–4; Jer. 2:21; Hos. 10:1.) God desired that his chosen vine bear fruit to feed the hungry nations around it. But it did not do so. In the fullness of time, therefore, God set aside this wild and wicked and wasted vine. Our Lord Jesus solemnly and sadly declared this rejection in a lecture to the wicked Pharisees. He said: "Therefore I say unto you, The kingdom of God shall be taken from you, and given to a nation bringing forth the fruits thereof" (Mt. 21:43).

While he was upon earth, the Lord Jesus was God's blessed vine (Isa. 53:2), and bore goodly fruit through his miracles, parables, prayers, and sermons. But then it came time for the crucified and resurrected vine to ascend back into his Father's heavenly vineyard. Who then would bear the Father's fruit on earth? This thrilling plan is spelled out in detail for us in John 15:1–8. The believer is therefore to do that which Israel would not do—to bear fruit, more fruit, much fruit. This can only be done through abiding in him (prayer) and allowing his words to abide in us (Bible study). He is the vine, we are the branches. A branch exists for one sole purpose—to bear fruit. It cannot produce it, it simply bears it. It is good for nothing else. Its wood is not used for building or furniture making, nor can it be employed for fuel material. It is simply to bear and share its fruit.

25. Psalm 81
Selection:
"I am the Lord thy God, which brought thee out of the land of Egypt; open thy mouth wide, and I will fill it. But my people would not hearken to my voice; and Israel would none of me. So I gave them up unto their own hearts' lust: and they walked in their own counsels. Oh that my people had hearkened unto me, and Israel had walked in my ways! I should soon have subdued their enemies, and turned my hand against their adversaries" (81:10–14).

Reflection:
Nearly ten centuries later the rejected Redeemer of Israel would stand on Mt. Olive overlooking Jerusalem and powerfully voice similar words. (See Mt. 23:37–39.)

26. Psalm 84
Selection:
"Blessed is the man whose strength is in thee; in whose heart are the ways of them. Who passing through the valley of Baca make it a well; the rain also filleth the pools. They go from strength to strength, every one of them in Zion appeareth before God" (84:5–7).

Reflection:
Verse 7 speaks of growing in strength. This word *strength* is very important in the biblical vocabulary of prayer and sanctification. Note the statement describing man's inward strength as opposed to God's imparted strength.

Man's strength:
"My strength is dried up . . ." (Ps. 22:15).
"My strength faileth because of mine iniquity . . ." (Ps. 31:10).
"I retained no strength" (Dan. 10:8).

God's strength:
"Hast thou not known? hast thou not heard, that the everlasting God, the Lord, the Creator of the ends of the earth, fainteth not, neither is weary? There is no searching of his understanding. He giveth power to the faint; and to them that have no might he increaseth strength. Even the youths shall faint and be weary, and the young men shall utterly fall: But they that wait upon the Lord shall renew their strength; they shall mount up with wings as eagles; they shall run, and not be weary; and they shall walk, and not faint" (Isa. 40:28–31).

"Fear thou not; for I am with thee: be not dismayed; for I am thy God: I will strengthen thee; yea, I will help thee; yea, I will uphold thee with the right hand of my righteousness" (Isa. 41:10).

(See also Ps. 27:1; 28:7; 29:11; 43:2; 46:1; 81:1; 118:14; 119:28; Phil. 4:13; 1 Pet. 5:10; Eph. 3:16; Rom. 5:6; 2 Tim. 4:17; 2 Cor. 12:9.)

27. Psalm 85

Selection:

"Wilt thou not revive us again: that thy people may rejoice in thee?" (85:6).

"I will hear what God the Lord will speak: for he will speak peace unto his people, and to his saints: but let them not turn again to folly. Surely his salvation is nigh them that fear him . . ." (85:8, 9).

"Mercy and truth are met together; righteousness and peace have kissed each other" (85:10).

Reflections:

Perhaps no other prayer is more welcome in the ears of God than the one for revival, as expressed here in verse 6. Only a child of God can be revived. Sinners cannot be revived; they need to be resurrected. A dead person cannot be revived; only a live person can be or should be revived. Later, Habakkuk would pray a similar prayer for himself and the Israelite remnant:

". . . O Lord, revive thy work in the midst of the years, in the midst of the years make known; in wrath remember mercy" (Hab. 3:2). As millions of Christians throughout church history have discovered, God will hasten to answer the prayer of that soul who desires revival. But as Korah suggests in the last few words of verse 8, a true desire for revival carries with it a determination to abandon that sin which necessitated it in the first place.

There are many revivals recorded in the Bible. All of them were prompted by either prayer or Bible study or both. Consider these scriptural reforms and revivals:

a. under Jacob (Gen. 35:2–4)
b. under Moses (Ex. 14:31—15:21)
c. under David (1 Chron. 15:25-28; 16:1-43; 29:10-25)
d. under Solomon (2 Chron. 7:4-11)
e. under Elijah (1 Ki. 18:21–40)
f. under Asa (1 Ki. 15:11-15)
g. under Jehu (2 Ki. 10:15-28)
h. under Jehoiada (2 Ki. 11:17-20)
i. under Josiah (2 Ki. 22, 23)
j. under Jehoshaphat (2 Chron. 20)
k. under Hezekiah (2 Chron. 29-31)
l. under Manasseh (2 Chron. 33:11-20)
m. under Ezra (Ezra 9, 10)
n. under Nehemiah (Neh. 13)
o. under Jonah (Jonah 3)
p. under Esther (Est. 9:17-22)
q. under John the Baptist (Lk. 3:2-18)
r. under the Savior (Jn. 4:28-42)
s. under Philip (Acts 8:5-12)
t. under Peter (Acts 9:32-35; 2:1-47)
u. under Paul (Acts 13:14-52; 17:10-12; 18:8; 19:18)

The amazing power of prayer is seen in verse ten. Here are two pairs of irreconcilables, mercy and truth, and righteousness and peace. Mercy looks at the sinner and says, "Spare him," but truth demands, "For the wages of sin is death." Peace viewed the troubled soul of the sinner and longed to soothe it, but righteousness pointed out that the soul that sinneth shall surely die. What could be done? Then came the miracle—love found a way, in Christ.

Thus these two opposites could be reconciled and kiss each other.

28. Psalm 88

Selection:

"For my soul is full of troubles: and my life draweth nigh unto the grave" (88:3).

Reflection:

This is by far the darkest and most despondent prayer in the entire Bible. Not one ray of hope appears.

29. Psalm 90

Selection:

"The days of our years are threescore years and ten; and if by reason of strength they be fourscore years, yet is their strength labour and sorrow; for it is soon cut off, and we fly away" (90:10).

"So teach us to number our days, that we may apply our hearts unto wisdom" (90:12).

Reflection:

This has often been called "The Psalm of Death" or "The Psalm of the First Adam." It was written by Moses. Note the seventy-year average span of man statement in verse 10, a tragic drop from the early patriarchal age found in Genesis 5. But as the first Adam would discover, one of the bitter fruits of sin is physical death. With this background, man's only logical conclusion is stated in verse 12. A sinner should accept Christ today (for this is the beginning of wisdom), and the believer should spend his days as wisely as he is exhorted to spend his money. In fact, more so, for wasted time can never be reclaimed.

30. Psalm 91

Selection:

"He that dwelleth in the secret place of the most High shall abide under the shadow of the Almighty" (91:1).

"For he shall give his angels charge over thee, to keep thee in all thy ways" (91:11).

"They shall bear thee up in their hands, lest thou dash thy foot against a stone" (91:12).

Reflection:

This is known as "The Psalm of Life," or "The Psalm of the Second Adam." It is primarily one which describes the keeping power of the Father concerning the Son while he walked this earth. Verse 11 speaks of giving "his angels charge over thee." Note the ministry angels performed for our Lord Jesus while he was upon this earth:

a. They worshiped him (Heb. 1:6).
b. They announced his birth (Lk. 1:26–38; 2:8–14; Mt. 1:20–23).
c. They ministered to him:
  (1) in the wilderness (Mt. 4:11)
  (2) in the garden (Lk. 22:43)
d. They rolled away the tombstone (Mt. 28:2).
e. They announced his resurrection (Mt. 28:6).
f. They were present at his ascension (Acts 1:10, 11).
g. They will accompany his Second Coming (2 Thess. 1:7, 8).

During Jesus' awful temptations, Satan quoted verse 11 of this Psalm (Mt. 4:6). Shakespeare was right when he declared, "The devil doth quote Scripture."

31. Psalm 94

Selection:

"When I said, my foot slippeth; thy mercy, O Lord, held me up" (94:18).

Reflection:

This verse, like others in the Psalms, teaches the eternal security of the believer. It describes not the child of God desperately "hanging on" to the Father for dear life, but rather having his frail hand securely clasped by that strong heavenly grasp. (See also Ps. 37:23, 24.)

32. Psalm 100
Selection:
"Make a joyful noise unto the Lord, all ye lands" (100:1).
Reflection:
This has been known as "The Old One Hundredth," and for style, beauty and content, deserves to be placed alongside Psalm 23.

33. Psalm 103
Selection:
"Bless the Lord, O my soul: and all that is within me, bless his holy name" (103:1).
Reflection:
This Psalm is possibly the greatest, grandest, and most glorious poem of praise to Jehovah God ever composed. In it David's zeal reaches its zenith. His reach is higher, his thoughts are deeper, his song is sweeter, and his heart is more moved than in any other prayer of praise in the Bible.

34. Psalm 107
Selection:
"For he satisfieth the longing soul, and the hungry soul he filleth with goodness. Such as sat in darkness and in the shadow of death, being bound in affliction and iron. . . . He maketh the storm a calm, so that the waves thereof are still" (vs. 9, 10, 29).
Reflection:
While he was upon this earth our Lord literally and lovingly fulfilled these verses:
   a. He fulfilled 107:9, 10, in Matthew 4:16 and Hebrews 2:14, 15.
   b. He fulfilled 107:29, in Matthew 8:26.

35. Psalm 111
Selection:
"The fear of the Lord is the beginning of wisdom . . ." (111:10).
Reflection:
The word "fear" in the Bible, especially in the Psalms, where it is used over a hundred times, is closely connected with prayer and praise. This particular kind of fear is not the sickening dread type, but that of reverential respect. This holy breed of fear is obviously missing in the world today. As Paul would say when describing the wickedness of the human race: "There is no fear of God before their eyes" (Rom. 3:18). Note the usage of the word fear as it relates to prayer and fellowship with God.

   "And now, Israel, what doth the Lord thy God require of thee, but to fear the Lord thy God, to walk in all his ways, and to love him, and to serve the Lord thy God with all thy heart and with all thy soul" (Deut. 10:12).
   "Now therefore fear the Lord, and serve him in sincerity and in truth . . ." (Josh. 24:14).
   "Serve the Lord with fear . . ." (Ps. 2:11).
   "In thy fear will I worship . . ." (Ps. 5:7).
   "Then they that feared the Lord spake often one to another: and the Lord hearkened, and heard it, and a book of remembrance was written before him for them that feared the Lord, and that thought upon his name" (Mal. 3:16).

36. Psalm 118
Selection:
"[Jehovah] hath chastened me sore: but he hath not given me over unto death. This is the Lord's doing; it is marvellous in our eyes. This is the day which the Lord hath made; we will rejoice and be glad in it" (Ps. 118:18, 23, 24).
Reflection:
The life and experiences of Job serve as an entire commentary on verse 18. Verses 23 and 24 can be rightfully claimed by all believers on the basis of Romans 8:28, even on the day of the funeral of a loved one.

37. Psalm 119
Selection:
"Thy word have I hid in my heart, that I might not sin against thee" (119:11).
   "It is good for me that I have been afflicted; that I might learn thy statutes" (119:71).
   "I know, O Lord, that thy judgments are right, and that thou in faithfulness hast afflicted me" (119:75).
   "For ever, O Lord, thy word is settled in heaven" (119:89).
   "I have more understanding than all my teachers: for thy testimonies are my meditation" (119:99).
   "Thy word is a lamp unto my feet, and a light unto my path" (119:105).
   "The entrance of thy words giveth light; it giveth understanding unto the simple" (119:130).
Reflection:
We now come to the longest Psalm and by far the most lengthy prayer in all the Bible. The sole theme of this prayer is the Word of God. It is referred to in every one of the 176 verses with the exception of five. The psalmist gives the Bible nine titles in this Psalm and ascribes some twelve ministries to it.
   a. The nine titles
      (1) his law (v. 1)
      (2) his testimonies (v. 2)
      (3) his ways (v. 3)
      (4) his precepts (v. 4)
      (5) his statutes (v. 5)
      (6) his commandments (v. 6)
      (7) his righteous judgments (v. 7)
      (8) his Word (v. 9)
      (9) his ordinances (v. 91)
   b. The twelve ministries
      (1) it cleanses (v. 9)
      (2) it quickens (v. 25)
      (3) it strengthens (v. 28)
      (4) it establishes (v. 38)
      (5) it defends (v. 42)
      (6) it comforts (v. 50)
      (7) it instructs (vs. 98, 99)
      (8) it enlightens (v. 105)
      (9) it assures (v. 114)
      (10) it upholds (v. 116)
      (11) it brings peace (v. 165)
      (12) it delivers (v. 170)
   Concerning verse 11, D. L. Moody said that the Bible would keep one from sin or sin would keep one from the Bible. Concerning verse 71, God often afflicts us with woes in order to acquaint us with his Word (see also Ps. 94:12). The author of the book of Hebrews builds upon verse 75. (See Heb. 12:5-15.)
   Concerning verse 89, our Lord once said:
"Heaven and earth shall pass away, but my words shall not pass away" (Mt. 24:35). (See also Mt. 5:18; 1 Pet. 1:23, 25.)

Concerning verse 99, the psalmist is not boasting of his brain-power, nor is he belittling all instructors. He is simply saying that in matters of God's will for his life, more can be gleaned from a study of the Scriptures than from all well-meaning, but nevertheless human, advisors. Sometimes even the godliest instructor can give another believer the wrong advice. A classic example of this was Nathan's encouragement concerning David's plan to build the Temple (see 1 Chron. 17:1-4). In his first letter, the Apostle John writes concerning this (see 1 Jn. 2:27).

Concerning verse 105, it can be pointed out that Satan too is described as a light-displayer of some type. But there is this difference: God's light is directed at the man's feet, thus guiding his eyesight. Satan's light is aimed at the man's eyes, thus blinding his eyesight. As Paul would later declare: "The god of this world hath blinded the minds of them which believe not, lest the light of the glorious gospel of Christ, who is the image of God, should shine unto them" (2 Cor. 4:4). (See also Ps. 97:11.)

Concerning verse 130, it can be pointed out that the Word of God is simple enough to bless the heart of the densest believer and at the same time profound enough to challenge the brain of the wisest believer. It is both milk for the babe and meat for the man.

38. Psalm 123
Selection:
"Unto thee lift I up mine eyes, O thou that dwellest in the heavens. Behold, as the eyes of servants look unto the hand of their masters, and as the eyes of a maiden unto the hand of her mistress; so our eyes wait upon the Lord our God, until that he have mercy upon us" (123:1, 2).
Reflection:
A citizen of Western civilization, whose society advocates (at least on paper) the equality of all men, who reads these words in this Psalm cannot but faintly comprehend their full meaning, as he knows nothing of the absolute submission and loyalty which existed in the oriental servant-master and maid-mistress relationships. We are told that when in the presence of his master, the servant should fix his gaze upon the hand of that master. Thus, the lightest movement or gesture from that hand would rouse the servant into immediate and total action. This eye-to-hand service was likewise true with the maid and her mistress. This meaning may certainly be attached to God's words to David in Psalm 32:8, 9: "I will instruct thee and teach thee in the way which thou shalt go: I will guide thee with mine eye. Be ye not as the horse, or as the mule, which have no understanding: whose mouth must be held in with bit and bridle, lest they come near unto thee." In Romans 1:1, Paul refers to himself as a bond-slave of Jesus Christ. This was no doubt the secret underlying his mighty works for God.

39. Psalm 136
Selection:
"O give thanks unto the Lord; for he is good: for his mercy endureth forever" (Ps. 136:1).
Reflection:
This is Scripture's great mercy refrain Psalm. The phrase, "for his mercy endureth forever," appears twenty-six times, once for each verse. Note other biblical prayers in which mercy is the outstanding element:

a. Jacob's prayer (Gen. 32:10)
b. Abraham's prayer (Gen. 24:27)
c. Moses' prayer (Ex. 15:13)
d. David's prayer (2 Sam. 22:26; 24:14)
e. the remnant's prayer (Neh. 9:19)
f. Jonah's prayer (Jonah 4:2)
g. the publican's prayer (Lk. 18:13)
h. other Psalms (25:6; 40:11; 51:1; 69:16; 79:8; 103:4; 119:77, 156; 145:9)

40. Psalm 139
Selection:
"O Lord, thou hast searched me, and known me" (139:1).
Reflection:
Within this Psalm of David is more about the omniscience of God than can be found in any other prayer in the Bible. According to David:
a. God knew when he sat or stood (v. 2).
b. God knew his every thought (v. 2).
c. God knew his every habit (v. 3).
d. God knew his every word (v. 4).
e. God knew his every step (v. 5).
f. God knew him before he was born (v. 16).
Because of this wonderful wisdom, David thanked God:
g. For creating him (vs. 13-16).
h. For keeping him.
   (1) Even if he ascended into heaven (v. 8).
   (2) Even if he descended into the grave (v. 8).
   (3) Even if he visited the furthest ocean (v. 9).
   (4) Even if he covered himself with the blackest night (vs. 11, 12).
i. For thinking about him (vs. 17, 18).

## The Penitential Psalms (6, 32, 38, 51, 102, 130, 143)

No less than five out of the seven penitential Psalms were written by David. He wrote 6, 32, 38, 51, and 143. We will here consider Psalms 32, 38, and 51.

1. Psalm 32
This Psalm should be connected with Psalm 51. The latter describes David's emotions as he confesses his sin of adultery and murder (2 Sam. 11), while this Psalm depicts his feelings before such confession was made, when the awful burden of guilt still bore heavy upon him. In the book of Romans (4:7, 8) Paul quotes the first two verses of this Psalm to illustrate one of Scripture's great doctrines, that of imputation. Imputation is that act of one person adding something to another person's account. There are three main imputations in the Bible:
   a. That of Adam's sin nature upon mankind (Rom. 3:23; 5:12).
   b. That of man's sin upon Christ (Isa. 53:5, 6; Heb. 2:9; 2 Cor. 5:14-21; 1 Pet. 2:24).
   c. That of Christ's righteousness upon the believing sinner (Phil. 3:9; Jas. 2:23; Rom. 4:6-24).

2. Psalm 51
We have already seen the background from which David wrote this Psalm.
   a. He begins this great confessional by doing what God expects every sinning saint to do—freely acknowledging his sin. The Father will accept our tears, but not our excuses. David refuses to blame his failure on society, heredity, poverty, or environment.

b. In verse 4 he states that he has sinned "against . . . thee only." In a technical sense, of course, this was not true. David had sinned against himself, against Bath-sheba, against Uriah, and against all Israel who looked up to their beloved king. But his sin against God was so serious and stupendous that all other parties involved faded away. The last part of this verse is quoted by Paul to prove the universal condemnation of mankind (Rom. 3:4).

c. In verse 7 David pleads to be purged (or cleansed) with hyssop. Perhaps his mind slipped back to his nation's first Passover night some five centuries before. Doubtless he had read the account many times:

"Then Moses called for all the elders of Israel, and said unto them, Draw out and take you a lamb according to your families, and kill the passover. And ye shall take a bunch of hyssop, and dip it in the blood that is in the bason, and strike the lintel and the two side posts with the blood that is in the bason. . . . For the Lord will pass through to smite the Egyptians; and when he seeth the blood . . . the Lord will pass over the door, and will not suffer the destroyer to come in unto your houses to smite you" (Ex. 12:21-23).

So God purged him. Later, David's greater Son would perform this ministry for all believers everywhere. We are told:

" . . . When he had by himself purged our sins, sat down on the right hand of the Majesty on high" (Heb. 1:3b).

David wanted this ministry that he might be whiter than snow. Some three centuries later God would use David's words in addressing sinful Israel. Through the mouth of Isaiah, Jehovah said: "Come now, and let us reason together, saith the Lord: though your sins be as scarlet, they shall be as white as snow . . ." (Isa. 1:18).

d. In verse 11 David prays a prayer, however, which no believer need or should request today. Regardless of the seriousness of our sin, we need not concern ourselves over losing the indwelling Holy Spirit. In the upper room our Lord promised:

"And I will pray the Father, and he shall give you another Comforter, that he may abide with you forever" (Jn. 14:16).

e. However, every child of God will sometime need to pray David's words in verse 12. The entire church at Ephesus needed to pray these words, as Jesus told them: "Nevertheless I have somewhat against thee, because thou hast left thy first love" (Rev. 2:4). When this joy and first love returns, the conversion of sinners will indeed take place as mentioned in verse 13.

f. This confession Psalm brings out many precious truths, but perhaps the greatest of all is found in verses 16 and 17. The reason for this was very simple—there existed no sacrifice for the sin of adultery. Rather, the one guilty of adultery was to be taken out and stoned to death (Lev. 20:10). So then, David bypasses the Levitical offerings and throws himself completely upon the mercy and grace of God.

3. Psalm 38

Surely this must rank among the most remarkable passages in the entire Bible, if for no other reason,

because of its absolute frankness. This pitiful prayer ought to demonstrate that the Bible is not only a Book that man could not write if he would, but would not write if he could! Here is David, the sweet singer of Israel, the anointed of the Lord, the man after God's own heart. Yet as one carefully studies the language of this prayer, it becomes impossible to escape the shocking possibility that David was plagued with that kind of disease which often accompanies immoral living and activities (see vs. 3-11).

## The Imprecatory Psalms
## (35, 55, 58, 59, 69, 83, 109, 137, 140)

A. The definition of these Psalms: To imprecate is to pray against, or to invoke evil upon someone or something.

B. The fact of these Psalms: There are many instances where the Psalmist calls down judgment upon his enemies, asking God to:

1. fight against them (35:1)
2. bring them into confusion (35:4)
3. scatter them as chaff (35:5)
4. allow the Lord's angel to chase and persecute them (35:5)
5. cause their way to be dark and slippery (35:6)
6. allow death to seize upon them (55:15)
7. pull them down into hell (55:15)
8. break their teeth (58:8)
9. cut up their defense (58:7)
10. withhold all mercy to them (59:5)
11. consume them in wrath (59:13)
12. set a trap for them (69:22)
13. darken their eyes (69:23)
14. make their loins to shake (69:23)
15. let their habitation be desolate (69:25)
16. blot them out of the book of the living (69:28)
17. make them as the dung of the earth (83:10)
18. persecute them (83:14)
19. give them over to Satan (109:6)
20. let their days be few (109:8)
21. let their children be beggars (109:10)
22. let burning coals fall upon them (140:10)
23. cast them into a deep pit (140:10)

C. The problems involved in these Psalms: How can we reconcile these phrases with the New Testament admonition of Jesus in Matthew 5:44:

"But I say unto you, love your enemies, bless them that curse you, do good to them that hate you, and pray for them which despitefully use you, and persecute you"?

D. The suggested answers for these Psalms. (The following material is taken from Dr. Roy L. Aldrich's booklet, *Notes for Lectures on the Psalms.*)

1. The Psalms are inspired and the Holy Spirit has a right to denounce sin and sinners.
2. This is in harmony with the law (Ps. 28:4; Jer. 50:15).
3. Such judgment against evil and evildoers is in harmony with the teachings of Christ and the epistles (Mt. 18:6; 23:33; 26:24; Gal. 1:8, 9; 5:12; Jas. 5:3; Jude 13, 15; 2 Pet. 2:12, 22; 2 Thess. 2:10-12; Rev. 14:10, 11).
4. The Scriptures pronounce maledictions against the Israelites also for falling into sin and idolatry (Lev. 26; Deut. 27-28; Isa. 5:24, 25; 28:13, etc.).

5. David in private exercised great forbearance, but in the Psalms he makes God's cause his cause (Ps. 5:10, 11).
6. The Oriental was accustomed to using stronger language than the Westerner. His denunciations were more exaggerated and his praise more vehement.
7. Many of the imprecations are uttered out of sympathy for the injured and the oppressed (Ps. 10:8-10).
8. Some of these Psalms are prayers for success on the battlefield (Ps. 144:5-7). Many of Israel's wars were definitely approved of God.
9. Some of the petitions have reference to scriptural predictions (Ps. 137:8, 9). The Psalmist has before him a direct prophecy where the fall of Babylon is predicted in these same terms (Isa. 13:16; also Jer. 50:15; 51:6, 36).
10. Some concern Christ and his betrayers (Ps. 40; 55; 60). Psalm 69:22-25 gives us the punishment meted out to Judas. Psalm 109 has been called the "Iscariot Psalm."
11. The wicked in the Psalms are looked upon as confirmed or apostate wicked. This is in keeping with the sovereignty of God and also with the prophetic character of the Psalms. Many of the Psalms look forward to the final earthly judgments against the wicked.
12. Grace is manifest in frank and repeated warnings to the wicked (Ps. 2:12).
13. The imperative may be changed to the future without violence to the Hebrew: Instead of, "Let them be confounded" we have, "They shall be confounded." The prayer thus becomes a prophecy. (See Ps. 109:8-10.)

E. A brief examination of these Psalms:
1. Psalm 35. This is the first of the nine imprecatory Psalms. (See vs. 1-8.) But it should also be kept in mind that David had at first fervently prayed for his fierce enemies in spite of their cruelty toward him. (See vs. 12-16.) This is also the first of four Iscariot Psalms, that is, Psalms which prophetically depict the treachery of Judas in the New Testament. The other three are: 41:9; 55:12-14; 109:6-8. See the following verses for the imprecatory prayer in each:
2. Psalm 55:9
3. Psalm 58:6-9
4. Psalm 59:11-15
5. Psalm 69:22-28
6. Psalm 83:9-17
7. Psalm 109:6-20
8. Psalm 137. Here is a twofold imprecatory prayer:
   a. That God would judge Edom for their treachery during the fall of Jerusalem by the Babylonians (v. 7).
   b. That God would judge Babylon. (See vs. 8, 9.) Note, however, that these words do not describe an army of Israelite "G.I. Joes" running around and bashing the bodies of little Babylonian babies, for, historically speaking, the Babylonians conquered Israel, and not the opposite. This may then be regarded as a prophecy referring to the Persians who did indeed defeat Babylon. (See Dan. 5; Isa. 12:16.) The divine law of retribution was involved here, as

it was in Exodus 32:34; Psalm 7:16; Proverbs 11:19, 21; and Galatians 6:7.
9. Psalm 140. See verses 8-10 for the imprecatory prayer.

## The Degree or Ascent Psalms

A. Who wrote them? A commonly held theory is that they were composed by three men.
   1. Hezekiah wrote ten of them (120, 121, 123, 125, 126, 128, 129, 130, 132, 134).
   2. Solomon wrote one of them (127).
   3. David wrote four of them (122, 124, 131, 133).
B. Why were they written? Many believe it was because of the following: Around 7 B.C., God healed a Judean king named Hezekiah of a fatal illness. Isaiah (ch. 38) records the prayer of thanksgiving of the grateful king, composed after his recovery. In verse 20 he exclaims:
   "The Lord was ready to save me: therefore we will sing my songs to the stringed instruments all the days of our life in the house of the Lord."
   Some scholars (including Thirtle, Lightfoot, Scroggie) believe that these songs of Hezekiah are the ten anonymous "Songs of Degrees" in the group of fifteen (120-134). These Psalms do have a certain similarity of style. Hezekiah may have written ten of these anonymous degree Psalms in memory of the ten steps of the shadow on the sundial (2 Ki. 20:9-11), and then added five appropriate hitherto unpublished Psalms from the pens of (David and) Solomon (see Prov. 25:1), to bring the total to fifteen, in honor of the fifteen years God added to his life. (See 2 Ki. 21:6.)
C. How were they to be sung? Here there are various theories:
   1. An old Jewish tradition explains that they were sung when the choir ascended the semicircular flight of stairs leading up to the court of men in the Temple.
   2. The ascents may have referred to the stages of pilgrimage to Jerusalem, to be sung along the way by travelers en route to the various annual feast days.
   3. Ascent means "a song in the higher choir," the singers being on the stairs of some high place.
   4. The reference may be musical, signifying that the notes rose by degrees in succession.

## The Hallel (Hallelujah) Psalms (113—118)

These six Psalms were sung on the night of the Passover.
A. Psalms 113 and 114 at the beginning of the meal.
B. Psalms 115 and 116 at the close. These were sung by the Savior and his disciples in Matthew 26:30. They are still recited in Palestine eighteen times a year at various occasions, and twenty-one times yearly by those Jews outside the Holy Land.

## The Historical Psalms (78, 105, 106)

These three Psalms, which depict the history of Israel, may be summarized as follows:
A. The sins of Israel.
   1. They refused to walk in God's law (78:10).
   2. They forgot his works (78:11, 42; 106:13).
   3. They spoke against him (78:19).

4. They didn't trust his salvation (78:22).
5. They lied to him (78:36).
6. They grieved him (78:40).
7. They limited him (78:41).
8. They worshiped graven images (78:58; 106:19).
9. They envied his leader Moses (106:16).
10. They despised the Promised Land (106:24).
11. They murmured in their tents (106:25).
12. They ate the sacrifices of the dead (106:28).
13. They mingled among the heathen (106:35).
14. They sacrificed their sons and daughters to devils (106:37).
15. They shed innocent blood (106:38).

B. The grace of God.
1. He remembered his covenant when they cried unto him (105:8–11).
2. He divided the sea (78:13).
3. He led them with a cloud by day (78:14).
4. He led them with a fire by night (78:14).
5. He provided water for them out of rocks (78:15).
6. He rained down manna for them (78:24).
7. He was full of compassion and forgave their iniquity (78:38).
8. He wrought signs for them in Egypt (78:43; 105:27–36).
9. He brought them to the border of the Promised Land (78:54).
10. He cast out the heathen before them (78:55).
11. He chose David to lead them (78:70, 71).
12. He allowed no man to hurt them (105:14).
13. He fed them (78:72).
14. He reproved kings for their sake (105:14).
15. He elevated them through Joseph (105:17).
16. He gave them the riches of Egypt (105:37).
17. He kept them all strong (105:37).
18. He continually forgave them (106:43).
19. He continually heard their cry (106:44).

## The Acrostic Psalms (9, 10, 25, 34, 37, 111, 112, 119, 145)

These nine Psalms are also called the alphabetical Psalms. This is so because each line of these Psalms begins with a successive letter of the twenty-two letters in the Hebrew alphabet.

Psalm 119 is of course the most famous of the acrostic Psalms. It has twenty-two stanzas. Each stanza has eight verses, for a total of 176. Each of these stanzas begins with one of the twenty-two Hebrew letters. Not all of these Psalms are complete in this arrangement; that is, some are missing a letter or more. Thus we find:

A. Psalms 9, 10, 25 are missing several letters.
B. Psalms 34, 45 have all but one letter.
C. Psalms 37, 111, 112, 119 have all the letters.

It is reasonable to suppose that the acrostic device was designed to assist the memory.

## The Messianic Psalms

We shall consider these all-important Psalms in a twofold manner. First, in the order that Christ fulfilled them in the New Testament. Second, in the order that they appear in the book of Psalms.

A. In the order that Christ fulfilled them in the New Testament.
1. his obedience (40:6–10).
"Sacrifice and offerings thou didst not desire . . . then said I, Lo, I come: In the volume of the book it is written of me" (compare Heb. 10:5–7).
2. his zeal (69:9).
"The zeal of thine house hath eaten me up" (Jn. 2:17).
3. his rejection (118:22).
"The stone which the builders refused is become the headstone of the corner" (see Mt. 21:42).
4. his betrayal.
"Yea, mine own familiar friend, in whom I trusted, which did eat of my bread, hath lifted up his heel against me" (41:9).
"For it was not an enemy that reproached me; then I could have borne it: neither was it he that hated me that did magnify himself against me . . . but it was thou, a man mine equal, my guide, and mine acquaintance. We took sweet counsel together, and walked unto the house of God in company" (55:12–14).
(See Mt. 26:14–16, 21–25.)
5. his sufferings (22:1, 6, 7, 8, 16, 18).
"They gave me also gall for my meat; and in my thirst they gave me vinegar to drink" (69:21). (See Mt. 27:34, 48.)
"Into thine hand I commit my spirit" (Ps. 31:5). (See Lk. 23:46.)
"He keepeth all his bones: Not one of them is broken" (34:20). (See Jn. 19:33–36; also 129:3.)
6. his false witnesses.
"For the mouth of the wicked and the mouth of the deceitful are opened against me: They have spoken against me with a lying tongue. They compassed me about also with words of hatred; and fought against me without a cause" (109:2, 3). (See Mt. 26:59–61; 27:39–44.)
7. his prayers for his enemies.
"[In return] for my love they are my adversaries: but I give myself unto prayer" (109:4). (See Lk. 23:34.)
8. his resurrection.
"For thou wilt not leave my soul in hell; neither wilt thou suffer thine Holy One to see corruption" (16:10; compare with Acts 13:35).
"I will declare thy name unto my brethren: in the midst of the congregation will I praise thee" (22:22; compare with Jn. 20:17).
9. his ascension.
"Thou hast ascended on high, thou hast led captivity captive: thou hast received gifts for men . . ." (68:18; compare with Eph. 4:8).
10. his triumphal entry.
"Lift up your heads, O ye gates; and be ye lifted up, ye everlasting doors; and the King of Glory shall come in. Who is this King of Glory? The Lord strong and mighty, the Lord mighty in battle" (24:7, 8). (See Acts 1.)
11. his high priestly work.
"The Lord hath sworn, and will not repent, thou art a priest forever after the order of Melchizedek" (110:4). (See Heb. 5–7.)
12. his marriage (45:2, 6, 8, 13, 15). (See Rev. 19.)
13. his destruction of the heathen.
"The Lord said unto my Lord, sit thou at my right hand, until I make thine enemies thy footstool" (Ps. 110:1). (See also Ps. 2.)
"He shall judge among the heathen . . ." (110:6). (See Rev. 6–19.)

Whither shall I go from thy spirit?
or whither shall I flee from thy presence?
If I ascend up into heaven, thou art there:
if I make my bed in hell, behold thou art there.
If I take the wings of the morning and dwell in the uttermost parts of the sea;
even there shall thy hand lead me,
and thy right hand shall hold me. PSALM 139:7-10

# PSALMS

## BY BOOK DIVISION

| CHAPTERS | HOW SIMILAR TO PENTATEUCH |
|---|---|
| 1-41 | Key word is man (corresponds to **Genesis**) |
| 42-72 | Key word is deliverance (corresponds to **Exodus**) |
| 73-89 | Key word is sanctuary (corresponds to **Leviticus**) |
| 90-106 | Key words are wandering, unrest (correspond to **Numbers**) |
| 107-150 | Key word is word of God (corresponds to **Deuteronomy**) |

## BY SUBJECT MATTER

| SUBJECT | PSALMS |
|---|---|
| **PENITENTIAL** | 6, 32, 38, 51, 102, 130, 143 |
| **IMPRECATORY** | 35, 55, 58, 59, 69, 83, 109, 137, 140 |
| **DEGREE OR ASCENT** | 120-134 |
| **HALLELUJAH** | 113-118 |
| **HISTORICAL** | 78, 105, 106 |
| **ACROSTIC** | 9, 10, 25, 34, 37, 111, 112, 119, 145 |
| **MESSIANIC** | 16, 22, 24, 31, 34, 40, 41, 45, 55, 68, 69, 89, 102, 109, 110, 118, 129 |

## BY AUTHORSHIP

| AUTHOR | PSALMS |
|---|---|
| **DAVID: 77** | Shepherd Psalms—**8, 19, 23, 29, 144**<br>Sinner Psalms—**32, 51, 38**<br>Suffering Psalms—**3, 4, 5, 6, 7, 11, 12, 13, 14, 17, 22, 25, 26, 27, 28, 31, 34, 35, 39, 40, 41, 53, 54, 55, 56, 57, 58, 59, 61, 62, 63, 64, 69, 70, 86, 109, 140, 141, 142, 143**<br>Satisfied Psalms—**2, 9, 15, 16, 18, 20, 21, 24, 30, 36, 37, 52, 60, 65, 68, 72, 95, 101, 103, 105, 108, 110, 122, 124, 131, 133, 138, 139, 145** |
| **KORAH: 10** | 42, 44, 45, 46, 47, 48, 49, 84, 85, 87 |
| **ASAPH: 12** | 50, 73, 74, 75, 76, 77, 78, 79, 80, 81, 82, 83 |
| **HEMAN: 1** | 88 |
| **ETHAN: 1** | 89 |
| **SOLOMON: 1** | 127 |
| **MOSES: 1** | 90 |
| **HEZEKIAH: 10** | 120, 121, 123, 125, 126, 128, 129, 130, 132, 134 |
| **ANONYMOUS: 37** | 1, 10, 33, 43, 66, 67, 71, 91, 92, 93, 94, 96, 97, 98, 99, 100, 102, 104, 106, 107, 111, 112, 113, 114, 115, 116, 117, 118, 119, 135, 136, 137, 146, 147, 148, 149, 150 |

## MESSIANIC PSALMS

| PSALM REFERENCE | FEATURE OF CHRIST DESCRIBED | NEW TESTAMENT FULFILLMENT |
|---|---|---|
| 40:6-10 | **His Obedience** | Hebrews 10:5-7 |
| 69:9 | **His Zeal** | John 2:17 |
| 118:22 | **His Rejection** | Matthew 21:42 |
| 41:9; 55:12-14 | **His Betrayal** | Matthew 26:14-16, 21-25 |
| 22:1, 6-8, 16, 18; 31:5; 34:20; 69:21; 129:3 | **His Sufferings** | Matthew 27:34, 48; Luke 23:46; John 19:33-36 |
| 109:2, 3 | **His False Witnesses** | Matthew 26:59-61; 27:39-44 |
| 109:4 | **His Prayer for His Enemies** | Luke 23:34 |
| 16:10 | **His Resurrection** | Acts 13:35 |
| 68:18 | **His Ascension** | Ephesians 4:8 |
| 24:7, 8 | **His Triumphal Entry into Glory** | Philippians 2:9-11 |
| 110:4 | **His High Priestly Work** | Hebrews 5-7 |
| 45:2, 6, 8, 13, 15 | **His Marriage to the Church** | Revelation 19:7-10 |
| 110:1, 6 | **His Destruction of the Heathen** | Revelation 6-19 |
| 89:27; 102:16-21; 72:17 | **His Millennial Reign** | Matthew 23:39; Revelation 11:15 |

14. his millennial reign (89:27; 102:16-21).

"Thou madest him to have dominion over the works of thy hands: thou hast put all things under his feet" (8:6; compare with Heb. 2).

"His name shall endure forever: his name shall be continued as long as the sun, and men shall be blessed in him. All nations shall call him blessed" (72:17). (See Mt. 23:39; Rev. 11:15.)

B. In the order they appear in the book of Psalms.

1. Psalm 2: Predicts the tribulational destruction of the heathen and the millennial reign of Christ. This Psalm is in four parts:

   a. the rebellion of man (vs. 1-3)
   b. the reaction of God (vs. 4-6)
   c. the rule of the Son (vs. 7-9)
   d. the recommendation of the Psalmist (vs. 10-12)

   Messianic passages:

   Verse 2: "The kings of the earth set themselves, and the rulers take counsel together, against the Lord, and against his anointed . . . ." (Quoted in Acts 4:26.)

   Verse 7: "I will declare the decree: The Lord hath said unto me, Thou art my Son; this day have I begotten thee." (Quoted in Acts 13:33.)

2. Psalm 8: Predicts the millennial reign of Christ. One may well compare the statement in this Psalm (v. 6) which says it took God's fingers to create man with Isaiah 53:1 where we are told it cost God his arms to redeem us! Thus, salvation is infinitely more costly than creation.

   Messianic passage:

   Verse 6: "Thou madest him to have dominion over the works of thy hands; thou hast put all things under his feet."

3. Psalm 16: Predicts the death and resurrection of Christ.

   Messianic passage:

   Verse 10: "For thou wilt not leave my soul in hell; neither wilt thou suffer thine Holy One to see corruption." (Quoted in Acts 2:27.)

4. Psalm 22: Predicts the intense sufferings of Christ. The Psalm is in two parts:

   a. the sob of the crucified (vs. 1-21)
   b. the song of the glorified (vs. 22-31)

   It has been suggested that Peter had this Psalm in mind when he wrote 1 Peter 1:10, 11:

   "Of which salvation that prophets have inquired and searched diligently, who prophesied of the grace that should come unto you: searching what, or what manner of time the Spirit of Christ which was in them did signify, when it testified beforehand the sufferings of Christ, and the glory that should follow."

   If this is true, then verses 1-21 speak of the sufferings, while verses 22-31 depict the glory.

   Messianic passages:

   Verse 1: "My God, my God, why hast thou forsaken me?" (Quoted by Christ on the cross, Mt. 27:46.)

   Verse 8: "He trusted in the Lord that he would deliver him: let him deliver him, seeing he delighted in him." (Quoted by the wicked Israelite rulers at the cross, Mt. 27:43.)

   Verse 16: "They pierced my hands and my feet." (Fulfilled by the Roman soldiers at the cross, Mt. 27:35.)

   Verse 18: "They part my garments among them, and cast lots upon my vesture." (Fulfilled by the Roman soldiers at the cross, Mk. 15:24.)

   Verse 22: "I will declare thy name unto my brethren: in the midst of the congregation will I praise thee." (Quoted in Heb. 2:12.)

5. Psalm 23: Predicts the tender shepherding ministry of Christ.

   Messianic passage:

   Verse 1: "The Lord is my shepherd; I shall not want." (Although this exact quotation does not appear in the New Testament, it is nevertheless referred to by Jesus himself in Jn. 10:1-18).

   This is known as the Pearl of the Psalms. It is in three parts:

   a. The Sheep and the Shepherd (vs. 1-3; speaks of provision).
   b. The Guide and the Traveler (vs. 3, 4; speaks of direction).
   c. The Host and the Guest (vs. 5, 6, speaks of communion).

6. Psalm 24: Predicts Christ's triumphal entry into heaven. This Psalm, although originally written to celebrate David's entrance into the newly captured city of Jerusalem, and his subsequent inauguration as King, may also speak of that victorious entry of the Savior into glory after he had finished his work of redemption and ascended from the Mount of Olives. The Psalm was sung by two choirs:

   a. Verses 1-6 were sung at the foot of the hill on which Jerusalem stood.
      (1) Choir A would sing 1-3.
      (2) Choir B would respond with 4-6.
   b. Verses 7-10 were sung in front of the gates of the city.
      (1) Choir A would sing verse 7.
      (2) Choir B would sing the first part of verse 8.
      (3) Choir A would sing the second part of verse 8.
      (4) Choir A would sing verse 9.
      (5) Choir B would sing the first part of verse 10.
      (6) Choir A would sing the second part of verse 10.
   c. Certain Psalms were sung at the morning service in the Temple worship each day of the week:
      (1) On Monday the choir sang Psalm 48. Then, each day as follows:
      (2) Tuesday, Psalm 82
      (3) Wednesday, Psalm 94
      (4) Thursday, Psalm 81
      (5) Friday, Psalm 93
      (6) Saturday, Psalm 92
      (7) Sunday, Psalm 24

   Messianic passages:

   Verses 7-10: "Lift up your heads, O ye gates; and be ye lift up, ye everlasting doors; and the King of glory shall come in. Who is this King of glory? The Lord strong and mighty, the Lord mighty in battle. Lift up your heads, O ye gates; even lift them up, ye everlasting doors; and the King of glory shall come in. Who is this King of glory? The Lord of hosts, he is the King of glory."

(Although these verses are not directly quoted in the New Testament, they are nevertheless generally spoken of in Acts 2:32, 33.)

7. Psalm 31: Predicts the Savior's thoughts and words on the cross.
   Messianic passage:
   Verse 5: "Into thine hand I commit my spirit . . . ."
   (This was directly quoted by Jesus just prior to his death on Calvary in Lk. 23:46.) The Apostle Paul would later refer to verse 19 of this Psalm in 1 Corinthians 2:9.

8. Psalm 40: Predicts the obedience of Christ while on this earth.
   Messianic passage:
   Verse 6: "Sacrifice and offerings thou didst not desire: mine ears hast thou opened. . . ." (Quoted in Heb. 10:5, 6.)
   Verse 7: "Then said I, Lo, I come: in the volume of the book it is written of me." (Quoted in Heb. 10:7.)

9. Psalm 41: Predicts the betrayal of the Savior by Judas. This is the first of three Psalms which speak of that treachery. The others are Psalms 55 and 109.
   Messianic passage:
   Verse 9: "Yea, mine own familiar friend, in whom I trusted, which did eat of my bread, hath lifted up his heel against me." (A reference to Judas. See Jn. 13:18.)

10. Psalm 45: Predicts the beauty and marriage of Christ. This Psalm probably had its historical roots in Solomon's marriage to the King of Egypt's daughter (1 Ki. 3:1), but it certainly lends itself to the marriage of Christ passage in Revelation 19:7-9. The Psalm is in two parts:
    a. Part one: The characteristics of the Bridegroom (1-8a).
       (1) He is the fairest of all.
       (2) His words are filled with grace.
       (3) He enjoys the fullest possible blessings of God.
       (4) He is a defender of truth, humility, and justice.
       (5) He defeats all his enemies.
       (6) His throne will exist forever.
       (7) Justice is his royal scepter.
       (8) He loves the good and hates the wrong.
       (9) His robes are perfumed with myrrh, aloes, and cassia.
    b. Part two: The privileges of the Bride (8b-17).
       (1) She will live in an ivory palace filled with lovely music.
       (2) She will be fitted with the finest of clothing and most costly jewelry.
       (3) She will be loved throughout all eternity by her Bridegroom.
           Messianic passage:
           Verse 6: "Thy throne, O God, is for ever and ever: The sceptre of thy kingdom is a right sceptre." (Quoted in Heb. 1:8.)
           Verse 7: "Thou lovest righteousness, and hatest wickedness: therefore God, thy God, hath anointed thee with the oil of gladness above thy fellows." (Quoted in Heb. 1:9.)

11. Psalm 68: Predicts the glorious victory of Christ and his triumphal entry into heaven.
    Messianic passage:
    Verse 18: "Thou hast ascended on high, thou hast led captivity captive: Thou hast received gifts for men." (Quoted in Eph. 4:8.) Where was the abode of the departed righteous prior to Calvary? It is held by a number of Bible students that before Jesus died, the souls of all men descended into an abode located somewhere in the earth known as Hades in the New Testament, and Sheol in the Old Testament. Originally, there were two sections of Hades, one for the saved and one for the lost. The saved section is sometimes called "paradise" (see Lk. 23:43), and other times referred to as "Abraham's bosom" (See Lk. 16:22).

    There is no name given for the unsaved section apart from the general designation of Hades. In Luke 16:19-31 the Savior relates the account of a poor believer who died and went to the unsaved section. However, many believe that all this changed after Christ made full payment for the believer's sins on Calvary. The *Scofield Bible* suggests that during the time of his death and resurrection, our Lord descended into Hades, depopulated paradise, and led a spiritual triumphal entry into the heavenlies with all the saved up to that time. Ephesians 4:8-10 is offered as proof of this. In his book, *Revelation,* the late Dr. Barnhouse writes:

    "When He ascended on High (Eph. 4:8) He emptied Hell of Paradise and took it straight to the presence of God. Captivity was taken captive. . . . From that moment onward there was to be no separation whatsoever for those who believe in Christ. The gates of Hell would never more prevail against any believer." (See Mt. 16:18.)

12. Psalm 69: Predicts the zeal and sufferings of Christ.
    Messianic passages:
    Verse 9: "For the zeal of thine house hath eaten me up." (Quoted in Jn. 2:17.)
    Verse 21: "They gave me also gall for my meat; and in my thirst they gave me vinegar to drink." (Fulfilled in Mt. 27:34, 48.)

13. Psalm 72: Predicts the millennial reign of Christ. It is not absolutely certain whether this Psalm is a prayer of Solomon to God or a prayer of David concerning Solomon. At any rate, it vividly describes the glorious millennial reign of David's greater Son, the Lord Jesus Christ. Note the following characteristics of his reign:
    a. The poor will receive righteousness (v. 2).
    b. The mountains and hills will flourish (v. 3).
    c. All oppressors will be crushed (v. 4).
    d. His rule will be as gentle and fruitful as the springtime rains upon the grass (v. 6).
    e. All good men will prosper exceedingly (v. 7).
    f. His reign will extend to the ends of the earth (v. 8).
    g. All nations will give him gifts and serve him (vs. 10, 11).
    h. All peoples will bless and praise him (v. 15).
    i. His name will be honored and will continue forever (v. 17).

Messianic passage:

Verse 8: "He shall have dominion also from sea to sea, and from the river unto the ends of the earth." (Referred to by John in Rev. 11:15.)

14. Psalm 89: Predicts the unchanging faithfulness of God upon David's dynasty through Christ, in spite of continued disobedience within that dynasty. This Psalm was written by Ethan the Ezrahite, who was a noted wise man during Solomon's reign (1 Ki. 4:31). While we cannot be certain, the Psalm may express the thoughts of Solomon during his latter years when, because of his sin, he underwent hard times. (See 1 Ki. 11.)

Messianic passage:

Verse 27: "Also I will make him my firstborn, higher than the kings of the earth." (Referred to by Paul in Phil. 2:9-11.)

15. Psalm 102: Predicts the eternality of Christ. This Psalm may be assigned to the closing years of the Babylonian exile, and its design was to encourage the Jews to return and rebuild Jerusalem. It also refers to the second coming of Jerusalem's great King. (See v. 16.)

Messianic passage:

Verses 25-27: "Of old hast thou laid the foundation of the earth: and the heavens are the work of thy hands. They shall perish, but thou shalt endure: yea, all of them shall wax old like a garment; as a vesture shalt thou change them, and they shall be changed: But thou art the same, and thy years shall have no end." (Quoted in Heb. 1:10-12.)

16. Psalm 109: Predicts the betrayal of Judas and his frightful punishment.

Messianic passage:

Verse 8: "Let his days be few; and let another take his office." (Quoted by Peter in Acts 1:20.)

17. Psalm 110: Predicts the eternal priesthood of Christ.

a. Note the fivefold description of Christ in this Psalm.

(1) He is God (v. 1).

(2) He is King (v. 2).

(3) He is a Priest (v. 4).

(4) He is a Judge (v. 6).

(5) He is a mighty Warrior (v. 6).

b. Note the twofold description of Christ's people in this Psalm.

(1) They are priests: "Thy people shall be willing" (literally, "They shall offer up freely offerings," v. 3). (Compare with Rev. 1:6.)

(2) They are soldiers: "In the day of thy power" (literally "Thy army," v. 3). (Compare with Eph. 6:11.)

Messianic passages:

Verse 1: "The Lord said unto my Lord, Sit thou at my right hand, until I make thine enemies thy footstool."

This verse is quoted more times in the New Testament than any other single Old Testament verse. On at least four occasions it is repeated.

(3) In Matthew 22:41-46 (to point out the deity of Christ).

(4) In Acts 2:34, 35 (to point out the identity of Christ).

(5) In Hebrews 1:13 (as a question, to point out the superiority of Christ).

(6) In Hebrews 10:12, 13 (to point out the finished work of Christ).

Verse 4: "The Lord hath sworn, and will not repent, Thou art a priest forever after the order of Melchizedek."

This verse is found no less than three times in the New Testament, and all three deal with his high priesthood.

(7) In Hebrews 5:6 (to give the qualifications of this High Priesthood after the order of Melchizedek).

(8) In Hebrews 6:20 (to give the immutability of this High Priesthood).

(9) In Hebrews 7:21 (to give the necessity for the High Priesthood).

18. Psalm 118: Predicts Christ to be the vital stone in God's building, rejected by men but chosen by the Lord. This Psalm, often used during the Feast of Tabernacles, may have been sung by the Savior en route to Gethsemane.

Messianic passages:

Verse 22: "The stone which the builders refused is become the headstone of the corner."

This "Supreme Stone of the Scriptures" is referred to in many Old Testament and New Testament passages.

a. It is the cornerstone (Mt. 21:42; Eph. 2:20).

b. It is the headstone (Zech. 4:7; Acts 4:11).

c. It is the smitten stone (1 Cor. 10:4).

d. It is the stumbling stone (1 Cor. 1:23).

e. It is the crushing stone (Dan. 2:34).

f. It is the living, chosen, and precious stone (1 Pet. 2:4-7).

Verse 26: "Blessed be he that cometh in the name of the Lord." (Quoted by the triumphal entry crowd in Mt. 21:9.)

In concluding this section, here are a few suggested names and titles for some of the Psalms.

1. Psalm of the Godly Man (1)
2. Psalms of Creation (8, 104)
3. The Good Shepherd Psalm (22)
4. The Great Shepherd Psalm (23)
5. The Chief Shepherd Psalm (24)
6. The Unity Psalm (133)
7. Psalms of Jerusalem (48, 122, 126, 132, 137)
8. Family Psalms (127, 128)
9. The Security Psalm (121)
10. Psalm of the Only True God (115)
11. Psalm of the Exodus (114)
12. Psalm of Refuge (46)
13. The Ladder of Faith Psalm (37)
14. Psalms of Supreme Praise (103, 148, 150)
15. The Psalm of Old Age (71)
16. The Old One Hundredth Psalm (100)
17. The Psalm of Death (90)
18. The Psalm of Life (91)
19. The Deliverance Psalms (31, 116)
20. The House of God Psalm (84)
21. The Wealth of God Psalm (50)
22. The Word of God Psalms (19, 119)
23. The Voice of God Psalm (29)
24. The Mercy of God Psalm (136)
25. The Goodness of God Psalms (27, 107)
26. The Omniscience and Omnipresence of God Psalm (139)

27. The Omnipotence of God Psalm (147)
28. The Psalm of the Davidic Covenant (89)
29. The History of Israel Psalms (78, 105, 106)
30. The Psalms of the "Why?" (42, 73)
31. Psalms of Deepest Despair (69, 88)

II. The Book of Proverbs.
   Introduction:
   1. A proverb is a short sentence drawn from long experience.
   2. There are several authors of the Book of Proverbs.
      a. Solomon (1–24). We are told in 1 Kings 4:32 that he wrote three thousand proverbs and composed over one thousand songs. However, chapters 1–24 contain only a fraction of this number.
      b. the men of Hezekiah (25–29)
      c. Agur (30)
      d. Lemuel (31)
   3. The book tells a story. It is a picture of a young man starting out in life. His first lesson is given in 1:7. Two schools bid for him and both send out their literature. One is the school of wisdom , and the other, the school for fools.
   4. The key word of Proverbs is, of course, wisdom.
      a. Wisdom will protect her students (2:8).
      b. Wisdom will direct her students (3:5, 6).
      c. Wisdom will perfect her students (4:18).
   5. There are several classic passages in this book.
      a. the warnings of wisdom (1:20–31)
      b. the rewards of wisdom (3:5, 6)
      c. the energy of wisdom (6:6–11)
      d. the godless whore (7:1–27)
      e. the godly wife (31:10–31)
      f. the sovereign Savior (8:22–31)
      g. fifteen famous facts (30:18–31)
      h. the riotous rebel (30:11–14)
   6. Proverbs is the Old Testament equivalent of the epistle of James. It is impossible to offer a chronological outline of this book. At least eleven main subjects are discussed.
      a. A good name:
         (1) "The memory of the just is blessed: but the name of the wicked shall rot" (10:7).
         (2) "A good name is rather to be chosen than great riches, and loving favour rather than silver and gold" (22:1).
      b. Youth and discipline:
         (1) A man with a level headed son is happy, but a rebel's mother is sad (10:1; 17:21, 25; 19:13).
         (2) A wise youth will listen to his father but a young mocker won't (13:1).
         (3) "He that spareth his rod hateth his son: but he that loveth him chasteneth him betimes" (13:24).
         (4) "Chasten thy son while there is hope, and let not thy soul spare for his crying" (19:18).
         (5) "Train up a child in the way he should go: and when he is old, he will not depart from it" (22:6).
         (6) "Foolishness is bound in the heart of a child; but the rod of correction shall drive it far from him" (22:15; 29:15, 17).

         (7) "Withhold not correction from the child: for if thou beatest him with the rod, he shall not die. Thou shalt beat him with the rod, and shalt deliver his soul from hell" (23:13, 14).
         (8) See 23:15–25.
         (9) See 30:11–14.
      c. Business matters:
         (1) God hates a dishonest scale and delights in honesty (11:1; 16:11; 20:10, 23).
         (2) Don't sign a note for someone you barely know (6:1–5; 11:15; 17:18).
         (3) Don't withhold repayment of your debts (3:27).
         (4) God will not let a good man starve to death (10:3).
         (5) Lazy men are soon poor; hard workers have an abundant supply (10:4; 22:29).
         (6) A lazy fellow is a pain to his employer— like smoke in his eyes or vinegar that sets the teeth on edge (11:26).
         (7) He that trusts in his riches shall fall (11:28).
         (8) It is wrong to accept a bribe to twist justice (17:23).
         (9) Develop your business first before building your house (24:27).
         (10) "Riches can disappear fast. And the king's crown doesn't stay in his family forever—so watch your business interests closely. Know the state of your flocks and your herds; then there will be lamb's wool enough for clothing, and goat's milk enough for food for all your household after the hay is harvested, and the new crop appears, and the mountain grasses are gathered in" (27:23–27, The Living Bible).
      d. Marriage:
         (1) Drink waters out of your own cistern (5:15).
         (2) Rejoice with the wife of your youth (5:18).
         (3) A beautiful woman lacking discretion and modesty is like a fine gold ring in a pig's snout (11:22).
         (4) He that troubles his own house shall inherit the wind (11:29).
         (5) A virtuous woman is a crown to her husband: but she that makes ashamed is as rottenness in his bones (12:4).
         (6) Every wise woman builds her house; but the foolish one plucks it down with her hands (14:1; 19:13).
         (7) Whoever finds a wife finds a good thing, and obtains favor of the Lord (18:22).
         (8) It is better to dwell in a corner of the housetop, than with a brawling woman in a wide house (21:9; 25:24).
         (9) It is better to dwell in the wilderness, than with a contentious and angry woman (21:19).
         (10) Who can find a virtuous woman?
            Note: The most detailed answer to this question is given in the last chapter of Proverbs (31).

e. Immorality:
   (1) It means to flout the law of God (2:17).
   (2) It leads along the road to death and hell (2:18; 7:27; 9:18).
   (3) It pollutes the conscience (5:4).
   (4) It causes one to groan in anguish and shame when disease consumes the body (5:11).
   (5) It leads to bitter remorse (5:12, 13).
   (6) It will be judged by God (5:21).
   (7) It will bring a man to poverty (6:26).
   (8) It will burn the soul as surely as fire burns the skin (6:27, 32).
   (9) It can be compared to (7:22, 23):
      (a) an ox going to the butcher
      (b) a trapped stag awaiting the death arrow
      (c) a bird flying into a snare

f. Evil companions:
   (1) Refuse them, for in attempting to trap others they only trap themselves (1:10–19).
   (2) Refuse them, for they eat the bread of wickedness and drink the wine of violence (4:17).
   (3) Refuse them, for their kindness is a trick; they want to use you as their pawn (23:6–8).
   (4) Refuse them, for a man's true character is reflected by the friends he chooses (27:19).

g. Wisdom:
   (1) The fear of God is its root (1:7; 9:10).
   (2) It will gain one many honors (1:9).
   (3) It will keep one from immorality (2:16).
   (4) It will direct all one's paths (3:6).
   (5) It will give one renewal, health, and vitality (3:8).
   (6) It will (as one wisely tithes) fill one's barns with wheat and barley and overflow the wine vats with the finest wines (3:9, 10).
   (7) It is better than silver, gold, and precious rubies (3:14; 8:11, 19).
   (8) It gives a long life, riches, honor, pleasure, and peace (3:16, 17; 9:11).
   (9) It was God's method in creation (3:19, 20).
   (10) It is the principal thing (4:7).
   (11) It should be loved like a sweetheart (7:4).
   (12) It brings the favor of God (8:35).

h. Self-control:
   (1) It is better to have self-control than to capture a mighty city (16:32).
   (2) An uncontrolled man often begins something he can't finish (25:8).
   (3) A man without self-control is as defenseless as a city with broken down walls (25:28).

i. Strong drink:
   (1) It gives false courage and leads to brawls (20:1).
   (2) It fills the heart with anguish and sorrow (23:29).
   (3) It causes bloodshot eyes and many wounds (23:29).
   (4) It bites like a poisonous serpent and stings like an adder (23:32).
   (5) It leads to hallucinations and delirium tremens (23:33).
   (6) It makes one say silly and stupid things (23:33).
   (7) It causes one to stagger like a sailor tossed at sea (23:34).
   (8) It allows one to be beat up without even being aware of it (23:35).
   (9) It causes leaders to forget their duties and thus pervert justice (31:5).

j. Friendship:
   (1) A true friend is always loyal and is born to help in time of need (17:17).
   (2) Wounds from a friend are better than kisses from an enemy (27:6).
   (3) Never abandon a friend—either yours or your father's (27:10).
   (4) Friendly suggestions are as pleasant as perfume (27:9).
   (5) A friendly discussion is as stimulating as the sparks that fly when iron strikes iron (27:17).
   (6) A man who would have friends must himself be friendly (18:24).
   (7) A true friend sticks closer than a brother (18:24).

k. Words and the tongue:
   (1) The tongue of the just is as choice silver (10:20).
   (2) He that refrains from speaking is wise (10:19; 11:12).
   (3) The lips of the righteous feed many (10:21).
   (4) A hypocrite with his mouth destroys his neighbor (11:9).
   (5) A talebearer reveals secrets; but one of a faithful spirit conceals the matter (11:13).
   (6) Some speak like the piercings of a sword; but the tongue of the wise is health (12:18).
   (7) He who keeps his mouth keeps his life; but he who opens wide his lips shall have destruction (13:3).
   (8) A true witness delivers souls (14:25).
   (9) A soft answer turns away wrath; but grievous words stir up anger (15:1).
   (10) A wholesome tongue is a tree of life; but perverseness is a breach in the spirit (15:4).
   (11) A word spoken in due season is good (15:23).
   (12) The heart of the righteous studies to answer (15:28).
   (13) Pleasant words are like a honeycomb: sweet to the soul, and health to the bones (16:24).
   (14) A froward man sows strife; and a whisperer separates chief friends (16:28; 17:9).
   (15) The beginning of strife is like letting out water. Therefore, leave off contention, before it is meddled with (17:14).

(16) He who has knowledge spares his words (17:27).

(17) The words of a talebearer are wounds (18:8).

(18) He who answers a matter before he hears it, it is folly and shame unto him (18:13).

(19) Death and life are in the power of the tongue (18:21).

(20) He that speaks lies shall not escape (19:5).

(21) A word fitly spoken is like apples of gold in pictures of silver (25:11).

(22) By long forebearing is a prince persuaded, and a soft tongue breaks the (hard) bone (25:15).

(23) He who passes by, and meddles with strife not belonging to him, is like one who takes a dog by the ears (26:17).

(24) Where no wood is, there the fire goes out; so where there is no talebearer, strife ceases (26:20).

(25) Let another man praise you, and not your own mouth (27:2).

# PROVERBS

## ELEVEN TIMELY THEMES

### A Good Name
10:7; 22:1

### Youth and Discipline
13:24; 19:18; 22:6, 15; 23:13, 14

### Business Matters
11:1; 6:6-11; 10:4, 26

### Marriage
5:15, 18; 11:22, 29; 12:4; 14:1; 19:13; 21:9, 19; 31:10

### Immorality
5:3-5; 6:24-32

### Evil Companions
1:10-19; 4:17; 23:6-8; 27:19

### Wisdom
3:13-18; 8:35

### Self-Control
16:32; 25:28

### Strong Drink
20:1; 23:29-32

### Friendship
17:17; 18:24; 26:6

### Words and the Tongue
15:1, 23, 28; 16:24; 17:27; 18:21; 25:11; 26:17, 20; 2

## CLASSICAL PASSAGES

*A WORD SPOKEN IN DUE SEASON, HOW GOOD IS IT!* (15:23).

| CHAPTER | VERSES | CHAPTER | VERSES |
|---------|--------|---------|--------|
| 1 | 24-28 | 24 | 16, 17, 28, 29 |
| 3 | 5, 6, 9, 10-12, 19-26 | 25 | 19-22 |
| 6 | 16-19 | 27 | 1 |
| 8 | 22-31 | 28 | 13 |
| 11 | 30 | 29 | 1, 18 |
| 14 | 12, 34 | 30 | 4-9, 11-14 |
| 16 | 3, 7, 18 | 31 | 10-12, 28, 30 |
| 18 | 10 | | |

l. Various groupings:

(1) Seven things that God hates (6:16-19):
  (a) a proud look
  (b) a lying tongue
  (c) hands that shed innocent blood
  (d) a wicked, plotting heart
  (e) eagerness to do wrong
  (f) a false witness
  (g) sowing discord among brothers

(2) Four things which are never satisfied (30:15, 16):
  (a) the grave
  (b) the barren womb
  (c) a barren desert
  (d) fire

(3) Four wonderful and mysterious things (30:18, 19):
  (a) how an eagle glides through the sky
  (b) how a serpent crawls upon a rock
  (c) how a ship finds its way across the ocean
  (d) the growth of love between a man and a woman

(4) Four things which the earth finds unbearable (30:21-23):
  (a) a slave who becomes a king
  (b) a fool when he is filled with meat
  (c) a bitter woman when she finally marries
  (d) a servant girl who marries her mistress' husband

(5) Four small but wise things (30:24-28):
  (a) ants (They aren't strong, but store up food for the winter.)
  (b) cliff badgers (delicate little animals who protect themselves by living among the rocks)
  (c) the locust (Though they have no leader, they stay together in swarms.)
  (d) spiders (They are easy to catch and kill, yet are found even in kings' palaces.)

(6) Four stately monarchs (30:29-31):
  (a) the lion, king of animals (He won't turn aside for anyone.)
  (b) the greyhound
  (c) the he-goat
  (d) a king as he leads his army

(7) Two things Agur requests of God (30:7-9):
  (a) Remove from me vanity and lies.
  (b) Give me neither poverty nor riches—feed me with food convenient for me:
    Lest I be full, and deny thee and say, who is the Lord?
    Lest I be poor, and steal, and take the name of my God in vain.

In addition to all this, there are a number of classical passages in this book. Some of the more important are as follows:

"Because I have called, and ye refused; I have stretched out my hand, and no man regarded; but ye have set at nought all my counsel, and would none of my reproof: I also will laugh at your calamity; I will mock when your fear cometh; when your fear cometh as desolation, and your destruction cometh as a whirlwind; when distress and anguish cometh upon you. Then shall they call upon me, but I will not answer; they shall seek me early, but they shall not find me" (1:24-28).

"Trust in the Lord with all thine heart; and lean not unto thine own understanding. In all thy ways acknowledge him, and he shall direct thy paths. Honour the Lord with thy substance, and with the first-fruits of all thine increase: So shall thy barns be filled with plenty, and thy presses shall burst out with new wine.

My son, despise not the chastening of the Lord; neither be weary of his correction: For whom the Lord loveth he correcteth; even as a father the son in whom he delighteth.

The Lord by wisdom hath founded the earth; by understanding hath he established the heavens. By his knowledge the depths are broken up, and the clouds drop down the dew.

My son, let not them depart from thine eyes: keep sound wisdom and discretion: So shall they be life unto thy soul, and grace to thy neck. Then shalt thou walk in thy way safely, and thy foot shall not stumble.

When thou liest down, thou shalt not be afraid: yea, thou shalt lie down, and thy sleep shall be sweet. Be not afraid of sudden fear, neither of the desolation of the wicked, when it cometh. For the Lord shall be thy confidence, and shall keep thy foot from being taken" (3:5, 6, 9-12, 19-26).

"These six things doth the Lord hate: yea, seven are an abomination unto him: A proud look, a lying tongue, and hands that shed innocent blood, an heart that deviseth wicked imaginations, feet that be swift in running to mischief, a false witness that speaketh lies, and he that soweth discord among brethren" (6:16-19).

"The Lord possessed me in the beginning of his way, before his works of old. I was set up from everlasting, from the beginning, or ever the earth was. When there were no depths, I was brought forth; when there were no fountains abounding with water.

Before the mountains were settled, before the hills was I brought forth: while as yet he had not made the earth, nor the fields, nor the highest part of the dust of the world.

When he prepared the heavens, I was there: when he set a compass upon the face of the depth: when he established the clouds above: when he strengthened the fountains of the deep: when he gave to the sea his decree, that the waters should not pass his commandment: when he appointed the foundations of the earth: then I was by him, as one brought up with him: and I was daily his delight, rejoicing always before him; rejoicing in the habitable part of his earth; and my delights were with the sons of men" (8:22-31).

"The fruit of the righteous is a tree of life; and he that winneth souls is wise" (11:30).

"There is a way which seemeth right unto a man, but the end thereof are the ways of death. Righteousness exalteth a nation: but sin is a reproach to any people" (14:12, 34).

"Commit thy works unto the Lord, and thy thoughts shall be established. When a man's ways please the Lord, he maketh even his enemies to be at peace with him. Pride goeth before destruction, and an haughty spirit before a fall" (16:3, 7, 18).

"The name of the Lord is a strong tower: the righteous runneth into it, and is safe" (18:10).

"For a just man falleth seven times, and riseth up again: but the wicked shall fall into mischief. Rejoice not when thine enemy falleth, and let not thine heart be glad when he stumbleth: Be not a witness against thy neighbour without cause; and deceive not with thy lips. Say not, I will do so to him as he hath done to me: I will render to the man according to his work" (24:16, 17, 28, 29).

"Confidence in an unfaithful man in time of trouble is like a broken tooth, and a foot out of joint. As he that taketh away a garment in cold weather, and as vinegar upon nitre, so is he that singeth songs to an heavy heart. If thine enemy be hungry, give him bread to eat; and if he be thirsty, give him water to drink: for thou shalt heap coals of fire upon his head, and the Lord shall reward thee" (25:19-22).

"Boast not thyself of tomorrow; for thou knowest not what a day may bring forth" (27:1).

"He that covereth his sins shall not prosper: but whoso confesseth and forsaketh them shall have mercy" (28:13).

"He, that being often reproved hardeneth his neck, shall suddenly be destroyed, and that without remedy. Where there is no vision, the people perish: but he that keepeth the law, happy is he" (29:1, 18).

"Who hath ascended up into heaven, or descended? who hath gathered the wind in his fists? who hath bound the waters in a garment? who hath established all the ends of the earth? what is his name, and what is his son's name, if thou canst tell? Every word of God is pure: he is a shield unto them that put their trust in him.

Add thou not unto his words, lest he reprove thee, and thou be found a liar. Two things have I required of thee; deny me them not before I die: Remove far from me vanity and lies: give me neither poverty nor riches; feed me with food convenient for me: Lest I be full, and deny thee, and say, Who is the Lord? or lest I be poor, and steal, and take the name of my God in vain. There is a generation that curseth their father, and doth not bless their mother. There is a generation that are pure in their own eyes, and yet is not washed from their filthiness.

There is a generation, O how lofty are their eyes! and their eyelids are lifted up. There is a generation, whose teeth are as swords, and their jaw-teeth as knives, to devour the poor from off the earth, and the needy from among men" (30:4-9, 11-14).

"Who can find a virtuous woman? for her price is far above rubies. The heart of her husband doth safely trust in her, so that he shall have no need of spoil. She will do him good and not evil all the days of her life. Her children arise up, and call her blessed; her husband also, and he praiseth her. Favour is deceitful, and beauty is vain: but a woman that feareth the Lord, she shall be praised" (31:10-12, 28, 30).

III. The Book of Ecclesiastes.
Introduction:
1. The meaning of the word is to address an assembly.
2. The purpose of the book:
  a. "To convince men of the uselessness of any world view which does not rise above the horizon of man himself. It pronounces the verdict of 'vanity of vanities' upon any philosophy of life which regards the created world of human enjoyment as an end in life." (Gleason L. Archer, *A Survey of Old Testament Introduction*, p. 459)
  b. "You do not have to go outside the Bible to find the merely human philosophy of life. God has given us in the book of Ecclesiastes the record of all that human thinking and natural religion has ever been able to discover concerning the meaning and goal of life. The arguments in the book, therefore, are not God's arguments, but God's record of man's arguments. This explains why such passages as 1:15; 2:24; 3:3, 4, 8, 11, 19, 20; 8:15 are at positive variance with the rest of the Bible." (*What the Bible Is All About*, Henrietta Mears, p. 200)
3. Did Solomon teach there is no life after death? The answer is no! (See 3:16; 11:9; 12:14.)
4. The key words in Ecclesiastes are man (used forty-seven times), labor (thirty-six), under the sun (thirty), and vanity (thirty-seven).
5. The book of Ecclesiastes may be summarized by two statements, one made by a sewer worker in Chicago, and the other by a well-known agnostic lawyer. Both statements were in response to a question concerning their personal philosophy of life.
  "There is a statement in the Bible which summarizes my life. It says, 'We have toiled all night, and have taken nothing . . . ' " [Lk. 5:5]. —Clarence Darrow
  "I digge de ditch to gette de money to buye de food to gette de strength to digge de ditch!" — Cook County Sewer Employee
A. The quest—man's problems stated (1-2). Even before he starts the search, Solomon has doubts. In his opinion:
  Everything seems so futile (1:2).
  Generations come and go, but it seems to make no difference (1:4).

The sun rises and sets, the wind twists back and forth, but neither seems to get any place or accomplish any purpose (1:5, 6).
The river runs into the sea, but the sea is never full. The water returns again to the rivers and flows again to the sea (1:7).
Everything appears so unutterably weary and tiresome (1:8).
No man seems satisfied, regardless of what he has seen or heard (1:8).
History merely repeats itself—absolutely nothing new ever occurs under the sun (1:9, 10).
One hundred years from now everything will have been forgotten, regardless what occurs today (1:11).
Was life truly this way everywhere? Could a wise and healthy man, by searching the length and breadth of the land, find peace and purpose? Solomon would try. This he diligently did by drinking deeply at the wells of the following:
1. Human wisdom.
  "I communed with mine own heart, saying, Lo, I am come to great estate, and have gotten more wisdom than all they that have been before me in Jerusalem: yea, my heart had great experience of wisdom and knowledge. And I gave my heart to know wisdom, and to know madness and folly: I perceived that this also is vexation of spirit" (1:16, 17).
  Solomon had more natural capacity to accumulate and apply raw facts than any man who ever lived (apart from Christ), but he sadly concluded:
  "For in much wisdom is much grief: and he that increaseth knowledge increaseth sorrow" (1:18).
2. Pleasure (2:1-3).
  "Philosophy has failed, says the preacher, so let merriment be tried. Music, dance, wine (not to excess), the funny story, the clever repartee: these are now cultivated. Clowns are now welcomed to the court where only grave philosophy had been. The halls of the palace resounded with laughter and gaiety." (Henrietta C. Mears, *What the Bible Is All About*, p. 201).
  But laughter and liquor could in no way soothe man's soul.
  Note the king's sad conclusion: "I said of laughter, It is mad: and of mirth, What doeth it?" (2:2). (See also 8:15.)
3. Alcohol (2:3).
  "I sought in mine heart to give myself unto wine . . . ."
4. Great building projects (2:4).
  "I made me great works; I builded houses . . . ."
  Solomon now attempts to plug that "hole in his soul" by inaugurating a great public works program. Aqueducts, pools, palaces, and gleaming buildings soon grace the Syrian skyland. The court comedians give way to the great architects. But all too soon the building campaign wears thin and is quietly dropped.

5. Beautiful gardens and parks (2:4–6).
"I planted vineyards; I made me gardens and orchards, and I planted trees in them of all kinds of fruits; I made pools of water, to water therewith the wood that bringeth forth trees" (2:4–6).

Now luscious vineyards, graceful gardens, exotic and rare flowers, tropical plants, and other gems of green suddenly sprout up. Jerusalem and the vicinity bloom like the original Garden of Eden. But, alas, before long the frost of disinterest puts the blight to this bloom also!

6. Personal indulgences (2:7).
"I got me servants and maidens, and had servants born in my house" (2:7).

The king now had an individual servant for every wish. But none could serve up his wish for inward peace and purpose.

7. Sex.
"And he had seven hundred wives, princesses, and three hundred concubines . . ." (1 Ki. 11:3).

8. Massive wealth.
"I had great possessions of herds and flocks above all that were in Jerusalem before me: I gathered also silver and gold, and the peculiar treasure of kings and the provinces . . ." (2:7, 8).

9. International reputation.
"And she [the Queen of Sheba] said to the king, it was a true report that I heard in mine own land of thy acts and of thy wisdom. Howbeit, I believed not the words, until I came, and mine eyes had seen it: and behold, the half was not told me: thy wisdom and prosperity exceedeth the fame which I heard" (1 Ki. 10:6, 7).

10. Cattle breeding (2:7).
Great herds of cows, sheep, oxen, goats, and other animals would now graze upon the green Palestinian pastures. But while the skin and meats of these animals might clothe and feed the outer man, the inner person remained naked and starving.

11. Music (2:8).
"I got me men singers and women singers, and the delights of the sons of men, as musical instruments, and that of all sorts."
But the missing chord of contentment was not to be found through music, however beautiful the song and talented the singers.

12. Literature.
"And he spoke three thousand proverbs, and his songs were a thousand and five" (1 Ki. 4:32).

13. Natural science.
"And he spake of trees, from the cedar tree that is in Lebanon even unto the hyssop that springeth out of the wall: he spake also of beasts, and of fowl, and of creeping things, and of fishes" (1 Ki. 4:33).

14. Military power.
"And Solomon had forty thousand stalls of horses for his chariots, and twelve thousand horsemen" (1 Ki. 4:26).

"And King Solomon made a navy of ships . . . on the shore of the Red Sea . . ." (1 Ki. 9:26).

B. The digest—man's problems studied (3–10).
After completing an exhaustive (and doubtless exhausting) journey, Solomon returns home (4:1) and contemplates his travels. He concludes the following about life apart from God:
1. It is utterly futile (2:11).
2. It is filled with repetition (3:1–8).
3. It is permeated with sorrow (4:1).
4. It is grievous and frustrating (2:17).
5. It is uncertain (9:11, 12).
6. It is without purpose (4:2, 3; 8:15).
7. It is incurable (1:15).
8. It is unjust (7:15; 8:14; 9:11; 10:6, 7).
9. It is on the level of animal existence (3:19).

C. The best—man's problem solved (11–12).
Solomon concludes that even with God, life is a mystery, but apart from him it becomes a horrible nightmare. Therefore, it is best if man:
1. Finds God early in his life (11:9, 10; 12:1, 2).
2. Fears God throughout his life (12:13, 14).

J. Vernon McGee aptly summarizes verses 1–7 in the following way:
Verse 2: "Failing eyesight makes it appear that the sun, moon, and stars are getting dimmer. Time flies and one sad experience follows another—clouds return after rain."
Verse 3: "Keepers of the house shall tremble" refers to the legs. The old person begins to totter. "Strong men" are the shoulders that are no longer erect. "Grinders" are the teeth. "Those that look out of the windows" refers to failing eyesight.
Verse 4: "Doors shut in the street" refers to being hard of hearing. "Sound of grinding is low" refers to the tongue. The voice of old age gets thin.
"Shall rise up at the voice of the bird"—it took an alarm clock to wake him before, now the chirping of a bird disturbs his sleep.
"Daughters of music shall be brought low" indicates that he can no longer sing in the choir, cannot carry a tune anymore.
Verse 5: "Afraid of that which is high"—things that formerly did not frighten him. "Fears shall be in the way"—he no longer enjoys traveling. "Almond tree shall flourish"—our senior citizen is getting gray-haired, if his hair has not fallen out. "Grasshoppers shall be a burden"—little things annoy him. "Desire shall fail"—romance is gone. "Man goeth to his long home"—death comes.
Verse 6: "Silver cord"—the spinal cord.
"Golden bowl"—the head.
"Pitcher"—the lungs.
"Wheel"—the heart.

IV. The Song of Solomon.
Background of the story:
A. Act One—The Shulamite Cinderella.
1. Solomon had a vineyard in the hill country of Ephraim, just outside the little town of Shunam, about fifty miles north of Jerusalem (8:11).

137

2. This vineyard was rented out to a family of sharecroppers consisting of a mother, two sons, and two daughters. The oldest of these girls was the Shulamite, and the youngest, her little sister (6:13; 8:8).

3. The Shulamite was the Cinderella of the family, having great natural beauty, but unnoticed by the world.

4. Her brothers made her work very hard tending the vineyards, so that she had little opportunity to care for her personal appearance (1:6).
   a. She pruned the vines.
   b. She set traps for the little foxes (2:15).
   c. She also kept the flocks (1:8).

5. From being out in the open so often, she became sunburned (1:6).

B. Act Two—The Shepherd Stranger.

1. One day a mysterious, handsome stranger comes to the vineyard and soon wins the heart of the Shulamite girl. Unknown to her, he is really Solomon, disguised as a lowly shepherd.

2. She asks about his flocks (1:7).

3. He answers evasively, but is very definite concerning his love for her (1:8-10).

4. He leaves her, but promises he will someday return to her.

5. During his absence she dreams of him on two occasions.
   a. First dream—that they are already married and that one night she awakens to find him missing from her bed. She quickly dresses and goes out looking for him (3:2-4).
   b. Second dream—that her beloved has returned and besought her to open the door and let him in. But she refuses for she is unwilling to reclothe herself and soil her feet going to the door. Soon however, her heart smites her for this shabby action and she leaps for the door. But alas, he has gone! We read:
      "My beloved put in his hand by the hole of the door . . . I rose up to open to my beloved; and my hands dropped with myrrh, and my fingers with sweet smelling myrrh, upon the handles of the lock" (5:4, 5).
      Dr. J. Vernon McGee informs us that a lovely custom of that day was for the lover to place sweet-smelling myrrh inside the handle of the bride's door. The bride then began her frantic search for the lover she had so carelessly ignored. During her search the guards of the city mistreated her, and the watchman on the wall tore off her veil. She then pleaded with the women of Jerusalem to aid her in finding her lover and informing him of her love for him (5:6-8).
      Suddenly and joyfully she discovers his whereabouts.
      "My beloved is gone down into his garden, to the beds of spices, to feed in the gardens, and to gather lilies. I am my beloved's and my beloved is mine: he feedeth among the lilies" (6:2, 3).

6. These then, are her two dreams concerning the mysterious shepherd lover of the Shulamite girl. But why did he leave her? Where did he go? Would he ever return?

C. Act Three—The Mighty Monarch.

1. One day the little town of Shunam receives some electrifying news. King Solomon himself is approaching their city. But the lovesick and lonely maiden is not interested, and takes no further notice until word is brought to her that the powerful potentate himself desires to see her.

2. She is puzzled until she is brought into his presence, where she recognizes him as her beloved shepherd. He then gently explains to her that although he has already gathered sixty wives, eighty concubines, and unnumbered virgins, that she will be his choice bride and true love (6:8). He invites her to come with him and promises to care for her little sister (8:8, 9).

3. The bride is then placed in the king's chariot, made from the wood of Lebanon, with silver posts, a golden canopy, and purple seating (3:9, 10).

4. Together they ride off to the royal palace in Jerusalem, accompanied by sixty mighty swordsmen and experienced body guards (3:7, 8).

D. The bride of the story (as described by the bridegroom).

1. She was the most beautiful girl in the world (1:8).

2. She was like a bouquet of flowers in a garden (1:14).

3. Her eyes were as soft as doves (1:15).

4. She was as a lily among the thorns as compared to his other wives (2:2).

5. Her hair fell across her face like flocks of goats which frisked across the slopes of Gilead (4:1).

6. Her teeth were as white as sheep's wool (4:2).

7. Her lips were like a thread of scarlet (4:3) and made of honey (4:11).

8. Her neck was as stately as the Tower of David (4:4).

9. Her bosom was as twin fawns of a gazelle, feeding among the lilies (4:5).

10. She was like a lovely orchard, bearing precious fruit (4:13).

11. She was as a garden fountain, a well of living water, refreshing as the streams from the Lebanon mountains (4:15).

12. Her thighs were like jewels, the work of the most skilled of craftsmen (7:1).

13. Her navel was as lovely as a goblet filled with wine (7:2).

14. Her waist was like a heap of wheat set about with lilies (7:2).

15. Her nose was shapely like the Tower of Lebanon overlooking Damascus (7:4).

16. He was completely overcome by a single glance of her beautiful eyes (4:9).

E. The bridegroom of the story (as described by the bride).
   1. He was as swift as a young gazelle leaping and bounding over the hills (2:9).
   2. He was ruddy and handsome, the fairest of ten thousand (5:10).
   3. His head was as purest gold, covered by wavy, raven hair (5:11).
   4. His eyes were as doves beside the water brooks, deep and quiet (5:12).
   5. His cheeks were like sweetly scented beds of spice (5:13).
   6. His lips were as perfumed lilies and his breath like myrrh (5:13).
   7. His arms were as round bars of gold set with topaz (5:14).
   8. His body was bright ivory encrusted with jewels (5:14).
   9. His legs were pillars of marble set in sockets of finest gold, like cedars of Lebanon (5:15).

# THE CHAOTIC KINGDOM STAGE

## THE CHAOTIC KINGDOM STAGE
### (1 Kings 12-22; 2 Kings 1-17; 2 Chronicles 10-36; Obadiah; Joel; Jonah; Amos; Hosea; Micah; Isaiah; Nahum; Zephaniah; Habakkuk; Jeremiah; Lamentations)

1. This stage covers a period of around 325 years, from 930 B.C. to 605 B.C. The key events take place in Jerusalem and Samaria.
2. The period begins with a tragic civil war which splits the nation Israel into two opposing kingdoms. The period ends with the capture of both these kingdoms by two enemy Gentile nations (1 Ki. 12; 2 Ki. 17, 25).
3. The chaotic stage would feature the following:
   a. One king (Josiah) discovering God's Word in the Temple and another king (Jehoiakim) attempting to destroy it in the fire (2 Ki. 22; Jer. 36).
   b. The writing of at least twelve Old Testament books by eleven human authors. These are: Obadiah, Joel, Jonah, Amos, Hosea, Micah, Isaiah, Nahum, Zephaniah, Habakkuk, and Jeremiah (who also wrote Lamentations).
   c. The second of four great miracle-working periods in the Bible.
      (1) The first was during the time of Moses and Joshua.
      (2) The second was during the time of Elijah and Elisha.
      (3) The third was during the time of Daniel and Ezekiel.
      (4) The fourth was during the time of Christ and the apostles.
   d. All three of the individuals who were raised from the dead in the Old Testament: (1) 1 Kings 17, (2) 2 Kings 4, and (3) 2 Kings 13.
   e. The only Old Testament man ever to be healed of leprosy (Naaman, 2 Ki. 5).
   f. The salvation of Samaria (northern capital) by four lepers, and the salvation of Jerusalem (southern capital) by the death angel (2 Ki. 7, 19).
   g. The beginning of the Samaritan race (2 Ki. 17).
   h. The second and third of three occasions when God rolled back the waters of the Jordan river (2 Ki. 2). (For the first, see Josh. 3.)
   i. The account of a singing choir defeating an enemy on a battlefield.
      "And they rose early in the morning, and went forth into the wilderness of Tekoa: and as they went forth, Jehoshaphat stood and said, Hear me, O Judah, and ye inhabitants of Jerusalem;

Believe in the Lord your God, so shall ye be established; believe his prophets, so shall ye prosper. And when he had consulted with the people, he appointed singers unto the Lord, and that should praise the beauty of holiness, as they went out before the army, and to say, Praise the Lord; for his mercy endureth for ever. And when they began to sing and to praise, the Lord set ambushments against the children of Ammon, Moab, and mount Seir, which were come against Judah; and they were smitten" (2 Chron. 20:20-22).

   j. The sight of water being burned by fire (1 Ki. 18). "Then the fire of the Lord fell and consumed the burnt-sacrifice, and the wood, and the stones, and the dust, and licked up the water that was in the trench" (1 Ki. 18:38).
   k. The sight of an axe head floating on water (2 Ki. 6).
   l. The second of two men who went to heaven without first dying (2 Ki. 2).
      "And it came to pass, as they still went on, and talked, that, behold, there appeared a chariot of fire, and horses of fire, and parted them both asunder; and Elijah went up by a whirlwind into heaven" (2 Ki. 2:11).
   m. The only time in the Old Testament where men are allowed to see God's mounted army of angels (2 Ki. 6).
      "And when the servant of the man of God was risen early, and gone forth, behold, an host compassed the city both with horses and chariots. And his servant said unto him, Alas, my master? how shall we do? And he answered, Fear not: for they that be with us are more than they that be with them. And Elisha prayed, and said, Lord, I pray thee, open his eyes, that he may see. And the Lord opened the eyes of the young man; and he saw: and, behold, the mountain was full of horses and chariots of fire round about Elisha" (2 Ki. 6:15-17).
   n. Seven prayers on a mountain, seven dips in a river, and seven sneezes on a bed (1 Ki. 18; 2 Ki. 5; 4).
      Elijah did the praying on Carmel.
      Naaman did the dipping in Jordan.
      A resurrected child did the sneezing in Shunem.

## THE CHAOTIC KINGDOM STAGE

This stage is the most interwoven, fast-moving, and detailed period in all the Bible. It will be considered under three main divisions.
   I. An Introduction to the Chaotic Kingdom Stage.
   II. The Rulers of the Chaotic Kingdom Stage.
      At this point we will employ a twofold method:

## THE CHAOTIC KINGDOM STAGE

1 Kings 12-22
2 Kings
2 Chronicles 10-36
Obadiah
Joel
Jonah
Amos
Hosea
Micah
Isaiah
Nahum
Zephaniah
Habakkuk
Jeremiah
Lamentations

### THE SOUTHERN KINGDOM

| | |
|---|---|
| REHOBOAM | JOTHAM |
| ABIJAM | AHAZ |
| ASA | HEZEKIAH |
| JEHOSHAPHAT | MANASSEH |
| JEHORAM | AMON |
| AHAZIAH | JOSIAH |
| ATHALIAH | JEHOAHAZ |
| JOASH | JEHOIAKIM |
| AMAZIAH | JEHOIACHIN |
| UZZIAH | ZEDEKIAH |

### THE NORTHERN KINGDOM

| | |
|---|---|
| JEROBOAM | JEHOAHAZ |
| NADAB | JEHOASH |
| BAASHA | JEROBOAM II |
| ELAH | ZECHARIAH |
| ZIMRI | SHALLUM |
| OMRI | MENAHEM |
| AHAB | PEKAHIAH |
| AHAZIAH | PEKAH |
| JEHORAM | HOSHEA |
| JEHU | |

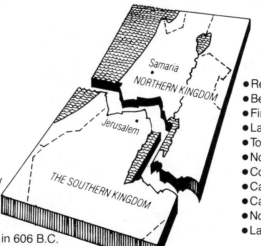

- Referred to as Judah
- Began in 931 B.C.
- First ruler was Rehoboam
- Last ruler was Zedekiah
- Total number of rulers: twenty
- Eight were saved
- Consisted of two tribes
- Capital was Jerusalem
- Captured by the Babylonians in 606 B.C.
- Three separate returns from captivity
- Lasted 325 years: 931—606 B.C.

- Referred to as Israel and Ephraim
- Began in 931 B.C.
- First ruler was Jeroboam
- Last ruler was Hoshea
- Total number of rulers: nineteen
- Not one was saved
- Consisted of ten tribes
- Capital was Samaria
- Captured by the Assyrians in 721 B.C.
- No return from captivity
- Lasted 210 years: 931—721 B.C.

A. The floodlight, shotgun approach. Here the reign of every king will be briefly outlined.

B. The spotlight, rifle approach. Here the reign of the more important kings will be expanded upon.

III. The Old Testament Books Written During the Chaotic Kingdom Stage.

I. An Introduction to the Chaotic Kingdom Stage.
After the death of Solomon, a tragic civil war split Israel into two opposing kingdoms, the north and the south.

A. The northern kingdom:
1. It began in 931 B.C. and lasted 210 years.
2. The first ruler was Jeroboam.
3. The last ruler was Hoshea.
4. The total number of kings was nineteen. Not one was righteous.
5. It consisted of ten tribes.
6. Its capital later became Samaria.
7. It was captured by the Assyrians in 721 B.C.
8. There was no return from captivity.

B. The southern kingdom:
1. It began in 931 B.C. and lasted 326 years.

## NORTHERN RULERS

### 1. Jeroboam
DATES **931-909**   DURATION **22 YEARS**
SCRIPTURE **1 KINGS 11:26—14:20;**
**2 CHRONICLES 9:29—13:22**

1. He served as a cabinet member under Solomon, but fled to Egypt to escape the king's wrath.
2. He led the revolt of the ten tribes at Shechem.
3. His false religion caused Israel to sin.
4. His pagan altar was destroyed, his arm paralyzed, and his son stricken by God due to his sin.
5. He was defeated in battle by Abijam, the second king of the south.
6. He was stricken with a plague from God and died.

### 2. Nadab
DATES **910-908**   DURATION **2 YEARS**
SCRIPTURE **1 KINGS 15:25-28**

1. He was the son of Jeroboam.
2. He was assassinated by a rebel named Baasha.

### 3. Baasha
DATES **909-885**   DURATION **24 YEARS**
SCRIPTURE **1 KINGS 15:27—16:7;**
**2 CHRONICLES 16:1-6**

1. He killed Nadab and thus fulfilled Ahijah the prophet's prediction. Compare 1 Kings 14:4 with 15:29.
2. He fought with Asa (third king of the south) and built a wall to cut off trade to Jerusalem.
3. His seed was predicted to suffer the same judgment as that of Jeroboam.

### 4. Elah
DATES **885-883**   DURATION **2 YEARS**
SCRIPTURE **1 KINGS 16:6-14**

1. He was the son of Baasha.
2. He was assassinated by a soldier rebel while drunk.

### 5. Zimri
DATES **885**   DURATION **7 DAYS**
SCRIPTURE **1 KINGS 16:9-20**

1. He fulfilled prophecy by slaughtering Baasha's seed.
2. He was trapped by rebel soldiers in his own palace, resulting in a fiery suicidal death.

### 6. Omri
DATES **885-873**   DURATION **12 YEARS**
SCRIPTURE **1 KINGS 16:15-28**

1. He made Samaria the northern capital.
2. He was the most powerful king up to his time.
3. He arranged the marriage of his son Ahab to Jezebel.

2. The first ruler was Rehoboam.
3. The last ruler was Zedekiah.
4. The total number of rulers was twenty: nineteen kings and one queen. Eight of the twenty were righteous.
5. It consisted of two tribes (Judah and Benjamin).
6. Its capital remained Jerusalem.
7. It was captured by the Babylonians in 606 B.C.
8. There were three separate returns from captivity.

   Note: The Chaotic Kingdom Stage may thus be divided into two time periods:
   a. The divided kingdom (both north and south) (931–721 B.C.).
   b. The single kingdom (only the south) (721–605 B.C.).

II. The Rulers of the Chaotic Kingdom Stage.
   *The Floodlight, Shotgun Approach:*
   Northern rulers:
   A. Jeroboam (1 Ki. 11:26—14:20; 2 Chron. 9:29—13:22).
      1. He served as a cabinet member under Solomon, but fled to Egypt for awhile to escape the king's wrath (1 Ki. 11:28, 40).
      2. He led the revolt of the ten tribes at Shechem.
      3. His false religion caused Israel to sin.
      4. His false altar was destroyed, his arm was paralyzed, and his son stricken by God, all as punishment for his sin.
      5. He was defeated in battle by Abijam, the second king of the South.
      6. He was stricken with a plague from God and died.
      7. He ruled for twenty-two years (931–909 B.C.).
   B. Nadab (1 Ki. 15:25-28).
      1. He was the son of Jeroboam.
      2. He was assassinated by a rebel named Baasha.
      3. Nadab was thus the first of six northern kings to be murdered while in office.
      4. He ruled for two years (910–908).
   C. Baasha (1 Ki. 15:27—16:7; 2 Chron. 16:1-6).
      1. He unknowingly fulfilled the prophecy given to Jeroboam's wife by Ahijah the prophet, in killing Nadab and his relatives. (Compare 1 Ki. 14:14 with 15:29.)
      2. He declared war on Asa (third king of Judah) and began building a wall fortress at Ramah to control the road to Judah, thus hoping to cut off all trade to Jerusalem (2 Chron. 16:1).
      3. He was rejected by God because of his sin. Jehu, the prophet, predicted that Baasha's descendants would suffer the same judgment God placed on Jeroboam.
      4. Baasha ruled for twenty-four years (909–885 B.C.).

      Note: It can be seen already that some of the reigns overlapped each other—that is, on occasion both father and son may have ruled at the same time. This explains the difference in the total number of years of all the northern kings *as given in the Bible*, which is 252 years; and the *actual time involved*, around 208 years (beginning with Jeroboam in 931 B.C., and ending with Hoshea in 721 B.C.).

D. Elah (1 Ki. 16:6-14).
1. He was the son of Baasha.
2. He was assassinated by the commander of his royal chariot troops, a man named Zimri.
3. Elah was drunk at the time.
4. He ruled for two years (885-883 B.C.).

E. Zimri (1 Ki. 16:9-20).
1. He fulfilled Jehu's prophecy by slaughtering all the seed of Baasha. (Compare 1 Ki. 16:7 with 16:12.)
2. Zimri was then trapped by Omri, Israel's new commander-in-chief, in the palace, which resulted in a fiery suicidal death.
3. He reigned but seven days (885 B.C.).

F. Omri (1 Ki. 16:15-28).
1. He moved the northern capital from Tirzah to Samaria.
2. He arranged the political marriage of his son Ahab to Jezebel, daughter of Ethbaal, king of the Sidonians.
3. He ruled for twelve years (885-873 B.C.).

G. Ahab (1 Ki. 16:28—22:40; 2 Chron. 18:1-34).
1. He married Jezebel.
2. He was allowed to defeat the Syrians on two occasions.
3. He was denounced often by Elijah.
   a. for encouraging Baal-worship
   b. for his part in the murder of Naboth
   c. for sparing the life of a godless Syrian king
4. He tricked godly king Jehoshaphat (fourth king of Judah) into a twofold compromise:
   a. a matrimonial alliance, whereby his wicked daughter, Athaliah, is given to Joram, son of Jehoshaphat
   b. a military alliance, whereby Jehoshaphat and Ahab go to war against Syria
5. The death of his wicked wife was predicted by Elijah.
6. His own death was predicted by both Elijah and the prophet Micaiah.
7. He was slain in battle with the Syrians.
8. He ruled for twenty-two years (874-852 B.C.).

H. Ahaziah (1 Ki. 22:40—2 Ki. 1:18; 2 Chron. 20:35-37).
1. He was the oldest son of Ahab and Jezebel.
2. He persuaded Jehoshaphat to enter into a shipbuilding enterprise with him at Ezion-geber (2 Chron. 20:35-37).
3. He suffered a severe (and later fatal) fall in his palace at Samaria.
4. He turned to the pagan god Baal-zebub for healing, but received instead the condemnation of Elijah, whom he unsuccessfully attempted to arrest.
5. He ruled for two years (853-851 B.C.).

I. Jehoram (2 Ki. 3:1—9:25; 2 Chron. 22:5-7).
1. He was the youngest son of Ahab and brother of Ahaziah.
2. He also (like father and brother) persuaded Jehoshaphat to enter into an alliance, this time a military campaign against the Moabites. The prophet Elisha at this time worked a miracle on the battlefield (for Jehoshaphat's

## NORTHERN RULERS

### 7. Ahab
DATES **874-852**   DURATION **22 YEARS**
SCRIPTURE **1 KINGS 16:28—22:40;**
          **2 CHRONICLES 18:1-34**
1. He married Jezebel.
2. His Baal-worshiping practices caused a great famine to fall upon the land.
3. He was allowed to defeat the Syrians on two occasions to prove a point.
4. He tricked godly King Jehoshaphat (fourth king of Judah) into a twofold compromise—matrimonial and military.
5. His death for his many sins was predicted by three prophets (1 Ki. 20:42; 21:19; 22:17, 28).
6. The death of Jezebel, his wife, was also predicted by Elijah.
7. He experienced a brief (but temporary) fox-hole type conversion (1 Ki. 21:29).
8. He was killed in a battle with Syria.

### 8. Ahaziah
DATES **853-851**   DURATION **2 YEARS**
SCRIPTURE **1 KINGS 22:40—2 KINGS 1:18;**
          **2 CHRONICLES 20:35-37**
1. He was the oldest son of Ahab and Jezebel.
2. He persuaded Jehoshaphat to enter into a ship-building enterprise with him at Ezion-Geber.
3. He suffered a severe fall (which proved fatal) in his palace in Samaria.
4. He turned to the pagan god Baal-Zebub for healing.
5. He was rebuked for this by Elijah, whom he unsuccessfully attempted to arrest.

### 9. Jehoram
DATES **852-840**   DURATION **12 YEARS**
SCRIPTURE **2 KINGS 3:1—9:25;**
          **2 CHRONICLES 22:5-7**
1. He was the youngest son of Ahab and Jezebel.
2. He persuaded Jehoshaphat to ally with him against Syria.
3. Elisha the prophet performed a miracle (for Jehoshaphat's sake) which won the battle.
4. Elisha later helped Jehoram by warning him of several planned Syrian ambushes.
5. Elisha would, however, prevent him from slaughtering some supernaturally blinded Syrian troops.
6. He was on the throne when Naaman came to be healed of leprosy.
7. He was on the throne when God used four lepers to save Samaria from starvation.
8. He was finally murdered by Jehu in the Valley of Jezreel.

### 10. Jehu
DATES **841-813**   DURATION **28 YEARS**
SCRIPTURE **2 KINGS 9:1—10:36;**
          **2 CHRONICLES 22:7-12**
1. He was anointed by a messenger from Elisha.
2. He was known for his bloodletting. He executed:
Judah's King Ahaziah (not to be confused with Ahab's oldest son), grandson of Jehoshaphat
The northern king Jehoram
Jezebel
Ahab's seventy sons, relatives, and friends
Forty-two royal princes of Judah
The Baal-worshipers

## NORTHERN RULERS

### 11. Jehoahaz
DATES **814-797**   DURATION **17 YEARS**
SCRIPTURE **2 KINGS 13:1-9**

1. He was the son of Jehu.
2. He saw his army almost wiped out by the Syrians.
3. He experienced a brief period of remorse over his sins, but apparently not genuine repentance.

### 12. Jehoash
DATES **798-782**   DURATION **16 YEARS**
SCRIPTURE **2 KINGS 13:10—14:16;**
**2 CHRONICLES 25:17-24**

1. He visited Elisha on his deathbed.
2. He defeated Amaziah (sixth king of Judah) on the battlefield.
3. He related one of the two Old Testament fables to ridicule the arrogant claims of Amaziah.
4. He plundered Jerusalem, taking many hostages and much wealth.

### 13. Jeroboam II
DATES **793-752**   DURATION **41 YEARS**
SCRIPTURE **2 KINGS 14:23-29**

41 years

1. He ruled longer than any other northern king.
2. He was one of the most powerful kings of the north.
3. He recovered much of Israel's lost territory.

### 14. Zechariah
DATES **753**   DURATION **6 MONTHS**
SCRIPTURE **2 KINGS 14:29—15:12**

6 months

1. He was the great-great-grandson of Jehu, and fourth ruler in his dynasty.
2. He was murdered by a rebel named Shallum, thus fulfilling God's prophecy against Jehu. See 2 Kings 10:30; 14:29; 15:8-12.

### 15. Shallum
DATES **752**   DURATION **1 MONTH**
SCRIPTURE **2 KINGS 15:10-15**

1 month

He was murdered by a cruel soldier named Menahem.

### 16. Menahem
DATES **752-742**   DURATION **10 YEARS**
SCRIPTURE **2 KINGS 15:14-22**

1. He was one of Israel's most brutal dictators.
2. He bought off Assyrian king Tiglath-Pileser with a two-million-dollar bribe.

### 17. Pekahiah
DATES **742-740**   DURATION **2 YEARS**
SCRIPTURE **2 KINGS 15:22-26**

2 years

1. He was the son of Menahem.
2. He was killed by his army commander, Pekah.

sake) which resulted in an allied victory over the Moabites.
3. Elisha later helped Jehoram by warning him of several planned Syrian ambushes.
4. Elisha then refused to allow him to slaughter some enemy Syrian soldiers who had been supernaturally blinded by God.
5. Jehoram was on the throne when God used the four lepers to save the city of Samaria from starvation.
6. He was also the king with whom the Syrian leper Naaman met.
7. He was later murdered by Jehu in the Valley of Jezreel.
8. He ruled for twelve years (852–840 B.C.).

J. Jehu (2 Ki. 9:1—10:36; 2 Chron. 22:7-12).
1. He was anointed by Elisha and ordered to execute the dynasty of Ahab, which included Jehoram and Jezebel.
2. He rode his chariot to the valley of Jezreel, where he executed both Jehoram and Ahaziah, the sixth king of Judah (not to be confused with the Ahaziah who was Jehoram's older brother).
3. He then made his way to the city of Jezreel and killed Jezebel.
4. After this he demanded and received the heads of the seventy sons of Ahab who were living in the city of Samaria.
5. He continued his blood purge by slaying even the descendants and friends of Ahab.
6. He finally, by trickery, assembled all the priests of Baal in a large convention hall in Jezreel, where he ordered the slaughter of each priest.
7. He ruled for twenty-eight years (841–813 B.C.).

K. Jehoahaz (2 Ki. 13:1-9).
1. He was the son of Jehu.
2. He was oppressed by the Syrian king Hazael during his entire reign, and his army was finally reduced to fifty mounted troops, ten chariots, and ten thousand infantry men.
3. He briefly displayed remorse (as Ahab had once done, see 1 Ki. 21:27-30), but apparently it was not true repentance.
4. He ruled for seventeen years (814–797 B.C.).

L. Jehoash (2 Ki. 13:10—14:16; 2 Chron. 25:17-24).
1. He was the son of Jehoahaz.
2. He visited Elisha on his deathbed.
3. He defeated Amaziah (sixth king of Judah) on the battlefield.
4. He related the second of two Old Testament fables to ridicule the arrogant claims of Amaziah.
5. He led Amaziah back to Jerusalem as a captive and left the city, taking both wealth and hostages.
6. He ruled for sixteen years (798–782 B.C.).

M. Jeroboam II (2 Ki. 14:23-29).
1. He was the son of Jehoash.
2. He ruled longer than any other northern ruler.
3. He was also one of the most powerful kings of the north.
4. He recovered the lost territories of Israel surrounding the Dead Sea. God thus allowed

him to prosper and enlarge his kingdom in spite of his wicked ways, because of divine mercy upon the pitiful condition of Israel at that time (2 Ki. 14:25, 26).

5. Jonah the prophet lived and ministered during this time.

6. Jeroboam II ruled for forty-one years (793-753 B.C.).

N. Zechariah (2 Ki. 14:19—15:12).
1. He was the son of Jeroboam II.
2. He was murdered by a rebel named Shallum.
3. Zechariah was the great-great-grandson of Jehu, and the fourth ruler in his dynasty. With his death the line would cease, thus fulfilling God's prophecy to Jehu. (See 2 Ki. 10:30; 14:29; 15:8-12.)
4. He ruled for six months (753 B.C.).

O. Shallum (2 Ki. 15:10-15).
1. He was murdered by a cruel warrior named Menahem.
2. He ruled for one month (752 B.C.).

P. Menahem (2 Ki. 15:14-22).
1. He was one of the most brutal dictators to sit upon the northern throne.
2. He rewarded any opposition on the part of his subjects by a wholesale slaughter, including the ripping open of pregnant women.
3. He bought off the Assyrian king Tiglath-pileser, who had invaded Israel at that time with a two-million-dollar bribe.
4. He ruled for ten years (752-742 B.C.).

Q. Pekahiah (2 Ki. 15:22-26).
1. He was the son of Menahem.
2. He was assassinated by his army commander, Pekah.
3. He ruled for two years (742-741 B.C.).

R. Pekah (2 Ki. 15:27-31; 2 Chron. 28:5-8).
1. He joined Syria in an unsuccessful attack against the Judean king Ahaz to punish the southern kingdom for refusing to team up with them in an effort to stop the growing Assyrian threat.
2. During his reign Tiglath-pileser, the Assyrian king, invaded Israel and captured some of its northern and eastern cities.
3. Pekah was assassinated by Hoshea.
4. He ruled for twenty years (740-732 B.C.).
   Note: It will be noted that only eight years are in view here (740-732). It is thought that the first twelve years (752-740) were shared by a co-regency arrangement with both Menahem and Pekahiah.

S. Hoshea (2 Ki. 15:20—17:6).
1. He was the last ruler of the northern kingdom.
2. After becoming a vassal to the Assyrian king, Shalmaneser, Hoshea joined with Egypt in rebelling against Assyria.
3. For this he was imprisoned and the people were exiled to Assyria (2 Ki. 17:4-6). Hoshea thus became the last of the northern kings. Eight died natural deaths, seven were murdered, one died a suicide, one in battle, one under judgment of God, one in a fall. Not a single ruler turned to God. From this captivity, the ten tribes have never been restored to Palestine. In fact, they would soon lose

## NORTHERN RULERS

### 18. Pekah
DATES **740-732**   DURATION **20 YEARS**
SCRIPTURE **2 KINGS 15:27-31;**
**2 CHRONICLES 28:5-8**

1. Only eight years are in view here (740-732). It is thought that the first twelve years (752-740) were shared by a co-regency arrangement with both Menahem and Pekahiah.
2. He joined Syria in an unsuccessful attempt to punish Judah for their refusal to team up against Assyria.
3. He saw Assyria capture some of Israel's northern and eastern cities.
4. He was assassinated by Hoshea.

### 19. Hoshea
DATES **732-721**   DURATION **9 YEARS**
SCRIPTURE **2 KINGS 15:30—17:6**

1. He was Israel's final king.
2. He joined with Egypt in rebelling against Assyria.
3. For this he was imprisoned in Assyria.

their very tribal identity (but not their ancestry). The future restoration of all twelve tribes of Israel will be consummated at the Second Coming of Christ. (See Mt. 24:27-31.) The righteous God had to cut off Israel for their sin. (See 2 Ki. 17:7-18.)

a. The King of Assyria then transplanted colonies of people from various foreign countries into the depopulated land of northern Israel (2 Ki. 17:24).
b. Soon after their arrival, a plague of man-eating lions, sent by God, terrified the land. In desperation, the colonists sent a message to the Assyrian ruler, asking for the ministry of a Jehovah prophet, that the plague be stopped (17:25, 26). This lion plague had been predicted by Moses centuries back. (See Ex. 23:29; Lev. 26:21, 22.)
c. A prophet arrived and began his ministry from Bethel. The lion plague disappeared and a form of Jehovah-worship appeared, but only in form, as the people continued with their idol-worship as well (2 Ki. 17:27-34). This is the beginning of the Samaritan race and religion which was prevalent in the time of Jesus. (See Jn. 4.)

4. Hoshea ruled for nine years (732-723 B.C.).
Southern rulers:

A. Rehoboam (1 Ki. 11:42—14:31; 2 Chron. 9:31—12:16).
1. He was the son of Solomon.
2. His stupidity caused the civil war of Israel.
3. He had eighteen wives and sixty concubines. They gave him twenty-eight sons and sixty daughters.
4. His favorite wife was Maachah, the evil daughter of Absalom.
5. He was invaded by Shishak of Egypt.
6. He ruled seventeen years (931-914 B.C.).

## SOUTHERN RULERS

### 1. Rehoboam
DATES **931-914**   DURATION **17 YEARS**
SCRIPTURE **I KINGS 11:42—14:31;**
   **2 CHRONICLES 9:31—12:16**

1. He was the son of Solomon.
2. His stupidity and tactlessness sparked the civil war.
3. He had eighteen wives and sixty concubines.
4. His favorite wife was Maachah, the evil daughter of Absalom.
5. He sees his capital, Jerusalem, invaded by Shishak, Pharaoh of Egypt.

### 2. Abijam
DATES **914-911**   DURATION **3 YEARS**
SCRIPTURE **1 KINGS 14:31—15:8;**
   **2 CHRONICLES 13:1-22**

1. He defeated (by supernatural intervention) the northern king Jeroboam on the battlefield.
2. In spite of God's help, he degenerated into a wicked king.

### 3. Asa
DATES **911-870**   DURATION **41 YEARS**
SCRIPTURE **1 KINGS 15:8-14;**
   **2 CHRONICLES 14:1—16:14**

1. He was Judah's first saved king.
2. He led Judah in a revival.
3. He was a great builder.
4. He saw God answer his prayer by delivering Jerusalem from a massive Ethiopian attack (2 Chronicles 14:11).
5. He deposed Maacah (his grandmother) because of her idolatry.
6. He later backslid and threw into prison a prophet who had rebuked his sin.
7. He died of a foot disease, which problem he refused to take to God.

### 4. Jehoshaphat
DATES **873-848**   DURATION **25 YEARS**
SCRIPTURE **1 KINGS 22:41-50;**
   **2 CHRONICLES 17:1—20:37**

1. He instituted a national religious education program by sending out teachers of the Word of God.
2. He later marred his testimony by compromising with three ungodly northern kings.
3. He appointed a religious director and a civil director, thus recognizing the separation of church and state.
4. When Jerusalem was threatened by a massive Moabite invasion, God heard his prayer and supernaturally intervened.

### 5. Joram
DATES **853-845**   DURATION **8 YEARS**
SCRIPTURE **2 KINGS 8:16-24;**
   **2 CHRONICLES 21:1-20**

1. He married Athaliah, daughter of Ahab and Jezebel.
2. He began his reign by murdering his six brothers.
3. He received a posthumous message from Elijah predicting judgment upon him because of his wicked and murderous reign.
4. He was attacked and defeated by the Philistines and Arabians.
5. He died of a horrible disease and was unmourned at the funeral.

B. Abijam (1 Ki. 14:31—15:8; 2 Chron. 13:1-22).
  1. He defeated (by supernatural intervention) the northern king, Jeroboam, on the battlefield.
  2. In spite of God's help at this time, he later degenerated into a wicked king.
  3. He ruled three years (914-911 B.C.).

C. Asa (1 Ki. 15:8-14; 2 Chron. 14:1—16:14).
  1. He was Judah's first righteous king.
  2. He led Judah in a revival and was a great builder.
  3. God answered his prayer and delivered him from a massive Ethiopian attack.
  4. He even deposed his own grandmother Maachah because of her idolatry.
  5. He later was rebuked by a prophet for his sin and responded by throwing him in prison.
  6. He died with a foot disease which problem he refused to take to God.
  7. He ruled forty-one years (911-870 B.C.).

D. Jehoshaphat (1 Ki. 22:41-50; 2 Chron. 17:1—20:37).
  1. He was the second righteous king of Judah.
  2. He instituted a nationwide Bible education program.
  3. He compromised with Ahab and his two sons, Ahaziah and Jehoram.
  4. He ruled for twenty-five years (873-848 B.C.).

E. Joram (2 Ki. 8:26-29; 2 Chron. 21:1-20).
  1. He married Athaliah, daughter of Jezebel and Ahab.
  2. He began his reign by murdering his six brothers.
  3. He received a posthumous message from Elijah predicting judgment upon him because of his wicked and murderous reign.
  4. He was attacked and defeated by the Philistines and Arabians.
  5. He died of a horrible disease and was unmourned at the funeral.
  6. He ruled for eight years (853-845 B.C.).

F. Ahaziah (2 Ki. 8:24—9:29; 2 Chron. 22:1-9).
  1. He was killed by Jehu (tenth northern king)
  2. He ruled for one year (841 B.C.).

G. Athaliah (2 Ki. 11:1-20; 2 Chron. 22:1—23:21).
  1. She was the mother of the slain Ahaziah.
  2. At his death she slaughtered all his children except one who was hidden from her.
  3. She herself was later executed.
  4. She ruled for six years (841-835 B.C.).

H. Joash (2 Ki. 11:1—12:21; 2 Chron. 22:10—24:27).
  1. He was the surviving heir of Athaliah's bloodbath.
  2. For awhile he lived for God but later became a cruel leader.
  3. He sanctioned the stoning of Zechariah, the godly Jewish high priest who had rebuked Judah's sin and called for national repentance.
  4. He was executed by his own palace guard.
  5. He ruled for forty years (835-795 B.C.).

I. Amaziah (2 Ki. 14:1-20; 2 Chron. 25:1-28).
  1. He was a good king for awhile, and executed the men who had assassinated his father, Joash. But he did not kill their children, obeying the Mosaic law which said the sons

were not to be killed for the sins of their fathers (Deut. 24:16; Ezek. 18:4, 20). (See 2 Chron. 25:1-4; 2 Ki. 12:21; 14:1-6).

2. Amaziah then organized the army of Judah and found he had an army of 300,000. He then hired 100,000 experienced mercenary soldiers from Israel for $200,000 to help him fight against Edom (2 Chron. 25:5, 6).

3. He was warned against this by a prophet. The king reluctantly sent these mercenaries home, bitterly resenting the lost money he had paid them. But the prophet reassured him, "The Lord is able to give thee much more than this" (2 Chron. 25:9). Here is a precious spiritual gem that should be carefully considered whenever God requires us to give up our time, talent, treasure, or anything close and precious to us. See Jesus' stirring words to Peter in Matthew 19:27-29.

4. The Israelite troops returned home, also angry and frustrated. On the way they raided several cities of Judah and killed 3000 people (2 Chron. 25:13).

5. Amaziah went into battle with only his own troops and soundly defeated Edom, killing 20,000 enemy soldiers (26:11). But the foolish king brought back with him some Edomite idols and began worshiping them. God warned the king, through a prophet, of his divine anger. Amaziah refused to listen and curtly dismissed him, but not before the king's doom was predicted (25:14-16).

6. The overconfident Amaziah then declared war on northern king Jehoash, for the disgraceful action of the returning Israelite mercenaries (25:17). Northern king Jehoash responded to Amaziah's challenge by relating the second (and final) Old Testament fable. (For the first one, see Jdg. 9:8-15.) Note the language of this fable:

> "The thistle that was in Lebanon sent to the cedar that was in Lebanon, saying, Give thy daughter to my son to wife: and there passed by a wild beast that was in Lebanon, and trode down the thistle" (2 Chron. 25:18).

7. Jehoash was at this point warning Amaziah not to let his Edomite victory blind him to reality but to withdraw his arrogant declaration of war. But the plea fell on deaf ears.

Amaziah was soundly defeated by Jehoash at Beth-shemesh and was led as a common prisoner back to his own capital in Jerusalem. Upon arriving, Jehoash dismantled 200 yards of the city walls to effect an impressive victory celebration. He then carried off all the treasures of the Temple and palace. Finally the northern king left, taking with him many hostages (2 Chron. 25:21-24).

8. He ruled for twenty-nine years (796-767 B.C.).

J. Uzziah (2 Ki. 15:1-7; 2 Chron. 26:1-23).
   1. He was a mighty warrior and builder.
   2. He attempted to intrude into the office of the priest.
   3. He was punished for this sin by leprosy.
   4. He ruled for fifty-two years (792-740 B.C.).

## SOUTHERN RULERS

### 6. Ahaziah
DATES **841**   DURATION **1 YEAR**
SCRIPTURE **2 KINGS 8:24—9:29;**
**2 CHRONICLES 22:1-9**

1. He was the son of Joram and Athaliah.
2. He was killed by Jehu (tenth northern king)

### 7. Athaliah
DATES **841-835**   DURATION **6 YEARS**
SCRIPTURE **2 KINGS 11:1-20;**
**2 CHRONICLES 22:1—23:21**

1. At the death of Ahaziah, her son, she took over the throne of Judah, slaughtering all the royal seed but one (Joash) who was hidden from her.
2. After a rule of six years, she herself was executed.

### 8. Joash
DATES **835-795**   DURATION **40 YEARS**
SCRIPTURE **2 KINGS 11:1—12:21;**
**2 CHRONICLES 22:10—24:27**

1. He alone had survived Athaliah's bloody purge.
2. For awhile he lived for God, but later became a cruel tyrant.
3. He sanctioned the stoning of Judah's own high priest, Zechariah, who had fearlessly rebuked the sin among the people.
4. He was executed by his own palace guard.

### 9. Amaziah
DATES **796-767**   DURATION **29 YEARS**
SCRIPTURE **2 KINGS 14:1-20;**
**2 CHRONICLES 25:1-28**

1. He was a good king for awhile, executing the killers of his father, Joash.
2. He was rebuked by a prophet for hiring some mercenary Israeli soldiers to help him fight against Edom.
3. He reluctantly dismissed these paid soldiers and, with God's help, defeated Edom with his own soldiers.
4. He foolishly brought back some of the Edomite gods for worshiping purposes.
5. The reckless king then declared war on northern Israel and was soundly defeated.

### 10. Uzziah
DATES **792-740**   DURATION **52 YEARS**
SCRIPTURE **2 KINGS 15:1-7;**
**2 CHRONICLES 26:1-23**

LEPER

1. He was a mighty warrior and builder.
2. He attempted, however, to intrude into the office of the priesthood and was punished for this by leprosy.

### 11. Jotham
DATES **750-736**   DURATION **16 YEARS**
SCRIPTURE **2 KINGS 15:32-38;**
**2 CHRONICLES 27:1-9**

1. He was a good king.
2. He built the upper gate of the Temple and erected fortresses and towers.
3. He defeated his enemies and received huge annual tribute from them.

## SOUTHERN RULERS

### 12. Ahaz
DATES **735-719**   DURATION **16 YEARS**
SCRIPTURE **2 KINGS 16:1-20;**
                      **2 CHRONICLES 28:1-27**

1. He was perhaps the second worst king of Judah.
2. He sacrificed his own children to devil gods.
3. He was the first person to hear about the virgin birth. (See Isa. 7:1-25.)
4. He ordered the construction of a pagan Assyrian altar and placed it in the Temple to appease Tiglath-Pileser.

### 13. Hezekiah
DATES **716-687**   DURATION **29 YEARS**
SCRIPTURE **2 KINGS 18:1—20:21;**
                      **2 CHRONICLES 29:1—32:33**

1. He was Judah's second best king and the richest of all.
2. He repaired the Temple, organized an orchestral group, and appointed a Levitical singing choir.
3. He carried out the greatest Passover celebration since Solomon.
4. He saw the death angel defeat the Assyrian enemies which had surrounded Jerusalem.
5. He was supernaturally healed of a terminal disease and given an additional fifteen years to live.
6. He added fifteen Psalms to the Old Testament Canon.
7. He foolishly showed the wealth of Judah to some nosy Babylonian ambassadors.

### 14. Manasseh
DATES **697-642**   DURATION **55 YEARS**
SCRIPTURE **2 KINGS 21:1-18;**
                      **2 CHRONICLES 33:1-20**

1. He ruled longer than any other king of north or south.
2. He was the most wicked king of all.
3. He experienced the new birth while in an enemy prison.

### 15. Amon
DATES **643-641**   DURATION **2 YEARS**
SCRIPTURE **2 KINGS 21:19-26;**
                      **2 CHRONICLES 33:21-25**

1. He was wicked like his father, Manasseh, but did not repent as did his father.
2. He was executed by his own household servants.

### 16. Josiah
DATES **641-610**   DURATION **31 YEARS**
SCRIPTURE **2 KINGS 22:1—23:30;**
                      **2 CHRONICLES 34:1—35:27**

1. He was the godliest king since David.
2. He was Judah's last godly king.
3. The book of Moses was accidentally discovered among the debris in the Temple at the beginning of his reign.
4. He used this to lead Judah in a great revival.
5. He also conducted a larger Passover celebration than that of Hezekiah his great-grandfather.
6. He fulfilled a three-hundred-year-old prophecy. Compare 1 Kings 13:1, 2 with 2 Kings 23:15.
7. He was killed in a battle with the Egyptians.

K. Jotham (2 Ki. 15:32-38; 2 Chron. 27:1-9).
  1. He was a good king (2 Chron. 27:6).
  2. He built the upper gate of the Temple and erected fortresses and towers.
  3. He defeated the Ammonites and received a huge annual tribute of silver and wheat from them.
  4. He ruled for sixteen years (750-732 B.C.).
L. Ahaz (2 Ki. 16:1-20; 2 Chron. 28:1-27).
  1. He was perhaps the second worst king of Judah.
  2. He sacrificed his own children to devilish gods.
  3. He was the first person to hear about the virgin birth.
  4. He ruled sixteen years (732-716 B.C.).
M. Hezekiah (2 Ki. 18:1—20:21; 2 Chron. 29:1—32:33).
  1. He was the second best king of Judah.
  2. He was also the richest of all.
  3. He organized the greatest Passover celebration since the days of Solomon.
  4. He saw the death angel defeat the Assyrian enemies which had surrounded Jerusalem.
  5. He was supernaturally healed and given an additional fifteen years to live.
  6. He ruled for twenty-nine years (716-687).
N. Manasseh (2 Ki. 21:1-18; 2 Chron. 33:1-20).
  1. He ruled longer than any northern or southern king.
  2. He was the worst of all the kings.
  3. He experienced the new birth prior to his death.
  4. He ruled fifty-five years (697-642 B.C.).
O. Amon (2 Ki. 21:19-26; 2 Chron. 33:21-25).
  1. He was, like his father Manasseh, a wicked sinner.
  2. He was, unlike his father Manasseh, unrepentant.
  3. He was executed by his own household servants.
  4. He ruled two years (643-641 B.C.).
P. Josiah (2 Ki. 22:1—23:30; 2 Chron. 34:1—35:27).
  1. He was the best king since David.
  2. The book of Moses was discovered in the Temple during his reign.
  3. He led his people in a great revival.
  4. He was the last good king of Judah.
  5. He was killed in a battle with the Egyptians.
  6. He ruled for thirty-one years (641-610 B.C.).
Q. Jehoahaz (2 Ki. 23:31-33; 2 Chron. 36:1-4).
  1. This middle son of Josiah had both a sinful (2 Ki. 23:32) and short-lived (2 Ki. 23:30, 31) reign. He was deposed by Pharaoh Necho (who had previously killed his father, Josiah, in battle), after but ninety days on the throne (2 Ki. 23:33). Necho then leveled a tax against Judah totaling $230,000. Jehoahaz was eventually carried into Egypt where he died in captivity (2 Ki. 23:34).
  2. Jehoahaz's younger brother, Eliakim (renamed Jehoiakim by Necho), was chosen by the Egyptian king to succeed him on the throne of Judah (2 Ki. 23:34). Things were now at rock bottom when the devil's man could pick the king over the Lord's people!
  3. He ruled for three months (609 B.C.).

R. Jehoiakim (2 Ki. 23:34—24:5; 2 Chron. 36:5-7).
1. He was the brother of Jehoahaz.
2. He was probably Judah's third worst king.
3. He persecuted Jeremiah the prophet.
4. He experienced the first of Nebuchadnezzar's fearsome "visits" to Jerusalem.
5. During this time Daniel and other Hebrew young people were taken to Babylon by Nebuchadnezzar.
6. He died, and as Jeremiah had predicted, received the burial of an ass.
7. He ruled for eleven years (609-598).

S. Jehoiachin (2 Ki. 24:6-16; 2 Chron. 36:8-10).
1. He was the son of Jehoiakim, and grandson of Josiah. Jehoiachin was also called Coniah (Jer. 22:24, 28; 37:1).
2. He began ruling at eighteen (2 Ki. 24:8). Note: There is a textual problem here, for 2 Chronicles 36:9 informs us he was eight years old.
3. He was an evil king (2 Ki. 24:9). Because of this:
   a. Both Ezekiel (19:5-9) and Jeremiah (22:24-26) predicted that he would be carried off into the Babylonian captivity.
   b. He was to be regarded as childless, as none of his children would ever sit upon the throne of David or rule in Judah.
   The *New Scofield Bible* observes:
   "This declaration does not mean that he would have no children, for in 1 Chron. 3:17, 18, some are named (Cf. Mt. 1:12). By divine judgment, this king was to be written childless, i.e., no physical descendant would occupy a place in the list of Israel's kings. Consequently, if our Lord Jesus, who is to occupy David's throne (Lk. 1:32, 33), had been begotten by Mary's husband, Joseph, who was of the line of Jeconiah (Mt. 1:12, 16), it would have contradicted this divine prediction. Christ's dynastic right to the throne came through his foster father, Joseph, from Jeconiah, but the physical descent of Jesus from David came through Mary, whose genealogy is traced to David through Nathan, rather than through Solomon." (Compare Lk. 3:31 with Mt. 1:17.) (pp. 793, 794)
4. Jehoiachin was captured during the eighth year of Nebuchadnezzar's reign (2 Ki. 24:12) and carried into Babylon, along with 10,000 other Jewish captives (Jer. 24:1; 29; 2 Ki. 24:14, 15). Ezekiel was also carried away at this time.
5. He then appointed Zedekiah (Jehoiachin's great uncle) to occupy the throne of Judea (2 Ki. 24:17).
6. Jehoiachin was placed in a Babylonian prison, where he remained for thirty-six years, until the death of Nebuchadnezzar. He was then released by the new Babylonian monarch, Evil-Merodach, who not only freed him, but gave him a seat at the king's own table and an allowance for his support (2 Ki. 25:27-30; Jer. 52:31-34).
7. He ruled for three months (598 B.C.).

## SOUTHERN RULERS

## 17. Jehoahaz
DATES **609**  DURATION **3 MONTHS**
SCRIPTURE **2 KINGS 23:31-33;**
**2 CHRONICLES 36:1-4**
1. He was the middle son of Josiah.
2. He was deposed after only ninety days by the Pharaoh who had killed his father.
3. He was carried into Egyptian captivity where he eventually died.

## 18. Jehoiakim
DATES **609-598**  DURATION **11 YEARS**
SCRIPTURE **2 KINGS 23:34—24:5;**
**2 CHRONICLES 36:5-7**
1. He was the oldest brother of Jehoahaz.
2. He was put on the throne by the Egyptian Pharaoh.
3. He was later made vassal by Nebuchadnezzar after the Babylonians had defeated the Egyptians.
4. He was totally materialistic and self-centered. He can be considered Judah's third worst king.
5. He murdered the innocent and often persecuted Jeremiah.
6. He burned a copy of a part of God's Word. (See Jer. 36:22-32.)
7. He experienced the first of three fearful "visits" Nebuchadnezzar made to the city of Jerusalem.
8. During this visit (606 B.C.) Daniel and other Hebrew young people were carried off into captivity.
9. At his death he received the burial of an ass, as Jeremiah had predicted.

## 19. Jehoiachin
DATES **598**  DURATION **3 MONTHS**
SCRIPTURE **2 KINGS 24:6-16;**
**2 CHRONICLES 36:8-10**
1. He was the son of Jehoiakim and grandson of Josiah.
2. He incurred a curse from God, stating that his sons would not sit upon Judah's throne.
3. Both Ezekiel (19:5-9) and Jeremiah (22:24-26) predicted he would be carried off into Babylonian captivity.
4. This happened during Nebuchadnezzar's second "visit" (597) to Jerusalem. Ezekiel was also carried away at this time.
5. He eventually died in Babylon.

## 20. Zedekiah
DATES **597-586**  DURATION **11 YEARS**
SCRIPTURE **2 KINGS 24:17—25:30;**
**2 CHRONICLES 36:11-21**
1. He was the youngest son of Josiah and uncle to Jehoiachin.
2. Jeremiah was persecuted during his reign.
3. He rebelled against Babylon along with Egypt.
4. He was captured, blinded, and carried off into Babylonian captivity by Nebuchadnezzar.
5. Jerusalem was burned to the ground and the Temple destroyed at this time.

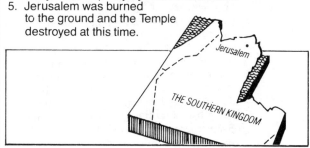

T. Zedekiah (2 Ki. 24:17—25:30; 2 Chron. 36:11-21).
   1. He was the youngest son of Josiah.
   2. He rebelled against Nebuchadnezzar. For this he was blinded and carried off as a captive to Babylon.
   3. He ruled for eleven years (597-586 B.C.).

*The Spotlight, Rifle Approach:*

The Chaotic Kingdom Stage can be best summarized by examining in some detail the lives of twenty individuals. This number does not include the writing prophets such as Jonah, whose life will be considered along with his book. Of the twenty, six are northern rulers, twelve are southern rulers, and two are prophets. These are: Jeroboam, Omri, Ahab, Jehu, Jeroboam II, Hoshea (northern), Rehoboam, Asa, Jehoshaphat, Athaliah, Joash, Uzziah, Ahaz, Hezekiah, Manasseh, Josiah, Jehoiakim, Zedekiah (southern), Elijah and Elisha (prophets).

*The important northern rulers:*

A. Jeroboam (first king). He began in 930 B.C. and ruled for twenty-two years.
   To properly consider the reign of Jeroboam, it is necessary to know something of the circumstances which put him into power. It all began with Solomon's arrogant young son named Rehoboam.
   1. Rehoboam comes to Shechem to be crowned king over all Israel (1 Ki. 12:1; 2 Chron. 10:1).
   2. He is issued an ultimatum by a delegation led by Jeroboam (who had returned from Egyptian exile after Solomon's death) which stated simply that the people demanded a better life under him than they had known under Solomon (1 Ki. 12:3, 4; 2 Chron. 10:2-4).
   3. Rehoboam asks for a three-day recess to consider their demands. During this period he consults with his arrogant young friends and, favoring their advice over the older and wiser men, retorts to waiting Israel at the end of the three-day period:
      "My Father made your yoke heavy, and I will add to your yoke: my Father also chastised you with whips, but I will chastise you with scorpions" (1 Ki. 12:14).
   4. Upon hearing this, ten of the twelve tribes heed Jeroboam's cry to strike their tents, and Israel's sorrowful secession story has begun (1 Ki. 12:16).
   5. Rehoboam's tax collector is stoned to death and the frightened king runs for his life to Jerusalem (12:21, 22). (Rehoboam would continually disobey this command throughout his reign; see 1 Ki. 15:6.)
   6. Jeroboam, the new leader of the ten-tribe confederation, is immediately faced with a serious threat. Three times a year, as commanded by God (see Lev. 23; Ex. 23:17), the entire nation is to go to Jerusalem and worship God. Jeroboam knows the priests will doubtless use these opportunities to bring all Israel back into the fold of Rehoboam. Jeroboam therefore attempts to resolve all this by adopting a fourfold plan.
      a. He changes the religious symbols of Israel. Instead of the two golden cherubims above the ark, he substitutes two golden calves. Here he could point to the action of the first high priest Aaron for a historical example. (In fact, he stole Aaron's text in introducing these calves to Israel. Compare Ex. 32:4 with 1 Ki. 12:28.)
      b. He changes the religious worship center from Jerusalem to Bethel and Dan. This is in direct disobedience to God's clear command to him. (See 1 Ki. 11:36.)
      c. He degrades the Levitical priesthood, by making "priests of the lowest of the people, which were not of the sons of Levi" (12:31). Because of this, the vast majority of priests and Levites flee southward to Judah, leaving behind them a situation of near-total apostasy. (See 2 Chron. 11:13-17.) (This explains the tragic fact that not one of the nineteen Israelite kings beginning with Jeroboam and ending with Hoshea—over a period of approximately 210 years—turned his heart and kingdom to God!)
      d. He changes the religious calendar, from October to November. According to Leviticus 23, Israel was to observe six main yearly feasts, beginning in April and ending in October. These six feasts, three of which would fall in October, foreshadowed the Cross (unleavened bread), the resurrection (firstfruits), Pentecost (feast of fifty days), the rapture (feast of trumpets), the tribulation (day of atonement), and the millennium (feast of tabernacles). It is evident, however, that Jeroboam has little use for any of this, for we are told that he devises this November feast after his own heart. (See 12:33.)
   7. Jeroboam visits the altar in Bethel to burn incense. He now becomes the second of three Israelite kings who dared to take upon themselves the office of a priest also. All three were severely punished. The other two were:
      a. Saul (1 Sam. 13:9-14)
      b. Uzziah (2 Chron. 26:16-21)
   8. For his idolatry, Jeroboam is prophesied against and punished by a man of God.
      a. The prophecy. That years later a king of Judah named Josiah would totally destroy Jeroboam's false religion, even burning the bones of his dead priests upon the very altar where Jeroboam stood sacrificing. This amazing prophecy was fulfilled exactly some 300 years later. (Compare 1 Ki. 13:2 with 2 Ki. 23:15, 16.)
      b. The punishment. Jeroboam's altar was destroyed and his arm was paralyzed, both supernaturally from God (1 Ki. 13:3-6). The prophet then prayed and the king's hand was restored.
   9. On his route home, the prophet foolishly heeds the words of a lying old prophet from Bethel, and thus forfeits his life for disobeying God.

a. God had told him to return home immediately.

b. The old Bethel prophet told him God had changed his mind and desired him to stay and eat in Bethel.

c. When he finally left for home he was attacked and killed by a lion.

10. Soon after this sad event, Jeroboam's son, Abijah, becomes very ill. Ahijah the prophet sadly relates God's message to Jeroboam's wife (who had attempted to disguise herself), which is that because of his extreme wickedness he will suffer terrible judgment (14:10-14). All this, of course, did take place. The child soon died (14:17) and a few years later Nadab, Jeroboam's son who succeeded him, was murdered along with all his relatives by a rebel named Baasha, who took over his throne (15:29). At this time God also issued the first chilling warning of the future Assyrian captivity, which occurred some 200 years later (14:15).

11. God strikes Jeroboam with a plague and he dies, after a wicked reign of twenty-two years. No less than twenty-one times it is recorded that he "made Israel to sin." He is succeeded by his son Nadab (1 Ki. 14:20; 2 Chron. 13:20). Nadab was murdered by a rebel named Baasha, after a reign of only two years. He thus became the first of six northern kings to be assassinated. These are: (2) Elah, (3) Jehoram, (4) Zechariah, (5) Shallum, and (6) Pekahiah. In killing him and his relatives, Baasha unknowingly fulfills the prophecy given to Jeroboam's wife by Ahijah the prophet. (Compare 1 Ki. 14:14 with 15:29.)

B. Omri (sixth king).
1. He began in 885 B.C. and reigned for twelve years.
2. Omri made the city of Samaria the new northern capital (1 Ki. 16:24).
3. He was the most wicked king of the north up to that time (16:25).

C. Ahab (seventh king).
1. He began in 874 and reigned for twenty-two years.
2. Ahab marries Jezebel and builds a temple to Baal in Samaria (1 Ki. 16:31, 32).
3. He was more wicked than his father Omri (16:33). (See also 21:25, 26.)
4. At the beginning of his reign a 500-year-old prophecy is fulfilled concerning the rebuilding of Jericho (16:34; compare with Josh. 6:26).
5. He is confronted by Elijah and warned that, due to his sin and Israel's wickedness, a three-and-a-half-year famine will occur (1 Ki. 17:1; Jas. 5:17).
6. Ahab sees his priests of Baal defeated and destroyed by Elijah on Mt. Carmel (18:40).
7. He is allowed by God to defeat the arrogant Syrians on two occasions to prove a point, the point being that Jehovah is Lord over all (20:23, 28).

At this time King Ben-hadad of Syria declares war on Ahab, who at first attempts to appease with a bribe to the greedy Syrian Monarch, but when this fails, Ahab is determined to fight (1 Ki. 20:1-11). A nameless prophet (perhaps Elijah) reassures Ahab of victory over the Syrians, which victory soon takes place (20:13-19). After their defeat, the Syrians conclude it was due to a geographical factor, as the battle had taken place on hilly ground, thus giving the Israeli troops a tremendous advantage. The Syrians believed that the God of Israel was a hill God. Plans were then made to fight again, but this time they would meet Israel on the plains. They could not have been more mistaken. Israel's God is indeed the God of the hills, but he is also:
a. the God of the valley (Ex. 17:8-13; 1 Sam. 17:3, 49)
b. the God of the mountain (1 Ki. 18:19, 40)
c. the God of the plain (Jdg. 11:33)
d. the God of the water (Ex. 14:27, 28)
e. the God of the fire (Dan. 3:19-26)

The Syrians attack and are again soundly defeated, losing 127,000 infantrymen. The victorious Ahab disobeys God's command and spares Ben-hadad's life (as Saul had once done with Agag, 1 Sam. 15:31-33). The prophet of God then announces that because Ahab has done this, the Lord will require his life for Ben-hadad's life (1 Ki. 20:32-43). This will happen some three years later (see 1 Ki. 22:29-37).

8. Ahab attempts unsuccessfully to purchase a choice vineyard near his palace owned by a man from Jezreel named Naboth. Years back Samuel had warned against land grabbing by Israel's kings. (See 1 Sam. 8:14.) Even had Naboth wanted to sell his vineyard, the Levitical law would have forbidden him. (See Lev. 25:23; Num. 36:7; Ezek. 46:18.)

Ahab returns home in a sullen mood. Jezebel is told of Naboth's refusal and informs her pouting potentate to cheer up, as he will soon possess that vineyard. She then writes letters in Ahab's name, seals them with his seal, and addresses them to the civic leaders of Jezreel where Naboth lives. She commands them to call the citizens together for prayer and fasting. They are then to summon Naboth and pay two lying witnesses to accuse him of cursing God and the king. He then is to be taken out and murdered. This horrible order is carried out to the letter (1 Ki. 21:4-14). His sons are also stoned. (See 2 Ki. 9:26.) Wicked Jezebel, herself a rabid worshiper of Baal, now cleverly appeals to the Mosaic law in obtaining two witnesses against the accused (Lev. 24:17).

This mock trial would have its ultimate counterpart some nine centuries later on an early Friday morning in April as the mighty Creator is judged by his miserable creatures. (See Mt. 26:59-68.) Jezebel is told the news, and Ahab gleefully goes down to the vineyard to claim it (1 Ki. 21:15, 16). God now orders Elijah to confront Ahab in Naboth's vineyard and pronounces heaven's curse upon him and his household. An angry and doubtless fearful Ahab then hears Elijah's stern words of judgment (21:19, 21-24). All this literally came true.

a. The dogs did lick Ahab's blood, as they had done with Naboth's blood (1 Ki. 22:38).

b. His descendants were destroyed. Ahaziah, his oldest son, died in a fall (2 Ki. 1:17), and Jehoram, his youngest son, was murdered by Jehu (2 Ki. 9:24), and his body thrown in the same field where Naboth was buried.

c. His wicked wife Jezebel was eaten by the wild dogs of Jezreel (2 Ki. 9:30-36).

Upon hearing these terrible prophecies, Ahab humbles himself, and God spares him from at least seeing his sons killed. But his repentance is only temporary and shallow (1 Ki. 21:27-29).

9. At this time Ahab desires the reigning Judean monarch of the southern kingdom (whose name was Hezekiah) to join with him in fighting against Syrian king Ben-hadad, who has betrayed a three-year convenant (1 Ki. 22:1), and is still stationing Syrian troops at Ramoth-gilead. Had Ahab executed him as God had commanded some time back, this serious situation would not have arisen. Jehoshaphat had nothing materially to gain, and much morally to lose. His response is tragic:

"I am as thou art, my people as thy people, my horses as thy horses" (1 Ki. 22:4). Jehoshaphat evidently has second thoughts concerning this alliance right away, for he desires Ahab to, "Enquire, I pray thee, at the word of the Lord today" (2 Chron. 18:4).

Ahab immediately summons 400 prophets, all of which were in his pay, and each possessing a spineless back and a lying tongue. They arrive and, to a man, loudly predict victory (2 Chron. 18:5, 6). These were the kind of men Jeremiah would later speak about. (See Jer. 23:21.) Jehoshaphat, still bothered with doubts, asks if there is any other prophet around. Ahab bitterly relates that, yes, "There is yet one man, Micaiah the son of Imlah, by whom we may enquire of the Lord: but I hate him; for he doth not prophesy good concerning me, but evil" (1 Ki. 22:8). Perhaps the greatest compliment that could be paid to Micaiah is that he was hated by Ahab. The wicked king hated this prophet the way a foolish man might despise the doctor who told him he had cancer!

At the gentle urging of the southern king, Ahab reluctantly sends for the imprisoned Micaiah, but privately instructs the messenger to warn his prison prophet not to contradict the majority report. Micaiah listens to the message and retorts: "As the Lord liveth, what the Lord saith unto me, that will I speak" (1 Ki. 22:14).

As the two kings await the arrival of Micaiah, Zedekiah, the puppy-dog prophet spokesman for the rest, performs a few little tricks for his master Ahab. He grabs some horns and prances around, attempting to demonstrate Ahab's victory over the Syrians. He may have learned this little act by taking Deuteronomy 33:17 completely out of context. Finally Micaiah stands before Ahab, and no doubt with a twinkle in his eye, and with sarcasm in his voice, imitates the other prophets: "Go, and prosper: for the Lord shall deliver it into the hand of the king" (1 Ki. 22:15). The dripping sarcasm must have been painfully evident to both, for Ahab turns livid with rage and screams out: "How many times shall I adjure thee that thou tell me nothing but that which is true in the name of the Lord?" (22:16). Ahab wanted this about as much as a guilty criminal desires to hear the judge pronounce sentence upon him. The words were doubtless said to impress Jehoshaphat.

The twinkle from Micaiah's eye suddenly disappears and the scorn turns to sobering words of judgment as he says: "I saw all Israel scattered upon the hills, as sheep that have not a shepherd: and the Lord said, These have no master: let them return every man to his house in peace" (22:17).

Upon hearing this, Ahab explodes again, saying to Jehoshaphat: "Did I not tell thee that he would prophesy no good concerning me, but evil?" (22:18).

Micaiah continues however, but stating that God has allowed a lying spirit to deceive Ahab's prophets, in order to kill the wicked king in battle. As he finishes this true prophecy, he is slapped by Zedekiah, Ahab's house pet. This stinging insult would later be experienced by both our Lord (Jn. 18:22) and the Apostle Paul (Acts 23:2). Ahab orders Micaiah back to prison and puts him on a diet of bread and water until he returns home safely from the battle. As he leaves, Micaiah states that if indeed Ahab returns safely, it will mean God has not spoken through him (1 Ki. 22:28).

10. Ahab and Jehoshaphat hurriedly proceed to Ramoth-gilead. On the eve of the battle, Ahab suggests that Jehoshaphat wear his royal robes, but that he, Ahab, put on the garment of an infantry soldier. The southern king agrees. Sometimes, it would seem, Jehoshaphat can be downright stupid (1 Ki. 22:29, 30).

Jehoshaphat is immediately spotted in battle and mistaken by the Syrians for Ahab. The foolish and frightened Judean king cries out to God for deliverance, and is unharmed by the Syrians when they realize he is not Ahab (1 Ki. 22:31-33; 2 Chron. 18:30-32). One of the Syrian soldiers, however, shoots an arrow haphazardly into the air at the Israeli troops and it strikes the disguised Ahab at the openings where the lower armor and the breastplate meet. The wound is a mortal one. At his gasping order, Ahab is propped up in his chariot and hurriedly driven home. Just as the sun sinks in the western skies, he dies (1 Ki. 22:34-37; 2 Chron. 18:33, 34). Ahab is buried in Samaria and his blood-caked chariot is taken down to be cleaned at a nearby pool, where it is licked by the dogs, just as Elijah predicted (1 Ki. 22:38, 39). Ahab is succeeded by his oldest son, Ahaziah, who continues in the evil ways of his father (1 Ki. 22:52, 53).

D. Jehu (tenth king).
 1. He began in 841 B.C. and reigned for twenty-eight years.
 2. Elijah had been commanded to anoint Jehu as king (1 Ki. 19:16), but for some reason had not done so. Therefore, Elisha anoints him, using the services of a young preacher boy (2 Ki. 9:1).
 3. Jehu becomes notorious for his chariot riding (9:20) and bloodletting. He would execute:
  a. the Judean king, Ahaziah, grandson of Jehoshaphat (9:27)
  b. the northern king, Jehoram, who was in power at the time (9:24)
  c. Jezebel (9:30-37)
  d. Ahab's seventy sons (10:1, 11)
  e. forty-two royal princes of Judah (10:14)
  f. the Baal worshipers (10:25)

God orders him to execute the dynasty of Ahab, including Jezebel, whom the dogs would later eat (2 Ki. 9:1-10), but does not sanction these other assassinations. Let us now consider his bloody activities in brief manner.

Upon being anointed, Jehu mounts his chariot and drives furiously toward Jezebel to execute King Jehoram, Ahab's youngest son, who was at this time recovering from some wounds he had received in a recent battle. On that fateful day he had received a visitor, the Judean king, Ahaziah, who was Jehoshaphat's grandson, and Jehoram's nephew. It is doubtful in all history that two conferring heads of state have had more wicked mothers than did this pair. Jehoram's mother was Jezebel, and Ahaziah's mother was Athaliah.

Jehu is spotted while still on the valley road, and both Jehoram and Ahaziah, fearing an impending rebellion, ride out to meet Jehu, hoping to settle any demands in a peaceful manner. Jehu spurns Jehoram's pleas and executes both uncle and nephew kings by a shower of deadly arrows. Jehoram's lifeless body is thrown into the field of Naboth, where Ahab (the dead king's father) had once dumped Naboth himself. The birds were indeed coming home to roost (2 Ki. 9:25-29).

Jehu enters Jezreel, spots the painted hag, Jezebel, taunting him from an upstairs window, and orders her cast down. She is immediately thrown to her death and soon eaten by the wild city dogs who leave only her skull, feet, and hands. Thus Elijah's sober

prophecy to Ahab is literally fulfilled. (Compare 1 Ki. 21:23 with 2 Ki. 9:30-36.)

Jehu then writes a letter to the city council of Samaria, demanding the heads (literally) of the seventy sons of Ahab who were all living in that city. The frightened officials immediately obey this bloody order, pack the separated heads into baskets, and deliver this gory mass to Jehu in Jezreel (10:11-14).

Jehu continues his blood purging by slaying every descendant and friend of Ahab, including forty-two kinsmen of Ahaziah who have just arrived in Jezreel to visit Jezebel (10:11-14). The brutal charioteer then orders all the priests of Baal to attend a special religious convention in Jezreel, pretending that he too has become a Baal worshiper. However, secret plans are laid to slaughter the whole bunch once they can be herded into a central meeting place.

Eventually the house of Baal in Jezreel is packed with pagan priests. It is then that Jehu gives the order and the false Phoenician god stands helplessly by while his worshipers are systematically slaughtered. Jehu then burns their altar, wrecks the temple, and converts it into a public toilet. Because of his obedience to God concerning the destruction of Ahab's dynasty, Jehu is promised a continuation of his own dynasty up through the fourth generation (2 Ki. 10:30).
 4. In spite of his reforms, Jehu continues worshiping the golden calves set up by Jeroboam (10:29-31), and dies an unsaved king.

E. Jeroboam II (thirteenth king).
 1. He began in 793 and reigned forty-one years.
 2. Jeroboam was the most powerful of all the northern kings.
 3. He restored much of Israel's land which previously had been taken by the Syrians (2 Ki. 3:5; 14:25-27).
 4. This was prophesied by Jonah, who lived during the reign of Jeroboam II (14:25).

F. Hoshea (nineteenth king).
 1. He began in 732 and reigned nine years.
 2. After becoming a vassal to the Assyrian king, Shalmaneser, Hoshea joined with Egypt in rebelling against that empire.
 3. For this he was imprisoned by Shalmaneser (2 Ki. 17:4, 5).
 4. It was at this time that Samaria fell and the citizens of the northern kingdom were carried away into Assyrian captivity (2 Ki. 17:6).

*The important southern rulers:*
A. Rehoboam (first king).
 1. He began in 930 B.C. and reigned seventeen years.
 2. His cruel and tactless answer to the demands of some of Israel's leaders help trigger the tragic civil war (1 Ki. 12:1-16).
 3. He is unknowingly helped by Jeroboam who has driven the faithful Levite priests from the north to Jerusalem. These godly men were responsible in the main for Judah's continuation a century after Assyria had captured the northern kingdom (2 Chron. 11:16, 17).

4. Rehoboam's failure doubtless began by his polygamous actions, which involved eighteen wives and sixty concubines; they bore him twenty-eight sons and sixty daughters. Another factor in his downfall was his favorite wife, whose name was Maachah. This woman, the daughter of Absalom, apparently exercised an evil influence upon both Rehoboam and Abijam, their son, who succeeded his father. Finally, her wicked power was curbed by her own grandson, King Asa, who deposed her for idol-worshiping (2 Chron. 11:18-23; 12:1, 14; 2 Ki. 15:13). As his power grew, so his evil increased. Judah built shrines and obelisks and idols on every high hill and under every green tree. In addition to all this, there was homosexuality throughout the land. This vile and perverted sexual crime had possibly been introduced to the inhabitants of Palestine by Canaan, grandson of Noah. (See Gen. 9:20-25.)

Now the people of Israel had allowed this sickness of the soul to degrade them also. In the New Testament the Apostle Paul lashes out against sodomy perhaps more severely than against any other single sin. (Read Rom. 1:18-32.)

5. During the fifth year of Rehoboam's reign, Judah is invaded by King Shishak of Egypt with a powerful force. Because of Rehoboam's wickedness, Jerusalem is now invaded by a foreign power for the first time in nearly 100 years. Shishak conquers the fortified cities of Judah and comes to Jerusalem. Shemaiah, the prophet, then leads Rehoboam and the frightened people in a revival. God thus spares Jerusalem, but allows the city to pay tribute to Shishak, that they might realize it is far better to serve their Heavenly King than an earthly one. Shishak plunders the Temple treasury, including the golden shields placed there by Solomon. Rehoboam then replaces them with bronze shields, symbolizing the rapidly deteriorating spiritual condition of Judah. Already the trace of Ichabod could be seen gathering over the southern kingdom (2 Chron. 12:2-12; 1 Sam. 4:21).

6. After a reign of seventeen years, Rehoboam dies and is succeeded by his son, Abijam (1 Ki. 14:31).

7. Abijam soon finds cause to do battle with his father's old enemy, Jeroboam. They meet in the field, but Abijam has only 400,000 troops, as opposed to Jeroboam's 800,000 Israeli soldiers. Just prior to the fighting, Abijam gives a long lecture to Jeroboam and his soldiers concerning the folly of rebelling against the house of David, and the wickedness of their golden calf worship. He contrasts all this to the true Temple worship still carried on in Jerusalem. Upon completing his message, however, Abijam discovers that Jeroboam has secretly outflanked him and they are surrounded. He immediately cries out to God for mercy and the priests blow their trumpets. God then turns the tide of battle their way and Jeroboam is dealt a severe defeat which costs him 500,000 men (2 Chron. 13:1-17).

8. In spite of his heaven-sent victory on the battlefield, Abijam degenerates into a wicked king (1 Ki. 15:3, 4). After a reign of three years, Abijam dies and is succeeded by his son Asa (1 Ki. 15:8).

B. Asa (third king).

1. He began in 911 B.C. and reigned forty-one years.

2. During the first ten years of his reign, the land was at peace. Asa used the time wisely.

   a. He led the people in a great revival (2 Chron. 14:2-5).

   b. He built up and fenced in the cities of Judah (14:6, 7).

3. This peace is suddenly shattered, however, when he is threatened with invasion by a million Ethiopian troops (14:9).

4. Hopelessly outnumbered, Asa cries out to God:

   "Lord, it is nothing with thee to help, whether with many, or with them who have no power: help us, O Lord our God; for we rest on thee, and in thy name we go against this multitude. O Lord, thou art our God; let not man prevail against thee" (14:11).

5. God graciously answers this prayer and personally smites the Ethiopians (14:12).

6. A thankful Asa returns home and continues his reforms (15:8-15).

   "And they entered into a covenant to seek the Lord God of their fathers with all their heart and with all their soul" (15:12).

7. The zealous king even deposes Maachah (his grandfather Rehoboam's wife) because of her idolatry (1 Ki. 15:13).

8. In the thirty-sixth year of Asa's reign, the northern king, Baasha, declares war on him and begins building a wall fortress at Ramah to control the road to Judah, thus hoping to cut off all trade to Jerusalem (2 Chron. 16:1). Instead of trusting God, as he did during the Ethiopian threat some years back, Asa bribes the Syrian king to ally with him against Israel (2 Chron. 16:2-6).

9. Asa is severely rebuked for this by the prophet Hanani and warned that he would be plagued with wars from that point on due to his faithlessness. He eloquently reminds the foolish king of past history (2 Chron. 16:8, 9).

   Hanani then says:

   "For the eyes of the Lord run to and fro throughout the whole earth, to show himself strong in the behalf of them whose heart is perfect toward him. Herein thou hast done foolishly: therefore, from henceforth thou shalt have wars" (16:9).

   Asa responds by throwing Hanani in prison (2 Chron. 16:10). This is a favorite but futile trick of sinful monarchs toward uncooperative preachers. Ahab had done it to Micaiah (2 Chron. 18:7), Zedekiah did it to Jeremiah (Jer. 32:3), and Herod did it to John the Baptist (Mt. 14:3). He then ended the good reign he began by oppressing the people. Two years prior to his death he became seriously diseased in his feet, but refused to take this problem to God. After a reign of forty-one years he died and was succeeded by his son Jehoshaphat (2 Chron. 16:10—17:1).

C. Jehoshaphat (fourth king).
1. He began in 873 and reigned twenty-five years.
2. He began by continuing the moral reforms and building projects his father Asa had started (2 Chron. 17:3-6).
3. During his third year in power he instituted a nationwide religious education program, sending out Bible teachers to all important Judean cities who lectured to the people from the Law of Moses (17:7-9).
4. He grew in power and accepted tribute from the Philistines (17:11).
5. In the latter years of his reign, however, he marred his testimony by compromising with three ungodly northern kings, Ahab and his two sons, Ahaziah and Jehoram.
   a. His matrimonial alliance with Ahab: He foolishly allowed his son Joram to marry Athaliah, the wicked daughter of Ahab and Jezebel (2 Chron. 18:1).
   b. His military alliance with Ahab against Syria (2 Chron. 18:2, 3).
   c. His trading alliance with Ahaziah, Ahab's oldest son (2 Chron. 20:35-37).
   d. His military alliance with Jehoram, Ahab's youngest son, against Moab (2 Ki. 3:6, 7).
6. Jehoshaphat returns home after the Syrian fiasco and is soundly rebuked for his foolishness and compromise by the prophet Jehu (2 Chron. 19:1-3).

   A chastened Jehoshaphat once again resumes his spiritual reforms, this time going out himself among the people, encouraging them to worship God, and appointing godly men to judge them. His admonition to these Jewish dispensers of justice is noteworthy indeed. (See 2 Chron. 19:6, 7.)
7. Jehoshaphat also appoints the high priest, Amariah, to act as a court of final appeal in religious matters, and Zebediah, a ruler of Judah, to determine all important civil cases. Here is another example of the "separation of church and state" principle often found in the Old Testament (as well as in the New Testament) (2 Chron. 19:11).
8. At this time the Moabites and their allies declare war upon Judah, and word reaches Jerusalem that a vast army is marching toward the Holy City. Jehoshaphat is badly shaken by this terrifying news and calls for a national time of fasting and praying. People from all across the nation flock to Jerusalem to join their king as he himself leads in public prayer beside the Temple. He prays:

"O Lord God of our fathers, art not thou God in heaven? And rulest not thou over all the kingdoms of the heathen? And in thine hand is there not power and might, so that none is able to withstand thee? O our God, wilt thou not judge them? for we have no might against this great company that cometh against us; neither know we what to do: but our eyes are upon thee" (2 Chron. 20:6, 12).

9. Suddenly the Spirit of God came upon a Levite named Jahaziel who proclaimed the following thrilling words:

   "Hearken ye, all Judah, and ye inhabitants of Jerusalem, and thou King Jehoshaphat, thus saith the Lord unto you, Be not afraid nor dismayed by reason of this great multitude; for the battle is not yours, but God's. Ye shall not need to fight in this battle: set yourselves, stand ye still, and see the salvation of the Lord with you, O Judah and Jerusalem. . . . Tomorrow go out against them: for the Lord will be with you" (2 Chron. 20:15, 17).

10. The king falls down and leads all the people in a worship and praise service to God. The service ends as the Levitical choir stands and sings joyful songs of thanksgiving (20:18, 19).

   Early the next morning the army of Judah marches forth to meet the enemy. After a consultation with his associates, Jehoshaphat determines to let the choir lead the march, clothed in sanctified garments and singing, "His mercy endureth for ever" (v. 21). And so they meet the enemy. Almost immediately God causes consternation among the troops of the foe, and they begin fighting among themselves. Surely no other battle in all history was won like this battle. Here songs defeated spears, and hosannas proved stronger than horses. Four days after the battle, after gathering all the immense loot discarded by their enemies (money, garments, jewels), all the Judeans gathered in a valley called Berachah, which means "blessings" and again had a heavenly hallelujah hour of praising God (20:26-30).

D. Athaliah (seventh ruler).
1. She began in 841 B.C. and reigned six years.
2. It has already been noted that Athaliah (Jezebel's daughter) has married Joram (Hezekiah's son). They had one son and named him Ahaziah. When he was killed by Jehu, Athaliah mounted the throne (2 Chron. 22:10).
3. This murderous woman then ordered the slaughter of all of the royal seed of the house of Judah.
4. But Athaliah's own daughter, Jehosheba (along with her husband Jehoiada, who was high priest at that time) hid one sole survivor of the bloodbath, a small boy named Joash (22:11).
5. After hiding the lad for six years, Jehoiada planned a coup to dethrone Judah's only queen. He was aided by the army and the Levitical priests. When all was ready, Joash

was brought out of hiding and publicly proclaimed king. When the astonished and infuriated queen rushed out to crush this revolt, she was arrested and executed. It is ironic to note that this murderous mother, who had once attempted to wipe out David's seed, was herself slain by one of David's own spears (2 Ki. 11:4-16).

E. Joash (eighth king).

1. He began in 835 B.C. and reigned forty years.
2. The young king first cooperates with Jehoiada the high priest in ushering in a time of revival, which includes, among other things, the destruction of the temples of Baal (2 Chron. 23:16-21; 24:1, 2).

   Joash then determines that the Temple of God needs repairs and orders Jehoiada to carry it out. Jehoiada constructs a special offering box to finance the work (2 Ki. 12:4-16). This was the first free-will offering taken since the construction of the tabernacle under Moses. (See Ex. 35 and Num. 7.)
3. After the death of Jehoiada, the high priest, Judah would experience difficult days. As long as Jehoiada was living, Joash walked the line, but with his death, a tragic transformation took place. It was doubtless in the grace of God that the high priest lived as long as he did—130 years. But now he was dead and without him Joash became as a Lot without an Abraham (2 Chron. 24:2, 15, 16).
4. We note with sadness the events which took place during the final years of Joash's reign.
   a. Soon after Jehoiada's funeral, the leaders of Judah induce the king to abandon God and worship idols. Joash now makes the same foolish and fatal error that his forefather, Rehoboam, once made; he allows himself to be counseled by the corrupt. (See 1 Ki. 12:8; 2 Chron. 24:17-19.)
   b. The Syrian king, Hazael, began a move to enlarge his throne by capturing the Philistine city of Gath. He then started toward Jerusalem, but was for awhile bribed away by Joash, who hurriedly sent him all the gold and treasuries of the Temple (2 Ki. 12:17, 18).
   c. The Spirit of God at this time came upon Zechariah, Jehoiada's son, and this fearless high priest boldly denounced Judah's idolatry and called for national repentance. Finally, at Joash's order, Zechariah was stoned to death. This is perhaps the darkest moment in Judah's history, the brutal murder of her own high priest. Our Lord would refer to this some eight-and-a-half centuries later. (See Mt. 23:35.)

      Zechariah thus becomes the Old Testament Stephen, as both of them were stoned for speaking the truth. (See Acts 7:51-59.) His last words were: "The Lord look upon it, and require it" (2 Chron. 24:22).

      Here the high priest asked that his death be avenged by God. We have already noted the favorable comparison between Zechariah and Stephen's ministry. But there is a significant difference in that Zechariah dies demanding that God judge his murderers, while Stephen asks the Lord to forgive them (see Acts 7:60). New Testament grace goes much further than Old Testament law.
5. A few months after the murder of Zechariah, God sent the Syrian army all the way into Judah. Jerusalem was captured, the chief leaders executed, and the Holy City looted and spoiled. Joash himself was severely wounded at this time and was finally murdered by his own palace officials.

F. Uzziah (tenth king).

1. He began in 790 B.C. and reigned for fifty-two years.
2. Uzziah had the second longest rule of all Judah's kings. Uzziah was a good ruler and was helped much by a godly prophet named Zechariah (2 Chron. 26:5). We marvel at his accomplishments:
   a. He rebuilt the city of Eloth and restored it to Judah.
   b. He subdued the strong cities of the Philistines.
   c. He was victorious against the Arabians.
   d. He made the Ammonites give him annual tribute.
   e. His fame spread down to Egypt and other nations.
   f. He built fortified towers in Jerusalem.
   g. He constructed forts in the Negeb.
   h. He built many water reservoirs.
   i. He raised great herds of cattle.
   j. He laid out many farms and vineyards.
   k. He organized his army into regiments. This army consisted of 307,500 men, all elite troops. These men were led by 2600 commanders.
   l. He equipped them with the finest weapons of war.
   m. He produced great engines of war which shot arrows and huge stones from the towers and battlements (2 Chron. 26:6-15).
3. But in the midst of his strength he was cut down by pride. We are told: "But when he was strong, his heart was lifted up to his destruction" (26:16). The first creature in God's universe who sinned had these same tragic words said against him. (See Isa. 14:12-15; Ezek. 28:12-17.)
4. His sin was intrusion into the office of the priesthood by burning incense upon the golden altar.
5. Caught in the very act of doing this, the king was soundly and severely rebuked by the high priest, Azariah, and eighty other brave priests. He was warned that this action was only to be done by the descendants of Aaron. Uzziah became furious and refused to budge. He suddenly was divinely struck with leprosy even as he held the incense burner (26:17-21). Uzziah was the third and final

biblical king to make the fatal error of assuming the office of the priesthood. God rejected the first (Saul; 1 Sam. 13:11-14), took the son of the second (Jeroboam; 1 Ki. 14:17), and here struck the third with leprosy.

6. Uzziah later died, still in this tragic condition. "And Uzziah, the king, was a leper unto the day of his death, and dwelt in a separate house . . . for he was cut off from the house of the Lord" (2 Chron. 26:21).

G. Ahaz (twelfth king).

1. He began in 735 B.C. and reigned sixteen years.

2. This young, arrogant twenty-year-old king experienced troubles almost from the start.

    a. He was threatened by an enemy alliance of Rezin (the Syrian king), and Pekah (the Israelite king) (2 Ki. 15:37; 16:5, 6).

    b. He was attacked separately, and then cojointly (2 Chron. 28:5, 6; 2 Ki. 16:5). They wanted to punish him for his refusal to join them in an alignment to stop the growing power of Assyria, Rezin, and Pekah.

    c. The terrified young king was visited by Isaiah, who assured him not to worry, for the Syrian-Israelite plot would fail and those nations themselves would soon (within sixty-five years) be destroyed (Isa. 7:1-9).

    d. God then (through Isaiah) invited Ahaz to ask him for a divine sign to prove his enemies would indeed be destroyed as prophesied. The unbelieving king refused (having apparently already determined to enlist Israel) and Isaiah then predicted that a sign would be forthcoming from God himself to the entire house of David (and not just to Ahaz), proving God's might and love to all Abraham's seed. Note the eloquent language:

    "Therefore the Lord himself shall give you a sign; Behold a virgin shall conceive, and bear a son, and shall call his name Immanuel" (Isa. 7:14).

    Thus did Isaiah predict the virgin birth of Christ! Seven centuries later the angel Gabriel would remind a heartbroken carpenter living in Nazareth concerning these words. (See Mt. 1:18-25.)

    e. Ahaz not only refused to heed God's word, but turned his wicked heart to Baal worship, which included offering up his own children as burnt sacrifices to this devil-god in the valley of Hinnom, right outside Jerusalem (2 Chron. 28:1-4).

    f. Because of all this, God allowed many enemies to spoil Ahaz's kingdom.

    g. In sheer desperation, Ahaz turned to the Assyrian king, Tiglath-pileser, for help against these foes. He bribed him by sending along the gold and silver of the Temple with his request (2 Chron. 28:16-21; 2 Ki. 16:7, 8).

    h. Tiglath-pileser agreed and captured Damascus, killing Rezin, one of Ahaz's enemies. The Judean king then hastened to Damascus to lick the hand of the Assyrian king. While he was there, he saw a special pagan altar. He jotted down its dimensions and sent it back to Urijah, the high priest, with orders to have a model ready for him upon his return. This false altar then replaced the old bronze one in the Temple (2 Ki. 16:10-16). He thus continued his vile pagan worship (2 Chron. 28:22).

    i. Tiglath-pileser continued his conquest by carrying away into captivity some of the cities of northern Israel, including the land east of Jordan (2 Ki. 15:29).

H. Hezekiah (thirteenth king).

1. He began in 715 B.C. and reigned for twenty-nine years.

2. His reforms. By God's estimation, Hezekiah was the best king of Judah up to his time. His spiritual record would only be exceeded by his grandson, Josiah (2 Ki. 18:5). He broke the shrines on the hills, destroyed the idols of Asherch and the serpent of brass made by Moses (Num. 21:9), which were being worshiped by the people.

3. His wealth. Among all the kings of both North and South, Hezekiah's vast wealth was exceeded only by Solomon (2 Chron. 32:27-30).

4. His Temple ministry. During the very first month of his reign, Hezekiah ordered the reinstitution of animal sacrifices, realizing that great Mosaic law which stated, "It is the blood that maketh an atonement for the soul" (Lev. 17:11; see also Heb. 9:22). The king then organized the Temple orchestral group consisting of harps, psalteries, cymbals, and a special trumpet corps of priests. A Levitical singing choir was also formed, which featured the Psalms of David in their repertoire. When all was ready, the public was invited to come (2 Chron. 29:20-30). This simply had to be one of the great worship services of all time.

5. His great Passover celebration. Hezekiah began planning for the grandest Passover celebration since Solomon's dedication of the Temple over three centuries back (2 Chron. 30:26). Letters were sent throughout all Judea and parts of Israel inviting people to repent, return, and rejoice, all of which could be accomplished by attending the Passover. Many of the northern peoples laughed and scorned such an invitation (for a New Testament example, see Luke 14:16-24), but others joyfully responded (2 Chron. 30:3-11).

The celebration was originally scheduled to last seven days, but it was unanimously decided to continue it for another seven days. A fantastic number of animals were offered during these days which included 20,000 young bulls and 17,000 sheep (2 Chron. 30:21-27). Eventually the worshipers returned home and the revival continued, as household idols were destroyed (2 Chron.

31:1). Hezekiah then organized his priests and Levites into service corps, appointing some to offer animal sacrifices to God, and others simply to thank and praise him (2 Chron. 31:2, 3). Years before, David had appointed a special choir numbering 288 to do nothing but praise and thank the Lord (1 Chron. 16:4; 6:31, 32.) Time and again we read of this consecrated choir:

a. As the Temple was dedicated under Solomon (2 Chron. 5:12, 13).
b. As the Lord defeated a great host of Israel's enemies under Jehoshaphat (2 Chron. 20:21).
c. As wicked Queen Athaliah was deposed under Jehoiada the high priest (2 Chron. 23:13).
d. During Hezekiah's revival (2 Chron. 29:25–28).
e. During the Passover celebration under Josiah (2 Chron. 35:15, 16).
f. As the returning remnant laid the Temple foundation under Ezra (Ezra 3:11, 13).

The tithes now began to roll in from God's revived people. Azariah, the high priest, put the surplus in specially prepared rooms in the Temple. Note his testimony:

"Since the people began to bring the offering into the house of the Lord, we have had enough to eat, and have left plenty: for the Lord hath blessed his people; and that which is left is this great store" (2 Chron. 31:10).

This glorious truth is further amplified in the final Old Testament book. (See Mal. 3:8–10.)

6. His military achievements. Under the reign of Ahaz, Judah had paid tribute to the Assyrians, but in the fourth year of his rule Hezekiah rebelled against the Assyrian monarch, Shalmaneser, and no longer did this (2 Ki. 18:7). He also conducted a successful Philistine campaign at this time (2 Ki. 18:8).

7. His sickness and recovery. Hezekiah was stricken with a fatal boil-like disease and told by God through Isaiah that he would not recover. The reason for this sickness may have been his pride (2 Chron. 32:24, 25; Isa. 38:17).

The broken king turned his face to the wall and pleaded for God to spare him. God heard and promised to add fifteen more years to his life (2 Ki. 20:1–6). Thus Hezekiah was the only human being who ever lived who could (for fifteen years) absolutely count on seeing another sunrise when he retired at night.

Isaiah prepared a fig paste to put upon Hezekiah. This plaster, of course, had no more healing power than did the clay with which Jesus anointed the eyes of the blind man (Jn. 9:6). Both healings were accomplished by faith in the power and promise of God's Word (2 Ki. 20:7). Hezekiah asked for a supernatural sign to prove this treatment would really work. God granted him this,

and, at the king's own request, moved the shadow on the royal sundial back ten points (2 Ki. 20:8–11). Dr. John Davis writes the following concerning this miracle:

"The sign that God gave to Hezekiah was certainly one of the most spectacular miracles in Old Testament history. In the courtyard of the palace there was apparently a series of steps (not necessarily a sundial as we would think of it) so arranged that the shadow cast by the sun would give an approximation of the time. At the request of the kings, and, doubtless, in the presence of a large group of officials (including foreign ambassadors?), the shadow moved backward ten steps (or degrees)! How did God actually accomplish this miracle? Did He cause the earth to stop its rotation and turn backwards a little? All true Christians would agree that He could have done such a thing, for by Him all things consist, or hold together (Col. 1:17). But the Bible makes it rather clear that this was not God's method; for, in referring to this miracle, 2 Chronicles 32:24 states that Hezekiah 'prayed unto Jehovah; and he spake unto him, and gave him a sign (Hebrew: *mopheth*).' But in verse 31 we are told that the Babylonians sent ambassadors to Hezekiah 'to inquire of the wonder (*mopheth*) that was done in the land.' Obviously, then, it was a geographically localized miracle, which did not involve a reversal of the earth's rotation, with shadows retreating ten degrees all over the Near East. Instead, the miracle occurred only 'in the land' (of Judea); and, to be even more specific, it was only in the king's courtyard that 'the sun returned ten steps of the dial whereon it was gone down' (Isa. 38:8). It is the writer's conviction that a proper understanding of the nature of this great miracle helps us to understand what happened in the miracle of Joshua's long day (Josh. 10:12–14). Since Joshua's need was a prolongation of light (not a slowing down of the earth's rotation), his need could be met by a supernatural continuation of sunlight and moonlight in central Palestine for 'about a whole day' until Joshua's army could follow up its great victory and completely destroy the enemy." (*Solomon to the Exile*, pp. 128–129)

In his book, the prophet Isaiah includes for us a page in Hezekiah's diary written during this terrible sickness. It makes a gloomy reading indeed. (See Isa. 38:9–20.)

Some believe that Hezekiah spent the last fifteen years of his life putting the Old Testament Scriptures in order, for we often find the Hebrew letters "H Z K" at the end of many Old Testament books in the Hebrew manuscripts.

8. His Babylonian visitors. Hezekiah received an envoy from a rising power which would

soon meet and defeat mighty Assyria. The Babylonians may have come for several reasons:

a. To pay their respects to a king who had been raised from his very deathbed.

b. To inquire as to how this happened. The Babylonians were indeed fascinated by astronomic signs, for their national life revolved around the movement of heavenly bodies. (See Isa. 47:13; Dan. 2:27; Jer. 10:2.)

c. To determine how much loot they could take from Jerusalem after coming into power (2 Ki. 20:12, 13).

Hezekiah foolishly showed them all his treasures. He was soundly rebuked by Isaiah for this. The prophet then predicted that years after the king's death, Judah would be carried into captivity by the Babylonians, partly to obtain the very wealth Hezekiah had so freely shown them. The king's answer is a classic study in total selfishness:

"Good is the word of the Lord which thou hast spoken. And he said, Is it not good, if peace and truth be in my days?" (2 Ki. 20:19). (See also Rom. 7:18.)

We are told that God allowed the Babylon visit as a test for Hezekiah. But he flunked. (See 2 Chron. 32:31.)

9. His ordeal with Sennacherib. As we have already observed, Hezekiah had rebelled against paying tribute to Assyria during the fourth year of his reign. But as he began his fourteenth year in office, the powerful successor of Shalmaneser began to threaten Jerusalem. Hezekiah attempted to patch up his previous rebellion by sending a $1,500,000 bribe to the Assyrian warrior. This sad attempt to appease the bloodthirsty Sennacherib reminds one of England's prime minister, Neville Chamberlain, meekly going to Munich in the late thirties to hand over to Hitler half of Europe! But it didn't work, as both Hezekiah and Chamberlain would sadly discover.

Sennacherib soon surrounded the city of Jerusalem (2 Ki. 18:17; Isa. 36:1). Hezekiah made a desperate effort to defend himself by reinforcing the walls and recruiting an army. He even delivered a challenging message to inspire them, but apparently the king had serious personal doubts concerning the outcome of the crisis (2 Chron. 32:1-8).

Sennacherib now sent his Rabshakeh (title for his chief of staff) who attempted at first to break down Jerusalem's walls by the sheer power of his big mouth alone. He spewed out his terrible threats near the water supply source of the city, a place where he knew the greatest number of Jews could be reached. He lists seven arguments why Jerusalem should surrender immediately (2 Ki. 18:17-35).

a. Their ally Egypt was powerless to help them (v. 21).

b. They had "offended" Jehovah their God by destroying all the worship places except in Jerusalem (v. 22).

Those Jews who heard this argument must have laughed out loud at its stupidity. It was quite true that Hezekiah had removed the high places (see 18:4), but only because these were centers of Baal worship.

c. Jerusalem had a weak army (v. 23). Rabshakeh even offered to furnish 2000 horses, but doubted if they would muster up the soldiers to ride them.

d. It was God's will that Jerusalem be conquered (v. 25). It is true that Isaiah did predict the invasion of Assyria into Palestine (Isa. 10:5, 6), but not because this was his perfect will. It was a divine punishment for their sins.

e. Assyria had a massive army (v. 24).

f. Pleasant surrender conditions were proposed (v. 31). No one but an absolute fool would swallow this lie, for the Assyrians treated their prisoners in a most horrible way.

g. The absolute inability of Jehovah to save Jerusalem was pointed out (v. 35). This loudmouth would soon learn firsthand just how "weak" Jehovah really was!

During all this Assyrian arrogance, Rabshakeh was interrupted only once by Hezekiah's three-man truce delegation. They timidly asked that the "peace talks" be conducted in Aramaic (Syrian), and not in Hebrew, to prevent the listening crowd from understanding. The Judean negotiators were afraid a panic would follow if the seriousness of the situation was fully realized. Rabshakeh not only refused, but lifted his voice to a shout, so all could hear. But a panic did not take place. The people remained silent. This was wise, for how does a sheep answer the grunts and snorts of a wild hog? (2 Ki. 18:27, 28, 36).

10. His prayer for the city of Jerusalem. The three-man delegation immediately reported all Rabshakeh's threats to Hezekiah. The king then earnestly besought God in prayer. Hezekiah immediately heard from that grand prophet Isaiah, who reassured him that God had already determined to slay Sennacherib; and that he had nothing to fear from the Assyrian sneers. (See 2 Ki. 19:1-7; also Phil. 4:6, 7.)

11. His answer from the Lord. God at this point addressed both Hezekiah and Sennacherib through the prophet Isaiah (2 Ki. 19:20-33).

To Hezekiah, God said:

a. I have heard you (v. 20). This by itself would have surely comforted the king's heart. (See Ps. 20:1; 34:4; 120:1; Jonah 2:2; 1 Jn. 5:14.) How different are the deaf idols of the pagan gods. (See Ps.135:15-21; 115:2-7.)

b. The fields which the Assyrians have destroyed will be resown and replanted (v. 29).

c. By the third year the normal agricultural cycle will function again (v. 29).

d. This time of testing will produce a strong remnant of spiritual believers in Jerusalem (v. 29).

To Sennacherib, God said:

e. My "daughter" Zion is not afraid of you (v. 21).

f. She scorns and mocks you (v. 21).

g. The only reason you have conquered anything is because I let you do so (v. 25).

h. I know every rotten thing you think, say, and do (v. 27).

i. I will put a hook in your nose and a bridle in your mouth and drag you from Jerusalem (v. 28).

Note: This was a cruelty which the Assyrians frequently inflicted upon their captives. Another pagan nation will suffer this same kind of judgment during the tribulation. (See Ezek. 38:4.)

j. You will not enter Jerusalem nor even shoot an arrow into the city (v. 32).

k. You yourself will be murdered by members of your own household (v. 7).

Note: Archaeological findings indicate that Sennacherib was crushed to death by his own sons. This they did by creeping into his private prayer chapel and pushing over upon him a gigantic statue of Nisrich, his god! Dr. John Davis writes: "And thus the great and proud king of Assyria, who boasted that Hezekiah's God was utterly helpless, not only lost his army at one flick of Jehovah's finger but was himself crushed to death by the idol of a non-existent deity to whom he had devoted his life." (*Solomon to the Exile*, p. 124)

l. I will save this city both for my sake, and for David's sake (v. 34).

m. All this will happen because when you mocked Jerusalem, you also mocked me.

God not only promised to save Jerusalem, but assured the king that not one enemy arrow would fall into it. That very night the angel of the Lord killed 185,000 Assyrian troops, and dead bodies were seen all across the landscape in the morning. Some believe this angel was Christ himself. At any rate, the powers of an angel are fantastic. In Matthew 26:53 our Lord said he could, if he so desired, even then call for twelve legions of angels to help him. A legion in those days was 6000 soldiers. Thus Christ had at his immediate disposal at least 72,000 heavenly warriors. The Assyrians now experienced that which the Egyptians had suffered some eight centuries previously. (See Ex. 12:29.) Sennacherib immediately returned to Nineveh and was soon murdered, just as God predicted (2 Ki. 19:36, 37). Hezekiah died after a glorious twenty-nine-year reign, and was succeeded by his son, Manasseh (2 Ki. 20:20, 21; 2 Chron. 32:32, 33).

I. Manasseh (fourteenth king).

1. He began in 695 B.C. and reigned for fifty-five years.

2. The fourteenth ruler of Judah was, without doubt, the most unique king ever to sit upon either the northern or southern throne. Note the following:

a. He was king longer than any other of either kingdom.

b. He had the godliest father up to that time of all Judean kings.

c. His grandson Josiah was finest of all.

d. He was the only wicked king to genuinely repent prior to his death.

e. He was the most wicked of all kings prior to his salvation!

3. The preconversion reign of Manasseh (as recorded in 2 Ki. 21:2-6; 2 Chron. 33:1-20) would probably have surpassed that of Stalin and Hitler in terms of sheer wickedness. Consider the following items of information:

a. He rebuilt all the altars of Baal his father had destroyed (2 Chron. 33:3).

b. He set up a Zodiac center for the heathen worship of the sun, moon, and stars in every house of God (2 Chron. 33:4, 5).

c. He sacrificed his own children to satanic gods in the Valley of Hinnom as his grandfather Ahaz had done (33:6).

d. He consulted spirit-mediums and fortune-tellers (33:6).

e. Tradition says he murdered Isaiah by having him sawn asunder (Heb. 11:37).

f. God said he was more wicked than heathen nations which had once occupied Palestine (2 Ki. 21:11).

g. He shed innocent blood from one end of Jerusalem to another (2 Ki. 21:16).

h. He totally ignored repeated warnings of God in all this (2 Chron. 33:10).

i. He was imprisoned temporarily by the king of Assyria.

j. He repented while in prison and was forgiven by God.

k. He was later allowed to return as king of Judah.

l. He ruled for fifty-five years and was succeeded by his son, Amon.

J. Josiah (sixteenth king).

1. He began in 640 B.C. and reigned for thirty-one years.

2. Josiah was the finest king since Solomon.

"And like him was there no king before him, that turned to the Lord with all his heart, and with all his soul, and with all his might, according to all the law of Moses; neither after him arose there any like him" (2 Ki. 23:25).

His achievements stagger the mind. One wonders just when he arranged to eat and sleep!

3. The reforms of Josiah.

a. He began to seek after God while he was yet very young, only sixteen (2 Chron. 34:3).

b. At the age of twenty, he began his massive reform work (34:3).

c. He destroyed all the altars of Baal (34:4).

d. He then ground them into dust and scattered it over the graves of those who had sacrificed to them (34:4).

e. He burned the bones of heathen priests upon their own altars (34:5).

f. He carried out these actions in distant Israelite cities as well as in his own kingdom (34:6).

g. At the age of twenty-six, he began to repair the Temple (34:8).

h. He led his people in a massive "repentance service" upon the discovery of the law of Moses (2 Ki. 23:1-3, 18-21, 29-32). He then had this book read to all his people.

i. He planned for and presided over one of the greatest Passover services of all time (2 Chron. 35:1, 18).

j. He killed heathen priests whom previous kings of Judah had appointed (2 Ki. 23:5).

k. He removed the shameful idol of Asherah from the Temple (23:6).

l. He tore down the houses of male prostitutes (23:7).

m. He brought back to Jerusalem the priests of God who were living in other cities in Judah (23:8).

n. He destroyed the altar of Topheth in the Hinnom Valley so no one could offer human sacrifices upon it (23:10).

o. He tore down the statue of horses and chariots (which were dedicated to the use of the sun god) located near the entrance of the Temple (23:11).

p. He tore down Ahaz's pagan altars on the palace roof (23:12).

q. He destroyed those altars which Manasseh had built in the two courts of the Temple (23:12).

r. He removed the shrines of Ashtoreth (god of Sidon), Chemosh (god of Moab), and Milcom (god of Ammon), which Solomon had built for his many wives (23:13).

s. He tore down the altar and shrine at Bethel which Jeroboam I had made (23:15), thus fulfilling a 300-year-old prophecy. (See 1 Ki. 13:1, 2.)

t. He demolished the shrines on the hills of Samaria (23:19).

u. He exterminated mediums, wizards, and soothsayers (23:24).

4. The scriptural ministry of Josiah.

a. In cleansing the Temple, Hilkiah the high priest discovered an old scroll which turned out to be a copy of the Law of Moses (2 Ki. 22:8).

b. Josiah was informed of this and tore his clothes in terror, realizing how the Old Testament laws had been so ridiculed and ignored during the wicked reign of both his father and grandfather (22:9-13). Apparently under Manasseh's wicked reign the Word of God had been all but totally destroyed. It was probably a capital offense to possess a copy of the Mosaic Law. Thus some faithful priest may have hidden a copy of this precious law in the Temple to await better days.

c. The young king then ordered Hilkiah to seek the counsel of a godly woman prophetess concerning all this. Her name was Huldah, and she may have been Jeremiah's aunt. (See 2 Ki. 22:14; Jer. 32:7.) God had often spoken to his people through a woman, and would do so after this also (22:14).

(1) He spoke through Miriam, the sister of Moses (Ex. 15:20).

(2) He worked through Deborah (Jdg. 5).

(3) Zacharias' wife was a prophetess (Lk. 2:36).

(4) Philip's four daughters were called prophetesses (Acts 21:9).

d. Huldah's message was a twofold prophecy. It stated that:

(1) Because of Judah's tragic and shameful spiritual failure, God had already determined to judge his people. She pronounced upon the Holy City the fearful divine words of the Lord (see 22:17).

(2) Because of Josiah's love of God, he would be spared all this, as judgment would not fall until after his death. He himself would be "gathered into thy grave in peace" (2 Ki. 22:20).

We are not to understand this to mean that Josiah would die a quiet death on his royal bed (he was actually killed in battle), but that he would be spared the wrath of the Babylonian capitivity and subsequent destruction of Jerusalem.

e. Josiah then gathered all his people at the Temple and personally read aloud the Law of Moses and urged them all to obey God's Word (2 Ki. 23:1-3).

5. The great Passover celebration of Josiah. This feast, which had begun in Egypt nearly 900 years back (Ex. 12) had evidently not been celebrated since the days of Hezekiah, over sixty years ago. But now Josiah determines to amend for this delay. We note with amazement the tremendous number of animals offered up at this time (2 Chron. 35:7, 8).

a. Animals.

(1) thirty thousand lambs

(2) three thousand young bulls

(3) seventy-six hundred sheep

(4) three hundred oxen

b. Ark of the Covenant.

According to 2 Chronicles 35:18, this was the greatest Passover of all time. During the Passover celebration, Josiah elevated the sacred Ark of the Covenant to its proper place in the Temple

(2 Chron. 35:3). Here is the final Old Testament mention of this, the most sacred piece of furniture ever built, the Ark of the Covenant. Its history makes fascinating reading indeed.

(1) It is first mentioned in Exodus 25:10.

(2) It was put in the tabernacle by Moses (Ex. 40:21).

(3) It was carried throughout Israel's forty-year wilderness experiences (Num. 10:35; 14:44).

(4) It followed the people of Israel across the Jordan River (Josh. 4:5).

(5) It was carried around Jericho (Josh. 6:13).

(6) It was placed beside Joshua on Mt. Ebal as he read the law to all Israel (Josh. 8:33).

(7) It was formally placed in the new tabernacle, set up at Shiloh (Josh. 18:1).

(8) It was carried into battle with the Philistines by wicked Hophni and Phinehas (1 Sam. 4:4).

(9) It was captured by the Philistines for seven months (1 Sam. 4:11; 6:1). During this time

(a) It was taken to Ashdod where it defeated Dagon (1 Sam. 5:1).

(b) It was taken to Ekron, where it caused a great plague (1 Sam. 5:10).

(10) It was carried by two "Milch Kine" into Bethshemesh. Here God smote a number of the citizens of this city for looking inside (1 Sam. 6:12).

(11) It was taken to Kirjath-jearim. Here it remained for twenty years (1 Sam. 7:1).

(12) It was brought to Gibeah by Saul. Here it saved Israel from the Philistines (1 Sam. 14:18).

(13) It was carried from Gibeah toward Jerusalem by David on a new cart. En route, Uzzah was slain for touching it (2 Sam. 6:3).

(14) It rested at the house of Obed-edom for three months (2 Sam. 6:11).

(15) It was brought into Jerusalem by David (2 Sam. 6:16).

(16) It was carried by Zadok the high priest over the brook Kidron to David during his escape from Absalom's rebellion (2 Sam. 15:24).

(17) It was carried back to Jerusalem by David's order (2 Sam. 15:25, 29).

(18) It was placed in Solomon's Temple (1 Ki. 8:1).

(19) We do not know what eventually became of it.

6. The tragic death of Josiah.

a. Necho, the king of Egypt, planned to lead an army through Judah to aid the Babylonians against the Assyrians at Carchemish (2 Chron. 35:20).

b. Josiah declared war upon Necho for this. In vain, the Egyptian king attempted to convince the Judean ruler that he had no quarrel with him whatsoever, and warned him not to interfere, lest God destroy him in battle (35:20, 21).

c. Josiah refused the peace offers and attacked Necho in the Valley of Megiddo. This particular encampment located in the plain of Esdraelon had already seen many battles.

(1) It was here that Deborah and Barak defeated the Canaanites (Jdg. 4–5).

(2) It was here that Gideon defeated the Midianites (Jdg. 7).

(3) It was here that David defeated Goliath (1 Sam. 17).

(4) It was here that the Philistines killed Saul (1 Sam. 31).

(5) It was here that Josiah was killed (2 Chron. 35:22).

(6) It will be in this area that the mighty battle of Armageddon will someday be fought (Zech. 12:11; Rev. 16:16).

d. Josiah was tragically slain in spite of an attempt to disguise himself (as did another king once). (See 1 Ki. 22:30.) He was carried back to Jerusalem and buried with much ceremony and sorrow. Jeremiah himself attended the funeral (1 Chron. 35:23–25). At his death, Judah would see no more good kings. It was all spiritual degeneration from this point on. Josiah was succeeded by his son, Jehoahaz (2 Chron. 36:1).

K. Jehoiakim (eighteenth king).

1. He began in 609 B.C. and reigned for eleven years.

2. With the exception of Manasseh (his great-great-grandfather), Jehoiakim may be regarded as Judah's most evil king. Note this sordid record:

a. He built a plush palace, with huge rooms, many windows, paneled throughout with a fragrant cedar, and painted a beautiful red. This he accomplished with forced slave labor while his own people were suffering (Jer. 22:13, 14).

b. He was full of selfish greed and dishonesty (22:17).

c. He murdered the innocent, oppressed the poor, and reigned with ruthlessness (22:17).

d. He butchered with a sword a godly and fearless prophet named Uriah, having him first tracked down in Egypt and brought back to Jerusalem (26:33).

e. He often attempted to silence the prophet, Jeremiah (26:24; 36:19, 26).

f. On one occasion he burned a scroll which contained the inspired writings and prophecies of Jeremiah. But this backfired, as the prophet rewrote all the king had burned and added a chilling prophecy against Jehoiakim (36:22, 23, 27–32).

3. Jehoiakim was made a vassal by Nebuchadnezzar after the Babylonians had defeated the Assyrians and Egyptians at the battle of Carchemish. During the last part of his reign, Nebuchadnezzar captured Jerusalem and took some of the sacred Temple vessels to Babylon. He also bound Jehoiakim, intending to carry him along, but apparently, for some reason, restored him to the throne of Judah as his puppet king (2 Ki. 24:1; Jer. 25:1; 2 Chron. 36:6, 7). He did, however, carry into captivity some royal Jewish youths, one of which was Daniel (Dan. 1:3, 4).
4. After three years of this, Jehoiakim was induced by the Egyptian party in his court to rebel against Nebuchadnezzar.
5. Although Nebuchadnezzar apparently could not rise up immediately at that time to crush this rebellion, God punished the wicked Judean king by allowing the land to be invaded by the Syrians, Moabites, and Ammonites (2 Ki. 24:2, 3).
6. Jehoiakim died, and, as prophesied by Jeremiah (22:18, 19; 36:30), received the burial of a wild animal. He was dragged out of Jerusalem and thrown on the garbage dump beyond the gate, unmourned even by his immediate family. He was succeeded by his son, Jehoiachin (2 Ki. 24:5, 6).

L. Zedekiah (twentieth king).
1. He began in 597 and reigned for eleven years. This youngest son of godly King Josiah was the last to rule, and, like his two brothers, Jehoahaz and Jehoiakim, Zedekiah was wicked. He has been called "the fickle puppet" (2 Ki. 24:18, 19; 2 Chron. 36:12).
2. At first, Zedekiah showed signs of an intention to obey the Law of Moses (Jer. 34:8-10).
3. He went to Babylon in his fourth year, probably to reassure Nebuchadnezzar of his loyalty (51:59).
4. He returned and was forced to muzzle the "loud-mouth" prophet, Jeremiah (27-29).
5. Jeremiah suffered much under the reign of Zedekiah.
   a. He was hated and plotted against because of his message of divine judgment (Jer. 11:8-10).
   b. He was arrested by the Temple priest Pashhur, whipped, and put in stocks for one night (20:1-3).
   c. He was almost murdered by a wild mob by Judah's false priests and prophets after one of his messages (26:7-9).
   d. In the fourth year of Zedekiah's reign, a false prophet named Hananiah publicly rebuked Jeremiah, saying Babylon would be overthrown in two years (28:1-4).
   e. He was arrested and thrown into prison, charged with treason (27:11-16).
   f. He was then removed from there and placed in the palace prison by the fickle Zedekiah (37:21).
   g. He was soon taken from here, however, and placed into an empty cistern in the prison yard by some Jewish hotheads.

There was no water in it, and Jeremiah sank down into the thick layer of mire at its bottom (38:1-6).
   h. He was again set free and, in vain, attempted to convince Zedekiah to submit to the Babylonian threat as God's divine punishment (38:14-26).
   i. During the final two years of Zedekiah's pitiful and perverted rule, Jeremiah was again confined to prison. At this time, he was ordered to purchase a farm from his cousin, Hanamel (32:6-15).
6. Zedekiah foolishly refused the counsel of Jeremiah and rebelled against Nebuchadnezzar, even though he had taken an oath of loyalty (2 Chron. 36:13). Rising to this revolt, Nebuchadnezzar came against him. For some thirty months, Jerusalem held out, but on July 18, 586 B.C., it totally collapsed. During the final night, Zedekiah attempted to escape, but was captured near Jericho and brought back to Nebuchadnezzar for punishment. He was forced to witness the execution of his own sons and then his eyes were gouged out. He was finally taken in chains to Babylon where he died (Jer. 52:4-11; 39:1-7).

   Note: Jeremiah had warned Zedekiah that he would look into the very eyes of Nebuchadnezzar (32:4; 34:3), but Ezekiel prophesied that he would not see Babylon with his eyes (12:6, 12, 13). These horrible prophecies came true.
7. During the latter part of July, 587, Nebuchadnezzar's captain of the guard, Nebuzaradan, burned the Temple, along with most private and public buildings. The walls of the city were torn down (Jer. 52:12-23).
8. Nebuchadnezzar then ordered the execution of Seraiah the high priest along with seventy-three other important officials. Judah's exile was now complete (Jer. 52:24-27). From this date on, until May 14, 1948 A.D., Israel as a nation would cease to exist.

*The important oral prophets:*

A. Elijah.
   The ministry of Elijah, one of the most colorful and courageous prophets who ever lived, will be considered first in outline subject-matter form, and then presented in actual chronological fashion.
   An outline, subject-matter consideration of his life:
1. Elijah and King Ahab:
   a. announcing the three-and-a-half year drought (1 Ki. 17:1)
   b. challenging him to a contest on Mt. Carmel (18:17-20)
   c. predicting the end of the drought (18:41-46)
   d. pronouncing the death sentence upon him and his wife (21:17-24)
2. Elijah and the ravens at Cherith (17:2-7)
3. Elijah and the widow at Zarephath (17:8-15)
4. Elijah and Obadiah (18:1-16)
5. Elijah and the people of Israel (18:20-24)

 Elijah

## ELIJAH AND KING AHAB
Announcing the three-and-a-half year drought (1 Ki. 17:1)
Challenging him to a contest on Mt. Carmel (17:17-19)
Predicting the end of the drought (18:41-46)
Pronouncing the death sentence upon him and his wife (21:17-24)

## ELIJAH AND THE RAVENS OF CHERITH
He is supernaturally fed by some ravens beside a drying brook (1 Ki. 17:2-7)

## ELIJAH AND A WIDOW AT ZAREPHATH
He is supernaturally fed by God through a widow (1 Ki. 17:8-16)
He raises the dead son of that widow (17:17-24)

## ELIJAH AND A BACKSLIDER NAMED OBADIAH
Obadiah was a secret believer who had ministered to 100 prophets (1 Ki. 18:1-15)
He reluctantly and fearfully arranges a meeting between Elijah and Ahab (1 Ki. 18:16)

## ELIJAH AND THE NATION ISRAEL
He rebukes and challenges Israel on Mt. Carmel (1 Ki. 18:20-24)

## ELIJAH AND THE PRIESTS OF BAAL
The priests of Baal are unable to pray down the fire (1 Ki. 18:25-29)
He has them killed for their paganism (18:40)

## ELIJAH AND THE LORD GOD
He flees Israel to escape Jezebel's revenge (1 Ki. 19:1-3)
He is ministered to by an angel (19:4-7)
He hears God's still small voice in a cave (19:8-18)

## ELIJAH AND ELISHA THE PROPHET
He calls Elisha to special service (1 Ki. 19:19-21)
He prepares Elisha for special service (2 Ki. 2:1-10)

## ELIJAH AND NORTHERN KING AHAZIAH
He predicts wicked Ahaziah will die from a fall (2 Ki. 1:1-18)
He prays down fire to destroy two companies of soldiers sent to arrest him (1:9-12)
He spares the third company, led by a captain who begs for mercy (1:13-16)

## ELIJAH AND A CHARIOT OF FIRE
He parts the River Jordan and stands on the eastern bank (2 Ki. 2:1-8)
He receives a last request from Elisha (2:9, 10)
He is carried into heaven without dying (2:11)

6. Elijah and the priests of Baal (18:25-40)
7. Elijah and God (19:1-18)
8. Elijah and Elisha
   a. calling him to special service (1 Ki. 19:19-21)
   b. preparing him for special service (2 Ki. 2:1-10)
9. Elijah and King Ahaziah (2 Ki. 1:1-17)
10. Elijah and the chariot of fire (2 Ki. 2:11)

*A chronological consideration of his life:*
1. Dr. John Whitcomb introduces this mighty Tishbite as follows:
   "Like a meteor suddenly flashing across the darkened sky, Elijah appears on the scene without historical background, and without warning!" (*Solomon to the Exile*, p. 50)
2. He announces to wicked King Ahab that a long drought can be expected as a punish-

ment for sin (1 Ki. 17:1). The New Testament writer James refers to this terrible drought as an example of the tremendous power of prayer (Jas. 5:17). James says the drought lasted three-and-a-half years. The lack of rain was a divine punishment for sin. (See Deut. 11:13-17; 28:24; 2 Chron. 7:12-15.)

3. God then orders his prophet to hide himself (from the king's wrath) by the Brook Cherith at a place east of where it enters the Jordan (17:2). Here he would be fed supernaturally by some ravens.

4. Elijah is now ordered to proceed to a city in Jezebel's own backyard, called Zarephath, where God has commanded a widow to feed him. After what must have seemed an eternity (possibly a year or longer), Elijah finally graduates from the D.B.I. (Drying Brook Institute). The brook experience almost always precedes the Mt. Carmel challenge in the plan of God for his chosen servants. Paul spent three years in the A.B.I. (Arabian Bible Institute, Gal. 1:18) and Moses passed some forty years on the campus of the S.B.I., Sinai Bible Institute. (See Ex. 3:1; 1 Ki. 17:8, 9.)

   Again God does the unexpected thing. His prophet who has been fed by some ravens now has his needs met by a lonely and poverty-stricken old widow. Elijah asks the starving widow and her son to share their last available meal with him and promises them that God himself will see to it that their oil and flour containers will always be full until it rains and the crops grow again. By faith the widow shares with him and finds God's promise to be true (17:10-16).

5. Suddenly, with no warning whatsoever, the widow's son dies. In her grief-stricken statement at this time, the widow brings out two significant things (1 Ki. 17:18):
   a. The testimony of Elijah. Note her phrase, "O thou man of God." Here was a woman who had seen the prophet out of his pulpit and before he had drunk his first cup of coffee in the morning. She saw him as he really was, and still could call him a man of God. The acid test of a man's true religion is the home test.
   b. Her own uneasy conscience. She asks him if he was sent to call her sin to remembrance. Perhaps some shameful and secret deed in her past had constantly plagued her conscience.

6. Elijah carries the lad upstairs, stretches himself upon the lifeless body three times, and prays that God will raise the boy. God hears his prayer. This marks the first of eight body resurrections in the Bible (not counting the resurrection of Christ). These are:
   a. Elijah raises the widow's boy (1 Ki. 17:22).
   b. Elisha raises the son of a Shunammite woman (2 Ki. 4:35).
   c. Elisha's bones raise a man whose dead body touches them during a graveyard burial (2 Ki. 13:21).

d. Christ raises the daughter of Jairus (Mt. 9:25).

e. Christ raises the son of a widow (Lk. 7:14).

f. Christ raises Lazarus (Jn. 11:43, 44).

g. Peter raises Dorcas (Acts 9:40, 41).

h. Paul raises Eutychus (Acts 20:12).

7. Elijah is promised by God that he will soon send rain and orders his prophet to confront Ahab again. En route to the palace, Elijah is met by Obadiah, a backslidden believer, who served as household administrator under Ahab. Obadiah attempts to impress Elijah with his good works (he has hidden 100 prophets in a cave from the murderous wrath of Jezebel) and reluctantly and fearfully agrees to inform Ahab of Elijah's presence (1 Ki. 18:1-16).

8. At their summit meeting, Ahab blames Elijah for all Israel's trouble.

9. Elijah, however, refuses to accept Ahab's stupid accusation and challenges Ahab and pagan priests of Baal to a "fire-consuming sacrifice" contest on Mt. Carmel, with the following rules:

a. Two bullocks would be sacrificed and laid upon two altars, one dedicated to Baal, the other to God.

b. Both deities would be prayed to, and the real god could prove himself by sending down fire from heaven to consume his sacrifice (1 Ki. 18:23-25).

10. The priests of Baal pray first, agonizing, screaming, dancing, and even cutting themselves to attract their god's attention, but all in vain. During this time Elijah mocks them. We read that about noontime, Elijah began mocking them.

"'You'll have to shout louder than that,' he scoffed, 'to catch the attention of your god! Perhaps he is talking to someone, or is out sitting on the toilet, or maybe he is away on a trip, or is asleep and needs to be awakened'" (1 Ki. 18:27, *The Living Bible*).

11. Then it was evening, and Elijah's turn. He took twelve stones and rebuilt an old torn-down altar of God in that very area. He then dug a three-foot wide trench around the altar and dumped twelve barrels of sea water into it. Finally, he stepped back and prayed (18:36, 37).

12. The fire immediately fell from heaven and consumed the sacrifice. Note the order in which the things at the altar were consumed:

a. The burnt-sacrifice. This speaks of ourselves! (See Rom. 12:1-3.)

b. The wood. This speaks of our efforts. It is tragically possible for a pastor on a Sunday morning to experience either fire without wood or wood without fire. The first occurs when he isn't studied up, and the second when he isn't prayed up.

c. The stones. This speaks of the difficult things in our lives.

d. The dust. This speaks of the useless things in our lives.

e. The water. This speaks of the impossible things in our lives (18:38).

13. Elijah then executed the prophets of Baal.

14. Finally, after a sevenfold prayer meeting, there was a great rain (18:45). God often works in a roundabout way, but he does so to accomplish certain specific things. Thus, through all this:

a. Elijah received valuable training for his future ministry.

b. A disrespectful king learned the fear of the Lord.

c. A heathen woman believed on the name of the Lord.

d. A young man was raised from the dead.

e. A backslidden believer was restored to fellowship.

f. The nation Israel experienced a temporary revival.

g. A large number of God's enemies were destroyed.

15. Upon hearing of Elijah's action, Jezebel vowed to kill him in twenty-four hours, and Elijah ran for his life (19:2). This points out two important spiritual truths:

a. The infallibility of the Word of God. No mere human author would have included the sad account we read here. This part in the life of a fearless man of God would have simply been denied or ignored.

b. The fallibility of the man of God. Elijah, like David, was a man who failed God in what was supposedly his strongest point. In David's case it was his purity and in Elijah's situation it was his courage. But both fell on their faces. They needed the lesson God taught Paul in 2 Corinthians 12:1-10.

16. Elijah fled eastward and after a day's journey he fell exhausted under a juniper tree, praying that God would kill him (19:4). This was prayed some twenty-eight centuries ago and God had yet to answer it. Elijah, like Enoch, participated in God's first and second space shot. (Compare Gen. 5:24 with 2 Ki. 2:11.) But someday the Lord will allow his prophet to lay down his life for Jesus. (Compare Mal. 4:5, 6 with Rev. 11:3-12.) Both Moses (Num. 11:15) and Jonah (4:3) had also prayed this despondent prayer.

17. As he slept, an angel touched him and fed him (19:5). God often allows his angels to participate in his dealing with man. (See Heb. 1:14; 1 Pet. 1:12.)

Elijah was by now totally exhausted, having traveled 150 miles from Jezreel to Beersheba. But now he desperately needed food. Our spiritual and physical natures are so closely entwined that one automatically affects the other. Part of his terrible soul depression was due to the mistreatment of his body. The stomach can affect the soul. (See Ps. 127:2.)

18. God himself finally spoke through a still, small voice to Elijah in a cave, perhaps the same one where Moses had viewed God's glory some five centuries before. (Compare 19:9 with Ex. 33:21-23.) In spite of his objections to the contrary, Elijah was ordered immediately to perform four tasks:
    a. Get back and start preaching again. Besides, he was not alone as he claimed, for God still had 7000 followers in Israel who had not bowed to Baal (19:15, 18).
    b. Anoint a man named Hazael to be king of Syria (19:15).
    c. Anoint a man named Jehu to be king of Israel (19:16).
    d. Begin training Elisha to succeed him (19:16). In passing, it should be noted (19:10) that Elijah's prayer here is the only example of an Israelite believer making intercession against his own beloved nation Israel. Paul specifically states that this was indeed the case. (See Rom. 11:1-4.) Needless to say, God has never and will never honor this kind of praying. James and John later expressed the same vindictive spirit concerning some unbelieving Samaritans. (See Lk. 9:55.)

19. Elijah returned and found Elisha plowing in a field. Elijah went over to him and threw his coat across his shoulders. Elisha thereupon prepared a farewell feast for his family and servants and followed Elijah (19:19-21).

20. Elijah confronted wicked Ahab in the vineyard of Naboth. There he predicted the divine death penalty judgment upon both Ahab and Jezebel for their part in the cold-blooded murder of godly Naboth (1 Ki. 21:17-24).

21. Sometime later, King Ahaziah, wicked northern ruler (and eldest son of Ahab) suffered a severe fall off the upstairs porch of his palace in Samaria. Fearing the worst, he sent messengers to the Philistine temple dedicated to Baalzebub at Ekron to ask this pagan god whether he would recover (2 Ki. 1:1-3). This ungodly son of Ahab was apparently unaware of Israel's history, for had he been aware, he certainly would not have trusted in a pagan god who was utterly powerless to save his own worshipers against the wrath of the Ark of God (in 1 Samuel 5:10-12). Elijah was instructed by God's angel to intercept these messengers and send them back to Ahaziah with his prophecy, that due to the king's idolatry, he would indeed soon die (1:3-6).

Ahaziah correctly guessed the identity of this fearless hairy man with the wide leather belt and sent out a captain with fifty men to arrest him. As the soldiers approached him, Elijah called down fire from heaven and they were consumed. Another fifty were sent out and suffered the same fate. The captain of the third group fell to his knees and begged Elijah to spare their lives and come with them. The prophet agreed and soon stood before the king where he repeated similar words he had once said to Ahab, Ahaziah's father. Shortly after this, Ahaziah died and was succeeded by his younger brother Jehoram (2 Ki. 1:7-17). He had reigned for but two short years.

22. Elijah's magnificent ministry had now come to a close and he would soon be taken heavenward by means of a whirlwind, without dying. He quickly traveled his circuit for the final time, moving rapidly from Gilgal to Bethel to Jericho to the Jordan River. At the first three stops he tested the determination of Elisha by suggesting that he might want to drop the hectic life of the prophet and return to his quiet farm. But on each occasion (2:2, 4, 6) he refused by uttering these five fearless words: "I will not leave thee!" Elisha, like Ruth, thus proved worthy for the blessings of God! (See Ruth 1:15-17.) Both at Bethel and Jericho Elisha spoke with the sons of the prophets living in those areas. These men may have been able to trace their heritage back to the prophetic schools of Samuel's day (1 Sam. 19:20). But what a sorry lot they were.
    a. They were cowardly (1 Ki. 18:4).
    b. They attempted to discourage Elisha (2 Ki. 2:3, 5)
    c. They lacked faith (2 Ki. 2:16-18).
    When they came to the Jordan River, Elijah folded his cloak together and struck the water with it; and the river divided, allowing them to cross on dry ground (2:8).

23. Elijah then asked Elisha what wish he would have granted before his heavenly departure. Elisha asked for a double portion of his master's power. He was told this was a hard thing, but that if he were present at Elijah's translation the request would be granted (2:9, 10).

24. Suddenly a chariot of fire, drawn by horses of fire, appeared and drove between them, separating them, and Elijah was carried by a whirlwind into heaven (2:11). He thus became the second of two individuals who saw glory without the grave. (See Gen. 5:24 for the other person.)

B. Elisha.
    1. Parting the waters at Jordan (2 Ki. 2:14). When Elijah had disappeared from view, Elisha picked up his master's cloak and returned to the Jordan River bank to see if his request for power had been granted. Striking the river with Elijah's cloak, he thundered out, "Where is the Lord God of Elijah?" Immediately the Jordan waters parted. This marked the third time such a miracle had happened in Israel's history. (Compare Josh. 3:17; 2 Ki. 2:8, 14.) Today, in our desperate world, the cry is: "Where are the Elijahs of the Lord God?"
    All this was watched by the students from the J.B.I. (Jericho Bible Institute), but these pessimistic prophets found it difficult to be-

lieve Elijah really went all the way to heaven and therefore suggested that some of their best athletes form a search party; "Lest peradventure the Spirit of the Lord hath taken him up, and cast him upon some mountain, or into some valley" (2 Ki. 2:16). After repeated urging, Elisha agreed to the search. After the fifty men combed the entire area for three days, the hunt was called off (2 Ki. 2:17, 18).

Elisha now employed his supernatural powers to their greatest extent. No other Old or New Testament individual (apart from the Savior), with the possible exception of Moses, could match the sheer number of his miracles.

2. Purifying the waters at Jericho (2:19-22).
At Jericho Elisha purified a polluted city well, which was believed by the citizens to be causing miscarriages, by pouring a bowl of salt into the noxious water (2 Ki. 2:19-22). Moses did a similar miracle at Marah centuries before. (See Ex. 15:23-25.)

3. Judging some hoodlums at Bethel (2:23, 24).
En route to Bethel he was surrounded by a gang of young hoodlums from that city who ridiculed his bald head and mocked the recent translation of Elijah. Elisha caused two female bears to appear, and forty-two of these arrogant rebels were clawed as a divine punishment (2 Ki. 2:23-25). The Hebrew word *yeled*, translated "little children," should doubtless be rendered "young lads." The same word is found in 1 Samuel 16:11, referring to David, and by then David had already established a reputation as "a mighty man of valor" (1 Sam. 16:18), having killed a lion and a bear (1 Sam. 17:34-37). Note their taunt, "Go up, thou bald head," an obvious effort to ridicule the rapture of Elijah. (See Lev. 26:21, 22.)

4. Causing some empty ditches to fill with water (2 Ki. 3:16-27).
This took place during the days of Jehoshaphat, king of Judah. Jehoshaphat was again tricked by the Ahab dynasty into an unholy alliance. This time (the fourth and final), King Jehoram, Ahab's youngest son, persuaded him into a fighting alliance to defeat the Moabites, who had rebelled against Israel by refusing to pay their tribute after Ahab's death (3:1-8).

The two allied armies met in the wilderness of Edom and immediately were faced with the problem of water. In desperation both kings turned to Elisha when it was discovered he was secretly traveling with them. Elisha utterly spurned the pleas of wicked Jehoram, but agreed to help for Jehoshaphat's sake. At his order, great trenches were dug and the next day God had filled them all with water (3:9-20).

The Moabites were now aware of the impending attack and began to marshal their forces along the frontier. On the day of the battle, the Moabites mistook the rays of the sun shining across the water-filled trenches for blood, and immediately attacked, concluding that their enemies were fighting a bloody battle among themselves (3:21-23).

This reckless action led them into a trap which resulted in their total defeat. The Moabite king made one last effort to break through the siege by leading an attack of 700 swordsmen. When this failed, he took his oldest son and, to the horror of the watching allied armies, killed and sacrificed him as a burnt offering to his pagan god (3:22-27).

5. Creating oil in empty vessels (4:1-7).
At Samaria he rescued a poverty-stricken widow of a God-fearing man from her creditor, who was threatening to enslave her two sons for non-payment. Elisha ordered the woman to borrow every possible container from her neighbors and then pour her remaining jar of olive oil into these vessels. She did this and every container was supernaturally filled, thus solving her indebtedness problem (2 Ki. 4:1-7). God loves to use little things.
   a. He used Moses' rod (Ex. 4:2).
   b. He used Aaron's rod (Num. 17:8).
   c. He used David's sling (1 Sam. 17:49).
   d. He used Gideon's trumpet (Jdg. 7:18).
   e. He used the widow's handful of meal (1 Ki. 17:12).
   f. He used a little boy's lunch (Jn. 6:9-11).

6. Raising a dead boy at Shunem (4:18-21, 32-37).
In Shunem he was given a sleeping room by a prominent woman of that city and her husband. To reward her kindness for his prophet's chamber, Elisha promised she would have a son. The son was born, but fell sick some years later and died. In desperation the mother found Elisha and begged him to do something. He then sent his carnal servant Gehazi who laid the prophet's staff upon the dead child's face, but all in vain. Elisha then arrived and stretched his body across the child. The lad became warm, sneezed seven times, and opened his eyes (2 Ki. 4:8-37). Elisha would later advise this woman to leave the land during a divinely sent seven-year famine. Upon return, she went to the northern king (Jehoram) to get her land back. Gehazi happened to be there and was relating to the king how Elisha had once raised a boy from the dead. At that very moment she walked in. The king was so impressed he restored all her land (2 Ki. 8:1-6).

7. Purifying a poisonous stew at Gilgal (4:38-41).
In Gilgal a student prophet had unknowingly prepared some harmful stew for the students' lunch hour by adding some poisonous wild gourds. Upon discovering this, Elisha purified the soup by throwing some meal into it (2 Ki. 4:38-41).

8. Feeding 100 men by supernaturally increasing twenty loaves of bread and a sack of corn (4:42-44).

Near Baal-shalishah he fed one thousand men supernaturally from a sack of fresh corn and twenty loaves of barley bread. Again the prophet's servant Gehazi displayed his carnality by doubting this could be done. He acted here as Philip and Andrew would later respond prior to the feeding of the 5000 performed by our Lord in John 6:5-13. (See 2 Ki. 4:42-44.)

9. Healing of Naaman (5:1-19).
The Syrian king at this time had an army commander whose name was Naaman. This general was honorable, brave, and successful, but he had a problem, for he was also a leper (2 Ki. 5:1). A little Israeli slave girl who was serving in the Naaman household told her master about the miraculous power of the prophet Elisha in Israel. Acting upon her testimony, the Syrian king sent Naaman to Jehoram (Israel's ruler) carrying $20,000 in silver, $60,000 in gold, and ten units of clothing, along with a personal royal letter requesting healing (5:2-6).

Jehoram was filled with both wrath and fear at this impossible request and concluded Syria demanded this as an excuse to invade the land again. However, Elisha soon learned the purpose of Naaman's visit, and bid the leprous general to visit him (5:7, 8). Naaman arrived and waited outside Elisha's home where he was instructed by a servant to wash seven times in the Jordan River, which would cure his leprosy. The Syrian soldier was furious at such "impersonal treatment" but finally was persuaded by his own servants to obey. This he did and was immediately healed (5:9-14).

Naaman arrived back at Elisha's home and was this time greeted by the prophet, but his offered reward was refused. Elisha's servant, Gehazi, coveted the money and later told Naaman that his master had changed his mind. Naaman gave him $4,000 and two expensive robes. Elisha discovered this, and Gehazi was divinely punished by being afflicted with the kind of leprosy of which Naaman was cured (5:15-27).

10. Predicting the judgment of leprosy upon Gehazi (2 Ki. 5:15-27).

11. Recovering a lost axehead (6:1-7).
At the river Jordan, Elisha caused an axehead which had accidentally fallen into the water to float on top (2 Ki. 6:1-7).

12. Revealing the secret war plans of Syria (6:8-12).
Elisha the prophet, who had once refused to help Jehoram, the northern king, now aided him by warning the monarch of several planned Syrian ambushes (2 Ki. 6:8-10).

The Syrian king concluded a traitor in his camp must be informing Israel of their plans, but was told by one of his officers that Elisha was supernaturally revealing these plans (6:11, 12). Syrian troops were immediately dispatched to arrest Elisha at Dothan. The prophet awakened the next day and found himself surrounded by a great army of chariots and horses (6:13-15).

13. Praying that his servant could see an invisible angelic army and blinding the Syrian army (6:15-23).
His servant, Gehazi, was terrified, but was soon reassured by Elisha.

"And he answered, Fear not: for they that be with us are more than they that be with them. And Elisha prayed, and said, Lord, I pray thee, open his eyes, that he may see. And the Lord opened the eyes of the young man; and he saw: and, behold, the mountain was full of horses and chariots of fire round about Elisha. And when they came down to him, Elisha prayed unto the Lord, and said, Smite this people, I pray thee, with blindness. And he smote them with blindness according to the word of Elisha" (6:16-18).

Elisha then led these sightless Syrian soldiers into Samaria, where their eyes were opened. King Jehoram (the northern king) determined to slay his helpless enemies, but was forbidden to do so by Elisha (6:19-23). This little account by itself totally refutes the devilish claim of liberals and unbelievers that the Old Testament is one huge bloody "eye-for-an-eye" slaughter story. Here an entire Syrian army was defeated by sheer kindness. (See Rom. 12:20, 21; Prov. 25:21, 22; Mt. 5:43-45.)

14. Blinding the entire Syrian army (2 Ki. 6:18-23).

15. Predicting the salvation of Samaria from starvation (2 Ki. 7).
Some years later (perhaps after Naaman's death) the Syrians invaded Israel and besieged the city capitol of Samaria, causing a great famine. This must have been indescribably horrible, for even a donkey's head sold for $50.00 and a pint of dove's dung brought $3.00. Things became so desperate that even cannibalism was practiced (6:29).

All this was tragically prophesied over five centuries before by Moses. (See Lev. 26:27-29.) The southern kingdom of Judah would later be reduced to this same pit of despair during the destruction of Jerusalem. (Compare Deut. 28:53 with Lam. 4:10; see 2 Kings 6:25-29.) The northern king, Jehoram, bitterly remembered how Elisha had once refused to allow him to kill the blinded Syrian soldiers some years back, and vowed to execute the prophet, blaming him for the present terrible situation (6:31). The unruffled Elisha ignored the king's threats and predicted that within twenty-four hours food would be so plentiful that two gallons of flour and four gallons of barley grain would only bring a dollar in the Samaritan market. He also prophesied that the king's chief officer, an especially arrogant man, would see this food but never live to eat it (7:1, 2).

Outside the gate of the city sat four starving lepers who decided in desperation to surrender to the Syrians and began walking toward their camp (7:3, 4). But God caused their very footsteps to resemble the clatter of speeding chariots and horses. In panic, the Syrians fled, concluding that Samaria must have hired the Hittites and Egyptians to attack them (7:5-7).

God had employed this method before. (See 2 Sam. 5:23, 24; Jdg. 7:16-21; 2 Chron. 20:20-25.) After looting the camp, the four lepers reported the good news to Samaria. Soon thousands of frantically happy men and women were rushing out from the main gate to gather food. In their mad drive, the king's official, attempting to control the traffic, was knocked down and crushed to death, just as Elisha had predicted. That very day two gallons of flour and four gallons of barley grain did indeed sell for a dollar (7:8-20).

16. Predicting the death of Ben-hadad, King of Syria, and the subsequent reign of Hazael over Syria (2 Ki. 8:7-15).

Elisha went to Damascus to visit Ben-hadad, the ailing Syrian king. En route he was greeted by Hazael, an important Syrian official who presented the prophet with forty camel loads of the best products of the land. Hazael was instructed to inquire whether Ben-hadad would recover from his illness. Elisha gave the strange answer that he would indeed get well, but would still die (2 Ki. 8:7-10).

Elisha then predicted that Hazael would become the next king of Syria and that his reign would shed much Israelite blood. Hazael denied this, but the very next day he smothered to death his master, Ben-hadad (8:11-15).

Hazael would later oppress Israel without mercy. (See 2 Ki. 13:22.) Elisha instructed one of his young prophets to locate a professional charioteer in Ramoth-gilead named Jehu and anoint him the next king over Israel. This was done and Jehu was ordered by God to execute the dynasty of Ahab, including Jezebel, whom the dogs would later eat (2 Ki. 9:1-10). Note: The anointing of both

# Elisha

## ELISHA AND EIGHTEEN EXCITING EVENTS

1. Parting the waters at Jordan—
**2 KINGS 2:14**

2. Purifying the waters at Jericho—
**2 KINGS 2:19-22**

3. Judging some hoodlums at Bethel—
**2 KINGS 2:23, 24**

4. Causing some empty ditches to fill with water—
**2 KINGS 3:16-27**

5. Creating oil in empty vessels—
**2 KINGS 4:1-7**

6. Raising a dead boy at Shunam—
**2 KINGS 4:18-21; 32-37**

7. Purifying a poisonous stew at Gilgal—
**2 KINGS 4:38-41**

8. Feeding 100 men by supernaturally increasing twenty loaves of bread and a sack of corn—
**2 KINGS 4:42-44**

9. Healing of Naaman from leprosy—
**2 KINGS 5:1-14**

10. Predicting the judgment of leprosy upon Gehazi—
**2 KINGS 5:15-27**

11. Recovering a lost axehead from the Jordan—
**2 KINGS 6:1-7**

12. Revealing the secret war plans of Syria to Israel—
**2 KINGS 6:8-12**

13. Praying that his servant would see an invisible angelic army—
**2 KINGS 6:13-17**

14. Blinding the entire Syrian army—
**2 KINGS 6:18-23**

15. Promising deliverance to the starving citizens of Samaria—
**2 KINGS 6:24—7:20**

16. Predicting the death of Benhadad, king of Syria, and the subsequent reign of Hazael over Syria—
**2 KINGS 8:7-15**

17. Predicting three victories by Israel over Syria—
**2 KINGS 13:14-19**

18. Raising a dead man years after Elisha himself had died—
**2 KINGS 13:20, 21**

Hazael and Jehu was ordered by God to be performed by Elijah, but for some reason he did not accomplish this. (See 1 Ki. 19:15, 16.)

17. Predicting Israel's three victories over Syria (2 Ki. 13:14–19).

On his deathbed Elisha was visited by Jehoash, a wicked northern king of Israel. In spite of his evil ways he did apparently have some affection for Elisha. Jehoash visited the dying prophet and wept over his impending death. Following Elisha's strange command, the king shot an arrow from his bedroom window. This was to symbolize Israel's victory over the Syrians. He was then instructed to strike the floor with some arrows, which he timidly did three times, thus angering Elisha, who told him he should have hit the ground five or six times, for each strike assured him of a victory over Syria (2 Ki. 13:14–19).

During the period that followed, Jehoash reconquered the cities his father had previously lost, and defeated the Syrians on three specific occasions, just as Elisha had predicted (13:22–25).

18. Raising a man from the dead years after the prophet himself had died (13:20, 21).

Elisha died and was buried. After some years, a corpse was being buried near the prophet's grave and was accidentally allowed to touch the bones of Elisha. The dead man suddenly revived and jumped to his feet (13:20, 21).

## OBADIAH (around 848 B.C.)

INTRODUCTION:

1. Obadiah is the shortest and smallest Old Testament book.
2. We know nothing about the author except his name, which means, "The servant of the Lord."
3. Obadiah has only one theme, and that concerns the destruction of the nation, Edom, for its treachery toward Judah.
4. There were at least four instances when Edom helped in the plunder of Jerusalem and Judah. These were:
   a. during the reign of Joram (853 B.C.) (2 Chron. 21:8, 16, 17; Amos 1:6)
   b. during the reign of Amaziah (796 B.C.) (2 Chron. 25:11, 12, 23, 24)
   c. during the reign of Ahaz (735 B.C.) (2 Chron. 28:16–21)
   d. during the reign of Zedekiah (597 B.C.) (2 Chron. 36:11–21; Ps. 137:7)

I. The House of Edom—to be reviled by God (1:1–16).
   A. Because of their thankless heart (1:1–9).
      1. They had become proud and arrogant because they lived in those high, inaccessible, mountainous cliffs, which surrounded their capital, the city of Petra.
         Note: These unique ruins, cut out of the solid cliffs of rose-colored rock and long hidden in the arid regions of the Dead Sea, were discovered in A.D. 1812.
      2. Esau had founded and fathered this proud people. (See Gen. 25:30; 36:1.)

## THE WRITING PROPHETS OF THE CHAOTIC KINGDOM STAGE

| AUTHOR | YEARS OF MINISTRY | DATES | DESTINATION |
|---|---|---|---|
| 1. Obadiah | 10 | 850-840 | EDOM |
| 2. Jonah | 35 | 785-750 | NINEVEH |
| 3. Nahum | 30 | 650-620 | NINEVEH |
| 4. Amos | 7 | 760-753 | NORTH (Israel) |
| 5. Hosea | 60 | 760-700 | NORTH |
| 6. Joel | 7 | 841-834 | SOUTH (Judah) |
| 7. Isaiah | 58 | 739-681 | SOUTH |
| 8. Micah | 35 | 735-700 | SOUTH |
| 9. Zephaniah | 20 | 640-620 | SOUTH |
| 10. Habakkuk | 3 | 609-606 | SOUTH |
| 11. Jeremiah | 32 | 627-575 | SOUTH |
| 12. Lamentations | — | 586 | SOUTH |

3. God prophesied every nook and cranny of Petra would be searched and robbed, and every treasure found and taken.
4. Edom's allies would turn against them.
5. Their wise men would be filled with stupidity. Edom was noted for her wise men. Eliphaz, the wisest of Job's three friends, was from Teman, five miles east of Petra in Edom. (See Job 2:11; Obad. 1:8.)
6. The mightiest soldiers of Teman would be confused and helpless to prevent this awful slaughter.

B. Because of their treacherous hand (1:10–16).
   1. They deserted their blood brothers (Judah) in time of great need. Both peoples were, of course, related, for two twin brothers, Jacob and Esau, were their forefathers.
   2. They stood aloof, refusing to lift even one finger to help.
   3. They actually rejoiced over Judah's agony.
   4. They mocked them.
   5. They occupied their lands after the captivity.
   6. They stood at the crossroads and killed those trying to escape.
   7. Those they did not murder were returned to Judah's enemies, or became prisoners of war.

II. The House of Jacob—to be revived by God (1:17–21).
   A. In spite of their terrible persecutions and punishments, some deserved and others undeserved, Judah will someday be fully restored to Palestine.
   B. The Israelites will then control tremendous land areas never before occupied, including the land of Edom.
   C. Judges will rule over Edom and Petra from Jerusalem during the millennium.
      Note: Some of these prophecies concerning Edom have already come to pass, at least in part.
      1. By 312 B.C., the Nabataeans, an Arab people, had displaced the Edomites living in Petra.

2. They then fled to Southern Palestine and were later subdued by the Jewish military hero, John Hyrcanus, during the Maccabean period (134–104 B.C.).
3. Wicked King Herod came from this displaced group of Edomites.
4. They were destroyed in A.D. 70, along with the Jews, when they revolted against the Roman empire.
5. Other Scripture verses which foretell the doom of Edom are:
Isaiah 34:5–15; Ezekiel 25:12–14; 35:1–15; Amos 1:11, 12.
6. In spite of the nation's sins, a gracious God will someday restore Edom. (See Isa. 11:14.)

# JOEL (835–796 B.C.)
INTRODUCTION:
1. As with Obadiah, almost nothing is known concerning the prophet Joel. He was the son of Pethuel, and his name means, "Jehovah is God."
2. Sometime during Joel's ministry, the land of Judah was struck by a ferocious locust plague, more intense than any experienced before.
3. Joel, under divine inspiration, compares that terrible locust plague to the coming tribulation period.
4. Joel is also known as the prophet of Pentecost, because his words about the Holy Spirit were later quoted by Simon Peter on the day of Pentecost.

I. Israel and God's Judgment: A review of the past (1:1–20).
A. The severity of the locust judgment.
"That which the palmer worm hath left hath the locust eaten; and that which the locust hath left hath the cankerworm eaten; and that which the cankerworm hath left hath the caterpillar eaten" (1:4).
Some expositors interpret these words as describing the four stages in the development of the caterpillar, while others consider them to be four different kinds of insects. Locusts were often sent as a judgment from God. (See Deut. 28:38–42; Ex. 10:12–15; 1 Ki. 8:37; Rev. 9:1–12.)
B. The title name for the locust judgment.
"Alas for the day! For the day of the Lord is at hand, and as a destruction from the Almighty shall it come" (1:15).
This is the second mention in the minor prophets of the term, "The day of the Lord." It can be found in many passages, both in the Old and New Testaments. (See Isa. 2:12; 13:6, 9; Ezek. 13:5; 30:3; Joel 2:1, 11, 31; 3:14; Amos 5:18, 20; Obad. 1:15; Zeph. 1:7, 14; Zech 14:1; Mal. 4:5; Acts 2:20; 1 Thess. 5:2; 2 Thess. 2:2; 2 Pet. 3:10.) The phrase is almost always a reference to the seven-year tribulation period, but here in Joel 1:15, the prophet uses it to refer to the judgment then going on.
II. Israel and God's Judgment: A preview of the future (2:1—3:21).
A. The identity of this invasion. What nation or enemy is Joel speaking of here in chapters 2 and 3? He may be referring to several in general, giving special emphasis to the last in particular.
1. The Assyrian invasion in 701 B.C., led by Sennacherib and crushed at the very gates of Jerusalem by God's death angel (2 Ki. 19). See Joel 2:20.
2. The Babylonian invasion in 586 B.C., led by Nebuchadnezzar (2 Ki. 24).
3. The Russian invasion, during the middle of the tribulation, to be led by Gog (Ezek. 38, 39).
4. The final invasion, at the end of the tribulation, to be led by the antichrist at the battle of Armageddon (Rev. 16:13–16; 19:11–21).
B. The gathering place of this invasion.
"I will also gather all nations, and will bring them down into the Valley of Jehoshaphat, and will judge them there" (3:2). (See also 3:9–14.)
Note: This battle, the biggest, boldest, bloodiest, and most brazen of all time, will stretch from the city of Megiddo on the north (Zech. 12:11; Rev. 16:16), to Edom on the south (Isa. 34:5, 6; 63:1), a distance of some 200 miles. It will reach from the Mediterranean Sea on the west to the hills of Moab on the east, a distance of 100 miles. Thus, the total fighting area will exceed twenty thousand square miles. The center of the action will apparently be the Valley of Jehoshaphat, located just east of Jerusalem, between the Holy City and the Mount of Olives. It is also known as the Kidron Valley.
C. The twofold purpose for this invasion gathering.
1. The purpose of the antichrist—to destroy Israel and her God. (See Ps. 2.)
2. The purpose of God—to destroy antichrist and his allies.
D. The outcome of this invasion.
"The sun and the moon shall be darkened, and the stars shall withdraw their shining. The Lord also shall roar out of Zion, and utter his voice from Jerusalem; and the heavens and the earth shall shake: but the Lord will be the

## Joel

### The prophet used an event contemporary in his day to describe coming events

**CONTEMPORARY EVENTS—Joel 1**
**A Review of Israel's Current Insect Invasion**
- Nature: A terrible locust plague had settled down upon the land **(1:4, 12)**
- Reason: Because of Israel's sin **(1:5)**
- Suggested cure: Call for a special meeting, pray, and repent **(1:14)**

**COMING EVENTS—Joel 2-3**
**A Preview of Israel's Coming Enemy Invasion**
- Identity: Probably twofold:
  1. The Russian invasion during the middle of the tribulation, led by Gog **(Ezek. 38-39)**
  2. The final invasion at the end of the tribulation, led by the antichrist **(Rev. 16:13-16; 19:11-21)**
- Location: Valley of Jehoshaphat **(3:2, 9-14)**
- Purpose:
  1. The purpose of Satan—to destroy Israel and her God **(Ps. 2)**
  2. The purpose of God—to destroy Satan and his allies **(Rev. 16:16)**
- Results:
  1. The salvation of Israel **(3:15-21)**
  2. The sanctification of Israel **(2:21-32)**

hope of his people and the strength of the children of Israel" (Joel 3:15, 16). (Also see Rev. 19:11-21.)
E. The blessings after this invasion has been crushed.
   1. God's Spirit will be poured out upon all flesh. (See 2:28-32.) It should be noted that this passage event will mark the fulfillment of Moses' desire. (See Num. 11:29.)
      Peter would later quote this passage in Joel on the day of Pentecost. (See Acts 2:16-21.) This he did, not to indicate that Pentecost was the *fulfillment* of Joel's prophecy (for it was not), but, rather, as an *example* of it.
   2. All human needs will be provided for (2:21-27).
   3. Nature itself will be transformed (3:18).
   4. Christ himself will reign in Zion (3:21). Mount Zion is the height which rises close to the southwest corner of the old walled city. It was once within the walls of ancient Jerusalem. It is held to be one of the most sacred places in Israel, because there is located the traditional tomb of King David. Above it is an upper room believed to be on the site of that upper room in which Jesus and his disciples ate the last Passover together and where he established the Communion service (Mk. 14:12-16; Lk. 22:7-13). This upper room has also been considered to be the place where the twelve disciples were gathered when the Holy Spirit came upon them on the day of Pentecost (Act 1:12-14; 2:1-4).

# JONAH (780-750)
INTRODUCTION:
A. The book of Jonah is one of three Old Testament books especially hated by Satan. These are:
   1. Genesis, which predicts the incarnation of Christ as the seed of the woman (Gen. 3:15).
   2. Daniel, which predicts the glorious Second Coming of Christ (Dan. 7:9-12) to destroy his enemies.
   3. Jonah, which predicts (in type form) the death and resurrection of Christ. (Compare Jonah 2 with Mt. 12:38-41.)
B. There are three basic interpretations of the book of Jonah.
   1. The *mythological* approach. This is the liberal view, which would look upon Jonah as it would Robinson Crusoe, Gulliver (of *Gulliver's Travels*), or Hercules.
   2. The *allegorical* (or parabolic) approach. In this view the book is merely an extended parable. Thus:
      a. Jonah is really Israel.
      b. The sea is Gentile nations in general.
      c. The fish is the Babylonian captivity.
      d. The regurgitation is the return during Ezra's time.
         "Surely this is not the record of actual historical events nor was it ever intended as such. It is a sin against the author to treat as literal prose what he intended as poetry . . . His story is thus a story with a moral, a parable, a prose poem like the story of the Good Samaritan." (Julius Bewer, *International Critical Commentary*)

3. The *literal-historical* approach. This, alone, is the correct view.
   a. The account presents itself as actual history.
   b. The Jews and early church believed it to be literal.
   c. The author of 2 Kings (14:25) refers to Jonah as a historical person. His hometown is given, along with the name of his father, and the king he served under.
   d. Jesus testified to the literal account of Jonah (Mt. 12:38-41; 16:4; Lk. 11:29-32).
4. Jonah was from Gath-heper of Zebulun (Josh. 19:13), north of Nazareth in Galilee. Thus, the Pharisees were in error concerning their statement recorded in John 7:52—"Search, and look; for out of Galilee ariseth no prophet."

I. Jonah Protesting (demonstrating God's patience)— chapter 1:
   A. The command of God—Go! (1:1, 2).
      God orders his prophet to proceed to Nineveh and preach out against the city's exceeding wickedness.
   B. The action of the minister—No! (1:3).
      1. The futility of his action. Jonah foolishly attempts the impossible—to flee from God's presence! (See Ps. 139:7-12.) He purchases a fare to Tarshish (ancient name for Spain) from the Port of Joppa. This port is significant, for some eight centuries later, another Jewish preacher would receive a similar command to share the Gospel with some Gentiles! (See Acts 10:5.)
      2. The reason for his action. Why did he disobey? Several reasons have been offered.
         a. Because he was a coward. This is definitely in error, as seen by 1:12.
         b. Because he was an extreme nationalist. This seems to be the logical answer. At this time in history, Assyria was on the rise and many felt it would only be a matter of time before her blood-covered boots came marching toward Palestine. The cruelty of the Assyrian armies was unparalleled in ancient history. Consider the following testimonies from various authors:
            "Some of the victims were held down while one of the band of torturers, who are portrayed upon the monuments gloating fiendishly over their fearful work, inserts his hand into the victim's mouth, grips his tongue, and wrenches it out by the roots. In another spot, pegs are driven into the ground. To these, another victim's wrists are fixed with cords. His ankles are similarly made fast, and the man is stretched out, unable to move a muscle. The executioner then applies himself to his task; and beginning at the accustomed spot, the sharp knife makes its incision, the skin is raised inch by inch till the man is flayed alive. These skins are then stretched out upon the city walls, or otherwise disposed of so as to terrify the people

and leave behind long-enduring impressions of Assyrian vengeance. For others, long, sharp poles are prepared. The sufferer, taken like all the rest from the leading men of the city, is laid down; the sharpened end of the pole is driven in through the lower part of the chest; the pole is then raised, bearing the writhing victim aloft; it is planted in the hole dug for it, and the man is left to die."

"Pyramids of human heads marked the path of the conqueror; boys and girls were burnt alive or reserved for a worse fate; men were impaled, flayed alive, blinded, or deprived of their hands and feet, or their ears and noses, while the women and children were carried into slavery, the captured city plundered and reduced to ashes, and the trees in its neighborhood cut down."

C. The hand of God—Blow! (1:4-12).
1. God suddenly flings a terrific wind over the sea, causing a great storm.
2. The frightened sailors pray to their various pagan gods and frantically throw the cargo they are carrying overboard to lighten the ship.
3. During this time, Jonah is sound asleep in the ship's hold. Upon hearing this, the captain awakes him and orders that he, too, make prayer to his God for salvation.
4. In desperation, the sailors cast lots to determine who among them had brought the storm by offending his God. The lot falls upon Jonah.
5. Jonah admits to them his nationality and sin of disobeying God. He then advises them to throw him overboard.

D. The action of the mariners—Throw! (1:13-17).
1. After further useless strugglings, the sailors cry out a prayer for forgiveness for what they have to do with Jonah and quickly throw him overboard into the boiling sea.
2. Immediately, the raging waters become calm as the storm ceases. The amazed sailors give thanks to Jehovah God.
3. Jonah is swallowed by a huge fish, which God had previously arranged for.

Of all the miracles in the Bible, none is better known or has raised more eyebrows, than this one.

Dr. J. Vernon McGee writes:

"The fish here is not the hero of the story, neither is it its villain. The book is not even about a fish. The fish is among the props and does not occupy the star's dressing room. Let us distinguish between the essentials and the incidentals. Incidentals are the fish, the gourd, the east wind, the boat, and Nineveh. The essentials are Jehovah and Jonah—God and man."

The question is often asked as to whether a whale could actually swallow a man. In the first place, it should be pointed out that nowhere in the original Old Testament or New Testament language does it say a whale swallowed Jonah. The word "whale" does not even appear in the King James Version in the book of Jonah. The Hebrew word for fish is *dag,* and refers to a great sea monster. In Matthew 12:40, the word translated *whale* by the King James Version is the Greek word, *ketos,* which again refers to a sea monster. In the second place, God *could* have used a whale, had he chosen to. Dr. Gleason Archer writes the following paragraph:

"Numerous cases have been reported in more recent times of men who have survived the ordeal of being swallowed by a whale. The *Princeton Theological Review* (Oct., 1927) tells of two incidents, one in 1758 and the other in 1771, in which a man was swallowed by a whale and vomited up shortly thereafter with only minor injuries.

One of the most striking instances comes from Francis Fox, *Sixty Three Years of Engineering* (pp. 298-300), who reports that this incident was carefully investigated by two scientists (one of whom was M. DeParville, the scientific editor of the *Journal Des Debats* in Paris). In February, 1891, the whaling ship, *Star of the East,* was in the vicinity of the Falkland Islands, and the lookout sighted a large sperm whale three miles away. Two boats were lowered and in a short time, one of the harpooners was enabled to spear the creature. The second boat also attacked the whale, but was then upset by a lash of its tail, so that its crew fell into the sea. One of them was drowned, but the other, James Bartley, simply disappeared without a trace. After the whale was killed, the crew set to work with axes and spades removing the blubber. They worked all day and part of the night. The next day they attached some tackle to the stomach, which was hoisted on deck. The sailors were startled by something in it which gave spasmodic signs of life, and inside was found the missing sailor, doubled up and unconscious. He was laid on the deck and treated to a bath of sea water, which soon revived him. At the end of the third week, he had entirely recovered from the shock and resumed his duties . . . His face, and neck and hands were bleached to a deadly whiteness and took on the appearance of parchment. Bartley affirms that he would probably have lived inside his house of flesh until he starved, for he lost his senses through fright and not through lack of air." (*A Survey of Old Testament Introduction*), p. 302

II. Jonah Praying (demonstrating God's pardon)—chapter 2:
A. The petition (2:1-8).
1. Jonah immediately begins an earnest and all-out one-man prayer meeting. His altar was

perhaps the strangest ever used, the slippery slopes of a fish's stomach!

2. Some believe Jonah's language seems to indicate he actually died and was later resurrected by God. Note his phrases:
   a. "Out of the belly of hell (*sheol*)" (v. 2).
   b. "Thou brought up my life from corruption" (v. 6).
   c. "My soul fainted within me" (v. 7).

   While there is no question that God could have done this, the simple context approach would suggest Jonah did not die, but was at the point of death.

3. On two occasions, Jonah refers to "thine holy temple." (See vs. 4, 7.) In fact, he points his prayer in this direction. Jonah was no doubt calling to remembrance Solomon's Temple dedication some 150 years back (1 Ki. 8:38, 39).

   "What prayer and supplication soever be made by any man, or by all thy people Israel, which shall know every man the plague of his own heart, and spread forth his hands toward this house: Then hear thou in heaven thy dwelling place, and forgive, and do, and give to every man according to his ways, whose heart thou knowest; (for thou, even thou only, knowest the hearts of all the children of men)."

4. One can almost picture the pathetic and praying prophet as he sloshed and slid around with the seaweeds wrapped around his head. The backslider is often forced to wear a strange halo!

5. Jonah mentions a scientific fact totally unknown by human resources in that day when he speaks of the mountains which rise from off the ocean floor (see v. 6). This is just another little proof that the Bible is, indeed, the very Word of God!

6. Jonah renounces his sin, remembers his vow of service, and reconsecrates his life to God (vs. 8, 9).

B. The pardon (2:9, 10).
   1. He ends his prayer with a five-word summary of the entire Bible and, indeed, the very plan and purpose of God: "Salvation is of the Lord!" (v. 9).
   2. He is then vomited up on dry land by the fish.

III. Jonah Preaching (demonstrating God's power)—chapter 3:
A. The warning —(3:1-4).
   1. His mission field:
      "Nineveh lay on the eastern side of the Tigris, and was one of the greatest—if not the greatest—of the cities of antiquity. It had 1,200 towers, each 200 feet high, and its wall was 100 feet high, and of such breadth that three chariots could drive on it abreast. It was 60 miles in circumference, and could, within its walls, grow corn enough for its population of 600,000. Zenophon says the basement of its wall was of polished stone, and its width 50

feet. In the city was a magnificent palace, with courts and walls covering more than 100 acres. The roofs were supported by beams of cedar, resting on columns of cypress, inlaid and strengthened by bands of sculptured silver and iron; its gates were guarded by huge lions and bulls sculptured in stone; its doors were of ebony and cypress encrusted with iron, silver, and ivory, and panelling the rooms were sculptured slabs of alabaster, and cylinders and bricks with cuneiform inscriptions. Hanging gardens were filled with rich plants and rare animals, and served with other temples and palaces, libraries and arsenals, to adorn and enrich the city; and all was built by the labor of foreign slaves."

2. His message:
   "Yet forty days and Nineveh shall be overthrown" (v. 4). Forty is often the number of testing in the Bible, as indicated by the following:
   a. The flood rains continued forty days in Noah's time (Gen. 7:17).
   b. Moses spent forty days on Mt. Sinai (Ex. 24:18).
   c. The twelve spies searched out Palestine for forty days (Num. 13:25).
   d. Israel wandered for forty years in the wilderness (Num. 14:33).
   e. Jesus was tempted for forty days (Mt. 4:2).
   f. Forty days elapsed between his resurrection and ascension (Acts 1:3).

B. The mourning—(3:5-9).
   1. This chapter describes the greatest revival in all recorded history. No other physical miracle in this book (or any other Old Testament book) compares with the marvel and extent of this spiritual miracle! In the New Testament, Jesus later warned that his entire generation (in general) would someday be drastically affected because: "The men of Nineveh shall rise in judgment with this generation and shall condemn it: because they repented at the preaching of Jonah; and behold, a greater than Jonah is here" (Mt. 12:41).
   2. The critic, however, always anxious to knock the Bible, has gleefully pointed out that secular history records no such revival in Nineveh as described here. Dr. H. Freeman writes:
      "The complaint that there is no record of Nineveh's repentance in secular history is not only a valueless argument from silence, but ignores the fact that the event *is* recorded in Biblical history in the book of Jonah. Remember the Hittites! They were an ancient people mentioned in more than a dozen Old Testament books. Of the Hittites no trace could be found, leading some critics to view these Old Testament references with suspicion. Archaeological discoveries in the early

part of the twentieth century, however, not only co⹁rmed the Biblical references as accurate, but also revealed the Hittites to be an important people with an extended empire during the fourteenth and thirteenth centuries B.C." *(Introduction to the Old Testament)*

However, secular history may, indeed, hint to this sacred revival recorded in Jonah after all. It is known that about this time there was a religious movement in Nineveh, which resulted in a change from the worship of many gods to that of one God whom they called Nebo. Nebo was the son in the Babylonian trinity. His name meant, "The Proclaimer, the Prophet."

He was the proclaimer of the mind and will of the trinity head. Nebo was the god of wisdom, the creator, the angelic overseer. Some believe Nebo had been worshiped in earlier days as the only supreme God. It is known that the Ninevite ruler Adal-Nirari III (810-783) had advocated a monotheistic worship system of some kind. *If* the revival took place at this time as a result of Jonah's preaching, then the use of their national name for the Son of God is what we might possibly expect. Jonah did not preach repentance to the Ninevites in the name of Yahweh (the Hebrew God of the Covenant), but in the name of Elohim (the triune Creator of the Universe; Gen. 1:1). Some believe, however, that the revival took place a little later, under the reign of King Assurdan III (771-754 B.C.) If so, then God had even more time to prepare the Ninevites, for:

   a. A great plague had occurred in 765 B.C.

   b. A total eclipse of the sun took place on June 15, 763 B.C..

   c. Another plague fell in 759 B.C.

C. The transforming (3:10).

"And God saw their works, that they turned from their evil way; and God repented of the evil that he had said that he would do unto them, and he did it not."

Two phrases in this verse deserve a brief comment:

1. "God repented"—that is, God changed his previously intended course of action. (See also Gen. 6:6; Ex. 32:14; 2 Sam. 24:16.)

2. "Of the evil." While it is true the Hebrew word *ra* (here translated evil) is usually connected with sin, it can also be (and is often) translated by such words as affliction, calamity, distress, grief, harm, trouble, and sorrow. The context would show that the latter meaning is meant here in Jonah 3:10. See also Jonah 1:7, 8 and Isaiah 45:7 for similar examples.

IV. Jonah Pouting (demonstrating God's pity)— chapter 4:

A. Lamenting over a city (4:1-5).

1. This chapter, along with 2 Samuel 11; 1 Kings 19; Genesis 9, 13, and others, demonstrates beyond any reasonable doubt that the Bible is not a book man would write if he could: Here God's chosen minister is presented as a petty and pouting prophet, sitting on a hill outside Nineveh and hoping the city will refuse his previous message and be destroyed! Surely Jeremiah's sober words apply here:

"The heart is deceitful above all things, and desperately wicked: who can know it?"

2. He reluctantly acknowledges the grace, mercy, and goodness of God, and then in brazen desperation and disappointment dares to pray:

"Therefore now, O Lord, take, I beseech thee, my life from me; for it is better for me to die than to live" (4:3).

See Numbers 11:15 (Moses); Jeremiah 20:14-18 (Jeremiah); 1 Kings 19:4 (Elijah) for similar requests.

3. God then attempted to reason with Jonah as he once did with Cain (Gen. 4:6, 7) and as he still does with sinners everywhere (Isa. 1:18).

B. Learning under a gourd (4:5-11).

1. Jonah makes a leafy lean-to shelter and continues to sit sulking on the hillside.

2. When the sun has withered the leafy shelter, to Jonah's surprise and relief, God arranges for a vine to grow quickly and shade him.

3. But God also prepares a worm, which soon eats through the vine's stem and kills it.

4. Finally, the Lord subjects his prophet to a scorching east wind, until he once again cries out for God to kill him.

5. Jonah is asked then if he regretted the destruction of the vine. The prophet loudly assures God he did, indeed, and the divine trap is sprung. God's final recorded words to Jonah must have softened his stubborn and carnal heart:

"Then said the Lord, Thou hast had pity on the gourd, for which thou hast not laboured, neither madest it grow; which came up in a night, and perished in a night: And should not I spare Nineveh, that great city, wherein are more than sixscore thousand persons that cannot discern between their right hand and their left hand; and also much cattle?" (4:10, 11).

# AMOS (765-750)

INTRODUCTION:

1. The name Amos means "burden." As Middle Eastern names are usually meaningful, this name may have referred to his unwelcome birth, or been given as a prophecy of his future ministry to describe his burdened heart over Judah and Israel's sin.

2. He was from the little town of Tekoa, some five miles from Bethlehem in Judea.

3. Amos was a herdsman (1:1; 7:14, 15) and a gatherer of sycamore fruit (7:14). He had not graduated from the school of the prophets, but was called by God to become a layman evangelist.

4. He was called to be a prophet to the whole house of Jacob (3:1, 13), but chiefly to the northern kingdom (7:14, 15) at the main sanctuary at Bethel (7:10). Here

he conducted his "Greater Samaritan Revival Campaign," and thundered away on the subjects of sin, separation, and sanctification.

5. Amos ministered during the reigns of Uzziah (King of Judah) and Jeroboam II (King of Israel), beginning his ministry some two years before a mighty earthquake had struck Palestine (1:1). This earthquake was so severe that Zechariah (a later Hebrew prophet) referred to it some 250 years later. (See Zech. 14:5.) Josephus, the Jewish historian, tells us the earthquake happened at the time when God punished King Uzziah with leprosy for his intrusion into the office of the priesthood. (See 2 Chron. 26:16-21.)

6. At the time of Amos' ministry, Israel, under powerful King Jeroboam II, was at its zenith of success. (See 2 Ki. 14:25.) But along with the nation's prosperity had come religious perversion!

I. Eight Nations Denounced (1-6).
   A. Syria—capital city, Damascus (1:1-5).
      1. This nation had often harassed Israel, especially under Ben-hadad I and King Hazael. (See 2 Ki. 10:32, 33; 1 Ki. 20:1; 2 Ki. 6:24.)
      2. God would thus:
         a. Burn down the palace of the capital city.
         b. Break down their strongholds.
         c. Cause many Syrians to die and others to be carried back into Kir, the land of their former slavery. (Compare 1:5 with 9:7.) Kir was located in Mesopotamia. See also 2 Kings 16:9.
   B. Philistia—capital city, Gaza (1:6-8).
      Philistia's four chief cities, Gaza, Ashdod, Ashkelon, and Ekron were to be judged because they sold Israelites into slavery to Edom. (See 2 Chron. 21:16, 17; Joel 3:4-8.)
   C. Phoenicia—capital city, Tyre (1:9, 10).
      1. They had broken their covenant of brotherhood with Israel (referring to the agreement David and Solomon had made with Tyre. See 1 Ki. 9:13).
      2. Israel had been attacked by Tyre and its citizens led into slavery to Edom. (See also Joel 3:4-8.)
      3. God would thus burn down the forts and palaces of Tyre.
   D. Edom—capital cities, Teman and Bozrah (1:11, 12).
      1. Teman was located southeast of Petra, and Bozrah was in north central Edom.
      2. Even though the Edomites and Israelites were closely related (one people from Esau, the other from Jacob, see Gen. 25:30), Israel had suffered grievously at the hands of Edom. (See also Mal. 1:2; Obad. 1:1-21.)
      3. Their strongholds would thus be burned.
   E. Ammon—capital city, Rabbah (1:13-15).
      1. The Ammonites, descendants of Lot's youngest daughter (Gen. 19:38) had committed cruel crimes, ripping open pregnant Israelite women with their swords during their expansion wars in Gilead.
      2. God would thus destroy their cities and enslave their people.
   F. Moab—capital city, Kirioth (2:1-3).
      1. These people (from Lot's older daughter, Gen. 19:37) had, among other crimes, dese-

crated the tombs of the kings of Edom, with no respect for the dead. (See 2 Ki. 3:26, 27.)
      2. Moab would be defeated in battle and its palaces burned.
   G. Judah—capital city, Jerusalem (2:4, 5).
      1. Judah had rejected the Word of God, and disobeyed the God of the Word.
      2. They had hardened their hearts as their fathers had done.
   H. Israel—capital city, Samaria (2:6-16).
      1. They had perverted justice by accepting bribes.
      2. They had sold the poor into slavery, trading them for a pair of shoes.
      3. Both fathers and sons were guilty of immorality with the same harlot.
      4. They were lounging in stolen clothing from their debtors at religious feasts.
      5. They had offered sacrifices of wine in the Temple, which had been purchased with stolen money.
      6. They were absolutely unthankful for God's past blessings.
      7. They caused Nazarites to sin by tempting them to drink wine.
      8. Because of all this, God would:
         a. Make them groan as a loaded-down wagon would groan.
         b. Cause their swiftest warriors to stumble in battle.
   I. The Whole House of Jacob (both Israel and Judah) (3:1—6:14).
      1. Jacob's punishment must equal her past privileges (3:1-3)
         "Hear this word that the Lord hath spoken against you, O children of Israel, against the whole family which I brought up from the land of Egypt, saying, You only have I known of all the families of the earth: therefore I will punish you for all your iniquities. Can two walk together, except they be agreed?"
      2. God was issuing them one final warning through his prophets (3:7).
      3. Jacob's enemies are called upon to attest to her wickedness (3:9).
         a. Her women had become cruel and demanding (4:1-3).
         b. Her formal and empty religious ceremonies had become an insult to divine holiness (4:4, 5; 5:21-26).
         c. They had surrounded themselves with gross luxury, with ivory beds to lie upon, and the choicest food to eat (6:4).
         d. They thought more of worldly music than their own Messiah (6:5).
         e. They had drunk wine by the bucketful, perfumed themselves with sweet ointments, and totally neglected the poor and needy (6:6).
      4. God had tried everything to bring his people to their senses (4:6-13). But they had refused. Thus, their former Savior would now become their Judge.
         "Therefore, thus will I do unto thee, O Israel; and because I will do this unto

thee, prepare to meet thy God, O Israel" (4:12).

5. One final invitation is extended by God (5:4–15).

"Seek him who maketh the . . . stars . . . and turneth the shadow of death into the morning, and maketh the day dark with night: that calleth for the waters of the sea, and poureth them out upon the face of the earth: The Lord is his name."

6. This invitation was rejected and judgment would fall.

a. Jacob would be consumed as a lion devours a sheep (3:12).

b. There would be crying in the streets and every road (5:16).

c. In that day they would be like a man who escaped from a lion, only to meet a bear. They would be as one who leans against a wall in a dark room and puts his hand upon a snake! (5:19).

d. Ninety percent of their soldiers would fall in battle (5:3).

II. Five Visions Announced (7–9).

A. The locust plague (7:1-3).

1. In a vision God revealed to Amos his intentions to destroy all the main crops that sprang up after the first mowing.

2. Amos interceded for Israel and a merciful God changed his course of action.

B. The vision of the great fire (7:4-6).

1. Amos saw a destructive fire, the heat from which was so fierce that it consumed the very waters of Palestine. This was to fall upon the land to punish sin.

2. Again the prophet pled for mercy, and again God set aside this deserved judgment.

C. The vision of the plumb line (7:7-16).

1. Amos viewed the Lord as he stood beside a wall built with a plumb line to see if it was straight.

2. God informed Amos:

a. That he would continue testing Israel with the plumb line of heavenly justice.

b. That he would no longer turn away from punishing.

c. That he would destroy the dynasty of Jeroboam II by the sword. This, of course, literally happened (as do all of God's prophecies). Jeroboam II was succeeded by his son Zechariah, who was assassinated by a rebel named Shallum after a reign of only six months. (See 2 Ki. 15:10-12.) God would later use this same plumb line on Judah during the days of wicked King Manasseh. (See 2 Ki. 21:13-15.)

3. At this point in his preaching ministry, Amos was confronted by Amaziah, the chairman of the Bethel ministerial association, who quickly issued two messages.

a. One was to King Jeroboam II, warning him against the "Bible banging" activities of Amos.

b. The other was to Amos himself, ordering him to leave Bethel and go back to his own land of Judah.

Amos quickly responded that, in spite of his lowly background (he was not a prophet, nor a prophet's son) he had been called by God and would not allow any middle-of-the-road spokesman to stop him. Amos then related to Amaziah from the Lord one of the most terrifying prophecies ever pronounced upon a human being, because of the false priest's attempts to silence God's true prophet.

(1) Amaziah's wife would become a common Bethel street prostitute.

(2) His sons and daughters would be killed.

(3) His land and possessions would be divided up.

(4) He, himself, would die as a captive in a heathen land.

D. The vision of the basket of summer fruit (8:1-14).

1. The meaning of this vision: God showed Amos a basket filled with ripe fruit, explaining that it symbolized Israel, which was now ripe for judgment.

2. The reason for this judgment vision. The cruel and totally materialistic merchants of the northern kingdom had:

a. robbed the poor (by selling them moldy food) and trampled upon the needy

b. longed for the Sabbath to end and various religious holidays to be over that they could once again start cheating, using their weighted scales and undersized measures

c. made slaves of the poor, buying them for their debt of a piece of silver or a pair of shoes

3. The results of this judgment vision:

a. The riotous sound of singing in the Temple would be turned to weeping.

b. Dead bodies would be scattered everywhere.

c. Fearful heavenly signs would occur:

"And it shall come to pass in that day, saith the Lord God, that I will cause the sun to go down at noon, and I will darken the earth in the clear day" (8:9). This frightening punishment will have its ultimate fulfillment during the coming great tribulation. (See Mt. 24:22, 29.)

d. There would be no comforting words from God (8:11, 12).

"Behold, the days come, saith the Lord God, that I will send a famine in the land, not a famine of bread, nor a thirst for water, but of hearing the words of the Lord: And they shall wander from sea to sea, and from north even to the east, they shall run to and fro to seek the word of the Lord, and shall not find it."

E. The vision of the Lord at the altar (9:1-15).

1. The condemnation of Israel's transgressors (9:1-10).

"Though they dig into hell [sheol] there shall mine hand take them; though they climb up to heaven, from there will I bring them down; and though they hide themselves in the top of [mount] Carmel, I will search and take them out from there; and though they be hidden from my sight in the bottom of the sea, there will I command the serpent and he shall bite them" (9:2, 3).

2. The restoration of David's Tabernacle (9:11-15).
   a. The Davidic monarchy was in a degraded condition with ten out of the twelve

# Amos

## PART ONE

## Eight Nations Denounced Amos 1-6

| NATION | CRIME | PUNISHMENT |
|---|---|---|
| **SYRIA** (1:1-5) | Had often harassed Israel | ● The capital at Damascus to be burned<br>● Their strongholds to be broken<br>● Their citizens to be enslaved |
| **PHILISTIA** (1:6-8) | Had sold Israelites into slavery to Edom | ● The burning of their four main cities: Gaza, Ashdod, Ashkelon, Ekron |
| **PHOENICIA** (1:9, 10) | Had broken their peace covenant with Israel | ● The burning down of the forts and palaces in Tyre, their chief city. |
| **EDOM** (1:11, 12) | Had murdered many Jews | ● The destruction of their cities |
| **AMMON** (1:13-15) | Had murdered Jewish women | Their cities to be burned<br>● Their citizens to be enslaved |
| **MOAB** (2:1-3) | Had desecrated the tombs of the dead | ● They would be defeated in battle |
| **JUDAH** (2:4, 5) | ● Had rejected the Word of God<br>● Had disobeyed the God of the Word | ● Their Temple in Jerusalem to be destroyed |
| **ISRAEL** (2:6-16) | ● Had accepted bribes<br>● Had enslaved the poor<br>● Had committed adultery<br>● Had stolen<br>● Were totally unthankful<br>● Had caused the innocent to sin | ● Their punishment would make them groan as a loaded-down wagon<br>● Their armies would stumble in battle |

Additional indictments upon the whole house of Israel —both southern and northern kingdoms **(3-6)**

## PART TWO

## Five Visions Announced Amos 7-9

**THE LOCUST PLAGUE** (7:1-3)

**THE GREAT FIRE** (7:4-6)

**THE PLUMB LINE** (7:7-16)

**THE BASKET OF SUMMER FRUIT** (8:1-4)

**THE LORD AT THE ALTAR** (9:1-15)

tribes refusing to give homage to it. But during the glorious millennium all this would change. James quotes Amos 9:11, 12 at the Jerusalem Council (Acts 15:14-17) and bases an important decision upon it, namely, should saved Gentiles be circumcised? His answer was a resounding *no!*

b. The blessings of this restored monarchy (under Christ, the rightful seed of David) would be manifold:
   (1) The harvest time will scarcely end before the farmer starts again to sow another crop.
   (2) The terraces of grapes upon the hills of Israel will drip sweet wine.
   (3) Israel's faithful will have their fortunes restored and be permanently regathered in the glorious land.

# HOSEA (755–715 B.C.)

INTRODUCTION:

1. Hosea's name means "salvation." He was a prophet to the northern kingdom, and wept over their sins, as Jeremiah later wept over Judah's sins.
2. Hosea is perhaps the strangest book in all the Bible, for God instructed his prophet to "take unto thee a wife of whoredoms."
   There were several reasons why God did this.
   a. The experimental reason. By marrying an unfaithful wife, Hosea could, as perhaps no other single prophet, understand somewhat the anguish in God's own heart over the northern kingdom, whose people were constantly committing spiritual fornication and adultery against Jehovah.
      God had often compared his relationship to Israel to that of a marriage. (See Isa. 62:5; Hos. 2:19; Jer. 3:14.)
   b. The illustrative reason. His own marriage would become a walking and visible example of his message to Israel.
   c. The prophetical reason. God would command him to name his children by those titles which would describe the future punishment and eventual restoration of all Israel.
3. He may have ministered longer than any other prophet.
4. Hosea predicted the Assyrian invasion, and later lived to see these prophecies fulfilled in 721 B.C.
5. In his book he refers to the northern kingdom as Ephraim constantly. Ephraim was the first of the twelve tribes of Israel to backslide.
6. Hosea is quoted more times for its size in the New Testament than any other Old Testament book, for a total of some thirty times. Compare:
   a. Hosea 11:1 with Matthew 2:15
   b. Hosea 6:6 with Matthew 9:13
   c. Hosea 10:8 with Luke 23:30
   d. Hosea 2:23 with Romans 9:25
   e. Hosea 13:14 with 1 Corinthians 15:55

I. A Grieving Husband and His Grievous Wife (Hosea vs. Gomer) (1-3).
   A. Hosea's wife, ill-famed. His wife Gomer was apparently a harlot before marriage and an adulteress after marriage. Hosea attempts in vain to save this marriage by:

1. Barring her from the markets of the world. "Therefore, behold I will hedge up thy way with thorns, and make a wall that she shall not find her paths" (2:6).

Hosea thought he could force her to remain home in this manner. He even sought the help of his first son, Jezreel, asking him to reason with his mother concerning the folly of her ways.

"Plead with your mother, contend; for she is not my wife, neither am I her husband. Let her, therefore, put away her harlotry out of her sight, and her adulteries from between her breasts" (2:2).

But all this was to no avail. Gomer apparently continues to run off at the first opportunity.

2. Buying her out of the markets of the world. It was not long before Gomer had been used, abused, and abandoned by her lustful lovers, and found herself in a slave market.

God ordered Hosea to find and redeem her from this market. "So I bought her for myself for fifteen pieces of silver, and for an homer of barley, and an half homer of barley" (3:2).

B. Hosea's children, ill-named. The prophet fathered three children through Gomer. Each child (at God's command) was given a name which carried with it prophetical meaning. The first child, a boy, named *Jezreel* (1:4), meaning "to be scattered," predicted two future events.

1. The setting aside of the dynasty of a northern king named Jehu. This brutal and bloody king had slain many in and around the city of Jezreel. Among his victims were:

   a. the northern king Jehoram and the Judean king Ahaziah on the same day (2 Ki. 9:14-28)

   b. Jezebel (2 Ki. 9:33)

   c. Ahab's seventy sons (2 Ki. 10:1-10)

   d. Ahab's distant relatives and political friends (2 Ki. 10:11, 17)

   e. the royal princes of Judah (2 Ki. 10:12-14)

   f. the priests of Baal (2 Ki. 10:18-28)

   While God did indeed order him to avenge Naboth, whose innocent blood Ahab had shed (1 Ki. 21), the brutal Jehu went too far in his bloodletting. Because of this, Jehu would be allowed only four generations upon Israel's throne (2 Ki. 10:30). These were:

   first generation, Jehoahaz, his son

   second generation, Jehoash, his grandson

   third generation, Jeroboam II, his great-grandson

   fourth generation, Zechariah, his great-great-grandson

   At the time of the birth of Hosea's son, Jehu's third generation was ruling, in the person of Jeroboam II. Thus, it would not be long until the dynasty would end. This, of course, happened in the days of Zechariah, who was murdered after a reign of but six months (2 Ki. 15:12).

2. The Assyrian invasion, at which time the entire northern kingdom would be scattered (1:5).

The second child, a girl, named *Lo-ruha-mah* (1:6). This name literally meant, "no more mercy," indicating that God's judgment was just around the corner. Along with this baby, however, came the promise that God would spare Judah, the southern kingdom, of this coming Assyrian invasion. (See 1:7.) This, of course, happened as recorded in 2 Kings 19:35.

The third child, a boy, named *Lo-ammi* (1:9). Here the name means "not my people."

II. A Grieving Husband and His Grievous Wife (God vs. Ephraim) (4:14).
   A. Ephraim denounced:
      1. Because of her ignorance:

         "My people are destroyed for lack of knowledge; because thou hast rejected knowledge, I will also reject thee, that thou shalt be no priest to me; seeing thou hast forgotten the law of thy God, I will also forget thy children" (4:6).

      2. Because of her idolatry:

         "My people ask counsel of their idols . . . they sacrifice upon the tops of the mountains, and burn incense upon the hills . . . Ephraim is joined to idols; let him alone" (4:12, 13, 17).

      3. Because of immorality:

         "I know Ephraim, and Israel is not hidden from me; for now, O Ephraim, thou committest whoredoms, and Israel is defiled" (5:3).

   B. Ephraim desired: In spite of her wickedness, God still loved her.

      "O Ephraim, what shall I do unto thee? O Judah, what shall I do unto thee? For your goodness is like a morning cloud, and like the early dew it goeth away" (6:4).

   C. Ephraim described:
      1. She was aflame with lust like a baker's hot oven (7:4). God said the hearts of the people smolder with evil plots during the night, and burst into flaming fire the next morning.
      2. They mingled with the heathen and had become as useless as a half-baked cake (7:8).
      3. They were as a silly dove, calling to Egypt, and flying to Assyria for help (7:11).
      4. They were as a crooked bow, always missing the target, which was God's glory (7:16).
      5. They lay among the nations as a broken pot (8:8).
      6. They were as a wandering and lonely wild ass (8:9).
      7. They were as a dried up root (9:16).
      8. They were as an empty vine (10:1).
      9. They were as a backsliding heifer (4:16).

   D. Ephraim disciplined: God declared,

      "For they have sown the wind, and they shall reap the whirlwind" (8:7). (See also 10:13.)

      1. God would therefore (for awhile) withhold his mercy from them (2:4).
      2. They would be many days without (3:4):
         a. A king: In 721 B.C. Hoshea, Israel's last king, was dethroned, and in 587 B.C.,

Zedekiah, Judah's final king, was deposed. Some six centuries later Israel's only true king was rejected (Jn. 19:15). Thus, this tragic situation will continue until he comes again (Rev. 19:11–16).

b. A prince: The next recorded prince in Israel's future will not minister until the millennium. (See Ezek. 44:3.)

c. A sacrifice: In A.D. 70 Titus destroyed the Temple and all animal sacrifices ceased. During the tribulation they will once again be instituted, only to be stopped by the antichrist (Dan. 9:27).

d. An image: This literally means, "the pillars," and may refer to the Temple. A temple will be rebuilt during the tribulation (Rev. 13), destroyed (Zech. 14:2), and again raised during the millennium (Ezek. 40:48).

e. An ephod: A reference to Israel's high priesthood. The ephod was a garment he wore. Her last high priest personally

planned the murder of the nation's own Messiah. (See Jn. 11:49–51; Mt. 26:57–68.)

f. Teraphim: These were normally figurines, or images in human form. (See Gen. 31:34.) It is not known what Hosea had in mind here.

3. They would go off as slaves into Assyria (10:6).

4. They would be (for awhile) swallowed up among the nations (8:8; 9:17).

E. Ephraim delivered. Someday this glorious event will indeed take place. Note the following passages:
1. Hosea 2:19, 23
2. Hosea 3:5
3. Hosea 6:1–3
4. Hosea 11:1, 4, 8, 9
5. Hosea 13:10, 14
6. Hosea 14:4–7

# MICAH (740–690 B.C.)

INTRODUCTION:

1. Micah lived on the Philistine border at a town called Moresheth, about twenty-five miles southwest of Jerusalem.

2. He was a contemporary with Isaiah. Micah was a country preacher, while Isaiah was a court preacher.

3. Micah was God's final prophet to the northern kingdom.

4. He was the only prophet sent to both the southern and northern kingdoms. He ministered especially to the capitals of these kingdoms, Jerusalem and Samaria.

5. He includes an amazing number of prophecies in his short book.
a. the fall of Samaria (1:6, 7)
b. the invasion of Judah by the Assyrians (1:9–16)
c. the eventual fall of Jerusalem and destruction of its Temple (3:12; 7:13)
d. the exile in Babylon (4:10)
e. the return from captivity and future restoration of Israel (4:1–8, 13; 7:11, 14)
f. the birth of Christ in Bethlehem (5:2)
g. the future reign of Christ (2:12, 13; 4:1, 7)

6. Micah is quoted on three occasions:
a. by the elders of Judah (Jer. 26:18, quoting Micah 3:12)
b. by the Magi coming to Jerusalem (Mt. 2:5, 6, quoting Micah 5:2)
c. by Jesus, when sending out the twelve (Mt. 10:35, 36, quoting Micah 7:6)

I. The Outward Look: Micah's public sermons (1–6).
A. Proclaiming the retribution upon Israel (1:3).
1. First sermon (1):
a. God himself would soon respond in judgment because of the sins found in Samaria and Jerusalem (1:1–5).
b. Samaria would be utterly destroyed (1:6). This, of course, happened during the Assyrian invasion. (See 2 Ki. 17:1–18.)
c. The enemy will come up to the very gates of Jerusalem (1:9). But God would spare his beloved city for yet another 115 years before allowing the Babylonians to destroy it. (See 2 Ki. 19:35.)

# Hosea

## A GRIEVING HUSBAND AND HIS GRIEVOUS WIFE

### HOSEA AND GOMER   HOSEA 1-3

**His Wife—Ill-Famed**
Gomer was a harlot before marriage and an adulteress after marriage.
Hosea attempts to save his marriage by:
1. Barring Gomer from the markets of the world.
2. Buying her out of the markets of the world.
3. Asking his own son to reason with his mother.

**His Children—Ill Named**

| NAME | MEANING |
|---|---|
| JEZREEL | "To be scattered" This predicted two things: 1. Scattering of Jehu's seed. 2. Scattering of the northern kingdom. |
| LO-RUHA-MAH | "No more mercy" |
| LO-AMMI | "Not my people" |

**Ephraim Denounced**
1. Because of her ignorance (4:6)
2. Because of her idolatry (4:12, 13, 17)
3. Because of her immorality (5:3)

**Ephraim Desired (6:4)**
In spite of all this, God still loved her!

**Ephraim Described**
1. A backsliding heifer (4:16)
2. A baker's hot oven (7:4)
3. A half-baked cake (7:8)
4. A silly dove (7:11)
5. A crooked bow (7:16)
6. A broken pot (8:8)
7. A wandering and lonely wild animal (8:9)
8. A dried up root (9:16)
9. An empty vine (10:1)

**Ephraim Disciplined (3:4)**
To be many days without:
1. A king
2. A prince
3. A sacrifice
4. An image
5. An ephod
6. Teraphim

**Ephraim Delivered**
1. 2:19, 23
2. 3:5
3. 6:1-3
4. 11:1, 4, 8, 9
5. 13:10, 14
6. 14:4-7

2. Second sermon (2):
   a. God condemns those who lie awake at night, plotting wickedness, and rise at dawn to perform it (2:1).
   b. He promises to reward their evil with evil (2:3).
   c. Israel rejects her true prophets, telling them God would never do such things (2:6).
   d. Their punishment will only end when the Messiah (the Breaker and King of 2:13) leads them out of exile through the gates of their cities of captivity, back to their own land.
3. Third sermon (3):
   a. Israel's leaders are especially rebuked by God. They were supposed to know right from wrong, but were themselves the vilest sinners of all (3:1–5).
   b. Their corrupt and crowd-pleasing messages would lead to the destruction of the people (3:6, 7).
   c. Micah alone of the prophets at that time was "full of power by the Spirit of the Lord, and of judgment, and of might, to declare unto Jacob his transgression, and to Israel his sin" (3:8).
   d. Because of those false prophets, Jerusalem would later be plowed as a field and become a heap of rubble. The very spot on Mt. Moriah where the Temple stood would be overgrown with brush (3:12).
B. Prophesying the restoration of Israel (4–5). In spite of her terrible sins, God would someday, after her punishment had been consummated, restore her to Palestine.
   1. The chronology leading to this restoration:
      a. Judah must first suffer the seventy-year Babylonian captivity (4:10). This was a remarkable passage indeed, for at the time Micah wrote, Babylon was anything but a world power. Assyria was the strong nation then.
      b. Judah's Messiah would be born in Bethlehem (5:2).
      c. God would set them aside awhile as a nation until their spiritual rebirth during the tribulation (5:3).
      d. The nations would gather together against Israel at Armageddon (4:11). (See also Rev. 16:13–16; 19:17.)
      e. These nations would be utterly destroyed (5:15).
   2. The final results of this restoration (Micah 4:1–6).
C. Pleading for the repentance of Israel (6). See Micah 6:3–8.
II. The Inward Look: Micah's personal contemplations (7:1–6).
   "Woe is me! For I am as when they have gathered the summer fruits, as the grape gleanings of the vintage; there is no cluster to eat; my soul desired the first ripe fruit" (7:1).
III. The Upward Look: Micah's prayerful petitions (7:7–20).
   A. His decision for God:

# Micah

## His Public Messages  MICAH 1-6

Proclaiming retribution upon Israel (three sermons) Chapters **1-3**
Prophesying restoration of Israel (1 prediction) Chapters **4-5**
1. Chronology of restoration
   ● Seventy-year captivity **(4-10)**
   ● Bethlehem **(5:2)**
   ● Divine rejection **(5:3)**
   ● Armageddon **(4:11)**
   ● Gentile destruction **(5:15)**
2. Results of restoration **(4:1-6)**
Pleading for repentance from Israel **(6:3-8)**

## His Personal Contemplations  7:1-6

*"Woe is me! For I am as when they have gathered the summer fruits, as the grape gleanings of the vintage; there is no cluster to eat; my soul desired the first-ripe fruit"* **(7:1)**.

## His Prayerful Petition  7:7-20

His decision for God **(7:7, 9)**
His description of God **(7:18-20)**

"Therefore, I will look unto the Lord; I will wait for the God of my salvation; my God will hear me" (7:7).

"I will bear the indignation of the Lord, because I have sinned against him, until he plead my cause, and execute judgment for me; he will bring me forth to the light, and I shall behold his righteousness" (7:9).

B. His description of God (7:18–20):
   "Who is a God like unto thee, that pardoneth iniquity, and passeth by the transgression of the remnant of his heritage? he retaineth not his anger for ever, because he delighteth in mercy. He will turn again, he will have compassion upon us; he will subdue our iniquities; and thou wilt cast all their sins into the depths of the sea. Thou wilt perform the truth to Jacob, and the mercy to Abraham, which thou hast sworn unto our fathers from the days of old."

# ISAIAH

INTRODUCTION:
1. The book of Isaiah may be compared to the Bible. The Bible has sixty-six books; Isaiah has sixty-six chapters. The Old Testament has thirty-nine books; the first section of Isaiah has thirty-nine chapters. The New Testament has twenty-seven books; the last section of Isaiah has twenty-seven chapters. The Old Testament covers the history and sin of Israel, as does Isaiah 1–39. The New Testament describes the person and ministry of Christ, as does Isaiah 40–66. The New Testament begins with the ministry of John the Baptist. The second section in Isaiah (chapter 40) begins by predicting this ministry. The New Testament ends by referring to

the new heavens and the new earth. Isaiah ends his book by describing the same things. (Compare Isa. 66:22 with Rev. 21:1-3.)

2. The book of Isaiah is generally regarded as one of the six greatest in the Bible. The others are: Romans, John, the Psalms, Genesis, and Revelation.

3. A copy of this book was among the famous Dead Sea scroll discovery in 1947 in cave one at Qumran. It was copied in the second century, B.C., and consisted of seventeen sheets which were twenty-four feet in length by ten inches high. This copy was amazingly similar to the standard masoretic text of the twelfth century, A.D.

4. Isaiah was the greatest of the Old Testament prophets, and one of the most eloquent writers who ever lived, at times even surpassing the literary abilities of a Shakespeare, a Milton, or a Homer.

5. He prophesied during the reigns of five kings of Judah (Uzziah, Jotham, Ahaz, Hezekiah, and Manasseh).

6. He is called the Messianic prophet. Only the Psalms have more material about Christ than Isaiah.

7. Jesus said Isaiah saw the glory of Christ, and "spoke of him" (Jn. 12:41).

8. Isaiah was married and had two sons.

9. It is believed that his father, Amoz, was the brother of King Amaziah of Judah. This then would make Isaiah of the royal seed.

10. Isaiah wrote other books which have not been preserved, such as:
    a. The life of Uzziah (2 Chron. 26:22).
    b. A book of the kings of Israel and Judah (2 Chron. 32:32).

11. Isaiah is quoted more times in the New Testament than any other Old Testament prophet. These passages quote his words in reference to:
    a. the ministry of John the Baptist (Mt. 3:3; Lk. 3:4; Jn. 1:23)
    b. the ministry of Christ to the Gentiles (Mt. 4:14, 15; 12:17, 18)
    c. the future rule of Christ over the Gentiles (Rom. 15:12)
    d. the healing ministry of Christ (Mt. 8:17)
    e. the blindness of Israel (Mt. 13:14; Acts 28:25-27)
    f. the hyprocrisy of Israel (Mt. 15:7)
    g. the disobedience of Israel (Rom. 10:16, 20)
    h. the saved remnant of Israel (Rom. 9:27, 29)
    i. the sufferings of Christ (Acts 8:28, 30)
    j. the anointing of Christ (Lk. 4:17)

## The Book of Isaiah
I. General Outline
II. A Summary of Isaiah's Prophecies
III. The Various Personalities Mentioned in Isaiah
IV. The Greatness of God
V. The Messiah
VI. The Sins of Israel
VII. The Gentile Nations
VIII. The Tribulation
IX. The Millennium

## General Outline
I. Israel, God's Faithless Servant (and her various enemies) (1-35).
   A. Her sins listed (1, 3, 5).
   B. Her future predicted (2, 4, 9, 11, 12, 25-35).

C. Her great prophet's vision (6).
D. Her wicked king's unbelief (7).
E. Her enemies judged (13-23).
   1. Babylon (Isa. 13, 14, 21)
   2. Assyria (14:24-27)
   3. Philistia (14:28-32)
   4. Moab (15-16)
   5. Damascus (17)
   6. Ethiopia (18)
   7. Egypt (19-20)
   8. Edom (Idumea) (34:5-15)
   9. Arabia (21:13-17)
   10. Tyre (23)
   11. The entire world (24-25)
II. Hezekiah, God's Frightened Servant (36-39).
   A. Hezekiah and the king of Assyria (36-37).
   B. Hezekiah and the King of heaven (38).
   C. Hezekiah and the king of Babylon (39).
III. Christ, God's Faithful Servant (40-66).
   A. The deliverance—the comfort of Jehovah (40-48).
      1. God and the idols (40-46).
      2. God and the nations (47-48).
   B. The Deliverer—the salvation of Jehovah (49-57).
   C. The delivered—the glory of Jehovah (58-66).

## A Summary of Isaiah's Prophecies
I. Prophecies Fulfilled During His Own Lifetime.
   A. Judah would be saved from the threatened Syrian and Israelite invasion (7:4, 16).
   B. Syria and Israel later to be destroyed by Assyria (8:4; 17:1-14; 28:1-4).
   C. Assyria would invade Judah (8:7, 8).
   D. Jerusalem would be saved during this invasion (37:33-35).
   E. Moab would be judged by the Assyrians within three years (15-16).
   F. Egypt and Ethiopia would be conquered by the Assyrians (18-20).
   G. Arabia would be destroyed (21:13-17).
   H. Tyre to be destroyed (23:1-12).
   I. Hezekiah's life would be extended by fifteen years (38:5).
   J. Assyria to be judged by God (10:5-34; 14:24-27; 30:27-33; 37:36).
II. Prophesies Fulfilled After His Lifetime.
   A. The Babylonian captivity (3:1-8; 5:26-30; 22:1-14; 39:5-7).
   B. Babylon to be overthrown by Cyrus (13:17-22; 14:1-23; 21:2; 46:11; 48:14).
   C. Babylon to suffer perpetual desolation (13:20-22; 47:1-15).
   D. The conquests of a Persian named Cyrus (41:2, 3; 44:28; 45:1-4).
   E. The return to Jerusalem decree of Cyrus (44:38; 45:13).
   F. The joy of the returning remnant (48:20; also compare with Ps. 126).
   G. The restoration of Tyre (23:13-18).
   H. The perpetual desolation of Edom (34:5-17).
   I. The birth, earthly life, sufferings, death, resurrection, ascension, and exaltation of Jesus Christ (7:14, 15; 9:1, 2, 6; 11:1, 2; 35:5, 6; 42:1-3; 50:4-6; 52:13-15; 53:2, 10-12, 15; 61:1, 2).
   J. The ministry of John the Baptist (Isa. 40:3-5).

III. Prophecies Yet to Be Fulfilled.
   A. The tribulation (Isa. 2:10-22; 13:6-13; 24:1-23; 26:20, 21; 34:1-10; 51:6).
   B. The battle of Armageddon (Isa. 34:1-10; 42:13, 14; 63:1-6; 66:15, 16).
   C. The millennium (Isa. 2:2-4; 4:2-6; 11:6-10, 12; 14:3, 7, 8; 19:18-25; 29:18; 30:19, 23-26; 32:18; 35:1-10; 40:4, 5; 42:13, 14, 16; 44:23; 49:10-13; 51:3, 11; 52:1, 6-10; 56:6-8; 59:20, 21; 60:1-3, 11-13, 19-22; 62:1-4; 63:1-6; 65:18-25; 66:10, 12, 15, 16, 23).

## The Various Personalities
I. Isaiah.
   A. The greatest Old Testament prophet and author of this book (1:1).
   B. He viewed the glory of God as few other men have ever experienced (6:1-13). For other experiences, see the accounts of:
      1. Moses (Ex. 33:18-23)
      2. Ezekiel (Ezek. 1:1-28)
      3. Daniel (Dan. 7:9-14)
      4. Zechariah (Zech. 3:1-9)
      5. Stephen (Acts 7:55-60)
      6. Paul (2 Cor. 12:1-4)
      7. John (Rev. 4-22)
   C. He was ordered to offer wicked King Ahaz a sign concerning God's faithfulness (7:3).
   D. He fathered two children (*Shear-jash-ub,* 7:3; and *Ma-her-shalal-hash-baz,* 8:3), giving them names which depicted coming events in prophecy.
   E. He was ordered to walk barefooted and naked (perhaps from the waist up) for three years to symbolize the troubles God would bring upon the Egyptians and the Ethiopians (20:1-6).
II. Ahaz—the wicked father of Hezekiah who refused God's gracious sign of his faithfulness to Judah in their hour of need (7:1-25).
III. Lucifer—that powerful and perverted angel, who rebelled against God, became known as Satan and the devil (Isa. 14:12-14).

   "How art thou fallen from heaven, O Lucifer, son of the morning! How art thou cut down to the ground, which didst weaken the nations! For thou hast said in thine heart, I will ascend into heaven, I will exalt my throne above the stars of God: I will sit also upon the mount of the congregation, in the sides of the north: I will ascend above the heights of the clouds, I will be like the most high" (14:12-14).

We note these five foolish and fatal "I wills" of the devil:
   A. "I will ascend into heaven"—obviously Satan had the third heaven in mind here, the very abode of God! (See 2 Cor. 12:1-4.)
   B. "I will exalt my throne above the stars of God"—this is probably a reference to angels. Satan desired the worship of angels!
   C. "I will sit also upon the mount of the congregation, in the sides of the north"—Lucifer now sought to enter God's "executive office" somewhere in the north and sit at God's very desk. He would attempt to control not only the angels, but the size and number of the starry galaxies.
   D. "I will ascend above the heights of the clouds"—this may well refer to that special Shekinah glory cloud of God found so frequently in the Bible.

   E. "I will be like the most high"—it is revealing to note the name for God that Satan uses here. He wanted to be like *El-Elyon,* the most High. This name literally means, "the strongest strong one." The devil could have picked other names for God. He could have used *El-Shaddai,* which means, "the breasted one, the one who feeds his children," but he didn't. He might have selected *Jehovah-Rohi,* which means, "the shepherd God," but he avoided this title also. The reason is obvious—Satan coveted God's strength, but was not the least bit interested in his feeding and leading attributes.
IV. Shebna (22:15-25).
He was the indulgent and utterly self-centered palace administrator (perhaps during Hezekiah's early reign) who was rebuked and set aside by God.
V. Eliakim (36:3).
He replaced the selfish Shebna and was Hezekiah's spokesman during the Assyrian crisis led by Sennacherib.
VI. Rabshakeh (36:2).
The personal (and arrogant) loudmouthed Assyrian spokesman during the siege of Sennacherib.
VII. Sennacherib (37:21).
The Assyrian Commander-in-chief whose efforts to destroy Jerusalem were totally blocked by God's death angel.
VIII. Hezekiah (36:1).
The thirteenth king of Judah who was on the throne when God saved Jerusalem, and also extended the king's own life by fifteen years.
IX. Mero-dach-bal-adan (39:1).
The King of Babylon who sent spies (disguised as good-will ambassadors) to congratulate Hezekiah after his recovery. Their real mission was to discover the amount and location of Jerusalem's wealth.
X. John the Baptist (40:3-5).
Compare these verses with: Matthew 3:1-3; Mark 1:2, 3; Luke 3:2-6; John 1:23.
XI. Cyrus (44:28; 45:1).
The Persian monarch whose name and ministry to the Jewish remnant (in allowing them to return and rebuild the Temple) Isaiah prophesied some two centuries before he was even born.

## The Greatness of God
I. Isaiah 1:18:
   "Come now, and let us reason together, saith the Lord; though your sins be as scarlet, they shall be as white as snow; though they be red like crimson, they shall be as wool."
   Scarlet—a reference to the deep-dyed character of sin. (See Num. 19:2, 6, 9.)
   Snow—Psalm 51:7
   Reason together
   God appeals to man's intellect as well as his emotions. We are not to simply put our brains into neutral in our dealing with God. (See Isa. 43:26; Rom. 12:1; Mt. 22:37; 2 Pet. 3:1.)
II. Isaiah 12:2-5:
   "Behold, God is my salvation; I will trust, and not be afraid: for the Lord Jehovah is my strength and my song; he also is become my salvation. Therefore with joy shall ye draw water out of the wells of salvation. And in that day shall ye say, Praise

the Lord, call upon his name, declare his doings among the people, make mention that his name is exalted. Sing unto the Lord; for he hath done excellent things; this is known in all the earth."

These blessed waters had formerly been rejected. (See 8:6. See also Jn. 4:10, 14.)

III. Isaiah 25:1, 4, 8, 9:

"O Lord, thou art my God; I will exalt thee, I will praise thy name; for thou hast done wonderful things; thy counsels of old are faithfulness and truth. For thou hast been a strength to the poor, a strength to the needy in his distress, a refuge from the storm, a shadow from the heat, when the blast of the terrible ones is as a storm against the wall. He will swallow up death in victory; and the Lord God will wipe away tears from off all faces; and the rebuke of his people shall he take away from off all the earth: for the Lord hath spoken it. And it shall be said in that day, Lo, this is our God; we have waited for him and he will save us: this is the Lord; we have waited for him, we will be glad and rejoice in his salvation."

Swallow up death. (See 1 Cor. 15:54; Hos. 13:14; Rev. 20:14.)

Wipe away tears. (See Rev. 7:17; 21:4.)

IV. Isaiah 40:1-31:

A. Concerning verses 1, 2.
  1. God orders the prophet to speak tenderly to and comfort the hearts of his people. The message of comfort is threefold.
    a. Their term of forced service is complete.
    b. Their guilt is pardoned.
    c. They had received ample punishment for their sins.
B. Concerning verses 3-5.
  1. This voice had its partial fulfillment at his first coming through the mouth of John the Baptist (Mt. 3:3), but will only see its ultimate consummation at his Second Coming. (See Isa. 35:2.) Note the main features of this proclamation:
    a. A straight highway in the desert was to be made for the King.
    b. Every valley was to be filled in.
    c. Every mountain and hill should be leveled off.
  2. When all this was accomplished (spiritually, in the hearts of Israelites), then the glory of the Lord would be revealed to all flesh.
C. Concerning verses 6-8.
  A heavenly voice orders an earthly voice to cry out concerning the greatness of God and the insignificance of man, saying:
  1. The beauty and duration of man is as a flower and grass, which would soon fade and wither away (Jas. 1:10; 1 Pet. 1:24, 25).
  2. The Word of our God by contrast would stand forever.
D. Concerning verses 9-11.
  The voice now orders Zion's messengers upon a high mountain where they are to boldly proclaim the following:
  1. Behold the coming of your mighty God!
  2. He comes as a King to rule over you and to reward you.
  3. He comes as a Shepherd to tenderly feed you and lead you.
E. Concerning verses 12-31.
  This coming King-Shepherd had all power.
  1. As seen in his dealing with nature (vs. 12-14).
    a. He holds the oceans in his hands.
    b. He measures off the heavens.
    c. He knows the weight of the earth and mountains.
    d. He needs no advice from angels, demons, or men. (See Rom. 11:34; 1 Cor. 2:16.)
  2. As seen in his dealing with the nations (vs. 15-17).
    a. All peoples are as a drop in the bucket and dust on the scales.
    b. He picks up the islands as if they had no weight at all.
    c. All of Lebanon's forests do not contain sufficient fuel to consume a sacrifice large enough to honor him, nor all its animals enough to offer God.
  3. As seen in his dealing with vain idols (vs. 18-20).
    a. God cannot be even remotely depicted by a wooden or golden idol.
    b. Man can create a false idol, but only God can create man. (See also 41:6, 7, 21-24, 29; 44:9-20; 46:1, 5-7.)
  4. As seen in his dealing with the mighty of this earth (vs. 21-24).
    a. Man's willful ignorance of God's greatness is inexcusable. (See Rom. 1:18-23; 2 Pet. 3:5.)
    b. God sits enthroned above the circle of the earth and views its inhabitants as grasshoppers. (Compare Num. 13:33.)
    c. He spreads out the heavens like a veil.
    d. He brings the great men of the world to naught (1 Cor. 1:26-29).
    e. They are scarcely planted until he removes them. (See Ps. 103:15, 16.)
  5. As seen in his dealings with the stars (vs. 25, 26).
    a. He originally created all the stars.
    b. He knows their number.
    c. He has named each one. (See Ps. 147:4.)
  6. As seen in his dealing with the elect (vs. 27-31).
    a. In light of all this, God's children are not to question his dealing with them. (See also Isa. 54:7, 8.)
    b. The eternal God has unending strength and unfathomable insight.
    c. He therefore gives power to the faint who wait upon him.
    d. This allows them to walk, run, and fly as eagles.
V. Isaiah 41:8-10.
  "But thou, Israel, art my servant, Jacob whom I have chosen, the seed of Abraham my friend. Thou whom I have taken from the ends of the earth, and called thee from the chief men thereof, and said unto thee, Thou art my servant; I have chosen thee, and not cast thee away. Fear thou not; for I am with thee: be not dismayed; for I am thy God: I will strengthen thee; yea, I will help thee, yea, I will uphold thee with the right hand of my righteousness."

"Israel . . . my servant." Scofield notes the following:

Three servants of the Lord mentioned in Isaiah: (1) David (Isa. 37:35); (2) Israel the nation (Isa. 41:8-16; 43:1-10; 44:1-8; 21; 45:4; 48:20); and (3) Messiah (42:1-12; 49:5-7; 50:4-6; 52:13-15; 53:1-12).

VI. Isaiah 42:8-12:

"The former things are come to pass"—a possible reference to the fall of Babylon (Isa. 13:17-22; 21:1-10) and destruction of Assyria (10:5-34; 14:24-27; 30:27-33; 31:8)

"New things do I declare"—the sufferings, death, resurrection, and ascension of Jehovah's Servant, Jesus Christ! (See 52:13-15; 53:1-12.)

"Let the inhabitants of the rock sing"—a possible reference to the hiding remnant in Petra during the tribulation. (See Zech. 14:5; Dan. 11:41.)

VII. Isaiah 43:2, 5, 6, 11, 25:

"When thou passest through the waters, I will be with thee; and through the rivers, they shall not overflow thee; when thou walkest through the fire, thou shalt not be burned; neither shall the flame kindle upon thee. Fear not: for I am with thee: I will bring thy seed from the east, and gather thee from the west: I will say to the north, Give up; and to the south, Keep not back: bring my sons from far, and my daughters from the ends of the earth; I, even I, am the Lord; and beside me there is no Saviour. I, even I, am he that blotteth out thy transgressions for mine own sake, and will not remember thy sins."

"through the waters" (Ex. 14:19-31).

"through the fire" (Ps. 66:12; Dan. 3:25-27).

"from the east . . . west . . . north . . . south." (See Mt. 24:31.)

"beside me there is no Saviour" (Acts 4:12).

"who blotteth out thy transgressions" (Isa. 44:22; Acts 3:19).

"and will not remember thy sins" (Ps. 103:10-12; Isa. 38:17; 44:22; Micah 7:19; Heb. 8:12).

VIII. Isaiah 44:3:

"For I will pour water upon him that is thirsty, and floods upon the dry ground: I will pour my spirit upon thy seed, and my blessing upon thine offspring."

(See Joel 2:28-32; Acts 2:16, 17.)

IX. Isaiah 45:5-12, 18-23:

"I girded thee" (v. 5). This passage describes the work of Cyrus, who would allow the Jews in Babylon to return. God reminds all here that he allowed Cyrus to capture Babylon.

"I . . . create evil" (v. 7). God is of course not the author of sin! (See Hab. 1:13; 2 Tim. 2:13; Titus 1:2; Jas. 1:13; 1 Jn. 1:5.) One of the meanings of the Hebrew word *ra* carries the idea of adversity or calamity, which is obviously the intended meaning here.

"Woe to him that striveth with his maker" (v. 9). (See Isa. 10:15; 29:16; Rom. 9:19-21.) Sinful Israel is here pictured as questioning God's dealing with her, accusing him of being all thumbs! (Note the expression, "He hath no hands.") This of course was sheer insanity, for God points out later that those same hands made the earth and created man (see v. 12).

"I have not spoken in secret" (v. 19). God never dealt in esoteric knowledge which was available only for a select few. (See Jn. 18:19, 20.)

"Look unto me, and be saved, all the ends of the earth" (v. 22). This was the verse that led the great Charles H. Spurgeon to Christ according to his testimony.

"Every knee shall bow." (See Rom. 14:11; Phil. 2:10.)

X. Isaiah 46:9, 10:

"Remember the former things of old: for I am God, and there is none else; I am God, and there is none like me. Declaring the end from the beginning, and from ancient times the things that are not yet done, saying, My counsel shall stand, and I will do all my pleasure."

"Remember the former things of old" (v. 9). Perhaps God had in mind those things such as the Passover salvation, the Red Sea deliverance, the sweetened waters of Marah, the heavenly manna, etc.

"Declaring the end from the beginning" (v. 10). Bible prophecy is simply history written in advance!

XI. Isaiah 49:13-16:

"Sing, O heavens; and be joyful, O earth; and break forth into singing, O mountains: for the Lord hath comforted his people, and will have mercy upon his afflicted. But Zion said, The Lord hath forsaken me, and my Lord hath forgotten me. Can a woman forget her sucking child, that she should not have compassion on the son of her womb? yea, they may forget, yet will I not forget thee. Behold, I have graven thee upon the palms of my hands; thy walls are continually before me."

XII. Isaiah 55:1-3:

This chapter may rightly be entitled, "The Incredible Invitation."

A. The Host of the invitation (v. 1):
God himself! Here the Father is depicted as standing behind a booth in an eastern market place, seeking the attention of those who pass by.

B. The guests of the invitation (v. 1):
Who are those invited? All the thirsty and penniless.

C. The menu of the invitation (vs. 1, 2).
These items constitute the original soul food of man.

1. Water and wine—a reference to the Spirit of God. (See Jn. 7:37-39; Eph. 5:18; 1 Thess. 1:6.)

2. Milk—a reference to the Word of God. (See 1 Pet. 2:2.)

3. Bread—a reference to the Son of God. (See Jn. 6:35.)

D. The terms of the invitation (vs. 6, 7):
1. Seek the Lord.
2. Call upon him.
3. Let the wicked forsake his way.
4. Let him return unto the Lord.

E. The time limit of the invitation (vs. 6, 7):
1. While he may be found.
2. While he is near.

F. The necessity of the invitation (vs. 8, 9):
"For my thoughts are not your thoughts, neither are your ways my ways, saith the Lord.

For as the heavens are higher than the earth, so are my ways higher than your ways, and my thoughts than your thoughts."

G. An example of the invitation (vs. 9, 10). Rain! "For as the heavens are higher than the earth, so are my ways higher than your ways, and my thoughts than your thoughts. For as the rain cometh down, and the snow from heaven, and returneth not thither, but watereth the earth, and maketh it bring forth and bud, that it may give seed to the sower, and bread to the eater."

H. The promise of the invitation.
1. To Israel:
   a. the blessings of the Davidic Covenant (v. 4)
   b. the acceptance of all nations (v. 5)
   c. the fullness of joy and peace (v. 12)
2. To nature:
   the removal of the curse (vs. 12, 13)
3. To all:
   a. sublime soul satisfaction (v. 2)
   b. mercy and abundant pardon (v. 7)

XIII. Isaiah 57:15, 19-21:
"For thus saith the high and lofty One that inhabiteth eternity, whose name is Holy; I dwell in the high and holy place, with him also that is of a contrite and humble spirit to revive the spirit of the humble, and to revive the heart of the contrite ones. I create the fruit of the lips; Peace, peace to him that is far off, and to him that is near, saith the Lord; and I will heal him. But the wicked are like the troubled sea, when it cannot rest, whose waters cast up mire and dirt. There is no peace, saith my God, to the wicked."

"A contrite and humble spirit" (v. 15). (See Ps. 34:18; 51:17; Isa. 66:2; 2 Cor. 7:10; 1 Pet. 5:6.)
"Peace to him . . . far off" (v. 19). (See Heb. 13:15; Acts 2:39; Eph. 2:17.)
"There is no peace . . . to the wicked" (v. 21). (See Isa. 48:22.)

XIV. Isaiah 61:10:
"I will greatly rejoice in the Lord, my soul shall be joyful in my God; for he hath clothed me with the garments of salvation, he hath covered me with the robe of righteousness, as a bridegroom decketh himself with ornaments, and as a bride adorneth herself with her jewels."

"robe of righteousness" (see Isa. 64:6; Gen. 3:21; Mt. 22:2-13; Rev. 19:8; Jer. 33:11; Rev. 21:2.)

XV. Isaiah 63:7-9:
"I will mention the loving kindnesses of the Lord, and the praises of the Lord, according to all that the Lord hath bestowed on us, and the great goodness toward the house of Israel, which he hath bestowed on them according to his mercies, and according to the multitude of his loving kindnesses. For he said, Surely they are my people, children that will not lie: so he was their Saviour. In all their affliction he was afflicted, and the angel of his presence saved them: in his love and in his pity he redeemed them; and he bare them, and carried them all the days of old."

"he was afflicted." (See Jdg. 10:16.)
"the angel of his presence." (See Gen. 16:9; 22:11; 48:16; Ex. 3:2; 14:19; Num. 22:22; Jdg. 2:4; 6:11; 13:3; 2 Ki. 19:35; Zech. 1:12; 12:8.)

## The Messiah

I. His Incarnation:
A. Isaiah 7:14, 15:
"Therefore the Lord himself shall give you a sign; Behold, a virgin shall conceive, and bear a son, and shall call his name Immanuel. Butter and honey shall he eat, that he may know to refuse the evil, and choose the good."

It should be noted that three children are mentioned in connection with Isaiah's visit to King Ahaz and the wicked ruler's refusal to ask God for a sign. Two of these children were yet unborn. The three are:
1. Immanuel, meaning, "God with us." There are six major implications within 7:14:
   a. This sign was to be given by God. (Note the phrase, "the Lord himself.")
   b. It was given to the entire house of David and not to Ahaz (the word "you" here is plural).
   c. It involved a miraculous sign (God had just invited Ahaz to ask of him any fantastic miracle he desired, whether "in the depth or in the height above." (See v. 11.)
   d. It concerned a virgin birth. The Hebrew word *almah* was a common term for an unmarried and sexually undefiled girl. (See Gen. 24:43; Ex. 2:8; Ps. 68:25; Song of Solomon 1:3; Prov. 30:19.) Were the promised babe not to have been virgin born, this could scarcely have been considered a mighty sign. (See Mt. 1:22, 23 for the fullfillment of this where the Greek word *parthenos* is used, a term depicting absolute virginity.
   e. This mighty miracle sign would result in the very incarnation of God himself into human flesh, for the baby's name was to be *Immanuel*, meaning "God with us."
   f. This divine baby would also be completely human, eating what other children ate, and growing to maturity like other children. (Compare Isa. 7:16 with Lk. 2:52.)
2. *Shear-jashub*, meaning, "a remnant shall return" (7:3). This tiny child was Isaiah's son who accompanied him to Ahaz's palace. Isaiah told the unbelieving king that before this young boy reached the age to know right from wrong, both of Ahaz's enemies, Pekah and Rezin, would be destroyed. This was literally fulfilled by the Assyrian monarch Tiglath Pileser, who slew the Damascus King Rezin in 732 B.C. (2 Ki. 16:9), and by Hoshea, who murdered Pekah shortly after this (2 Ki. 15:30).
3. *Maher-shalal-hash-baz*, meaning "hasten to the booty, hurry to the prey" (8:1-4). This child, also the son of Isaiah, was called by this name to indicate the Assyrian captivity of the northern Israelite kingdom.

B. Isaiah 9:6:
"For unto us a child is born, Unto us a son is given, and the government shall be upon his shoulder; and his name shall be called Won-

derful, Counsellor, The mighty God, the everlasting Father, The Prince of Peace."

1. Both his humanity and deity are seen here.
   a. The phrase, "A child is born" refers to his humanity (Lk. 2:7; Heb. 2:14; 1 Jn. 4:9).
   b. The phrase, "a son is given" refers to his deity (Jn. 3:16).
2. Five great names are ascribed to this child-son of Mary and God.
   a. "Wonderful"—this is a noun in the Hebrew, and therefore a real name. (See Jdg. 13:18 where it is translated "secret.")
   b. "Counsellor." This child-son would never need an advisory board, for, "Who hath known the mind of the Lord? or who hath been his counsellor?" (Rom. 11:34). (See also Jn. 2:24, 25.)
   c. "The mighty God"—here is *El-Gibbohr,* "God's strong Hero"!
   d. "The everlasting Father"—literally, Avi-ad, "The Father of eternity." (See Jn. 1:3; Col. 1:16; Heb. 1:2.)
   e. "The Prince of Peace"—this is *Sar-Sha-lohim,* as described in Isaiah 57:15-19.
3. From the very dawn of history this wicked world has desperately sought to employ the services of someone (or something) who could heal the hurt of the human soul and usher in the long dream of universal righteousness. Many persons have applied for this position, and numerous methods have been employed, but all have led to bitter disappointment and despair. But here the prophet Isaiah introduces a special candidate. What are his qualifications? Can he satisfy the five key questions?
   a. What about his personality and character? Answer—it is *wonderful.*
   b. What about his education? Answer—he knows all things and is therefore the supreme *Counselor.*
   c. What about his nationality? Answer—he is the *mighty God,* and the only Son of the living God.
   d. What about his previous work experience? Answer—he both planned for and carried out the creation of this universe and is therefore the *Father of eternity.*
   e. What is his special talent? Answer—as the God-man, he is able to reconcile man with God, and is therefore the *Prince of Peace.*
      In view of all this, Isaiah (along with Peter, Paul, John, and a host of others) earnestly exhorts all sinners to hire this heavenly Candidate immediately. (See Isa. 1:18.)

II. His Lowliness and Youth in Nazareth:
   A. Isaiah 11:1, 2:
      "And there shall come forth a rod out of the stem of Jesse, and a Branch shall grow out of his roots; and the Spirit of the Lord shall rest upon him, the Spirit of Wisdom and Understanding, the Spirit of Counsel and Might, the Spirit of Knowledge and of the Fear of the Lord."

1. This passage describes what is left of a once mighty tree after it has been cut down—a stump. That mighty tree, the kingdoms of David and Solomon, would be cut to the ground by the Assyrian and Babylonian axemen.
2. But this stump stands in obvious contrast to the vast number of dead stumps that covered the ground after God had hewn down the huge Assyrian forest described by Isaiah in chapter 10 (as he will eventually do to all ungodly nations). But there is an important difference in that this stump is not dead! First, a rod (or sprig) will spring from that supposed dead stump, and then that rod will branch out into fruit. (See Rev. 5:5.)
3. The Hebrew word for branch is *netser,* and was probably what Matthew referred to when he stated that Christ, "Came and dwelt in a city called Nazareth: that it might be fulfilled which was spoken by the prophets, He shall be called a Nazarene" (Mt. 2:23).
4. The Holy Spirit of God was to rest upon this Babe of Bethlehem and citizen of Nazareth, thus giving to him:
   a. The spirit of wisdom—that ability to discern the nature of things.
   b. The spirit of understanding—the ability to discern their differences.
   c. The spirit of counsel—the ability to adopt right conclusions.
   d. The spirit of power—the ability to carry them out.
   e. The spirit of knowledge—the ability to personally know the very essence of the Father himself. This characteristic can be considered the *root* of his ministry, and the first four its *fruit.*
   f. The spirit of the fear of the Lord—because of this knowledge, the ability to always refrain from displeasing him. (See Jn. 8:29.)

Thus these seven (counting the Holy Spirit and his gifts) correspond to the seven-lighted lampstand, with its main shaft and the three pairs of branches from its side (Ex. 25:31, 32; Rev. 1:4; 4:5; 5:6).

   B. Isaiah 53:2:
      "For he shall grow up before him like a tender plant, and like a root out of a dry ground; he hath no form nor comeliness, and when we shall see him, there is no beauty that we should desire him."
      (This verse is only quoted here. It will be dealt with under the aspect of his suffering in connection with Isaiah 53.)
   C. Isaiah 7:15:
      "Butter and honey shall he eat, that he may know to refuse the evil, and choose the good."
      This refers to the relative poverty of the Savior's family. Thickened milk and honey were the food of desert wanderers. They were, of course, not the only articles of food, but provided the staples.

III. His Relationship to the Father:
  A. Beloved by the Father
      "Behold my servant, whom I uphold; mine elect in whom my soul delighteth; I have put my Spirit upon him; he shall bring forth justice to the nations" (Isa. 42:1).
      This was quoted in Matthew 12:18 and demonstrated in Matthew 3:17 and 17:5.
  B. Obedience to the Father
      "The Lord God hath given me the tongue of the learned, that I should know how to speak a word in season to him who is weary; he awakeneth morning by morning; he waketh mine ear to hear like the learned. The Lord God hath opened mine ear, and I was not rebellious, neither turned backward" (Isa. 50:4, 5).
      (See Jn. 7:16; 8:28, 38; 12:49; 14:10. 24; Phil. 2:8; Heb. 10:5.)
IV. His Specific Ministry to the Gentiles:
  "Nevertheless, the dimness shall not be such as was in her vexation, when at the first he lightly afflicted the land of Zebulun and the land of Naphtali, and afterward did more grievously afflict her by the way of the sea, beyond Jordan, in Galilee of the nations. The people that walked in darkness have seen a great light; they that dwell in the land of the shadow of death, upon them hath the light shined" (Isa. 9:1, 2).
  Here Isaiah points out that the very region where Assyrian armies brought darkness and death would be the first to rejoice in the light brought by the preaching of Christ. Matthew refers to the fulfillment of this prophecy. (See Mt. 4:12–16.)
V. His Gracious Ministry to All:
  "He shall not cry, nor lift up, nor cause his voice to be heard in the street. A bruised reed shall he not break, and the smoking flax shall he not quench; he shall bring forth justice in truth" (Isa. 42:2, 3).
  Here we are told three things God's righteous servant would *not* do during the course of his ministry:
  A. He would not scream out in the streets. Unlike other worldly and noisy warriors, this gentle conqueror would not allow his voice to be shouted out in the streets. Our Lord would bear absolutely no similarity to wild-eyed, shrieking rebels.
  B. He would not break the bruised reed. This he demonstrated when he freely forgave and restored an immoral woman whose sin had twisted and torn her soul. (See Jn. 8:1–11.)
  C. He would not quench the smoking flax. This he demonstrated by releasing an army of evil spirits which had all but snuffed out the light of sanity and hope from the maniac of Gadara. (See Mk. 5:1–20.)
      The fulfillment of this prophecy is recorded in Matthew 12:14–21 and amplified in 11:28–30.
VI. His Miracles:
  "Then the eyes of the blind shall be opened, and the ears of the deaf shall be unstopped. Then shall the lame man leap as an hart, and the tongue of the dumb sing . . ." (Isa. 35:5, 6).
  Although this passage will have its ultimate fulfillment in the millennium, it does nevertheless refer in part to the first earthly ministry of Christ.

  A. The eyes of the blind were opened. (See Mt. 9:29; Mk. 8:25; Jn. 9:7; Mt. 12:22; Mt. 20:34.)
  B. The ears of the deaf were unstopped. (See Mt. 11:5; Mk. 7:34.)
  C. The crooked limbs of the lame were straightened. (See Mt. 9:2; Mk. 12:13; Jn. 5:8.)
VII. His Message:
  "The Spirit of the Lord God is upon me, because the Lord hath anointed me to preach good tidings unto the meek; he hath sent me to bind up the brokenhearted, to proclaim liberty to the captives, and the opening of the prison to those who are bound; to proclaim the acceptable year of the Lord, and the day of vengeance of our God; to comfort all that mourn" (Isa. 61:1, 2).
  Scofield has the following helpful note at this point:
  "Observe that the Lord Jesus suspended the reading of this passage in the synagogue at Nazareth (Lk. 4:16–21) with the words 'Year of the Lord.' The first advent, therefore, opened the day of grace, 'the acceptable year of the Lord,' but does not fulfill the day of vengeance that will be accomplished when Messiah returns."
  (See 2 Thess. 1:7–10 and compare with Isa. 34:8; 35:4.)
VIII. His Sufferings and Death:
  In three key passages Isaiah describes in accurate and awesome detail the crucifixion of Christ some 700 years before it took place.
  A. Isaiah 50:6:
      "I gave my back to the smiters, and my cheeks to them that plucked off the hair; I hid not my face from shame and spitting."
      This was, of course, literally fulfilled:
      1. the smiters—see Matthew 27:26, 30; John 18:22
      2. the spitters—see Matthew 26:67; 27:30; Mark 14:65; 15:19
  B. Isaiah 52:14:
      "As many were astounded at thee—his visage was so marred more than any man, and his form more than the sons of men."
      Scofield notes:
      "The literal rendering presents a shocking picture: so marred from the form of man was his aspect that his appearance was not that of a son of man, i.e., not human. This was the effect of the brutalities described in Matthew 26:67, 68; 27:27–30."
      If this passage be taken at face value it means that Christ suffered more on the cross than any other human being ever suffered anywhere, anytime.
  C. Isaiah 53:1–10a:
      1. Concerning verses 1–3.
          a. These opening statements may be the voices of the believing Israelite remnant of all ages as they discuss his death. The first verse is literally, "Who believed what we heard?"
              Leupold writes:
              "So to speak, here we seem to hear two disciples standing on a street-corner in Jerusalem reviewing the things that happened on Good Friday in the

light of the better insight that came after Pentecost. They express especially their amazement at the complete misunderstanding they were guilty of in regard to the remarkable figure that appeared as the great Sufferer in their midst . . . they still marvel as they reflect on this blindness." (*Exposition on Isaiah*, p. 225)

An example of this can be seen through the testimony of the two Emmaus disciples as they comment on their former unbelief. See Luke 24:13-32.

b. The question, "And to whom is the arm of the Lord revealed?" should be compared with Psalm 8:3. In this passage David says it took only the fingers of God to create us, but Isaiah states it took his arms to redeem us.

c. Verses 2 and 3 tell the life story of the Savior from the cradle to the cross.
   (1) He was despised (counted as nothing) because of his lowly background (v. 2). See also John 1:46.
   (2) He was rejected because of his message (v. 3). See also Luke 4:16-30.
   (3) He was a man of sorrows and acquainted with grief because of his earthly mission (v. 3). See also Luke 19:10.

d. His humble beginning seemed so unimportant. Who really noticed him as a stripling lad in Nazareth? He could be likened to an insignificant "shoot," a bit of vegetation that is scarcely noticed.

e. What about the personal appearance of Christ? There is no biblical description of our Lord, for there was no need of this. He came as the suffering Servant of Jehovah and the only qualification of a servant is that he be able to do the job. This is why Mark's Gospel account (which pictures Christ as the ox-servant of God) has no genealogy. We may conclude that our Lord was humble, healthy, wholesome, but not handsome. He probably did not exude charisma, nor display a flashy and striking life style. The late-night talk show hosts never would have considered booking him for an interview.

2. Concerning verses 4-6.
   a. *The Scofield Bible* notes the following about verse 4:

   "Because Matthew quotes this passage and applies it to physical disease (8:17) it has been conjectured by some that disease as well as sin was included in the atoning death of Christ. But Matthew asserts that the Lord fulfilled the first part of Isaiah 53:4 during the healing ministry of his service on earth. Matthew 8:17 makes no reference to Christ's atoning death for sin" (p. 759).

   b. The last part of verse 4 informs us that the nation Israel in general looked upon the cross as a righteous sentence imposed

by God himself upon a blasphemer named Jesus Christ! (See Mt. 27:38-44.) Thus Israel here looked upon Jesus as Job's wife and friends looked upon Job, as a man suffering for his sins. (See Job 2:9; 4:7; 8:3.)

   c. Verse 5 tells us he was wounded (translated tormented by *Lang's Commentary*) and bruised (crushed) for our iniquities. These two words "wounded" and "bruised" are the strongest terms to describe a violent and agonizing death.

   d. Verse 6 is the "all" verse, as it begins and ends with this word. "*All* we like sheep have gone astray . . . the Lord hath laid on him the iniquity of us *all*." Thus Christ took our hell that we might partake of his heaven. The blessed Son of God became the Son of Man that sons of men might become sons of God.

3. Concerning verses 7-9.
   a. Some might ask how we can know that Isaiah is really referring to Christ in chapter 53, since the Savior is not mentioned by name. But his identity is clearly brought out in two New Testament passages which link him directly to Isaiah 53.
      (1) The testimony of John the Apostle—John 12:37, 38. (Here Isa. 53:1 is quoted.)
      (2) The testimony of Philip—Acts 8:32, 33. (Here Isa. 53:7, 8 is quoted.)

   b. We are told that although he was oppressed (treated unsparingly), yet he opened not his mouth. Not once during his seven unfair trials before Annas, Caiaphas, the Sanhedrin, Pilate, Herod, Pilate again, and the Roman soldiers did our Lord attempt to justify himself, or demand a mistrial. (See v. 7.) John the Baptist was doubtless thinking of the phrase "as a lamb to the slaughter" when he first introduced Jesus as "the Lamb of God" (Jn. 1:29).

   c. Verse 8 might be rendered: "By oppression and an unjust sentence he was taken away; and as to his fate, who gave it any thought?"

   d. Verse 9 tells us the religious officials planned to dump him into a potter's field along with the two thieves. Of course, God stepped in and he was placed in a new tomb owned by a rich man (see Mt. 27:57). Scofield notes the following concerning verse 9:

   "In the Hebrew the word rendered 'death' is an intensive plural. It has been suggested that it speaks of the violence of Christ's death, the very pain of which made it like a repeated death" (p. 759).

4. Concerning verse 10a.
   Who really killed Christ? Many of course played a part in his death. This would include Judas, Caiaphas, Annas, the wicked Jewish religious leaders, Pilate, Herod, the

Roman soldiers, the devil, and the sins of all sinners! But who actually masterminded the original plan? Here we are told it was God himself! See the following: Acts 2:23; 1 Peter 1:18-20; Revelation 13:8.

IX. His Resurrection, Ascension, and Exaltation:
    A. Isaiah 52:13:
        "Behold, my servant shall deal prudently; he shall be exalted and extolled, and be very high."

The word "prudent" here means to prosper, to be successful (see Josh. 1:7, 8; Jer. 23:5, where the same Hebrew word occurs) and what a success story we have here in this verse.

Note the predicted threefold accomplishments of God's Servant:

1. He would be exalted (literally, to be high). This is a reference to his resurrection. (See Mt. 28:1-10.)
2. He would be extolled (meaning, to be lifted up). This is a reference to his ascension. (See Acts 1:9, 10.)
3. He would be very high (or, greatly exalted). This is a reference to his exaltation. (See Phil. 2:5-11.)

All this is even more significant because of what follows in Isaiah 53, for here we see the Servant of the Lord resurrected, ascended, and exalted even before he was crucified! Who but God himself could possess that kind of glorious confidence?

    B. Isaiah 53:10b-12; 52:15:
        "When thou shalt make his soul an offering for sin, he shall see his seed, he shall prolong his days, and the pleasure of the Lord shall prosper in his hand. He shall see of the travail of his soul, and shall be satisfied; by his knowledge shall my righteous servant justify many; for he shall bear their iniquities. Therefore will I divide him a portion with the great, and he shall divide the spoil with the strong, because he hath poured out his soul unto death; and he was numbered with the transgressors; and he bore the sin of many, and made intercession for the transgressors" (53:10b-12).
        "So shall he sprinkle many nations; the kings shall shut their mouths at him; for that which had not been told them shall they see, and that which they had not heard shall they consider" (52:15).

These final verses give us a grand summary of both the sufferings and the ultimate satisfaction of Jehovah's servant. Doubtless Peter had this in mind when he wrote:

"Of which salvation the prophets have inquired and searched diligently, who prophesied of the grace that should come unto you: Searching what, or what manner of time the spirit of Christ which was in them did signify, when it testified beforehand the sufferings of Christ, and the glory that should follow" (1 Pet. 1:10, 11).

1. The sufferings of God's Servant.
    a. He poured out his soul unto death as a trespass offering unto God. (See Jn. 10:11, 15, 18.)
    b. He was counted as a common criminal.
    c. In spite of this, he bore the sins of the world and prayed for his tormentors. (See Heb. 2:9; Lk. 23:34.)
2. The satisfaction of God's Servant.
    a. He shall see the spiritual children he died to save. (Compare Heb. 12:1, 2 with Jude 1:24.)
    b. He would fulfill the will and pleasure of his Father.
    c. He will receive from his Father the spoils of victory. (See Rev. 11:15.)
    d. He will be the supreme source of blessing to many nations. (See Rev. 21:22-26.)

# CHRIST in ISAIAH

1. His Incarnation  **7:14, 15; 9:6**

2. His Youth in Nazareth
   **11:1, 2; 53:2; 7:15**

3. His Relationship with the Father
   **42:1; 50:4, 5**

4. His Miracles  **35:5, 6**

5. His Message  **61:1, 2**

6. His Specific Ministry to the Gentiles
   **9:1, 2**

7. His Gracious Ministry to All  **42:2, 3**

8. His Suffering and Death
   **50:6; 52:14; 53:1-10**

9. His Resurrection, Ascension, and Exaltation  **52:13; 53:10-12**

10. His Millennial Reign
    **9:7; 42:4-7; 59:16-21; 11:3-5; 49:1-12; 32:1; 33:22**

e. He will enjoy this satisfaction throughout all eternity. (See Rev. 1:8; 1 Pet. 1:1, 2; Heb. 10:22.)

X. His Millennial Reign:
   A. Isaiah 9:7:
   "Of the increase of his government and peace there shall be no end, upon the throne of David, and upon his kingdom, to order it, and to establish it with judgment and with justice from henceforth even for ever. The zeal of the Lord of hosts will perform this."
   B. Isaiah 42:4-7
   C. Isaiah 59:16-21:
      1. These verses describe God's search for a man, and his choice of Christ as the only acceptable Redeemer. Isaiah here depicts a sight later described by the Apostle John in Revelation 5:1-14.
      2. Paul informs us that the armor pieces worn by this Warrior-Redeemer are now available to all his redeemed warriors. (See Eph. 6:13-17.)
   D. Isaiah 11:3-5:
   "And shall make him of quick understanding in the fear of the Lord: and he shall not judge after the sight of his eyes, neither reprove after the hearing of his ears: But with righteousness shall he judge the poor, and reprove with equity for the meek of the earth: and he shall smite the earth with the rod of his mouth, and with the breath of his lips shall he slay the wicked. And righteousness shall be the girdle of his loins, and faithfulness the girdle of his reins."
   E. Isaiah 49:1-12
   F. Isaiah 32:1:
   "Behold, a king shall reign in righteousness, and princes shall rule in judgment."
   G. Isaiah 33:22:
   "For the Lord is our judge, the Lord is our lawgiver, the Lord is our king; he will save us."

## The Sins of Israel

I. Her Stupidity.
   A. She did not even have the common sense of a brute animal (1:3).
   B. God had to tell them everything over and over again (line upon line; here a little, there a little) and still they could not understand (28:9-13).
II. Her Hypocrisy.
   A. God was sick of their sacrifices which were offered without any sorrow for sins (1:11-14).
   B. Because of this, he would refuse to see their outstretched hands or hear their pious words during prayer time (1:15).
   C. Israel's worship services amounted to mere words learned by rote memory (29:13).
III. Her Women (3:16-26).
   A. Before God judged them (3:16-23):
      1. They were haughty with their noses in the air.
      2. They had wanton eyes.
      3. They wore ornaments about their feet and chains around their ankles.
      4. They had necklaces and bracelets.

5. They had veils of shimmering gauze.
6. They wore head bands.
7. They wore nose jewels and earrings.
8. They sported party clothes, negligees, and capes.
9. They wore ornate combs and carried purses. How far removed all this was from Peter's description of real beauty and adornment. (See 1 Pet. 3:1-4.)
   B. After God judged them (3:24-26):
      1. Instead of sweet fragrance, there would be rottenness.
      2. Instead of a girdle (sash), a rope.
      3. Instead of well-set hair, baldness.
      4. Instead of beauty, shame, disgrace, and widowhood.
IV. Her Fruitlessness (5:1-7). The parable of the Lord's vineyard.
   This parable employs one of the two figures taken from the botanical world to represent the nation Israel. The other figure is a fig tree. (See Mt. 21:33-46.)
   A. What God did for his vineyard (5:1, 2).
      1. He planted it on a very fertile hill with the choicest vine.
      2. He plowed it and took out all the rocks.
      3. He built a watchtower and cut a winepress in the rocks.
      4. He waited patiently for the harvest.
   B. What God received from his vineyard—nothing but wild and sour grapes (5:2).
   C. What God would do to his vineyard (5:3-7).
      1. He would tear down the fences and let the vineyard go to pasture, to be trampled by cattle and sheep.
      2. He would not prune nor hoe it, but let it be overgrown with briars and thorns.
      3. He would even command the clouds not to rain on it anymore.
V. Her Six-Count Indictment (5:8-22).
   A. She denied others their own property rights.
   B. She had become a nation of drunkards. (See also 28:1-8.)
   C. She had mocked God and dared him to punish her.
   D. She had called right wrong, and wrong right. Her black was white, her white was black, her bitter was sweet, and her sweet was bitter! Here is a classic example of today's "new morality" practiced by Israel some seven centuries B.C.
   E. She was wise and shrewd in her own eyes.
   F. She took bribes which resulted in freeing the guilty and imprisoning the innocent.
VI. Her False Leaders.
   A. 9:15, 16:
   "The ancient and honourable, he is the head; and the prophet that teacheth lies, he is the tail. For the leaders of this people cause them to err; and they that are led of them are destroyed."
   B. 28:14, 15:
   "Wherefore hear the word of the Lord, ye scornful men, that rule this people which is in Jerusalem. Because ye have said, We have a covenant with death, and with hell are we at agreement; when the overflowing scourge shall pass through, it shall not come unto us:

for we have made lies our refuge, and under falsehood have we hid ourselves."

VII. Her Dependence upon Egypt (Isa. 30:1-7; 31:1-3).
31:1, 3:
"Woe to them that go down to Egypt for help; and stay on horses, and trust in chariots, because they are many; and in horsemen because they are very strong; but they look not unto the Holy One of Israel, neither seek the Lord! Now the Egyptians are men, and not God; and their horses flesh, and not spirit. When the Lord shall stretch out his hand, both he that helpeth shall fall, and he that is holpen shall fall down, and they all shall fail together."

VIII. Her Tragic Overall Condition.
A. 1:5, 6:
"Why should ye be stricken any more? Ye will revolt more and more: the whole head is sick, and the whole heart faint. From the sole of the foot even unto the head there is no soundness in it; but wounds, and bruises, and putrifying sores: they have not been closed, neither bound up, neither mollified with ointment."

B. 59:1-8

C. 64:6:
"But we are all as an unclean thing, and all our righteousnesses are as filthy rags; and we all do fade as a leaf; and our iniquities, like the wind, have taken us away."

D. 65:2, 3:
"I have spread out my hands all the day unto a rebellious people, which walketh in a way that was not good, after their own thoughts; A people that provoketh me to anger continually to my face; that sacrificeth in gardens, and burneth incense upon altars of brick."

## The Gentile Nations

I. Babylon (Isa. 13-14, 21).
The *New Scofield Bible* notes the following:
"This prophecy concerning Babylon announces the doom of the nation and city at the hands of the Medes (13:17-22), but applies the word Babylon to the totality of Gentile world power beginning with Nebuchadnezzar (Dan. 2:31, 32, 37, 38) and culminating in the fourth world empire (Dan. 2:34, 35, 40-45) at the return of Jesus Christ to the earth as the Smiting Stone. This is the time of the Gentiles. See Luke 21:24."

A. Babylon was to be destroyed by the Medes (13:17-22).

B. Their armies would be chased back to their own land as a wild dog would pursue a frightened deer (13:14).

C. Their soldiers would be butchered, their children murdered, and their wives raped (13:15, 16).

D. The prophet Isaiah is horrified and becomes physically ill at God's description of Babylon's punishment (21:3-5).

The last passage was no doubt fulfilled to a T when Darius took Babylon. (See Dan. 5.) This all reads as if it were an eyewitness account of the destruction as recorded by Daniel. Yet Isaiah wrote about this some 200 years before it actually transpired. (See also Jer. 51:8, 9.)

Isaiah also vividly describes the watchman as he brings word to the king that the city had fallen. (See 21:6-10. Also see Jer. 51:31-33.)

E. Babylon was to become a desolate land of porcupines and swamps (14:23); the wild animals would make it their home, and demons would come there to dance (13:21).

F. Babylon was never to be rebuilt on that site. Here it should be pointed out that some believe the ultimate fulfillment of these verses must await the tribulation period, when ancient Babylon will be rebuilt on the Euphrates. (See Rev. 18.) This is advocated because some of the prophecies concerning Babylon's destruction were not all fulfilled when the city fell to the Medes. (See also Jer. 25:17-26; 51:26.)

G. The rulers of two Gentile nations are used by God as a basis of describing the person and ministry of Satan. One is Tyre (Ezek. 28:1-19) and the other is Babylon (Isa. 14:12-16).
For other examples of this addressing Satan through another, see the following:
1. Genesis 3:15, where Satan is addressed through the serpent.
2. Matthew 16:22, 23 where Satan is addressed through Simon Peter.

II. Assyria (14:24-27).
A. God had determined to crush the Assyrian army on the mountains of Israel (14:25).
B. This would be done to remove the awful Assyrian yoke from his people.

III. Philistia (14:28-32).
A. Philistia was warned not to rejoice over the death of King Ahaz of Judah, who had smote them while alive (14:29).
B. His son (Hezekiah) would be even more demanding (14:29).
C. Finally, Philistia was to suffer total doom under the cruel attack of Sargon, the Assyrian king.

IV. Moab (15-16).
A. Moab was the nation which came from Lot through the incestuous relationship with his eldest daughter. The illegitimate son of this sordid affair was the father of the Moabites. Their people became the persistent enemies of the nation Israel. Balak, their king, hired Balaam, the prophet, to curse them. But Ruth also came from this land! (See Num. 22:2-4; Ruth 1:4.)
B. Moab was to be punished by God, with its chief cities destroyed in one night (15:1).
C. The whole land would be filled with weeping from one end to another (15:8).
D. Lions would hunt down the survivors (15:9).
E. Moab's refugees were invited by God to avail themselves of his mercies. They were enjoined to pay tribute to Israel according to their past arrangement (2 Ki. 3:4-9; Isa. 16:1).
F. However, pride kept Moab from doing this (16:6).
G. Isaiah wept because of God's judgment upon this stubborn pride (16:11).
H. Judgment was officially set to fall within three years. The Assyrians at that time invaded Moab (16:14).

V. Damascus (17).
A. Damascus was the capital of Syria and is the oldest living city in the world today. Ephraim (an-

other title for the Israelite northern kingdom) and Damascus had allied together against Judah, thus linking that kingdom with the divine judgment. Partners in crime meant partners in punishment (17:3).

B. Both allies were later besieged by Tiglath-Pileser (2 Ki. 15:29) and were finally deported by Shalmaneser (2 Ki. 17:6).

VI. Ethiopia (18).

A. This "land shadowing with wings" is thought to be African Ethiopia (18:1). Missionaries to that land tell us that it is known as the land of birds and is called "the Land of Wings."

B. This nation marches against Israel (historically or prophetically?) but is cut off by God himself. Their army will be left dead on the field for the birds and animals to eat (18:4-6).

C. After this (the tribulation?) Ethiopia will bring gifts to the Lord of Hosts in Jerusalem (18:7).

VII. Egypt (19-20).

A. No nation is so prominent in the Bible as Egypt. It is first mentioned when Abraham visited there (Gen. 12). Later Joseph lived and died there (Gen. 39-50). There Israel became a nation.

B. Egypt was to be severely punished because of her idolatry (19:1). Her people were originally monotheistic but gradually lapsed into the basest idolatry. They worshiped the bull, the frog, the

fish, and various birds. The contest in Exodus was a battle of the gods versus Jehovah. (See Ex. 7-12. Note Isaiah's prophecies in chapters 19-20.)

1. Egypt was to be given over to a cruel ruler (19:4) who may have been the Ottoman Turk who reduced Egypt to a poverty-stricken nation.

2. Egyptian would fight against Egyptian (19:2). A pharaoh arose about the time of Isaiah who could not control this great kingdom and the army no longer obeyed him.

3. The channels along the Nile River would be filled and fouled with rotting reeds. This is true even today.

4. The paper reeds by the brooks would wither away (19:7), a reference to the papyri which was used in that day as paper. This was one of the main industries of Egypt and afforded a great volume of wealth. It disappeared, though, and no longer grows along the banks where Moses was once hidden.

5. Egypt's fishing industry was to disappear (19:8, 10).

6. Her linen industry was also to disappear (19:9). The linen of Egypt was world-renowned. The linen taken from mummies is superior to any linen that is made by the mills of Ireland. The fine twined byssus linen

## PROPHECIES CONCERNING GENTILE NATIONS IN ISAIAH

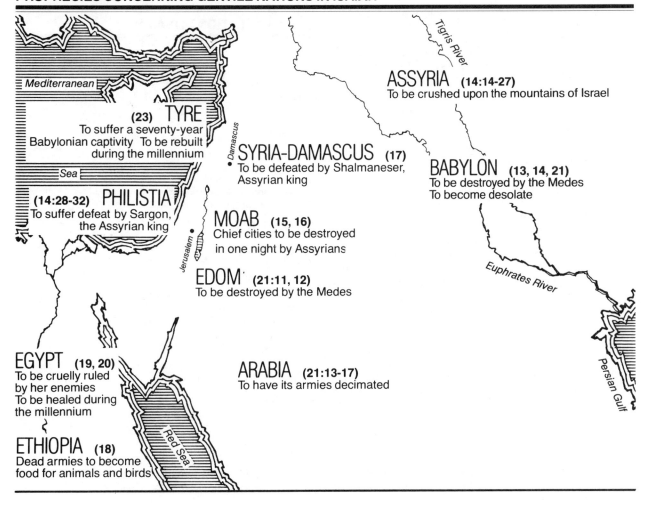

was used in the construction of the tabernacle. All this, however, has gone.

7. Egypt was to stagger along in world history as a "drunken man staggereth in his vomit" (19:14).
8. Judah would be a terror to Egypt (19:17).
9. Egypt was to be invaded within three years by Assyria (20:1-6).

C. But all this would someday gloriously change.
1. God would smite Egypt in the tribulation, but would then graciously heal her (19:22).
2. Egypt and Iraq will be connected by a highway, thus allowing both nations to freely travel to Jerusalem to worship God (19:23-25).

VIII. Edom (21:11, 12). This passage includes a question and an answer:
A. The question: "Watchman, what of the night?"
B. The answer: "The morning cometh, and also the night."

Both morning and night are coming. What will be glory for some (the Medes, who would overrun Edom), would be shame for others (the Edomites). The New Testament likewise presents Christ's glorious coming as night for some (the unsaved, see Jn. 9:4) and morning for others (the saved, see Rom. 13:11, 12).

IX. Arabia (21:13-17).
A. Arabia was the land of the Ishmaelites, the Bedouin tribes of the desert, the modern Arabs.
B. They would be so severely judged that only a few of their stalwart archers would survive (21:17).

X. Tyre (23).
This is the tenth and last burden against the nations. J. Vernon McGee suggests that each of these great nations represents or symbolizes some principle, philosophy, or system which God must judge.
Thus:
Babylon—false religion, idolatry
Assyria—utter ruthlessness
Philistia—extreme pride
Moab—a formal religion
Damascus—compromise
Ethiopia—an industrial-military complex
Egypt—the world
Edom—the flesh
Arabia—war
Tyre—big business

Tyre and Sidon were the two great cities of the Phoenicians. Their ships entered all ports of the Mediterranean Sea; they even penetrated the uncharted ocean beyond the pillars of Hercules. Their vessels brought tin from Great Britain. They settled the North African city of Carthage.

A. Tyre was to be destroyed by the Babylonians and carried into captivity for seventy years (23:15).
B. This was to be done because of its pride and utter materialism (23:8). (For several remarkable similarities in the history of Judah and the life of Nebuchadnezzar, see Jer. 25:11; 29:10; Dan. 9:24; 4:28-37.)
C. Nebuchadnezzar would lay siege to the coastland city, raze its palaces, and make it a heap of ruins (23:13).
D. Egypt, its ally, would sorrow over its swift destruction, along with its own sailors, who would

not even be able to return home to port (23:5-7). For another remarkable similarity, see the sorrow of this world over the destruction of Babylon during the tribulation (Rev. 18).

E. After seventy years Tyre would be rebuilt (as was Jerusalem), but would soon degenerate into the same gross materialism and pride of former days (23:17).

Note: At this point the student should carefully examine Ezekiel 26 where the historical account is completed. Alexander the Great utterly destroys both the coastal and the island cities of Tyre in 332 B.C.

F. In the millennium, Tyre will be rebuilt and be blessed by God (23:18). (See also Ps. 45:12.)

## The Tribulation

I. The Main Passages:
A. Isaiah 2:10-22
B. 13:6-13
C. 24:1-23
D. 26:20, 21
E. 34:1-10
F. 42:13, 14
G. 51:6
H. 63:1-6
I. 66:15, 16

II. The Main Action:
A. The earth.
1. Shall be terribly shaken (2:21).

## THE TRIBULATION IN ISAIAH

# EARTH

**MAIN PASSAGES**

| 2:10-22 | 13:6-13 | 24:1-23 |
|---|---|---|

**MAIN ACTION**

To be shaken
To be moved out of its place
To be made waste and turned upside down
To be burned with fire
To be broken and dissolved
To reel to and fro like a drunkard
To be unable to cover its dead

# HEAVENS

**MAIN PASSAGES**

| 26:20, 21 | 34:1-10 | 42:13, 14 |
|---|---|---|

**MAIN ACTION**

Stars, sun, and moon to be darkened
Hosts of heaven to be dissolved and rolled up like a scroll
Stars to fall as figs from a tree when shaken

# SINFUL MANKIND

**MAIN PASSAGES**

| 51:6 | 63:1-6 | 66:15, 16 |
|---|---|---|

**MAIN ACTION**

To hide in caves and holes of the earth
To faint with fear and hearts to melt
To suffer the pain of childbirth
To experience no joy whatsoever
To cover the mountains with their dead
To overpower the valleys with their stench
To be trampled by God like overripe grapes

2. To be moved out of its place (13:13).
3. To be made waste and turned upside down (24:1).
4. To be burned with fire (24:6).
5. To be broken down and dissolved (24:19).
6. To reel to and fro like a drunkard (24:20).
7. To be unable to cover its dead (26:21).

B. The heavens.
1. The stars, sun, and moon to be darkened (13:10).
2. The hosts of heaven to be dissolved and rolled up as a scroll (34:4; 51:6).
3. The stars shall fall as figs from a tree when shaken (34:4).

C. Sinful mankind.
1. To hide in the caves and holes of the earth (2:19).
2. Will faint with fear and their hearts will melt (13:7; 24:17).
3. To suffer the agonies of childbirth (13:8).
4. To experience no joy whatsoever (24:8-10).
5. To cover the mountains with their blood and to overpower the valleys with the stench of their dead (34:3).
6. To be utterly trampled by a wrathful God like overripe grapes (63:3).

## The Millennium.

I. The Salvation of Gentile Nations:
A. Isaiah 2:2-4:
"And it shall come to pass in the last days, that the mountain of the Lord's house shall be established in the top of the mountains, and shall be exalted above the hills; and all nations shall flow into it. And many people shall go and say, Come ye, and let us go up to the mountain of the Lord, to the house of the God of Jacob; and he will teach us of his ways, and we will walk in his paths: for out of Zion shall go forth the law, and the word of the Lord from Jerusalem. And he shall judge among the nations, and shall rebuke many people: and they shall beat their swords into plowshares, and their spears into pruninghooks: nation shall not lift up sword against nation, neither shall they learn war any more."

Isaiah 2:4 is inscribed upon the foundation of the U.N. building in New York City. This glorious truth will, of course, be literally realized during the millennium. But until that day, the fearful words of Joel 3:9, 10, the exact reverse of this passage, will hold true.

B. 11:10:
"And in that day there shall be a root of Jesse, which shall stand for an ensign of the people; to it shall the Gentiles seek: and his rest shall be glorious."

C. 19:18-25:
Israel suffered perhaps more under the various brutal reigns of Assyria and Egypt than any other two nations. But during the millennium God will supernaturally unite these three into a beautiful trio of fellowship.
1. The Egyptians will speak the Hebrew language.
2. They will build an altar and monument to the Lord.

3. God will answer their prayers and heal them.
4. Both Egypt and Assyria (Iraq) will be connected by a highway.
5. Both shall worship Jehovah and receive his rich blessings.

D. 52:10:
"The Lord hath made bare his holy arm in the eyes of all the nations; and all the ends of the earth shall see the salvation of our God."

E. 56:6-8

F. 66:23:
"And it shall come to pass, that from one new moon to another, and from one sabbath to another, shall all flesh come to worship before me, saith the Lord."

These glorious verses are condensed by John in Revelation 21:23-27.

II. The Salvation of Israel and Jerusalem:
A. 4:2-6
1. They will be washed and rinsed of all their moral filth.
2. They will once again be blessed by the fiery and cloudy pillar.

B. 11:12:
"And he shall set up an ensign for the nations, and shall assemble the outcasts of Israel, and gather together the dispersed of Judah from the four corners of the earth."

C. 14:3:
"And it shall come to pass in the day that the Lord shall give thee rest from thy sorrow, and from thy fear, and from the hard bondage wherein thou wast made to serve."

D. 30:19:
"For the people shall dwell in Zion at Jerusalem: thou shalt weep no more: he will be very gracious unto thee at the voice of thy cry; when he shall hear it, he will answer thee."

E. 32:18:
"And my people shall dwell in a peaceable habitation, and in sure dwellings, and in quiet resting places."

F. 44:23:
"Sing, O ye heavens; for the Lord hath done it: shout, ye lower parts of the earth: break forth into singing, ye mountains, O forest, and every tree therein: for the Lord hath redeemed Jacob, and glorified himself in Israel."

G. 49:10-13

H. 51:3, 11:
"For the Lord shall comfort Zion: he will comfort all her waste places; and he will make her wilderness like Eden, and her desert like the garden of the Lord; joy and gladness shall be found therein, thanksgiving, and the voice of melody. Therefore the redeemed of the Lord shall return, and come with singing unto Zion; and everlasting joy shall be upon their head: they shall obtain gladness and joy; and sorrow and mourning shall flee away."

I. 52:1, 6-9
J. 59:20, 21:
"And the Redeemer shall come to Zion, and unto them that turn from transgression in Jacob, saith the Lord. As for me, this is my covenant with thee, saith the Lord; my spirit that

is upon thee, and my words which I have put in thy mouth, shall not depart out of thy mouth, nor out of the mouth of thy seed, nor out of the mouth of thy seed's seed, saith the Lord, from henceforth and for ever."

    K. 60:1–3, 11, 12, 13, 19–22
    L. 62:1–4
    M. 65:18–24
    N. 66:10, 12:

> "Rejoice ye with Jerusalem, and be glad with her, all ye that love her: rejoice for joy with her, all ye that mourn for her: For thus saith the Lord, Behold, I will extend peace to her like a river, and the glory of the Gentiles like a flowing stream: then shall ye suck, ye shall be borne upon her sides, and be dandled upon her knees."

These glorious verses are condensed by Paul in Romans 11:1, 26, 27.

III. The Salvation of the Afflicted:
    A. 29:18:

> "And in that day shall the deaf hear the words of the book, and the eyes of the blind shall see out of obscurity, and out of darkness."

    B. 35:3–6
    C. 42:16:

> "And I will bring the blind by a way that they knew not; I will lead them in paths that they have not known: I will make darkness light before them, and crooked things straight. These things will I do unto them, and not forsake them."

These glorious verses are condensed by John in Revelation 22:1–5.

IV. The Salvation of All Nature
    A. 11:6–9
    B. 14:7, 8:

> "The whole earth is at rest, and is quiet: they break forth into singing. Yea, the fir trees rejoice at thee, and the cedars of Lebanon, saying, Since thou art laid down, no feller is come up against us."

    C. 30:23–26
    D. 35:1, 2, 7–10:

> "The wilderness and the solitary place shall be glad for them; and the desert shall rejoice, and blossom as the rose. It shall blossom abundantly, and rejoice even with joy and singing: the glory of Lebanon shall be given unto it, the excellency of Carmel and Sharon, they shall see the glory of the Lord, and the excellency of our God. And the parched ground shall become a pool, and thirsty land springs of water: in the habitation of dragons, where each lay, shall be grass with reeds and rushes. And an highway shall be there, and a way, and it shall be called The way of holiness; the unclean shall not pass over it; but it shall be for those: the wayfaring men, though fools, shall not err therein. No lion shall be there, nor any ravenous beast shall go up thereon, it shall not be found there; but the redeemed shall walk there: And the ransomed of the Lord shall return, and come to Zion with songs and everlasting joy upon their heads: they shall obtain joy and gladness, and sorrow and sighing shall flee away."

## THE MILLENNIUM IN ISAIAH

# Fourfold Salvation

## Of Gentile Nations
**2:2-4; 11:10; 19:18-25; 52:10; 56:6-8**

## Of Israel and Jerusalem
**4:2-6; 11:12; 14:3; 30:19; 32:18; 44:23; 49:10-13; 51:3, 11; 52:1, 6-9; 59:20, 21; 60:1-3, 11-13, 19-22; 62:1-4; 65:18-24; 66:10, 12**

## Of the Afflicted   **29:18; 35:3-6; 42:16**

## Of All Nature
**11:6-9; 14:7, 8; 30:23-26; 35:1, 2, 7-10; 40:4, 5; 65:25**

    E. 40:4, 5:

> "Every valley shall be exalted, and every mountain and hill shall be made low: and the crooked shall be made straight, and the rough places plain: And the glory of the Lord shall be revealed, and all flesh shall see it together: for the mouth of the Lord hath spoken it."

    F. 65:25:

> "The wolf and the lamb shall feed together, and the lion shall eat straw like the bullock; and dust shall be the serpent's meat. They shall not hurt nor destroy in all my holy mountain, saith the Lord."

These glorious verses are condensed by Paul in Romans 8:18–25.

## NAHUM (630–612 B.C.)

INTRODUCTION:
1. The name Nahum means "the comforter."
2. The New Testament Galilean headquarters of Jesus was a city named Capernaum, which literally means, "the village of Nahum." Many thus believe Capernaum was named after this prophet.
3. The book has only one theme, the terrible and total coming destruction of Nineveh. At the time of this prophecy, Nineveh appeared to be impregnable, with its walls 100 feet high and broad enough for chariots to drive upon them. It had a circumference of some sixty miles and was adorned by more than 1200 towers.

4. Nineveh fell in 612 (some eighteen years after this prophecy), being completely destroyed by the Medes from the north and the Babylonians from the south.

5. Nahum not only predicted the fall of Nineveh, but the very manner in which it would fall. (Note 1:8: "an overrunning flood he will make an utter end of the place.")

History tells us that Nabopolassar, King of the Babylonian invasion forces, besieged the city for three years, leading three massive attacks against it, and failing each time. Because of this, the Assyrians inside Nineveh rejoiced and began holding drunken parties. But suddenly the Tigris River overflowed its banks and sent its wildly churning waters against the walls of the city. Soon it had washed a hole, into which rushed Babylonians, and the proud city was destroyed.

6. The destruction of Nineveh was so great that Alexander the Great marched his troops over the same desolate ground which had once given support to her mighty buildings and did not even know there had once been a city there! The city itself was not excavated until as recently as A.D. 1845.

7. God had once used Jonah (150 years before) to ward off his judgment. But now because of the city's relapse into gross sin, he calls upon Nahum to pronounce judgment.

I. The Patience of God (1:1-8).
"The Lord is slow to anger, and great in power . . ." (see Gen. 15:16; Ps. 103:8.)
For over 500 years Nineveh and the Assyrians were feared as the terror of Western Asia. But while God's patience is infinite in depth, it is not eternal in duration. The time for judgment would soon come.

II. The Pride of Sennacherib (1:9-14).
"There is one come out of thee, that imagineth evil against the Lord, a wicked counselor" (1:11).
It is generally agreed that the wicked counselor here is Sennacherib, the evil Assyrian king who invaded Judah and surrounded Jerusalem in 701 B.C. Although Sennacherib's armies had been smashed at Jerusalem's gates and the monarch himself murdered years before (see 2 Ki. 19:35-37), the arrogant ruler seemed to symbolize the pride of Nineveh, and is therefore used here.

Sennacherib had made Nineveh a truly magnificent city, laying out its streets and squares, and built within a famous "palace without a rival." The dimensions of this palace were fantastic, 600 × 630 feet! It comprised at least eighty rooms, many of which were lined with sculpture.

III. The Promise of Judah (1:15).
"Behold upon the mountains the feet of him that bringeth good tidings, that publisheth peace! O Judah, keep thy solemn feasts, perform thy vows: for the wicked shall no more pass through thee; he is utterly cut off."
Judah would need no longer fear this cruel nation.

IV. The Punishment of Nineveh (2-3).
A. The certainty of this terrible punishment (3:11-19).
Nahum compared Nineveh to Thebes (No-Amon, see 3:8), that great capital of upper Egypt. It too boasted that no power on earth could subdue it. However, both Jeremiah (46:25) and Ezekiel (30:14-16) predicted its destruction, which

# Nahum

**THE DESTRUCTION OF NINEVEH**

## Source of the Destruction—
**GOD HIMSELF**

## Reason for the Destruction—
**SIN**

Cruelty   Wickedness   Evil

## Tool used in the Destruction—
**BABYLON**

1. ## The Patience of God (1:8)
God had once stayed his hand of judgment upon Nineveh through Jonah's ministry. But now his patience was exhausted.

2. ## The Pride of the Assyrian King (1:9-14)

3. ## The Promise to Judah (1:15)
Judah need no longer fear this cruel nation.

4. ## The Punishment of Nineveh (2-3)
The certainty of it (3:11-19)
The description of it (2:3-9)

was fulfilled later by Sargon of Assyria in his campaign against Egypt. Now Nineveh's hour had come.

B. The description of this terrible punishment.
"Shields flash red in the sunlight! The attack begins! See their scarlet uniforms! See their glittering chariots moving forward side by side, pulled by prancing steeds! Your own chariots race recklessly along the streets and through the squares, darting like lightning, gleaming like torches. The king shouts for his officers; they stumble in their haste, rushing to the walls to set up their defenses. But too late! The river gates are open! The enemy has entered! The palace is in panic! The queen of Nineveh is brought out naked to the streets, and led away, a slave, with all her maidens weeping after her; listen to them mourn like doves, and beat their breasts! Nineveh is like a leaking water tank! Her soldiers slip away, deserting her; she cannot hold them back. 'Stop, stop,' she shouts, but they keep on running. Loot the silver! Loot the gold! There seems to be no end of treasures. Her vast, uncounted wealth is stripped away. Soon the city is an empty shambles; hearts melt in horror; knees quake; her people stand aghast, pale-faced and trembling" (Nahum 2:3-10, *The Living Bible*).

# ZEPHANIAH (625–610 B.C.)

INTRODUCTION:
1. The name Zephaniah means, "the Lord hides or protects."
2. He was the great-great-grandson of King Hezekiah and, therefore, of royal blood.

3. He ministered during the days of King Josiah, Judah's last godly ruler. The prophet was kin to Josiah.
4. His ministry may well have helped prepare for the great revival of 621 B.C., which occurred under Josiah's reign when the law of Moses was rediscovered during the repair of the Temple. (See 2 Chron. 34-35.)

I. A Bad Day—The prophet pronounces judgment (1:1—3:8).
   A. Upon the land of God:
      1. The fact of this judgment: God would sweep away everything in the land and destroy it to the ground. This would include man, birds and even fish (1:2-4).
      2. The reason for this judgment: Judah had worshiped Baal (the great god of the Canaanite pantheon), and Milcom (chief Ammonite deity), thus ignoring the only true God (1:5, 6).
      3. The name of this judgment: the prophet calls it "the day of the Lord." This term is used no less than seven times. See 1:7, 8, 14, 18; 2:2, 3.
      4. The results of this judgment (1:14-18).
      Note: Zephaniah evidently had in mind not only the historical Babylonian invasion of 605-586 B.C., but also the yet future Great Tribulation. (See Rev. 6:12-17.)
   B. Upon the enemies of God:
      1. The Philistine cities of Gaza, Ashkelon, Ashdod, and Ekron would be rooted out and left in desolation (2:4-6).
      2. Moab and Ammon would be destroyed as Sodom and Gomorrah, for mocking Judah and invading her land (2:8-11). (See Gen. 19.)
      3. Ethiopia would be slain by God's avenging sword (2:12).
      4. Assyria and its capital Nineveh were to be made utterly desolate (2:13-15).
   C. Upon the city of God:
      1. A cry of alarm would begin at the fish gate in Jerusalem. It would be heard from gate to gate until it reached the highest part of the city (1:10).
      2. God planned to search with lanterns in Jerusalem's darkest corners to find and destroy all sinners (1:12, 13).
      3. The city's leaders were like roaring lions and ravenous wolves, devouring any and all victims (3:1-7).
II. A Glad Day—the prophet announces justice (3:8-20).
   A. Upon the (once) enemies of God (3:9, 10):
      "For then will I turn to the people a pure language, that they may call upon the name of the Lord, to serve him with one consent. From beyond the rivers of Ethiopia my suppliants, even the daughters of my dispersed, shall bring mine offering."
      Note: The "pure language" of 3:9 may refer to two things:
      1. It may indicate a reversal of the language curse at Babel (Gen. 11:9), thus allowing redeemed man to once again enjoy a universal language, perhaps composed of the best from all known existing human languages.

# Zephaniah

## Judgment

**The Prophet Pronounces Judgment (1:1—3:8)**

**UPON THE LAND OF GOD**
The facts of **(1:2-4)**
The reason for **(1:5, 6)**
The name of **(1:7, 8, 14, 18; 2:2)**
The results of **(1:14-18)**

**UPON THE ENEMIES OF GOD**
Philistia **(2:4-6)**
Moab and Ammon **(2:8-11)**
Ethiopia **(2:12)**
Assyria **(2:13-15)**

**UPON THE CITY OF GOD**
Its gates **(1:10)**
Its citizens **(1:12, 13)**
Its leaders **(3:1-7)**

## Justice

**The Prophet Announces Justice (3:9-20)**

**UPON THE (FORMER) ENEMIES OF GOD**
During the millennium all nations will worship God **(3:9)**

**UPON THE LAND OF GOD**
Israel will dwell in peace **(3:13)**

**UPON THE CITY OF GOD**
Jerusalem to be filled with singing **(3:14, 15)**
God himself to lead the songs **(3:17)**

      2. It doubtless carries with it a morality purity. In other words this new language will have no filthy four-letter words.
   B. Upon the land of God (3:13):
      "The remnant of Israel shall not do iniquity, nor speak lies; neither shall a deceitful tongue be found in their mouth: for they shall feed and lie down, and none shall make them afraid."
   C. Upon the city of God (3:14-20):
      1. Jerusalem will once again be filled with singing, for the theme of their song, the King of Israel will be there (3:14, 15).
      2. God himself will lead this happy song (3:17).

## HABAKKUK (620-610 B.C.)

INTRODUCTION:
1. His name means, "embrace."
2. Habakkuk was the last of the minor prophets writing to the southern kingdom before the Babylonian captivity in 606 B.C., just as Micah was the final prophet to the northern kingdom prior to the Assyrian captivity in 721 B.C.
3. He was apparently one of the Levitical choristers in the Temple. His closing statement, "for the chief musicians on my stringed instrument" reveals that this is actually a song.
4. It is a book of deepest doubt. Habakkuk has been called the Doubting Thomas of the Old Testament. His doubts centered around two painful problems.
   a. How could God allow the sins of Israel to go unpunished? God then tells him Judah would indeed be punished by the Babylonians.

b. How then, he asks, could God justify allowing a godless nation to punish Judah, which nation at least believed in God and had some good men left?

5. Habakkuk sees one of the greatest manifestations of God's glory and power in all the Bible (3:1-16). It is reminiscent of that at Mount Sinai as viewed by Moses. (See Ex. 19.)

6. Habakkuk's great theological declaration, "the just shall live by faith" (2:4) is quoted no less than three times in the New Testament. (See Rom. 1:17; Gal. 3:11; Heb. 10:38.)

7. It has been noted that the book opens with gloom but ends with glory. The doubts of the prophet turn into shouts.

I. The Doubts (1-2).
   A. His question: "Will you punish our nation?" The prophet was grieved over the wickedness of Judah.
      1. Wherever he looked he saw oppression and bribery (1:3).
      2. The laws were not enforced and in the courts unrighteousness prevailed (1:4).
   B. God's answer: "I will, through Judah's foes." This would be done even during Habakkuk's lifetime (1:5).
      1. He was raising a new force on the world scene, the Chaldeans, a tribe of Semites living between Babylon and the Persian Gulf who began to assert themselves against the Assyrians around 630 B.C. (1:6).
      2. They would become notorious for their cruelty (1:7).
         a. Their horses were swifter than leopards (1:8).
         b. Their warriors were more fierce than wolves at dusk (1:8).
   C. His question: "Will you punish these Chaldeans also?" Habakkuk could not comprehend why God would let this pagan nation punish his own people, even though they were admittedly guilty of gross sin (1:12-17).
      "Thou art of purer eyes than to behold evil, and canst not look on iniquity: wherefore lookest thou upon them that deal treacherously, and holdest thy tongue when the wicked devoureth the man that is more righteous than he?"
      Habakkuk continues to probe for answers. He wants to know:
      1. Will God's people be caught and killed like fish? (1:14).
      2. Would they be strung upon hooks and dragged along in nets? (1:15).
      God then answers his question concerning whether he would punish the Chaldeans.
   D. God's answer:, "I will, through my woes!" Habakkuk climbs upon his watchtower to await God's answer. Soon it comes.
      1. God tells him the Chaldeans would indeed be punished, but only at his appointed time (2:3). This later took place, for some seventy-five years later Babylon fell to the Medes and Persians. (See Dan. 5.)
      2. Babylon was to be judged for their many sins.

# Habakkuk

## The Doubts   (HABAKKUK 1-2)
HIS QUESTIONS *Will you punish our nation?*
GOD'S ANSWERS *I will, through your foes!*
Habakkuk wonders if God will allow Judah's sins to go unpunished. *The Babylonian captivity was the answer.*
HIS QUESTIONS *Will you punish our foes?*
GOD'S ANSWERS *I will, through my woes!*
God informs Habakkuk that Babylon, Judah's foe, would herself be punished for her sins.

"The just shall live by faith"   **2:4**

## The Shouts   **(3)**
The soul of the prophet is revived **(3:2).**
The eyes of the prophet are reassured **(3:3-16).**
The heart of the prophet is rejoiced **(3:18).**
The feet of the prophet are renewed **(3:9).**

a. They had destroyed many nations without a shred of pity (2:8).
b. They had degenerated into a nation of drunkards (2:5).
c. They had worshiped various pagan idols (2:18, 19).
d. All this would surely take place, for "The Lord is in his holy temple; let all the earth keep silence before him" (2:20). In other words, the trial is to begin, the Judge is on his bench, therefore, let the court remain silent!

II. The Shouts (3).
   A. The soul of the prophet is revived. Habakkuk had even before this, concluded that, "the just shall live by faith" (2:4).
      But now he probes deeper into the grace and glory of God.
      "O Lord, I have heard thy speech, and was afraid; O Lord, revive thy work in the midst of the years, in the midst of the years make known; in wrath remember mercy" (3:2).
   B. The eyes of the prophet are reassured. In 3:3-16 Habakkuk sees an awesome manifestation of God's majestic glory.
      1. He sees him moving across the deserts from Mount Sinai.
      2. His brilliant splendor fills the earth and sky.
      3. From his hands flash rays of brilliant light.
      4. Habakkuk sees him stop for a moment, gazing upon the earth. He then shakes the nations, scattering the everlasting mountains.
      5. He sees him (in a historical vision) part the waters of the Red Sea. (See Ex. 14.)
      6. He sees him lead Israel across the hostile desert into Palestine.
   C. The heart of the prophet rejoices.
      "Yet I will rejoice in the Lord, I will joy in the God of my salvation" (3:18).
   D. The feet of the prophet are renewed.
      "The Lord is my strength, and he will make my feet like hinds' feet, and he will make me to walk upon mine high places" (3:19).

# JEREMIAH (Destination southern kingdom)

I. The Rulers Under Whom Jeremiah Ministered.
  A. Josiah. Jeremiah was called by God during the reign of Josiah, Judah's last good king.
  B. Jehoiakim. This wicked king burned Jeremiah's original written prophecy scroll.
  C. Jehoiachin. This ninety-day wonder is soundly condemned by Jeremiah.
  D. Zedekiah. The prophet suffered much under the reign of Zedekiah, Judah's final king.
  E. Nebuchadnezzar. Jeremiah is treated with respect by the great Babylonian conqueror.
  F. Gedaliah. He was appointed by Nebuchadnezzar to govern the fallen city of Jerusalem.
  G. Johanan. He took over after the tragic assassination of Gedaliah and later forced Jeremiah to accompany a Jewish remnant to Egypt.

II. The Threefold Ministry of Jeremiah.
  A. He warned the majority still in Judah about the coming Babylonian captivity.
  B. He comforted the minority already captive in Babylon (ch. 29). Jeremiah wrote a letter of encouragement to the Jewish exiles in Babylon (29:1-32).
    1. They were to settle down for a long seventy-year stay.
    2. They were to pray for the peace and prosperity of Babylon, that their own lives might be peaceful.
    3. They were to ignore the lies of these false prophets and mediums in Babylon, lest they be punished along with them.
    4. Jeremiah pronounced God's death sentence upon two of these prophets named Ahab and Zedekiah for their lying messages and their sin of adultery (29:20-23).
    5. He also warned the exiles concerning a man named Shemaiah, who was sending poison pen letters from Babylon to the influential leaders in Jerusalem against Jeremiah (29:23-32).
    6. God still loved them and would someday bring them back to Jerusalem (29:14).
  C. He pronounced judgment upon nine Gentile nations (46-51). These nations were:
      Egypt (46:1-27)
      Philistia (47:1-6)
      Moab (48:1-47)
      Ammon (49:1-6)
      Edom (49:7-22)
      Damascus (49:23-27)
      Kedar and Hazor (49:28-33)
      Elam (49:34-39)
      Babylon (50-51)
    After listing these nations, Jeremiah dealt with each one in a specific way:
    1. Egypt (46:1-27).
      a. Egypt would be defeated by Nebuchadnezzar at the Battle of Carchemish (46:2).
      b. Their armies would flee in terror and fill the Euphrates with corpses (46:5, 6).
      c. Their sin wound (like Judah's) was incurable (46:11).
      d. Pharaoh Hophra, the Egyptian leader, is ridiculed as a man of plenty of noise, but no power (46:17).
      e. Egypt would be occupied by Nebuchadnezzar (46:26).
    2. Philistia (47:1-6).
      a. It was to be overrun by the Egyptians. This occurred in 606 B.C., the year King Josiah died (47:1).
      b. Strong Philistine men would scream and fathers would flee, leaving behind their helpless children (47:2, 3).
      c. Philistia's allies, Tyre and Sidon, would be destroyed at the same time (47:4).
      d. The two chief Philistine cities of Gaza and Ashkelon would be totally destroyed (47:5).
    3. Moab (48:1-47).
      a. Nebuchadnezzar's armies would overrun Moab (48:1, 2).
      b. Their god Chemosh was to be carried away with priests and princes (48:7).
      c. Prior to this time, Moab had been relatively undisturbed, from various invasions (48:11).
      d. In the end, Moab will be as ashamed of her national idol god Chemosh as Israel was of her calf-god at Bethel (48:13).
      e. The ancestor of the Moabites (Moab) was born in a cave (Gen. 19:37). During the fearful Babylonian invasion, the Moabites will once again flee into caves (48:28).
    4. Ammon (49:1-6).
      a. This nation would be punished for occupying the cities of Israel after the captivity and worshiping the false god Milcom (49:1).
      b. Milcom, along with the Ammonite princes and priests, would be carried away (49:3).
      c. Ammon will be reestablished during the millennium (49:6).
    5. Edom (49:7-22).
      a. Edom's cities would become as silent as Sodom and Gomorrah (49:18).
      b. Their cry will be heard as far away as the Red Sea (49:21).
      c. God will, however, be merciful to her widows and orphans (49:11).
    6. Damascus (49:23-27).
      a. Her entire army would be destroyed in one single day (49:26).
      b. A fire would start at the edge of the city and eventually burn up the palaces of Benhadad (49:27).
    7. Kedar and Hazor (49:28-34).
      a. Kedar was the name of an Arab tribe living in the desert east of Palestine which was to be destroyed by Nebuchadnezzar (49:28).
      b. God himself ordered Nebuchadnezzar to destroy these wealthy, materialistic, and arrogant Bedouin tribes (49:31).
      c. Hazor, another Arabian tribe located nearby, was to be leveled also, never again to be rebuilt (49:33).

8. Elam (49:34-39).
   a. Elam was east of the Tigris-Euphrates country, with its capital at Susa and over-run by Nebuchadnezzar in the winter of 596 B.C. Zedekiah, Judah's last king, began ruling in Jerusalem at that time (49:34).
   b. Elam is to be reestablished during the millennium (49:39).
9. Babylon (50:1—51:64).
   a. Two Babylons seem to be referred to in these verses. One is the historical Babylon, captured by Darius the Persian in October of 539 B.C. (see Dan. 5) and the other is future Babylon, which will be destroyed by God himself. (See Rev. 18:18.)
   b. After the destruction of both Babylons, Israel would seek their God. This happened historically (Ezra 1) and it will occur in the future (Zech. 13:9-11).
   c. After the final destruction of Babylon (Rev. 18) the city will never be inhabited again (51:26).
   d. The ungodly nations would weep over the destruction of both Babylons (Rev. 18; Jer. 50:46).
   e. The Israelites were to flee from both Babylons (Rev. 18:4; Jer. 51:6).
   f. Both cities are depicted as golden cups filled with iniquities from which the nations have drunk and become mad (Rev. 17:1-6; Jer. 51:7).
   g. All heaven rejoices over the destruction of both (Jer. 51:10, 48; Rev. 18:20).
III. A Personal History of Jeremiah.
   A. He is called into full-time service during the reign of Josiah (1:1-10). He was to remain unmarried (16:2).
      1. Jeremiah was the son of Hilkiah, a priest living in Anathoth, some three miles northeast of Jerusalem in the land of Benjamin (1:1).
      2. He received his call to full-time service during the thirteenth year of godly King Josiah (1:6).
         a. Jeremiah at first protested this call (as Moses once did—see Ex. 3-4) pleading his youth as an excuse (1:6).
         b. He was quickly reassured by God, however, that:
            (1) The Lord had already chosen him prior to his birth as a divine spokesman to the nations (1:5).
            (2) God would therefore give his chosen messenger the message (1:7-10).
      3. Because of his fearless sermons on the coming judgment, Jeremiah was persecuted by his own family (12:6), the townspeople of Anathoth (11:21), and eventually the entire nation of Judah.
      4. As he began his ministry, God showed him two things which underlined the nature and importance of his call.
         a. He was shown an almond tree rod (1:11). Because it flowers earlier than the other trees, the almond signified the near fulfillment of God's proposed judgment.
         b. He saw a pot of boiling water, tipping southward from the north. This symbolized the Babylonian invasion (1:13).
      5. Jeremiah weeps over Judah's coming destruction (4:19-21). He would often do this (see 8:18, 21; 9:1, 2, 10; 13:17; 14:17).
      6. He is commanded (like the Greek Diogenes who once ran through the streets of Athens with a lantern trying to find an honest man) by God to "run to and fro through the streets of Jerusalem, and see now, and know, and seek in its broad places, if ye can find a man, if there be any that executeth justice, that seeketh the truth, and I will pardon her" (5:1). God had once made a similar arrangement with Abraham concerning Sodom (see Gen. 18:23-33).
      7. Jeremiah admits that this dreadful condition existed among the poor and ignorant, but that he felt he could find honest men within the ranks of Judah's educated and rich rulers. However, they too had utterly rejected God (5:4, 5).
      8. After a fruitful thirty-one-year reign, Josiah dies. A weeping prophet attends his funeral (2 Chron. 35:25). Judah's last good king had gone and it would be downhill spiritually from that point on.
   B. He pleads with Judah to return to God (3:12-14; 26:1-7).
      1. God would repeatedly invite Israel back to himself (2:9).
      2. He would receive Israel even after her immorality with other lovers (3:1). This was prohibited under the Mosaic Law (see Deut. 24:1-4).
      3. Jeremiah pleaded with them to plow up the hardness of their hearts, lest all be choked up by thorns (4:3, 4).
      4. They could still escape judgment by cleansing their hearts and purifying their thoughts (4:14).
      5. To repent meant they could remain in the land (7:3).
      6. To refuse meant to be covered by thick darkness (13:16).
   C. He fearlessly pronounces coming judgment at the hands of the Babylonians. He then lists Judah's sins.
      1. Judah had forsaken the fountain of divine water and built broken cisterns which could not hold water (2:13).
      2. The nation had become a race of evil men (2:21).
      3. No amount of soap or lye could make them clean (2:22).
      4. The rulers had stained their clothes with the blood of the innocent and poor (2:34).
      5. They were as an unashamed prostitute (3:3).
      6. They worshiped false gods upon every hill and under every shade tree (3:6).
      7. They had killed their prophets as a lion would slaughter his prey (2:30).
      8. They were as insolent as brass, and hard and cruel as iron (6:28).

9. They had set up idols right in the Temple and worshiped the pagan "queen of heaven" goddess (7:18; 44:17).
10. They had actually sacrificed their little children as burnt offerings to devil gods (7:31; 19:5).
D. He finally warns them concerning the terrible results of their disobedience.
   1. Great armies would march upon Jerusalem.
   2. Neither Assyria or Egypt could help Judah against Babylon (2:18, 36).
   3. People will flee from Judah's cities as one runs from a hungry lion (4:5-7).
   4. Jerusalem will be surrounded as by hunters who move in on a wild and wounded animal (4:17; 6:3-5).
   5. They will cry out as a woman in delivery (4:31; 6:24; 13:21).
   6. Jerusalem's own trees would be cut down and used against her walls as battering rams (6:6).
   7. The Temple would be destroyed (7:14).
   8. Enemy troops would then move among the people like poisonous snakes (8:17).
   9. Many would die by sword (15:3), disease (16:3, 4), and starvation (21:9).
   10. Some would be scattered as chaff by the fierce desert winds (13:24).
   11. Unburied corpses would litter the valleys outside Jerusalem, and become food for wild animals and birds (7:32, 33; 9:22; 12:8, 9).
   12. Judah's enemies would break open the sacred graves of her kings, priests, and prophets, and spread out their bones on the ground before the sun, moon, and stars (8:1, 2).
   13. Thousands would be carried away into Babylon for a period of seventy years (7:15; 25:11; 29:10).
   14. The severity of Judah's punishment would astonish the onlooking pagan Gentile nations (19:8; 22:8; 25:11).
E. When the people ridicule and reject his message, the warning prophet becomes the weeping prophet (4:19; 8:21; 9:1, 2, 10; 13:17; 14:17).
F. Because of his sermons and stand, Jeremiah suffers much.
   1. He is persecuted by his own family (12:6).
   2. He is plotted against by the people of his hometown (11:21).
   3. He is rejected and reviled by his peers in the religious world.
      a. Pashhur, the chief Temple priest, has him whipped and put in stocks (20:1-3).
      b. He is almost murdered by a wild mob of priests and prophets after one of his messages (26:7-9).
      c. He is ridiculed by a false prophet named Hananiah (28).
   4. He is threatened by King Jehoiakim (28:21-24; 36:26).
   5. He is arrested, flogged, and accused of treason (37:11-16). Zedekiah sends to Jeremiah asking for his prayers after Nebuchadnezzar had declared war on Judah (21:1, 2). Jeremiah sends word back to the wicked king stating

prayers were useless on this subject, for God would use the Babylonians to punish Jerusalem, and Zedekiah himself was to be given over to Nebuchadnezzar (21:3-7). Jeremiah tells Zedekiah that Jerusalem will be burned and he is to be captured and carried into Babylon (34:1-5).

Jeremiah rebukes those rich Jewish home owners who violated the Mosaic Law which demanded all Hebrew servants to be set free after serving six years (34:8-16).

Pharaoh Hophra's Egyptian armies had arrived to aid Judah in fighting Nebuchadnezzar. Jeremiah warns Zedekiah that their political alliance would fail, for Nebuchadnezzar would defeat the Egyptians (37:5-10).

Jeremiah attempts to visit the land of Benjamin at this time to inspect some property he had bought (37:11, 12). However, a guard named Irijah arrests him at the city gate and accuses him of defecting to the Babylonians (37:13). Jeremiah denies this, but is flogged and thrown into prison (37:14-16). He is soon secretly sent for by Zedekiah, and once again predicts the defeat of Jerusalem (37:17). Zedekiah places him in the palace prison instead of returning him to the dungeon he was formerly in (37:21).

In the palace, however, pressure from the religious officials who despised Jeremiah eventually force Zedekiah to return the prophet to a more crude confinement. This time he is lowered by ropes into an empty cistern in the prison yard where he soon sinks down into a thick layer of mire at the bottom (38:1-6). Eventually, an Ethiopian friend, Ebed-melech, persuades Zedekiah to remove him from this filthy place. It takes thirty men to haul him from the cistern. He is returned to the palace prison (38:7-13). Jeremiah again predicts the fall of Jerusalem (38:14-17). See also 32:1-5. He would remain in prison until the city was taken (38:28).

6. He sees his original manuscript burned by wicked King Jehoiakim (36:21-23). He is ordered to have his scribe Baruch write down all those oral messages he had been given for the past twenty-three years (36:1, 2). Baruch does this and reads them to the people in the Temple (36:8). He then is invited to read them to the religious officials. When he finishes, they are badly frightened and decide King Jehoiakim should also hear them (36:14-16).

An official named Jehudi thereupon reads them to Jehoiakim as the sullen king sits in front of his fireplace. As Jehudi finishes reading three or four columns, Jehoiakim will take his knife, slit off the section of the roll, and throw it into the fire. Finally, the entire scroll is destroyed (36:21-23). Jeremiah is then commanded to rewrite the burned sections plus a good deal of additional material, including these fearful words about Jehoiakim:

"Therefore thus saith the Lord of Jehoiakim king of Judah; he shall have none to sit upon the throne of David: and his dead body shall be cast out in the day to the heat, and in the night to the frost. And I will punish him and his seed and his servants for their iniquity; and I will bring upon them, and upon the inhabitants of Jerusalem, and upon the men of Judah, all the evil that I pronounced against them; but they hearkened not. Then took Jeremiah another roll, and gave it to Baruch the scribe, the son of Neriah; who wrote therein from the mouth of Jeremiah all the words of the book which Jehoiakim king of Judah had burned in the fire: and there were added besides unto them many like words."

After Jehoiakim burns the scroll, Baruch becomes despondent. It had probably taken him a year to write the material. God then both warns and encourages him through Jeremiah (45:1-5).

7. He is now commanded by God not to pray for Judah (7:16, 11:14; 14:11; 16:5).
8. He experiences frustration and depression (20:7-9, 14-18). Jeremiah had become so frustrated over his inability to call Judah back to God that he determines to quit the ministry!

> "Then I said, I will not make mention of him, nor speak any more in his name. But his word was in mine heart like a burning fire shut up in my bones, and I was weary with forebearing, and I could not refrain" (20:9). (See also 1 Ki. 19:3, 4; Jonah 1:1-3; 1 Cor. 9:16.)

At this time he utters one of the most despondent prayers in all the Bible (see also Job 3):

> "Cursed be the day wherein I was born: let not the day wherein my mother bare me be blessed. Cursed be the man who brought tidings to my father saying, A man child is born unto thee; making him very glad. And let that man be as the cities which the Lord overthrew, and repented not: and let him hear the cry in the morning, and the shouting at noontide. Because he slew me not from the womb; or that my mother might have been my grave, and her womb to be always great with me. Wherefore came I forth out of the womb to see labour and sorrow, that my days should be consumed with shame?" (20:14-18).

9. He writes a letter of encouragement to those Jewish exiles already in Babylon (29).
10. While in prison, he is ordered by God to buy a field from his cousin Hanamel. This was to illustrate that in spite of the advancing Babylonian armies, "Houses and fields and vineyards shall be possessed again in this land" (32:15). The background of all this is interesting: God tells Jeremiah that his cousin, Hanamel, was soon to visit him, attempting to sell the prophet a farm he owned in Anathoth. Jeremiah was to buy it for seventeen shekels of silver (32:6-13). Baruch was then to place the sealed deed in a pottery jar and bury it. All this was to demonstrate that someday people would once again own property in Judah, and buy and sell (32:14, 15).

Jeremiah is comforted during this time in prison by God's gracious promise:

> "Call unto me, and I will answer thee, and show thee great and mighty things, which thou knowest not" (33:3).

These tremendous and thrilling "things" are listed in chapters 30, 31, and 33. They include the following:

a. In spite of the impending Babylonian captivity, the time was coming when God would heal Jerusalem's hurt and give her prosperity and peace (33:4-6).
b. He still loved Israel with an everlasting love (31:3).
c. Israel would be gathered into Palestine from the earth's farthest ends (31:8). See also 30:3, 10, 11.

> "They shall come with weeping, and with supplications will I lead them; I will cause them to walk by the rivers of water in a straight way, in which they shall not stumble; for I am a father to Israel. . . . Therefore they shall come and sing in the height of Zion . . . to the goodness of the Lord . . . and their soul shall be like a watered garden, and they shall not sorrow any more at all" (31:9, 12).

Note: In 31:15, 16, Jeremiah predicts that the loud wails and bitter weeping of Rachel for her children in Ramah will disappear. Ramah is an ancient reference to the area in and around Bethlehem. It was here that Nebuchadnezzar killed many sick and feeble exile captives who would not be able to endure the long trip to Babylon. Rachel, who was the wife of Jacob, is of course symbolic of all weeping Israelite mothers. In Matthew 2:18 this sad verse is linked to that occasion when Herod murdered the babies of Bethlehem in an attempt to kill Christ.

d. During the millennium Israel will understand the necessity for and the purpose of all their sufferings (31:18, 19).
e. The cities of Israel will be rebuilt and Jerusalem is to become the praise and power center of all the earth (33:7-9; 31:38, 39; 30:18-21).

11. Jeremiah sees two baskets of figs in the Temple. One basket has fresh, well-ripened figs, but the other contains rotten ones (24:1-3). God explains that the fresh figs represent the Jewish exiles in Babylon (men such as Daniel and Ezekiel), while the rotten fruit depicts Zedekiah and his corrupt officials (24:4-8).

Jeremiah is ordered to make a yoke and fasten it upon his neck with leather thongs. He is then to send messages to the kings of Edom, Moab, Ammon, Tyre, and Sidon, through their ambassadors in Jerusalem,

# Jeremiah

## HIS PERSONAL LIFE

1. Was the son of a priest **(Jeremiah 1:1)**
2. Was commanded to remain unmarried **(16:2)**
3. Protested his call by God at first, pleading youth as an excuse **(1:6)**
4. Was assured that God had already chosen him prior to birth **(1:5)**
5. Attempted to find one honest man in Jerusalem **(5:1-5)**
6. Pleaded with Judah to return to God **(3:12-14; 26:1-7)**
7. Fearlessly denounced Judah's sin and was persecuted by:
    - His family **(12:6)**
    - Hometown people **(11:21)**
    - Religious world **(20:1-3; 26:7-9; 37:11-16)**
8. Listed Judah's many sins
    - Their worship of the queen of heaven **(7:18; 44:17)**
    - Their sacrifice of their own children to devil gods **(8:31; 9:15)**
    - Their murder of Judah's own prophets **(2:30)**
9. Warned them about coming Babylonian captivity
    - Jerusalem to be surrounded **(4:17; 6:3-5)**
    - Her own trees to be used against her **(6:6)**
    - Temple to be destroyed **(7:14)**
    - Corpses to feed animals **(7:32; 9:22; 12:8, 9)**
    - Captivity for seventy years **(7:15; 25:11; 29:10)**
10. Wept over this captivity **(4:19-21; 8:18, 21; 9:1, 2, 10; 13:17; 14:17)**
11. Had his original manuscript burned by King Jehoiakim **(36:21-23)**
12. Threatened to resign **(20:7-9, 14-18)**
13. Ordered to buy a field while in prison to prove a point **(32:6-15)**
14. Was freed by Nebuchadnezzar **(40:1-6; 39:14)**
15. Helped newly appointed governor Gedaliah **(40:6)**
16. Advised Johanan when Gedaliah was killed **(42:1-5)**
17. Was carried by force to Egypt by Johanan **(43:1-7)**
18. Continued to preach out against sin **(43-44)**
19. Probably died in Egypt

---

*"I ordained thee a prophet*

*unto the nations"*

**Jeremiah**

---

## RULERS HE MINISTERED UNDER

**JOSIAH** Judah's last godly king

**JEHOIAKIM** Ungodly, Bible-burning king

**JEHOIACHIN** A ninety-day wonder judged by God

**ZEDEKIAH** Judah's final king

**NEBUCHADNEZZAR** Great Babylonian conqueror

**Gedaliah** Babylonian appointed governor of occupied city of Jerusalem

**JOHANAN** Successor of Gedaliah who was assassinated.

## PEOPLE HE MINISTERED TO

1. To the majority in Judah about the coming captivity—a warning 2. To the minority already captive in Babylon—an encouragement (see chapter **29**)

## NATIONS HE PROPHESIED AGAINST

**EGYPT** 46:1-27
To be defeated by Nebuchadnezzar at battle of Carchemish

**PHILISTIA** 47:1-6
To be overrun and destroyed by the Egyptians

**MOAB** 48:1-47
To be conquered by Babylon

**AMMON** 49:1-6
To be destroyed for sinning against Israel
To be reestablished d ring the millennium

**EDOM** 49:7-22
To become as Sodom and Gomorrah

**DAMASCUS** 49:23-27
To be destroyed in a single day

**KEDAR AND HAZOR** 49:28-35
To be destroyed by Nebuchadnezzar

**ELAM** 49:34-39
To be overrun by Nebuchadnezzar
To be reestablished during the millennium

**BABYLON** 50:1—51:64
These prophecies concern two Babylons. (See next outline.)

warning them that God has given their nations over to Babylon. Those who submit and wear the yoke of punishment with true repentance will be spared, but those who refuse will be destroyed (23:1-11). After God had used Nebuchadnezzar to punish Judah and his neighbor nations, he would chastise Babylon itself (27:7). Judah is reassured that after the Babylonian captivity she will be gathered back to Jerusalem (27:22).

Jeremiah is accused of lying by a false prophet named Hananiah who had predicted the Babylonian captivity would last for only two years and that those already in exile (such as King Jehoiachin, Daniel, Ezekiel, etc.) would be returned along with all the Temple treasury which had been taken (28:1-4). To dramatize his accusation, Hananiah breaks the yoke worn by Jeremiah (28:10, 11).

Jeremiah predicts Hananiah's death by God's hand in the near future because of the prophet's lying ministry. Within two years he was dead (28:13-17).

12. Jeremiah visits the settlement where the Rechabite families live. These individuals belonged to a religious order founded by Jonadab, son of Rechab, during the reign of Jehu (841-814 B.C.). They assisted in the eradication of Baalism from Israel. Avoiding city life, they lived as shepherds, drinking no wine (35:2).

   a. Jeremiah is commanded to test the people by offering them wine. They immediately refuse, saying:

> "We will drink no wine; for Jonadab, the son of Rechab, our father, commanded us, saying, Ye shall drink no wine, neither ye, nor your sons forever" (35:6).

   b. Jeremiah then relates this sterling example to Judah, and contrasts the obedience of the Rechabites to the disobedience of Jerusalem (35:12-19).

13. He preaches a sermon at the Temple gate and is nearly killed by an angry mob for predicting the Temple will be destroyed (26:6-9). He is defended by some of Judah's wise old men, who remind the angry mob that Jeremiah's message is like that of the prophet Micah (Micah 3:12). See Jeremiah 26:17-19.

G. Jeremiah under Nebuchadnezzar.

1. Zedekiah attempts to escape the doomed city, but is captured near Jericho and brought back to Jerusalem. Here he is forced to witness the execution of his own sons, and then submit to the agony of his eyes being gouged out (39:4-7; 52:6-11).

2. Nebuchadnezzar instructs his chief-of-staff, Nebuzaradan, to treat Jeremiah with kindness (39:11, 12).

3. Jeremiah is released from prison and taken by Nebuzaradan to Ramah. Here he is offered his choice of going on to Babylon, or returning to Jerusalem. Jeremiah chooses to return and is placed under the protection of the new Jewish governor of Jerusalem, a man named Gedaliah (40:1-6; 39:14).

H. Jeremiah under Gedaliah.

1. Gedaliah attempts to institute a moderate post-war administration over the devastated city of Jerusalem (40:7-12).

2. This soon arouses the fury of a Jewish rebel leader named Ishmael, who plots to assassinate Gedaliah. The governor is warned of this plot by a man named Johanan, but refuses to take it seriously (40:13-16).

3. Gedaliah is murdered by Ishmael, along with many other Jewish officials, pilgrims, and some Babylonian soldiers. Some of their bodies are hurled down an empty cistern (41:1-9).

4. Johanan arrives upon the scene of the massacre and soon restores order (41:11-17).

I. Jeremiah under Johanan.

1. Johanan asks Jeremiah to determine God's will for the tiny Jewish remnant still in Jerusalem (42:1-5).

2. After a ten-day prayer session with God, Jeremiah is told the Lord desired the remnant to remain in Jerusalem and not go to Egypt, as some were already planning to do (46:6-22).

3. Upon hearing this unwelcome report, Johanan and other leaders accuse Jeremiah of lying. They then disobey the clearly revealed word of God by going to Egypt. Jeremiah is forced to accompany them (43:1-7).

4. Upon reaching Egypt, many of the Jews resort to their old habits of idolatry. They begin burning incense to the "queen of heaven" (this was another name for Ishtar, the pagan Mesopotamian goddess of love and war, 44:8-10, 15-19).

5. Jeremiah pronounces the divine death penalty upon all who refuse to repent and return to Jerusalem (44:7-14, 28).

6. To dramatize this bitter truth, he buries some large rocks between the pavement stones at the entrance of Pharaoh's palace. This signified that Nebuchadnezzar would occupy Egypt and set his throne upon those stones. Jeremiah predicted he would then kill many of the Jewish remnant who refused to return. The others would die of various plagues or be enslaved (43:9-13).

IV. The Prophecies of Jeremiah.

A. The fall of Jerusalem (1:14-16; 3; 4:5-9; 5:15-17; 6:1-6; 32:2, 3; 38:17, 18).

B. The destruction of the Temple (7:11-15; 26:6-9).

C. The death of the deposed Judean king, Jehoahaz, in Egypt (22:10-12).

D. The ignoble and unlamented death of King Jehoiakim (36:27-30). He soundly condemns Jehoiakim for his wicked reign (22:13-19). He was constructing an extravagant palace with forced labor. He had murdered the innocent and oppressed the poor. He was filled with selfish greed and dishonesty.

About this time one of Jeremiah's fellow prophets, Uriah, is murdered by Jehoiakim for his fearless preaching (26:20-23). Therefore, Jeremiah predicts that the king will die unlamented and be buried like a dead donkey, dragged out of Jerusalem, and thrown on the garbage dump beyond the gate.

E. The cutting off from the royal line of King Jehoiachin (22:24-30).

1. This young son of Jehoiakim ruled only three months, but so aroused the divine wrath of heaven that, Jeremiah is told, had he been the signet ring of God's right hand, he would still have been cast off and given to the Babylonians (22:24, 25).

2. Jeremiah predicted that this ninety-day wonder would:
   a. Be given over to Nebuchadnezzar.
   b. Be cast out of the land along with his mother.
   c. Die in a foreign land.
   d. Be regarded as a discarded and broken dish.
   e. Be considered childless (even though he had offspring) as far as the throne of David was concerned (22:25-29).

F. The death of two false prophets (Zedekiah and Ahab) and the punishment of another (Shemiah) who were ministering among the first Jewish captive exiles in Babylon (29:20-32).

G. The death of a false Jerusalem prophet named Hananiah (28:13-17).

H. The captivity of Seraiah.
Jeremiah warns a man named Seraiah that he will be taken captive by Nebuchadnezzar at a later date. (This literally happened some six years later, 51:59.) Seraiah is then given a scroll containing Jeremiah's prophecies against Babylon. When he arrives there the prophet commands him to publicly read it and then tie a rock to the scroll and throw it into the Euphrates River. This symbolized that Babylon would sink, never to rise again (51:60-64).

I. The failure of the Egyptian-Judean military alliance against Babylon (37:5-10).

J. The defeat of Egypt by Babylon (46:1-26).
Jeremiah describes in vivid detail the world-famous battle at Carchemish at the very moment when it is being fought. Egypt suffers a resounding defeat at the hands of Nebuchadnezzar (46:1-12).

K. The eventual occupation of Egypt by Babylon (43:9-13).

L. The seventy-year captivity of Judah into Babylon (25:11; 29:10).

M. The restoration after the seventy years to Jerusalem (27:19-22; 30:3, 10, 11, 18-21; 31:9, 12, 38, 39; 33:3-9).
Jeremiah promises ultimate restoration.

1. Israel will be gathered back from all over the world (3:14; 31:10; 32:37-43).

2. God will appoint leaders after his own heart (3:15).

3. Palestine will once again be filled with the glory of God, and the people of God (3:16-18). This will be a far greater event than the original Exodus, when God brought them out of Egypt (16:14, 15; 23:7).

4. A righteous Branch (the Savior) will occupy King David's throne, ruling with wisdom and justice (23:5, 6; 30:21; 33:17).

5. Jerusalem will be rebuilt and filled with joy and great thanksgiving (38:18-20; 31:4, 7-9, 12-14, 23-25; 33:10-12).

N. The defeat of Babylon after the seventy years (25:12; 27:6).
Note: The punishment Babylon would receive from God as found in Jeremiah 50-52 evidently refers not only to the historical judgment (see Dan. 5), but also that future judgment (see Rev. 18).

## THE TWO BABYLONS OF JEREMIAH 50-51

### Historical Babylon
Was captured by Darius the Persian in 539 B.C.

### Future Babylon
Will be destroyed by God the Father during the tribulation **(See Rev. 18:18.)**

- After the final destruction of Babylon (Rev. 18) the city will never be inhabited again **(51:26).**
- The ungodly nations would weep over the destruction of both Babylons **(Rev. 18; Jer. 50:46).**
- The Israelites were to flee from both Babylons **(Rev. 18:4; Jer. 51:6).**
- Both cities are depicted as golden cups filled with iniquities from which the nations have drunk and become mad **(Rev.17:1-6; Jer. 51:7).**
- All heaven rejoices over the destruction of both **(Jer. 51:10, 48; Rev. 18:20).**
- After the destruction of both Babylons, Israel would seek their God. This happened historically (Ezra 1) and it will occur in the future **(Zech. 13:9).**

## THE EIGHTEEN PROPHECIES OF JEREMIAH

1. Fall of Jerusalem **(1:14-16; 4:5-9; 5:15-17; 6:1-6; 32:2, 3; 38:17, 18)**
2. Destruction of the Temple **(7:11-15; 26:6-9)**
3. Death of deposed King Jehoahaz in Egypt **(22:10-12)**
4. Unlamented death of King Jehoiakim **(36:27-30)**
5. Cutting off of the royal line of King Jehoiachin **(22:24-30)**
6. Death of two false prophets and punishment of another—all three living in Babylon **(29:20-32)**
7. Death of a false Jerusalem prophet **(28:13-17)**
8. Capture and exile of a friend named Seraiah **(51:59)**
9. Failure of the Egyptian-Judean military alliance against Babylon **(37:5-10)**
10. Defeat of Egypt by Babylon at Carchemish **(46:1-12)**
11. Babylonian occupation of Egypt **(43:9-13)**
12. Seventy-year captivity of Judah in Babylon **(25:11; 29:10)**
13. Restoration to Jerusalem after the seventy years **(27:19-22; 30:3, 10, 11, 18-21; 31:9, 12, 38, 39; 33:3-9)**
14. Defeat of Babylon after the seventy years **(25:12; 27:7)**
15. Capture of Zedekiah **(21:3-7; 34:1-5; 37:17)**
16. Kindly treatment of the godly exiles in Babylon **(24:1-7)**
17. Final regathering of people of Israel **(30:3, 10; 31:8-12)**
18. Final rebuilding of the land of Israel **(30:18-21; 31:38, 39; 33:7-9)**

O. The capture of Zedekiah (21:3-7; 34:1-5; 37:17). (See 39:4-7; 52:6-11 for fulfillment.)

P. The kindly treatment of the godly exiles in Babylon (24:1-7).

V. The New Covenant of Jeremiah.

A. The nature of the new covenant (31:31-34).

1. It would embrace the entire house of Israel.

2. It would be totally unlike the old Mosaic Covenant.

3. God would inscribe his laws upon their hearts. Israel had always suffered with self-inflicted spiritual heart trouble. Note the divine diagnosis:

> "The sin of Judah is written with a pen of iron and with the point of a diamond; it is engraved upon the tablet of their hearts . . ." (Jer. 17:1).

But under the new covenant the heavenly Physician would offer them perfect and guaranteed successful heart transplants.

4. This nation with the new hearts would then once again become God's people, and he their God.

B. The time of the new covenant. It will go into effect "after those days" (31:33), and following the "time of Jacob's trouble" (30:7). Both these terms refer to the coming great tribulation. Thus, the new covenant will begin to function after the time of Jacob's trouble, at the start of the glorious millennium.

C. The superiority of the new covenant. It will be immutable, unconditional, and eternal, as opposed to the Mosaic Covenant (Ex. 19:5-8). M. F. Unger writes:

> "The Old Covenant was the law covenant grounded in legal observance. The New Covenant (Heb. 8:8-12) will be entirely on the basis of grace and the sacrificial blood of Christ, which will be the foundation of Israel's future inward regeneration and restoration to God's favor. Israel's entering into the blessings of the New Covenant (Rom. 11:1-26) will insure her being an everlasting nation." (*Unger's Bible Dictionary*, p. 352)

God himself assures Israel of the duration of this new covenant when he declares: "If the heaven above can be measured, and the foundations of the earth searched out beneath, I will also cast off all the seed of Israel . . ." (31:37). (See also 33:20-26.)

D. The Mediator of the new covenant: the Son of David himself (33:15-18; 30:9).

VI. Classic Passages in Jeremiah.

A. "They have healed also the hurt of the daughter of my people slightly, saying, Peace, peace; when there is no peace" (6:14).

B. "Is this house, which is called by my name, become a den of robbers in your eyes? Behold, even I have seen it, saith the Lord" (7:11).

C. "The harvest is past, the summer is ended, and we are not saved. Is there no balm in Gilead; is there no physician there? why then is not the health of the daughter of my people recovered?" (8:20, 22).

D. "Who would not fear thee, O King of nations? for to thee doth it appertain: forasmuch as among all the wise men of the nations, and in all their kingdoms, there is none like unto thee. He hath made the earth by his power, he hath established the world by his wisdom, and hath stretched out the heavens by his discretion" (10:7, 12).

E. "But I was like a lamb or an ox that is brought to the slaughter; and I knew not that they had devised devices against me, saying, Let us destroy the tree with the fruit thereof, and let us cut him off from the land of the living, that his name may be no more remembered" (11:19).

F. "Can the Ethiopian change his skin, or the leopard his spots? then may ye also do good, that are accustomed to do evil" (13:23).

G. "Then said the Lord unto me, Though Moses and Samuel stood before me, yet my mind could not be toward this people: cast them out of my sight, and let them go forth. Thy words were found, and I did eat them; and thy word was unto me the joy and rejoicing of mine heart: for I am called by thy name, O Lord God of hosts" (15:1, 16).

H. "Therefore, behold, the days come, saith the Lord, that it shall no more be said, The Lord liveth, that brought up the children of Israel out of the land of Egypt; but, the Lord liveth, that brought up the children of Israel from the land of the north, and from all the lands whither he had driven them; and I will bring them again into their land that I gave unto their fathers" (16:14, 15).

I. "Thus saith the Lord; Cursed be the man that trusteth in man, and maketh flesh his arm, and whose heart departeth from the Lord. For he shall be like the heath in the desert, and shall not see when good cometh; but shall inhabit the parched places in the wilderness, in a salt land and not inhabited. Blessed is the man that trusteth in the Lord, and whose hope the Lord is. For he shall be as a tree planted by the waters, and that spreadeth out her roots by the river, and shall not see when heat cometh, but her leaf shall be green; and shall not be careful in the year of drought, neither shall cease from yielding fruit. The heart is deceitful above all things, and desperately wicked: who can know it? I the Lord search the heart, I try the reins, even to give every man according to his ways, and according to the fruit of his doings" (17:5-10).

J. "The word which came to Jeremiah from the Lord saying, Arise and go down to the potter's house, and there I will cause thee to hear my words. Then I went down to the potter's house, and, behold, he wrought a work on the wheels. And the vessel that he made of clay was marred in the hand of the potter; so he made it again another vessel, as seemed good to the potter to make it. Then the Lord came to me saying, O house of Israel, cannot I do with you as this potter? saith the Lord. Behold, as the clay is in the potter's hand, so are ye in mine hand, O house of Israel" (18:1-6).

K. "O Lord, thou hast deceived me, and I was deceived: thou art stronger than I, and hast prevailed: I am in derision daily, everyone mocketh me. For since I spake, I cried out, I cried violence and spoil; because the word of the Lord was made a reproach unto me, and a derision, daily. Then I said, I will not make mention of him, nor speak any more in his name. But his word was in mine heart as a burning fire shut up in my bones, and I was weary with forebearing, and I could not stay" (20:7-9).

"Sing unto the Lord, praise ye the Lord: for he hath delivered the soul of the poor from the hand of evildoers. Cursed be the day wherein I was born: let not the day wherein my mother bare me be blessed. Cursed be the man who brought tidings to my father, saying, A man child is born unto thee; making him very glad" (20:13-15).

L. "And unto this people thou shalt say, Thus saith the Lord; Behold, I set before you the way of life, and the way of death" (21:8).

M. "Is not my word like as a fire? saith the Lord; and like a hammer that breaketh the rock in pieces?" (23:29).

N. "For I know the thoughts that I think toward you, saith the Lord, thoughts of peace, and not of evil, to give you an expected end. Then shall ye call upon me, and ye shall go and pray unto me, and I will hearken unto you. And ye shall seek me, and find me, when ye shall search for me with all your heart. And I will be found of you, saith the Lord: and I will turn away your captivity, and I will gather you from all the nations and from all the places whither I have driven you, saith the Lord; and I will bring you again into the place whence I caused you to be carried away captive" (29:11-14).

O. "Alas! for that day is great, so that none is like it; it is even the time of Jacob's trouble; but he shall be saved out of it" (30:7).

P. "The Lord hath appeared of old unto me, saying, Yea, I have loved thee with an everlasting love: therefore with loving kindness have I drawn thee. Behold, I will bring them from the north country, and gather them from the coasts of the earth, and with them the blind and the lame, the woman with child and her that travaileth with child together; a great company shall return thither. They shall come with weeping, and with supplications will I lead them: I will cause them to walk by the rivers of waters in a straight way, wherein they shall not stumble: for I am a father to Israel, and Ephraim is my firstborn. Thus saith the Lord: A voice was heard in Ramah, lamentation, and bitter weeping; Rachel weeping for her children refused to be comforted for her children, because they were not. How long wilt thou go about, O thou backsliding daughter? for the Lord hath created a new thing in the earth, a woman shall compass a man" (31:3, 8, 9, 15, 22).

Q. "Ah Lord God! behold, thou hast made the heaven and the earth by thy great power and stretched out arm, and there is nothing too hard for thee: Behold, I am the Lord, the God of all flesh: is there anything too hard for me?" (32:17, 27).

R. "Call unto me, and I will answer thee, and shew thee great and mighty things, which thou know-

est not. As the host of heaven cannot be numbered, neither the sand of the sea measured: so will I multiply the seed of David my servant, and the Levites that minister unto me" (33:3, 22).

S. "But fear not thou, O my servant Jacob, and be not dismayed, O Israel: for, behold, I will save thee from afar off, and thy seed from the land of their captivity; and Jacob shall return, and be in rest and at ease, and none shall make him afraid" (45:27).

T. "O thou sword of the Lord, how long will it be ere thou be quiet? put up thyself into thy scabbard, rest, and be still" (47:6).

## LAMENTATIONS (586 B.C.)
INTRODUCTION:

1. This book is composed of five elegies, all of them lamenting the tragic destruction of Jerusalem by the Babylonians.

2. The literary form is alphabetical, somewhat like Psalm 119.
   a. A different Hebrew letter of the alphabet begins each of the twenty-two verses of chapters 1, 2.
   b. In chapter 3 there are sixty-six verses, arranged in twenty-two groups of three verses, each of which in succession begins with a different letter.

3. Tradition says Jeremiah sat weeping outside Jerusalem's north wall under the knoll called Golgotha, where our Lord was later to die.

4. J. Vernon McGee writes:
   "The book is filled with tears and sorrow. It is a paean of pain, a poem of pity, a proverb of pathos, a hymn of heartbreak, a psalm of sadness, a symphony of sorrow. . . . It is the wailing wall of the Bible." (*Briefing the Bible*, p. 232)

I. The Provocation Against God (Lam. 1). Around 1000 B.C. David had established his capital in Jerusalem. (See 2 Sam. 6.) Thus, God had blessed this beloved city for nearly 400 years. He had allowed the northern kingdom to be carried away by the Assyrians in 721 B.C. But Jerusalem had been spared for another 115 years. All this mercy and longsuffering, however, had been in vain, for Judah continued provoking the Holy One of Israel through constant sinning. The end had now come.

Note the following verses of indictment.

A. 1:1:
   "How doth the city sit solitary, that was full of people! how is she become as a widow! She that was great among the nations, and princess among the provinces, how is she become tributary!"

B. 1:3:
   "Judah is gone into captivity because of affliction, and because of great servitude: she dwelleth among the heathen, she findeth no rest: all her persecutors overtook her between the straits."

C. 1:8:
   "Jerusalem hath grievously sinned; therefore she is removed: all that honoured her despise her, because they have seen her nakedness: yea, she sigheth, and turneth backward."

D. 1:9:
   "Her filthiness is in her skirts; she remembereth not her last end; therefore she came down

wonderfully: she had no comforter. O Lord, behold my affliction: for the enemy hath magnified himself."

E. 1:17:

"Zion spreadeth forth her hands, and there is none to comfort her: the Lord hath commanded concerning Jacob, that his adversaries should be round about him: Jerusalem is as a menstrous woman among them."

II. The Punishment from God (Lam. 2).

A. He had destroyed every home in Judah (2:2).

B. Every fortress and wall was broken (2:2).

C. He bent his bow of judgment across the land (2:4).

D. He allowed his own Temple to fall as though it were a booth of leaves and branches in a garden (2:6).

E. Judah's enemies were given full freedom to ridicule and destroy her citizens (2:16).

F. Her people, old and young alike, choked the streets of Jerusalem with their lifeless bodies (2:21).

III. The Prophet of God (Lam. 3). The tears of Jeremiah fell like a spring rain over the destruction of Jerusalem and its suffering people.

A. The affliction of the prophet. All through Lamentations, Jeremiah shares the agony of his soul with us, as the following verses bring out.

1. 1:12:

"Is it nothing to you, all ye that pass by? behold, and see if there be any sorrow like unto my sorrow, which is done unto me, wherewith the Lord hath afflicted me in the day of his fierce anger."

2. 1:16:

"For these things I weep; mine eye, mine eye runneth down with water, because the comforter that should relieve my soul is far from me: my children are desolate, because the enemy prevailed."

3. 2:11:

"Mine eyes do fail with tears, my bowels are troubled, my liver is poured upon the earth, for the destruction of the daughter of my people; because the children and the sucklings swoon in the streets of the city."

4. 3:1–19:

Jeremiah then relates the sufferings he endured at the hands of his own countrymen even prior to the Babylonian invasion. (See 3:52–66.)

B. The assurance of the prophet. In the midst of the terrible storm there shines a ray of reassurance.

"This I recall to my mind, therefore have I hope. It is of the Lord's mercies that we are not consumed, because his compassions fail not. They are new every morning: great is thy faithfulness. The Lord is my portion, saith my soul; therefore will I hope in him. The Lord is good unto them that wait for him, to the soul that seeketh him. It is good that a man should hope and quietly wait for the salvation of the Lord. It is good for a man that he bear the yoke in his youth; for the Lord will not cast off for ever: But though he cause grief, yet will he have compassion according to the multitude of his mercies. For he doth not afflict willingly nor grieve the children of men" (3:21, 22, 23, 24, 25, 26, 27, 31, 32, 33).

C. The advice of the prophet (3:40, 41).

"Let us search and try our ways, and turn again to the Lord. Let us lift up our heart with our hands unto God in the heavens."

IV. The People of God (Lam. 4).

A. The children's tongues stuck to the roof of their mouths for thirst (4:4).

B. The cream of Judah's youth were treated as earthenware pots (4:2). See also 5:13.

C. The rich and pampered were in the streets begging for bread (4:5).

D. Their mighty princes, once lean and tan, were now but skin and bones, and their faces black as soot (4:7, 8). See also 5:12.

E. Tender-hearted women had cooked and eaten their own children (4:10).

F. The false prophets and priests were blindly staggering through the streets, covered with blood (4:14).

G. The king, himself (Zedekiah), had been captured, blinded, and carried off into captivity (4:20).

V. The Prayer to God (Lam. 5). Jeremiah's prayer contained four elements:

A. That of remembrance

"Remember, O Lord, what is come upon us; consider, and behold our reproach" (5:1).

B. That of repentance

"The crown is fallen from our head; woe unto us, that we have sinned" (5:16).

C. That of recognition

"Thou, O Lord, remainest forever, thy throne from generation to generation" (5:19).

D. That of renewal

"Turn thou us unto thee, O Lord, and we shall be turned; renew our days as of old" (5:21).

# THE CAPTIVITY STAGE

## INTRODUCING
## THE CAPTIVITY STAGE

1. Psalm 137 describes the beginning of this period, while Psalm 126 describes the end.
2. Israel is cured of the *sin* of idolatry while in the *city* of idolatry.
3. Two eyewitnesses write of this era. One was a prime minister, the other a priest.
4. This historical period includes:
   a. Three men who wouldn't bend or burn (Dan. 3).
   b. A *review* of Babylon's greatest king (Nebuchadnezzar, Dan. 1–4) and a *preview* of Greece's greatest king (Alexander the Great, Dan. 7:6; 8:5–8, 21, 22; 11:3, 4).
   c. A fight between a Persian ram and a Greek goat (Dan. 8).
   d. An aimless hand (of God) that wrote and a lifeless band (of men) that walked (Dan. 5; Ezek. 37).
   e. The only description of God the Father in the Bible (Dan. 7:9–14).
   f. Great prophecies revealed through the falling of a stone (Dan. 2) and the felling of a tree (Dan. 4).
   g. The second of three attempts to consolidate religion around an image (1) Genesis 11 (2) Daniel 3 (3) Revelation 13.
   h. The real story of when the Bear comes over the mountain (Ezek. 38–39).
   i. The future and final earthly temple (Ezek. 40–48).
5. God blesses a basic diet and curses a blasphemous feast (Dan. 1, 5).
6. Both archangels, Gabriel and Michael, are referred to during this period (Dan. 8, 12).
7. This era has more to say about the ministry of the heavenly cherubim than any other period (Ezek. 1, 10).
8. This era has more to say about the ministry of the hellish antichrist than any other period (Dan. 7, 8, 9, 11).
9. Ezekiel denounces the materialistic city of Tyre (ch. 26) and describes the millennial city of God (ch. 48).
10. Ezekiel begins by describing the removal of God's glory cloud (Ezek. 10:18), and concludes by predicting the return of this glory cloud (Ezek. 43:2).

## THE CAPTIVITY STAGE
### Ezekiel (around 597 B.C.)

INTRODUCTION:
1. Ezekiel was the son of a Zadokite priest. He was deported to Babylon in 597 B.C. with King Jehoiachin. His wife died the day the siege began in 588 B.C. (Ezek. 24:1, 15–18).

2. He was thirty when he began writing and resided at a town on the Chebar, a canal which flowed from the Euphrates River.
3. His ministry was twofold, to *remind* the exiles of their sins and to *encourage* them concerning God's future blessings.
4. Ezekiel may be compared with other Old Testament books as follows:
   a. Isaiah speaks of God's salvation.
   b. Jeremiah speaks of God's judgment.
   c. Daniel speaks of God's kingdom.
   d. Ezekiel speaks of God's glory.

I. The Sanctification of the Man of God—Ezekiel (1, 2, 33).
   A. Ezekiel sees the vision of the living creatures (1:1–28).
      1. The description of these creatures. (See 1:4–28.)
      2. The identity of these living creatures. Who are they? These magnificent beings are identified later by Ezekiel (10:20) as the cherubim, angels of high ranking order. They make their appearance on three distinct occasions in the Word of God.
         a. In the Garden of Eden, to keep Adam from the Tree of Life after his sin (Gen. 3:22–24).
         b. To Ezekiel here in Babylon (1:4–28).
         c. In heaven, during John's vision (Rev. 4:6–8).
      3. The duties of these living creatures.
         a. To guard and vindicate the righteousness of God (Gen. 3:24; Ex. 26:1; 36:8, 35).
         b. To symbolize the mercy of God (Ex. 25:22; 37:9).
         c. To aid in the administration of the government of God (1 Sam. 4:4; Ps. 80:1; 99:1; Ezek. 1:22, 26).
         d. To be eternal reminders of the blessed earthly ministry of the Lord Jesus Christ. This is seen by the following summary of the four gospel accounts:
            (1) Matthew (writing to the Jews), pictures Christ as a Lion, the Messiah.
            (2) Mark (writing to the Romans), pictures Christ as an Ox, the Servant.
            (3) Luke (writing to the Greeks), pictures Christ as the perfect Man.
            (4) John (writing to the whole world), pictures Christ as the Eagle, the mighty God.

(For a description of another kind of special angelic beings, called the seraphim, see Isaiah 6:1–7.)

B. Ezekiel hears the voice of the living God (2:1—8:27; 33:1–22).

1. He was commissioned as Israel's watchman in Babylon.

2. He was to warn the wicked that if they abandoned their wicked ways, God would not physically destroy them.

3. He was to warn the righteous that if they abandoned their righteous ways, God would physically destroy them.

4. He was to do all this without fear or favor.

5. He was to totally absorb the message of God (3:1, 2). (See also Rev. 10:8–11.)

II. The Desolation of the City of God—Jerusalem (4–24). There were three distinct phases in the Babylonian captivity and the siege of Jerusalem.

In 605 B.C. At this time Daniel and other individuals of noble birth were carried away (Dan. 1:3, 4; 2 Chron. 36:6, 7).

In 597 B.C. During this phase both King Johoiachin and Ezekiel, along with many others, were taken into Babylon (2 Ki. 24:10–16).

In 586 B.C. At this final time Judah's last king, Zedekiah, was carried away, the walls of Jerusalem were destroyed, and both Temple and city were burned (2 Ki. 25:1–7).

The events recorded here in Ezekiel 4–24 took place between the second and third phase. Apparently there were false prophets, both in Jerusalem and in Babylon, who brazenly assured the Jews that God would not dare destroy his own city, even though it had already suffered two bitter sieges. But Ezekiel knew otherwise and he attempted through symbolism, parables, visions, and messages to warn all that the Holy City would indeed suffer desolation and destruction.

A. Ezekiel's twelve symbolic acts.

1. He drew a map of Jerusalem on a large flat tablet of soft clay, showing siege mounds being built against the city. He then added more details, portraying the enemy camps around it, and the placement of the battering rams. He finally placed an iron plate between the map and himself. This was to indicate the impenetrable wall of the Babylonian army, and also to show the impossibility of escape (4:1–3).

2. He lay on his left side a few hours each day for 390 days, to symbolize the iniquity of the northern kingdom. Each day was to represent a year (4:4, 5).

3. He then lay on his right side a few hours each day for forty days, to depict the iniquity of Judah, the southern kingdom. Again, each day was to represent a year (4:6). It must be admitted that the full meaning of these time periods cannot be known. Unger writes:

"His discomfort for 390 days on his left side and 40 days on his right side (total 430 years, symbolically a year for a day), recalled the Egyptian servitude (Ex. 12:40, 41). A similar captivity would engulf both Israel and Judah. The captivity of the Northern Kingdom was to be longer, however." (Unger's Bible Handbook, p. 367)

4. He prepared bread made with mixed grains and baked it over dried cow dung which had been set afire. This was to indicate the scarcity of food in Jerusalem (4:9–17).

5. He shaved his head and beard with a sharp sword, and then divided the hair into three equal parts (5:1–4).

a. One third he burned.

b. One third he cut up with the sword.

c. One third he scattered to the wind.

All this was to indicate what was in store for Judah and Jerusalem. One third of her citizens would die by fire in the Jerusalem siege. One third of her citizens would fall by the sword, and the remaining third would be scattered to the wind.

6. He was to stamp his feet and clap his hands to get their attention (6:11).

7. He set some scant baggage outside his home. Then, in the evening he dug an entrance through the city wall. As he went through it carrying the baggage, he also covered his face. This was to vividly symbolize the following (12:1–16):

a. The few articles of baggage represented the exiles hurriedly departing their homes.

b. The entrance in the wall symbolized their desperation to leave the doomed city of Jerusalem.

c. The covered face depicted Zedekiah, Judah's last king, who was blinded by Nebuchadnezzar because of his rebellion, and led captive into Babylon (2 Ki. 25:1–7).

8. He was to tremble as he ate his food and to ration out his water as though it were his last (12:17–20).

9. He was to slash about in the air a gleaming sword, and with sobbings, beat upon his thigh (21:9–17).

10. He drew a map of the Middle East and traced two routes for the King of Babylon to follow. One led to Jerusalem, and the other to Rabbath-Ammon. Both cities had rebelled against Nebuchadnezzar in 593 B.C. Ezekiel pictured the king here at the crossroads. Which city would be destroyed first? The sad answer is immediately forthcoming (21:18–22):

"He will call his magicians to use divination; they will cast lots by shaking arrows from the quiver; they will sacrifice to idols and inspect the liver of their sacrifices. They will decide to turn toward Jerusalem!" (21:21, 22, TLB).

11. He filled a pot of boiling water with the choicest meats and cooked it until the flesh fell off the bones. He then threw it all out and allowed the pot to bake itself dry to eliminate the scum and rust (24:1–14). Here, of course, the symbolism is clear. The judgment fire of God would utterly consume even the rich and noble of Jerusalem. All of

its citizens would be cast out of the land, that his holy city might be cleansed of their moral scum and rust.

12. He was forbidden to express any outward sorrow over the sudden death of his beloved wife (24:15-18). Charles Feinberg has written:

"The covered head (2 Sam. 15:30); the bare feet (Isa. 20:2); and the covered lip (Lev. 13:45; Micah 3:7) were prohibited Ezekiel. Priests could mourn for their near kin (Lev. 21:1-3), but Ezekiel was an exception for a special purpose. It was customary in ancient times to have a funeral feast; the friends of the bereaved sent the food as a token of sympathy (Deut. 26:14; Jer. 16:7; Hosea 9:4). Faced with this directive, Ezekiel exhibits complete subordination of his own will and feelings to his prophetic office in the will of God. In spite of the fact that he knew his wife's hours were numbered, he went about the ministry committed to Him. What an example of obedience!" (*The Prophecy of Ezekiel*, pp. 139, 140)

One of the most emotion-filled verses in all the Bible is his testimony at this time:

"So I spoke unto the people in the morning and at evening my wife died; and I did in the morning as I was commanded" (24:18).

God ordered him not to mourn over the death of his wife to emphasize that he, the Lord, would not mourn over Jerusalem's death. It is especially significant to observe that she died the very day that Nebuchadnezzar began his third and final assault upon Jerusalem (24:2).

B. Ezekiel's twelve judgment messages.

A brief summary of Ezekiel's main points in these sermons would include:

1. God had often held back his divine wrath in spite of Israel's brazen disobedience (20:7-10, 14, 21, 22).
2. God took no joy in judging his people even at this desperate stage and again called for Judah's repentance (18:31, 32).
3. But Judah would not listen and her hour of doom was now at hand (7:6, 12).
4. Judah would then be destroyed, *not* because of the sins of their fathers, but because of their own vile wickedness (18:1-4, 20).
5. Even the presence of such godly men as Noah, Daniel, and Job could not spare the City of Jerusalem (14:14, 20).
6. Her armies would be absolutely helpless in defending her (7:14).
7. Her wealth could not purchase one additional minute of freedom (7:19).
8. The Holy City of God had now become the harlot city of Satan.
9. God would therefore bring into Jerusalem the worst of nations and people to occupy their lands and homes (7:24).
10. Judah's cities would be burned and her idols smashed (6:4, 6).

11. Four great punishments would fall upon her citizens, that of war, famine, ferocious beasts, and plagues (14:21).

C. Ezekiel's six parables.

1. A fruitless vine tree (15:1-8).
   a. The vine is a common symbol for the nation of Israel in the Bible. (See Deut. 32:32; Ps. 80:8-12; Isa. 5:1-7; Jer. 2:21; Hosea 10:1; Mt. 21:33.)
   b. The only value and purpose of a vine is to bear fruit. It is not good for house building (the wood is too crooked), or furniture making (the wood is too soft), or for fuel (the wood burns too rapidly).
   c. Because the vine had refused to perform its only prescribed duty, it would be burned. (See Jn. 15:6.)
2. The adopted girl who became a harlot (16:1-63).

Dr. Charles Feinberg writes the following to introduce this parable:

"Here, in the longest chapter in Ezekiel, the story is told in detail in all its sordid, loathsome character, so that God's infinite abhorrence of Israel's sin may be clearly seen. According to Rabbi Eleizer ben Hyrcanus in the mishna, the chapter was not to be read nor translated in public." (*The Prophecy of Ezekiel*, p. 85)

   a. God had found in a field an abandoned, despised, and dying baby girl. Her name was Israel (16:1-5). This is a reference to Israel's bondage to the Egyptians in the first few chapters of Exodus. (See especially Ex. 1:13, 14; 2:23; 3:7.)
   b. God graciously adopted this ragged little girl. When she became of age, he entered into the sacred rite of marriage with her, and she legally became his elected wife (16:8). This, of course, all took place at Mt. Sinai when God ratified his covenant with Israel. (See Ex. 19:5. Also, compare Ezek. 16:9 with Ex. 19:14.)
   c. After the marriage God dressed her in the most beautiful clothes, adorned her with the most costly jewels, and provided the finest food available for his beloved (16:10-14). This occurred in Israel's history during the reign of David and Solomon. (See 2 Sam. 8:11; 1 Ki. 3:13; 10:4-7.)
   d. But this little ex-orphan soon spurned all his love and faithfulness and became a common harlot of the streets (16:15-34).
   e. This intolerable action could not continue unpunished, for the beloved Husband was also the righteous Judge. He would, therefore, turn her over to her own murderous lovers to be abused and punished (16:36-41).
   f. Her wickedness by this time had surpassed even that of her older sister (Samaria, the capital of the northern kingdom) and that of her younger sister (Sodom). (See Ezek. 16:46-50.)
   g. After he had chastened her, God would once again restore her to himself (along

with her two sinning sisters) because of his love for her and his promise to Abraham (16:53, 60, 63).

3. The two eagles (17:1-21). The events mentioned in this parable narrate the international affairs of Judah, Babylon, and Egypt between 597 and 588 B.C. The figures involved are Jehoiachin, Zedekiah, and Nebuchadnezzar. For the recorded history of this period, see 2 Kings 24:8-20; 2 Chronicles 36:9-13; Jeremiah 37; 52:1-7.

4. The tender twig (17:22-24).
   a. God himself stated he would someday plant the finest and most tender twig of all upon Israel's highest mountain (17:22).
   b. This twig would grow into a noble tree, blessing all who came near it by its fruit and shade (17:23).
   c. Through all this, the entire world would know the plan and power of God (17:24).
   d. These verses without question introduce a messianic prophecy. (See Isa. 2:2-4; Micah 4:1-4.) The tender twig is the Messiah (see Isa. 11:1; 53:2; Jer. 23:5, 6; 33:15; Zech. 6:12; Rev. 22:16) and the high mountain is Mount Zion. (See Ps. 2:6.)

5. The mother lioness and her cubs (19:1-9).
   a. A mother lioness had some cubs. One of her whelps grew up and learned to devour men. For this he was trapped and taken into Egypt (19:1-4).
   b. Another of her cubs did the same thing. He also was captured and carried away into Babylon (19:5-9).
   c. Some believe the mother lioness here was Hamutal, the wife of Josiah, and mother of three Judean kings. The first cub was Jehoahaz (2 Ki. 23:31-34) who was carried away into an Egyptian prison by Pharaoh Necho. The other cub was Zedekiah (Hamutal's youngest son). He was Judah's last king and was carried away by Nebuchadnezzar into Babylon (2 Ki. 24:18).

6. Two harlot sisters (23:1-49).
   a. Two sisters begin their sad history of prostitution by engaging in immorality with the Egyptians (23:1-3).
   b. The names of these girls are Aholah and Aholibah and are identified as Samaria and Jerusalem (23:4).
   c. The word *Aholah* means "her tent" and may be a reference to the fact that God never approved of the false religion of Samaria (capital of the northern kingdom) as instituted by its first king, Jeroboam. (See 1 Ki. 12:25-33.) Thus, "her tent" meant she had her own religion which did not include God.
   d. The word *Aholibah* means "my tent is in her," indicating perhaps that God's presence still dwelt in the Jerusalem Temple in spite of Judah's sin.
   e. It is said here both these girls became harlots because of their Egyptian immo-

rality. This may refer to the fact that both cities were impressed with the religious and political structures of Egypt.
   f. Aholah then began illicit relations with Assyria (23:5). This happened under northern king Menahem, who allied himself with Assyria. (See 2 Ki. 15:13-20.)
   g. Aholibah did the same thing with Babylon (23:11). King Hezekiah treated the Babylonian representatives almost as if they were gods. (See 2 Ki. 20:12-19; 2 Chron. 32:31.)
   h. God therefore determined to turn both these sisters over to the full brutality of their respective lovers (23:9, 22, 24).

D. Ezekiel's extended Temple vision (8:1—11:25).
   1. The departure of Judah from the glory of God.
      a. Ezekiel is caught away in a vision and transported from Babylon to the Jerusalem Temple during September of 592 B.C. Here he witnesses those things which are transpiring in the Holy City at that very moment (8:1-3).
      b. He first sees an idol just north of the altar gate (8:5).
      c. He then enters into a hidden room in the Temple court, where he sees the walls covered with pictures of all kinds of snakes, lizards, and hideous creatures. In this room are seventy Israelite elders who stand, each with his censer of burning incense, and worshiping these vile drawings. They are being led in their depraved devotions by a Jew named Jaazaniah, the son of Shaphan. Ezekiel must have gasped in shock, for it was Shaphan who had read the book of the law to King Josiah during the great Jerusalem revival some thirty years back (2 Ki. 22:8-11). But his son now led in this awful apostasy (Ezek. 8:7-11). (See also Rom. 1:21-23.)

   Dr. Feinberg writes:
   "The seventy men were obviously not the Sanhedrin which was not organized until the restoration from Babylon. The reference is probably to the pattern given in Exodus 24:9, 10 and Numbers 11:16. These seventy, in the time of Ezekiel, represented the laity . . . the Lord had appointed seventy leaders in years past and their chief duties were to guard against idolatry. What a perversion this was of their high calling!" (*The Prophecy of Ezekiel*, p. 51)
      d. After this repulsive experience, the prophet goes to the northern gate of the Temple. Here he sees Jewish women weeping for Tammuz, their god (8:14). A history of the religion of Tammuz makes sordid reading indeed:
         (1) Satan's church began officially at the tower of Babel in Genesis 11:1-9, nearly twenty-four centuries B.C.

Here, in the fertile plain of Shinar, probably very close to the original Garden of Eden, the first spade of dirt was turned for the purpose of devil-worship.

(2) The first full-time minister of Satan was Nimrod, Noah's wicked and apostate grandson (Gen. 10:8-10).

(3) Secular history and tradition tell us that Nimrod married a woman who was as evil and demonic as himself. Her name was Semerimus. Knowing God's promise of a future Savior (Gen. 3:15), Semerimus brazenly claimed that Tammuz, her first son, fulfilled this prophecy.

(4) Semerimus thereupon instituted a religious system which made both her and her son the objects of divine worship. She herself became the first high priestess. Thus began the mother-child cult which later spread over the world.

(5) What was the teaching of Semerimus' satanic church?

(a) That Semerimus herself was the way to God. She actually adopted the title "queen of heaven."

(b) That she alone could administer salvation to the sinner through various sacraments, such as the sprinkling of holy water.

(c) That her son Tammuz was tragically slain by a wild boar during a hunting trip.

(d) That he was, however, resurrected from the dead forty days later. Thus, each year afterward the temple virgins of this cult would enter a forty-day fast as a memorial to Tammuz's death and resurrection.

(e) After the forty-day fast, a joyful feast called Ishtar took place. At this feast colored eggs were exchanged and eaten as a symbol of the resurrection. An evergreen tree was displayed and a yule log was burned. Finally hot cakes marked with the letter "T" (to remind everyone of Tammuz) were baked and eaten.

Jeremiah also spoke against this vile religion. (See Jer. 7:18; 44:25.)

e. Ezekiel continues his journey and views twenty-five men with their backs to the Temple, facing east and worshiping the sun (8:16). Again, Dr. Feinberg writes:

"Ezekiel saw the crowning insult to the Lord of heaven and earth. Twenty-five men in that hallowed place were worshiping the sun, the object of Persian idolatry. Moses had warned them against this ever present

danger (Deut. 4:19) . . . The twenty-five men represent the twenty-four Levitical priestly courses with the high priest at their head. The apostasy of the laity and of the women has already been noted; now it is revealed in the ranks of the priesthood. Like priests, like people. Think of it! That which was intended best to manifest the glory of God in creation (Ps. 19), is perverted to detract from the glory of God . . . while they faced toward the sun in adoration, they turned their backs toward the temple of God. It was an attitude of defiance toward God and rejection of his worship. This was as complete a repudiation of the Lord as possible (see 2 Chron. 29:6), the cup of their iniquity had been filled to the brim." (*The Prophecy of Ezekiel*, p. 52)

f. As he stands there shocked by all this blasphemy, which literally surrounds him, he sees six heavenly beings appear, each one carrying a sword. They were led by another being dressed in linen clothing and carrying a writer's case (9:1, 2). This leader-angel may have been God's recording angel, and the writing case the Book of Life. (See Ex. 32:32; Ps. 69:28; 139:16; Isa. 4:3; Dan. 12:1; Phil. 4:3.)

g. The leader is commanded by God to walk through Jerusalem's streets and mark the forehead of those individuals whose hearts are grieved over Judah's sin (9:3, 4). Their sealing was for the purpose of insuring safety. (See also Rev. 7:1-3; Gal. 6:17; Rev. 13:16-18; 14:1; 2 Tim. 2:19.)

h. The sword-bearing angels are then commanded to follow this leader and slay all those unmarked individuals (9:5-11). They were to begin at the Temple. This is where God's judgment starts. (See 1 Pet. 4:17.)

i. Ezekiel prays over Jerusalem (as Abraham once did over Sodom. Compare Gen. 18:23-33 with Ezek. 9:8), but is told the situation is now beyond the praying stage (9:8-10).

j. The leaders of Judah have ignored all God's warnings and actually convinced themselves that those already taken captive (including Daniel and Ezekiel) were removed because of their sins (11:14, 15).

2. The departure of the glory of God from Judah.

a. Ezekiel views the glory cloud over the mercy seat (9:3).

b. It then stood over the door of the Temple (10:4).

c. From there it moved to the east gate (10:18, 19).

d. Finally it hovered over the Mount of Olives and disappeared (11:23).

From this point on, that terrible word Ichabod could have been written across the Jerusalem skies —The glory of the Lord is departed from Israel. (See 1 Sam. 4:22.) But, from those blackened skies of despair and doom, comes a dazzling beam of hope, for the prophet hears the voice of God. (See 11:17-20.)

III. The Condemnation of the Enemies of God (25:1—32:32; 35:1-15).
  A. Ammon (25:1-7).
    1. The nation Ammon (occupying that area east of the Jordan and north of Moab) came from the incestuous relationship between Lot and his youngest daughter. (See Gen. 19:38.)
    2. Ammon had often displayed its hostility toward Judah. (See 2 Sam. 10; Amos 1:13-15.) It had joined the Babylonians against Judah about 600 B.C. (2 Ki. 24:2). Previous to this, it had seized the territory belonging to the tribe of Gad after the Assyrian captivity (Jer. 49:1).
    3. Ammon's chief sin, however, was the devilish glee it openly displayed over the destruction of the Jerusalem Temple, the slaughter and enslavement of Judah's citizens (Lam. 2:15).
    4. Because of this, God would allow various fierce Bedouin desert tribes to overrun her land. Their capital city, Rabbath (the present day Amman) would be turned into a pasture for camels.
  B. Moab (25:8-11).
    1. These people originated from Lot and his oldest daughter. Their child was named Moab (Gen. 19:37).
    2. Their main sin was in degrading Judah's Jehovah as just another national and tribal god.
    3. The same desert tribes which overran Ammon would also occupy the main Moabite cities.
  C. Edom (25:12-14; 35:1-15).
    1. This nation stemmed from Esau, the brother of Jacob (Gen. 25:33). Because of their common ancestry, Israel was not to fight with Edom en route to the Promised Land (Deut. 23:7). The Edomites settled that territory south of Moab from the Dead Sea to the Gulf of Aqaba.
    2. In spite of their common heritage, Edom was considered as Israel's most bitter enemy. (See Obad. 1:10; Mal. 1:2-5.)
    3. Their sins were manifold:
      a. They had rejoiced over Judah's fall (Ps. 137:7; Lam. 4:21, 22; Obad. 1:10-14). See also Ezekiel 35:15.
      b. They butchered helpless Jews during the Babylonian invasion (35:5).
      c. They planned to occupy the entire land of Palestine and drive the Lord God from it (35:10).
    4. God would punish them by allowing various nations to fill the land with unburied Edomite corpses (35:5-9).
  D. Philistia (25:15-17).
    1. If Edom topped Israel's enemy list, Philistia would certainly rank a close second. This hostile nation is mentioned in the Old Testament more than any other.
    2. They constantly harassed and oppressed Israel until the reign of King David. (See 1 Sam. 13-14.)
    3. Because of this long-standing hatred and persecution, God would execute terrible vengeance upon them (25:17).
  E. Tyre (26:1—28:19).
    1. The history of Tyre.
      a. Tyre was the ancient city of the Phoenicians, appearing for the first time in the Bible in Joshua 19:29. It was the greatest commercial city in Old Testament times. Tyre means "rock" and was the center of the Mediterranean world.
      b. According to both Ezekiel (26:13), and Isaiah (23:16), Tyre was a city of great music lovers and musicians.
      c. The city exerted great influence during the reigns of David and Solomon. Hiram, King of Tyre was a devoted friend of David (2 Sam. 5:11). He later helped both David and Solomon in their building operations, especially that of the Temple (1 Ki. 5:1-12; 1 Chron. 14:1; 2 Chron. 2:3, 11).
      d. Perhaps here it should be noted that Tyre was actually two cities, one on the coastline, some sixty miles northwest from Jerusalem, and the other on an island, a half mile out in the Mediterranean Sea.
      e. At the time of Ezekiel's prophecy, the Tyrians were in open revolt against Babylon.
    2. The sin of Tyre.
      a. Tyre had rejoiced over the fall of Judah (26:2). The reason was that this meant free passage for her trade caravans going from north to Egypt in the south. With Judah's demise, she need no longer pay an interstate tax.
      b. She had sold Jews as slaves to the Greeks and Edomites (Joel 3:4-8; Amos 1:9, 10).
        (1) The ruler at this time was Ithobal II, who boasted he was as strong as a god and wiser than a Daniel (28:2, 3). History of course is filled with others whose pride became their downfall. See especially the examples of Sennacherib (2 Ki. 18:33-35), Nebuchadnezzar (Dan. 3:15; 4:30), and Herod (Acts 12:21-23).
        (2) In his claim to be a god, the Tyrian ruler becomes a foreshadow of the future antichrist. (See 2 Thess. 2:4.)
      c. The city was totally corrupted with gross materialism (27:4-25).
    3. The punishment of Tyre.
      a. Various nations were to come up against Tyre like ocean waves (26:3).
        (1) The Assyrian king, Sennacherib, in 701-696 B.C. had taken part of the city on the mainland, but did not capture the island fortress.

(2) The Babylonian king, Nebuchadnezzar, also tried to take both cities for thirteen years (585–573 B.C.), but like Sennacherib, failed to take the island.

b. In spite of this strong watery protection, Ezekiel predicted her walls would be torn down, her very soil would be scraped, making her as bare as a rock, and both cities would become a place for the spreading of fishing nets (26:4, 5).

Over 225 years passed without this prophecy being fulfilled. But in 332 B.C., Alexander the Great arrived upon the scene and the island city was doomed. He built a land bridge leading from the coastline to the island by throwing the debris of the old city into the water. In doing this, he literally scraped the coastline clean. Some years ago an American archaeologist named Edward Robinson discovered forty or fifty marble columns beneath the water along the shores of ancient Tyre. After a seven-month siege, Alexander took the island city and destroyed it. From this point on, the surrounding coastal area has been used by local fishermen to spread and dry their nets.

c. Ezekiel furthermore stated the city would never again be inhabited (26:20, 21). Tyre has never been rebuilt, in spite of the well-known nearby fresh water springs of Roselain, which yields some 10,000 gallons of water daily.

d. Many of her ships would be destroyed by fierce hurricanes (27:26, 27).

e. The entire known western world would lament and wail over her destruction (26:16–18; 27:28–36). In the tribulation, the world will do the same over the destruction of Babylon. (See Rev. 18.)

4. The sinister force behind Tyre (28:11–19).

a. The identity of this force. We have already noted that in 28:1–10 Ezekiel describes the pride of Ithobal II, who was ruler of Tyre at that time. But the prophet now moves beyond the earthly scene and describes for us the creation and fall of a vile and vicious non-human angelic creature. This fearful being is Satan himself, the real force behind the wickedness of Tyre. God often speaks to Satan through another indirect source. For example:

(1) He spoke to the devil through the serpent (Gen. 3:14, 15).

(2) He spoke to the devil through Simon Peter (Mt. 16:23).

b. The characteristics of this force.

(1) The perfection of wisdom and beauty (v. 12).
No human being is ever described in these terms, but rather the contrary! (See Rom. 3:23.)

(2) You were in Eden, the garden of God (v. 13).

Some have speculated that Ezekiel had Adam in mind here, but the Genesis account nowhere speaks of Adam's clothing being "bejeweled with every stone," and then fitted "in beautiful settings of finest gold."

(3) "The workmanship of thy tabrets and of thy pipes" (v. 13, as translated by the KJV).
Here Dr. J. Dwight Pentecost writes: "Musical instruments were originally designed to be means of praising and worshiping God. It was not necessary for Lucifer to learn to play a musical instrument in order to praise God. If you please, he had a built-in pipe organ, or, he was an organ. That's what the prophet meant when he said 'the workmanship of thy tabors and of thy pipes. . .' Lucifer, because of his beauty, did what a musical instrument would do in the hands of a skilled musician, bring forth a paean of praise to the glory of God. Lucifer didn't have to look for someone to play the organ so that he would sing the doxology—he was a doxology!" (*Your Adversary, the Devil,* p. 16)

(4) The anointed guardian cherub (v. 14).

(a) He was anointed—in the Old Testament, there were three anointed offices, that of the prophet, priest, and king. Here is a suggestion that Lucifer may have originally been created to function (under Christ) as heaven's prophet-priest and king but he failed! This may be the reason why God separated these offices. (See 1 Sam. 13; 2 Chron. 26.)

(b) He was a guardian cherub—a cherub was a special kind of angelic being whose purpose was to protect God's holiness. (See Gen. 3; Ex. 25; 1 Ki. 6; Ezek. 1; Rev. 4.) Both archaeological and biblical evidences suggest they bore the likeness of a lion, calf, eagle, and man. Apparently Lucifer was created (among other purposes) to demonstrate the earthly work of Christ, as pictured by the four Gospel writers.

Matthew—presents Christ as the lion-like king.

Mark—presents him as the calf-like servant.

Luke—presents him as the perfect man.

John—presents him as the eagle-like God.

(5) Your heart was filled with pride because of all your beauty (v. 17). Here is the first sin and the self-creation of the first sinner in all the universe.

F. Sidon (28:20–24).
1. Sidon was twenty miles north of Tyre and was founded by Canaan's firstborn (Gen. 10:15).
2. This city seemed to be the headquarters of the Baalite idolatry. The princess Jezebel, Scripture's most vicious woman, was a fanatical Baal-worshiper from Sidon. (See 1 Ki. 16:31–33.) In addition, Sidon was the center of Ashtaroth and Tammuz worship.
3. Because of her horrible influence, Sidon was likened to a pricking brier and a hurting thorn to the house of Israel.
4. God would thus punish Sidon by sending an epidemic of disease and an army to destroy her. This occurred in 351 B.C., at which time the city was put to the torch by the Persians.

G. Egypt (29:1—32:32).
1. Her historical punishment (by Nebuchadnezzar).
a. Egypt's sin, like that of so many other nations, was pride (29:3).
b. Pharaoh Hopha (the king referred to here in Ezek. 29) of the twenty-sixth dynasty had apparently convinced Judean King Zedekiah that Egypt could be of more help against Nebuchadnezzar than God himself (29:6). (See also 30:21–26.)
c. Ezekiel, therefore, pronounces doom upon Pharaoh, people, and even the animals (29:8–12).
d. In chapter 31 Egypt is described as a mighty cedar of Lebanon, towering above all other trees. The birds rested in its branches, and animals gave birth under its shade. But soon the tree was corrupted by pride and God ordered the Babylonian wood choppers to hew it down.

# Ezekiel
## THE DESOLATION OF THE CITY OF GOD

## JERUSALEM (4-9, 11-24)

### Twelve Symbolic Acts
Drawing a map of Jerusalem (Ezekiel 4:1-3)
Lying on his left side for a portion of 390 days (4:4, 5)
Lying on his right side for a portion of 40 days (4:6)
Preparing a scant meal (4:9-17)
Shaving his head and beard (5:1-4)
Stamping his feet and clapping his hands (6:11)
Digging through a wall (12:1-16)
Trembling as he ate his food (12:17-20)
Slashing about with a sword (21:9-17)
Drawing a map of the Middle East (21:18)
Boiling a pot of water dry (24:1-14)
Remaining tearless at his wife's funeral (24:15-18)

### Six Parables
A fruitless vine tree (15:1-8)
The adopted girl who became a harlot (16:1-63)
The two eagles (17:1-21)
The tender twig (17:22-24)
The mother lioness and her cubs (19:1-9)
The two harlot sisters (23:1-49)

### His Extended Temple Vision 8-11
He sees the departure of Judah from the glory of God.
He sees the departure of the glory of God from Judah.

### Twelve Messages

| | | |
|---|---|---|
| 6:1-14 | 14:13-23 | 21:1-7 |
| 7:1-27 | 18:1-32 | 22:1-16 |
| 13:1-23 | 20:1-44 | 22:17-22 |
| 14:1-12 | 20:45-49 | 22:23-31 |

NOTE: While in exile, Ezekiel warns his fellow captives that Jerusalem, already occupied by the Babylonians, will later be totally destroyed. He uses drama, parables, and sermons to emphasize this warning.

## TYRE (26-28)

| | |
|---|---|
| HISTORY | Was the greatest commercial city in Old Testament times |
| | The king of Tyre helped both David and Solomon during their reigns |
| LOCATION | Tyre was actually two cities, one on the Mediterranean, and the other nearly a mile out on an island |
| SIN | Pride and gross materialism |
| RULER | Ethbaal II (during Ezekiel's time) |
| PUNISHMENT | Both cities to be destroyed, never to be rebuilt |
| | Areas then to become bare, a place for the spreading of fishing nets |
| SINISTER FORCE BEHIND TYRE | Many believe God is actually condemning and describing Satan in 28:11-19 |
| | He was the real power behind its sin |

## EGYPT (29-32)

To be desolate for forty years
To remain a minor kingdom
To never be sought out by Israel for help again
To be punished during the tribulation

e. Ezekiel informs us that Nebuchadnezzar conquered Egypt for its wealth in order to pay his soldiers after their long siege of Tyre (Ezek. 29:17-21).

f. Egypt was to be desolate for forty years (29:9, 11); the period when the Babylonians held sway over Egypt was about this length of time. Berosus, historian of Babylon, states that Nebuchadnezzar took great numbers of Egyptians into captivity after he occupied their land.

g. After the forty-year punishment period, Egypt would be restored somewhat, but would forever remain a minor kingdom (Ezek. 29:13-15).

h. Israel would never again depend upon Egypt (29:16).

2. Her future punishment (30:1-19).

a. Although the name Nebuchadnezzar appears once in this passage (v. 10), it is thought that the final fulfillment of the judgments mentioned here would transpire during the tribulation. Ezekiel indicates this when he uses the prophetical term "the day of the Lord" (see v. 3). This phrase almost always refers to the seven-year tribulation. (See Isa. 13:6, 9; Joel 1:15; 2:1, 11; 3:14; Amos 5:18; Obad. 1:15; Zeph. 1:7, 14; Zech. 14:1; 1 Thess. 5:2; 2 Thess. 2:2; 2 Pet. 3:10.)

b. According to Daniel 11:40-43, Egypt will indeed be destroyed during the tribulation.

c. At that time she will experience God's judgments. (See 30:4-17.)

To complete this section, it may be observed that Ezekiel's words in 32:17-21 have been characterized as the most solemn eulogy over a heathen people ever composed. In it he pictures Egypt slowly descending into the dark and fearful underworld of Sheol in the heart of the earth. She will then make her bed next to various other once-powerful, but now crumbling and decaying people, such as Assyria, Elam, the Hittites, Edom, and Sidon.

IV. The Presentation of the Shepherd of God—Jesus Christ (34).
A. The many false shepherds.
1. They fed themselves instead of the flock (34:2, 3).
2. They had not taken care of the weak, nor tended the sick, nor bound up the broken bones, nor sought the lost (34:4).
3. The sheep were then scattered, having no shepherd (34:5).
4. They had become prey to the wild animals (34:5).
5. Therefore, the shepherds would be punished (34:9).
   a. Their positions as shepherds would be removed (34:10).
   b. They would themselves not be fed by the Great Shepherd (34:9, 10).
   c. They would be judged and destroyed (34:16).

B. The only true Shepherd. (See Ps. 23; Jn. 10:11; Heb. 13:20; 1 Pet. 5:4.)
1. He would search out the lost sheep (34:11).
2. He would deliver them from their enemies (34:12).
3. He would gather them from all nations (34:13).
4. He would feed them upon the mountains of Israel (34:14).
5. He would give them rest in green pastures (34:15).
6. He would put splints and bandages upon their broken limbs (34:16).
7. He would heal their sick (34:16).
8. He would establish David as his trusted undershepherd (34:23). (See also Ezek. 37:24; Jer. 30:9; Hos. 3:5.)
9. He would make an eternal pact with them (34:25).
10. He would guarantee their safety and place them in a perfect paradise (34:25-28).

V. The Restoration of the Nation of God—Israel (36-37).
A. The necessity of this restoration. Israel had previously been driven from Palestine because of her sin (36:17-19).
B. The reasons for this restoration.
1. To shame those Gentile nations which had sneered at Israel's tragedy (36:1-7).
2. To exonerate the great name of God (36:20-23, 32). The rumor was being spread around that the God of Israel was unable (or unwilling) to protect and purify his own people.
C. The vision of this restoration (37:1-14).
1. Ezekiel is commanded to prophesy over a valley filled with old dry human bones, scattered everywhere (37:1-6).
2. Suddenly there was a rattling noise from all across the valley and the bones of each body came together and attached to the other as they had once been (37:7).
3. After this, the muscles and flesh formed over the bones, and skin covered them (37:8).
4. But the completed bodies had no breath. Ezekiel was then commanded to:
   "Prophesy unto the wind, prophesy, son of man, and say to the wind, thus saith the Lord God: Come from the four winds, O breath, and breathe upon these slain, that they may live. So I prophesied as he commanded me, and the breath came into them, and they lived, and stood up upon their feet, an exceedingly great army" (37:9, 10).
D. The symbol of this restoration (37:15-22).
1. Ezekiel was to carve the following words on two wooden sticks:
   a. The first stick read: "For Judah, and for the children of Israel, his companions."
   b. The second stick read: "For Joseph, the stick of Ephraim, and for all the house of Israel, his companions."
2. Dr. Charles Feinberg writes the following concerning these two sticks:
   "The sticks are here equivalent to scepters, reminiscent of those in the days of

*"The thief cometh not, but for to steal, and to kill, and to destroy: I am come that they might have life, and that they might have it more abundantly.*

*I am the good shepherd . . ."*

**JOHN 10:10, 11**

**THE PRESENTATION OF THE
SHEPHERD OF GOD
—JESUS CHRIST (EZEK. 34)**

## The Many False Shepherds

They fed themselves instead of the flock **(34:2, 3)**

They had not taken care of the weak, tended the sick, bound up the broken bones, nor sought the lost **(34:4)**

The sheep were then scattered, having no shepherd **(34:5)**

They had become prey to the wild animals **(34:5)**

Therefore, the shepherds would be punished **(34:9)**

Their positions as shepherds would be removed **(34:9)**

They would not themselves be fed by the Great Shepherd **(34:9, 10)**

They would be judged and destroyed **(34:16)**

## The Only True Shepherd

He would search out the lost sheep **(34:11)**

He would deliver them from their enemies **(34:12)**

He would gather them from all nations **(34:13)**

He would feed them upon the mountains of Israel **(34:14)**

He would give them rest in green pastures **(34:15)**

He would put splints and bandages upon their broken limbs **(34:16)**

He would heal the sick **(34:16)**

He would establish David as his trusted undershepherd **(34:23)** (see also **Ezek. 37:24; Jer. 30:9; Hos. 3:5**)

He would make an eternal pact with them **(34:25)**

He would guarantee their safety and place them in a perfect paradise **(34:25-28)**

Moses (see Num. 17:1-2). 'Judah, and . . . his companions' (v. 16) showed that the southern kingdom included, in addition to Judah, the greater part of Benjamin and Simeon, the tribe of Levi, and godly Israelites who had come at different times from the northern kingdom with its idolatry and false priesthood into the kingdom of Judah (see 2 Chron. 11:12; 15:9; 30:11, 18; 31:1). In connection with the other stick, Joseph was mentioned. In all probability he was chosen because the house of Joseph, comprising the two powerful tribes of Ephraim and Manasseh, formed the main body of the northern kingdom." (*The Prophecy of Ezekiel*, p. 215)

## THE RESTORATION OF THE NATION OF GOD

# ISRAEL EZEKIEL 36, 37

## NECESSITY OF

Israel was out of the Promised Land because of sin **(36:17-19)**

## REASONS FOR

To punish the foes of Israel **(36:1-7)**
To exonerate the name of God **(36:20-23)**

## VISION EXPLAINING

Ezekiel speaks to a valley filled with dried Israeli bones **(37:1-6)**

The bones join together and are covered with flesh **(37:7, 8)**

He speaks again and the breath of life enters their bodies **(37:9-14)**

## SYMBOL OF

Ezekiel carves the name Judah on one stick and Ephraim on another **(37:15, 16)**

He then holds both sticks in one hand, indicating God would someday reunite all twelve tribes **(37:17-20)**

## RESULTS OF

Israel to once again become God's people **(36:28; 37:27)**

To be sprinkled with clear water **(36:25)**

To possess the indwelling Holy Spirit **(36:27)**

To be given new hearts **(36:26)**

To have a new Temple **(37:26, 28)**

To be ruled over by David **(37:24)**

To be justified among the nations **(36:30)**

To have abundant crops **(36:29; 30, 34, 35)**

To repopulate Jerusalem and other waste cities **(36:38)**

To occupy the Holy Land forever **(37:25)**

3. Ezekiel was then to hold both sticks together in one hand, indicating that God intended to reunite once again in Palestine the divided kingdoms of Israel (37:17-20).

E. The results of this restoration.
1. To once again become God's people (36:28; 37:27).
2. To be sprinkled by clear water (36:25, 29, 33). This, of course, is an allusion to the Mosaic rite of purification. (See Num. 19:17-19.)
3. To possess the ministry of the indwelling Holy Spirit (36:27; 37:14). (See also Ezek. 39:29; Isa. 44:3; 59:21; Joel 2:28, 29; Acts 2:16-18.)
4. To be given new hearts and right desires (36:26).
5. To enjoy the blessings of the new Temple (37:26, 28).
6. To be ruled over by David (37:24).
7. To be justified among the nations (36:30).
8. To have abundant crops (36:29, 30, 34, 35). (See also Isa. 35:1, 2; 55:13; Zech. 8:12.)
9. To repopulate the cities of Israel, especially Jerusalem (36:38).
10. To occupy the Holy Land forever (37:25).

VI. The Demonstration of the Wrath of God— Russia (38, 39).

In these two remarkable chapters, Ezekiel describes for us an invasion into Palestine by a wicked nation north of Israel in the latter days.

A. The identity of the invaders. Where is the land of Magog? It seems almost certain that these verses in Ezekiel refer to none other than that Red Communistic bear, the U.S.S.R. Note the following threefold proof of this.
1. Geographical proof.
Ezekiel tells us in three distinct passages (38:6, 15; 39:2) that this invading nation will come from the "uttermost part of the north" (as the original Hebrew renders it). A quick glance at any world map will show that only Russia can fulfill this description.
2. Historical proof.
The ancient Jewish historian Josephus (first century A.D.) assures us that the descendants of Magog (who was Japheth's son and Noah's grandson) migrated to an area north of Palestine. But even prior to Josephus, the famous Greek historian Herodotus (fifth century B.C.) writes that Meshech's descendants settled north of Palestine (Gen. 10:2).
3. Linguistic proof.
Dr. John Walvoord writes concerning this:
"In Ezekiel 38, Gog is described as 'the prince of Rosh' (ASV). The Authorized Version expresses it as the 'chief prince.' The translation 'the prince of Rosh' is a more literal rendering of the Hebrew. 'Rosh' may be the root of the modern term 'Russia.' In the study of how ancient words come into modern language, it is quite common for the consonants to remain the same and the vowels to be changed. In the word 'Rosh,' if the vowel 'o' is changed to 'u' it becomes the root of the modern word 'Russia' with the suffix

added. In other words, the word itself seems to be an early form of the word from which the modern word 'Russia' comes. Gesenius, the famous lexicographer, gives the assurance that this is a proper identification, that is, that Rosh is an early form of the word from which we get Russia. The two terms 'Mesheck' and 'Tubal' also correspond to some prominent words in Russia. The term 'Mesheck' is similar to the modern name 'Moscow' and 'Tubal' is obviously similar to the name of one of the prominent Asiatic provinces of Russia, the province of Tobolsk. When this evidence is put together, it points to the conclusion that these terms are early references to portions of Russia; therefore the geographic argument is reinforced by the linguistic argument and supports the idea that this invading force comes from Russia." (*The Nations in Prophecy*, p. 107, 108)

B. The allies in the invasion.

Ezekiel lists five nations who will join Russia during her invasion. These are Persia, Ethiopia, Libya, Gomer, and Togarmah. These may (although there is some uncertainty) refer to the following present-day nations:

1. Persia—modern Iran
2. Ethiopia—black African nations (South Africa)
3. Libya—Arabic African nations (North Africa)
4. Gomer—East Germany
5. Togarmah—southern Russia and the Cossacks, or perhaps Turkey.

C. The reasons for the invasion.

1. To cash in on the riches of Palestine (Ezek. 38:11, 12). To control the Middle East. Ancient conquerors have always known that he who would control Europe, Asia, and Africa must first control the Middle East bridge which leads to these three continents.
2. To challenge the authority of the antichrist (Dan. 11:40-44).

D. The chronology of the invasion.

Here it is utterly impossible to be dogmatic. The following is therefore only a suggested possibility, based on Ezekiel 38 and Daniel 11:40-44.

1. Following a preconceived plan, Egypt attacks Palestine from the south (Dan. 11:40a).
2. Russia thereupon invades Israel from the north by both an amphibious and a land attack (Dan. 11:40b).
3. Russia does not stop in Israel, but continues southward and double-crosses her ally by occupying Egypt also (Dan. 11:42, 43).
4. While in Egypt, Russia hears some disturbing news coming from the East and North and hurriedly returns to Palestine. We are not told what the content of this news is. Several theories have been offered:
   a. That it contains the electrifying news that the antichrist has been assassinated, but has risen from the dead! (See Rev. 13:3.)
   b. That it concerns itself with the impending counterattack of the western leader (the antichrist).
   c. That it warns of a confrontation with China and India ("kings of the East"), who may be mobilizing their troops.

It should be noted at this point, however, that some Bible students identify the "he" of Daniel 11:42 as being the antichrist, and not the Russian ruler. If this is true, then the above chronology would have to be rearranged accordingly.

E. The destruction of the invaders.

Upon her return, Russia is soundly defeated upon the mountains of Israel. This smashing defeat is effected by the following events, caused by God himself:

1. A mighty earthquake (Ezek. 38:19, 20).
2. Mutiny among the Russian troops (Ezek. 38:21).
3. A plague among the troops (Ezek. 38:22).
4. Floods, great hailstones, fire, and brimstone (Ezek. 38:22; 39:6).

F. The results of the invasion.

1. Five-sixths (83 percent) of the Russian soldiers are destroyed (Ezek. 39:2).
2. The first grisly feast of God begins (Ezek. 39:4, 17, 18, 19, 20). A similar feast would seem to take place later, after the battle of Armageddon (Rev. 19:17, 18; Mt. 24:28).
3. The communistic threat will cease forever.
4. Seven months will be spent in burying the dead (Ezek. 39:11–15).
5. Seven years will be spent in burning the weapons of war (Ezek. 39:9, 10).

Dr. John Walvoord writes the following concerning this seven-year period:

"There are some . . . problems in the passage which merit study. A reference is made to bows and arrows, to shields and chariots, and to swords. These, of course, are antiquated weapons from the standpoint of modern warfare. The large use of horses is understandable, as Russia today uses horses a great deal in connection with their army. But why should they use armor, spears, bows and arrows? This certainly poses a problem. There have been two or more answers given. One of them is that Ezekiel is using language with which he was familiar—the weapons that were common in his day—to anticipate modern weapons. What he is saying is that when this army comes, it will be fully equipped with the weapons of war. Such an interpretation, too, has problems. We are told in the passage that they used the wooden shafts of the spears and the bow and arrows for kindling wood. If these are symbols, it would be difficult to burn symbols. However, even in modern warfare there is a good deal of wood used . . . A second solution is that the battle is preceded by a disarmament agreement between nations. If this were the case, it would be necessary to resort to primitive

**THE DEMONSTRATION OF THE WRATH OF GOD**

# RUSSIA EZEKIEL 38, 39

## 1. IDENTITY OF THE INVADERS
- Geographical proof
- Historical proof
- Linguistic proof

## 2. ALLIES IN THE INVASION

| | |
|---|---|
| **PERSIA** | Modern Iran |
| **ETHIOPIA** | South African Nations |
| **LIBYA** | North African Nations |
| **GOMER** | Eastern Europe |
| **TOGARMAH** | Turkey |

## 3. REASONS FOR THE INVASION
- To cash in on the riches of Israel **(38:11, 12)**
- To challenge the authority of the antichrist **(DAN. 11:40-44)**

## 4. RESULTS OF THE INVASION
- Russia totally defeated by God **(38:21-23)**
- Five-sixths of the Russian troops destroyed on the mountains of Israel **(39:2)**
- Seven years to be spent in burning the war weapons **(38:9)**
- Seven months to be spent in burying the dead **(38:12)**

weapons easily and secretly made if a surprise attack were to be achieved. This would allow a literal interpretation of the passage. A third solution has also been suggested based on the premise that modern missile warfare will have developed in that day to a point where missiles will seek out any considerable amount of metal. Under these circumstances, it would be necessary to abandon the large use of metal weapons and substitute wood such as is indicated in the primitive weapons." (*The Nations in Prophecy*, pp. 115, 116)

VII. The Manifestation of the Glory of God—the Temple (40-48).
  A. Its biblical order.
  The millennial temple is the last of seven great scriptural temples. These are:
  1. the tabernacle of Moses—Exodus 40 (1500-1000 B.C.)
  2. the Temple of Solomon—1 Kings 5-8 (1000-586 B.C.)
  3. the Temple of Zerubbabel (rebuilt later by Herod)—Ezra 6; John 2 (516 B.C. TO A.D. 70)

4. the Temple of the Body of Jesus—John 2:21 (4 B.C. to A.D. 30)
5. the spiritual temple, the church—Acts 2; 1 Thess. 4 (from Pentecost till the rapture)
  a. the whole church (Eph. 2:21)
  b. the local church (1 Cor. 3:16, 17)
  c. the individual Christian (1 Cor. 6:19)
6. the tribulational temple—Revelation 11 (from the rapture till Armageddon)
7. the millennial temple—Ezekiel 40-48; Joel 3:18; Isaiah 2:3; 60:13; Daniel 9:24; Haggai 2:7, 9

  B. Its holy oblation.
  Palestine will be redistributed among the twelve tribes of Israel during the millennium. The land itself will be divided into three areas. Seven tribes will occupy the northern area and five the southern ground. Between these two areas there is a section called "the holy oblation," that is, that portion of ground which is set apart for the Lord. Dr. J. Dwight Pentecost quotes Merrill F. Unger on this:
  "The holy oblation would be a spacious square, thirty-four miles each way, containing about 1160 square miles. This area would be the center of all the interests of the divine government and worship as set up in the Millennial earth . . . The temple itself would be located in the middle of this square (the holy oblation) and not in the City of Jerusalem, upon a very high mountain, which will be miraculously made ready for that purpose when the temple is to be erected. (See Isa. 2:3; Micah 4:1-4; Ezek. 37:26.) (*Things to Come*, pp. 510, 514)
  C. Its dimensions (40:1—42:20; 46:21-24).
  D. Its purpose:
  1. To provide a dwelling place for the cloud of glory (43:1-17).
  2. To provide a center for the King of glory (43:7). (See also Isa. 2:2, 3; Micah 4:2.)
  E. Its priesthood (44:5-31).
  On four specific occasions, we are told that the sons of Zadok will be assigned the priestly duties (Ezek. 40:46; 43:19; 44:15; 48:11).
  Zadok was a high priest in David's time (the eleventh in descent from Aaron). His loyalty to the king was unwavering. Because of this, he was promised that his seed would have this glorious opportunity (1 Sam. 2:35; 1 Ki. 2:27, 35).
  F. Its prince (45:7, 8, 17; 46:1-20).
  In his description of the temple, Ezekiel refers to a mysterious "prince" some seventeen times. Whoever he is, he occupies a very important role in the temple itself, apparently holding an intermediary place between the people and the priesthood. We are sure that he is not Christ, since he prepares a sin offering for himself (Ezek. 45:22), and is married and has sons (Ezek. 46:16). Some suggest that the prince is from the seed of King David, and that he will be to David what the false prophet was to the antichrist.
  G. Its unique features.
  Several articles and objects present in the temples of Moses, Solomon, and Herod will be absent from the millennial temple.

1. There will be no veil. This was torn in two from top to bottom (Mt. 27:51) and will not reappear in this temple. Thus there will be no barrier to keep man from the glory of God.
2. There will be no table of shrewbread. This will not be needed, for the Living Bread himself will be present.
3. There will be no lampstands. These will not be needed either, since the Light of the World himself will personally shine forth.
4. There will be no Ark of the Covenant. This will also be unnecessary, since the Shekinah Glory himself will hover over all the world, as the glory cloud once did over the ark.
5. The east gate will be closed. Observe the words of Ezekiel: "This gate shall be shut, and no man shall enter in by it; because the Lord, the God of Israel, hath entered in by it; therefore, it shall be shut" (Ezek. 44:2).

    This gate, it has been suggested, will remain closed for the following reasons:
a. This will be the gate by which the Lord Jesus Christ enters the temple. As a mark of honor to an eastern king, no person could enter the gate by which he entered.
b. It was from the eastern gate that the glory of God departed for the last time in the Old Testament (Ezek. 10:18, 19). By sealing the gate, God reminds all those within that his glory will never again depart from his people.

H. Its sacrifices.

As we have already seen, several pieces of furniture in the Old Testament Temple will be missing in the millennial edifice. However, the brazen altar of sacrifice will again be present. There are at least four Old Testament prophecies which speak of animal sacrifices in the millennial temple: Isaiah 56:6, 7; 60:7; Zechariah 14:16-21; Jeremiah 33:18. But why the need of these animal blood sacrifices during the golden age of the millennium?

To answer this, one must attempt to project himself into this fabulous future period. Here is an age of no sin, sorrow, sufferings, sickness, Satan, or separation. During the millennium even the vocabulary will be different. For example, today respectable and decent society shuns certain filthy four-letter words, and well they should! This will doubtless also be practiced during the millennium. But how the words will change! Below is a sampling of some four-letter words to be shunned during the thousand-year reign: fear, pain, jail, hate, dope. These words are so much a part of our sinful society that it is utterly impossible to avoid or ignore them. The point is simply this: during the millennium millions of children will be born and reared by saved Israelite and Gentile parents who survived the tribulation. In spite of their perfect environment, however, these "kingdom kids" will need the new birth. As sons and daughters of Adam they, too, like all others, will require eternal salvation (Rom. 3:23; Jn. 3:3). But how can these children be reached? What object lessons can be used?

Here is a generation which will grow up without knowing fear, experiencing pain, witnessing hatred, taking dope, or seeing a jail.

This is one reason that the sacrificial system will be reinstituted during the millennium. These sacrifices will function as:
1. A reminder to all of the necessity of the new birth.
2. An object lesson of the costliness of salvation.
3. An example of the awfulness of sin.
4. An illustration of the holiness of God.

I. Its business office.
1. General business, such as standard weights and measurements, temple tax, etc. (45:9-16).

## THE MANIFESTATION OF THE GLORY OF GOD

# THE TEMPLE EZEKIEL 40-48
## DISTRIBUTION OF THE LAND

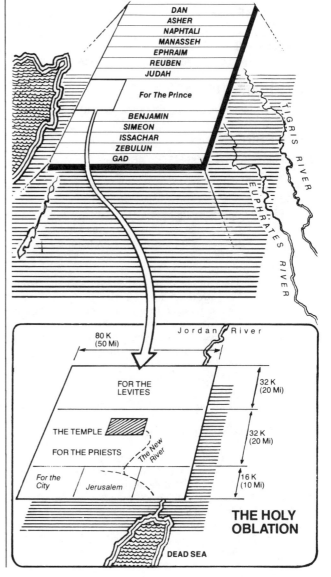

## FACTS ON THE MILLENNIAL TEMPLE

### ●ITS BIBLICAL ORDER

1. The tabernacle of Moses (**Ex. 40**)
   *Dates:* 1444—1100 B.C.
2. The Temple of Solomon (**1 Ki. 6**)
   *Dates:* 959—586 B.C.
3. The Temple of Zerubbabel (**Ezra 6**)
   Note: This was later greatly enlarged by Herod. (**See Jn. 2.**)
   *Dates:* 516 B.C.—A.D. 70
4. The temple of Christ's body (**Jn. 2**)
   *Dates:* 4 B.C.—A.D. 30
5. The spiritual temple, the church (**Acts 2**)
   *Dates:* Pentecost—rapture
   ● The whole church (**Eph. 2:21**)
   ● The local church (**1 Cor. 3:16, 17**)
   ● The individual believer (**1 Cor. 6:19**)
6. The tribulational temple (**Rev. 11**)
   *Dates:* Rapture—Armageddon
7. The millennial temple (**Ezek. 40-48**)
   *Dates:* Through the millennium

### ●ITS PURPOSE

1. To provide a place for the glory cloud of God (**Ezek. 43**)
2. To provide a center for the King of glory (**43:7**)

### ●ITS PRIESTHOOD

Those priests from the line of Zadok (**40:46**)

### ●ITS PRINCE

1. Definitely not Christ (**45:22; 46:16**)
2. Perhaps someone from the line of David.

### ●ITS UNIQUE FEATURES

1. No veil
2. No table of shewbread
3. No lampstands
4. No Ark of the Covenant
5. East gate to be closed (**44:2**)

### ●ITS SACRIFICES
(**Isa. 56:7; 60:7; Jer. 33:18; Zech. 14:16-21**)

1. As a *reminder* to all of the necessity of the new birth
2. As an *object lesson* of the costliness of salvation
3. As an *example* of the awfulness of sin
4. As an *illustration of the* holiness of God

### ●ITS RIVER
(**47:1-12**)

1. The *source:* proceeding from beneath the temple
2. The *course:* flows to Dead Sea and Mediterranean Sea
3. The *force:* waters to swim in

### ●ITS CITY

1. Circumference: six miles (**48:35**)
2. Name: the millennial Jerusalem will be named "Jehovah-Shammah," meaning, "the Lord is there" (**48:35**)

---

2. Specific affairs, such as land allotment (47:13—48:34). This total area land is about the size God promised Abraham. (See Gen. 15:18-21.)

J. Its river (47:1-12).
   1. The source of the river—proceeding from beneath the temple (47:1).
   2. The course of the river—flowing eastward and then south through the desert and Jordan River to the Dead Sea where its sweet waters will purify that lifeless body of polluted water (47:2, 6, 12).
   3. The force of the river—at first it reached Ezekiel's ankles, then his knees, after this his waist, and finally he swam across its unknown depths (47:3-5).

K. Its glory cloud (43:1-5).

L. Its city.
   1. Jerusalem will become the worship center of the world and will occupy an elevated site (Zech. 14:10). (See also Isa. 2:2, 3.)
   2. The city will be six miles in circumference (Ezek. 48:35). In the time of Christ the city was about four miles.
   3. The city will be named "Jehovah-Shammah," meaning "The Lord is there" (Ezek. 48:35).

## DANIEL (605-536 B.C.)

INTRODUCTION

1. Daniel was a teenager taken captive by Nebuchadnezzar during the first siege of Jerusalem in 605 B.C.
2. He was of royal blood.
3. While in captivity without the slightest compromise he faithfully served under the administration of three kings, Nebuchadnezzar, Belshazzar, and Darius.
4. He was himself ministered to by both of heaven's recorded archangels, Gabriel and Michael (9:21; 10:13).
5. He has more to say about the coming antichrist than any other Old Testament writer.
6. One of his contemporaries, Ezekiel, refers to:
   a. The righteousness of Daniel, comparing him with Noah and Job (Ezek. 14:14).
   b. The wisdom of Daniel (Ezek. 28:3).
7. Jesus quoted Daniel during his Mt. Olivet discourse (Mt. 24:15).
8. The unusual feature of his book is that Daniel wrote the central portion (2:4—7:28) in the Aramaic language.
9. He may be compared to Joseph, for both men had the gift of interpreting dreams. (Compare Gen. 37:5, 9; 40:8; 41:25 with Dan. 2:24; 4:19.)
10. His book marks the third of five great periods of miracles in the Bible. The periods are:

a. the time of Moses and Joshua
b. the time of Elijah and Elisha
c. the time of Daniel
d. the time of Christ and his disciples
e. the time of Peter and Paul

11. Daniel's life may be characterized by purpose, prayer, and prophecy.

I. A Divine Diet
   A. The resolution of Daniel (1:1-8).
      1. Nebuchadnezzar had selected some choice Hebrew youths to enroll in the special three-year B.D. course (Babylonian Development). Daniel and his three friends were a part of that student body (v. 4).
      2. These youths were assigned the best of the king's food and wine (1:5).
      3. Their brainwashing began when the superintendent changed their names (v. 7).
         a. *Hananiah* (the Lord is gracious) becomes *Shadrach* (illumined by the sun-god).
         b. *Mishael* (who is the Lord) becomes *Meshach* (who is Ishtar).
         c. *Azariah* (the Lord is my help) becomes *Abednego* (the slave of Nabu). Nabu was the Babylonian god of wisdom and education.
         d. *Daniel* (God is Judge) becomes *Belteshazzar* (Bel's prince). Bel was ruling god of the Babylonian pantheon, equivalent to Zeus or Jupiter.
      4. Daniel submits to his new name, but determines not to accept the king's menu (1:8). Three factors may have entered into his decision:
         a. The meat and wine had probably been sacrificed to false gods.
         b. The food may have been prohibited under Mosaic Law (Lev. 11:44-47).
         c. He may have previously taken the Nazarite vow (Num. 6:3).
      5. Satan doubtless attempted to get Daniel to rationalize through various ways. He may have considered:
         a. The king had ordered it, therefore it was a law.
         b. To disobey might bring severe punishment.
         c. It would probably spoil all chances of advancement.
         d. When in Rome (or Babylon), simply do as the natives do.
         e. He was a long way from home and no one would ever know.
         f. God had failed him anyway in permitting his capture.
   B. The recommendation of Daniel (1:8-14).
      1. Daniel seeks permission of the superintendent to eat other food instead. But in spite of his great affection for Daniel, the request is denied for fear of what Nebuchadnezzar might do.
      2. Daniel then proposes a test to the steward under the superintendent. He suggests a ten-day diet of only vegetables and water. At the end of this short time the steward could compare Daniel and his friends with the oth-

ers who ate the king's rich food (1:11-13). The terms of this test are granted.
   C. The rewards of Daniel (1:15-21).
      1. At the hand of God.
         a. Daniel and his friends look healthier and better nourished at the end of the ten-day period. This is the first of a number of miracles in the book of Daniel (1:15).
         b. Daniel and his friends are ten times smarter at the end of the three-year period. In addition to this, God imparts to Daniel the supernatural ability to understand dreams and visions, a gift he will greatly use (see Dan. 2:31; 4:19).
      2. At the hand of Nebuchadnezzar (1:21). This Babylonian king appoints Daniel to a political career which will span some seventy years under the reign of various Babylonian and Persian kings.

II. A Statue and a Stone.
   A. The frustration of the Babylonians (2:1-13).
      1. Nebuchadnezzar has a terrifying nightmare and calls in his entire cabinet to interpret his dream (2:1-3).
      2. The king is assured that if he will but relate the details of the dream, an interpretation will immediately be given (2:4). From this verse on through 7:28, the book of Daniel is written in Aramaic, the language spoken at Nebuchadnezzar's court. (Daniel wrote this section in Aramaic because it was a Gentile language and that part of his book deals with four great Gentile world powers.)
      3. Nebuchadnezzar refuses to tell them about his dream, and retorts: "the thing is gone from me" (v. 5). Here it should be noted that he is not telling them he has forgotten the dream, that it has gone from his mind, but rather that the command has gone from him and he wants action.
      4. He then issues his decree of punishment if they fail, but promises great rewards if they succeed (2:5, 6).
      5. The frightened cabinet admits its total inability to perform this, sadly concluding that: "There is no other that can show it before the king, except the gods, whose dwelling is not with flesh" (v. 11).
         Some six centuries later an amazing event transpiring in Bethlehem would gloriously and forever change all this (see Jn. 1:14; Gal. 4:4).
      6. Nebuchadnezzar, his face purple with rage, orders his entire State Department slaughtered for this shameful failure (2:12, 13). This, of course, included Daniel and his three friends who had only recently entered the Babylonian diplomatic service.
   B. The revelation of God (2:14-30).
      1. Daniel learns of this insane decree and immediately assures Arioch (head of the Babylonian F.B.I.) that the king's bloody order need not be carried out, for his dream will soon be revealed.
      2. Daniel then relates the same information to the king (2:14-16).
      3. He returns home and leads his three friends

in a prayer and praise service (2:17-23). We note here for the first time the phrase "the God of heaven," as found in 2:18. This expression is peculiar to the books of the captivity (see Neh. 1:4). Now that Jerusalem was destroyed and the Temple burned, God no longer dwelt between the cherubim. Ezekiel saw the departure of the Shekinah glory to heaven (see Ezek. 9:3; 10:4, 18; 11:23). He is now the God of heaven.

4. That very night God allows Daniel to see in a vision the same events Nebuchadnezzar had previously dreamed (2:19).

5. Daniel then offers praise to the God of heaven (2:21-23).

6. Daniel is ushered into Nebuchadnezzar's presence. Before he interprets the dream he makes it perfectly understood that:

"There is a God in heaven who revealeth secrets, and maketh known to the king . . . But as for me, this secret is not revealed to me for any wisdom that I have more than any living . . . " (2:28, 30).

C. The interpretation of Daniel (2:30-45).

1. A chronology of the dream (what did the king see?) (2:31-35).

a. He saw a huge and powerful statue of a man. It was made up of various materials.

(1) Its head was gold.

(2) Its breast and arms were silver.

(3) Its belly and thighs were brass.

(4) Its legs were iron and its feet part iron and clay.

b. This statue was then utterly pulverized into small powder by a special rock, supernaturally cut from a mountainside, which fell upon it.

c. The rock then grew until it filled the entire earth (2:34, 35).

2. A theology of the dream (what did this all mean?) (2:36-45).

a. The statue represented four Gentile world powers.

(1) The golden head was Babylon.

(2) The silver chest and arms were Persia.

(3) The brass belly and thighs were Greece.

(4) The iron legs and iron and clay feet were Rome.

b. In the days of the final world power, the God of heaven would shatter all earthly kingdoms through his Rock (the Lord Jesus Christ) and set up an eternal kingdom (2:44, 45).

c. The final Gentile power (Rome) will be revived during the tribulation and will consist of ten nations. This is implied, for the great prophecies concerning the fourth power were not fulfilled in the history of ancient Rome. The smiting Rock did not shatter those earthly kingdoms. On the contrary, he was put to death by the sentence of an officer of the fourth empire. During his Olivet discourse our Lord uttered the following words concerning Jerusalem. His message was both historical and prophetical in its scope. He proclaimed:

" . . . and Jerusalem shall be trodden down of the Gentiles until the times of the Gentiles be fulfilled" (Lk. 21:24). Concerning this, Scofield observes:

"The 'times of the Gentiles' began with the captivity of Judah under Nebuchadnezzar (2 Chron. 36:1-21), since which time Jerusalem has been under Gentile overlordship." (*Scofield Bible*, p. 1106)

The same powers that Nebuchadnezzar dreamed about were later depicted in the prophecy of Daniel (7:1-27) as four wild animals.

(1) Babylon was a winged lion.

(2) Persia was a bear.

(3) Greece was a winged leopard.

(4) Rome was an indescribably brutal and vicious animal.

Thus God views man in a far different light than man views himself.

3. A summary of the dream (important dates in the history of the four kingdoms).

Babylon (key dates: 626-556 B.C.).

a. The religious roots of Babylon were sown at the tower of Babel by Nimrod and his followers (Gen. 11:9).

b. By 1830 B.C. the city began its rise to prominence.

c. Hammurabi (1704-1662 B.C.) would later make it world famous through his code of law.

d. Babylon was controlled by the Assyrians from 900-722 B.C.

e. Around 722 B.C. a Babylonian named Merodach-Baladan (mentioned in 2 Ki. 20:12 and Isa. 39:1) revolted against the Assyrians.

f. In 626 B.C. another strong man named Nebopalassar founded the dynasty which was flourishing in Daniel's day.

g. In 612 he finished off the remaining Assyrian threat near the city of Haran.

i. In 605 B.C. he sent his world-famous son Nebuchadnezzar to do battle with the Egyptians at a place called Carchemish. The Babylonians emerged the masters of the world.

j. Nebuchadnezzar (who reigned from 606-561 B.C.) was a vigorous and brilliant commander and the greatest man of his time in the non-Jewish world. He was a soldier, statesman, and architect. He married a Median princess named Amyhia and built for her the famous Hanging Gardens of Babylon, considered by the Greeks the seventh wonder of the ancient world.

k. Nebuchadnezzar pursued the fleeing Egyptians as far west as Jerusalem. His first visit to Jerusalem was short, for he hurried home in 605 B.C. because of the sudden death of his father. But before he finished, he would lay siege to the Holy City on at least three occasions and ultimately burn it to the ground. These occasions were:

(1) 605 B.C. He occupies the city, allows Jehoiakim (Josiah's son) to rule as his puppet king, takes some of the Temple treasures, and key royal seed to Babylon. Among this group of teenagers were Daniel and his three friends (2 Chron. 36:6, 7; Dan. 1:1-3).

(2) 597 B.C. He comes again and takes the rest of the treasures to Babylon along with Ezekiel the prophet, King Jehoiachin (Jehoiachim's son), and 10,000 princes, officers, and chief men (2 Ki. 24:14-16).

(3) 586 B.C. He once more returns to punish the rebellion led by Zedekiah, Judah's last king. This time the walls are broken, the Temple destroyed, and the city burned. Zedekiah's sons are killed and he himself is blinded and carried into Babylon where he dies.

l. Nebuchadnezzar dies in 562 B.C.

m. Evil-merodach, his son, begins a short rule in 562 B.C. (2 Ki. 25:27). He released King Jehoiachin and treated him as a royal foreign guest.

n. In 556 an Assyrian nobleman named Nabonidus somehow managed to gain the throne. After a short while, however, he semi-retired and put up his young son Belshazzar as Babylonian co-regent.

o. Belshazzar ruled until the fateful night of October 13, 556 B.C., when the Medes and Persians entered Babylon and took the city (Dan. 5).

Persia (key dates: 539-331 B.C.).

a. Cyrus the Great founded the mighty Persian Empire in 559 B.C. He is mentioned often in the Old Testament (Ezra 1-5; Isa. 44:28; 45:1; Dan. 1:21; 6:28; 10:1).

b. In 546 he defeated King Croesus of Lydia, a ruler of fantastic wealth.

c. In 539 he took the city of Babylon and had Belshazzar executed.

d. Cyrus allowed the Jewish remnant to return a few years later.

e. He died in battle in 529 B.C.

f. He was then succeeded by his son Cambyses II (529-522) who conquered Egypt. Soon after this, he committed suicide. A civil war then began.

g. Darius the Great (522-486) succeeded Cambyses II and saved the crumbling empire by restoring law and order.

h. Darius was defeated by the Greeks during the great sea battle at Marathon in 490 B.C.

i. Xerxes (486-465), the son of Darius, then reigned. He was the King Ahasuerus of the book of Esther. Xerxes, like his fa-

ther, also suffered defeat by the Greeks in 480 at Salamis.

j. Artaxerxes I (465-423) was king during Nehemiah's palace service.

k. Darius III (335-331)—the Persian Empire was destroyed by Alexander the Great during his short reign.

Greece (key dates: 331-323 B.C.).

a. From 546-479 B.C. the Greek states were constantly threatened by Persian invasions. But all this ended after the victorious battles of Salamis and Platoea.

b. Shortly after these battles, Greece entered into its Golden Age, led by an Athenian democratic leader named Pericles (461-429 B.C.) A number of its citizens would become some of the most famous who ever lived.

(1) Herodotus (485-425), the father of history

(2) Hippocrates (460-370), the father of modern medicine

(3) Socrates (469-399), philosopher

(4) Plato (427-347), philosopher

(5) Aristotle (384-322), philosopher

(6) Demosthenes (385-322), one of history's greatest composers of oration

c. However, the Golden Era was short lived, for two of the leading Greek city states, Sparta and Athens, began fighting among themselves. Their three armed conflicts are known as the Peloponnesian wars (from 459-404 B.C.). Sparta came out ahead after these wars.

d. In 338 B.C. a man from Macedonia conquered Greece. He was assassinated two years later, in 336 B.C. His name was Philip of Macedon (380-336 B.C.).

e. Philip was succeeded by his son, Alexander the Great, who would soon become one of the world's most famous conquerors. He was twenty at the time. He immediately prepared to carry out his father's orders to invade Persia.

f. In 334 B.C. he crossed the Hellespont (which separated Asia Minor from the Middle East).

(1) He defeated the Persians at Granicus in 334 B.C.

(2) He routed them again at Issus in 333 B.C.

(3) He destroyed Tyre, spared Jerusalem, and was welcomed by Egypt. Here he founded the city of Alexandria.

(4) He forever crushed the Persians at Arbela in 331 B.C.

g. In 327 he invaded India. At this time he also laid plans to rebuild the city of Babylon to its former glory. But in India he died in 323 B.C. at the age of thirty-two.

h. His mighty empire was soon divided by his four generals.

(1) Ptolemy—who ruled Egypt. Cleopatra came from this line.

## THE CAPTIVITY STAGE

# Daniel, Ezekiel

## 1. The Divine Diet

**Resolution:**
Not to eat the king's food
**Recommendation:**
That a ten-day diet be conducted
**Reward:**
Daniel graduates ten times smarter

## 2. A Statue and a Stone

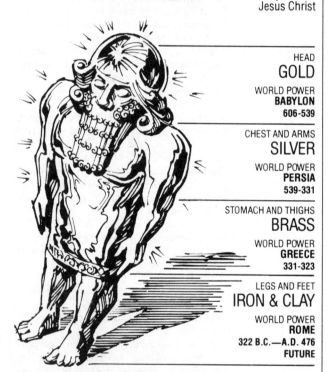

Statue is destroyed by a great stone, which represents Jesus Christ

HEAD
**GOLD**
WORLD POWER
**BABYLON**
606-539

CHEST AND ARMS
**SILVER**
WORLD POWER
**PERSIA**
539-331

STOMACH AND THIGHS
**BRASS**
WORLD POWER
**GREECE**
331-323

LEGS AND FEET
**IRON & CLAY**
WORLD POWER
**ROME**
322 B.C.—A.D. 476
**FUTURE**

- The frustration of the Babylonians: the king's aides cannot interpret his dream and are sentenced to death.
- The revelation of the Lord: God reveals the dream to Daniel.
- The interpretation of the prophet: Daniel explains the dream.
- The prostration of the king: upon hearing their interpretation, Nebuchadnezzar falls down and worships Daniel.

In Daniel 7 the same four nations are described, but from a heavenly view, which looks upon them as four wild animals.

| WORLD POWER | DESCRIPTION |
| --- | --- |
| Babylon | Lion |
| Persia | Bear |
| Greece | Leopard |
| Rome | Monster |

(2) Seleucus—who took Syria. From here came the notorious Antiochus Epiphanes IV (176-163 B.C.)
(3) Cassander—who took Greece and Macedonia.
(4) Lysimachus—who ruled Asia minor.

Rome (key dates: 58 B.C. to A.D. 476).
a. The traditional date for the founding of Rome is April 21, 753 B.C. Cicero says the name came from its founder, Romulus. He ruled for thirty-nine years and then mysteriously disappeared, having been supposedly taken up into heaven.
b. By the year 338 B.C. Rome controlled central Italy.
c. Then came the historic Punic Wars between Rome and Carthage, with the latter being destroyed in 146 B.C.
 (1) First war (264-241 B.C.)
 (2) Second war (218-202 B.C.): Hannibal appeared during this war. He terrified the Romans when he marched a herd of elephants over the Alps in 218 B.C. and defeated two large Roman armies. He also routed his enemy at Cannae in 216 B.C. Finally a Roman general named Scipio defeated Hannibal at Zama in 202 B.C. Rome then became the mistress of the Mediterranean.
 (3) Third war (149-146): The city of Carthage was taken and burned.
d. Pompey, the famous Roman General, conquered Palestine in 63 B.C. This was followed by a period of civil wars and uncertainty.
e. The empire was then saved and consolidated by Julius Caesar during his famous Gallic wars (58-51 B.C.). On the Ides of March, 44 B.C., Caesar was assassinated in Rome.
f. The empire was then taken over by Octavius (also known as Augustus) Caesar. He defeated Brutus and Cassius (two of the rebels who murdered Julius Caesar) at Philippi in 42 B.C. In 31 B.C. Octavius defeated the forces of Antony and Cleopatra at Actium, and made Egypt into a Roman province. The Roman empire now entered its zenith of power and glory. It was during Octavius' rule that our Lord was born (Lk. 2:1). Octavius ruled from 31 B.C. to A.D. 14.
g. Octavius was succeeded by Tiberius Caesar (A.D. 14-37). The ministries of both John the Baptist and the Savior took place at this time.
h. Caligula (A.D. 37-41), also known as Little Boots. He became a ruthless maniac and was assassinated. Caligula was in power during the early part of the book of Acts.
i. Claudius (41-54) was poisoned by his own wife. Paul conducted his great missionary trips during his reign.
j. Nero (54-68)—after a normal eight-year reign Nero degenerated into an insane

monster. He had Rome burned and murdered many Christians by falsely blaming them for the fire. Peter and Paul were martyred during his reign. In A.D. 68 Nero committed suicide.

k. The Roman General Vespasian (68–79) became ruler. He ordered his son Titus to destroy Jerusalem. This was done in A.D. 70.

l. Upon his death, Titus took the throne. He ruled from 79–81. During his rule Pompeii was destroyed by Mt. Vesuvius.

m. In 81 Domitian ascended into power. He banished John the apostle to the Isle of Patmos (Rev. 1:9).

n. The ten or more Roman emperors had one thing in common—they all hated Christians.

o. Finally in 284 Diocletian came into power. He is known as the last emperor to persecute believers, but also the most ruthless. Diocletian separated the Eastern empire from the Western and appointed a man named Maximian to rule the eastern part. In 305 he resigned.

p. When Diocletian left the throne two men immediately began contending for it. One was the son of Maximian, and the other was Constantine. The issue as to who would rule Rome was settled in 312 just outside the city at a place called Milvian Bridge. Here Constantine soundly defeated his rival to power.

q. In 313 Constantine issued the famous Edict of Toleration which in effect made Christianity his state religion. He also presided over the Council of Nicaea in 325.

r. Julian the apostate, the nephew of Constantine, became ruler after the death of his uncle. He attempted to replace Christianity but failed. His dying words on a battlefield in 363 were: "Oh Galilean, thou hast conquered at last!"

s. Theodosius the Great (378–395), a champion of Christianity, once more divided the empire into Eastern and Western sections (as Diocletian had previously done).

t. During the years of 450–455 Attila the Hun and the Vandals plundered Italy and Rome.

u. In 476 Romulus Augustulus, the last Roman Emperor, was dethroned.

D. The prostration of Nebuchadnezzar (2:46–49).
 1. The king bows down to Daniel and commands his people to offer sacrifices and burn sweet incense before him (2:46).
 2. He acknowledges the God of Daniel as being "God of gods" (2:47).
 3. He elevates Daniel to the highest office in Babylon, as chief magistrate in the king's court (2:48).

III. A Fiery Furnace.
 A. The king's command (3:1–7).
 1. Nebuchadnezzar constructs a golden statue ninety feet high and nine feet wide. This is set up in the Plain of Dura near Babylon.

## 3. A Fiery Furnace

The king's command: That all his leaders fall down and worship a ninety-foot golden image. Reasons for this:
1. To elevate his person
2. To consolidate his empire

The Hebrews stand: Shadrach, Meshach, and Abednego refuse to kneel and are thrown into the fiery furnace.

The Lord's own man: Christ himself joins the trio and delivers them out unhurt.

## 4. A Tree in Turmoil

The tree (Nebuchadnezzar) corrupted through vanity
1. Nebuchadnezzar relates his dream to Daniel
2. Daniel reveals the dream to Nebuchadnezzar

The tree (Nebuchadnezzar) corrected through insanity
1. The pride of Nebuchadnezzar
2. The punishment of Nebuchadnezzar
3. The praise from Nebuchadnezzar

## 5. The Heavenly Hand

| | |
|---|---|
| The Ball **DANIEL 5:1** | The Call **DAN. 5:7-23** |
| The Gall **DAN. 5:2-4** | The Scrawl **DAN. 5:24-29** *(writing)* |
| The Wall **DAN. 5:5, 6** | The Fall **DAN. 5:30, 31** |

## 6. The Lions and the Lion-Hearted

**AN EVIL PLAN (6:1-9)**
A plan is instigated by some jealous Chaldeans to trap Daniel by his daily prayer life.

**A KNEELING MAN (6:10-20)**
Daniel continues to pray and is cast into a den of hungry lions.

**A HEAVENLY BAN (6:21-28)**
Daniel is delivered by God's angel, who shuts the mouths of the lions.

There were several reasons behind this project.

   a. To elevate Nebuchadnezzar. Daniel had designated Nebuchadnezzar as the head of gold as he explained the meaning of his statue dream in chapter two. But the vain king wanted to be the whole thing! Bible teacher Bob Thieme writes the following:

"Let us assume for a moment that the image was half as thick as it was wide, or four and a half feet. Using these three dimensions (90 × 9 × 4 ½), we find the volume to be 3645 cubic feet or 4,400,000 pounds! Even at the pre-inflation price of $33 an ounce, this spectacular statue would have cost about $2,315,000,000! Not only does this give us an idea of the fantastic wealth of Nebuchadnezzar's empire, but it reveals the extent of his egomania." (*Daniel*, p. 3)

   b. To consolidate his empire through a common religion. This is the second of three great attempts of man to institute a one-world religion. The first occurred at the Tower of Babel (Gen. 11) and the last will take place in Jerusalem during the tribulation (Rev. 13).

2. The king then requires every VIP in all the empire to assemble in the Plain of Dura on a scheduled day (3:2).

3. When dedication day arrived, an orchestra was on hand (3:5).

4. At the sound of the music, all those assembled were commanded to fall down and worship the statue (3:4, 5).

5. Failure to comply would result in instant death by being thrown into a burning furnace. There is little doubt that the entire crowd could see this furnace and watch it belch forth its fierce yellow and orange flames high into the Babylonian sky. The Romans executed criminals through crucifixion, the Jews by stoning, and the Babylonians by burning. (See Jer. 29:22.) This doubtless was the most persuasive altar call of all times—bow or burn.

B. The Hebrews' stand (3:8–23).

1. Shadrach, Meshach, and Abednego remain standing during the "invitation." This was immediately reported to the king by some jealous petty Babylonian officials (3:8–12).

2. The three young men are brought to Nebuchadnezzar himself and offered a final chance to bow down. (Daniel apparently was not present at the dedication service. His duties as prime minister doubtless required him to travel extensively.) All three refuse, saying:

"O Nebuchadnezzar, we are not careful to answer thee in this matter. If it be so, our God whom we serve, is able to deliver us from the burning fiery furnace, and he will deliver us out of thine hand, O king. But if not, be it known unto thee, O king, that we will not serve thy gods, nor worship the golden image which thou hast set up" (3:16–18).

Especially noteworthy are the words "our God . . . is able." This phrase is often found in the New Testament. (See Heb. 7:25; 2:18; Jude 1:24; Eph. 3:20; 2 Tim. 1:12.) Their testimony was similar to that of Job. (See Job 13:15.)

The three youths were no doubt aware of the many excuses available to them for bowing down at this private meeting.

For example:

   a. Why not join the system. You can't fight city hall!

   b. We'll cooperate with old Neb and win him to Christ!

   c. A living dog is better than a dead lion—better red than dead! "He who fights and runs away lives to fight another day!"

   d. Daniel our leader is not here to make the right decision for us.

All these excuses *could* have been used. But they weren't, for Shadrach, Meshach, and Abednego had been brought up on the Ten Commandments of Moses. Especially burned in their minds was the second law:

"Thou shalt not make unto thee any graven image . . . Thou shalt not bow down thyself to them, nor serve them . . ." (Ex. 20:4, 5).

3. In an insane rage Nebuchadnezzar (who has now totally lost control of himself) orders the furnace to be heated seven times hotter and the three Hebrew heroes bound and cast in (3:19–21).

4. The horrible decree is done, resulting in the deaths of those soldiers who are accidentally burned themselves while throwing the three men in (3:22).

5. All three are seen falling headlong into the hellish fires.

C. The Lord's own man (3:24–30).

1. Finally the furnace has cooled down somewhat and the angry monarch sees something that nearly shocks him senseless. In utter amazement he turns and asks his counselors.

"Did not we cast three men, bound, into the midst of the fire?" (3:24).

Upon being immediately assured that this is indeed the case, the baffled Babylonian then exclaims:

"Lo, I see four men loose, walking in the midst of the fire, and they have no hurt; and the form of the fourth is like the Son of God" (3:25).

Here we note the following:

   a. He sees them walking. Thus the only thing the fire burned was their shackles, for they were all bound when thrown in.

   b. He sees one like the Son of God, or literally, "One like a son of the gods." Nebuchadnezzar was unaware of the Trinity, but he was looking upon the Son of God himself, the Lord Jesus Christ.

IV. A Tree in Turmoil.
  A. The tree (Nebuchadnezzar) corrupted through vanity (4:1-27).
    1. Nebuchadnezzar relates his dream to Daniel (4:1-18)
      a. This chapter could rightly be entitled "Nebuchadnezzar's Tract," as it contains his personal testimony of those events which led him to repentance.
      b. The tree-dream of Nebuchadnezzar occurred probably during the thirtieth and thirty-fifth year of his reign. Daniel was around forty-eight at the time. Some twenty-eight years had elapsed since the fiery furnace event.
      c. "I thought it good" (v. 2), literally, "It was beautiful before me." The king wanted all to know what had happened. (See Isa. 52:7.)
      d. I . . . was at rest (v. 4). The Hebrew here is *raan,* and is an idiom for prosperity. It literally means, "to grow green, to be covered with leaves."
      e. It was during this peaceful time that he experienced this fearful dream. The main features are as follows:
        (1) He saw a large and leafy tree increasing in size until it reached the heavens and was viewed by all. The wild animals and birds were shaded and sheltered by its leafy branches and the entire world was fed from its generous fruit supply (4:10-12).
        (2) Suddenly a heavenly figure appeared and ordered the tree cut down and its fruit scattered. Only the stump was to be left, banded with a chain of iron and brass. This felled tree represented a man who would be given the mind of an animal and remain in this pitiful condition for seven years (4:13-16).
        (3) This all was to be done so the entire world might know that "the most High ruleth in the kingdom of men, and giveth it to whomsoever he will, and setteth up over it the basest of men" (4:17).
    2. Daniel reveals the dream to Nebuchadnezzar (4:19-27).
      a. The interpretation was so frightful that Daniel observed an hour of shocked silence (4:19).
      b. He then revealed the details:
        (1) The tree indeed stood for a man, and that man was Nebuchadnezzar. (Compare Dan. 4:22 with 2 Sam. 12:7.) Often in the Bible trees symbolize various things. A tree can represent a man (Ps. 1:3; Jer. 17:8; Isa. 56:3). It can represent Christendom (Mt. 13:31, 32). It can represent judgment (Deut. 21:23; Gal. 3:13; Heb. 12:2; 1 Pet. 2:24).
        (2) The heavenly visitor was a reconnaissance angel which pronounced judgment upon the tree. (Compare 4:23 with Mt. 3:10; Lk. 13:7.)
        (3) The destruction, however, was not to be total, for the tree was ordered banded about with iron and brass. In the ancient world this was done to keep the stump of a felled tree from splitting, thus making it possible for the tree to grow again. God still had a purpose for Nebuchadnezzar.
        (4) The king would nevertheless suffer a seven-year period of insanity for his pride. During this time he would act and think like a wild animal. This mental illness is not uncommon and is known as zoanthropy or lycanthropy. Often the victim pictures himself as a wolf. As has already been observed, this psychosis would last seven years. The word "times" (Dan. 4:25) is used for units of years both in Daniel (7:25; 12:7) and in Revelation (12:14).
        (5) This affliction would only end when Nebuchadnezzar realized "the powers that be are ordained of God." (Compare 4:25 with Rom. 13:1.)
      c. Daniel then begs the proud monarch to "break off thy sins," but all to no avail (4:27).
  B. The tree (Nebuchadnezzar) corrected through insanity (4:28-37).
    1. The pride of Nebuchadnezzar (4:28-30).
      a. Twelve months after the dream the king is strolling on the roof of the royal palace in Babylon. We note his arrogant boast.
        "Is not this great Babylon, that I have built for the house of the kingdom by the might of my power, and for the honor of my majesty?" (4:30).
        Certainly the ancient city of Babylon was all this, as the following description (taken from Lehman Strauss and others) will bear out:
        Babylon was founded by Nimrod, the great-grandson of Noah (Gen. 10:8-10). Surviving a series of conflicts, it became one of the most magnificent and luxurious cities in the known world. Superbly constructed, it spread over an area of fifteen square miles, the Euphrates River flowing diagonally across the city. The famous historian Herodotus said the city was surrounded by a wall 350 feet high and eighty-seven feet thick—extending thirty-five feet below the ground to prevent tunneling, and wide enough for six chariots to drive abreast.
        Around the top of the wall were 250 watchtowers placed in strategic locations. Outside the huge wall was a large ditch, or moat, which surrounded the city and was kept filled with water from the Euphrates River. The large ditch was meant to serve as an additional protection

against attacking enemies, for any attacking enemy would have to cross this body of water first before approaching the great wall. Within this wall were one hundred gates of brass. But in addition to being a bastion for protection, Babylon was a place of beauty. The famous hanging gardens of Babylon are on record yet today as one of the seven wonders of the world. Arranged in an area 400 feet square, and raised in perfectly cut terraces one above the other, they soared to a height of 350 feet. Viewers could make their way to the top by means of stairways, which were ten feet wide.

From a distance these hanging gardens presented an imposing sight. The tower itself sat on a base 300 feet in breadth and rose to a height of 300 feet. The great temple of Marduk, adjoining the Tower of Babel, was the most renowned sanctuary in all the Euphrates Valley. It contained a golden image of Bel and a golden table which together weighed not less than 50,000 pounds. At the top were golden images of Bel and Ishtar, two golden lions, a golden table forty feet long, fifteen feet wide, and a human figure of solid gold eighteen feet high. Babylon was literally a city of gold! (See Isa. 14:4.) The city had fifty-three temples and 180 altars to Ishtar.

2. The punishment of Nebuchadnezzar (4:31-33).
   a. Even while the king spoke his proud words, the judgment of God fell from heaven and he was driven from the palace (4:31).
   b. We note the sad results of his vanity:
      "He was driven from men, and did eat grass like oxen, and his body was wet with the dew of heaven, till his hairs were grown like eagles' feathers, and his nails like bird claws" (4:33).
      In spite of his helpless condition, he was not harmed during those years of insanity. This was doubtless due to the divine protection of God. In addition to this, it was considered bad luck in the ancient world to kill an insane person. Nebuchadnezzar's malady protected him from physical injury, just as David's feigned madness at Gath spared his life. (See 1 Sam. 21:10-15.)
   c. The king's insanity is corroborated by history. Josephus quotes from a Babylonian historian named Berasus who mentions a strange malady suffered by the king. There is also the testimony of Abydenus, the Greek historian of 268 B.C.

3. The praise of Nebuchadnezzar (4:34-37). Nebuchadnezzar humbles himself and receives the manifold blessings of God. Note these heavenly gifts.
   a. His reason returns ("my reason returned").

   b. His reign is returned ("the glory of my kingdom").
   c. His reputation is returned ("mine honor").
   d. His resplendence is returned ("mine . . . brightness").
   e. His rapport is returned ("my counselors sought unto me").
   f. His rhetoric is returned ("now I, Nebuchadnezzar praise, and extol, and honor").
   g. His redemption is accomplished. (Was Nebuchadnezzar a saved man? The three words praise, extol, and honor are active verbs, indicating continued action. In other words, Nebuchadnezzar continued praising and glorifying God long after his restoration. This would hardly be the action of a pagan.)

V. A Heavenly Hand.
   A. The ball (5:1).
      1. Belshazzar the king stages a huge dinner and drinking party and invites his top 1000 officers to attend. For many years the historical fact of Belshazzar's very existence was doubted by historians. According to the known records, the last king of Babylon was Nabonidus. But recent findings have definitely authenticated Belshazzar's reign over Babylon. Here are the findings of archaeologist Sir Herbert Rawlinson who confirmed Belshazzar's existence in A.D. 1854.
         a. Nebuchadnezzar's only son Amel-Marduk (also called Evil-Merodach in 2 Ki. 25:27; Jer. 52:31-34) succeeded him in 562 B.C.
         b. He was murdered by his brother-in-law Nergal-Sharezer (Jer. 39:3, 13) in August of 560 B.C.
         c. Nergal-Sharezer died and was succeeded by his young son Labashi-Marduk in 556 B.C.
         d. This boy was murdered shortly after his ascension by Nabonidus. Nabonidus married one of Nebuchadnezzar's daughters. Belshazzar was born of this union. Nabonidus, who ruled from 556-539 B.C., for some reason chose not to make Babylon his capital, but left that dazzling city and resided in Tema of Arabia. Belshazzar was thus made the co-regent of Babylon by his father. This fact is brought out several times in Daniel 5 when Belshazzar offers to elevate Daniel to third ruler in the kingdom (see 5:7, 16, 29).
      2. His feast was ill-timed, to say the least, for Babylon had been under attack by the Medes and Persians for some time. Perhaps the feast was to build morale.
   B. The gall (5:2-4).
      1. Belshazzar sits at his table, drunk, depraved, and demon-possessed. Suddenly he is seized with a wild and wicked idea. He is reminded of the gold and silver cups taken by his grandfather Nebuchadnezzar from the Jerusalem Temple. He orders them brought to

the feast and proposes to his guests that they drink wine from them and praise the Babylonian gods.

2. These sacred vessels were originally made by Solomon (1 Ki. 7:48-51), shown by Hezekiah (2 Ki. 20:13), and taken by Nebuchadnezzar (2 Chron. 36:10).

C. The wall (5:5, 6).

1. Suddenly in the midst of this drunken toast, they see the fingers of a man's hand writing on the wall next to the king's table. Belshazzar is terrified! We are told: "Then the king's countenance was changed" (5:6). This is, literally, "his brightness changed." In other words he immediately turned from a drunken pink to a frightened white!

2. Belshazzar "cried aloud" (literally, "in great earnest") for some kind of help, but it was already too late. He would soon experience the fearful warning of Proverbs 1:24-27. Some ten centuries before this a group of Egyptian magicians had testified concerning this heavenly hand in connection with the terrible plagues which had befallen them.

We read:

"Then the magicians said unto Pharaoh, this is the finger of God!" (Ex. 8:19).

D. The call (5:7-23).

1. In his hour of great need, Belshazzar turns to astrology. How little human nature has changed. The United States alone has over fifteen million serious students of astrology.

2. But Belshazzar soon discovers that astrology is no balm in Gilead. No horoscope ever written can heal the hurt in the human heart. His wise men could not help him. This marks their third failure in the book of Daniel.

3. Finally at the suggestion of the queen (probably his mother, Nitocris) Belshazzar summons Daniel (5:10-15).

4. The king offers him the third ruling position if he will interpret the mysterious writing (5:16).

5. Daniel agrees to do so, but spurns the king's bribe. However, before he interprets the message, the aged prophet reviews Belshazzar's wicked past.

a. Belshazzar's grandfather, Nebuchadnezzar, had set a good example for his young grandson when he turned to God after his period of insanity (5:18-21).

b. Belshazzar knew all this, but had deliberately rejected and hardened his heart (5:22, 23). (See also Prov. 29:1.)

c. Belshazzar was thus gambling with his immortal soul, for the very air he breathed came from this God he had so recklessly spurned (5:23).

E. The scrawl (scroll) 5:24-29.

1. The writing contained a threefold message from God to Belshazzar.

a. "Mene, Mene"—God has numbered your kingdom and finished it! His number was up. Belshazzar had not followed the wise advice of Moses when he prayed: "So teach us to number our days, that we may apply our hearts unto wisdom" (Ps. 90:12). Belshazzar's sad end here should be contrasted to Paul's thrilling testimony before his death. (See 2 Tim. 4.)

b. "Tekel"—You are weighed in the balances, and found wanting. Again, by way of contrast, see David's testimony in Psalm 23:1. The words "found wanting" mean literally "found too light." Belshazzar's morality didn't weigh enough!

c. "Peres" ("Upharsin" is the plural of this word)—your kingdom is divided and given to the Medes and Persians.

F. The fall (5:30, 31).

1. The Greek historian Herodotus tells us that the Babylonian armies at first moved north to challenge the advancing Persian troops, but were soon driven back behind the walls of Babylon. Cyrus then proceeded to divert the Euphrates River from its normal bed, under the walls of the city, channeling the waters to a nearby reservoir he had dug. Another Greek historian, Xenophon, states that entrance was made into the city at a time when the Babylonians were feasting at a drunken orgy.

2. Belshazzar is slain that very night and the city is ruled by a sixty-two-year-old Mede named Darius.

3. The prophet Isaiah predicted the fall of Babylon over two hundred years in advance. (See Isa. 21:1-10.)

VI. The Lions and the Lion-hearted.

A. An evil plan (6:1-9).

1. Darius, the Mede, immediately sets about to reorganize and consolidate his fantastic new kingdom called Babylon. He divides the kingdom into 129 provinces, each under a governor. These governors are accountable to three presidents, with Daniel being one of the three. There has been some historical question raised concerning the identity of Darius. Three main explanations have been offered:

a. That he was really Cyrus under a different name.

b. That he was Cambyses, the son of Cyrus.

c. That he was a special "presidential assistant" named Gubaru, who was appointed by the great Persian king, Cyrus, to rule over this city for him. The third view seems the most logical one.

2. Daniel, now over eighty, was still blessed with so much skill and ability that Darius was considering elevating him over the other two presidents (6:3).

3. This so infuriated both the presidents and the governors that they plotted to take away his life (6:4).

4. Being unable to see the slightest flaw in his secular life, they determine to trap him in his religious life (6:5).

5. Darius is tricked into signing a thirty-day decree which says that all praying during that time is to be directed to the king himself (6:6-9).

B. A kneeling man (6:10–20).
1. Daniel learns of this and doubtless immediately sees through its clumsy effort to trap him. But the old warrior continues worshiping God as before. We note:
   a. He kept his windows opened. To close them would have been cowardly. To open them (had this not been his custom) would have been foolhardy.
   b. He continued praying three times a day, in the morning, at noon, and in the evening.
   c. He knelt down. This is perhaps the most common prayer posture depicted in the Bible.
   d. He faced Jerusalem. Solomon had given this procedure in his dedicatory prayer of the Temple. (See 1 Ki. 8:44–48; 2 Chron. 6:36–39.)
2. Those vicious hunters who had set their trap now see the prey inside and gleefully rush to Darius to deliver the death blow. Darius realizes he has been had and desperately seeks to find a loophole in the immutable law of the Medes and Persians, but all to no avail (6:11–15).
3. Daniel is arrested and thrown down into a den of hungry man-eating lions. In the Bible the devil is often likened to a lion. (See Ps. 10:9; 57:4; 2 Tim. 4:17; 1 Pet. 5:8; Dan. 6:16.)
4. After sealing the mouth of the den with his own signet ring, Darius returns and spends a sleepless and miserable night in the royal palace (6:17, 18).
5. At daybreak the next morning he rushes to the den, orders the cap stone removed, and calls out in anguish:
   "O Daniel, servant of the living God, is thy God, whom thou servest continually, able to deliver thee from the lions?" (6:20).
C. A heavenly ban (6:21–28).
1. Out of the blackness of that den of doom there comes a cheerful and clear voice:
   "O king, live for ever. My God hath sent his angel, and hath shut the lions' mouths, that they have not hurt me; forasmuch as before him innocency was found in me; and also before thee, O king, have I done no hurt" (6:21, 22).
   Peter and Paul doubtless had this thrilling event in mind when they later wrote:
   "Who, through faith, subdued kingdoms, wrought righteousness, obtained promises, stopped the mouths of lions" (Heb. 11:33).
   "Wherefore, let them that suffer according to the will of God commit the keeping of their souls to him in well-doing, as unto a faithful Creator" (1 Pet. 4:19).
   That same heavenly messenger who had saved Daniel's three friends in the furnace now protected the prophet in the den.
2. The king's reaction to all this was twofold; he was both glad and mad!
   a. He rejoiced at the salvation of Daniel and issued a decree ordering all the citizens of his kingdom to consider this almighty Judean God (6:23, 25–27).
   b. He took immediate vengeance upon those who had tricked him in the first place and ordered them along with all their families thrown into this same den. Their bodies were instantly torn apart by the lions (6:24). Persian law was much more cruel than Hebrew law. (See Ezek. 18:20; Deut. 24:16; 2 Ki. 14:6; 2 Chron. 25:4; Jer. 31:29, 30.)

VII. Godless Kingdoms and the Kingdom of God.
A. Nebuchadnezzar, the Babylonian lion (7:4)—also the head of gold in 2:32.
1. In this vision Daniel sees the same four godless kingdoms and the final kingdom of God that Nebuchadnezzar had dreamed of in chapter 2. But he sees it from an entirely different viewpoint. As has already been brought out, man may see his kingdoms as gleaming metals such as gold and silver, but God looks upon them as wild and ravenous beasts.
2. Daniel sees a great storm on a mighty ocean with four winds blowing from every direction. (See Rev. 7:2; Eph. 2:2; 6:12.) These winds may indicate satanic forces.
3. The first beast symbolized Nebuchadnezzar and Babylon.
   a. It was like a lion. (See Jer. 4:7; 49:19; 50:17, 43, 44.)
   b. It had eagle's wings. (See Jer. 48:40; 49:22; Lam. 4:19; Ezek. 17:3; Hab. 1:8.) Nebuchadnezzar showed these wings at the Battle of Carchemish in 605 B.C.
   c. Those wings were plucked. See Daniel 4:33 (Nebuchadnezzar's wings), and Daniel 5:31 (Babylon's wings).
B. Cyrus, the Persian bear (7:5)—also the silver breast and arms in 2:32.
1. This bear raised itself up on one side, probably referring to the stronger Persian part of the Mede and Persian dual alliance.
2. It had three ribs in its mouth, a reference to Babylon, Egypt, and Lydia, three nations Persia had just conquered.
3. It would devour much flesh. The Persian King Xerxes led a force of over one and one half million men and 300 ships into Greece alone.
C. Alexander, the Grecian leopard (7:6)—also the bronze stomach and thighs of 2:32.
1. It was like a leopard. Alexander traveled faster and conquered more land than any other man in all recorded history.
2. It had four heads. After his untimely death at 32, his kingdom fell to four of his generals.
D. Little horn, the Roman monster (7:7, 8)—also the iron legs and clay and iron feet of 2:33.
1. In A.D. 476 this monster "retired" to its den for awhile to hibernate.
2. It will awaken in the form of ten nations during the tribulation by the little horn, who is none other than the antichrist! He is called

the man of sin in 2 Thessalonians 2:3, 4 and the sea beast in Revelation 13:1.

3. The antichrist will defeat three of these ten kingdoms (horn) in his rise to power (7:8).

4. He will have a universal rule during the final three-and-a-half years of the tribulation (7:25). (See also Rev. 13:5; Mt. 24:21.)

5. He will shed blood upon his earth in an unprecedented manner (7:7, 19).

6. He will wear out the saints of God (Israel) (7:25). (See also Rev. 12:13.)

7. He will attempt to change seasons and laws (7:25).

8. He will blaspheme God (7:25). (See also Rev. 13:5, 6.)

9. He will be defeated at the coming of Christ and his body given over to the flames of hell (7:11).

E. Jesus Christ, the King of kings (7:13, 14)—also the smiting Stone of 2:34.

1. He comes in the clouds to claim his rightful earthly inheritance (7:13). Our Lord warned Israel's wicked high priest of this very coming during the unfair trial that led him to Calvary. (See Mk. 14:61, 62.)

2. He is given his universal and eternal throne by his Father, the Ancient of Days (7:9, 13, 14). This is the only description of the Father in the Bible, and corresponds to John's description of Jesus in Revelation 1:9-18. Both David (Ps. 2:6-9) and the angel Gabriel (Lk. 1:32) predict this throne Christ receives from his Father.

3. Daniel sees a continuous river of fire gushing from the throne (7:10). This stream of judgment (Heb. 12:29; Isa. 66:15, 16; 2 Thess. 1:8) will later turn into a fountain of blessing after the Great White Throne Judgment is completed. (See Rev. 22:1.)

4. Millions of angels stand and minister to the Ancient of Days and his Son (7:10). (A similar immense number of angels is mentioned in Rev. 5:11; Ps. 68:17; Heb. 12:22.)

5. Hundreds of millions stand before him ready to be judged and the books are opened (7:10). (See also Rev. 20:11-15.)

VIII. The Horns of the Heathen.

A. A two-horned ram (Persia, as represented by Darius III) (8:1-4).

1. In this vision Daniel sees himself in the fortress of Shushan (or Susa), a city some 230 miles east of Babylon and 120 miles north of the Persian Gulf.

2. He sees a victorious ram, coming from the east, and pushing its way westward, northward, and to the south. This, of course, represented the Persian conquests which included Syria (west), Armenia (north), and Egypt (south). Marcellinus, a fourth-century historian, states that the Persian ruler bore the head of a ram as he stood in front of his army.

B. A one-horned goat (Greece, as represented by Alexander the Great) (8:5-8).

1. Daniel then sees a goat from the west which rushes toward the ram, smashes it to the ground, and stomps it to pieces.

## 7. Godless Kingdoms and the Kingdom of God

*"And four great beasts came up from the sea . . ."* (7:3)

*"Behold, one like the Son of man came with the clouds . . ."* (7:13)

| KINGDOM | SYMBOL | REPRESENTATIVE |
|---|---|---|
| **BABYLON** 7:4 (2:37, 38) | A LION | Nebuchadnezzar |
| **PERSIA** 7:5 (2:39) | A BEAR | Cyrus |
| **GREECE** 7:6 (2:39) | A LEOPARD | Alexander the Great |
| **ROME** 7:7, 8 (2:40-43) | A ONE-HORNED MONSTER WITH TERRIBLE TEETH | HISTORICAL: Roman Caesars  PROPHETICAL: Antichrist |
| **EVERLASTING KINGDOM** 7:9-14 (2:44, 45) | THE SON OF MAN | The Lord Jesus Christ |

2. This prophecy of the ram and goat places a microscope down on the conflict between the second and third world empire in the struggle of East and West, of Orient and Occident, of Asia and Europe. Historical drawings have been discovered which depict a one-horned goat as the symbol for the ancient Greek armies.

3. We are told the goat was "moved with choler" against the ram. The driving energy and holy crusade of Alexander was to crush the hated Persian who had invaded Greece. As we have previously seen, he totally routed the Persians on three separate occasions:

a. at Granicus, in 334 B.C.

b. at Issus, in 333 B.C.

c. at Arbela, in 331 B.C.

An interesting footnote of history may be added here. Josephus tells us that Alexander was met outside Jerusalem by Juddua, Israel's high priest, who came dressed in all his magnificent apparel, and showed the Greek conqueror how a Hebrew prophet, Daniel by name, had predicted his defeat over the Persians some 225 years ago. The high priest then proceeded to read Daniel 8, whereupon Alexander fell down and worshiped him.

4. Daniel sees this powerful horn suddenly broken and its might divided fourfold. Alexander died in Babylon during a drunken orgy at the age of thirty-two, in 323 B.C. His kingdom was then divided among his four leading generals.

a. Ptolemy took the southern part, Egypt
b. Seleucus, the eastern section, Syria
c. Cassander, the western division, Greece
d. Lysimachus, the northern area, Asia Minor

C. Two little-horned kings (Syria and the revived Roman Empire and represented by Antiochus Epiphanes and the antichrist) 8:9–27. We note that the archangel Gabriel interpreted all this to Daniel. This is the first mention of him in the Bible. (See also 9:21; Lk. 1:19, 26.)

1. The historical little horn—Antiochus Epiphanes.

a. He was a Syrian.
b. He came to the throne in 175 B.C. and ruled until 164 B.C.
c. He was anti-Semitic to the core. He assaulted Jerusalem, murdering over 40,000 in three days, and selling an equal number into cruel slavery. It is thought that on September 6, 171 B.C., he began his evil actions toward the Temple.
d. On December 15, 168, his Temple desecration reached its ultimate low, for on that day this idolater sacrificed a giant sow on an idol altar he had made in the Jewish Temple. He then forced the priests to swallow its flesh, made a broth of it, and sprinkled all the Temple. He finally carried off the golden candlesticks, table of shrewbread, altar of incense, various other vessels, and destroyed the sacred books of the Law. A large image of Jupiter was placed in the Holy of Holies. All this was termed by the horrified Jews as "the abomination of desolation," and is referred to by Jesus in Matthew 24:15 as a springboard to describe the activities of the future antichrist.
e. All through Palestine altars to Jupiter were set up and the Jews were forced to sacrifice on them. But at a little Jewish town called Modin (seventeen miles northwest of Jerusalem) there lived a Jewish priest named Mattathias, of the House of Hasmon. He had five sons and this brave old man not only refused to worship Antiochus' idols, but boldly slew the king's religious ambassador. The Jewish revolt was on. One of his sons was named Judas and he was called the Maccabee (meaning, the hammer).

For the next few years Judas successfully led an army of Jews against the Syrians. Their brave exploits are described in two Apocrypha books, first and second Maccabees. On December 25, 165 B.C., the Jewish patriots cleansed and rededicated the Temple Antiochus had defiled. This later became a Jewish holiday known as the Feast of Dedication (see Jn. 10:22).

Note: In 8:14 there is a time period of 2300 days mentioned. This apparently began on September 6, 171 B.C. and ended on December 25, 165 B.C. It was, however, on the basis of this period that William Miller, founder of the modern Seventh Day Adventist movement, went astray. He made the days stand for years and arrived at the date of October 22, 1844, for the return of Christ!

f. Antiochus died in Babylon in 164 B.C. after being soundly defeated in battle.

2. The prophetical little horn—the antichrist. The future enemy of Israel will do all his forerunner did and much more. The following comparisons can be seen between the two:

a. Both would conquer much (Dan. 8:9; Rev. 13:4).
b. Both would magnify themselves (Dan. 8:11; Rev. 13:15).

---

# 8. The Horns of the Heathen

| KINGDOM | SYMBOL | REPRESENTATIVE |
|---|---|---|
| **MEDES AND PERSIANS** | A TWO-HORNED RAM 8:1-4, 20 | Darius III |
| **GREECE** | A ONE-HORNED GOAT 8:5-8, 21, 22 | Alexander |
| PAST **SYRIA** | TWO LITTLE HORNED KINGS 8:9-20, 23-27 | Antiochus Epiphanes |
| FUTURE **REVIVED ROMAN EMPIRE** | | Antichrist |

**Darius III and Alexander**

Some 250 years in advance, Daniel predicts the resounding defeat of Darius III at the hands of Alexander in 332 B.C.

At Alexander's death (age 32) his kingdom was divided by his four generals.

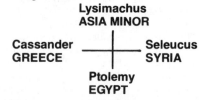

Lysimachus
ASIA MINOR

Cassander
GREECE

Seleucus
SYRIA

Ptolemy
EGYPT

Both to conquer much **(Dan. 8:9; Rev. 13:4)**
Both to magnify themselves **(8:11; Rev. 13:15)**
Both deceitful **(8:25; 2 Thess. 2:10)**
Both offer a false peace program **(8:25; 1 Thess. 5:2)**
Both hate and persecute Israel **(8:25; Rev. 12:13)**
Both profane the Temple **(8:11; Mt. 24:15)**
Both energized by Satan **(8:24; Rev. 13:2)**
Both active in Middle East for seven years **(8:14; 9:27)**
Both to speak against God **(8:25; 2 Thess. 2:4)**
Both to be destroyed by God **(8:25; Rev. 19:19, 20)**

c. Both would be masters of deceit (Dan. 7:25; 2 Thess. 2:10).

d. Both would offer a false "peace program" (Dan. 8:25; 1 Thess. 5:2, 3).

e. Both would hate and persecute Israel (Dan. 8:25; Rev. 12:13).

f. Both would profane the Temple (Dan. 8:11; Mt. 24:15).

g. Both would be energized by Satan (Dan. 8:24; Rev. 13:2).

h. Both would be active in the Middle East for about seven years (Dan. 8:14; 9:27).

i. Both would speak against the Lord God (Dan. 8:25).

j. Both would be utterly destroyed by God (Dan. 8:25) (Rev. 19:19, 20).

IX. The Secret of the Seventy Sevens

A. Daniel—the prayer of a prophet (9:1-19).

1. This is one of the greatest chapters in all the Bible. It has a double theme, that of prayer and prophecy. At this time Daniel was about eighty-five.

2. Daniel was reading from the book of Jeremiah (the old prophet had probably become the official custodian of various Old Testament books after the destruction of the Temple) and was reminded that God had determined Jerusalem must lie desolate for seventy years. (See Jer. 25:11; 29:10.)

3. He then began an intense and prolonged prayer to God, concerning both his personal sins and those national sins of Israel which had caused the captivity in the first place. His prayer was accompanied by fasting, sackcloth, and ashes (9:1-3). These three actions were customary for the day when genuine contriteness of heart was felt. (See Ezra 8:23; Neh. 9:1; Est. 4:1, 3, 16; Job 2:12; Jonah 3:5, 6.)

4. He reminds God of his covenants (9:4), possibly thinking of the Abrahamic Covenant (which promised Israel the land of Palestine forever) (Gen. 12:7; 13:14, 15-17; 15:7; 18-21; 17:8), and the Davidic Covenant (which guaranteed Israel an everlasting king and kingdom) (2 Chron. 13:5; 2 Sam. 7:12-16; 23:5).

5. He contrasts the grace and goodness of God with the immorality and idolatry of Israel (9:5, 7, 8, 9).

6. He mentions Judah's kings (9:8). Two of them had been carried off into the Babylonian captivity along with the Jewish people.

7. He fully agreed that Judah had gotten just what she deserved and that God meant just what he said when he warned them about disobedience and punishment (9:12-14). (See Lev. 26.)

8. He ends his prayer by throwing both himself and his people completely upon the manifold grace of God:

"For we do not present our supplications before thee for our righteousness, but for thy great mercies" (9:18).

B. Gabriel—the prophecy of an angel (9:20-27). Even while Daniel was praying, God sent Gabriel the archangel to both minister to him and ex-

plain the most important, the most amazing, and the most profound single prophecy in the entire Word of God! For another example of God answering even while his child was praying, see Genesis 24:15. Note the message of this mighty angel in 9:24-27. We will now consider this prophecy by asking and attempting to answer six key questions.

1. To whom does this prophecy refer? It refers to Israel.

2. What is meant by the term "seventy weeks"? In his correspondence course on the book of Daniel, Dr. Alfred Martin of Moody Bible Institute writes the following helpful words:

"The expression translated 'seventy weeks' is literally 'seventy sevens.' Apart from the context one would not know what the 'sevens' were. One would have to inquire, 'seven' of what? This expression in Hebrew would be as ambiguous as if one were to say in English, 'I went to the store and bought a dozen.' A dozen of what? One of the basic principles of interpretation is that one must always interpret in the light of the context, that is, in the light of the passage in which a given statement occurs. As one searches this context, remembering that the vision was given in answer to the prayer, one notes that Daniel had been reading in Jeremiah that God would 'accomplish seventy years in the desolations of Jerusalem' (Dan. 9:2). This is the clue. Daniel is told in effect, 'Yes, God will accomplish seventy years in the captivity; but now He is showing you that the whole history of the people of Israel will be consummated in a period of seventy sevens of years.'" (*Daniel, the Framework of Prophecy*, pp. 85, 86)

To further clarify the meaning of the seventy weeks, it should be noted that Israel had in its calendar not only a week of seven days (as in Ex. 23:12) but also a "week" of seven years (Lev. 25:3, 4, 8-10; Gen. 29:27, 28). In other words, God is here telling Daniel that he would continue to deal with Israel for another 490 years before bringing in everlasting righteousness.

To summarize this particular point:

a. Israel was to allow its land to remain idle every seventh year (Lev. 25:1-4).

b. This command was disobeyed (Lev. 26:33-35; Jer. 34:12-22; 2 Chron. 36:21).

c. Finally, over a total period of 490 years, the nation had built up a land rest debt of seventy years.

d. Daniel knew of all this and was praying about it. He recognized that the seventy years of captivity represented seventy sevens of years in which those violations had transpired.

e. Gabriel now tells him that another period, similar in length (490 years) to that which had made the exile necessary, was coming in the experience of the people.

3. When was the seventy-week period to begin? It was to begin with the command to

rebuild Jerusalem's walls. The first two chapters of Nehemiah inform us that this command was issued during the twentieth year of Artaxerxes' accession. The *Encyclopedia Britannica* sets this date on March 14, 445 B.C.

4. What are the distinct time periods mentioned within the seventy-week prophecy and what was to happen during each period?

# 9. The Secret of the Seventy Sevens

## DANIEL: THE PRAYER OF A PROPHET

| | |
|---|---|
| TIME OF THE PRAYER | First year of Persian rule 538 B.C. **(9:2)** |
| OCCASION FOR THE PRAYER | Daniel's understanding of Jeremiah's prophecy **(9:2)** |
| BASIS FOR THE PRAYER | The promise of God **(9:4)** The mercy of God **(9:9, 18)** |
| CONFESSION IN THE PRAYER | "We have sinned!" **(9:5, 8, 9, 11, 15, 16)** |
| REQUESTS IN THE PRAYER | That God would bring them out of Babylon as he once did out of Egypt **(9:15)** That God would forgive **(9:19)** That God would allow the Temple to be rebuilt in Jerusalem **(9:16, 17)** |
| ANSWER TO PRAYER | "Yea, while I was . . . in prayer . . . Gabriel . . . touched me . . ." **(9:21)**. |

## GABRIEL: THE PROPHECY OF AN ANGEL

| QUESTIONS | ANSWERS | |
|---|---|---|
| TO WHOM DOES THE PROPHECY REFER? | Israel **(9:24)** | |
| WHAT ARE THE SEVENTY WEEKS? | They refer to seven years of years, or 490 years. | |
| WHEN WOULD THIS PERIOD BEGIN? | At the rebuilding of Jerusalem's walls. March 14, 445 B.C. | |
| WHAT ARE THE THREE TIME PERIODS WITHIN THE SEVENTY WEEKS? WHAT HAPPENED DURING EACH PERIOD? | Seven "weeks" or forty-nine years | **FROM 445-396 B.C.** Walls of Jerusalem to be rebuilt in troublous times. |
| | Sixty-two "weeks" or 434 years | **FROM 396 B.C. TO 32 A.D.** Messiah to be crucified |

### CHURCH AGE

| | |
|---|---|
| One "week" or seven years | From rapture to Armageddon Ministry of antichrist and return of true Christ. |

(Taken from *Daniel's Prophecy of The Seventy Weeks,* By A. J. McClain, pages 30-31)

a. First period.
Seven weeks (forty-nine years), from 445 B.C. to 396 B.C. The key events during this time were the building of the streets and walls of Jerusalem "even in troublous times." This literally took place! (See Neh. 2-6.)

b. Second period.
Sixty-two weeks (434 years), from 396 B.C. to A.D. 30. At the end of this second period the Messiah was crucified! (See Mt. 27; Mk. 15; Lk. 23; Jn. 19.)
The brilliant British scholar and Bible student, Sir Robert Anderson, has reduced the first two periods into their exact number of days. This he has done by multiplying 483 (the combined years of the first two periods) by 360 (the days in a biblical year, as pointed out in Gen. 7:11, 24; 8:3, 4).
The total number of days in the first sixty-nine weeks (or 483 years) is 173,880. Anderson then points out that if one begins counting on March 14, 445 B.C., and goes forward in history, these days would run out on April 6, A.D. 32.
It was on this very day that Jesus made his triumphal entry into the city of Jerusalem! Surely our Lord must have had Daniel's prophecy in mind when he said:
"If thou hadst known, even thou, at least in this thy day, the things which belong to thy peace! But now they are hid from thine eyes" (Lk. 19:42).
Of course, it was on this same day that the Pharisees plotted to murder Christ (Lk. 19:47).
Thus Daniel, writing some five and one-half centuries earlier, correctly predicted the very day of Christ's presentation and rejection.

c. Third period—one week (seven years) from the rapture until the millennium. At the beginning of this period the antichrist will make his pact with Israel and will begin his terrible bloodbath. At the end of the last week (and of the entire seventy-week period), the true Messiah will come and establish his perfect millennium.

5. Do the seventy weeks run continuously? This is to say, is there a gap somewhere in these 490 years, or do they run without pause until they are completed?
Dispensational theology teaches that these "weeks" do not run continuously, but that there has been a gap or parenthesis of nearly 2000 years between the sixty-ninth and seventieth week. The chronology may be likened to a seventy-minute basketball game. For sixty-nine minutes the game has been played at a furious and continuous pace. Then the referee for some reason calls time out with the clock in the red and showing one final minute of play. No one knows for sure when the action will start again, but at some point the referee will step in and blow

his whistle. At that time the teams will gather to play out the last minute of the game.

God has stepped in and stopped the clock of prophecy at Calvary. This divine "time out" has already lasted some twenty centuries, but soon the Redeemer will blow his trumpet and the final "week" of action will be played upon this earth.

6. Does the Bible offer any other examples of time gaps in divine programs? It does indeed. At least three instances come to mind in which gaps of many centuries can be found in a single short paragraph.
   a. Isaiah 9:6, 7.
      In the first part of verse 6 a gap of at least twenty centuries is separated by a colon. The phrase "unto us a son is given" refers to Bethlehem, while the words "and the government shall be upon his shoulder" look forward to the millennium.
   b. Zechariah 9:9, 10.
      Verse 9 is a clear reference to the triumphal entry of our Lord, but verse 10 looks ahead to the millennium.
   c. Isaiah 61:1, 2.
      In verse 2 of this passage Christ's earthly ministry (to "proclaim the acceptable year of the Lord") and the tribulation (the "day of vengeance of our God") are separated by only a comma. It is extremely important to note that when Jesus read this passage during his sermon in Nazareth, he ended the reading at this comma, for "the day of vengeance" was not the purpose of his first coming. (See Lk. 4:18, 19.)

As a final brief review of the seventy weeks, we may note:

7. The six main accomplishments of the seventy weeks.
   a. To bring to an end all human transgressions and sins, especially those of the nation Israel (Acts 3:13-16; 28:25-31; Ezek. 37:23; Rom. 11:26, 27).
   b. To make reconciliation for iniquity. This was done at Calvary when the Messiah was cut off (2 Cor. 5:18-20).
   c. To vindicate by fulfillment all true prophets and their prophecies.
   d. To prove the inability of the devil to rightfully rule this world.
   e. To destroy him and his chief henchman, the antichrist (Rev. 19:20; 20:10).
   f. To usher in the millennium (Ps. 45:3-7; Isa. 11:3-5; Jer. 23:3-8).
8. The three main time-periods of the seventy weeks (490 years).
   a. First period—(forty-nine years, or seven weeks) from 445 to 396 B.C.
   b. Second Period—(434 years, or sixty-two weeks) from 396 B.C. to A.D. 32.
   c. A time out period (which has already lasted almost twenty centuries). This time gap between the sixty-ninth and seventieth week was unrevealed and therefore unknown to the Old Testament

prophets. (See Eph. 3:1-10; 1 Pet. 1:10-12.)
   d. Third period (seven years, or one week) from the rapture until the millennium.
9. The two main individuals of the seventy weeks.
   a. Messiah—the Lord Jesus Christ.
   b. The prince that shall come—the wicked antichrist.

X. The Conflict Above the Clouds.
   A. A man in mourning (10:1-4).
      1. Daniel had set aside a period of three weeks to be alone with God. During that time, he refrained from eating food, drinking wine, and anointing himself. The latter was usually done daily with oil to guard oneself against the fierce desert sun.
      2. There may have been several reasons which prompted this season of sorrow.
         a. because of the sins of his people
         b. because of the long period (490 years) of suffering his people must still go through (chapter 9)
         c. because of the paltry few (around 40,000) Jews who had elected to return under Zerubbabel. Some two years had already gone by since Cyrus issued his decree (Ezra 1:1-4) allowing them to return to Jerusalem.
         d. because of the hardships those returning Jews were experiencing.
            Note: God had apparently denied Daniel this opportunity to return. This was due perhaps to his advanced age (around ninety) and also the fact that his high governmental position could be used in helping the returning remnant.
   B. An angel in attendance (10:5-21).
      1. The description of the angel (10:5-9).
         a. Daniel immediately grows pale and weak with fright at such a dazzling sight. Some believe this angel to have been Jesus.

# 10. The Conflict Above the Clouds

**A MAN GREATLY BELOVED**
**THE MAN OF GOD**

- Daniel had been fasting and praying for three weeks on the banks of the River Tigris.
- Several possible reasons for this:
1. Because so few were elected to go back to Jerusalem.
2. Because of the heartaches of those who did go back.
3. Because of Israel's future sufferings, implied in the seventy-week prophecy.

**A MAN CLOTHED IN LINEN**
**THE ANGEL OF GOD**

- The description of the angel **(10:5-9)**
- The declaration of the angel **(10:10-17)**
1. He had been *hindered* by the prince of Persia.
2. He had been *helped* by the archangel Michael.
- The duty of the angel **(10:18, 19)**—to strengthen and to encourage Daniel.
- The determination of the angel **(10:20, 21)**—to again fight against the prince of Persia.

While a similar description is found in Revelation 1:12-16, it would not appear that the angel in Daniel can be identified with Christ. In 10:13 the angel had to call upon Michael, another angel, to help him. It is obvious that the Savior would have needed no help.

b. The men with Daniel were also filled with terror, although they did not actually see the vision as did Daniel (10:7). (See a similar event in Acts 9:7, 8.)

2. The declaration of the angel (10:10-19).

a. He had been hindered by the prince of Persia (10:13). Who was this prince? We quickly note that:

(1) He was powerful—he singlehandedly blocked one of heaven's mightiest angels for twenty-one days.

(2) He was perverted—he withstood God's divinely appointed messenger. Thus, he must have been a high ranking demon assigned by Satan to Persia to control the demonic activities in that kingdom. (See also Jn. 12:31; 14:30; 16:11; Mt. 9:34; 12:24; Isa. 24:21.)

b. He had been helped by the archangel Michael (10:13). This is the other archangel mentioned in the Bible. He is mentioned three times in the Old Testament (Dan. 10:13, 21; 12:1) and twice in the New Testament (Jude 1:9; Rev. 12:7). This was a mutual thing, however, for the angel here had once helped Michael. (See Dan. 11:1.)

Here the veil is momentarily lifted upon the heavenly warfare which believers, demons, and angels are engaged in. (See the following passages: 2 Cor. 10:3-5; Eph. 6:12; Rom. 8:38; Eph. 1:21; 3:10; Col. 2:15.)

This angel then proceeds to comfort, reassure, strengthen, and instruct Daniel concerning the end times.

3. The duty of the angel (10:18, 19).

4. The determination of the angel (10:20, 21). As he returned to God, the angel was aware that not only would he be once again confronted by the Persian demon, but also the demon of Greece. Apparently Satan was throwing in new support by sending into battle his future appointee over the Grecian empire. But the angel was confident, knowing he could again count on the help of Michael.

XI. A Chronology of Ungodly Kings. This chapter gives the most detailed account of history in all the Bible. It covers events occurring from approximately 529 to 164 B.C. It also describes many things which will yet transpire during the future tribulation. But the amazing thing is that Daniel wrote it all down in 540 B.C.

A. Alexander the Great (11:1-20), including his predecessors and successors.

1. Four Persian kings would rule after Cyrus (who was ruling when Daniel wrote this) and the fourth would be the richest of all. This happened (11:2).

a. Cambyses (529-522)

b. Smerdis (522-521)

c. Darius Hystaspes (521-486)

d. Xerxes (486-465) (He was by far the richest, see Est. 1:1-12)

2. After this, a mighty king would rule (11:3). This was Alexander the Great (336-323).

3. This king would suddenly die in his prime. His kingdom would not be given to his posterity, but would be divided up by outsiders into four sections (11:4). This is what happened. Shortly after his death, Philip, his half-brother; Alexander II, his legitimate son; and Hercules, his illegitimate son, were all three murdered and Alexander's four generals took over.

4. One of the generals, Ptolemy, would begin a southern dynasty in Egypt, and another general, Seleucus, would do the same through a northern dynasty in Syria. Ptolemy ruled from 323-283 B.C. and Seleucus from 304-281 B.C. (11:5).

5. These two kings would fight but later their countries would enter into an alliance (11:6). Egypt and Syria did make an alliance in 250 B.C. It happened after both generals had died when Ptolemy II Philadelphus (283-246), the son of Ptolemy I, gave his daughter Bernice in marriage to Antiochus II Theos (262-246), the grandson of Seleucus.

6. Two years later her father, Ptolemy II, died, and her husband Antiochus divorced her and remarried his former wife, whose name was Laodice.

7. Laodice, still bearing a grudge, poisoned Antiochus and had Bernice murdered. She then appointed her son, Seleucus II to become King of Syria.

8. Meanwhile, in Egypt, Bernice's brother, Ptolemy III, succeeded his father on the throne. He ruled from 246-221 B.C.

9. Ptolemy III invaded Syria and revenged his sister's death by executing Laodice. Seleucus II hid out in Asia Minor during this Egyptian invasion.

10. Ptolemy III then carried away much Syrian loot, including 40,000 talents of silver, and 2500 precious vessels (11:8-11).

11. In 240 B.C. Seleucus II attempted unsuccessfully to counterattack Ptolemy III in Egypt. Seleucus died and was succeeded by his son Antiochus III (also known as the Great). Antiochus ruled Syria from 223-187 B.C.

12. Ptolemy III died and was succeeded by his son, Ptolemy IV Philopaton (221-204).

13. These two kings (Antiochus III and Ptolemy IV) met head on in a crucial battle at Raphia in 217 B.C. This battle, where both sides used massive elephants, was won by Ptolemy IV.

14. In 203 B.C. Ptolemy IV died and was succeeded by Ptolemy V Epiphanes (203-181).

15. In 198 B.C. Antiochus the Great wrestled control of Palestine from Ptolemy V at a battle outside Sidon.

16. In 193 Antiochus the Great gave his daughter Cleopatra to marry Ptolemy V. (Note: This was not the famous Cleopatra of history, for

she would not come along until 69 B.C.) The reason for this marriage was to keep Egypt off his flank when he pursued warfare against Rome. Antiochus the Great also hoped Cleopatra would foster Syrian interests in Egypt, for he still secretly planned to conquer Egypt. But Cleopatra turned out to be a loyal wife.

17. Antiochus the Great was at this point joined by the renowned self-exiled Hannibal from Carthage. Together they invaded Greece, but in 188 B.C. were completely driven out of that part of the world by Rome.

18. Antiochus' grandiose plans failed utterly. He died in 187 B.C. (11:19).

19. His older son, Seleucus IV Philopator (187-176), then ruled, but was later murdered by his own prime minister (11:20).

B. Antiochus Epiphanes (11:21-35).

1. He was the youngest son of Antiochus the Great and is immediately classified as a vile (or contemptible) person by the Word of God (11:21).

2. He was nicknamed "Epimanes" ("madman") by those who knew him best.

3. He practiced deceit and pretended to be a second century Robin Hood (1 Macc. 3:29-31).

4. In 170 he defeated the Egyptian King Ptolemy Philometor (181-145) at a battle just east of the Nile delta. This young king was his own nephew, for his mother, Cleopatra, was Antiochus' sister.

5. Ptolemy lost this battle because he was betrayed by some of his friends who sat at his own table (11:26).

6. Antiochus then took his young nephew to Syria and pretended to befriend him. But neither the uncle nor the nephew trusted each other (11:27).

7. Antiochus had hoped to capture Egypt, but was stopped coldly by the mighty Romans (11:30).

8. He took out his insane rage on the city of Jerusalem (11:28-35).

C. Antichrist (11:36-45).

1. He shall do everything according to his own selfish will (11:36). (See also Rev. 13:7; 17:13.)

2. He shall magnify himself and malign God (11:36). (See also 2 Thess. 2:4; Rev. 13:6.) The word meaning "marvelous things" in this verse is literally "astonishing, unbelievable." The antichrist will scream out unbelievable blasphemies against God, insults no one else could ever think of, or would dare say if they could!

3. He will be allowed by God to prosper (given full rope) during the tribulation (the indignation) 11:36. (See also Rev. 11:7; 13:4, 7, 10.) The phrase "that which is determined shall be done," however, reminds us that God is still in absolute control, even during the terrible reign of this monster.

4. He will not regard "the gods of his fathers" (11:37). The word for God is plural. The antichrist will carry out a vendetta against all organized religion. In fact it is he who will

destroy that great harlot, bloody Babylon, which is the super world church. (See Rev. 17:5, 16.)

5. He will not have the desire for (or of) women (11:37). Here three theories are offered to explain this phrase.

   a. the normal desire for love, marriage, sex (see 1 Tim. 4:3)

   b. those things characteristic of women, such as mercy, gentleness, and kindness

   c. that desire of Hebrew women to be the mother of the Messiah (1 Tim. 2:15)

# 11. A Chronology of Ungodly Kings

## DANIEL 11:1-20
## Alexander and Predecessors

This amazing chapter contains no less than thirty-eight fulfilled prophecies. Some are as follows:

The rule of four Persian kings (v. 2)

The war of the fourth with Greece

The rise and fall of Alexander (v. 3, 4)

The fourfold division of his empire (v. 4)

The eventual alliance of two of these two kingdoms (v. 6)

The Egyptian plunder of Syria (v. 8)

The unsuccessful retaliation of Syria (v. 9)

The civil war in Egypt (v. 14)

The Syrian occupation of Palestine (v. 16)

The Temple desecration by a Syrian king (vs. 31, 32)

The Maccabean revolt (v. 32)

The eventual defeat of the Maccabeans (v. 33)

## DANIEL 11:21-35
## Antiochus Epiphanes

He was a cruel, Jew-hating Syrian king who occupied Jerusalem for awhile, ruling from 175-164 B.C.

On September 6, 171 B.C., he began his blasphemous actions against the Temple.

The supreme insult took place on December 15, 168, when he sacrificed a huge sow on the Jewish Temple altar.

In three days he murdered over 40,000 Jews.

On December 25, 165 (2300 days after the September 6, 171, date; see Dan. 8:9-14) some Jewish heroes called the Maccabees recaptured Jerusalem and the Syrian occupation ended.

## DANIEL 11:36-45
## Antichrist

Will be totally self-willed

Will magnify himself and malign God

Will prosper for awhile

Will not regard the gods of his fathers

Will have no desire for women

Will honor the god of fortress

Will be attacked by two southern and northern kings

Will occupy the Holy Land

Will occupy Egypt

Will hear frightful news while in Egypt

Will return to the Holy Land and wage war

Will be destroyed by Christ on Mt. Zion

6. His god will be the god of fortresses (11:38). The antichrist will spend all his resources on military programs.

7. In the latter days of the tribulation, he shall be attacked by the king of the south (Egypt) and the king of the north (Russia—11:40). According to Ezekiel (38–39) these two nations, especially Russia, are destroyed upon the mountains of Israel by God himself.

8. After the defeat of Russia, the antichrist will occupy Palestine (11:41). Edom and Moab will not be occupied by him. Some believe God will not allow him dominion over these areas, because Petra is located there, the mountainous city where the Jewish remnant will take shelter from the antichrist during the last part of the tribulation. (See Rev. 12:14.)

9. Upon establishing control in Palestine, the antichrist marches into Egypt and controls that land (11:42, 43).

10. While he is in Egypt he hears alarming rumors from the east and the north (11:44). The exact nature of these rumors is uncertain. Several suggestions have been offered:
   a. This concerns a report about a Jewish uprising. Dr. Leon Wood advocates this position in his book, *A Commentary on Daniel* (p. 313).
   b. It concerns an invasion of a vast horde of some 200,000,000 warriors from the far east (Rev. 9:16) under the leadership of "kings of the east" (Rev. 16:12), who now challenge him for world leadership. These nations would include China, India, and others. Dr. J. Dwight Pentecost suggests this possibility (*Things to Come*, p. 356).
   c. It concerns a report that thousands of Jews are escaping Jerusalem and fleeing into Petra. This theory is offered as a possibility by the author.

11. He quickly returns and in great fury destroys many (11:44). Here again the identity of those who are destroyed cannot be dogmatically stated.

12. He apparently successfully deals with the threat and establishes his worldwide headquarters on Mt. Zion. Here he remains until his total destruction by the King of kings at the end of the tribulation (11:45). (See also Rev. 19:11–21.)

XII. Closing Conditions.
A. The ministry of Michael (12:1).
   1. Michael is Israel's guardian angel.
   2. He will help deliver Israel through the worst period of human history since the creation of the world. Jesus quoted this verse when he spoke of that future hellish hour. (See Mt. 24:21, 22.) It is Michael who will cast Satan out of the heavenlies during the middle of the tribulation (Rev. 12:7), and then this heavenly hero apparently helps the escaping one-third Israelite nation into Petra. (See Zech. 13:8, 9; Rev. 12:14.)
   3. These Israelites already have their names in the Lamb's Book of Life. (See also Ex. 32:32; Ps. 69:28; Lk. 10:20; Mt. 24:22; Rev. 20:12.)
B. The two resurrections (12:2, 3). Other Old Testament and New Testament passages make it clear that these two resurrections are not at the same time, but rather are separated by a period of 1000 years. Neither resurrection here refers to the rapture.
   1. The resurrection of those to eternal life. This will occur at the beginning of the millennium and will include all Old Testament and martyred tribulational saints. (See Job 19:25, 26; Ps. 49:15; Isa. 25:8; 26:19; Hosea 13:14; Heb. 11:35; Rev. 20:4, 6.) The reward of all righteous soul-winners is mentioned in Daniel 12:3.
   2. The resurrection of those to shame and everlasting contempt. This will transpire after the millennium and will include all unsaved people who have ever lived. (See Rev. 20:5.) Our Lord summarizes these two resurrections in John 5:28, 29.
C. The two prophecies (12:4).
   "But thou, O Daniel, shut up the words, and seal the book, even to the time of the end: many shall run to and fro, and knowledge shall be increased."
   After reading this passage many years ago, the great scientist (and Christian), Sir Isaac Newton, is reported to have said:
   "Personally I cannot help but believe that these words refer to the end of the times. Men will travel from country to country in an unprecedented manner. There may be some inventions which will enable people to travel much more quickly than they do now."
   This was written around A.D. 1680. Newton went on to speculate that this speed might actually exceed fifty m.p.h. Some eighty years later, the famous French atheist, Voltaire, read Newton's words and retorted:
   "See what a fool Christianity makes of an otherwise brilliant man! Here a scientist like Newton actually writes that men may travel at the rate of 30 or 40 m.p.h. Has he forgotten that if man would travel at this rate he would be suffocated? His heart would stand still!"
   One wonders what Voltaire would have said had he known that some two centuries after he wrote this, an American astronaut, Edward H. White, on June 3, 1965, would climb out of a space craft a hundred miles in the sky and casually walk across the continental United States in less than fifteen minutes, strolling along at 17,500 m.p.h.? Or that during the moon landings, man exceeded a speed some twelve times faster than a twenty-two-caliber rifle bullet travels? In this same prophecy, Daniel predicted an intensification of knowledge. Our country is just over two hundred years old. Yet, during this time, we have developed the public educational system from absolutely nothing to its present level. We have now over sixty million students in America alone, attending some 72,000 public elementary schools, 27,000 secondary schools, and 1200 colleges and universities. Each year we spend thirty-six billions of dollars to finance all this.

D. The three time periods (12:5-13).
  1. 1260 days ("a time, times and a half." See 12:7.)
    a. Daniel sees two other angels who had been listening to this private prophecy conference the mighty angel was conducting for the old statesman. Angels are very much interested in God's program of salvation (1 Pet. 1:12) and one of the two suddenly asks how long this terrible tribulational period will last (12:6). Neither of these angels had apparently overheard the details of the seventy-week vision in 9:24-27.
    b. The mighty angel informs them that the duration of this final horrible half of the tribulation will last as long as it takes for the pride and power of the Jews to be broken, or three-and-a-half years (12:7).
  2. 1290 days (12:11). This period refers to the same as mentioned above, but includes an additional thirty days. Although we cannot be dogmatic, it would seem reasonable to conclude that an additional month will be needed here to carry out the sheep and goat judgment mentioned in Matthew 25:31-46.
  3. 1335 days (12:12). Here again a period of time is added, forty-five days. What will be the need of these forty-five days? It may be the time necessary for setting up the governmental machinery for carrying on the rule of Christ. Dr. Franklin Logsdon has written the following helpful words concerning the seventy-five additional days beyond the three-and-a-half year period.

    "We in the United States have a national analogy. The President is elected in the early part of November, but he is not inaugurated until January 20. There is an interim of 70 plus days. During this time, he concerns himself with the appointment of cabinet members, foreign envoys and others who will comprise his government. In the period of 75 days between the termination of the Great Tribulation and the Coronation, the King of Glory will likewise attend to certain matters." (*Profiles in Prophecy*, p. 81)

E. The four final conclusions
  1. The mighty angel raises both hands into heaven as he attests to the veracity of all this (12:7). The regular gesture of raising one's hand to heaven showed solemnity and importance (see Gen. 14:22; Deut. 32:40), but here both hands are raised. (See also Rev. 10:1-6.)
  2. Many shall be cleansed (saved) during the tribulation (12:1); this includes both Jews and Gentiles. (See Rev. 7:1-17.)
  3. The wicked, however, will continue their evil ways (12:10). (See Rev. 9:20, 21; 11:9, 10.)
  4. Daniel was to carefully preserve his writings (12:4), but all their meaning would not be revealed to him until that glorious day when he would stand alongside the righteous awaiting his inheritance lot (12:9, 13).

# 12. Closing Conditions

" . . . *A time of trouble, such as never was . . ."*  (12:1)

● **THE HELPER IN THE TRIBULATION**

Michael the Archangel **(12:1)**

● **THE LENGTH OF THE TRIBULATION**

There are three specific time periods listed here concerning the tribulation and following events.

**1260 DAYS (12:7)**

A reference to the final and worst part of the tribulation, some three-and-a-half years.

**1290 DAYS (12:11)**

A reference to the first time period plus thirty days. This time may be needed to conduct the various Jewish, Gentile, and angelic judgments.

**1335 DAYS (12:12)**

A reference to the second time period plus forty-five days. This may be spent in preparing for the millennial government.

● **THE INTEREST CONCERNING THE TRIBULATION**

Both angels and Old Testament prophets **(12:5-8)**

● **THE SALVATION DURING THE TRIBULATION**

" . . . Every one . . . written in the book" **(12:1)**.
"Many shall be purified, and made white . . ." **(12:10)**.

● **THE SIGNS PRECEDING THE TRIBULATION**

An Increase in Speed **(12:4)**

An Increase in Knowledge **(12:4)**

● **THE RESURRECTIONS FOLLOWING THE TRIBULATION (12:2, 3)**

At the Beginning of the Millennium
Resurrection of Old Testament and tribulation saints
At the End of the Millennium
Resurrection of all unsaved dead

## INTRODUCING THE RETURN STAGE

1. This period describes Satan's attempts to harass the Jews in Palestine (the book of Nehemiah) and hang them in Persia (the book of Esther).
2. It covers the construction of the second Old Testament Temple, and the completion of the Old Testament canon.
3. Its duration is approximately 140 years.
4. It begins with the historical ministry of Ezra the scribe (Ezra 7:6-10), and ends with the prophetical ministry of Elijah the prophet (Mal. 4:5, 6).
5. We read of the spirit-induced midnight mission of Nehemiah (Neh. 2) and the satanic-induced midnight mission of Haman (Est. 6).
6. We are told of a plot against a pagan king (Est. 2:21-23) and one against the King of kings (Zech. 11:12, 13).
7. This era includes the restoration of the feast of tabernacles (Neh. 8:13-18) and the institution of the feast of Purim (Est. 9:20-32).

## THE RETURN STAGE
## EZRA; ESTHER; NEHEMIAH;
## HAGGAI; ZECHARIAH; MALACHI

## EZRA (445 B.C.)

INTRODUCTION:

1. Zedekiah, Judah's last king, was carried away into captivity by Nebuchadnezzar in 597 B.C. The city of Jerusalem was destroyed and the Temple burned on July 18, 586, B.C. (see 2 Ki. 24).
2. Many citizens of Judah along with Daniel and Ezekiel were also transported to Babylon. Both ministered and wrote there. One was a priest, the other a prime minister.
4. On October 29, 539 B.C., Babylon fell to the invading armies of the Medes and Persians, led by Cyrus the Great. The Babylonian king at that time, Belshazzar, was executed. (See Dan. 5.)
5. Cyrus then placed his able general, Darius the Mede (also the Gobryas of history) as king over the city of Babylon.
6. During Cyrus' first year reigning, he issued the decree which permitted the Jews to return and rebuild their temple at Jerusalem.
   a. Jeremiah had predicted the length of the captivity. (See 25:11, 12; 29:10.)
   b. Isaiah had actually called Cyrus by name some 170 years before. (See Isa. 44:28; 45:1.)
7. There were three separate returns by the Jewish remnant.

a. Zerubbabel led the first in 536 B.C.
b. Ezra led the second in 455 B.C.
c. Nehemiah led the third in 445 B.C.
8. In 535 B.C. the construction on the Temple began. For a while it was halted by various satanic activities.
9. During this time Haggai and Zechariah ministered to the discouraged remnant.
10. In October of 516 the Temple was completed and dedicated.
11. There were at least five Persian kings associated in some way with the period of the return. They are:
   a. Cyrus the Great (539-530), the victor over Babylon, and king who issued the decree (Ezra 1:1-4).
   b. Cambyses (530-522 B.C.), the son of Cyrus.
   c. Smerdis (522-520 B.C.).
   d. Darius the Great (520-486 B.C.). This was not the same as Darius the Mede. Darius the Great established order and saved the Persian empire after the chaos which followed Cambyses' death. He allowed the Temple work to continue.
   e. Xerxes I (486-465 B.C.). He was the son of Darius the Great, and also the Ahasuerus of the book of Esther.
   f. Artaxerxes (465-424). He was the son of Xerxes I, and on the throne when both Ezra and Nehemiah returned (Ezra 7:1, 8; Neh. 2:1).

I. The Period Under Zerubbabel (Ezra 1-6).
   A. The king, proclaiming.
      1. The writing (1:1-4)
         a. God places a desire in Cyrus' heart to issue his return decree.
         b. The king freely acknowledges God's sovereignty in giving him his kingdom.
         c. The language of the decree suggests that Daniel himself may have drafted it for Cyrus.
      2. The rising (1:5-11)
         a. God plants a holy desire in the hearts of many Hebrew people to return. Although only three tribes are mentioned (Judah, Benjamin, and Levi), we know from other passages that there were doubtless representatives from all twelve who returned.
            Note:
            (1) In 2 Chronicles 11:13-17 we are told at the time of Israel's civil war that various individuals from all twelve tribes moved to Jerusalem.
            (2) Jesus said he came to minister to the entire house of Israel (Mt. 10:6).
            (3) The tribes of Zebulun and Naphtali are referred to in Matthew 4:13, 15.

# THE RETURN STAGE

Ezra      Esther

Nehemiah   Haggai

Zechariah  Malachi

*"For thus saith the Lord, after seventy years are accomplished at Babylon, I will visit you, and perform my good word toward you, in causing you to return even unto this place"*

Jer. 29:10.

## A CHRONOLOGY OF THE RETURN STAGE

| FOREIGN KING | DATE | EVENT | SCRIPTURE | OLD TESTAMENT BOOK | LOCATION |
|---|---|---|---|---|---|
| **Cyrus the Great** | **539—530** | Conquers Babylon | **Dan. 5** | **● Ezra 1-6** | |
| | | Issues return decree | **Ezra 1-3** | | |
| **Cambyses** | **530-522** | Not referred to in Old Testament | — | **● Haggai** | **Jerusalem** |
| **Smerdis** | **522-520** | Stops work on the Temple | **Ezra 4:1-23** | **● Zechariah** | |
| **Darius the Great** | **520-486** | Orders work to continue | **Ezra 4:24; 6:1-22** | **(See Ezra 5:1; 6:14)** | |
| **Ahasuerus** | **486-465** | Makes Esther his queen | **Esther 1-10** | **● Esther** | **Persia** |
| **Artaxerxes** | **465-424** | Allows Ezra to return | **Ezra 7-12** | **● Ezra 7-12** | **Jerusalem** |
| | | Allows Nehemiah to return | **Nehemiah 1-13** | **● Nehemiah** | |

(4) Anna was from the tribe of Asher (Lk. 2:36).

(5) Paul speaks of "our twelve tribes" (Acts. 26:7).

These verses alone refute the false doctrine of British Israelism, which teaches the ten "lost tribes" are really Americans and Englishmen.

b. Those Hebrews remaining in Babylon contributed toward this venture.

c. King Cyrus donated the golden vessels Nebuchadnezzar had taken from the Jerusalem Temple some sixty years before. This totaled 5,469 gold and silver items.

B. The people, reclaiming.

1. Their genealogy (2:1-57). The family trees of those who returned were carefully recorded for posterity. Especially to be noted was their leader, whose name was Zerubbabel. This humble man was the grandson of Jehoiachin (Ezra 3:2; 1 Chron. 3:19). He faced a difficult task in rebuilding the Temple and was often personally encouraged by God himself. (See Hag. 1:14; 2:4, 21, 23; Zech. 4:6, 7, 9, 10.) The total number of those returning was 42,360.

2. Their theology (3:1-13).

a. After they reached Jerusalem the altar was built and the sacrificial system reinstituted, led by Jeshua, grandson of Israel's last high priest before the Babylonian captivity. This Jeshua (called Joshua by Haggai and Zechariah) became the first high priest of the return period.

b. The first sacred feast to be observed was the Feast of the Tabernacles.

c. In June of 535 B.C. work was begun on the Temple.

d. When the foundation was laid a great ceremony was held. It may be concluded, however, that this ground-breaking program was different from any other either before or after. Note the unusual account in 3:10-13.

C. The devil, defaming. Satan tried his best to prevent the Temple from going up.

1. He tried compromise (4:1-3). Judah's enemies suggested they all have a part in building some kind of universal house of worship. Zerubbabel and Jeshua refused.

2. He tried slander (4:4, 5). Their enemies then wrote lies concerning them to the Persian officials. They reminded the king (Cambyses)

## SIX SOVEREIGN TRIPS

*"By the rivers of Babylon, there we sat down, yea, we wept, when we remembered Zion"* **(Ps. 137:1).**

## Three Trips from Jerusalem to Babylon

| DATE | CAPTIVES | OLD TESTAMENT PROPHETS | | FOREIGN KINGS | |
|------|----------|------------------------|--|---------------|--|
| 606 | **Daniel** | In Babylon | **Daniel** | Before 539 | Nebuchadnezzar |
| 597 | **Ezekiel** | | **Ezekiel** | | Belshazzar |
| 586 | **Zedekiah** | In Jerusalem | **Jeremiah** | After 539 | King Cyrus and his General Darius |

*"When the Lord turned again the captivity of Zion, we were like them that dream"* **(Ps. 126:1).**

## Three Trips from Babylon to Jerusalem

| DATE | LEADER | FOREIGN KING | OLD TESTAMENT PROPHET |
|------|--------|--------------|------------------------|
| 536 | **Zerubbabel** and **Joshua** | • Cyrus the Great<br>• Cambyses<br>• Smerdis<br>• Darius the Great | **Haggai**<br><br>**Zechariah** |
| 455 | **Ezra** | Artaxerxes | **Ezra** |
| 445 | **Nehemiah** | Artaxerxes | **Nehemiah** |

of Jerusalem's history as a hotbed of rebellion and suggested he stop all building action. Cambyses agreed and issued the order to halt (4:18-23).

D. The Lord, sustaining. In spite of all this, God was at work!

1. Both Haggai and Zechariah begin their comforting ministry at this time (5:1, 2).
2. The new Persian king, Darius the Great, takes a personal interest in the matter. A search soon reveals the original title decree of Cyrus, which gave the Jews permission to rebuild their Temple. Darius therefore orders the work to continue and decrees the construction cost to be paid from the treasury of some of his own officials (6:1-12).
3. On February 18, 516 B.C., the Temple was completed (6:15). In April the Passover was celebrated in Jerusalem, the first time in over sixty years (6:19).

II. The Period Under Ezra (Ezra 7-10). Between chapters 6 and 7 of Ezra there is a period of some sixty years. We have no biblical record concerning those events which transpired during this time. J. Vernon McGee writes the following about Ezra:

"He is one of the characters who has not received proper recognition. Ezra was a descendant of Hilkiah, the high priest (Ezra 7:1), who found a copy of the law during the reign of Josiah (2 Chron. 34:14); Ezra, as a priest, was unable to serve during the captivity, but he gave his time to a study of the Word of God—he was 'a ready scribe in the law of Moses' (Ezra 7:6). Ezra was a revivalist and reformer. The revival began with the reading of the Word of God by Ezra (see Neh. 8). Also, he probably was the writer of 1st and 2nd Chronicles and of Psalm 119, which exalts the Word of God. He organized the synagogue, and was the founder of the order of scribes, helped settle the canon of Scripture and arranged the Psalms." (*Through the Bible*, p. 117)

A. The cooperation from the king (Ezra 7). The Persian monarch Artaxerxes greatly aided Ezra in his plans to leave Babylon and lead a pilgrimage to Jerusalem. The king issued an official letter addressed to three parties.

1. To all Jews in Babylon: Artaxerxes invited as many as desired to return to Jerusalem with Ezra. He also encouraged them to give liberally to the special offering Ezra was collecting (7:11-20).
2. To all Persian officials west of the Euphrates River: They were to furnish Ezra with all he needed.
3. To Ezra himself: He was to select and appoint his own officials, and to rule the Jewish people west of the Euphrates River (7:25, 26).

B. The preparation for the trip (8).

1. Ezra leaves from Babylon in mid-March of 455 B.C. with approximately 1500 men and their families.
2. En route the group assembles at the Ahava River (a tributary of the Euphrates River) for a roll call. Ezra is amazed to discover that not one Levite has volunteered to come (8:15).
3. He then hurriedly sends a delegation to return and persuade some Levites to make the trip. God's Spirit works, for soon nearly 300 Levites join the group (8:16-20).
4. Ezra then proclaims a fast there by the river, praying God will grant them a safe journey. His confession here is interesting (8:22).
5. Ezra then appoints twelve leaders to be in charge of transporting the monies received from the offering he had taken in Babylon. This was a considerable sum, totaling over

# Ezra

## Period under Zerubbabel EZRA 1-6

**THE KING**

### PROCLAIMING

● Cyrus signs the return decree **(1:1-4)**.

● A spiritual Jewish minority responds to this **(1:5-11)**. Some 40,000 now leave for Jerusalem

**THE PEOPLE**

### RECLAIMING

● They reclaim their genealogy **(2)**.

● They reclaim their theology **(3)**.
Upon reaching Jerusalem they build the altar and keep the feasts.

**THE DEVIL**

### DEFAMING

● He attempts compromise **(4:1-3)**.

● He attempts slander **(4:4-24)**.

**THE LORD**

### SUSTAINING

● Through the ministry of Haggai and Zechariah **(5:1; 6:14)**.

● Through the title deed search by King Darius **(6)**.

---

**FIFTY-YEAR GAP**

Events in the book of
**ESTHER** take place

---

## Period under Ezra EZRA 7-10

**COOPERATION**

### FROM THE KING (7)

● Ezra is helped by King Artaxerxes, who encourages the Jews to go and writes letters in their behalf.

**PREPARATION**

### FOR THE TRIP (8)

● Ezra gathers 1500 families plus 300 Levitical priests.

● He collects five million dollars.

● He observes a time of prayer and fasting.

**SUPPLICATION**

### BY THE SCRIBE (9)

● He learns that the people have already compromised their testimony.

● He pours out his soul in prayer to God over their sin.

**PURIFICATION**

### OF THE PEOPLE (10)

● They are convicted of their sins.

● The people put away their sins.

---

five million dollars in gold and silver (8:24-29).

6. In August of 455 B.C., the little group arrives safely in Jerusalem (7:9; 8:31, 32).

C. The supplication of the scribe (9:1-15).

   1. Ezra soon learns that the Jews already in the Holy City have compromised their testimony by practicing heathen customs and even marrying their pagan women (9:1, 2).

   2. The great Bible teacher immediately goes into deep mourning and pours out his soul to God concerning this tragic situation. Ezra's prayer in 9:5-15 may be favorably compared to that of Daniel (Dan. 9) and also Nehemiah (Neh. 9).

D. The purification of the people (Ezra 10).

   1. Soon conviction of sin settles down upon the hearts of the leaders and they agree something must be done immediately.

   2. A proclamation goes out throughout all Judah, ordering all male citizens to appear in Jerusalem on the fifth day of December.

   3. Upon hearing Ezra's sermon, the men agree to dismiss their heathen wives. Ezra appoints various leaders to handle the legal matters connected with this. By March 15 of the following year the thing had been resolved.

## NEHEMIAH (445 B.C.)

INTRODUCTION:

1. The year was 445 B.C. The Jews had already been in Jerusalem for some ninety years. A number had remained in Babylon and Persia.

2. One of the Jews still living in Persia was Nehemiah. This capable man had been elevated to the position of cup bearer (personal press secretary and valet) to King Artaxerxes, monarch of all Persia.

3. Upon being saddened and then challenged concerning the desperate need about Jerusalem's wall-less and defenseless city, Nehemiah goes to the Holy City and builds the necessary walls.

4. Nehemiah was a younger contemporary of Ezra.

   a. Ezra was a priest and Bible teacher. His main job concerned the purification of the people of Jerusalem.

   b. Nehemiah was a politician and builder. His main job concerned the protection of the people of Jerusalem.

5. King Artaxerxes had shown kindness to Ezra some ten years before, and would also honor Nehemiah's request to return to Jerusalem. This king was the son of Xerxes and therefore the stepson of Esther. His stepmother no doubt had much influence upon Artaxerxes' attitude toward Ezra and Nehemiah.

6. Nehemiah is the last historical book in the Old Testament.

7. The book of Nehemiah is the autobiography of his "call to the wall."

I. The News Concerning the Wall (Neh. 1).

A. In December of 446 B.C., Nehemiah learns from a returning Jew named Hanani (and his own brother—see 1:2; 7:2) of the pitiful state of Jerusalem. The report breaks his heart (1:3).

B. Upon hearing this, Nehemiah begins a time of:
1. Confession to God over the deeds of his people (1:6, 7).
2. Intercession to God over the needs of his people (1:8–11).

II. The Request to Build the Wall (2:1–8).

A. In April of 445 B.C., after a prayer period of four months, Nehemiah asks the king to "send me unto Judah, unto the city of my fathers' sepulchers, that I may build it" (2:5).

B. Artaxerxes agrees and gives Nehemiah two letters.
1. One was to the Persian officials west of the Euphrates, giving him passport permission.
2. The other was to Asaph, manager of the king's forest, instructing him to issue the necessary timber for the construction job.

III. The Necessity for the Wall (2:9–20). Soon after reaching Jerusalem, Nehemiah makes a secret midnight ride around the city itself. The next morning he assembles Judah's leaders and shares with them the burden of his heart (2:17, 18).

It may be concluded that there were at least two compelling reasons for building the wall.

A. It was necessary for protection, that is, to keep the outsiders out. This would protect against sneak attacks.

B. It was necessary for separation, to keep the insiders in. This would cut down upon the growing worldliness of the Jews who had been associating freely with the surrounding pagan people.

IV. The Gates in the Wall (Neh. 3). The various gates mentioned here are in themselves a beautiful picture summary of the Christian life. Note:

A. The sheep gate (3:1). This speaks of the cross. (See Jn. 10:11.)

B. The fish gate (3:3). This speaks of soul-winning. (See Mt. 4:19.)

C. The old gate (3:6). This speaks of our old nature. (See Rom. 6:1–23.)

D. The valley gate (3:13). This speaks of sufferings and testing. (See 2 Cor. 1:3–5.)

E. The dung gate (3:14). This speaks of the works of the flesh. (See Gal. 5:16–21.)

F. The fountain gate (3:15). This speaks of the Holy Spirit. (See Jn. 7:37–39.)

G. The water gate (3:26). This speaks of the Word of God. (See Jn. 4:10–14.)

H. The horse gate (3:28). This speaks of the believer's warfare. (See Eph. 6:10–17.)

I. The east gate (3:29). This speaks of the return of Christ. (See Ezek. 43:1, 2.)

J. The Miphkad gate (3:31). This was thought to be the judgment gate and therefore speaks of the judgment seat of Christ. (See 1 Cor. 3:9–15; 2 Cor. 5:10.)

V. The Opposition to the Wall. A work for God will always be met by both human and satanic opposition. These combined forces did their perverted best to halt the wall building. Many methods were employed to accomplish this.

A. Ridicule (2:19; 4:1–3). Nehemiah had but begun when he was opposed by a hellish trinity. This consisted of:
1. Sanballat (the governor of Samaria)
2. Tobiah (an Ammonite leader)
3. Geshem (an Arab chief)

These troublemakers scoffed at the work. Tobiah sneered, "Even that which they build, if a fox go up, he shall break down their stone wall" (4:3). But Nehemiah took his case before God and continued the good work (4:4, 5).

B. Wrath (4:1, 6–9). In spite of this ridicule, however, the wall was soon half its intended height all around the city. The sneers of this terrible trio soon disappeared. In their fury they plotted to lead an army against Jerusalem. But once again Nehemiah would testify: "We made our prayer unto our God, and set a watch against them day and night, because of them" (4:9).

C. Discouragement (4:10). After awhile many of the workers became weary in the heavy work of removing the debris which had piled up for so many years.

D. Fear (4:11–23). The builders were aware of the impending attack planned by their combined enemies to murder them en masse. Once again the mighty Nehemiah was equal to the occasion.
1. He stationed armed guards behind the walls.
2. He inspired them with his own confidence in God.
3. He appointed a trumpeter to sound an alarm if needed.
4. He prepared his men by issuing both weapons and working tools to every man. Then the wall was constructed.
5. He scheduled the work from sunrise to sunset. During that hectic but heroic period neither the guards or the workers ever removed their clothes.

E. Internal strife (5:1–5). Some of the rich Jews were profiteering at the expense of their poorer brethren by forcing them into slavery and acquiring their properties. Nehemiah was furious upon hearing of this and called a public trial to deal with those materialistic men. At this hearing he demanded and received their promise to restore their dishonest gain to their victims (5:6–13).

F. Laziness (4:10). We are told that some of the leaders were lazy and of no help whatsoever.

G. Satanic subtlety (6:1–8). On four separate occasions Nehemiah's enemies attempted to set up a "dialogue" session with him. But he refused, knowing they actually were planning to kill him. Note:
1. Their invitation of compromise:
"Come now, therefore, and let us take counsel together" (6:7).
2. His answer of conviction:
"I am doing a great work, so that I cannot come down. Why should the work cease, while I leave it, and come down to you?" (6:3).

H. Lying prophets (6:10–14). A false prophet named Shemaiah, in the hire of Sanballat, attempted to frighten Nehemiah into hiding by claiming God had revealed to him Nehemiah would be murdered that very night.

VI. Blessings of the (Completed) Wall. In spite of all the persecution and hardships, Nehemiah had the wall up and completed in early September, just fifty-two days after they had begun (6:15). This project resulted in many blessings, including:

A. The reading of the Word of God (8:1–8; 9:3).

B. The restoration of the feast of tabernacles (8:13–18).

1. This feast had not been properly observed since the time of Joshua, over 900 years back.

2. The feast was instituted in Leviticus 23. Its purpose and method of observation are found in 23:40–43.

3. With great joy the people carried this out. Ezra read from the scroll on each of the seven days of the feast.

C. The prayer recitation of Israel's History (9:6–38). In this remarkable public prayer, Ezra summarized the entire history of the faithfulness of God bestowed upon Israel.

D. The ratification of a special covenant (9:38; 10:1–29).

E. The repopulating of the city of David (11:1, 2).

F. The denouncing of sins:

1. of ungodly alliances (9:1, 2; 10:30; 13:3)

2. untithed possessions (10:32–39; 12:44–47; 13:10, 11)

3. unlawful Sabbath work (10:31; 13:15–22)

4. unequal marriages (13:23, 24)

5. unauthorized usage of the Temple (13:1–9)

Nehemiah's fantastic zeal and fearless actions helped bring into being all this repentance over sin.

1. He had gone back to Persia for awhile (13:6), but upon returning he discovered several very disquieting things.

a. The Temple custodian had actually converted a storage room into a beautiful guest room for (of all people) his friend Tobiah.

b. Nehemiah ordered him to leave and threw out all his belongings from the room (13:9).

c. He then had to regather the Temple choir which had dissolved during his absence (13:10).

2. His zeal simply knew no limits, as the following account brings out. (See 13:23–25.)

3. His last recorded act was to excommunicate Joiada (the very son of Eliashib, the high priest) because of his unlawful marriage to Sanballat's daughter (13:28).

G. The rejoicing of all the remnant. When God's work is done in God's way, joy will follow. Note the various references to this.

1. The people sent presents to each other and ate festive meals (8:12).

2. The Levitical choir sang and played with cymbals, psalteries, and harps (9:4; 12:27, 28).

3. Nehemiah divided the people into two groups. Each walked in opposite directions upon the completed wall singing their songs of praise to God (12:31–34).

4. Ezra led a special corps of trumpet-playing priests (12:35–37).

5. The result of all this was that "the joy of Jerusalem was heard even afar off" (12:43).

# ESTHER (478–464 B.C.)

INTRODUCTION:

1. Esther is one of the two Old Testament books named after a woman. (The other is Ruth.)

2. The name Esther means "star."

3. The books give the story of those Jews living in Persia who did not return to Jerusalem after Cyrus' decree. To pinpoint the historical account here, consider the following:

a. The Jews first went back to Jerusalem under Zerubbabel in 536 B.C.

b. The Temple was completed in 516 B.C.

c. Esther became queen in 478 B.C.

d. She saved her people in 473 B.C.

e. Ezra returned to Jerusalem in 455 B.C.

f. Nehemiah returned in 445 B.C.

Thus Esther appears upon the scene about sixty years after the decree of Cyrus and approximately thirty-five years before Nehemiah returned.

4. The name of God never appears in this book. It is also not to be found in the Song of Solomon. For this reason the early church at first was somewhat reluctant to accept the book of Esther as a part of the inspired canon, but soon it was regarded as such.

5. In spite of the omission of any name for deity, there is no other book in all the Bible where God is more evident, working behind the scenes, than in this book.

6. The key in understanding Esther is the word "providence," literally meaning, "to provide in advance." Providence has been defined by the great theologian Strong as follows:

"Providence is that continuous agency of God by which He makes all events of the physical and moral world fulfill the original design with which He created it."

Providence has also been defined as "the hand of God in the glove of history." Providence is the last of three great facts which make up the sovereignty of God as witnessed by man. These are:

a. Creation—which accounts for the existence of this universe (Gen. 1:1).

b. Preservation—which accounts for the continuation of this universe (Heb. 1:3; Col. 1:16, 17).

c. Providence—which accounts for the progress and development of this universe (Ps. 135:6–10; Dan. 4:35).

7. One may with full justification pen the words of Romans 8:28 across the book of Esther.

I. The Rise of Esther (Est. 1–2).

A. The rejection of Vashti (1:2–21).

1. In the third year of his reign, the Persian monarch Ahasuerus (Xerxes) gave a fantastic feast which lasted 180 days. It was attended by thousands of his kingdom officials, coming from every one of the 127 provinces, stretching from India to Ethiopia (1:1–4).

2. Although it is not specifically stated so, the probable reason for the festivities was to raise the morale of his leaders and psychologically prepare them for his planned expedition against Greece. Here a little background is necessary.
   a. In 490 B.C., Xerxes' father, Darius the Great, had led a huge fleet of 600 ships carrying some 60,000 Persian crack cavalry and foot soldiers to capture Athens and subdue the Greek civilization. But he was soundly defeated on a small plain called Marathon by the brilliant Greek general Miltiades. In spite of the vastly numerical superiority of the Persians, the Greeks out-circled their foes and cut them down as overripe wheat.
   b. The battle of Marathon is listed as number six in the book, *History's 100 Greatest Events*, by William A. DeWitt.
3. During the final week of the feasting the king called for his wife, Vashti, to come in and parade her beauty before some of his important, but half-drunk friends. The queen curtly refused to display herself in this cheap manner (1:5-12).
4. Burning with anger, the king acted upon the advice of his crony friends and banished his wife forever from his presence, lest the other women of the kingdom get ideas from her insubordination (1:13-21).

B. The selection of Esther (2:1-20).
1. After his anger had cooled, the king regretted his hasty action, but was unable to change the strict Persian law even though he himself had decreed it (2:1).
2. At the suggestion of his aides, he allowed an empire-wide beauty search to begin, with the winner of the contest to become his new wife (2:2-4).
3. Among the beauties brought to the palace was a Jewish girl named Hadassah, also known as Esther. The beautiful young maiden had been raised by her older cousin, whose name was Mordecai, of the tribe of Benjamin (2:5-8).
4. Esther gained immediate favor with Hegai, the headmaster of the Miss Persian pageant. However, upon the advice of Mordecai, Esther did not reveal her Jewish identity at this time (2:9-11).
5. The contest lasted some four years, but after the king had seen all the available "finalists," he wholeheartedly chose Esther to become his next queen (2:12-17).
6. To celebrate this event, Ahasuerus threw another big party, and even went so far as to lower taxes in his province.

   Note: The reason for all this was also, in part, to compensate for his recent defeat at the hands of the Greeks. It should be understood that a period of some four years elapsed between the divorce of Vashti and the marriage to Esther. The following is a summary of the events which took place during that period.

   a. In the spring of 480 B.C., Xerxes crossed the Dardanelles with over 100,000 men and hundreds of ships. History tells us Xerxes wept while watching the dazzling display of his smartly marching armies, all carrying their brightly colored flags and banners. When asked why he wept, the king replied, "Because I know all this military glory is but for a moment and will soon fade away forever. Because in much less than one hundred years from now every man present here today will have died, myself included."
   b. Disaster struck soon after, for he lost 400 ships in a severe spring storm at sea. In blind frustration and anger, Xerxes beat upon the stormy waters with his belt.
   c. Upon landing in Greece, his proud Persian troops were stopped for an entire day at the mountainous pass called Thermopylae. Here, a Greek captain named Leonidas and his 300 brave Spartan soldiers held back the entire invading army for twenty-four hours, inflicting great losses on them, and allowing the much smaller Greek army to carry out an orderly retreat to safety.
   d. Xerxes eventually broke through and burned Athens to the ground. But most of its citizens had escaped to the island of Salamis. The king then set sail for Salamis, confident of victory, for he outnumbered his enemy at least three to one. But the smaller and swifter Greek fighting boats had mastered the art of ramming. Soon, before his horrified eyes, Xerxes viewed the slaughter of his proud navy.
   e. He left for Persia a defeated man. The remaining troops were put under the command of General Nardonius. One year later, Nardonius was defeated and killed in a pitched battle at Plataea in 479 B.C. The Persian Empire was then dealt the final death blow. J.F.C. Fuller's well-known book, *The Decisive Battles of the Western World*, lists the battles at Salamis and Plataea among the most important in recorded history.

C. The detection of Mordecai (2:19-23).
1. Mordecai, who had become a palace official, overhears at the gate a plot of two guards to assassinate Xerxes.
2. He reports this to Queen Esther, who in turn informs the king. Both guards are executed. This was all duly recorded in the book of the history of King Xerxes' reign. Note: Later, in 465 B.C., Xerxes would be assassinated in a similar plot.

II. The Lies of Haman (3-5).
A. Infernal servitude.
1. Soon after Esther had become queen, Xerxes appointed as his prime minister a vicious politician named Haman. Haman was an Amalekite, and a descendant from a former king of that nation named Agag, who ruled in the days of Saul and Samuel. It will be

remembered that Saul disobeyed God and spared King Agag in battle. (See 1 Sam. 15.) The Amalekites had been the bitter enemies of Israel. They had attacked them while en route to the Promised Land (Ex. 17:14; Deut. 25:17-19).

2. The arrogant Haman soon learned a Jew named Mordecai was refusing to bow before him, as had been commanded. Mordecai had simply stood for his faith, as once did three other Jewish captives in a foreign land (see Dan. 3).

3. Haman hatched a plot to exterminate not only Mordecai, but every other Jew living in the Persian Empire. Here is the ultimate of anti-Semitic action in the Old Testament. In his satanic strategy, he approached the king with the following "recommendations."

   a. That there is a "certain people scattered abroad and dispersed among the people in all the provinces of thy kingdom, and their laws are different from all people; neither keep they the king's laws. Therefore, it is not for the king's profit to tolerate them" (3:8). This, of course, was a brazen lie!

   b. That he, Haman, would be happy to contribute the sum of twenty million dollars into the royal treasury for the expense involved in this purge (3:9). Haman had doubtless counted on confiscating far more than this sum, which would be taken from those hundreds of thousands of innocent people he planned to butcher like cattle.

   c. The careless and heartless king agreed to this, without even checking the identity of this "certain people," to say nothing of their guilt (3:10, 11).

   d. Several weeks later Haman had prepared his murderous manifestation in the various languages and dialects of each province in the empire. Royal riders were sent forth to announce this edict of execution which decreed that all Jews would be killed on February 28 of the following year—473 B.C. (3:12-15).

B. Intestinal fortitude (4-5).

  1. As seen in Mordecai (4:1-14).

   a. Upon learning of the decree of death, Mordecai immediately identified with his people and went into deep mourning.

   b. Unaware of the new law, Esther learned of her cousin's sorrow and inquired concerning the reason behind it.

   c. Mordecai informed her and advised that she visit the king immediately.

   d. Esther pointed out to him that she had not been summoned to Xerxes' inner court for thirty days and to walk in uninvited would very possibly bring instant death.

   e. Mordecai answered with what is, perhaps, the key statement in the entire book. (See 4:13, 14.)

   f. Two phrases are especially significant here:

   (1) "Then shalt . . . deliverance arise to the Jews from another place." Even though the name God as such is not mentioned in Esther, surely Mordecai had his deliverance in mind here.

   (2) "Thou art come to the kingdom for such a time as this." This would indeed be the case. Not only did Esther later save the Jews in Persia, but also those living in Palestine, for the death decree included them too. In addition to this, Esther no doubt exercised a great influence upon her step-son, Artaxerxes, who later proved to be so kindly disposed toward Ezra and Nehemiah.

2. As seen in Esther (4:15—5:14).

   a. Esther immediately ordered a three-day fast among the Jews, and determined that she would "go in unto the king, which is not according to the law. And if I perish, I perish" (4:16). (See also Dan. 3:17, 18.)

   b. Three days later Esther entered the king's inner court, uninvited, but to her relief, she was warmly received. Xerxes, realizing his wife must have been desperate to take such a risk, said:

    "What wilt thou, queen Esther? And what is thy request? It shall be even given thee to the half of the kingdom" (5:3).

    (See Dan. 5:16 and Mk. 6:22, 23. See also Prov. 21:1; 19:12.)

   c. The queen did not reveal her request at this time, but simply asked that both the king and Haman attend a banquet she was preparing the next day. Xerxes quickly agreed.

   d. Upon learning of his invitation, the vain Haman became puffed up with pride. But when he saw Mordecai standing at the palace gate, still refusing to bow, he was furious.

   e. He related both his joy and frustration to Zeresh and his friends at home. Note the following account which revealed perhaps the true character of Haman (and indeed his wife) in the strongest light possible. (See 5:12-14.)

III. The Prize of Faith (6-10).

A. The execution of a beast—Haman (6-8).

  1. Scene one—the king's bedroom (6).

   a. Xerxes experienced a case of royal insomnia and ordered the reading of some historical records, hoping perhaps that this dull material would put him to sleep (6:1).

   b. The reader, by "chance," just happened to begin reading at the place which related how Mordecai had once saved the king's life by exposing an assassination plot. The king, now fully awake, asked: "What honor and dignity hath been bestowed upon Mordecai for this?" (6:3). The answer from his advisor was: "There has nothing been done for him."

c. At this exact moment Haman arrived at Xerxes' palace, seeking the king's permission to hang Mordecai. The king, still determined to reward Mordecai (neither Xerxes nor Haman, of course, knew what the other was thinking) used Haman as a sounding board and inquired:

"What shall be done for the man whom the king delighteth to honor?" (6:6).

d. The arrogant and self-centered Haman immediately thought Xerxes had him in mind and brazenly suggested the following:

(1) That the man to be honored be clothed in the king's own royal robes.

(2) That he be placed upon Xerxes' personal horse.

(3) That he be allowed to wear the king's crown.

(4) That the king's most noble prince lead this hero, seated upon the horse, through the streets of the city, shouting his praises for all to hear (6:7-9).

e. The king quickly agreed to all this and then turned to Haman and ordered his wicked prime minister to perform all this for Mordecai. The totally dumb-struck Haman stumbled out to obey Xerxes' command and later hurried home, utterly humiliated! Even there he received no comfort, but heard his wife say:

"If Mordecai is of the seed of the Jews, before whom thou hast begun to fall, thou shalt not prevail against him, but shalt surely fall before him" (6:13).

f. While they yet spoke, he received the message to attend Esther's banquet (6:14).

2. Scene two—the king's banquet hall (7).

a. The treachery learned (7:1-6).

(1) Esther warned the king that a plot was underway to slaughter both her and all her people. The king, filled with astonishment and then anger, asked: "Who is he, and where is he, who would presume in his heart to do so?" (7:5).

(2) Esther pointed to Haman and replied: "The adversary and enemy is this wicked Haman" (7:6). (See also 1 Pet. 5:8; 1 Jn. 2:13; 2 Thess. 2:8.)

b. The tables turned (7:7—8:17).

(1) Xerxes, unable to speak because of his fury, walked outside into his palace garden for a moment (7:7).

(2) Filled with horrible fear, the cowardly Haman begged Esther to intercede to the king for him. In his terrible fright he accidentally fell upon the couch where Esther was reclining (7:8).

(3) At this point Xerxes walked back in and viewed what he interpreted to be a rape attempt on the part of Ha-

man. Upon learning of the nearby gallows that Haman had built for Mordecai, the king roared out in his wrath for Haman himself to be hanged that very night. The order was immediately carried out (7:9, 10).

Note: Haman had violated that fearful warning of God to Abraham which said:

"And I will bless them that bless thee, and curse him that curseth thee" (Gen. 12:3).

For this violation he would forfeit his life. (See Prov. 26:27; Gal. 6:7, 8; Isa. 54:17.) Pharaoh learned that Esther's people couldn't be drowned (Ex. 14). Nebuchadnezzar learned

# Esther

## The Rise of Esther
### CHAPTERS 1-2

| | |
|---|---|
| The rejection of Vashti: | King Ahasuerus divorces his wife Vashti. |
| The selection of Esther: | Esther is the winner of a beauty contest and becomes his new queen. |
| The detection of Mordecai: | He overhears and reports a plot to assassinate the king. |

## The Lies of Haman
### CHAPTERS 3-5

| | |
|---|---|
| Infernal servitude: | Haman is appointed prime minister and instigates a plot to kill all the Jews. |
| Intestinal fortitude: | Upon hearing of this wicked plot, both Mordecai and Esther display great courage and wisdom.<br>• As seen by Mordecai's advice to Esther.<br>• As seen by Esther's appearance before the king. |

## The Prize of Faith
### CHAPTERS 6-10

The execution of a "beast"—Haman
• Scene one: The king's bedroom. He learns of Mordecai's loyalty.
• Scene two: The king's banquet hall. He learns of Haman's treachery.
The institution of a feast—Purim

they couldn't be burned (Dan. 3). Darius learned they couldn't be eaten (Dan. 6). Haman learned they couldn't be hanged (Est. 7).

(4) After his execution, Xerxes gave Esther Haman's estate and appointed Mordecai his new prime minister (8:1, 2).

(5) Both now begged the king to reverse Haman's order. But the law of the Medes and Persians once made, was immutable, and not even Xerxes himself could change it. Xerxes then did the next best thing. He ordered the Jews to defend themselves. Mordecai immediately sent copies of this new decree to all of the 127 provinces (8:3–14).

B. The institution of a feast—Purim (9–10).

1. The Jews prepared themselves and were able to slaughter their enemies on February 23, execution day (9:1–19).

2. Mordecai and Esther then instituted a new memorial feast called Purim, to commemorate yearly their great salvation from Haman (9:20–32).

3. Mordecai became a great and godly statesman, respected by both Jews and Gentiles for his abilities and actions (10).

Note: Some 1400 years after the events in the book of Esther had transpired, an amazing twentieth century replay was enacted in Russia:

On March 1, 1953—a bare eight years after the holocaust that took the lives of six million Jews—Josef Stalin unveiled a proposal to liquidate the Jews of the Soviet Union—another three million. The proposal was due to go into effect on March 9, but it never did, for a day after Stalin presented it, he unexpectedly dropped dead of a stroke.

The amazing story, often rumored, has been officially confirmed by a non-Jewish Soviet librarian, Ludmila Lufanov, who worked for years in top-secret Soviet archives in Moscow. She managed relatively recently to leave the USSR and now lives in the United States. A short while ago, in a Soviet Russian language journal, she told the incredible story and a copy reached the Jewish Press in Jerusalem.

Stalin, a paranoid Jew-hater, had liquidated thousands of Jews in the 1930s, including many who had been his most loyal and trusted comrades from the beginning of the Bolshevik movement. He liquidated not only the infamous Jewish community party section—Yevesektzia—which did more to wipe out Judaism and Jewish culture than anyone else, but also exterminated the heads of the Yevesektzia. After the war, which interrupted his plans for the Jews, Stalin was infuriated at the reception given to Israel's first ambassador to Moscow, Golda Meir, by Soviet Jews. He moved ruthlessly.

Jewish poets, writers, and artists were liquidated (most of whom had been loyal communists who had never complained when Stalin liquidated religious and Zionist Jews). He demanded that the satellite states do the same and the world was stunned to see Czechoslovak Community Party boss—Slansky—a loyal Stalinist, and a number of other top Jews, tried on charges of "cosmopolitanism" and "treason" and hanged. But it was the infamous "doctor's plot" that was to mark the climactic moment of Jewish genocide.

In 1953 Stalin suddenly announced that a "plot" had been discovered to kill him. It was a devious and clever one, planned by doctors—all of whom happened to be Jewish. The controlled press gave the "plotters" and the "plot" non-stop first-page treatment. Denunciations from puppet Communists came in from all over the Soviet Union. It was clear that the key word here was "Jewish" or the code names "Cosmopolitanism" and "Zionism." Stalin decided that the hanging of the doctors would serve as a pretext for mass rioting on the part of Soviet masses that would last three days and would eliminate two thirds of the three million Soviet Jews. The rest would be sent to Siberia to concentration camps where they would also die.

On March 1, 1953, at 12 noon, Stalin called a meeting of the Politburo in the Kremlin and read to the Soviet leaders his plan for the extermination of the Jews. According to the secret transcript, he said:

"The murderers in the white jackets have admitted their guilt. On the ninth of March they will be hanged in Red Square before all to see, but not even this punishment will satisfy our people. . . . The masses' anger will not be satisfied and there will be three days when we will be unable to stem the righteous wrath of the people who will pour out their fury on the Jewish heads."

Stalin concluded by saying that after three days, the heads of the Jewish community will admit in writing their collective guilt against the Russian people and will plead with the government to save them from total annihilation.

"After receiving this request to intervene, the government will not be able to remain aloof, and in order to separate the racist Jews from the Russian people, the Jews will be placed on special railroad cars and sent to the Far North and the Siberian plains. However, only a third of the passengers on the special trains will arrive at their destinations. The other two-thirds will fall victim to the anger of the masses at every stop along the way."

According to the librarian, when Stalin finished reading the proposal there was dead silence in the room. Stalin, furious, cursed his cabinet minister and walked out, slamming the door.

On March 2, the day after outlining the plans and exactly a week before the extermination of the three million Jews was to have taken place—Stalin died of a stroke. He lay in state for a week and was buried on March 9, which was the Jewish holiday—Purim.

# HAGGAI (520 B.C.)

INTRODUCTION:

1. The name Haggai means, "my feast."

2. His book is the second smallest in the Old Testament (Obadiah is the shortest), and consists of but thirty-eight verses.

3. Haggai was a contemporary of Zechariah. Both are mentioned in the book of Ezra (5:1; 6:14) as that dynamic duet who functioned as God's spiritual cheerleaders in erecting the Temple under Zerubbabel.

4. Haggai's prophecies are the most precisely dated ones in all the Bible.

5. His book has been compared to the epistle of James in the New Testament.

6. A chronology of this period may be seen by the following:

   a. 536 B.C.: 50,000 Jews under Zerubbabel return to Jerusalem.

   b. 536 B.C.: seventh month, they build the altar and offer sacrifice.

c. 535 B.C.: second month, work on the Temple begins, and is stopped.
d. 520 B.C.: sixth month (September), first day, Haggai's call to build.
   (1) sixth month, twenty-fourth day, building begins
   (2) seventh month (October), twenty-first day, Haggai's second appeal
   (3) eighth month (November), Zechariah's opening address
   (4) ninth month (December), twenty-fourth day, Haggai's third and fourth
   (5) eleventh month (February), twenty-fourth day, Zechariah's visions
e. 518 B.C.: ninth month (December), fourth day, Zechariah's visions
f. 516 B.C.: twelfth month (March), third day, the Temple is completed.
g. 515 B.C.: first month (April), fourteenth—twenty-first days, joyful Passover.
h. 455 B.C.: Ezra comes to Jerusalem and makes certain reforms.
i. 445 B.C.: Nehemiah rebuilds the wall. Period of Malachi.
7. Thus, his book is actually a record of four sermons.
   a. His first is found in 1:1-11.
   b. His second, in 2:1-9.
   c. His third, in 2:10-19.
   d. His fourth, in 2:20-23.
8. The New Testament passage found in 1 Corinthians 15:58 may appropriately be written over the book of Haggai.

I. A September Message: Directed to the hands of the people. It said, "Perform!" (1:1-15).
   A. The people had just about given up concerning the building of their Temple. After fifteen years it remained unfinished. Their lame excuse was, "The time is not yet come, the time that the Lord's house should be built" (1:2).
   Because of this carelessness, God could not and would not bless them with either spiritual or financial prosperity.
   B. God's advice to them was therefore to: "Go up to the mountain, and bring wood, and build the house; and I will take pleasure in it, and I will be glorified, saith the Lord" (1:8).
   C. The spirits of Zerubbabel (the governor) and Joshua (the high priest) were then stirred up by the Lord. This godly pair thus led the people to finish building the Temple.
II. An October Message: Directed to the hearts of the people. It said, "Patience!" (2:1-9).
   A. In spite of the insignificant Temple they had just built, as we have already seen (Ezra 3:8-13), there was weeping as well as joy at the dedication during Zerubbabel's time as some of the old men remembered the glories of Solomon's Temple. The new Temple was far inferior in size and cost.
   B. Patience was needed because of the magnificent temple that would someday be built.
   "The glory of this latter house shall be greater than of the former, saith the Lord of hosts; and in this place will I give peace, said the Lord of hosts" (2:9).

# Haggai

## PERFORM:
- DON'T GIVE UP—on the Temple.
- DO GO UP—on the mountain.
- GET ALL STIRRED UP—about the Lord.

## PATIENCE:
- IN SPITE OF the insignificant Temple they had just built
- BECAUSE OF the magnificent Temple they someday would build

## PONDER:
- THE FACT OF JUDAH'S CONTAMINATION (2:10-17)
- THE FACT OF GOD'S DETERMINATION (2:18, 19)
- THE FACT OF THE GREAT TRIBULATION (2:20-22)
- THE FACT OF ZERUBBABEL'S ELEVATION (2:23)

This, of course, is a reference to the beautiful new millennial temple, yet to be built. (See Ezek. 40-48.)

III. A December Message: Directed to the head of the people. It said, "Ponder!" (2:10-23).
   A. The fact of Judah's contamination (2:10-17). God asked Judah to answer two questions.
      1. "If one of you is carrying a holy sacrifice in his robes, and happens to brush against some bread, or wine, or meat, will it too become holy?" (2:12, *The Living Bible*).
      The answer of course, was, "No holiness does not pass to other things that way."
      2. "If someone touches a dead person, and so becomes ceremonially impure, and then brushes against something, does it become contaminated?" (2:13).
      Here the answer was yes! The point God was making here is that whatever righteousness the nation Israel might have once possessed was not automatically transferred upon them at this time. But their own unrighteousness was affecting both them and their children.
   B. The fact of God's determination (2:17-19). God promised them that because of their decision to finish the Temple, he would bless them from that day on, even before the structure was completed.
   C. The fact of the great tribulation (2:20-22). Someday God would destroy all those Gentile nations which had afflicted Israel throughout the years.
   ". . . I will shake the heavens and the earth; and I will overthrow the throne of kingdoms, and I will destroy the strength of the kingdoms of the nations; and I will overthrow the chariots, and those who ride in them; and the horses and their riders shall come down, every one by the sword of his brother" (2:21, 22). (See also Heb. 12:26; Rev. 16:18-20.)
   D. The fact of Zerubbabel's elevation (2:23).
   "In that day, saith the Lord of hosts, will I take thee, O Zerubbabel, my servant . . . and will make thee as a signet; for I have chosen thee. . . ."
   Some believe that Zerubbabel will be God's prime minister during the millennium.

## ZECHARIAH (520 B.C.)

INTRODUCTION:
1. Zechariah means, "Jehovah remembers." He was of priestly descent (as were Jeremiah and Ezekiel).
2. Josephus tells us he was later slain in the Temple, thus becoming a martyr for Christ.
3. He was a younger contemporary of Haggai (see 2:4).
4. Zechariah's writings resemble those of Daniel. Note also:
   a. Daniel was born in Palestine but wrote his prophecies in Babylon.
   b. Zechariah was born in Babylon, but wrote his book in Palestine.
5. Zechariah also reminds one of the book of Revelation.
6. His book contains more messianic passages than any other minor prophet. He speaks of the following:
   a. Christ as the Branch (3:8)
   b. Christ as God's Servant (3:8)
   c. Christ as God's smitten Shepherd (13:7)
   d. The triumphal entry (9:9)
   e. The betrayal for thirty pieces of silver (11:12, 13)
   f. The piercing of Jesus' hands and feet (12:10)
   g. His return to Mount Olivet (14:3–8)

I. The Visions of the Prophet (1–6). Zechariah receives ten visions, all apparently during the same night.
   A. The rider on the red horse (1:7–17).
      1. Zechariah sees a heavenly rider on a red horse, surrounded by other riders, all mounted also upon various colored horses.
      2. This special rider on the red horse is probably Christ.
      3. The other riders are angels who have been sent by God to "walk to and fro through the earth" (1:10). Thus, it is comforting to know that God also has his "spiritual spies" out checking upon this old sinful earth, as does Satan (see Job 1:7; 2:2; 1 Pet. 5:8).
      4. The angel of the Lord (Jesus) then prays over the troubled state of Jerusalem and is reassured by the Father that "the Lord shall yet comfort Zion, and shall yet choose Jerusalem" (1:17).
   B. The four horns (1:18, 19). Zechariah sees four animal horns and is told that they represent the four world powers that have scattered Judah, Israel, and Jerusalem. These horns may have symbolized the following:
      1. Assyria—which captured the northern kingdom of Israel. (See 2 Ki. 17.)
      2. Babylon—which captured the southern kingdom of Judah. (See 2 Ki. 24.)
      3. Persia—which planned on one occasion to destroy all Jews. (See the book of Esther.)
      4. Rome—which controlled and heavily taxed the city of Jerusalem during the days of Christ.
      These horns could, of course, also symbolize the four world powers mentioned by Daniel. (See 2:37-45; 7:2-8, 17-28.) Here they would be identified as Babylon, Persia, Greece, and Rome.
   C. The four artisans (1:20, 21). An artisan is a worker in wood, stone, or metal.
      1. The identity of these artisans: two suggestions have been offered here.
         a. That they refer to the four judgments spoken of by both Ezekiel (14:21) and John (Rev. 6:1-8). These judgments are war, famine, wild animals, and pestilence.
         b. That they refer to the powers which defeated those four nations.
            (1) Cyrus would be one, for he defeated Babylon (Dan. 5).
            (2) Alexander the Great would be one, for he defeated Persia (Dan. 8).
            (3) The various Roman generals would be one, for they subdued Greece.
            (4) Christ is one, for he will totally destroy the revived Roman Empire (Rev. 19).
      2. The purpose of the artisans:
         "These are come to terrify them, to cast out the horns of the nations, which lifted up their horn over the land of Judah to scatter it" (1:21).
   D. The man with a measuring line (2:1-13).
      1. Zechariah sees a man carrying a yardstick in his hand en route to measure Jerusalem. This is the second of four instances in the Bible in which either Jerusalem or its Temple is measured. Note:
         a. The Temple is measured in Jerusalem during the tribulation. (See Rev. 11:1, 2.)
         b. The Temple and city are measured during the millennium. (See Ezek. 40:3, 5; 37:26.)
         c. The eternal New Jerusalem is measured after the millennium. (See Rev. 21:15.)
      2. Zechariah is assured of the following thrilling facts concerning the millennial Jerusalem.
         a. That Jerusalem would someday be so full of people that some would have to live outside its city walls, yet dwelling in perfect safety.
         b. That God himself would be a wall of fire protecting them.
         c. That he would be the glory of the city.
         d. That the one who harmed them, touched the apple of his eye! (See also Deut. 32:7, 10; Ps. 17:8.)
      3. In verses 8, 9 of this chapter we have a remarkable Old Testament proof concerning the Trinity. Here the Lord of Hosts says he was sent by the Lord of Hosts.
      4. Palestine is referred to as "the holy land" in verse 12. This is the only place in Scripture where it is called by this name.
   E. The confrontation in heaven (3:1-10). The clothing of Joshua, the high priest. This is undoubtedly the greatest single chapter on the subject of salvation in all the Old Testament. In this vision Zechariah sees Joshua, the high priest, dressed in filthy clothing, and standing before God in heaven. He is being accused by Satan because of his soiled clothing. Christ, however, rebukes Satan, removes Joshua's dirty clothing, and dresses him in clean apparel. Joshua then is challenged to serve God with his whole heart. He is promised that someday God's Branch will appear to

255

cleanse the land of its sin. The following facts concerning salvation are brought out here:

1. The enemy of salvation. Contrary to popular opinion, Satan is not in hell today, but has accesss to God's very throne, where he constantly makes accusations against believers. (See also Job 1, 2; Rev. 12.)
2. The Person of Salvation. He is, of course, the Savior. Again in verse 2 we have proof of the Trinity, for the Lord (Jesus) calls upon the Lord (the Father) to rebuke Satan.
   a. His names: the Branch (3:8). He is called by this title in four Old Testament passages.
      (1) The branch of David. (Isa. 11:1; Jer. 23:5; 33:15). This corresponds to Matthew, who presents him as the King of the Jews.
      (2) My servant the Branch (Zech. 3:8). This corresponds to Mark, who presents him as the lowly slave.
      (3) The Man whose name is the Branch (Zech. 6:12, 13). This corresponds to Luke, who presents him as the perfect Man.
      (4) The Branch of Jehovah (Isa. 4:2). This corresponds to John, who presents him as the mighty God.
      (5) The Cornerstone (3:9). (See Isa. 28:16; Ps. 118; 22; Mt. 21:42; Acts 4:11; Eph. 2:20, 21.) Thus:
         (a) To the Gentiles, he is the Stone of crushing (Dan. 2:34, 35, 44, 45).
         (b) To Israel, he is the stumbling Stone (Rom. 9:31-33).
         (c) To the believer, he is the salvation Cornerstone (Eph. 2:19-22).
   b. His ministry:
      (1) To clothe all believers in robes of righteousness. (See Prov. 30:12; Isa. 64:6; 4:3, 4; Rom. 10:1-4; Phil. 3:9.)
      (2) To make intercession for the believer against Satan's lies. (See Lk. 22:31; Rom. 8:34; Heb. 7:25; 9:24; 1 Jn. 2:1.)
      (3) To bring in and rule over the millennium. (See Rev. 11:15-19.)
3. The purpose of salvation (3:6, 7). These verses may be paraphrased as follows: "If you will walk in my ways and keep my charge, you [Joshua] shall not only have the honor of judging my house, and keeping my courts, but when your walk on earth is done, you shall be transplanted to higher service in heaven, and have places to walk among these pure angelic beings who stand by me, harkening unto the voice of my word." (See also Ps. 103:20, 21; Eph. 2:4-10.)

F. The golden lampstand and the two olive trees (4:1-14). Here Zechariah sees a sevenfold golden lampstand, supplied by a reservoir of olive oil. On either side of the lampstand was a carved olive tree.

1. A lampstand in the Bible represents God's witnesses in this world.

   a. It can refer to Israel (as it does here).
   b. It can refer to the church (as it does in Rev. 1-3).
2. The olive oil is, of course, a symbol for the Holy Spirit. (See Lk. 4:18; Acts 10:38; Heb. 1:9; 1 Jn. 2:20.) We note the words of God in Zechariah 4:6 at this point:
   "Not by might, nor by power, but by my Spirit, saith the Lord of Hosts."
3. The olive trees refer to two famous teams:
   a. The historical team of Zerubbabel and Joshua.
   b. The prophetical team of Elijah and Moses. (See Rev. 11.)

G. The flying scroll (5:1-4). Zechariah sees a flying scroll, fifteen feet wide by thirty feet long. This represented the words of God's curse going out over the entire land of Israel.

1. The scope of this judgment. Although only two of the original commandments are mentioned here, that of swearing (the third, Ex. 20:7) and stealing (the eighth, Ex. 20:15), they nevertheless covered the entire moral code of God.
   a. The sin of swearing (using God's name falsely) represents all crimes against God and is vertical in nature.
   b. The sin of stealing represents all crimes against man, and is horizontal in nature.
2. The accused at this judgment. All unsaved Israelites throughout history. (See Rom. 9:6; Mt. 23; 1 Thess. 2:15, 16; Ezek. 11:21; 20:38.)
3. The time of this judgment. After the tribulation and just prior to the millennium. (See Mt. 25:1-30.)
4. The penalty of this judgment. It will apparently include both physical and spiritual death.

H. The woman in the ephah (5:5-11). The prophet views a flying bushel basket (ephah) covered by a heavy lead top piece. When the lid is lifted he sees a woman seated inside. He is then told:

1. The woman inside represents sin and wickedness. Often in the Bible iniquity is symbolized by a woman. (See Mt. 13:33; Rev. 2:20; 17:1-7.)
2. The heavy lead cover probably symbolizes the restraining power of God over evil.
3. The destination is said to be Babylon where it (evil and wickedness) would "be established, and set there upon its own base" (5:11). This statement may carry with it both historical and prophetical implications. Thus:
   a. Historical—the Tower of Babel, where organized rebellion against God began. (See Gen. 11:1-9.)
   b. Prophetical—the city of Babylon, which may actually be rebuilt during the tribulation. (See Rev. 18.)

I. The four chariots (6:1-8). Zechariah sees four chariots driven by four heavenly spirits proceeding from two brass mountains. Each chariot is pulled by a different colored team of horses. These colors are red, white, black, and gray. The various symbols here would seem to be as follows:

# Zechariah

- ● The Tenfold
**Vision** of the Prophet Zechariah 1-6
- ● The Manifold
**Vanities** of the People Zechariah 7-8
- ● The Twofold
**Visitation** of the Prince Zechariah 9-13

## THE TEN VISIONS

### 1. RIDER ON A RED HORSE (1:7-17)

● An appearance of Christ himself, along with some angels, keeping watch over Jerusalem.

### 2. THE FOUR HORNS (1:18, 19)

● May represent the four Gentile world powers which scattered (or would scatter) Israel

1. Assyria (Captured northern kingdom.)
2. Babylon (Captured southern kingdom.)
3. Persia (Plot against all Jews. See **Esther**.)
4. Rome (Has scattered and will scatter Israel.)

### 3. THE FOUR ARTISANS (1:20, 21)

● A probable reference to the first four sealed judgments in **Revelation 6:1-8**

### 4. MAN WITH A MEASURING LINE (2:1-13)

● Reference to the measuring of Jerusalem during the millennium **(Ezek. 40:1-5; 48:30-35)**

### 5. THE CONFRONTATION IN HEAVEN (3:1-10)

| | |
|---|---|
| The Charge | The wearing of filthy garments |
| The Charged | Joshua and the people of Jerusalem |
| The Prosecutor | Satan |
| The Defender | The Branch—called this four times in the Old Testament |

| | |
|---|---|
| The Branch of David **(Isa. 11:1; Jer. 23:5; 33:15)** | Gospel fulfillment—Matthew |
| My Servant, the Branch **(Zech. 3:8)** | Gospel fulfillment—Mark |
| Joshua Cleansed and Reassured | The man Branch **(Zech. 6:12)** | Gospel fulfillment—Luke |
| | The Branch of Jehovah **(Isa. 4:2)** | Gospel fulfillment—John |

### 6. THE GOLDEN LAMPSTAND AND THE TWO OLIVE TREES (4:1-14)

| | |
|---|---|
| ● Historical meaning | May refer to the anointed team of Zerubbabel and Joshua. |
| ● Prophetical meaning | May refer to the anointed team of Elijah and Moses. **(See Rev. 11:3-12.)** |

### 7. THE FLYING SCROLL (5:1-4)

| | | | |
|---|---|---|---|
| ● Meaning | God's judgment upon the land. Man had broken his entire moral law. | | |
| ● Reason | Sin of swearing | Against God | Vertical |
| | Sin of stealing | Against man | Horizontal |

### 8. THE WOMAN IN THE EPHAH (5:5-11)

| | |
|---|---|
| ● The woman | A type of sin and rebellion |
| ● The cover | A type of God's restraining power |
| ● The destination | To establish itself in Babylon |

| | |
|---|---|
| Organized rebellion | Had begun here **(Gen. 11)** |
| Organized rebellion | May end here **(Rev. 18)** |

### 9. THE FOUR CHARIOTS (6:1-8)

● Four heavenly spirits (angels) are driving these chariots, proceeding from two brass mountains

● The chariots may represent the first four plagues of **Revelation 6** and the mountains the judgment of God

### 10. THE CROWNING OF JOSHUA (6:9-15)

● Zerubbabel does this to illustrate the threefold ministry of the coming Messiah

1. He would build the Temple
2. He would minister as a Priest
3. He would rule as a King

---

1. The two brass mountains speak of God's judgment. (See Num. 21:9; John 3:14.)
2. The angel-driven chariots represent God's agents to effect various judgments upon Gentile nations. (See Rev. 7:1-3; 8:2, 7, 10, 12; 9:14, 15; 11:15; 15:1; 16:1-3.)
3. The various colored horses doubtless tie in with those mentioned in Revelation 6.
   a. The red ones speak of war and bloodshed. (See Rev. 6:4.)
   b. The black ones speak of famine and starvation. (See Rev. 6:5, 6.)
   c. The white ones speak of false peace. (See Rev. 6:2.)
   d. The gray ones speak of death. (See Rev. 6:8.)

   Note: We are told that those who proceeded "toward the north country have quieted my spirit . . ." (6:8).

   This may be a reference to the future divine judgment upon Russia during the tribulation. (See Ezek. 38, 39.)
J. The crowning of Joshua (6:9-15).
   1. Zechariah is told that three Jewish exiles will soon return to Jerusalem from Babylon, carrying gifts of silver and gold from the remnant there. Zechariah is instructed to make a golden crown from these gifts and place it upon Joshua, explaining to him that he rep-

resents the future Branch of Israel, the Messiah himself.

2. This blessed Messiah will someday function both as Priest and King. He will also build the Temple of God.

3. Zechariah is told the three returning exiles represent many others who will someday come from distant lands back to Palestine. (See also Isa. 56:6-8.)

II. The vanities of the people (7-8).

A. A group of Jews had come to Jerusalem from Bethel to ask the priests there if they could set aside their traditional custom of fasting and mourning each year during the month of August. The *New Scofield Bible* (p. 969) says in a footnote: "The mission of these Jews of the Captivity concerned a fast day instituted by the Jews in commemoration of the destruction of Jerusalem, wholly of their own will and without warrant from the Word of God. In the beginning there was doubtless sincere contrition in the observance of the day; now it had become a mere ceremonial. The Jews of the dispersion would be rid of it, but seek authority from the priests. The whole matter, like much in modern pseudo-Christianity, was extra-Biblical, formal and futile."

B. God tells them through the priests that it doesn't really make much difference what they do, for their hearts are insincere. He admonishes them to be honest in their dealings with both their God and their neighbors.

C. He promises that, because of his grace, their fast days will someday be feast days, and their sorrow turned into singing. (See 8:3, 4, 5, 8, 22, 23.)

III. The Visitation of the Prince (9-14).

A. The first coming of the Prince.

1. He came to feed the flock as his Father had instructed him to do (11:7).

2. The false shepherds of Israel, however, rejected him (11:8).

3. He thus broke one of his two staffs and set Israel aside for awhile (11:10). (See also Mt. 21:19, 42-46; 23:37-39.)

4. He finished his ministry by the triumphal entry into Jerusalem. "Rejoice greatly, O daughter of Zion; shout, O daughter of Jerusalem; behold, thy King cometh unto thee; he is just, and having salvation; lowly, and riding upon an ass, and upon a colt, the foal of an ass" (9:9). This was dramatically fulfilled, of course, in Matthew 21:1-11.

5. He was sold for thirty pieces of silver (11:12), the price of a slave which had been gored by an ox. (See Ex. 21:32.) This was fulfilled in Matthew 26:15.

6. This price, contemptuously given, was then cast aside with additional contempt, for the word "cast" used here is a gesture of disgust (as seen from Ex. 22:31; Isa. 14:19; 2 Sam. 18:17; 2 Ki. 23:12). This prophecy was fulfilled in Matthew 27:3-10.

7. He then broke his second staff, signifying perhaps the destruction of Jerusalem by Titus in 70 A.D. This tragedy ended all unity which existed in Israel.

8. He was finally crucified (12:10).

B. The Second Coming of the Prince:

1. The blood-letting of the false shepherd.

a. Because they rejected their Good Shepherd at his first coming, Israel will be given over for awhile to the cruel antichrist shepherd just prior to the second appearing of their glorious shepherd (11:15-17).

b. Two out of three will die in this horrible purge (13:8).

2. The bereavement of Israel (12:10-14). When he comes again, Israel will finally recognize him and mourn their heinous national crime of rexicide, the killing of one's own King. "And they shall look upon me whom they have pierced, and they shall mourn for him, as one mourneth for his only son . . ." (12:10).

3. The battle of Armageddon (12:1-9; 14:1-3, 12-15).

4. The bow of victory (10:4). This bow is, of course, the Son of God. We are assured of his deity because of the Father's statement in 13:7: "The man who is my fellow, said the Lord of hosts." This is literally translated, "the man who is my *equal*." From the bow of God this avenging arrow comes to earth.

## ZECHARIAH AND THE PRINCE

# The Two Visitations of the Prince

## HIS FIRST COMING

- He comes to feed the flock of God (11:7)
- He is rejected by Israel's leaders (11:8)
- He thus set aside Israel **(11:10)**
(Possible meaning of his breaking the staff called beauty)
- He makes his triumphal entry into Jerusalem **(9:9)**
- He is sold for thirty pieces of silver **(11:12)**
- He predicts the destruction of Jerusalem **(11:14)**
(Possible meaning of his breaking the staff called band)
- He is crucified **(12:10)**

## HIS SECOND COMING

- The cruel reign of the antichrist **(11:16)**
- Jerusalem to be surrounded and taken **(14:2)**
- Two thirds of the Jews to perish **(13:8)**
- One third of the Jews to be saved **(13:9)**
- Christ to appear upon the Mount of Olives **(14:4, 8)**
- Armageddon to be fought **(12:3; 14:2, 3)**
- God's enemies to be destroyed **(12:4, 9; 14:12-15)**
- Israel to recognize Christ **(12:10-14)**
- Israel to be cleansed **(13:1)**
- Israel to be settled in the land **(10:6-12; 8:8)**
- Gentiles to worship the Lord **(14:16-19)**
- Jerusalem to be filled with happy boys and girls **(8:5)**
- Christ to build the temple **(6:13)**
- Christ to rule as the Priest-King over all the world **(6:13; 9:10)**

a. He punishes those nations which have persecuted Israel. (See 9:1–8, 12–16.)
b. He will then strengthen the house of Judah, and "hiss [whistle] for them, and gather them" (10:8).

Note: God had previously said he would summon their enemies against them by hissing (Isa. 7:18, 19). Now, in the same way, he summons his people back to their own land.

c. He will finally "speak peace unto the nations; and his dominion shall be from sea even to sea, and from the river even to the ends of the earth" (9:10).
d. He will personally and visibly perform all this (14:4, 8).
5. The blessings of God (9:16, 17; 13:1, 9; 14:9, 10, 11, 16, 20, 21).

# MALACHI (435-396 B.C.)

INTRODUCTION:
1. Malachi means "my messenger."
2. Absolutely nothing is known of Malachi beyond his name and the fact that he was the last Old Testament prophet.
3. Malachi may be looked upon as a miniature summary of the entire Old Testament, for the prophet briefly covers those five key truths found in the other books. These are:
   a. The *selection* of Israel by God (1:2; 2:4–6, 10).
   b. The *transgression* of Israel against God (1:6; 2:11, 17).
   c. The *manifestation* of the Messiah (3:1; 4:2).
   d. The *tribulation* upon the nations (4:1).
   e. The *purification* of Israel at last (3:2–4, 12, 16–18; 4:2–6).
4. Malachi may be compared to Moses.
   a. Moses gives us the first Old Testament prophecy concerning the Messiah. (See Gen. 3:15.)
   b. Malachi lists the last Old Testament prophecy concerning the Messiah. (See 4:2.)
5. Malachi's book may be considered as a partial fulfillment of Daniel's prophecy in 9:24–27. This great prediction, known as the seventy-weeks (actually a 490-year period) began in 445 B.C. and was divided into three main segments. The first covered a period of forty-nine years. This would thus bring it to 396, or the approximate date many feel Malachi completed his book.

I. The Love of God Stated (1:1–5).
   A. In the second verse of his book Malachi lists the first of seven rather flippant questions the carnal Israelites had required of God. Each question was the result of a previous clear statement from God. These were:
      1. In what way hast thou loved us? (1:2).
      2. In what way have we despised thy name? (1:6).
      3. In what way have we polluted thee? (1:7).
      4. In what way have we wearied thee? (2:17).
      5. In what way shall we return? (3:7).
      6. How have we robbed thee? (3:8).
      7. What have we spoken so much against thee? (3:13).
   B. S. Franklin Logsdon writes the following concerning this first question:
      "The question, "Wherein hast thou loved us?" indicates an irritation on the part of the people which led them to accuse the Lord of failure to prove his love. They had a bitter recollection of the attitudes and actions of the Edomites when Jerusalem was plundered by the Philistines and Arabians (2 Chron. 21:16, 17). These descendants of Esau were there aiding and abetting the enemy in the defeat of their brethren, and the Lord did not restrain them (Obad. 11).
      They showed sadistic pleasure over Judah's misfortune by mocking at her calamities (Obad. 12). They shared the spoils with the enemy when the city was captured (Obad. 13). They assisted the enemy by blocking the retreat of refugees (Obad. 14). They turned over to the insurgents those that could not escape (Obad. 14). Thus, in Judah's trying hours, the Edomites looked, laughed, insulted, robbed, trapped, and murdered because of their inherited hatred toward Jacob (and his posterity) for fraudulently obtaining the blessing.
      The Lord's people carried a painful grievance concerning this. It was a festering sore in their memory. They recalled how their fathers, as captives, sitting along the rivers of Babylon, cried out, 'Remember, O Lord, the children of Edom in the day of Jerusalem; who said, Rase it, rase it, even to the foundation thereof' (Ps. 137:7). The question in Malachi's day is, in substance. 'Why did God permit this if He loved us?' " (*Malachi, or, Will a Man Rob God?* pp. 14, 15)
   C. God answers their first question by pointing out two facts.
      1. He would never allow Edom to prosper because they had mistreated the apple of his eye, Israel.
      2. He had already preferred Israel over Esau. Some have been greatly troubled over God's statement that he *loved* Jacob and *hated* Esau. Here several factors must be observed.
         a. The Genesis account which gives us the history of both boys never records that God actually and personally hated Esau and loved Jacob. (See Gen. 25, 27.)
         b. The statement may have well referred to those *nations* founded by the two men. God definitely did abhor the sinful attitudes and actions of the Edomites, as spoken of by the prophet Obadiah.
         c. The name *Jacob* here is a plural noun, which may indicate the entire nation of Israel.
         d. The Hebrew word for hate is *sane*, and sometimes is used to indicate preference or priority instead of abhorrence. This is also the case with the Greek word for hate which is *misco*. Note the following example:
            (1) "And when the Lord saw that Leah was *hated*, he opened her womb: but Rachel was barren" (Gen. 29:31). In no way does the record indicate that Jacob hated his first wife, but simply that he preferred his second.

(2) "The poor is *hated* even by his own neighbor, but the rich hath many friends" (Prov. 14:20).

"If any man come to me, and *hate* not his father, and mother, and wife, and children, and brethren, and sisters, yea, and his own life also, he cannot be my disciple" (Lk. 14:26).

Here it is perfectly obvious that our Lord was not teaching an individual to despise and abhor his own flesh and blood, but simply that God must be given first priority in a believer's life!

e. The real problem in Malachi's passage, however, is probably not the fact that God "hated" Esau, but that he could *love* Jacob. The fact is that he did indeed love his sinful nation. During his final address to Israel, Moses reminds them of this love no less than seven times. (See Deut. 4:37; 7:8, 13; 10:15; 15:16; 23:5; 33:3. Other passages stating this fact are: Isa. 43:4; 48:14; 63:9; Jer. 31:3; Hosea 3:1; 11:1, 4; 14:4.)

II. The Love of God Scorned.
   A. By the prophets.
      1. Who cheated the Lord through their shabby offerings (1:6—2:9).
         a. They had offered lame and sick animals to God. These cheap sacrifices were refused by the Lord, who challenged them if they dared to "offer it now unto thy governor; will he be pleased with thee, or accept thy person?" (1:8).
            (See also David's testimony in 2 Sam. 24:24.)
         b. They had not offered that proper honor and respect to God that:
            (1) a child should give to his father (1:6)
            (2) a servant should render to his master (1:6)
            (3) a citizen should pay to his king (1:14)
      2. Who cheated the people through their shabby example (2:7-9).
   B. By the people.
      1. through their *inequalities* (2:10)
      2. through their *intermarriages* (2:11)
      3. through their *immorality* (2:14)
      4. through their *insincerity* (2:17)
      5. through their *indebtedness* (3:8-10)
      6. through their *incriminations* (3:13-15)
III. The Love of God Shown.
   A. By remembering his own saints (3:16, 17). Especially to be noted are the last five words in 3:16, "that thought upon his name." This no doubt included the various names for God given in the Old Testament, along with their meanings. A summary of God's names would include:
      1. *Elohim*—used 2,570 times, refers to God's power and might (Gen. 1:1; Ps. 19:1).
      2. *El*—four compounds of this name—
         a. *Elyon*, the strongest strong One (Gen. 14:17-20; Isa. 14:13, 14)

b. *Roi*, the strong One who sees (Gen. 16:13)
c. *Shaddai*, the breasted One (used forty-eight times in Old Testament; see Gen. 17:1; Ps. 91:1)
d. *Olam*, the everlasting God (Isa. 40:28)
   3. *Adonai*—Master, Lord. God owns all his creation (Mal. 1:6).
   4. *Jehovah*—most common name. Occurs 6,823 times. The Self-existent One, the God of the covenant (Gen. 2:4).
      There are nine compound names of this name:

# Malachi

## The Love of God
### HIS LOVE STATED

"I have loved you, saith the Lord . . . I loved Jacob, and I hated Esau" **MALACHI 1:2, 3.**

A twofold problem is seen in these verses:

● WHY GOD "HATED" ESAU. NOTE:

1. The Genesis account **(25, 27)** never records God hating Esau.

2. The Hebrew word here translated hate can also mean preference (see **Gen. 29:31; Prov. 14:20; Lk. 14:26**).

3. The name Esau also doubtless stood for the entire wicked nation of Edom, whose ways God did indeed hate.

● WHY GOD LOVED JACOB: THIS IS THE REAL PROBLEM IN THE PASSAGE.

### HIS LOVE SCORNED

● BY THE PROPHETS:

1. Who cheated *the Lord* through their shabby offerings **(1:7, 8)**.
2. Who cheated *the people* through their shabby example **(2:7-9)**.

● BY THE PEOPLE:

1. Through their inequalities **(2:10)**
2. Through their intermarriages **(2:11)**
3. Through their immorality **(2:14)**
4. Through their insincerity **(2:17)**
5. Through their indebtedness **(3:8-10)**
6. Through their incriminations **(3:13-15)**

### HIS LOVE SHOWN

● BY REMEMBERING HIS SAINTS **(3:16).**
● BY SENDING HIS OWN SON.

1. His first coming was introduced by John the Baptist **(3:1a).**
2. His Second Coming will be introduced by Elijah the prophet **(4:5).**

**THE PURPOSE OF HIS SECOND COMING**
● REGARDING THE GENTILES:
To consume them as chaff in his oven **(4:1, 3).**
● REGARDING THE JEWS:
They will accept Christ **(3:1b).**
They will be gathered by Christ **(3:17).**
They will be purified by Christ **(3:2, 3).**
They will be healed by Christ **(4:2).**

a. *Jireh*—the Lord will provide (Gen. 22:13, 14)

b. *Nissi*—the Lord, my banner (Ex. 17:15)

c. *Shalom*—the Lord is Peace (Jdg. 6:24)

d. *Sabbaoth*—the Lord of Hosts (1 Sam. 1:3; Isa. 6:1–3)

e. *Maccaddeshoem*—the Lord thy Sanctifier (Ex. 31:13)

f. *Rohi (Raah)*—the Lord my Shepherd (Ps. 23:1)

g. *Tsidkenu*—the Lord our Righteousness (Jer. 23:6)

h. *Shammah*—the Lord who is present (Ezek. 48:35)

i. *Rapha*—the Lord our Healer (Ex. 15:26)

B. By sending his own Son

1. His first coming was introduced by John the Baptist (3:1). The *New Scofield Bible* observes: "The first part of verse one is quoted by John the Baptist (Mt. 11:10; Mk. 1:2; Lk. 7:27) but the next words, 'The Lord, whom ye seek,' etc., are nowhere quoted in the New Testament" (p. 980).

The reason for this omission is tragically apparent—Israel did not anticipate nor accept Christ at his first coming. (See Jn. 1:11.)

J. Vernon McGee writes:

"Malachi announced the coming of John the Baptist as my messenger. John was the Malachi of the New Testament and began where Malachi of the Old Testament left off. Malachi was the first radio announcer who said, 'The next voice you will hear will be that of the Lord's messenger.'"

2. His Second Coming will be introduced by Elijah the prophet (4:5, 6). (See also Rev. 11:3–14.)

Elijah thus will be awarded the privilege of preparing this cruel, corrupt, and cursed old world for its greatest, grandest, and most glorious moment—the personal and visible appearance of the King of kings and Lord of lords!

a. He shall come to punish the Gentiles (4:1, 3).

b. He shall come to purify Israel (3:2–4).

## IMPORTANT EVENTS BETWEEN THE TESTAMENTS

### YEAR B.C.

1. **334 B.C.**—Alexander crosses the Hellespont
2. **331 B.C.**—Alexander defeats the Persians
3. **323 B.C.**—Alexander dies at age thirty-two in Babylon
4. **260 B.C.**—The translation of the Septuagint
5. **214 B.C.**—The Great Wall of China begun
6. **175 B.C.**—Apocryphal literature completed
7. **169 B.C.**—Epiphanes defiles the Temple on December 15
8. **166 B.C.**—The revolt of the Maccabees

9. **165 B.C.**—The cleansing of the Temple on December 25

10. **146 B.C.**—Destruction of Carthage by Rome and the end of the Punic Wars
11. **63 B.C.**—Pompey conquers Jerusalem
12. **44 B.C.**—Julius Caesar is assassinated in March
13. **37 B.C.**—Herod is appointed to govern Jerusalem
14. **20 B.C.**—The rebuilding and enlargement of the Temple

# ACKNOWLEDGMENTS

*I am grateful to the following publishers for the kind permission to quote from the books listed below.*

**Baker Book House, Grand Rapids, Michigan**
James L. Boyer, *For a World Like Ours*, 1971.
Reginald M. Daly, *Earth's Most Challenging Mysteries*, 1972.
John Davis, *Conquest and Crisis*, 1969.
————, *Moses and the Gods of Egypt*, 1971.
Frederick A. Filby, *The Flood Reconsidered*, 1971.
John Whitcomb, *The Early Earth*, 1972.
————, *Solomon to the Exile*, 1971.

**Brethren Missionary Herald, Winona Lake, Indiana**
John Davis, *The Birth of a Kingdom*, 1970.
Herman A. Hoyt, *The End Times*, 1967.
————, *Revelation*, 1966.
Homer Kent, *The Epistle to the Hebrews*, 1972.
————, *From Jerusalem to Rome*, 1972.

**Creation-Life Publishers, San Diego, California**
Viola Cummings, *Noah's Ark*, 1973.
Duane T. Gish, *Evolution? The Fossils Say No*, 1973.
Henry Morris, *The Bible Has the Answers*, 1976.
————, *The Genesis Record*, 1976.
————, *The Remarkable Birth of Planet Earth*, 1972.
————, *Scientific Creationism*, 1974.

**William B. Eerdmans Publishing Company, Grand Rapids, Michigan**
Donald G. Barnhouse, *God's Remedy*, Vol. III, 1952.
Erich Sauer, *The Dawn of World Redemption*, 1955.
Merrill C. Tenney, *New Testament Survey*, 1953.
Kenneth S. Wuest, *Ephesians and Colossians*, 1953.
————, *First Peter*, 1953.
————, *In These Last Days*, 1952.

**Gospel Light Publications, Glendale, California**
Henrietta C. Mears, *What the Bible Is All About*, 1966.
Ray Stedman, *What More Can God Say?* 1975.

**Moody Press, Chicago, Illinois**
Gleason L. Archer, *A Survey of Old Testament Introduction*, 1964.
Maxwell Coder, *Jude, the Acts of the Apostates*, 1958.
Allen Johnson, *The Freedom Letter*, 1974.
Homer Kent, *Glory of the Church*, 1971.

Rene Pache, *The Return of Jesus Christ*, 1955.
J. D. Pentecost, *Prophecy for Today*, 1969.
————, *Will Man Survive?* 1971
John Phillips, *Exploring Romans*, 1969.
————, *Revelation*, 1974.
Charles Ryrie, *Balancing the Christian Life*, 1969.
————, *Dispensationalism Today*, 1955.
————, *First and Second Thessalonians*, 1959.
————, *Revelation*, 1968.
Merrill Unger, *Unger's Bible Handbook*, 1977.
John Walvoord, *Revelation*, 1966.

**Through the Bible Publications, Pasadena, California**
J. Vernon McGee, *Genesis, Exodus, Numbers, Deuteronomy, Ruth, Psalms, Luke, Ephesians, Second Timothy, Jude, Revelation*, 1971–77.

**Victor Books, Wheaton, Illinois**
Richard DeHaan, *Good News for Bad Times*, 1975.
Warren Wiersbe, *Be Free*, 1978.

**Zondervan Publishing House, Grand Rapids, Michigan**
Donald G. Barnhouse, *Genesis*, 1970.
————, *Revelation*, 1971.
W. A. Criswell, *Revelation*, 1969.
Arthur C. Custance, *Genesis and Early Man*, 1975.
————, *Noah's Three Sons*, 1975.
Henry H. Halley, *Halley's Bible Handbook*, 1965.
S. F. Lodgson, *Profiles in Prophecy*, 1971.
John Walvoord, *The Holy Spirit*, 1970.
————, *The Thessalonian Epistles*, 1973.
Leon Wood, *A Survey of Israel's History*, 1970.

*Also, I acknowledge permission to reprint from:*
J. Sidwell Baxter, *Explore the Book*, Marshall, Morgan, & Scott, London, England, 1958.
L. Strauss, *Daniel*, Loizeaux, Neptune, N.J., 1969.
J. Patten, *The Biblical Flood and the Ice Epoch*, Pacific Meridian Publishing Co., Seattle, Washington, 1966.
Tim LaHaye, *Revelation*, Publishers of Scriptural Truth, La-Mesa, California, 1968.
Hal Lindsey, *There's a New World Coming*, Vision House, Santa Ana, California, 1973.
W. McDonald, *Letters to the Thessalonians*, Walterick Publishers, Kansas City, Kansas, 1969.